STARTING OUT WITH

First Edition

App Inventor for Android

STARTING OUT WITH

First Edition

App Inventor for Android

Tony Gaddis
and
Rebecca Halsey

PEARSON

Boston   Columbus   Indianapolis   New York   San Francisco
Upper Saddle River   Amsterdam   Cape Town   Dubai   London   Madrid   Milan
Munich   Paris   Montréal   Toronto   Delhi   Mexico City   São Paulo   Sydney
Hong Kong   Seoul   Singapore   Taipei   Tokyo

Vice President and Editorial Director, ECS	*Marcia J. Horton*
Acquisitions Editor	*Matt Goldstein*
Editorial Assistant	*Kelsey Loanes*
Program Manager	*Carole Snyder*
Project Manager	*Rose Kernan, RPK Editorial Services, Inc.*
Project and Program Manager Team Lead	*Scott Disanno*
Media Team	*Steve Wright*
R&P Project Manager	*Rachel Youdelman*
Operations Specialist	*Vincent Scelta*
Inventory Manager	*Bruce Boundy*
Marketing Manager	*Demetrius Hall*
Product Marketing Manager	*Bram Van Kempen*
Marketing Assistant	*Jon Bryant*
Cover Designer	*Joyce Wells, Creative Circle*

The author and publisher of this book have used their best efforts in preparing this book. These efforts include the development, research, and testing of theories and programs to determine their effectiveness. The author and publisher make no warranty of any kind, expressed or implied, with regard to these programs or the documentation contained in this book. The author and publisher shall not be liable in any event for incidental or consequential damages with, or arising out of, the furnishing, performance, or use of these programs.

Pearson Education Ltd., London
Pearson Education Australia Ply. Ltd., Sydney
Pearson Education Singapore, Pte. Ltd.
Pearson Education North Asia Ltd., Hong Kong
Pearson Education Canada, Inc., Toronto
Pearson Education de Mexico, S.A. de C.V.
Pearson Education–Japan, Tokyo
Pearson Education Malaysia, Pte. Ltd.
Pearson Education, Inc., Upper Saddle River, New Jersey

Microsoft and/or its respective suppliers make no representations about the suitability of the information contained in the documents and related graphics published as part of the services for any purpose. All such documents and related graphics are provided "as is" without warranty of any kind. Microsoft and/or its respective suppliers hereby disclaim all warranties and conditions with regard to this information, including all warranties and conditions of merchantability, whether express, implied or statutory, fitness for a particular purpose, title and non-infringement. In no event shall microsoft and/or its respective suppliers be liable for any special, indirect or consequential damages or any damages whatsoever resulting from loss of use, data or profits, whether in an action of contract, negligence or other tortious action, arising out of or in connection with the use or performance of information avaliable from the services. The documents and related graphics contained herein could include technical inaccuracies or typographical errors. Changes are periodically added to the information herein. Microsoft and/or its respective suppliers may make improvements and/or changes in the product(s) and/or the program(s) described herein at any time. Partial screen shots may be viewed in full within the software version specified.

Microsoft® Windows®, and Microsoft Office® are registered trademarks of the Microsoft Corporation in the U.S.A. and other countries. This book is not sponsored or endorsed by or affiliated with the Microsoft Corporation.

Library of Congress Cataloging-in-Publication Data on File

V011
10 9 8 7 6 5 4 3 2 1

www.pearsonhighered.com

ISBN-13: 978-0-13-295526-3
ISBN-10:   0-13-295526-1

Brief Contents

Contents

Chapter 12   **Sensors   531**

Chapter 13   **Other App Inventor Capabilities   561**

Appendix A   **Setting Up App Inventor   597**

Appendix B   **Connecting an Android Device to App Inventor   603**

Preface

Cell phones have become an important part of most students' lives. Even students with limited computer experience have no trouble using their phones to send text messages, check their email, and update their Facebook statuses. Of course, the typical cell phone today is much more than a mere phone. It's a powerful computer with many unique capabilities, including the ability to run thousands of available programs, or apps.

Even though students regularly download, install, and use apps on their phones, they do not typically think of their phones as computers. In fact, students have a unique relationship with their phones that is different, and more personal, than the relationship they have with their laptop computers. When students learn that they can create their own mobile apps—especially apps that take advantage of a phone's unique capabilities (such as text messaging, location sensing, etc.)—they become excited and motivated to learn.

This book capitalizes on that excitement and motivation by using App Inventor 2 to teach introductory programming skills. App Inventor 2 is a free, cloud-based development platform that is provided by The MIT Center for Mobile Learning. It allows users with no prior programming experience to make their own Android apps. It is extremely easy to use, and it combines a visual GUI designer with a drag-and-drop code editor. An on-screen Android emulator or an actual Android device that is connected to the computer (either wirelessly or with a USB cable) runs apps as they are created. Because App Inventor 2 allows students to create apps and see them running on a phone, programming becomes a personally meaningful skill.

Programming With Blocks

For many beginning students, learning the syntax of a programming language can be a daunting task. Precious time that should be devoted to learning the fundamentals of programming is often spent tracking down missing semicolons or unbalanced braces.

Syntax errors in App Inventor are never a problem, because they never happen! You build an app by dragging and dropping "blocks" into an editor. The blocks, which represent actions and data, can be snapped together, like the pieces of a puzzle, to create fully functional programming statements. Because you don't have to spend time locating and fixing syntax errors, you can concentrate on planning the actions that you want your app to perform and arranging them into the proper sequence.

Runtime and logic errors can still occur, of course, because the student can use the wrong instruction or get instructions out of order. But because syntax is not an issue, the student devotes his or her time to developing and debugging algorithms.

Using the Emulator or Android Devices

You use a Windows, Mac, or Linux computer to develop apps with App Inventor 2, but to test your apps, you use either the Android emulator, which is included with App Inventor, or an actual Android device such as a smartphone or a tablet. An Android device can be connected to the computer either wirelessly (via Wi-Fi) or with a USB cable. This book can be used with either approach.

The emulator, which is shown in Figure P-1, is a simulated Android phone. As you are using App Inventor to develop an app, the app appears and runs on the emulator's screen. You can interact with the emulator in many of the same ways that you interact with an actual smartphone. Although the emulator is limited (for example, it does not have a GPS sensor to report its location, and it cannot make phone calls), it does provide many of the basic features of an actual smartphone.

Most of the topics that are covered in Chapters 1 through 11 can be taught using the emulator. The topics covered in Chapters 12 and 13 require an Android device.

Figure P-1 The Android Emulator

App Inventor in the Classroom

App Inventor can be used in a variety of ways in the classroom, and this text is designed to accommodate all of them. Here are some examples:

- You can use this text with App Inventor 2 for the first part of an introductory programming course, and then switch to a traditional programming language. Depending on the amount of time you want to devote to App Inventor, you can use the entire book, or you can omit some of the latter chapters.
- You can use this text with App Inventor 2 for a brief introduction to programming in a computer concepts course or an introduction to technology course. The latter chapters can be omitted to fit the amount of time that you have.
- You can use this text by itself in a semester-long course that uses only App Inventor 2 to teach programming fundamentals.
- You can use this text in short courses or summer programs that use App Inventor 2 to teach programming.

VideoNotes to Accompany This Book

A full set of VideoNotes has been developed to accompany each tutorial in the book. Students can follow along with the authors as they work through tutorials in the videos. Also, one exercise or programming project at the end of each chapter has an accompanying VideoNote that shows the student how to create the solution. To access these supplements, go to www.pearsonhighered.com/gaddis and click on the image of this book's cover.

Brief Overview of Each Chapter

Chapter 1: Introduction Programming and App Inventor 2

This chapter explains what algorithms and programs are, and why we use programming languages. App Inventor 2 is introduced and the student learns the fundamental steps for creating an app's user interface, using the Blocks Editor to program the app, and using the emulator to test an app.

Chapter 2: Working With Media

In this chapter, the student learns to create apps that use images and sound. Topics include setting the background image for the device's screen and displaying images in image components, as well as on buttons (to create clickable images). The Sound component is introduced for playing sound effects, and techniques for working with colors are presented. The chapter discusses the visual arrangement of components in the app's user interface and the importance of commenting code.

Chapter 3: Input, Variables, and Calculations

In this chapter, the student learns to use TextBox components to read user input. Variables are introduced as a way to store data in memory. App Inventor's math operator blocks are introduced, and the student learns to create math expressions. The Slider component is also discussed.

Chapter 4: Decision Blocks and Boolean Logic

In this chapter, the student learns about App Inventor's decision structures: the `if then` block, the `if then else` block, and the `if then else if` block. The relational operators are introduced, as well as logical operators. The chapter discusses random numbers, their applications, and how to generate them in App Inventor. The Screen component's `Initialize` event is introduced. The chapter concludes with a discussion of the ListPicker and CheckBox components.

Chapter 5: Repetition Blocks, Times, and Dates

This chapter shows the student how to use loops to create repetition structures. App Inventor's `while` and `for each` loops are presented. Counters, accumulators, and running totals are also discussed. The chapter introduces the Clock component as a way to work with dates and times, and also as a way to create a timer. The chapter concludes with a discussion of the DatePicker component.

Chapter 6: Procedures and Functions

In this chapter, the student first learns how to write procedures. The chapter shows the benefits of using procedures to modularize programs and discusses the top-down design approach. Then, the student learns to pass arguments to procedures. Finally, the student learns to write functions, or procedures that return a result.

Chapter 7: Lists

This chapter introduces lists. The student learns to create lists, insert and append items, select items at specific and random positions, remove items, replace items, search for items, and more.

Chapter 8: Storing Data on the Device

This chapter discusses the File component and the TinyDB component. The File component allows you to read and write text files on the device or emulator. TinyDB is a simple database component that allows you to store data as tag-value pairs.

Chapter 9: Graphics and Animation

App Inventor provides components for creating graphics and animations. In this chapter, the student first learns to draw primitive graphics with the Canvas component. Then, the Ball and ImageSprite components are discussed. Simple games are created that use collision detection, the Clock component, and sprites.

Chapter 10: Working with Text

In this chapter, the student learns to process strings at a detailed level. Various text-processing capabilities are discussed, such as concatenation, comparing strings, trimming strings, converting case, finding, replacing, and extracting substrings, and string splitting.

Chapter 11: Text to Speech and Text Messaging

This chapter begins with an introduction to the TextToSpeech component, which converts text to spoken words. (The component reads text aloud.) Next, the student learns to use the Texting component to send and receive text messages.

Chapter 12: Sensors

This chapter focuses on the sensors that are found on an Android device. The sensors that are introduced are: The LocationSensor, for determining the device's physical location, the OrientationSensor, for determining the device's orientation in 3D space, and the AccelerometerSensor, for determining the device's acceleration in 3D space. This chapter concludes with a discussion of using the ActivityStarter component to launch Google Maps.

Chapter 13: Other App Inventor Capabilities

This chapter presents various components that work on Android devices. The components that are covered in this chapter give capabilities such as recording audio, taking photos, selecting images from the device's gallery, playing videos, selecting entries from the contact list, scanning barcodes, using voice recognition, connecting to a Twitter account, and storing data on a Web server with a TinyWebDB component.

Appendix A: Setting Up App Inventor

Appendix B: Connecting an Android Device to App Inventor

Appendix C: Uploading Your Application to App Inventor Gallery and Google Play Store

Appendix D: Component Reference

Appendix E: Answers to Checkpoints

Features of the Text

Concept Statements

The major sections of the text starts with a concept statement. This statement concisely summarizes the main point of the section.

Example Apps

The text has an abundant number of complete and partial example apps, which are each designed to highlight the topic currently being studied.

Tutorials

Each chapter has several hands-on tutorials that lead the student through the process of developing or completing an app. These tutorials give the student experience performing the tasks discussed in the chapters.

VideoNotes

Online videos developed specifically for this book are available for viewing at www. pearsonhighered.com/gaddis. Icons appear throughout the text, alerting the student to videos about specific topics.

Notes

Notes appear at several places throughout the text. They are short explanations of interesting or frequently misunderstood points relevant to the topic at hand.

Tips

Tips advise the student on the best techniques for approaching different programming problems.

Checkpoints

Checkpoints are questions placed at intervals throughout each chapter. They are designed to query the student's knowledge quickly after learning a new topic.

Review Questions

Each chapter presents a thorough set of multiple-choice and short-answer review questions.

Exercises

Each chapter offers a set of exercises for developing apps. The exercises are designed to solidify the student's knowledge of the topics presented in the chapter.

Online Resources

This book's online resource page contains numerous student supplements. To access these supplements, go to www.pearsonhighered.com/gaddis and click on the image of this book's cover. You will find the following items:

- A link to the App Inventor site
- The book's example apps
- Graphics and audio files that can be used in student projects
- Access to the book's companion VideoNotes

Instructor Resources

The following supplements are available to qualified instructors only:

- Answers to the Review Questions
- Solutions for the exercises
- PowerPoint presentation slides for each chapter

Visit the Pearson Instructor Resource Center (www.pearsonhighered.com/irc) or send an e-mail to computing@pearson.com for information on how to access them.

Acknowledgements

The authors would like to thank Dr. Hal Abelson of MIT for his inspiring work, and particularly for creating App Inventor. We want to thank the entire App Inventor team at MIT for the amazing job they are doing. We also want to thank everyone at Pearson Education for making this book possible. We are extremely grateful that Matt Goldstein is our editor. He and Kelsey Loanes, editorial assistant, guided us through the process of writing this book. We are also fortunate to have Demetrius Hall and Bram Van Kempen as marketing managers. They do an amazing job of getting computer science books out to the academic community. The production team, lead by Camille Trentacoste, worked tirelessly to make this book a reality. We could not have done it without their patience and hard work. Thanks to you all!

About the Authors

Tony Gaddis

Tony Gaddis is the author of the *Starting Out with* series of textbooks. Tony has nearly twenty years of experience teaching computer science courses, primarily at Haywood Community College. He is a highly acclaimed instructor who was previously selected as the North Carolina Community College "Teacher of the Year" and has received the Teaching Excellence award from the National Institute for Staff and Organizational Development. The *Starting Out with* series includes introductory books covering C++, Java™, Microsoft® Visual Basic®, Microsoft® C#®, Python, Programming Logic and Design, and Alice, all published by Pearson Education.

Rebecca Halsey

Rebecca Halsey is an Associate Professor at Guilford Technical Community College where she teaches classes in Computer Science and Mobile Application Development. She is also developing and leading the new Mobile Application Development curriculum at GTCC. She also has twenty years of industry experience as a software developer.

VideoNotes

1 Introduction to Programming and App Inventor

1.1 Introduction

This book teaches fundamental programming skills using an exciting application known as App Inventor 2. (We will refer to it simply as App Inventor.) App Inventor allows you to quickly and easily create applications, or "apps," for Android smartphones and tablets. It is not necessary to have prior programming experience or knowledge to use this book. App Inventor was created for beginners who have never programmed before.

You might find it surprising that with no previous programming experience, you can learn to create apps for a smartphone or a tablet. Perhaps you have heard that you need to know a lot about programming in languages such as Java to create mobile apps. While it is true that apps are typically created with high-level programming languages, App Inventor takes a different approach. With App Inventor, you use a screen designer to visually create an app's screen, as shown in Figure 1-1. Then, you use a special editor known as the Blocks Editor to create the actions that the app performs. With the Blocks Editor, you do not have to know a language such as Java to program the app. Instead, you visually assemble *code blocks* to create the app's actions. Figure 1-2 shows an example of the Blocks Editor.

With App Inventor, you use a standard computer, like a Windows PC, a Mac, or a Linux system, to create an app. You can connect a supported Android smartphone or tablet to the computer either wirelessly or with a USB cable. As you develop the app, you will see it running on the connected device. (See Appendix B for more information about connecting your Android device to App Inventor.)

Figure 1-1 The App Inventor Designer *(Source:* MIT App Inventor 2, Pearson Education, Inc.)

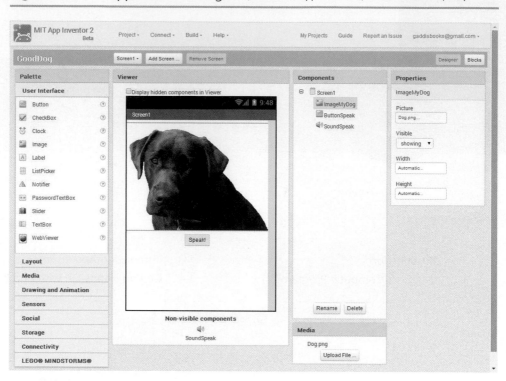

Figure 1-2 The Blocks Editor *(Source:* MIT App Inventor 2)

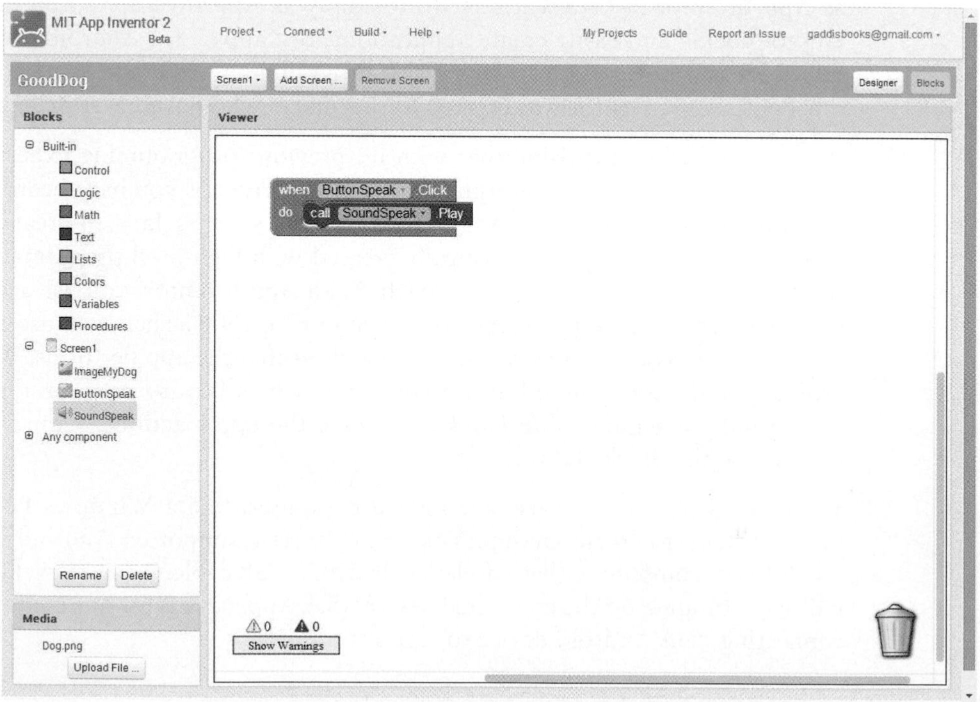

If you do not have a supported Android device to connect to your computer, App Inventor provides an Android emulator that runs on your computer. The emulator, which is shown in Figure 1-3, is a simulated Android phone. As you are using App Inventor to develop an app, the app appears and runs on the emulator's screen. You can interact with the emulator in many of the same ways that you interact with an actual smartphone. Although the emulator is limited (for example, it does not have a GPS sensor to report its location, and it cannot make phone calls), it does provide many of the basic features of an actual smartphone.

Figure 1-3 The Android Emulator (*Source:* MIT App Inventor 2, Pearson Education, Inc.)

App Inventor Runs in the Cloud

Although you will need to install a program on your computer to run the Android emulator, App Inventor runs in the *cloud*. This simply means that it runs on a remote server that you are accessing over the Internet. App Inventor is part of MIT's Center for Mobile Learning, so it is hosted on servers that are managed by MIT. Additionally, the projects that you create with App Inventor are stored on the remote servers.

There are several advantages to this cloud-based approach. For example, you can access App Inventor and your projects from any computer that is properly set up and connected to the Internet. In addition, the files that you create with App Inventor are maintained and backed up by the host. Also, you can be sure that you are always running the most recent version of App Inventor. Of course, this approach requires that you have an Internet connection to use App Inventor.

Setting Up App Inventor

Before you can work through the tutorials in this book, you must set up App Inventor to work with either the Android emulator or an actual Android device. If you haven't already done so, turn to Appendix A and follow the instructions to set up App Inventor. Appendix A also has an accompanying VideoNote that demonstrates the set up process. You can access the VideoNote from the book's companion website at www.pearsonhighered.com/gaddis. If you have an Android device that you want to connect to App Inventor, read Appendix B after you have set up App Inventor on your computer.

1.2 What Is a Computer Program?

CONCEPT: A computer program is a set of instructions that a computer follows to perform a task.

Before jumping straight into App Inventor, you should take a moment to learn some basic concepts about computer programming. The concepts that we discuss in this section apply to all types of computer programming, regardless of whether the computer is a laptop, a supercomputer, or a mobile device.

The title of this section poses the question "What is a computer program?" Before we can answer that, first we should answer the question "What is a computer?" To learn programming, you do not need a deep understanding of how computers work, but you do need to understand in the most basic terms what a computer is. Here's a definition that we can start with:

A computer is a device that follows instructions.

A computer doesn't know how to do anything on its own. It only follows the instructions that are given to it. Having said that, you must realize that a computer cannot follow just any kind of instruction. For example, you can't wake up in the morning and say to your computer, "Make an omelet and serve it to me in bed." That's not an instruction that a computer can understand. That's the kind of instruction that a human (like a butler, if you're lucky enough to have one) can understand. Unfortunately, common computers like the ones you and I have on our desktops don't make breakfast. Their purpose is to work with data. They do things like adding and multiplying numbers, displaying data on the screen, storing data so it can be retrieved later, and so forth. Knowing this, we can expand our definition of what a computer is, as follows:

A computer is a device that follows instructions for manipulating and storing data.

When a computer is designed, it is equipped with a set of operations that it can perform on pieces of data. Most of the operations are very basic in nature. For example, the following are typical operations that a computer can do:

- Add two numbers
- Subtract one number from another number
- Multiply two numbers
- Divide one number by another number
- Move a number from one memory location to another
- Determine whether one number is equal to another number
- And so forth . . .

A computer instruction is merely a command for the computer to perform one of the operations that it knows how to do.

Although an instruction exists for each operation that a computer is able to perform, the individual instructions aren't very useful by themselves. Because the computer's operations are so basic in nature, a meaningful task can only be accomplished if the computer performs many operations. For example, if you want your computer to calculate the amount of interest that you will earn from your savings account this year, it will have to perform a large number of instructions, carried out in the proper sequence. Now we can understand what a computer program is:

A computer program is a set of instructions that the computer follows to perform a task.

So, if we want the computer to perform a meaningful task, such as calculating our savings account interest, we must have a *program*, which is a set of instructions. The instructions in a program must be carefully written so they follow a logical sequence. When a computer is performing the instructions in a program, we say that the computer is *running* or *executing* the program.

Algorithms and Programming Languages

Computer programmers do a very important job. Their job is important because without programs, computers would do nothing! When a programmer begins the process of writing a program, one of the first things he or she does is develop an algorithm. An *algorithm* is a set of well-defined, logical steps that must be taken in order to perform a task. For example, suppose we are writing a program to calculate an employee's gross pay. Here are the steps that should be taken:

1. Get the number of hours that the employee worked, and store it in memory.
2. Get the employee's hourly pay rate, and store it in memory.

3. Multiply the number of hours worked by the hourly pay rate and store the result in memory.
4. Display a message on the screen that shows the amount of money earned. The message must include the result of the calculation performed in Step 3.

Notice that the steps in this algorithm are sequentially ordered. Step 1 should be performed before Step 2, and so forth. It is important that these instructions are performed in their proper sequence.

The steps shown in the pay-calculating algorithm are written in English. Although you and I might easily understand the algorithm, it is not ready to be executed on a computer. The instructions have to be translated into *machine language,* which is the only language that computers understand. In machine language, each instruction is represented by a binary number. A *binary number* is a number that has only 1s and 0s. Here is an example of a binary number:

```
1011010000000101
```

When you or I look at this number, we see only a series of 1s and 0s. To the computer, however, this number is an instruction, which is a command to perform some operation. A computer program that is ready to be executed by the computer is a stream of binary numbers representing instructions.

As you can imagine, the process of translating an algorithm from English statements to machine language instructions is very tedious and difficult. To make the job of programming easier, special programming languages have been invented. *Programming languages* use words instead of numbers to represent instructions. A program can be written in a programming language, which is much easier for people to understand than machine language, and then be translated into machine language. Programmers use special software called *compilers* or *interpreters* to perform this translation.

Over the years, many programming languages have been created. If you are working toward a degree in computer science or a related field, you are likely to study languages such as Java, Python, C++ (pronounced "C plus plus"), and Visual Basic. These are only a few of the languages that are used by professional programmers to create software applications. Each of these languages has its own set of words that the programmer must learn in order to use the language. The words that make up a programming language are known as *keywords.* For example, the word `print` is a keyword in the Python 2 language. It prints a message on the screen. Here is an example of how the `print` keyword might be used to form an instruction in a Python 2 program:

```
print "Hello Earthling!"
```

This causes the message *Hello Earthling!* to be displayed on the computer screen. Compare this instruction to the binary number we saw earlier. You can see from this simple example why programmers prefer to use programming languages instead of machine language. Using words to write a program is much easier than using binary numbers.

In addition to keywords, programming languages have *operators* that perform various operations on data. For example, all programming languages have math operators that perform arithmetic. In Java, as well as most other languages, the + sign is an operator that adds two numbers. The following would add 12 and 75:

```
12 + 75
```

In addition to keywords and operators, each language also has its own *syntax*, which is a set of rules that must be strictly followed when writing a program. The syntax rules dictate how keywords, operators, and various punctuation characters must be used in a program. When you are learning a programming language, you must learn the syntax rules for that particular language.

When you write a program with a traditional programming language, you convert your algorithm into a series of *statements*. A programming statement consists of keywords, operators, punctuation, and other allowable programming elements, arranged in the proper sequence to perform an operation. Programmers call these statements *code*. Typically, you type your programming statements into a text editor, save them to a file, and then use a compiler to translate the statements into an executable program. An *executable program* is a file containing machine language instructions that can be directly executed by the computer.

Programming with App Inventor

One way that App Inventor makes programming easy to learn is by eliminating many of the errors that beginning students commonly make. With a traditional programming language, like Java or C++, beginners frequently make typing mistakes that result in misspelled keywords, missing punctuation characters, and other such errors. These types of mistakes are known as *syntax errors*. If a program contains even one syntax error, it cannot be translated into an executable program. As a result, students and professional programmers alike spend a lot of time tracking down syntax errors and fixing them. In App Inventor, however, syntax errors never happen, because you do not type programming statements.

Instead, you drag and drop *code blocks*, which are graphical building blocks, into an editor. The blocks, which represent actions and data, can be "snapped" together, like the pieces of a puzzle, to create fully functional programming statements. Because you don't have to spend time locating and fixing syntax errors, you can concentrate on planning the actions that you want your app to perform, and arranging them into the proper sequence.

Perhaps the greatest reason that programming is easy with App Inventor is that it's fun! Rather than writing boring programs that perform calculations or analyze data, you will be creating mobile apps that you can run on your own smartphone or tablet, assuming it is a supported Android device. So if you have a great idea for an app, you can create it and install it on your device. If you want to share your apps with others, you can upload them to the Google Play Store or the App Inventor Gallery. (For more information about submitting your App Inventor apps to the Google Play store and the App Inventor Gallery, see Appendix C.)

Checkpoint

1.1 What is a computer?

1.2 What is a program?

1.3 What is an algorithm?

1.4 What is the only language that computers understand?

1.5 Why were programming languages invented?

1.3 Introducing App Inventor

App Inventor is a Web application that runs in your browser. The following browsers work with App Inventor:

- Google Chrome 4.0 or higher
- Apple Safari 5.0 or higher
- Mozilla Firefox 3.6 or higher

Each time you work with App Inventor to create or modify an app, you will perform the following general steps:

- You will open your browser and go to the App Inventor website.
- You will either create a new project or open an existing project.
- You will open the Blocks Editor.
- You will connect either the Android emulator or an actual Android device to App Inventor.

In Tutorial 1-1, you will perform these steps, using the Android emulator. Before performing this tutorial, make sure you have set up App Inventor on your computer. (If you have not already set up App Inventor, see Appendix A for instructions.)

VideoNote
Starting App Inventor and Creating a New Project

Tutorial 1-1:
Starting App Inventor and Creating a New Project

Step 1: Open your Web browser and go to the following address:

```
http://appinventor.mit.edu
```

Step 2: You will see a screen similar to the one shown in Figure 1-4. Click the *Create* button that appears in the upper right area of the screen.

Step 3: If you are not currently signed into your Google account, you will see a screen similar to the one shown in Figure 1-5. (If you are already signed into your Google account, skip to Step 4.) Enter your email address and Google account password, and then click *Sign In*.

Figure 1-4 App Inventor Main Screen (*Source:* MIT App Inventor 2)

Figure 1-5 Login to Your Google Account (*Source:* Google and the Google logo are registered trademarks of Google Inc., used with permission.)

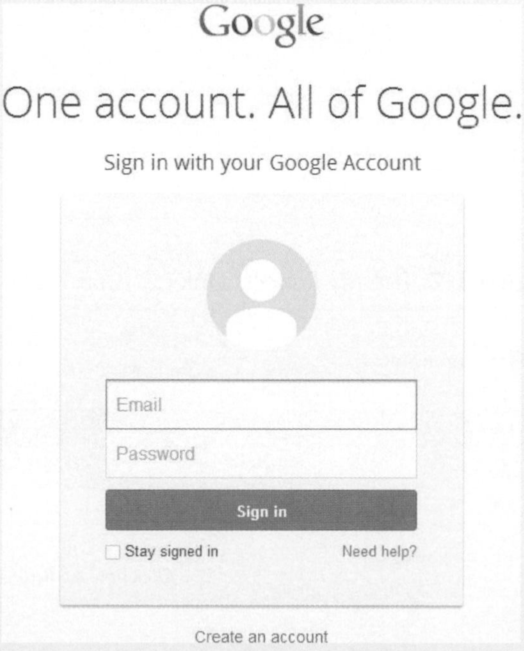

NOTE: If this is the first time you have used App Inventor with the Google account that you are signed in as, you will see a screen indicating that App Inventor is requesting permission to access your Google account. Click the *Allow* button.

Step 4: Next, you will see the *My Projects* screen, as shown in Figure 1-6. This screen normally displays a list of all the App Inventor projects that you have created. From this screen, you can open a project, delete a project, download and upload projects, and perform other actions. There are no projects listed in the screen shown in Figure 1-6 because we haven't created any yet. Any time that you want to display this screen, you simply click the *My Projects* link, as shown in Figure 1-7.

Figure 1-6 The *My Projects* Screen (*Source:* MIT App Inventor 2)

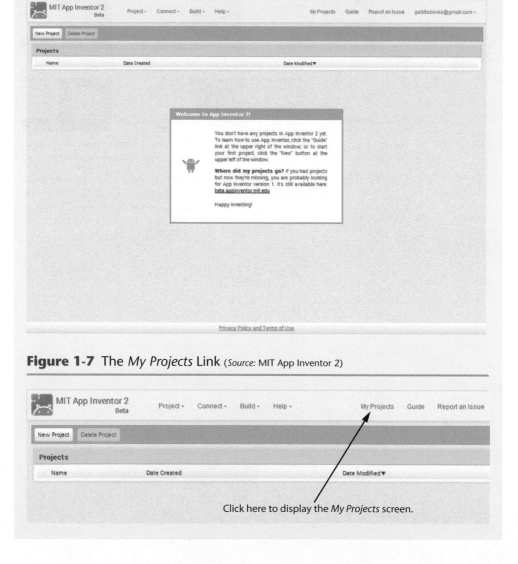

Figure 1-7 The *My Projects* Link (*Source:* MIT App Inventor 2)

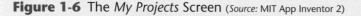

Click here to display the *My Projects* screen.

Step 5: To create a new project, click the *New Project* button, as shown in Figure 1-8. This will display the dialog box shown in Figure 1-9, prompting you to enter the name of the project that you are creating. You must follow these rules when naming a project:

- The project name must begin with an alphabetical letter.
- After the first letter, the remaining characters can be alphabetical letters, numbers, or underscore characters (_).
- You cannot have spaces in a project name.

When you create a project, you should give it a name that describes it. Because this is your first project, enter *MyFirstProject* as the name, and then click the *OK* button.

Figure 1-8 Click the *New* Button to Start a New Project (*Source:* MIT App Inventor 2)

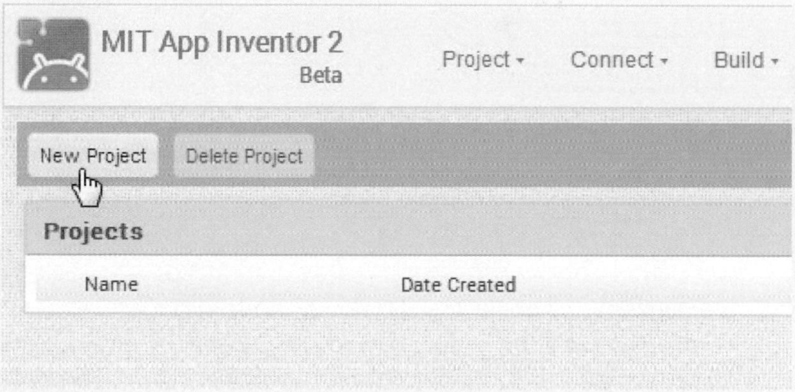

Figure 1-9 Specify a Project Name (*Source:* MIT App Inventor 2)

Step 6: You should now see the screen shown in Figure 1-10. This screen is known as the Designer. When you are developing an app, you will use the Designer to create the app's screen. We will discuss the Designer in greater detail later in the chapter.

Next you will open the Blocks Editor. Click the *Blocks* button in the upper-right area of the screen, as shown in Figure 1-11. The Blocks Editor will appear as shown in Figure 1-12.

Figure 1-10 The *Designer* (*Source:* MIT App Inventor 2)

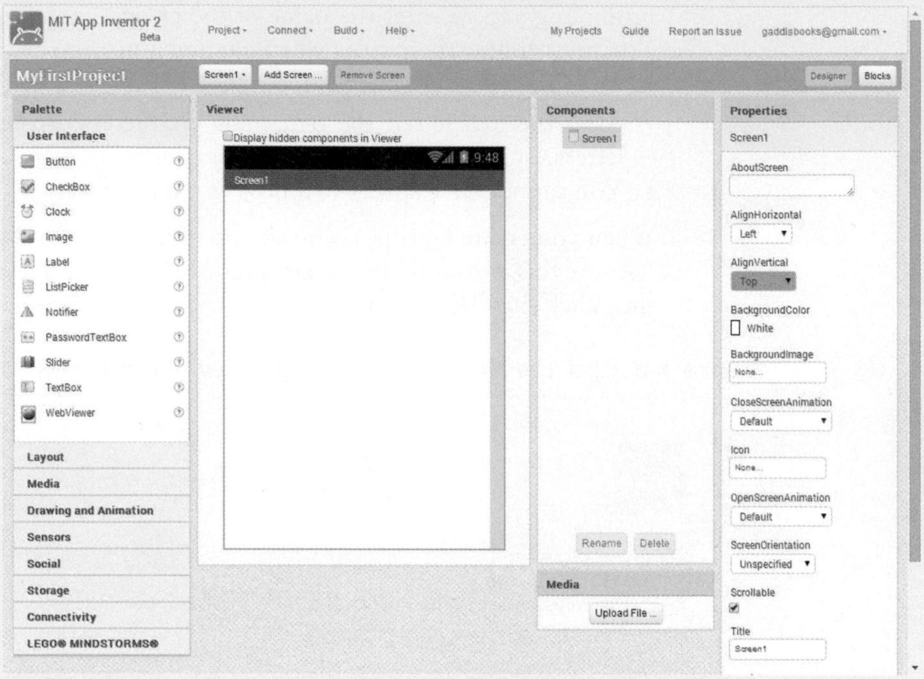

Figure 1-11 Click the *Open the Blocks Editor* Button (*Source:* MIT App Inventor 2)

Click here to open
the *Blocks editor*.

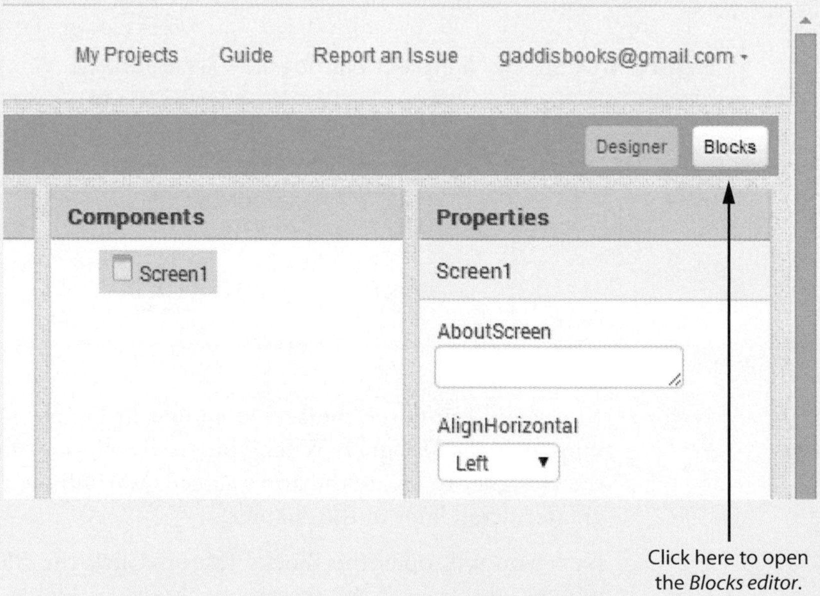

Step 7: The next step is to create a new Android emulator. As shown in Figure 1-13, click *Connect* at the top of the screen, and then click

Figure 1-12 The *Blocks Editor* (*Source:* MIT App Inventor 2)

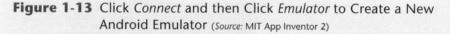

Figure 1-13 Click *Connect* and then Click *Emulator* to Create a New Android Emulator (*Source:* MIT App Inventor 2)

Emulator on the menu that appears. It might take several minutes for the emulator to be created in the computer's memory. Once the emulator has been created and initialized, it will appear as shown in Figure 1-14.

NOTE: In the Windows task bar, the emulator will be represented by an Android Icon ( ).

Figure 1-14 The Android Emulator (*Source:* Microsoft Corporation)

Step 8:   If you plan to continue with the next tutorial at this time, leave App Inventor open in your browser and the emulator running. If you plan to continue with the next tutorial at a later time, close the emulator and sign out of App Inventor by clicking your account email, which appears in the upper-right corner of the window, and then clicking *Sign out*. This is shown in Figure 1-15.

Figure 1-15 Signing Out (*Source:* MIT App Inventor 2)

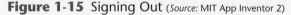

Let's take a closer look at the various parts of App Inventor.

The Designer

When you create an app with App Inventor, you will use the Designer to create the app's screen. The Designer is organized into the following columns, which are identified in Figure 1-16:

- The Palette column
- The Viewer column
- The Components column
- The Media column
- The Properties column

Figure 1-16 The Designer (*Source:* MIT App Inventor 2)

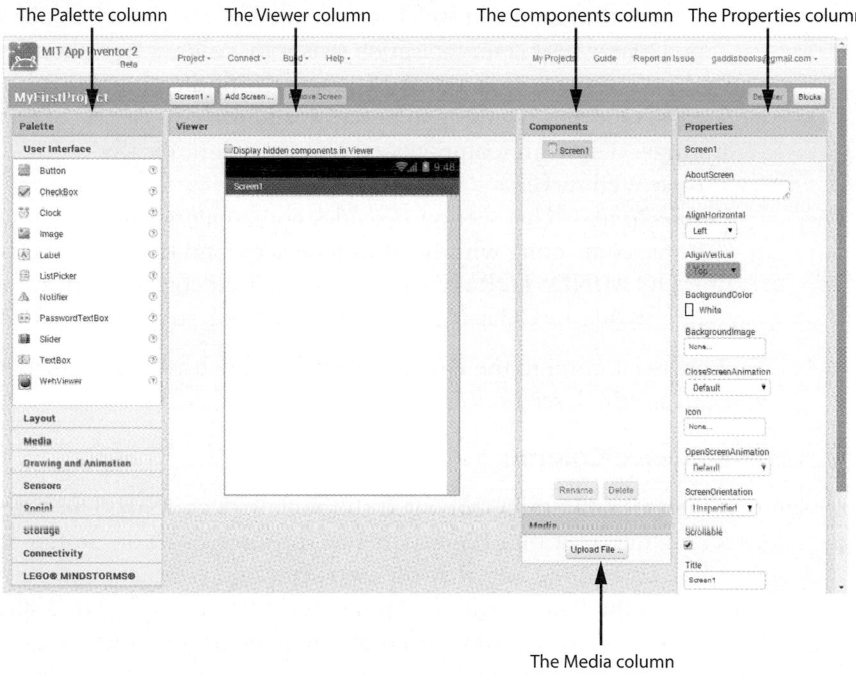

The Palette column   The Viewer column   The Components column   The Properties column

The Media column

Let's take a closer look at each of these columns.

The Palette Column

The leftmost column in the Designer is known as the Palette. The Palette provides a list of components that you can use to build your app. A *component* is an item that performs a specific purpose within an app. For example, an Image component displays an image on the screen, a Button component appears as a button that the user can touch, a Texting component sends and receives text messages, a PhoneCall component causes the phone to dial a number, and so forth. When you are creating an app, you select the components that you need from the Palette, and insert them into the app.

The Palette is divided into sections that each contain a group of components. Each section represents a category of components. The different sections, or categories, are:

> *User Interface*—These are the fundamental components for building an app's screen. If you want the app to have a button that the user can click, an image

that is displayed on the app's screen, a text box that the user can type input into, or various other basic components, you will find them here.

Layout—This section provides components for organizing other components on the app's screen. They provide ways to arrange components horizontally, vertically, or in rows and columns.

Media—This section provides components for taking photos, recording and playing videos, recording and playing sounds, picking images from the phone's gallery, recognizing speech, and converting text to speech.

Drawing and Animation—This section provides components for creating simple drawings and animations.

Sensors—These components allow your app to access the device's accelerometer (to detect shaking and movement), location sensor (to detect the device's location via GPS and/or network data), and orientation sensor (to detect the device's orientation, or the manner in which it is tilted). There is also a barcode scanner component and a near field communication sensor that allows two phones to exchange data.

Social—These are components that work with the phone's contact list, make phone calls, send and receive text messages, and perform certain operations with Twitter.

Storage—These are components that store data locally on the device or remotely on a Web server.

Connectivity—This section provides components for launching external applications, connecting with Bluetooth devices, and browsing the Web.

LEGO® MINDSTORM®—These specialized components are used to connect an app with a LEGO® MINDSTORM® NXT robot using Bluetooth.

You open a section in the Palette column simply by clicking its name. In Figure 1-16, you can see the *User Interface* section is open.

The Viewer Column

The Viewer column appears next to the Palette column. The Viewer column shows a rectangular area that represents the app's screen. You design an app's *user interface* (the part of the app that the user sees, and interacts with) by dragging components from the Palette and dropping them onto the simulated screen in the Viewer. Figure 1-17 shows a Button component being created by dragging it from the Palette to the Viewer. You can arrange the components on the simulated screen to make the app's interface look the way you want it.

Figure 1-17 Creating a Component by Dragging it from the Palette to the Viewer (*Source:* MIT App Inventor 2)

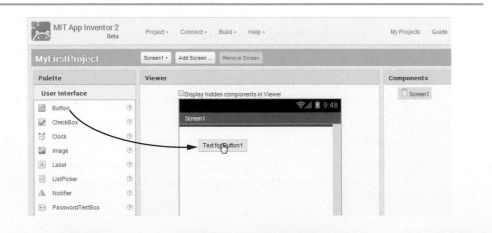

> **NOTE:** A subtle, but important concept to keep in mind is that the icons that are shown in the Palette are the *types* of components that you can create. When you drag a component from the Palette, you are selecting the type of component that you want. When you drop it into the Viewer, an actual component of the selected type is created.

Keep in mind, however, that the Viewer column does not truly show a *WYSIWYG* (*What You See Is What You Get*) display. The components that you place on the simulated screen in the Viewer might appear slightly different on the emulator screen, or on the device that you have connected to your system. You will be aware of any differences quickly because the components that you drop onto the simulated Viewer screen appear immediately on the emulator or the connected device. For example, Figure 1-18 shows an app screen in the Viewer, and the same screen displayed in the emulator. Notice that the shapes of the text boxes (the rectangles that let the user enter data) and the button are slightly different between the two screens, and the spacing between the components is also different. Think of the Viewer as a tool for arranging components on an app's screen, but always compare your layout with the actual display on the emulator or your connected device.

Figure 1-18 A Screen in the Viewer and the Emulator (*Source:* MIT App Inventor 2)

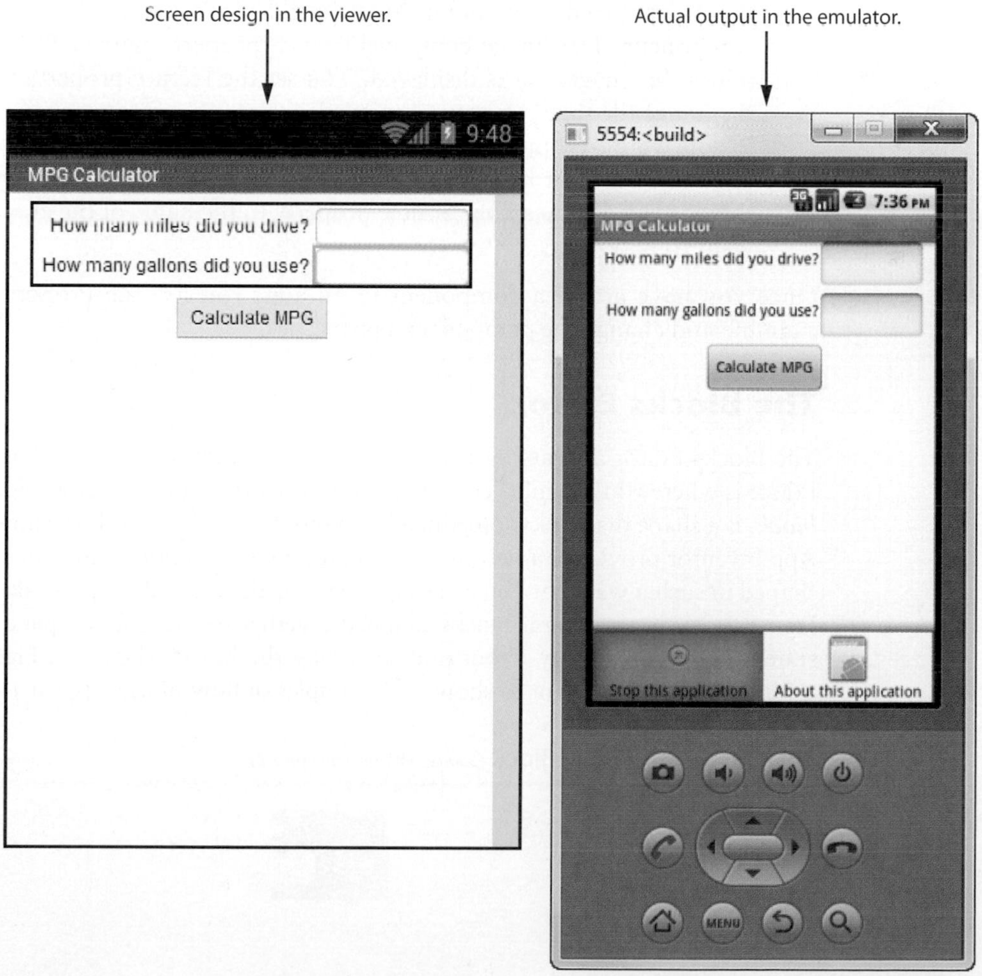

The Components Column

The Components column shows a hierarchical tree listing all of the components that you have placed in your app. Each time you drag a component from the Palette and drop it onto the Viewer, an entry representing that component appears in the Component column. You can use the Component column to select any component in your app.

The Media Column

Just below the Components column is the Media column. The Media column allows you to manage the media files (images, videos, and audio files) that you want to use in your app. Because App Inventor stores your apps in the cloud, you have to upload any media files that you want to use in an app. The Media column allows you to upload such files to the App Inventor server, download them from the server to your computer, and delete them from the server when they are no longer needed.

The Properties Column

A component's appearance and other characteristics, are determined by the component's properties. Here are just a few examples:

- If you want to display text on your device's screen, you will use a Label component. The Label component has a property named Text. You set the Label component's Text property to the text that you want to display.
- If you want to display an image on your device's screen, you will use an Image component. The Image component has a property named Picture that determines the image that is displayed. You set the Picture property to the name of the image file that you want displayed.
- If you want an app to play a sound, you will use a Sound component. The Sound component has a property named Source that determines the audio file that is played. You set the Source property to the name of the audio file that you want to play.

Once you have added a component to an app, you use the Properties column to examine and change the component's properties.

The Blocks Editor

The Blocks Editor appears in its own window, separate from the Designer. The Blocks Editor is where you assemble code blocks that perform actions. A code block, or simply a *block*, is a shape that looks something like a puzzle piece. Figure 1-19 shows an example. App Inventor provides numerous blocks that represent actions and data. The blocks are shaped in such a way that you can snap them together to make a program. For example, Figure 1-20 shows several blocks snapped together to make a complete programming statement. (Don't worry about understanding the blocks shown in Figures 1-19 and 1-20. They are just meant to show you examples of how blocks appear.)

Figure 1-19 A Code Block (*Source:* MIT App Inventor 2)

Figure 1-20 A Programming Statement Constructed from Code Blocks
(*Source:* MIT App Inventor 2)

The Blocks Editor is shown in Figure 1-21. Notice that a workspace is provided for assembling blocks. You drag blocks onto the workspace, and snap them together to create programming statements.

The column on the left side of the Blocks Editor provides access to the blocks that you can use. Notice in Figure 1-22 that the Blocks column is organized in the following manner: Built-In, Screen1, and Any component. Each of these provides a separate set of blocks that you can use in your app. Here is a summary of each:

Built-In—The blocks that you find here are the basic blocks that make up the App Inventor language. You have the built-in blocks available to you in every app.

Screen1—Each time you add a component to Screen1 in the Designer, a set of component blocks are added to this section. Component blocks are blocks that perform an action on a specific component that you have added to the app.

Any component—This section contains advanced blocks that allow us to work with any component in the app.

Figure 1-21 The Blocks Editor (*Source:* MIT App Inventor 2)

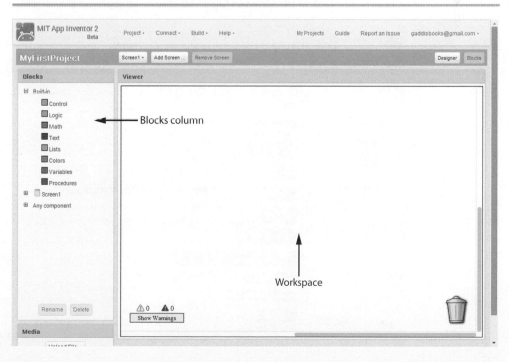

Figure 1-22 The Blocks Column (*Source:* MIT App Inventor 2)

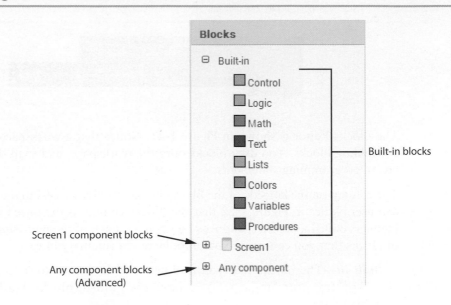

The Built-In Blocks

Notice in Figure 1-22 that the Built-in Blocks section is organized into the following categories: *Control*, *Logic*, *Math*, *Text*, *Lists*, *Colors*, *Variables*, and *Procedures*. When you click one of the categories, a *drawer* containing blocks opens. For example, Figure 1-23 shows what happens when you click *Math*. A drawer containing various math blocks opens. When you open a drawer, you can click and drag a block onto the workspace.

Figure 1-23 The Math Drawer Opened (*Source:* MIT App Inventor 2)

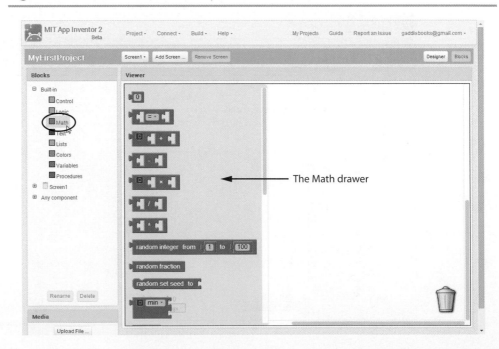

The topmost area of the App Inventor screen is shown in Figure 1-24. The bar at the top shows the following items:

Project—When you click this item, a menu appears. The Project menu allows you to start, save, import, and export projects.

Connect—When you click this item, a menu appears. The Connect menu allows you to connect to an Android device or the Android emulator.

Build—When you click this item, a menu appears. The Build menu allows you to package an app so it can be shared with others.

Help—When you click this item, a menu appears. The Help menu provides access to documentation, tutorials, and the App Inventor forum.

My Projects—When you click this item, the My Projects screen is displayed. (The screen was previously shown in Figure 1-6.) The My Projects screen displays a list of all the App Inventor projects that you have created. From this screen, you can open a project, delete a project, download and upload projects, and perform other actions.

Guide—Clicking this item opens a separate Web page containing the App Inventor documentation.

Report an Issue—Clicking this item takes you to the App Inventor support forum.

Figure 1-24 Top Part of the App Inventor Screen (*Source:* MIT App Inventor 2)

A trash can icon appears in the lower-right corner of the Blocks Editor, as shown on the left in Figure 1-25. You can delete blocks that you no longer need by dragging them onto the trash can, as shown on the right in Figure 1-25.

Figure 1-25 The Trash Can Icon (*Source:* MIT App Inventor 2)

 TIP: You can also delete a block by selecting it and then pressing the Delete key on the keyboard.

Checkpoint

1.6 True or false: *My First Project* is a legal project name in App Inventor.

1.7 What part of App Inventor do you use to create an app's screen?

1.8 What is a user interface?

1.9 Does the Viewer show a *WYSIWYG* (*What You See Is What You Get*) representation of an app's screen?

1.10 What is the Palette column?

1.11 What is the Viewer column?

1.12 What is the Components column?

1.13 What is the Media column?

1.14 What is the Properties column?

1.15 What is the Blocks Editor?

1.16 What is a code block (or simply, a block)?

1.17 How do you create an emulator and connect to it?

 ## 1.4 Getting Hands-On with App Inventor

You are almost ready to create your first app with App Inventor. There are a few more fundamental concepts and procedures that we need to discuss, however. We will cover those, and then in Tutorial 1-2 and Tutorial 1-3, you will create the Hello World app.

Managing Projects

You manage all of your App Inventor projects from the My Projects screen, which is shown in Figure 1-26. When you go to appinventor.mit.edu and click the *Create* button, you will be taken to the My Projects screen, unless you were actively working on a project the last time you used App Inventor. If that is the case, you will be

Figure 1-26 The My Projects Screen (*Source:* MIT App Inventor 2)

MIT App Inventor 2 Beta	Project ▾	Connect ▾	Build ▾	Help ▾		My Projects	Guide	Report an Issue	gaddisbooks@gmail.com ▾

New Project   Delete Project

Projects

	Name	Date Created	Date Modified ▾
☐	**MilesPerGallon**	2014 May 1 11:23:52	2014 May 1 11:23:52
☐	**Guitar**	2014 May 1 11:23:40	2014 May 1 11:23:40
☐	**GoodDog**	2014 May 1 11:23:30	2014 May 1 11:23:30
☐	**MyFirstProject**	2014 Apr 24 14:14:36	2014 Apr 30 17:01:13
☐	**Test**	2014 Apr 30 16:49:00	2014 Apr 30 16:49:10

taken directly to your most recent project in the Designer. From the Designer or the Blocks Editor, you can click the *My Projects* link at the top of the screen, as shown in Figure 1-27, to go to the My Projects screen.

Figure 1-27 The My Projects Link at the Top of the App Inventor Screen
(*Source:* MIT App Inventor 2)

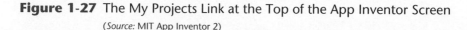

Notice that near the top of the My Projects screen (shown in Figure 1-26) there are buttons labeled *New Project* and *Delete Project*. The *New Project* button creates a new project. You used this in Tutorial 1-1, when you created the project named MyFirstProject. The *Delete Project* button deletes the project or projects that are currently selected in the project list. (You select a project by checking the checkbox that appears next to its name in the project list.)

Below these buttons, you see a list of your projects. The list shows each project's name and the date and time that it was created. To open a project, you simply click its name, and it is opened in the Designer. If you want to select a project (so you can delete it, or download its source), you click the checkbox that appears to the left of the project's name.

The App's `Screen1` Component

In App Inventor, the most fundamental type of component that an app can have is a Screen. In fact, every app *must* have a Screen component, which acts as a container for all the other components making up the app's user interface. When you start a new project, App Inventor automatically creates an empty Screen component.

Each component in an app must have a unique name that identifies it. When a component is added to an app, App Inventor automatically gives the component a default name. The empty Screen component that is automatically created in an app is named `Screen1`. Figure 1-28 shows the `Screen1` component, as displayed in the viewer.

Each time you add a component to an app, the component's name appears in the Component column. You can see in Figure 1-28 that `Screen1` is listed in the Component column. If you need to work with a particular component, you can select its name in the Component column.

NOTE: The Component column allows you to rename components. Normally, you will want to change the default name that App Inventor gives a component, because the default name does not indicate the component's purpose. The only exception is the `Screen1` component. App Inventor does not allow you to change the name of the `Screen1` component.

Figure 1-28 An App's Screen in the Viewer (*Source:* MIT App Inventor 2)

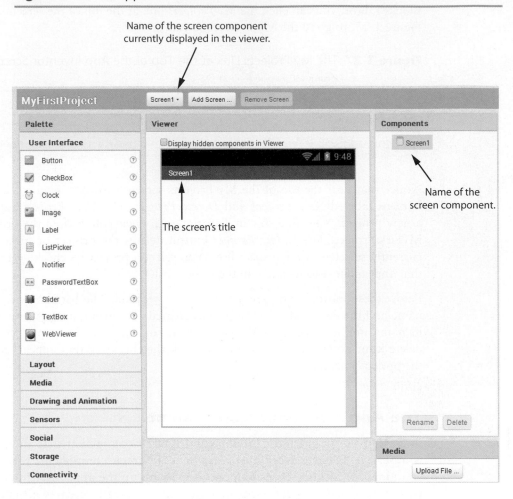

Working with the Properties Column

The appearance and other characteristics of a component are determined by the component's properties. When you select a component (either by clicking the component in the Viewer, or clicking its name in the Components column), that component's properties are displayed in the Properties column. For example, when the Screen1 component is selected, its properties are displayed in the Properties column as shown in Figure 1-29.

For example, look at the Properties column in Figure 1-29 and notice that one of Screen1's properties is named Title. The Title property determines the text that is displayed in the screen's title bar (the bar that appears at the top of the screen). As you can see from the figure, the default value of this property is *Screen1*. The text that is entered for the Screen1 component's Title property is displayed in the screen's title bar, both in the Viewer, and in the emulator or other connected device. This is shown in Figure 1-30.

In most cases, you will want to change the value of the Screen1 component's Title property to something that makes more sense to the user. For example, Figure 1-31 shows the Viewer, the Properties Column, and the emulator after we have changed the Title property to *My First App*. (The Screen1 component has several other properties, and a summary of all of them appears at the end of this chapter.)

Figure 1-29 The Properties Column, Showing the Selected Component's Properties (*Source:* MIT App Inventor 2)

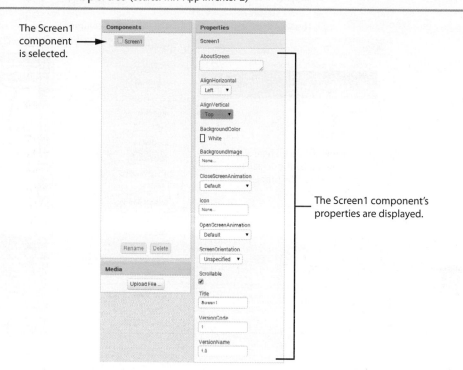

The Screen1 component is selected.

The Screen1 component's properties are displayed.

Figure 1-30 The Screen1 Component's Title Property Set to the Text *Screen1* (*Source:* MIT App Inventor 2)

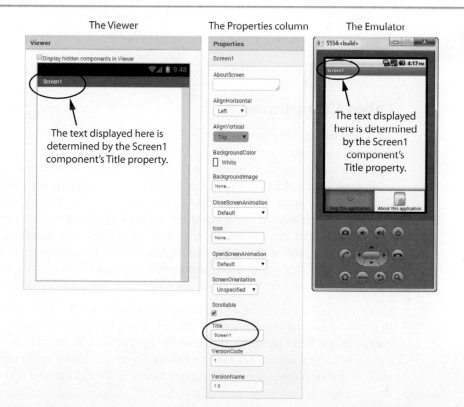

The Viewer

The Properties column

The Emulator

The text displayed here is determined by the Screen1 component's Title property.

The text displayed here is determined by the Screen1 component's Title property.

Figure 1-31 The `Screen1` Component's Title Property Set to the Text *My First App* (*Source:* MIT App Inventor 2)

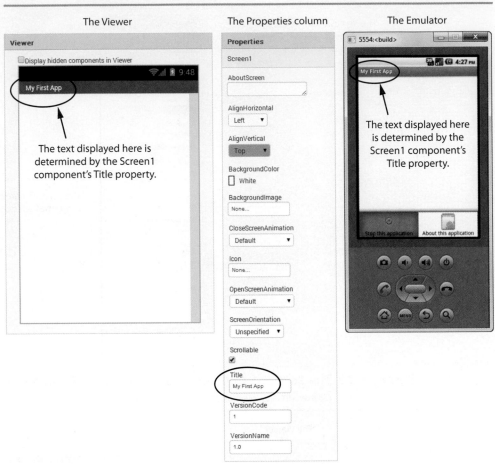

Label Components

Another basic component is the Label. A Label component displays text on the app's screen. You create a Label component by dragging it from the User Interface section of the Palette and onto the app's screen in the Viewer, as shown in Figure 1-32. When you create Label components in an app, they are given default names such as `Label1`, `Label2`, and so forth. For example, Figure 1-33 shows the Components column after a Label component has been created in an app. As you can see in the figure, the name of the component is `Label1`. (Also, notice that the name `Label1` is highlighted in the Components column, and in the Viewer, the component is outlined with a green border. This indicates that the component is currently selected.)

Once you have created a Label component, you set its Text property to the text that you want the component to display. For example, in Figure 1-34, the `Label1` component's Text property (look in the Properties column) is set to the value *Text for Label1*. As a result, *Text for Label1* is displayed on the app's screen in the viewer and on the emulator or other connected device. To change the text that is displayed

Figure 1-32 Creating a Label Component (*Source:* MIT App Inventor 2)

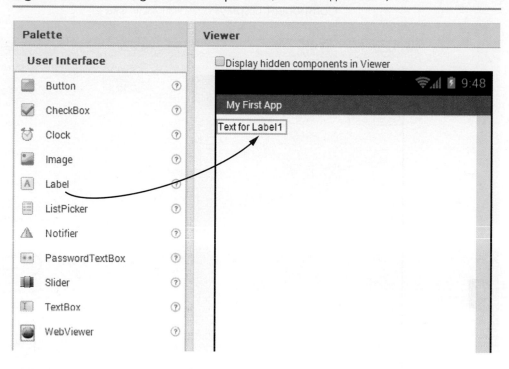

Figure 1-33 The Name of the Component Shown in the Components Column
(*Source:* MIT App Inventor 2)

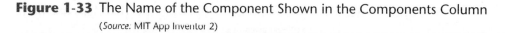

by a Label component, just make sure the component is selected in the Components tree, and then change the value of the component's Text property in the Properties column. (If the component is not currently selected, simply click its name in the Components column to select it.)

For example, Figure 1-35 shows an app with a Label component, with its Text property set to *Apps are fun to create!* The text is displayed by the component in the Viewer and on the emulator.

Figure 1-34 A Label Component's Text Property Determines the Text that the Component Displays (*Source:* MIT App Inventor 2)

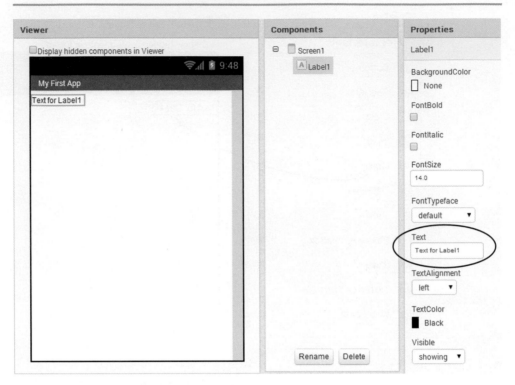

Figure 1-35 A Label Component Displaying the Text *Apps are fun to create!* (*Source:* MIT App Inventor 2)

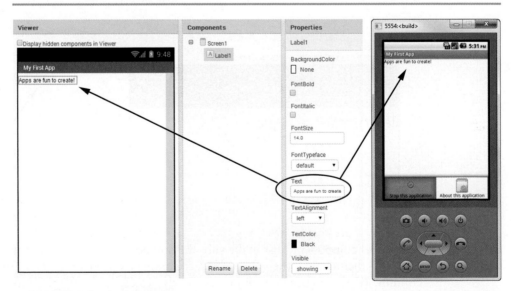

Label Width and Height

Label components have two properties, Width and Height, that determine the label's size on the app's screen. Figure 1-36 shows where a Label component's Width and Height properties are located in the Properties column. Notice that both properties are set to the value *Automatic* by default.

Figure 1-36 The Label Component's Width and Height Properties
(*Source:* MIT App Inventor 2)

When you click the Width or the Height properties, a small dialog box appears, as shown in Figure 1-37. (The dialog box is the same for both the Width and the Height properties.) The possible values that you can set the Width and Height properties to are:

Automatic—When a component's Width property is set to *Automatic*, the component's width will automatically adjust to accommodate the size of the label's text.

When a component's Height property is set to *Fill Parent*, the label's height will automatically adjust to accommodate the size of the label's text.

Fill parent—When a component's Width property is set to *Fill Parent*, the component will be as wide as the container (such as the Screen1 component) that it is enclosed in. When a component's Height property is set to *Fill Parent*, the component will be as high as the container (such as the `Screen1` component) that it is enclosed in.

A Specified Number of Pixels—You can specify a specific number of pixels for a component's width and/or height. You should avoid this in most cases, because different devices have different screen sizes. Specifying a specific number of pixels for a component's width or height will cause the component to appear differently on different devices.

Figure 1-37 Dialog Box to Set the Width Property *(Source:* MIT App Inventor 2)

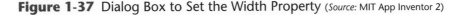

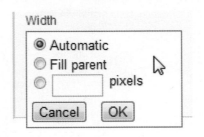

Changing a Component's Name

A component's name identifies the component in blocks that make up the app's code, and in the App Inventor environment. When you create a component, App Inventor automatically gives it a name (we refer to this as the default name). For example, suppose you created three Label components in an app. App Inventor would name these components `Label1`, `Label2`, and `Label3`. Default names are not very descriptive, so you should always change a component's name to something that is more meaningful. A component's name should reflect the purpose of the component.

For example, suppose you are creating an app that has several Label components, and one of them is used to display a phone number. A default name such as `Label1` does not convey the component's purpose. A name such as `LabelPhoneNumber` would be much better. When you are working with the app's code blocks, and you see the name `LabelPhoneNumber`, you will know precisely which Label component the code block is referring to.

In the Designer, you can use the Components column to change the name of any component (except the `Screen1` component). Here are the steps:

1. Click the name of the component in the Components column to select it.
2. Click the *Rename* button at the bottom of the Components column.
3. The *Rename Component* dialog box shown in Figure 1-38 will appear. Enter the component's new name and click OK.

In Figure 1-38, we are changing the name of the `Label1` component to `LabelMessage`. Figure 1-39 shows the Components column after the component's name has been changed.

Figure 1-38 Rename Component Dialog Box (*Source:* MIT App Inventor 2)

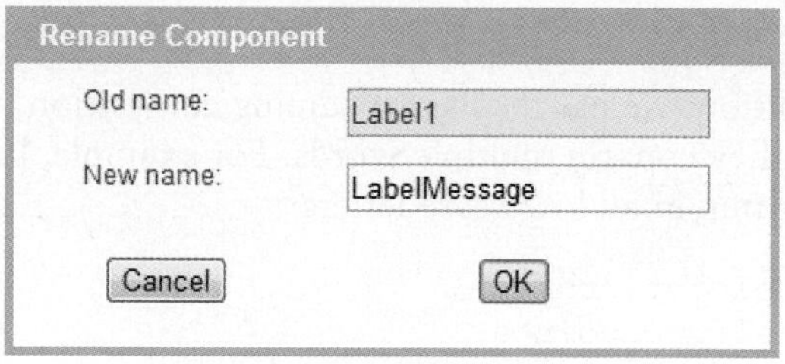

Figure 1-39 The Component's Name is Changed to `LabelMessage`
(*Source:* MIT App Inventor 2)

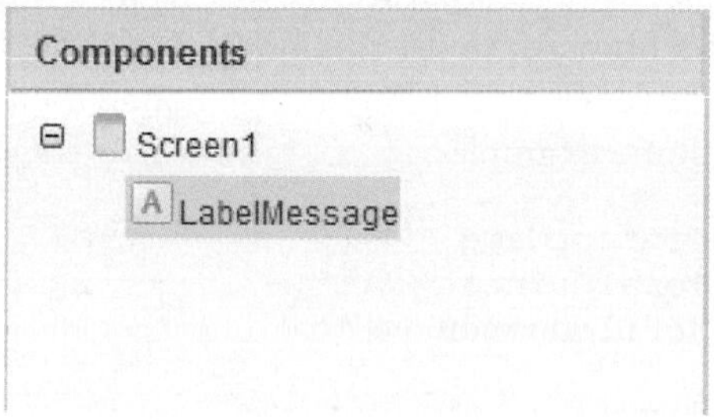

Rules and Conventions for Naming Components

When naming a component, you must follow these simple rules:

- Component names can contain only letters, numbers, and underscores (_).
- The first character of a component name must be a letter.
- Component names cannot contain spaces.

Table 1-1 lists some example component names and indicates whether each one is legal or illegal.

Table 1-1 Legal and illegal component names (*Source:* Pearson Education, Inc.)

Name	Legal or Illegal?
`3rdTestScoreLabel`	Illegal because component names must start with a letter
`Label*Mobile*Number`	Illegal because the * character is not allowed. Component names can contain only letters, numbers, and underscores.
`Label Contact Name`	Illegal because component names cannot contain spaces
`Label_Contact_Name`	Legal

Optional Conventions Used in this Book

Because a component's name should reflect the component's purpose, programmers often find themselves creating names that are made of multiple words. In this book, we always begin a component's name with a word that indicates the type of component. For example, a Label component's name will always begin with the word *Label*. This is not a requirement, but rather a convention that we follow in this book.

In addition, we use the Pascal naming convention, which makes names easier to read when they contain multiple words. For example, look at the following names, which are written in all lowercase letters:

```
labelcontactname
labeltotalpoints
labelmobilenumber
```

Unfortunately, these names are not easily read by the human eye because the words are not separated. Because we cannot have spaces in component names, we need to find another way to separate the words in a multiword name to make it more readable to the human eye. In this book, we address this problem using the Pascal case naming convention. In a Pascal case name, the first letter of each word is capitalized. Here are some examples:

```
LabelContactName
LabelTotalPoints
LabelMobileNumber
```

Deleting Components

If you add a component to an app and later decide that you don't want the component, it's easy to delete it. Just click on the component's name in the Components column to select it, and then click the *Delete* button that appears at the bottom of the Components column.

Button Components

Buttons are common components in mobile apps, as well as desktop applications. The user can click a button to make some action take place. In App Inventor, you create a Button component by dragging it from the User Interface section of the Palette to the app's screen in the Viewer. This is shown in Figure 1-40.

Button components have a Text property, which holds the text that is displayed on the face of the button. When you create a Button component, it is given a default name such as `Button1`, `Button2`, and so forth, and its Text property will be set to *Text for Button1*, *Text for Button2*, and so forth. Once you create a Button component, you should change its name to something that is more descriptive. You should also change the component's Text property to indicate what the button will do when it is clicked. For example, a button that calculates an average might have the text *Calculate Average* displayed on it. To change a Button component's Text property, just select the component in the Components tree, and then change the value of the component's Text property in the Properties column.

Figure 1-41 shows an example of an app with a Button component. Notice in the figure that we have renamed the component to `ButtonExample`, and we have changed its Text property to *Click Me!* The value of the Text property is displayed on the face of the button in both the viewer and the emulator.

Figure 1-40 Creating a Button Component (*Source:* MIT App Inventor 2)

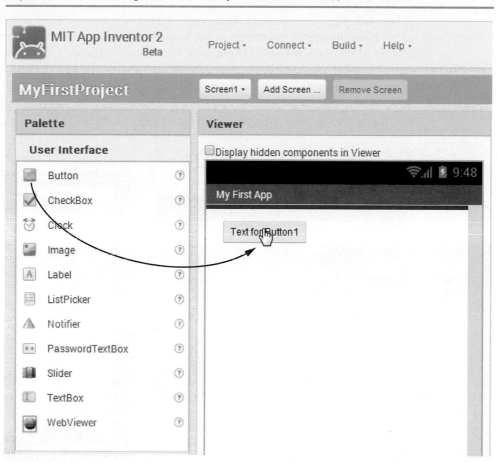

Figure 1-41 A Button Component Displaying the Text *Click Me!* (*Source:* MIT App Inventor 2)

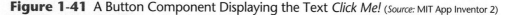

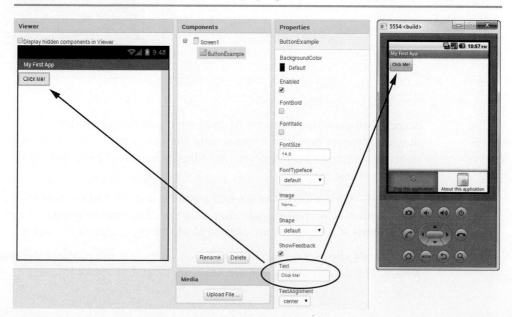

Screen Alignment

When you place components on an app's screen, the components are arranged vertically, from the top of the screen to the bottom of the screen. By default, they are also aligned along the left edge of the screen. For example, Figure 1-42 shows an app with three Button components. The image on the left shows the app's screen in the Viewer, and the image on the right shows the app in the emulator.

Figure 1-42 An App with Three Button Components (*Source:* MIT App Inventor 2)

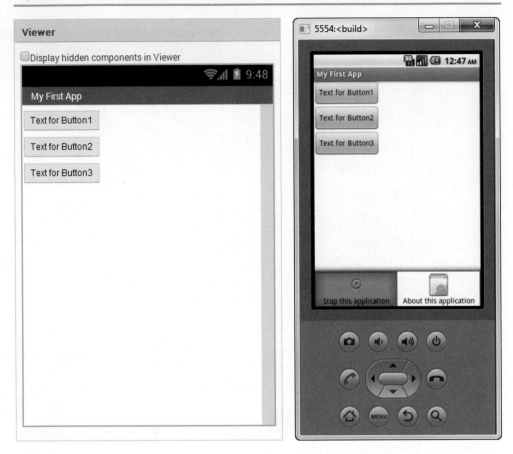

Screen components have an AlignHorizontal property (shown in Figure 1-43) that determines how the components that are contained in the screen are horizontally aligned. You can set the AlignHorizontal property to one of the following values:

- **Left**—Components are aligned along the left edge of the screen
- **Center**—Components are aligned in the center of the screen
- **Right**—Components are aligned along the right edge of the screen

Figure 1-44 shows examples of how each of these settings affect the contents of the screen. The default setting for the AlignHorizontal property is Left.

Figure 1-43 The AlignHorizontal Property (*Source:* MIT App Inventor 2)

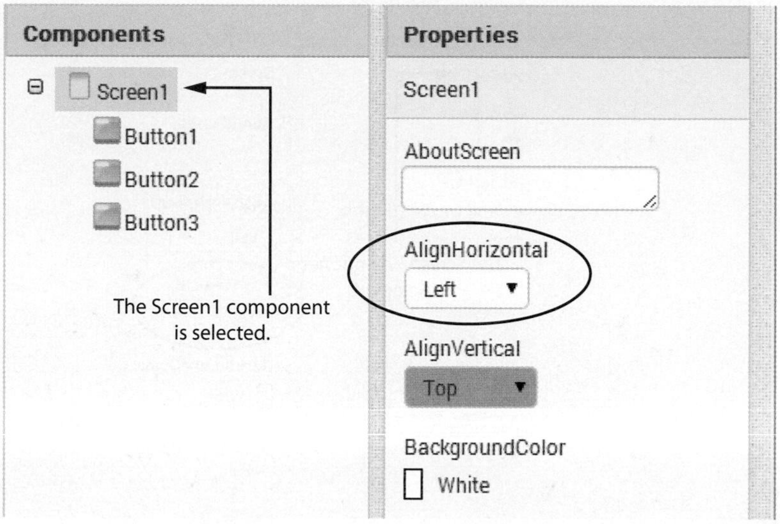

Figure 1-44 Examples of the AlignHorizontal Property Settings (*Source:* MIT App Inventor 2)

Screen components also have an AlignVertical property (shown in Figure 1-45) that determines how the components that are contained in the screen are vertically aligned. You can change the AlignVertical property only if the screen is not scrollable (the Scrollable property is not checked). If this is the case, you can set the AlignVertical property to one of the following values:

- **Top**—Components are aligned along the top of the screen
- **Center**—Components are aligned in the center of the screen
- **Bottom**—Components are aligned along the bottom of the screen

Figure 1-46 shows examples of how each of these settings affect the contents of the screen. (In each example, the AlignHorizontal property is set to *Center*.) The default setting for the AlignVertical property is *Top*. If the Scrollable property is checked, the components are automatically aligned to the top of the screen.

Figure 1-45 The AlignVertical Property (*Source:* MIT App Inventor 2)

Components
Screen1
Button1
Button2
Button3
The Screen1 component is selected.
Rename
Delete
Media
Upload File ...
Properties
Screen1
AboutScreen
AlignHorizontal
Left
AlignVertical
Top
BackgroundColor
White
BackgroundImage
None...
CloseScreenAnimation
Default
Icon
None...
OpenScreenAnimation
Default
ScreenOrientation
Unspecified
Scrollable
The Scrollabe property is not checked.
Title
My First App

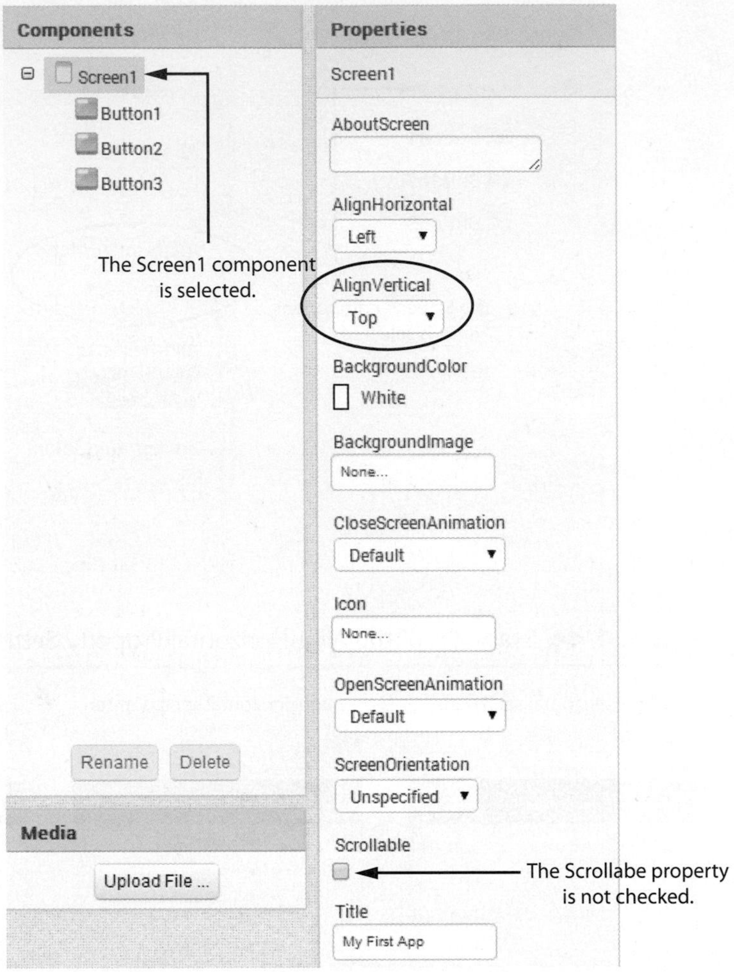

Figure 1-46 Examples of the AlignVertical Property Settings (*Source:* MIT App Inventor 2)

AlignHorizontal set to Center
AlignVertical set to Top
AlignHorizontal set to Center
AlignVertical set to Center
AlignHorizontal set to Center
AlignVertical set to Bottom
Viewer
Display hidden components in Viewer
9:48
My First App
Text for Button1
Text for Button2
Text for Button3

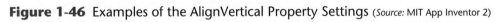

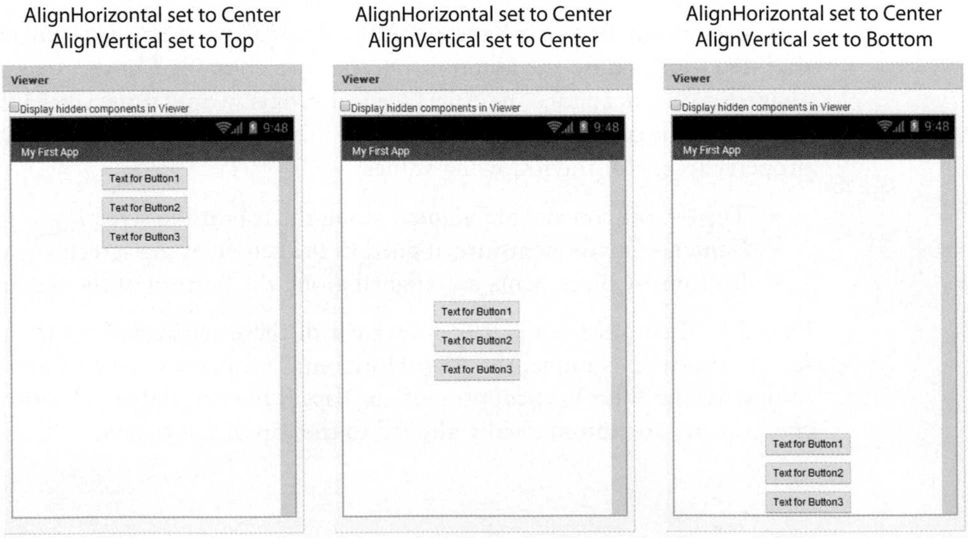

At this point, you know enough to design the screen for your first app. Tutorial 1-2 leads you through the steps to create the screen for the Hello World app.

Tutorial 1-2:
Creating the Screen for the Hello World App

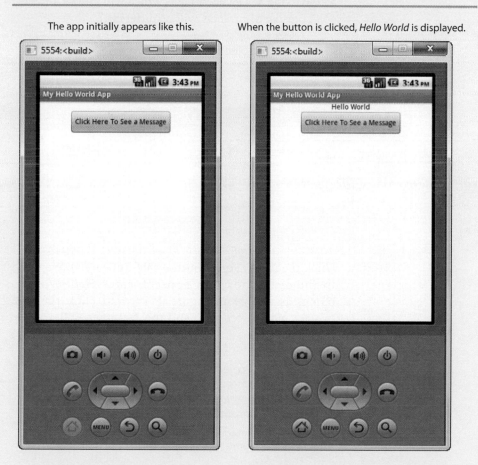

VideoNote
Creating the
Screen for the
Hello World App

When a student is learning computer programming, it is traditional to start by learning to write a *Hello World* program. A *Hello World* program is a simple program that merely displays the words *"Hello World"* on the screen. In this tutorial and the next, you will use App Inventor to create a *Hello World* app. The app will initially appear as the image on the left in Figure 1-47. Notice that

Figure 1-47 The Completed App (*Source:* MIT App Inventor 2)

The app initially appears like this.

When the button is clicked, *Hello World* is displayed.

the screen contains a button that reads *Click Here To See a Message*. When you click the button, the message *Hello World* will appear, as shown in the image on the right in the figure.

The process of creating this app is divided into two parts. In this tutorial you will create the app's screen. In the next tutorial you will use the Blocks Editor to write code that displays the *Hello World* message to appear when the user clicks the button.

Step 1: If App Inventor is already running on your computer, go to the *My Projects* page, which will appear similar to Figure 1-48. (Your list of projects will be different.)

If App Inventor is not running on your computer:

- Go to `appinventor.mit.edu` with your browser.
- Click the *Create* link that appears on that page.
- If prompted, log into your Google account.
- Go to the My Projects page, which will appear similar to Figure 1-48. (Your list of projects will be different.)

Figure 1-48 The My Projects Page *(Source: MIT App Inventor 2)*

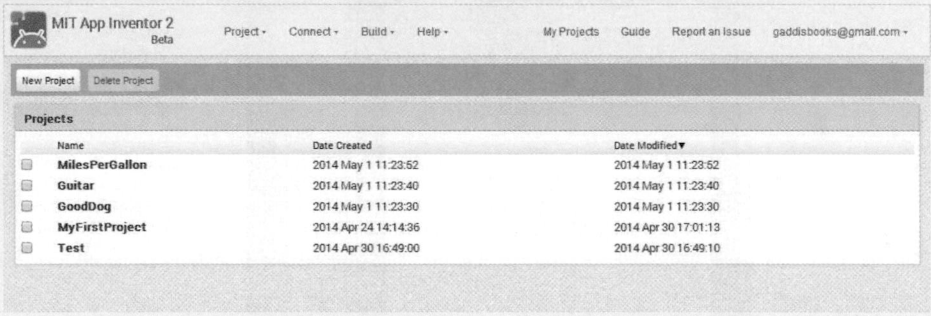

Step 2: Click the *New Project* button that appears above the list of projects. In the dialog box that appears, enter *HelloWorld* as the project name, as shown in Figure 1-49, and click the *OK* button. The project will be created, and the Designer will appear, as shown in Figure 1-50.

Figure 1-49 Enter the Project Name *(Source: MIT App Inventor 2)*

Figure 1-50 The HelloWorld Project in the Designer (*Source:* MIT App Inventor 2)

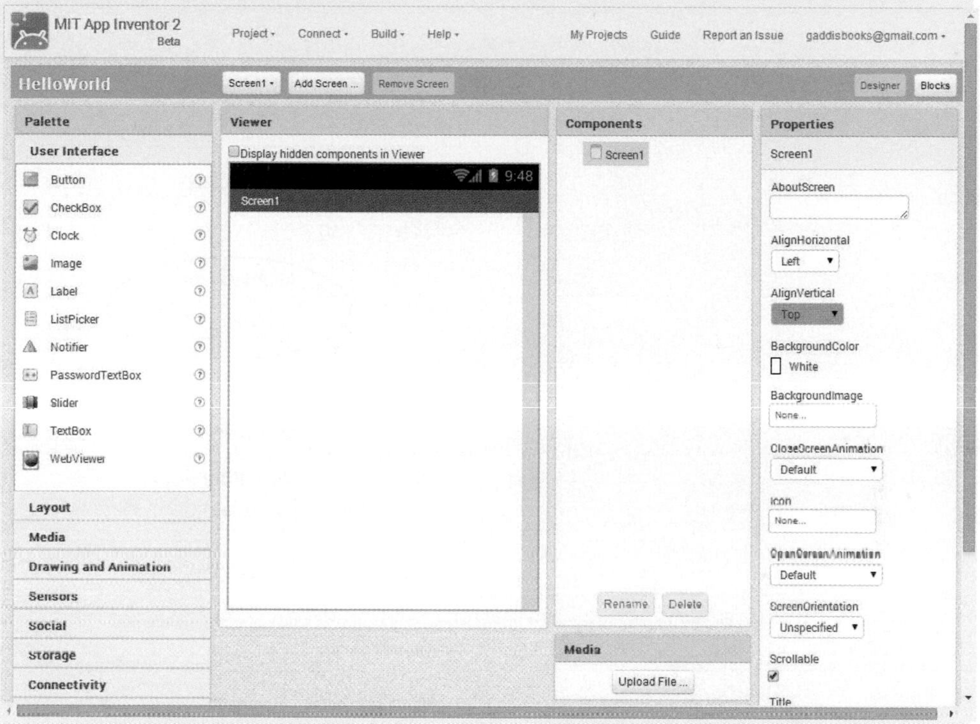

Step 3: The `Screen1` component should already be selected in the Components column. In the Properties column, change the AlignHorizontal property to *Center*, and change the Title property to read *My Hello World App*. This is shown in Figure 1-51.

Step 4: Drag a Label component from the Palette to the Viewer, as shown in Figure 1-52. This creates a Label component named `Label1`, with its Text property set to *Text for Label1*.

Step 5: Because the name `Label1` is not very descriptive, you should change the component's name. Make sure the `Label1` component is selected in the Components column, and click the *Rename* button (which appears at the bottom of the Components column). The dialog box shown in Figure 1-53 will appear. Enter `LabelMessage` as the component's new name, and click *OK*. The component's new name should now appear in the Components column, as shown in Figure 1-54.

Step 6: Make sure the `LabelMessage` component is selected in the Components column, and in the Properties column, delete the contents of the Title property. (The Title property should appear empty.) This is shown

Figure 1-51 Setting the `Screen1` Component's Properties
(*Source:* MIT App Inventor 2)

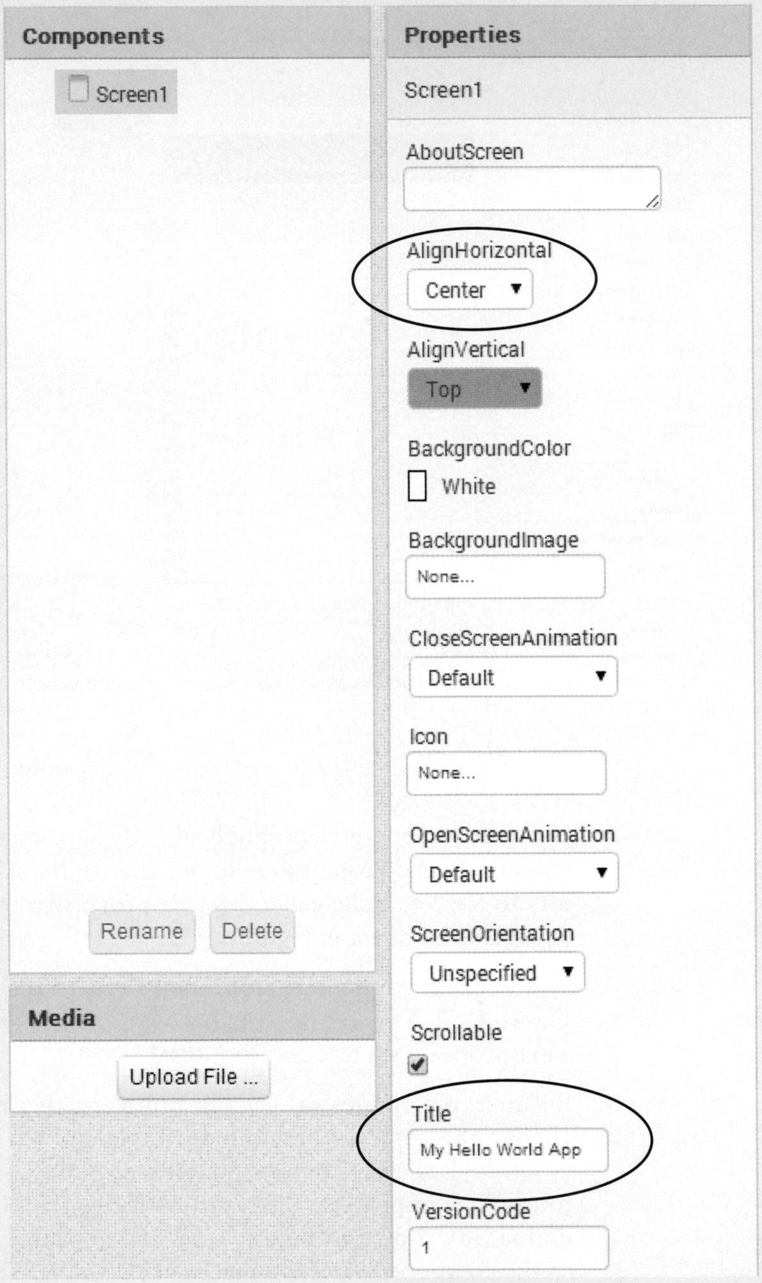

in Figure 1-55. Notice that the label now appears as a small dot in the viewer. This is because the label's Width and Height properties are both set to *Automatic*. Recall that this means the label's size will automatically

Figure 1-52 Creating the Label Component (*Source:* MIT App Inventor 2)

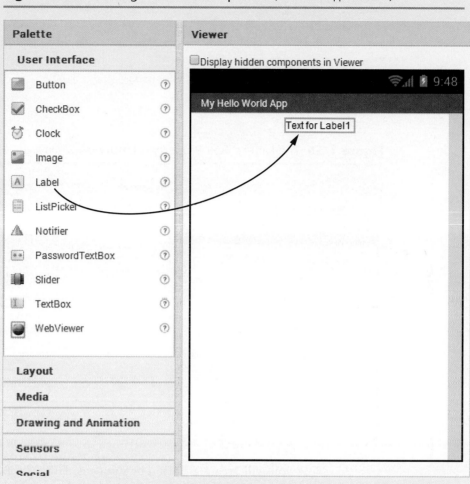

adjust to match the size of the text that it displays. Because the Text property is now empty, the label displays nothing, and its size automatically shrinks down to nothing. In fact, the only way that you can see the label in the Viewer is to select it in the Components column. The green border that indicates the component is selected will appear as a dot.

Figure 1-53 Renaming the `Label1` Component (*Source:* MIT App Inventor 2)

Rename Component	
Old name:	Label1
New name:	LabelMessage
Cancel	OK

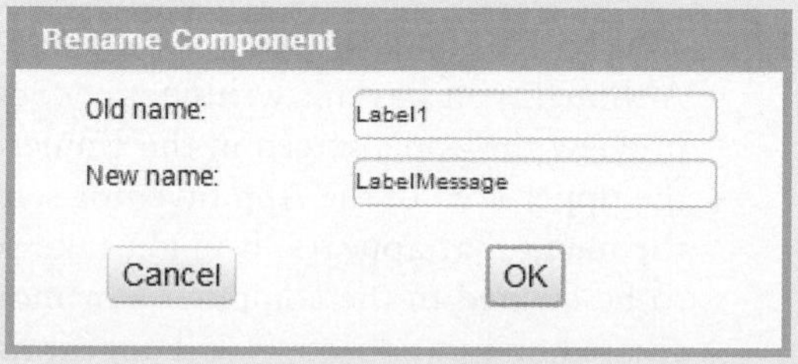

Figure 1-54 The Component Renamed (*Source:* MIT App Inventor 2)

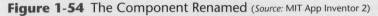

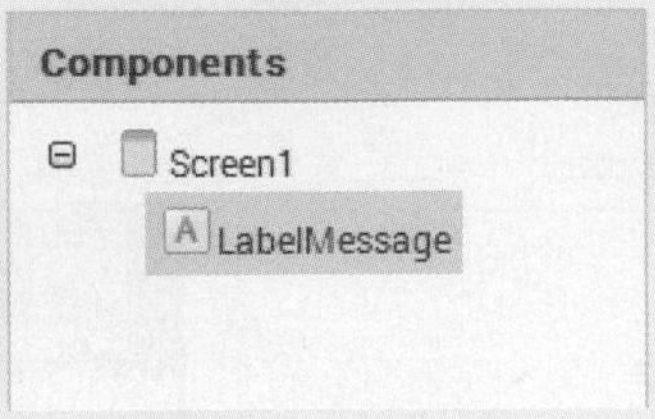

Figure 1-55 The Label's Text Property is Empty (*Source:* MIT App Inventor 2)

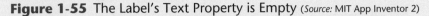

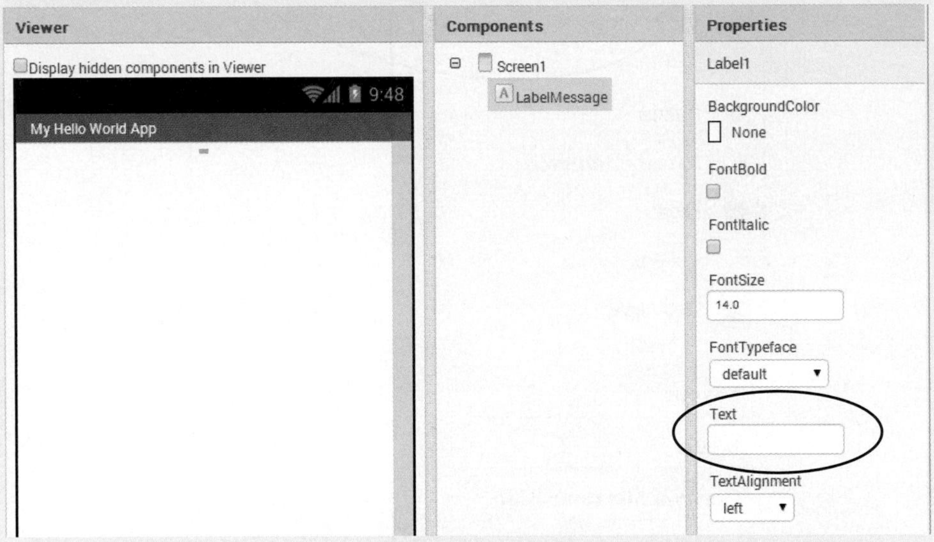

Step 7: Now you will create a Button component. Drag the Button component from the User Interface section of the Palette to the Viewer. Notice that as you drag the component, a thin blue line appears in the viewer, showing where the component will be inserted. You want the blue line to appear below the Label component, as shown in Figure 1-56, when you release the mouse button. This creates a Button component named `Button1`, with its Text property set to *Text for Button1*.

Step 8: Make sure the `Button1` component is selected in the Components column, and change the component's name to `ButtonDisplayMessage`. Then, in the Properties column, change the Text property to *Click Here To See a Message*. This is shown in Figure 1-57.

Step 9: You've added all of the components that you will need for this app. Although you haven't written any code, this would be a good time to preview the app's screen in the emulator. Click the *Connect* button in the upper area of the App Inventor screen, and then click *Emulator* on the menu that appears. It might take several minutes for the emulator to be created in the computer's memory. Once the emulator has been created and initialized, it will appear as shown in Figure 1-58.

Figure 1-56 Creating a Button Component (*Source:* MIT App Inventor 2)

The blue line shows where the component will be inserted.

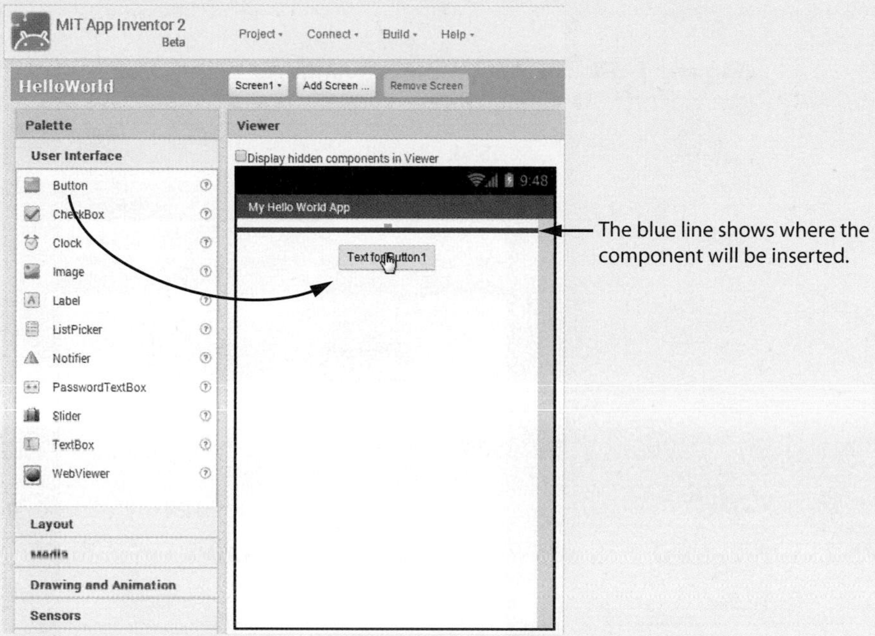

Figure 1-57 The Button Renamed and its Text Property Changed
(*Source:* MIT App Inventor 2)

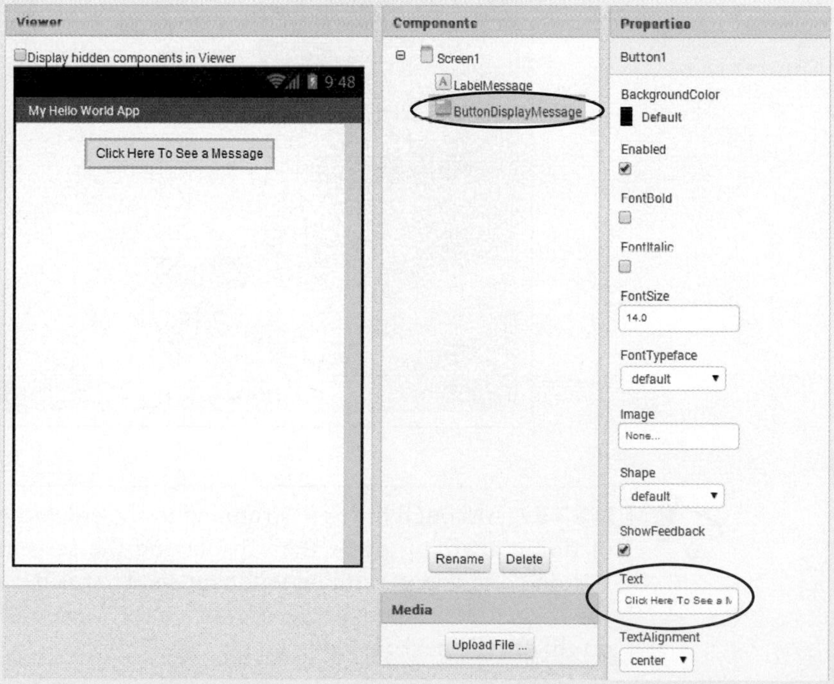

If possible, leave the project open in App Inventor. You will finish the app in the next tutorial.

Figure 1-58 The App in the Emulator *(Source:* MIT App Inventor 2)

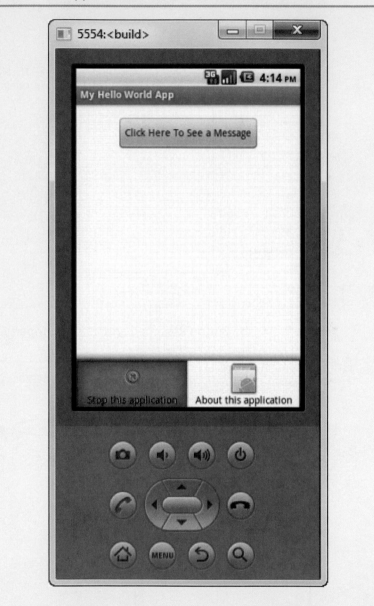

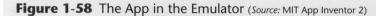 **NOTE:** Although the app is running in the emulator, it is not capable of doing anything other than displaying the screen. If you click the Button component, nothing will happen. That is because you have not yet written the code that executes when the button is clicked. You will do that in the next tutorial.

Programming with Blocks

Before you continue with the next tutorial, we will discuss the steps that you must take to complete the Hello World app. Carefully read this section, and then perform the steps in Tutorial 1-3.

First, you need to understand that apps are *event-driven* programs. This means that when an app is running, it waits for specific events to happen, and then it responds to those events. What do we mean by event? An event is an action that takes place, such as the user clicking a button, or sliding his or her finger across the device's screen. An incoming text message is also an event, as well as when the user tilts or shakes the phone. When you are creating an app, you decide which events the app will respond to, and then you write the code that executes when those events take place. (Obviously, there are limitations to the events that the emulator can respond to, because it isn't a physical device. For example, emulators can't receive incoming phone calls, and they can't be tilted or shaken.)

Recall that the Hello World app has a Button component named `ButtonDisplay Message`, and a Label component named `LabelMessage`. We want the app to display *Hello World* in the label when the user clicks the button. So, we need a block that executes when the user clicks the `ButtonDisplayMessage` component.

Assuming the HelloWorld project is currently open in the Blocks Editor, notice that the Blocks column has entries for `Screen1`, `LabelMessage`, and `ButtonDisplayMessage`. This is shown in Figure 1-59. Because you want to create a block that executes when the `ButtonDisplayMessage` component is clicked, you need to click `ButtonDisplayMessage` entry. This causes a "drawer" to open, revealing blocks that are related to the `ButtonDisplayMessage` component, as shown in Figure 1-60.

Figure 1-59 The Component Entries in the Blocks Column (*Source:* MIT App Inventor 2)

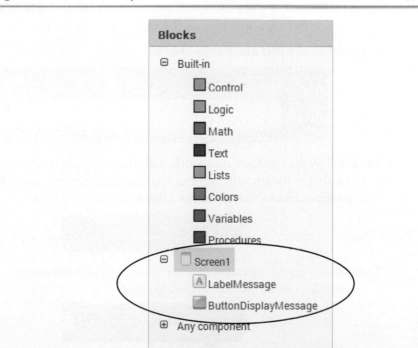

Figure 1-60 The `ButtonDisplayMessage` Drawer Open (*Source:* MIT App Inventor 2)

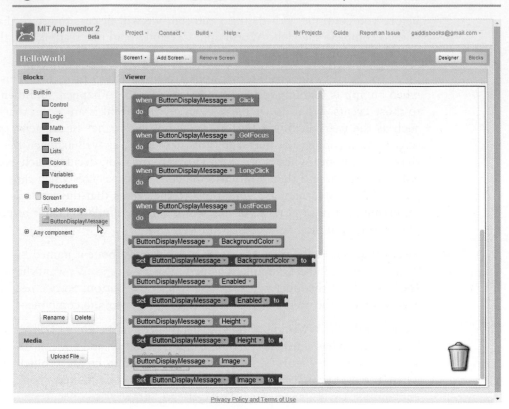

There are numerous blocks in this drawer. If you scroll through the drawer's contents, you will see that some of the blocks are brown, some are light green, and some are dark green. Here is a summary of the meaning of the colors:

- Brown blocks that are shaped like this:

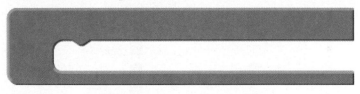

These are event handlers that work with the component. An *event handler* is a block that automatically executes when a specific event takes place.

- Light green blocks that are shaped like this:

These blocks represent values that are related to the component.

- Dark green blocks that are shaped like this:

These blocks are commands that perform actions with the component.

Figure 1-61 shows the topmost block inside the drawer (an event handler). Look at it carefully and notice that it reads:

```
when ButtonDisplayMessage.Click do
```

This block is the event handler that executes when the `ButtonDisplayMessage` component is clicked. The notation `ButtonDisplayMessage.Click` is simply a way of referring to the event of the `ButtonDisplayMessage` component being clicked. So, when you read the title of this block, think *when* `ButtonDisplayMessage` *is clicked, do this block*.

Figure 1-61 The `when ButtonDisplayMessage.Click do` Block

(*Source:* MIT App Inventor 2)

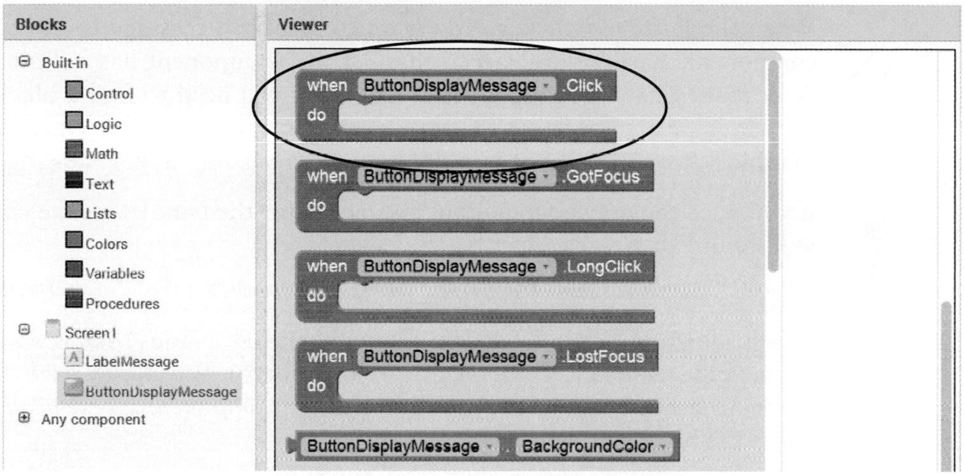

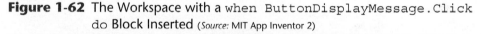

To insert the block into the workspace, simply click and drag it from the drawer. The workspace will appear similar to Figure 1-62. (It does not matter where you place the block in the workspace.)

Figure 1-62 The Workspace with a `when ButtonDisplayMessage.Click do` Block Inserted (*Source:* MIT App Inventor 2)

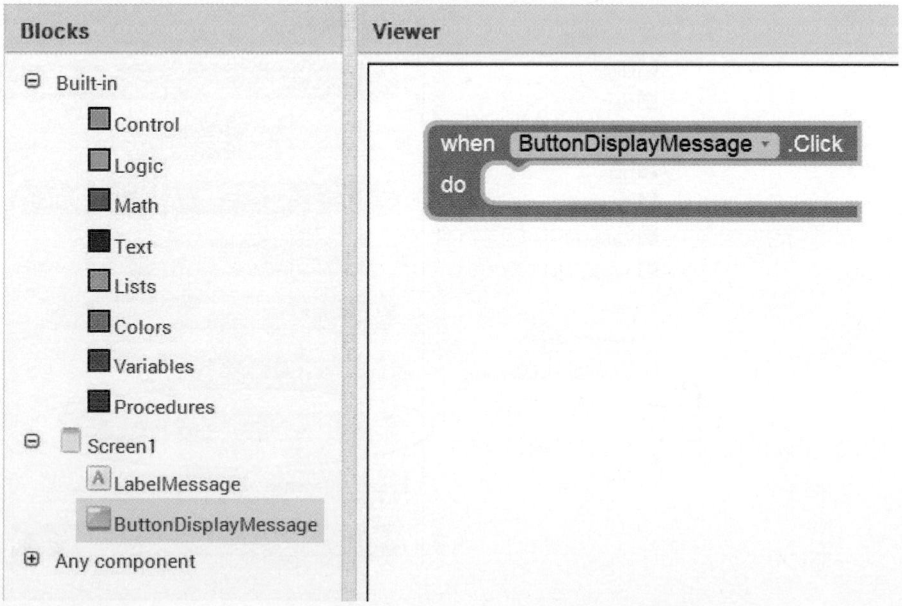

Notice that the `when ButtonDisplayMessage.Click do` block has an odd-shaped empty space in its middle, as shown in Figure 1-63. You can snap another block or a set of blocks into this space. Then, when the `ButtonDisplayMessage` component is clicked, the block or blocks that are snapped into this space will execute.

Figure 1-63 You Complete the Block by Snapping Other Blocks into the Empty Space. (*Source:* MIT App Inventor 2)

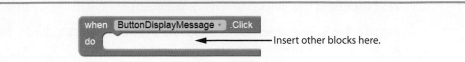

When the button is clicked, you want to display a message in the `LabelMessage` component. Earlier you learned that a Label component has a Text property that determines what the component displays. So, you need to find a block that sets the `LabelMessage` component's Text property to a specified value. Once you have found that block, you can snap it into the `when ButtonDisplayMessage.Click do` block.

If you open the drawer containing the blocks for the `LabelMessage` component, you will see one that reads

```
set LabelMessage.Text to
```

This is shown in Figure 1-64. The notation `LabelMessage.Text` is a way of referring to the `LabelMessage` component's Text property. When you read the title of this block, you should think *set the* `LabelMessage` *component's Text property to* . . . So, this is the block that you are looking for.

To insert the block, you simply click and drag it to the empty space inside the `when ButtonDisplayMessage.Click do` block. There will be an audible click

Figure 1-64 The `set LabelMessage.Text to` Block (*Source:* MIT App Inventor 2)

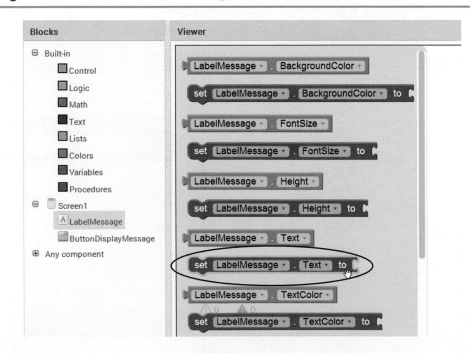

indicating that the blocks are snapped together. The workspace will appear similar to Figure 1-65.

Figure 1-65 The `set LabelMessage.Text to` Block Inserted
(*Source:* MIT App Inventor 2)

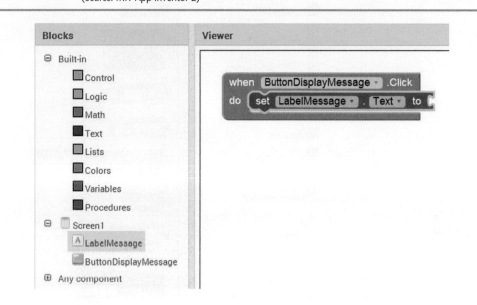

The `set LabelMessage.Text to` block is not a complete instruction until you specify the value that you want to set the property to. Notice the opening on the right edge of the `set LabelMessage.Text to` block, as shown in Figure 1-66. This opening is known as a *socket*. A socket is a place where another block can be snapped. To make this block a complete instruction, you need to snap another block specifying a value into the socket. In this case, you want to set the property to the text *Hello World*.

Figure 1-66 An Empty Socket (*Source:* MIT App Inventor 2)

If you click *Text* under *Built-in* in the Blocks column, a drawer will open, as shown in Figure 1-67. The topmost block shown in the figure is the *text string* block. (It appears with a set of quotation marks.) You use the text string block any time you need to specify a text value. Click and drag the block to the workspace, and snap it into the socket of the `set LabelMessage.Text to` block. You will hear a click indicating that the blocks are snapped together, and the workspace should appear similar to Figure 1-68.

Take a closer look at the text string block that you just inserted. Notice that it shows a set of quotation marks with an empty space between them. You need to insert the message *Hello World* in the empty space. To do this, simply click the empty space, type *Hello World*, and press Enter. This changes the value of the block to *Hello World*, as shown in the image on the right in Figure 1-69.

At this point, the instruction is complete. In Tutorial 1-3, you will perform the steps that we just discussed.

Figure 1-67 The Built-in `text string` Block (*Source:* MIT App Inventor 2)

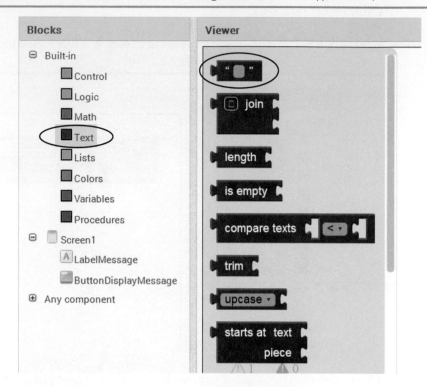

Figure 1-68 The Text String Block Snapped into the Socket of the `set LabelMessage.Text to` Block (*Source:* MIT App Inventor 2)

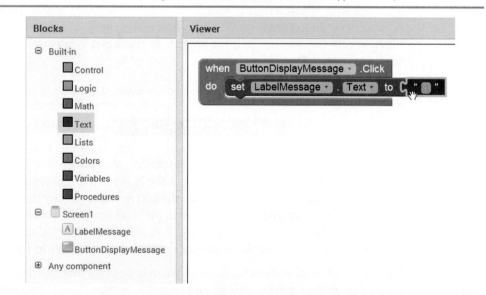

Figure 1-69 Changing the Value of the Text String Block to *Hello World* (*Source:* MIT App Inventor 2)

Click the empty space in the text string block.   Change the value to *Hello World*.

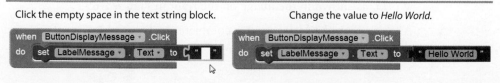

Tutorial 1-3:
Completing the Hello World App

VideoNote
Completing the
Hello World App

Step 1:   This tutorial resumes where Tutorial 1-2 ended. Make sure the Hello World project is open in App Inventor, the Blocks Editor is opened, and an emulator is created and connected to App Inventor.

Step 2:   In the Blocks column, click `ButtonDisplayMessage`. As shown in Figure 1-70, a drawer will open, containing blocks related to the `ButtonDisplayMessage` component. Click and drag the `when ButtonDisplayMessage do` block to the workspace. The workspace should now appear as shown in Figure 1-71.

Figure 1-70 The Blocks for the `ButtonDisplayMessage` Component
(*Source:* MIT App Inventor 2)

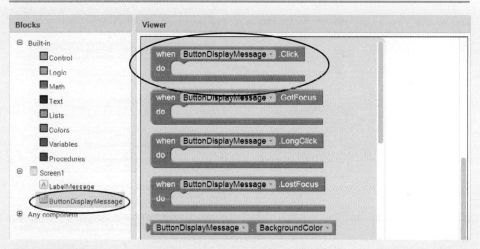

Figure 1-71 The `when ButtonDisplayMessage.Click do` Block Created
(*Source:* MIT App Inventor 2)

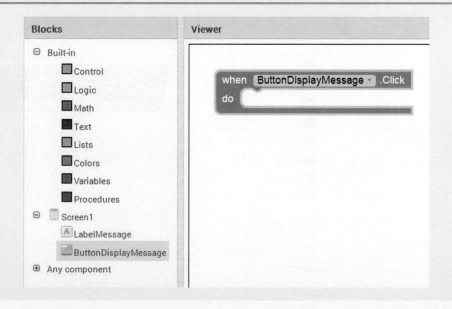

Step 3: In the Blocks column, click `LabelMessage`. As shown in Figure 1-72, a drawer will open, containing blocks related to the `LabelMessage` component. Drag the `set LabelMessage.Text to` block into the empty space inside the `when ButtonDisplayMessage do` block. There will be an audible click indicating that the blocks are snapped together. The workspace will appear similar to Figure 1-73.

Figure 1-72 The Blocks for the `LabelMessage` Component
(*Source:* MIT App Inventor 2)

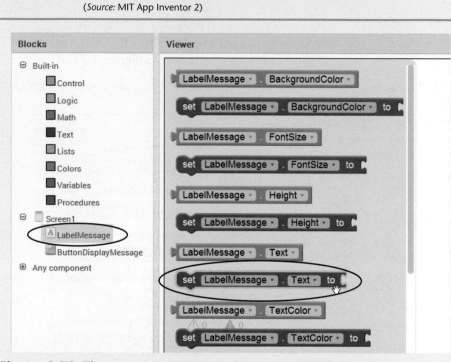

Figure 1-73 The `set LabelMessage.Text to` Block Created
(*Source:* MIT App Inventor 2)

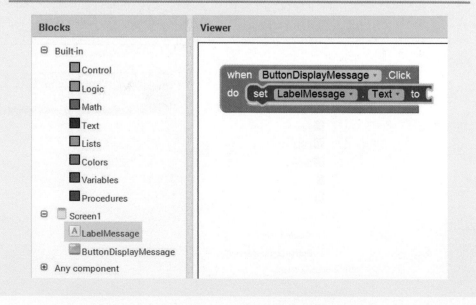

Step 4: In the Blocks column, click *Text* (which appears under *Built-in*). A drawer will open, as shown in Figure 1-74. Drag the text string block to the workspace, and snap it into the socket of the set LabelMessage.Text to block. You will hear a click indicating that the blocks are snapped together, and the workspace should appear similar to Figure 1-75.

Figure 1-74 The Built-in Text Blocks (*Source:* MIT App Inventor 2)

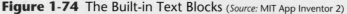

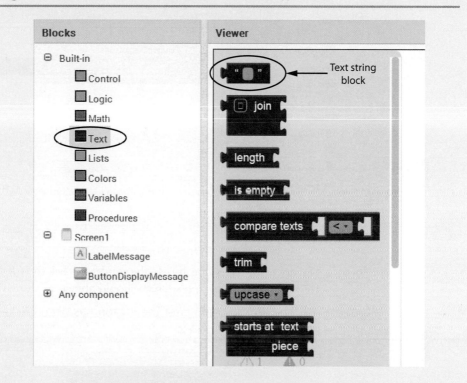

Figure 1-75 The Text String Block Inserted (*Source:* MIT App Inventor 2)

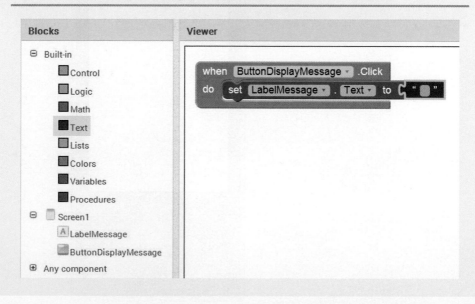

Step 5:   Now you will change the value of the text string block to *Hello World*. Click the empty space that appears between the quotation marks, type *Hello World*, and press Enter. The block should now appear as shown in Figure 1-76.

Figure 1-76 The Value of the Text String Block Changed to *Hello World*
(*Source:* MIT App Inventor 2)

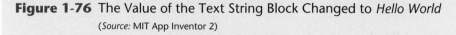

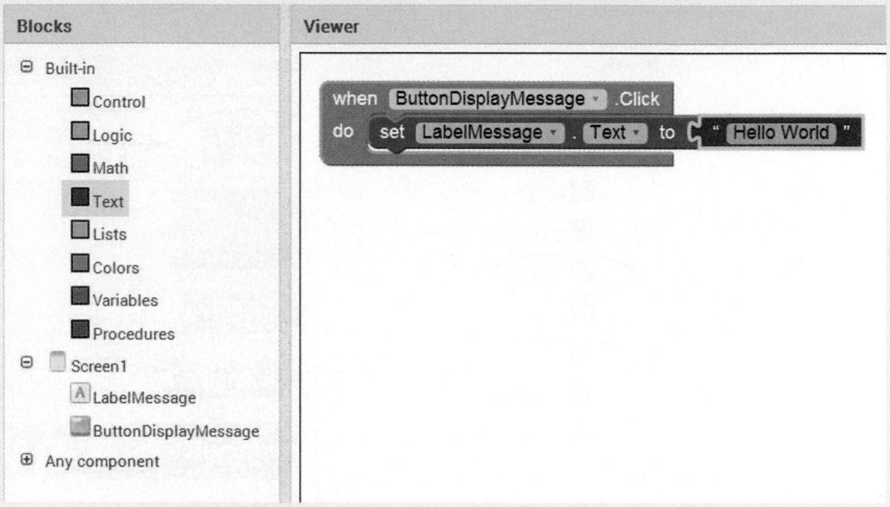

Step 6:   You are ready to test the app. In the emulator, click the *Click Here To See a Message* button. The app's screen should appear as shown in Figure 1-77.

Figure 1-77 The App's Screen after the Button has been Clicked
(*Source:* MIT App Inventor 2)

NOTE: In this chapter, you've learned that you write code in the Blocks Editor by snapping blocks together. You have probably noticed that each type of block has its own shape, like a puzzle piece. Just like real puzzle pieces, only certain shapes fit together. This is shown in Figure 1-78.

Because only certain shapes fit together, you cannot connect blocks that do not belong together. This makes programming in App Inventor much easier for beginners than programming in a traditional language, where you have to type the correct words in the correct order and use correct punctuation. With App Inventor, you only need to determine which blocks to use and snap them together!

Figure 1-78 Certain Shapes Fit Together (*Source:* MIT App Inventor 2)

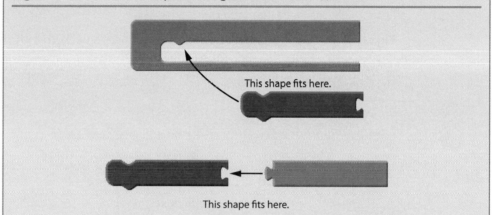

This shape fits here.

This shape fits here.

You should be getting more comfortable with the Designer and the Blocks Editor, so it's time to move on to a more interesting project. In Tutorial 1-4, you will create an app that displays the phrase "Good Morning" in different languages. In the process, you will explore additional component properties. Here is a summary of what you will do in the tutorial:

- You will change the `Screen1` component's BackgroundColor property to change the color of the app's screen.
- You will insert a Label component, and change its FontSize property to make the component's text larger.
- You will insert three Button components. Each one, when clicked, will cause a different phrase to be displayed in the Label component.

Tutorial 1-4:
Creating the Good Morning Translator App

In this tutorial, you will create an app that displays the phrase *Good Morning* in different languages. The app's screen will have three buttons: one for Italian, one for Spanish, and one for German. When the user clicks any of these buttons, the translated phrase will appear in a Label component.

Step 1:   Start App Inventor and begin a new project named *GoodMorning*. Create a new emulator.

Step 2:   In the Designer, change the Screen1 component's AlignHorizontal property to *Center* and change the Title property to *Good Morning App*.

Step 3:   The Screen1 component's BackgroundColor property determines the background color of the app's screen. By default, it is set to *White*. Click the property's current setting and select a color from the list that appears, as shown in Figure 1-79. (In the example, we will use the color light gray, but you can pick another color if you wish.) Figure 1-80 shows all of the Screen1 properties that we have changed.

Figure 1-79 Changing the Screen1 Component's BackgroundColor Property *(Source:* MIT App Inventor 2)

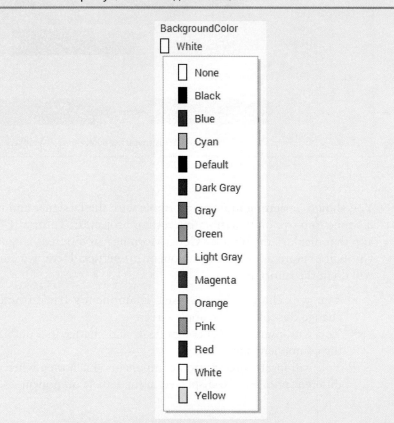

Step 4:   Insert a Label component onto the screen and change the component's name to LabelPhrase. Set the component's Text property to *Good Morning*. Because we want the label's text to appear larger on the app's screen and easier to read, you will make it boldface and increase its size. Enable the FontBold property to make the label's text boldface, and change the FontSize property to 24 to make the label's text larger. All of these settings are shown in Figure 1-81.

Figure 1-80 The `Screen1` Component's Properties that We have Changed
(*Source:* MIT App Inventor 2)

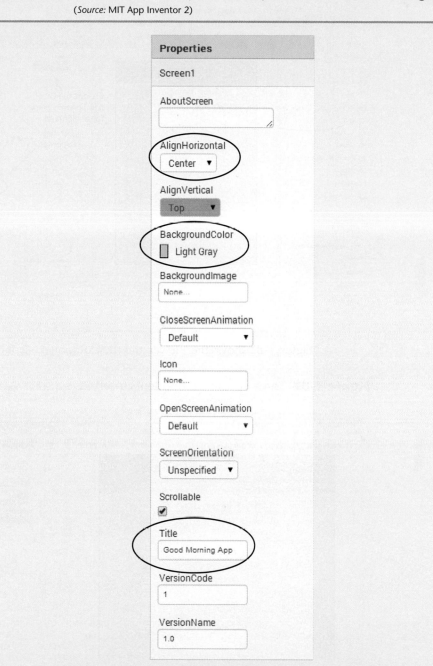

Step 5: Insert the following components, and set their properties as described:

- Insert a Button component, change its name to `ButtonItalian`, and set its Text property to *Italian*.
- Insert another Button component, change its name to `ButtonSpanish`, and set its Text property to *Spanish*.
- Insert another Button component, change its name to `ButtonGerman`, and set its Text property to *German*.

Figure 1-81 The `LabelPhrase` Component's Property Settings
(*Source:* MIT App Inventor 2)

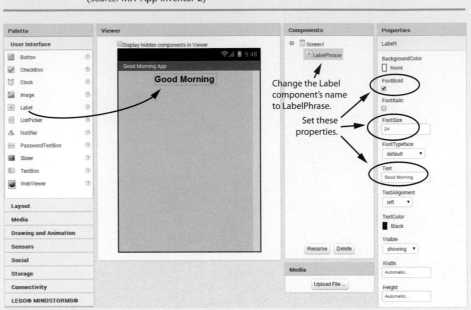

Figure 1-82 shows the Viewer and the Components column at this point.

Figure 1-82 Three Button Components Inserted (*Source:* MIT App Inventor 2)

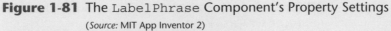

Step 6: Now you will write the app's code. These are the actions the app will perform:

- When the user clicks the `ButtonItalian` component, the `LabelPhrase` component's Text property will change to *Buongiorno*.

- When the user clicks the `ButtonSpanish` component, the `LabelPhrase` component's Text property will change to *Buenos Dias*.
- When the user clicks the `ButtonGerman` component, the `LabelPhrase` component's Text property will change to *Guten Morgen*.

Open the Blocks Editor, and click `ButtonItalian` in the Blocks column (it appears under `Screen1`). Drag the `when ButtonItalian do` block from the drawer and drop it into the workspace, as shown in Figure 1-83.

Figure 1-83 The `when ButtonItalian do` Block Inserted

(*Source:* MIT App Inventor 2)

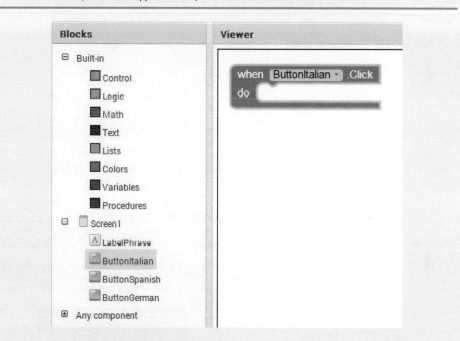

Step 7: In the Blocks column, click `LabelPhrase` (it appears under `Screen1`). Drag the `set LabelPhrase.Text to` block from the drawer and drop it inside the `when ButtonItalian do` block, as shown in Figure 1-84.

Step 8: In the Blocks column, click *Text* (which appears under *Built-in*). Drag the text string block to the workspace, and snap it into the socket of the `set LabelPhrase.Text to` block. You will hear an audible click indicating that the blocks are snapped together, and the workspace should appear similar to Figure 1-85.

Step 9: In the text string block, click the empty space that appears between the quotation marks, and type *Buongiorno*. The blocks should appear as shown in Figure 1-86. That completes the `Click` event handler for the `ButtonItalian` component.

Figure 1-84 The `set LabelPhrase.Text to` Block Inserted
(*Source:* MIT App Inventor 2)

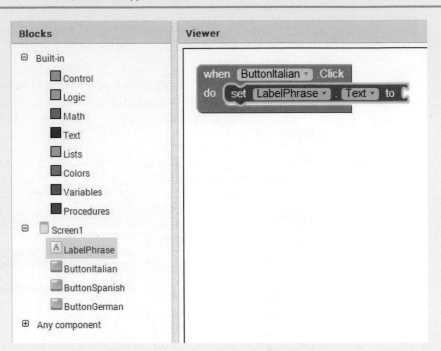

Figure 1-85 The Text String Block Snapped to the `set LabelPhrase.Text to` Block (*Source:* MIT App Inventor 2)

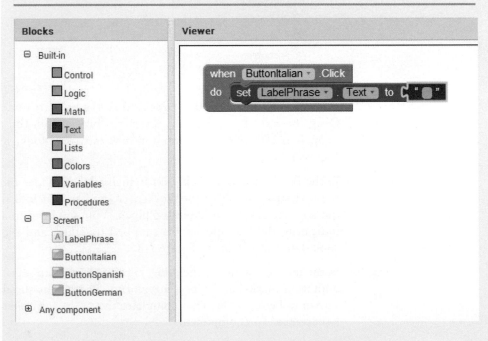

Figure 1-86 The Value of the Text String Block Changed to *Buongiorno*
(*Source:* MIT App Inventor 2)

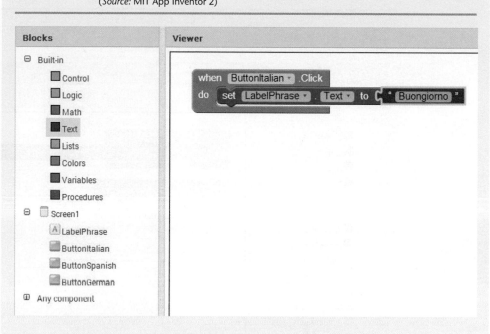

Step 10: Now you will complete the `Click` event handler for the `ButtonSpanish` component. Perform the following actions:

- In the Blocks column, click `ButtonSpanish` (it appears under `Screen1`). Drag the `when ButtonSpanish do` block from the drawer and drop it into the workspace.
- In the Blocks column, click `LabelPhrase` (it also appears under `Screen1`). Drag the `set LabelPhrase.Text to` block from the drawer and drop it inside the `when ButtonSpanish do` block.
- In the Blocks column, click *Text* (which appears under *Built-in*). Drag the text string block to the workspace and snap it into the socket of the `set LabelPhrase.Text to` block's socket.
- In the text string block, click the empty space that appears between the quotation marks and type *Buenos Dias*.

That completes the `Click` event handler for the `ButtonSpanish` component. The workspace should appear similar to Figure 1-87.

Step 11: Now you will complete the `Click` event handler for the `ButtonGerman` component. Perform the following actions:

- In the Blocks column, click `ButtonGerman` (it appears under `Screen1`). Drag the `when ButtonGerman do` block from the drawer and drop it into the workspace.
- In the Blocks column, click `LabelPhrase` (it also appears under `Screen1`). Drag the `set LabelPhrase.Text to` block from the drawer and drop it inside the `when ButtonGerman do` block.

Figure 1-87 The Workspace with `Click` Event Handlers for the `Button-Italian` and `ButtonSpanish` Components (*Source:* MIT App Inventor 2)

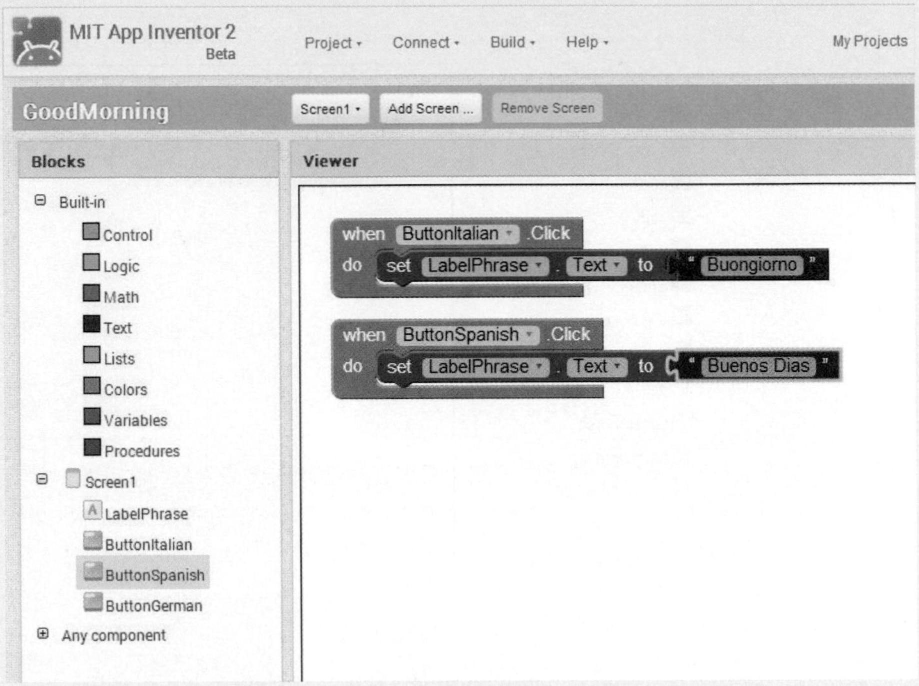

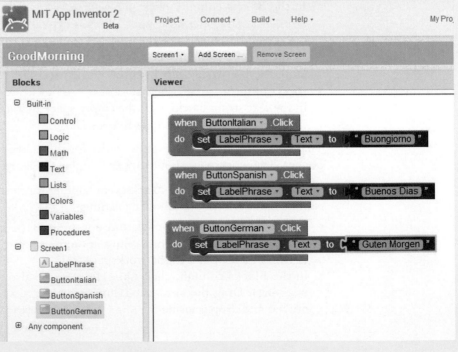

Figure 1-88 The Workspace with `Click` Event Handlers for the `Button-Italian`, `ButtonSpanish`, and `ButtonGerman` Components (*Source:* MIT App Inventor 2)

- In the Blocks column click *Text* (which appears under *Built-in*). Drag the text string block to the workspace, and snap it into the socket of the the `set LabelPhrase.Text to` block's socket.
- In the text string block, click the empty space that appears between the quotation marks, and type *Guten Morgen*.

That completes the `Click` event handler for the `ButtonGerman` component. The workspace should appear similar to Figure 1-88.

Step 12: Test the app in the emulator. Figure 1-89 shows how the app's screen should appear when you click each button.

Figure 1-89 Output of the App (*Source:* MIT App Inventor 2)

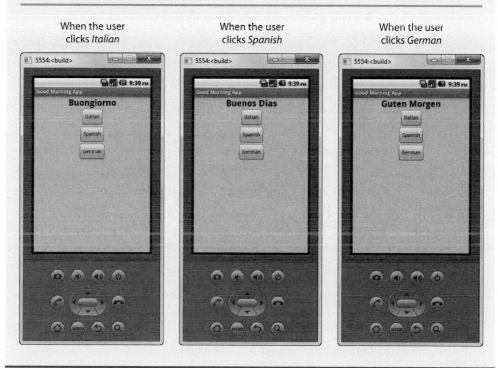

When the user clicks *Italian* — Buongiorno; When the user clicks *Spanish* — Buenos Dias; When the user clicks *German* — Guten Morgen.

 Checkpoint

1.18 What App Inventor screen do you go to when you want to start a new project or manage existing projects?

1.19 In App Inventor, what component must every app have?

1.20 What Screen component property sets the text that is displayed in the screen's title bar?

1.21 What does a Label component do?

1.22 What Label component property determines the text that the component displays?

1.23 What are the possible values for a Label component's Width and Height properties?

1.24 How do you rename a component? Why would you want to change a component's name from the default name that App Inventor gives it?

1.25 What rules must you follow when naming a component?

1.26 What Button component property determines the text that is displayed on the button?

1.27 What are the possible values for a Screen component's AlignHorizontal property?

1.28 What are the possible values for a Screen component's AlignVertical property?

1.29 What is an event-driven program?

1.30 In the Blocks column of the Blocks Editor, where do you find the blocks for the components that you have added to a project?

1.31 In the Blocks Editor, what is a drawer?

1.32 What Screen property do you use to change the background color of the screen?

1.33 What Label component property do you set to change the size of the text displayed by the component?

1.34 What Label component property do you set to make the component's text boldface?

Review Questions

Multiple Choice

1. This is what a computer device does.
   a. Has its own human-like intelligence
   b. Gives commands to humans
   c. Follows instructions to perform a task
   d. Understands languages such as English

2. This is a set of instructions that the computer follows.
   a. Language
   b. Program
   c. Binary number
   d. Compiler

3. This is a set of well-defined logical steps that must be taken in order to perform a task.
   a. Algorithm
   b. Programming language
   c. Compiler
   d. Execution

4. This is the only language that a computer understands.

   a. Java
   b. Machine language
   c. Keywords
   d. Android

5. This is a number that consists of only 1s and 0s.

   a. Binary
   b. Decimal
   c. Floating-point
   d. Unary

6. A program written in this is much easier for people to understand than a program written in machine language.

   a. Binary
   b. A programming language
   c. Decimal
   d. Hieroglyphics

7. This translates a program into machine language.

   a. An entry-level programmer
   b. Microprocessor
   c. Disk drive
   d. Compiler

8. These are the words that make up a programming language.

   a. Implied words
   b. External words
   c. Keywords
   d. Synthetic words

9. This is a set of rules that must be strictly followed when writing a program.

   a. Rules of order
   b. Syntax
   c. Procedural rules
   d. Rules of thumb

10. If a program contains even one of these, it cannot be translated into an executable program.

    a. Syntax error
    b. Keyword
    c. Compiler
    d. Binary number

11. Which is not a legal character in an App Inventor project name?

    a. Letter
    b. Number
    c. Space
    d. Underscore (_)

12. You use this screen to design a component's user interface.

   a. The Viewer
   b. The Blocks Editor
   c. The Screen Editor
   d. The Emulator

13. This column in the Designer provides a list of components that you can use to build your app.

   a. The Components column
   b. The Palette column
   c. The Properties column
   d. The Viewer

14. This column in the Designer shows a rectangular area that represents the app's screen.

   a. The Components column
   b. The Palette column
   c. The Properties column
   d. The Media column

15. This column in the Designer shows a hierarchical tree listing all of the components that you have placed in your app.

   a. The Components column
   b. The Palette column
   c. The Properties column
   d. The Blocks Editor

16. This column in the Designer allows you to manage the media files (images, videos, and audio files) that you want to use in your app.

   a. The Components column
   b. The Palette column
   c. The Properties column
   d. The Media column

17. This column in the Designer allows you to examine and change a component's properties.

   a. The Components column
   b. The Palette column
   c. The Properties column
   d. The Viewer

18. Each time you add a component to an app in the Designer, a set of component blocks is added to this part of the Blocks Editor.

   a. The Blocks column
   b. The Components column
   c. The Workspace
   d. The Designer column

19. The basic blocks that make up the App Inventor language are found in the Blocks column, under _____.

    a. Built-in
    b. Screen1
    c. AI components
    d. Any component

20. To create an emulator, you click this button on the App Inventor screen.

    a. Build
    b. Project
    c. Create Emulator
    d. Connect

21. Every app must have this component.

    a. `Button1`
    b. `Label1`
    c. `Screen1`
    d. `Title1`

22. When you want to display text on an app's screen, you use this type of component.

    a. Button
    b. Message
    c. Output
    d. Label

23. Which property of a Button component determines the text that is displayed on the button?

    a. Title
    b. Text
    c. Output
    d. Message

24. This is a block that automatically executes when an event takes place.

    a. Value block
    b. Command block
    c. Procedural block
    d. Event handler

25. This Screen component property changes the screen's background color.

    a. BackgroundColor
    b. Color
    c. BackColor
    d. BgColor

26. This Label component property changes the size of the text displayed by the component.
    a. Size
    b. TextSize
    c. Font
    d. FontSize

27. This Label component property makes the component's text boldface.
    a. Bold
    b. FontBold
    c. Boldface
    d. Font

Short Answer

1. What is a computer?

2. Why were programming languages invented?

3. What is an algorithm?

4. What rules must you follow when naming a project in App Inventor?

5. How do you rename a component?

6. Why should you change the name of a component from its default name?

7. What rules must you follow when changing a component's name?

8. Suppose you have the Designer open and you want to create a Button component on the app's screen. Describe how this is done.

9. How do you specify the text that a Label component displays on the screen?

10. What effect does the Automatic setting have on a component's Width and Height properties?

11. What are the possible settings for a Screen component's AlignHorizontal property?

12. What are the possible settings for a Screen component's AlignVertical property?

13. What is an event-driven program?

14. Assume an app has a Button component named ButtonClickMe and a Label component named LabelOutput. Describe what the blocks shown in Figure 1-90 do.

Figure 1-90 Blocks in an App (*Source:* MIT App Inventor 2)

Exercises

1. Use the Designer to create the screen shown in Figure 1-91.

Figure 1-91 Screen for Exercise 1 *(Source:* MIT App Inventor 2*)*

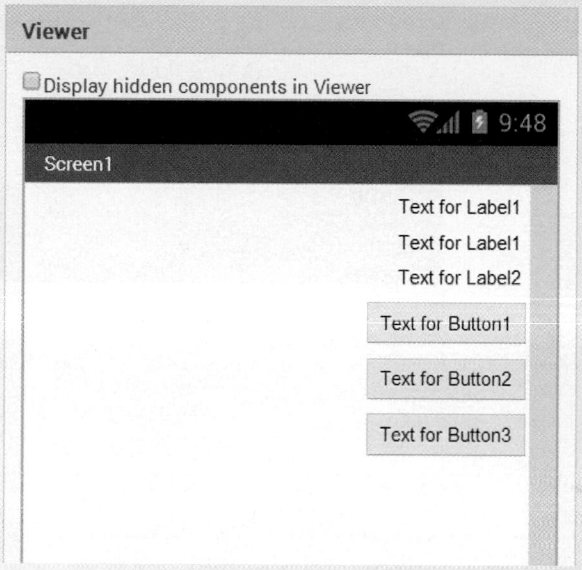

2. Use the Designer to create the screen shown in Figure 1-92. The font size for the topmost Label component is 24. For the middle Label component, it is 32, and for the bottom Label component, it is 38.

Figure 1-92 Screen for Exercise 2 *(Source:* MIT App Inventor 2*)*

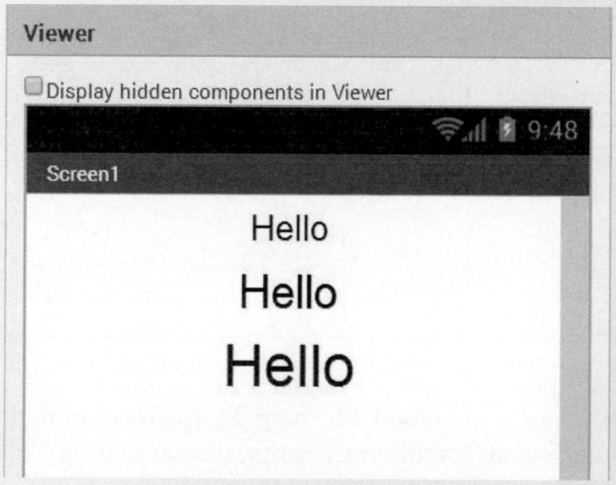

3. Use the Designer to create the screen shown in Figure 1-93. Here are some specific property settings for the components:
   - The `Screen1` component's Scrollable property is unchecked.
   - The topmost Button component's Width property is set to *Fill Parent*, and its Height property is set to *Automatic*.

- The middle Button component's Width property is set to *Automatic*, and its Height property is set to *50 pixels*.
- The bottom Button component's Width property is set to *Fill Parent*, and its Height property is set to *Fill Parent*.

Figure 1-93 Screen for Exercise 3 *(Source:* MIT App Inventor 2*)*

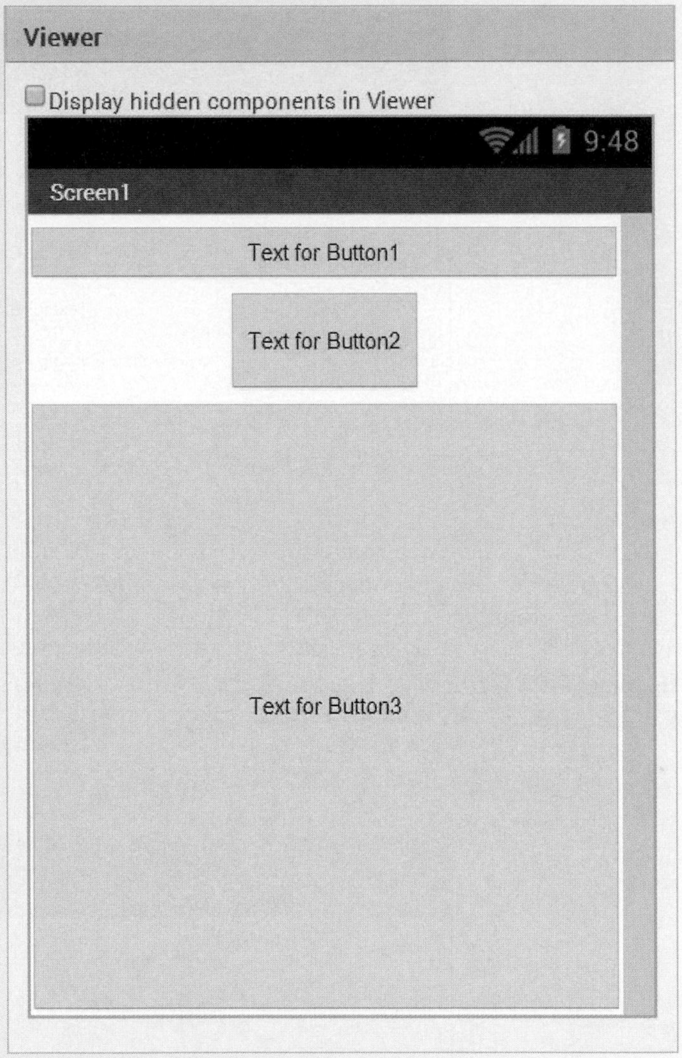

4. Enhance the Good Morning Translator app that you created in Tutorial 1-4 by adding an English button that displays *Good Morning* when the user clicks it.

Programming Projects

1. Presidential Trivia App

Create the app shown in Figure 1-94. The app initially appears as the image on the left, displaying the question *Who was the 4th U.S. president?* When the user

VideoNote
The Presidential Trivia App

clicks the *Show Answer* button, the answer is displayed as shown in the image on the right.

Figure 1-94 Presidential Trivia App *(Source:* MIT App Inventor 2)

2. **Latin Translator**

Look at the following list of Latin words and their meanings.

Latin	English
sinister	left
dexter	right
medium	center

Create an app that translates the Latin words to English. The app's screen should have three buttons, one for each Latin word. When the user clicks a button, the application should display the English translation in a Label component.

3. **Joke and Punch Line**

A joke typically has two parts: a setup and a punch line. For example, this might be the setup for a joke:

How many programmers does it take to change a light bulb?

And this is the punch line:

None. That's a hardware problem.

Think of your favorite joke and identify its setup and punch line. Then, create an app that has two Button components. One of the buttons should read *Setup* and the other button should read *Punch line*. When the *Setup* button is clicked, display the joke's setup in one or more Label components. (If the setup contains a large amount of text, you might need more than one Label component.) When the *Punch line* button is clicked, display the joke's punch line in the Label component(s).

2 Working with Media

 ## 2.1 Displaying Images

CONCEPT: There are various ways to display an image in an App Inventor app. An image can be displayed as the background for a screen, in an Image component, or on a Button component. An image must be uploaded to a project on the App Inventor server before it can be displayed. The Media column in the Designer lets you manage the image files that you have uploaded for a project.

Displaying an Image as a Screen Background

App Inventor gives you a variety of ways to display images on your app's screen. If you want to display an image as the background for an app's screen, you can use the Screen component's BackgroundImage property. Before you can display an image, however, it must be uploaded to your project on the App Inventor server. App Inventor supports a variety of graphics file formats, but the recommended formats are .png and .jpg.

To display an image as a screen's background image, make sure the Screen1 component is selected in the Components column. In the Properties column, set the BackgroundColor property to *None*. (In the emulator, the BackgroundColor property will override the BackgroundImage property. So, if you want to display a background image, you need to make sure you are not also displaying a background color.)

Then, as shown in Figure 2-1, in the Properties column, click the BackgroundImage property. The dialog box in the center of the figure appears, allowing you to select a previously uploaded image or upload a new image. In the example shown in the

Figure 2-1 Changing the BackgroundImage Property (*Source:* MIT App Inventor 2, Pearson Education, Inc.)

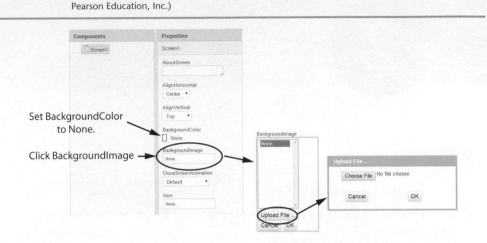

figure, no files have been uploaded, so you would click the *Upload File . . .* button to upload a file. This causes the *Upload File . . .* dialog box shown on the right side of the figure to appear. You would click the *Choose File* button to select a file from your local computer and then click the *OK* button to upload it. The file will automatically be set as the screen's background image.

Figure 2-2 shows Screen1 in the Viewer, Screen1's properties in the Properties column, and the emulator after a file named Boston01.png has been uploaded as the screen's background image.

Figure 2-2 An Image Set as the Screen's Background (*Source:* MIT App Inventor 2)

You can continue to place components on the screen after setting the screen's BackgroundImage property. For example, Figure 2-3 shows a screen with a background

Figure 2-3 A Screen with a Background Image and Four Button Components
(*Source:* MIT App Inventor 2, Pearson Education, Inc.)

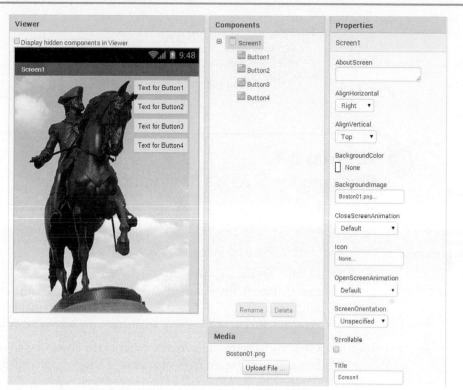

image and four Button components. (Notice in the figure that the Screen1 component's AlignHorizontal property is set to *Right*, which causes the buttons to appear on the right edge of the screen.)

Using the Media Column to Upload Files

When you upload an image to a project, the image file's name will appear in the Media column, which is at the bottom of the Components column. Figure 2-4 shows an example. As you can see in the figure, we have uploaded a file named Boston01.png.

Notice that the Media column has an *Upload File* . . . button. This button allows you to select and upload media files to your project without assigning them to any specific property. For example, you could use this button to upload all of a project's media files, and later select those files for their intended purposes.

Figure 2-4 The Media Column (*Source:* MIT App Inventor 2)

Media
Boston01.png
Upload File ...

If you click the name of a file in the Media column, you see the menu pop up as shown in Figure 2-5. The menu lets you delete the file (if you no longer need it in the project), or download the file to your local computer.

Figure 2-5 Using the Media Column to Delete or Download a File
(*Source:* MIT App Inventor 2)

Media

Boston01.png

Upload File ...

Delete...

Download to my computer

VideoNote
Changing the
Screen's
Background Image

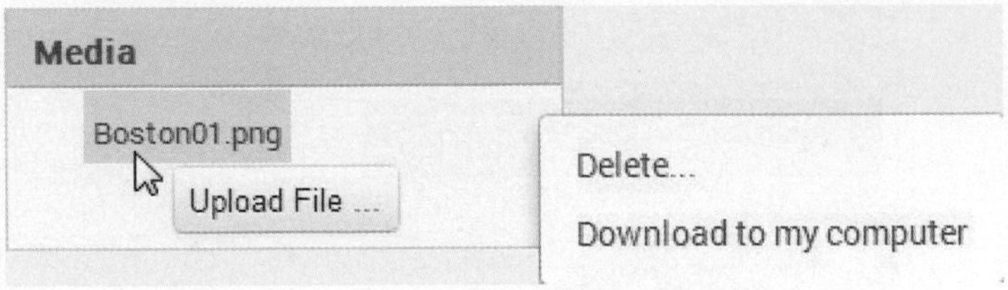

Tutorial 2-1:
Changing the Screen's Background Image

Step 1: Make sure you have downloaded the media files from this book's companion website at www.pearsonhighered.com/gaddis.

Step 2: Start a new App Inventor project named *ScreenBackground*.

Step 3: In the Designer, the Screen1 component will be selected in the Components column. In the Properties column, change the BackgroundColor to *None*. (You don't want to display a background color because you are going to display an image instead.)

Step 4: Click the BackgroundImage property in the Properties column. The dialog box shown in Figure 2-6 will appear. Click the *Upload File . . .* button.

Figure 2-6 Upload a File to Change the BackgroundImage Property
(*Source:* MIT App Inventor 2)

BackgroundImage

None

Upload File ...

Cancel   OK

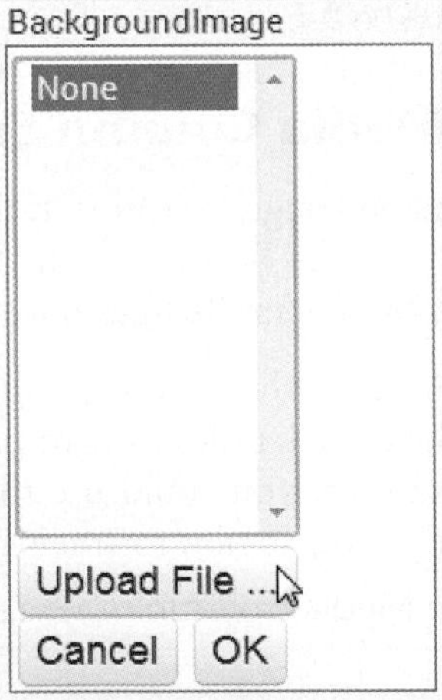

Step 5: The *Upload File . . .* dialog box shown in Figure 2-7 will appear. Click the *Choose File* button.

Navigate to the location on your system where the book's media files are located. You will find a folder named *Gradients* that contains several .png files. Select the Gradient01.png file.

The *Upload File . . .* dialog box will now look like Figure 2-8, showing that you have selected the Gradient01.png file. Click the *OK* button.

Figure 2-7 The *Upload File . . .* Dialog Box (*Source:* MIT App Inventor 2)

> Upload File...
>
> [Choose File] No file chosen
>
> [Cancel]   [OK]

Figure 2-8 The *Upload File . . .* Dialog Box Showing the Name of the Chosen File (*Source:* MIT App Inventor 2)

> Upload File...
>
> [Choose File] Gradient01.png
>
> [Cancel]   [OK]

Step 6: You will see the message *Uploading Gradient01.png to the App Inventor server* displayed momentarily at the top of the Designer. It will take a moment for the file to upload. Once it has uploaded, you will see it displayed in the Viewer as the screen's background, as shown in Figure 2-9. Notice in the Properties column that the filename is shown for the value of the BackgroundImage property and the BackgroundColor property is set to *None*. Also notice that the filename is listed in the Media column, indicating that it has been uploaded to the project on the App Inventor server.

Step 7: Create a new emulator (click *Connect* at the top of the App Inventor screen and then click *Emulator*). The background image should be displayed in the emulator, as shown in Figure 2-10. (Alternatively, you can connect to an Android device and see the background image displayed on its screen.)

Figure 2-9 The `Gradient01.png` File Displayed as the Screen's Background (*Source:* MIT App Inventor 2)

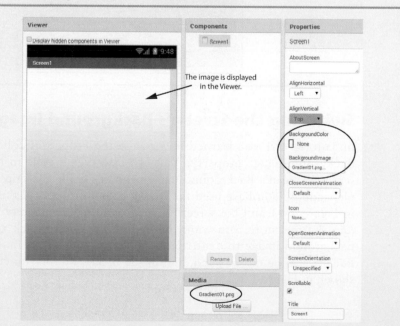

Figure 2-10 The Background Image Displayed in the Emulator
(*Source:* MIT App Inventor 2)

Switching the Screen's Background Image in Code

In Tutorial 2-1 you learned how to use the Properties column to set the screen's BackgroundImage property. You can also create code in the Blocks Editor that sets the screen's BackgroundImage property while the app is running. For example, suppose you have used the Media column to upload the two .png files shown in Figure 2-11 and the screen's BackgroundImage property is set to Gradient01. png. Furthermore, you want the user to be able to click a button to change the background image to Gradient02.png. So, you add a Button component named ButtonChangeBackground, and in the Blocks Editor you create the event handler shown in Figure 2-12.

Figure 2-11 Two .png Files Uploaded (*Source:* MIT App Inventor 2)

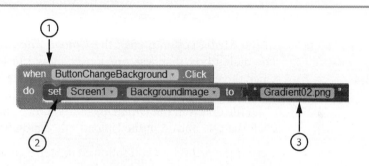

Figure 2-12 The Click Event Handler for the ButtonChangeBackground
Button (*Source:* MIT App Inventor 2)

Let's take a closer look at the blocks shown in Figure 2-12:

1. This is the when ButtonChangeBackground.Click do event handler. It executes when a Click event occurs for the ButtonChangeBackground component (In other words, when the user clicks the button).

2. This is the set Screen1.BackgroundImage to block. The purpose of this block is to set the Screen1 component's BackgroundImage property to a value. This block has a socket that receives another block, specifying the value.

3. This is a text string block and its value is set to *Gradient02.png*. This block is plugged into block 2, so this is the value that we are setting the screen's BackgroundImage property to.

The result of this set of blocks is as follows:

When the ButtonChangeBackground button is clicked, set the Screen1 component's BackgroudImage property to Gradient02.png.

 NOTE: In this example, the Gradient02.png file must already be uploaded to the App Inventor server before the user clicks the button. If the Gradient02.png file has not been uploaded, an error will occur when the button is clicked.

In Tutorial 2-2 you will create an application that uses this technique to switch the screen's background image among three images that you will upload to the App Inventor server.

VideoNote
Switching the Screen's Background Image in Code

Tutorial 2-2:
Switching the Screen's Background Image in Code

Step 1: Make sure you have downloaded the media files from this book's companion website at `www.pearsonhighered.com/gaddis`.

Step 2: Start a new App Inventor project named *MultipleBackgrounds*.

Step 3: In the Designer, the `Screen1` component will be selected in the Components column. In the Properties column, change the BackgroundColor to *None*. (You don't want to display a background color because you are going to display an image instead.)

Step 4: Set `Screen1`'s Title property to *Multiple Backgrounds* and set the AlignHorizontal property to *Center*.

Step 5: In the Media column, click the *Upload File . . .* button. The *Upload File* dialog box that was previously shown in Figure 2-7 will appear. Click the *Choose File* button, and then navigate to the location on your system where the book's media files are located. Select the `Gradient01.png` file that is in the *Gradients* folder. Once you have selected the file, click the *OK* button in the Upload File dialog box to upload the file.

Step 6: Repeat the procedure you followed in Step 5 to upload the `Gradient02.png` and `Gradient03.png` files. Once these files are uploaded, the Media column should appear as shown in Figure 2-13. (Note that you have uploaded these files to your project on the App Inventor server, but none of them are displayed at this time. Uploading them makes them available to your project.)

Figure 2-13 The Media Column Showing the Three Files Uploaded
(*Source:* MIT App Inventor 2)

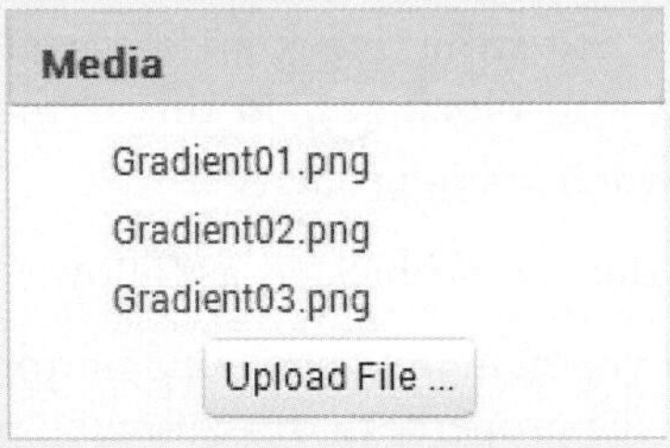

Step 7: Add three Button components to the screen. The Button components' names will be `Button1`, `Button2`, and `Button3`. Perform the following:

- Change the `Button1` component's name to `ButtonBackground1` and change its Text property to *Show Background 1*.
- Change the `Button2` component's name to `ButtonBackground2` and change its Text property to *Show Background 2*.
- Change the `Button3` component's name to `ButtonBackground3` and change its Text property to *Show Background 3*.

The Viewer and the Components column should appear as shown in Figure 2-14

Figure 2-14 Buttons Added to the Screen (*Source:* MIT App Inventor 2)

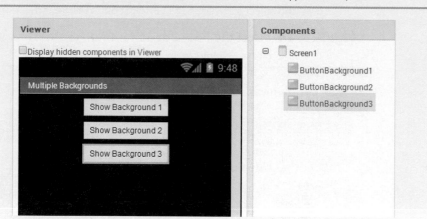

Step 8: Now you will program the `Click` event handlers for the buttons. The idea is that each button will display a different image as the screen's background:

- When the user clicks the `ButtonBackground1` button, the app will display the `Gradient01.png` image.
- When the user clicks the `ButtonBackground2` button, the app will display the `Gradient02.png` image.
- When the user clicks the `ButtonBackground3` button, the app will display the `Gradient03.png` image.

First you will program the `Click` event handler for `ButtonBackground1`. Open the Blocks Editor and in the Blocks column click `ButtonBackground1`. Select the `when ButtonBackground1.Click do` event handler, as shown in Figure 2-15.

Figure 2-15 Create a `Click` Event Handler for `ButtonBackground1` (*Source:* MIT App Inventor 2)

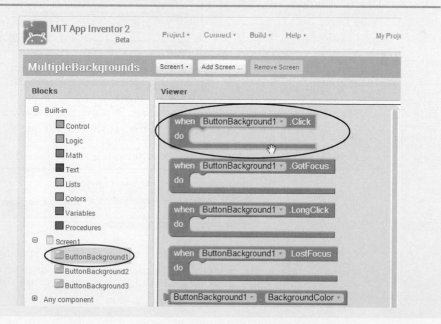

Step 9:   In the Blocks column, click `Screen1`, and then scroll down in the drawer and select `set Screen1.BackgroundImage to`, as shown in Figure 2-16.

Figure 2-16 Select the `set Screen1.BackgroundImage to` Block
(*Source:* MIT App Inventor 2)

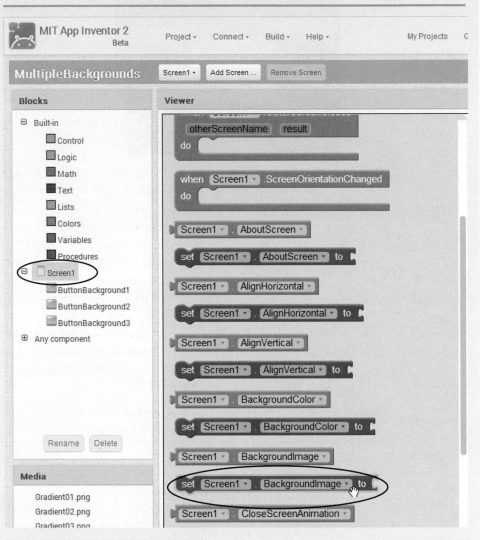

Step 10:   In the workspace, snap the `set Screen1.BackgroundImage to` block inside the `Click` event handler, as shown in Figure 2-17.

Figure 2-17 Snap the Blocks Together (*Source:* MIT App Inventor 2)

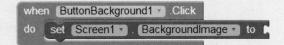

Step 11:   Now you will create a text string block that specifies the name of an image file. Select *Text* (under *Built-in*). A drawer will open, and as shown in Figure 2-18, click the text string block.

Figure 2-18 Select the Text String Block (*Source:* MIT App Inventor 2)

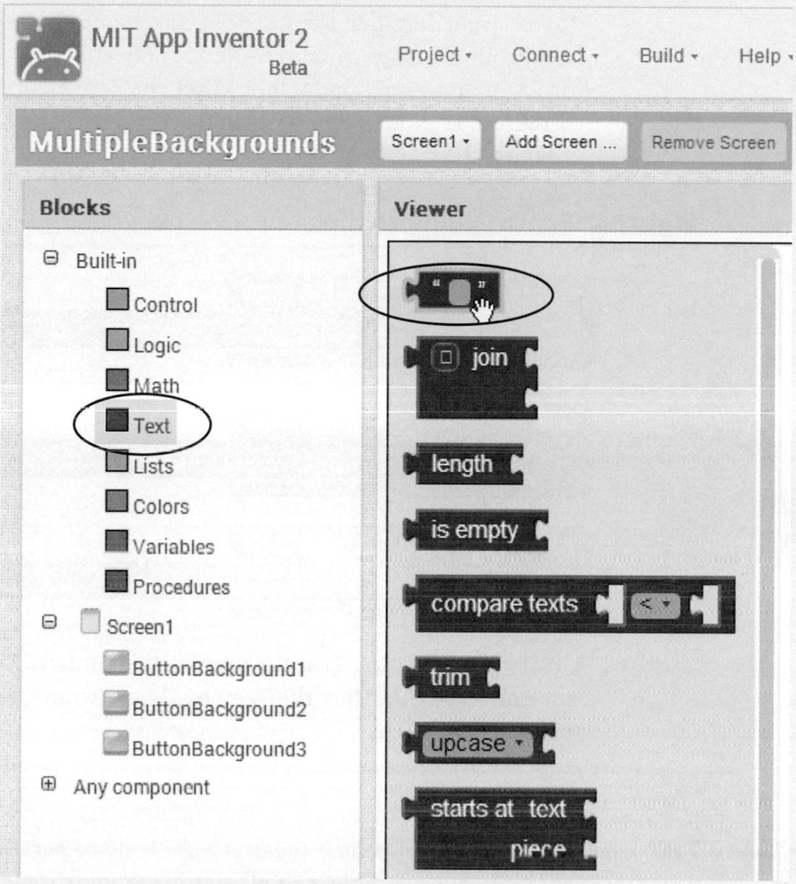

Step 12: Now you will change the value of the text string block that you just created. Click the empty space that appears between the quotation marks and type *Gradient01.png*, as shown in Figure 2-19.

Figure 2-19 Change the Value of the Text String Block to *Gradient01.png*
(*Source:* MIT App Inventor 2)

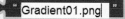

Step 13: Snap the text string block into the empty socket of the set Screen1. BackgroundImage to block, as shown in Figure 2-20. This completes the Click event handler for the ButtonBackground1 component. As a result, when the user clicks the button, the screen's background image will be set to the Gradient01.png file.

Figure 2-20 The Completed Click Event Handler for ButtonBackground1
(*Source:* MIT App Inventor 2)

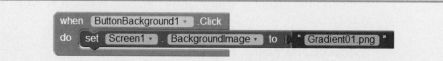

Step 14: Repeat steps 8 through 13 to create the `Click` event handlers for the `ButtonBackground2` and `ButtonBackground3` components. The `Click` event handler for `ButtonBackground2` should set the screen's background image to `Gradient02.png` and the `Click` event handler for `ButtonBackground3` should set the screen's background image to `Gradient03.png`. The completed workspace should appear as shown in Figure 2-21.

Figure 2-21 The Completed Workspace (*Source:* MIT App Inventor 2)

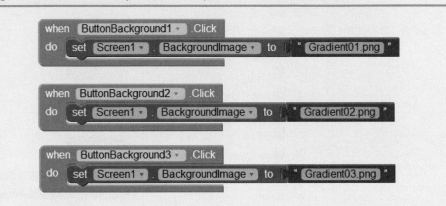

Step 15: Create an emulator. Test the app in the emulator by clicking each button and verifying that the screen's background image changes when you click each one.

> **TIP:** The term *programmatically* means to use code to perform something while a program is running. For example, in Tutorial 2-2 you created an app that programmatically changes the screen's background image when the user clicks a button.

The Image Component

When you use the screen's `BackgroundImage` property to display an image, the image occupies the entire screen and components are placed on top of the image. Another way to display an image is with the Image component, which is found in the *User Interface* section of the Designer's palette. The Image component allows you to specify the image's size with its Width and Height properties. Because it is a component, it is positioned on the screen like any other component.

The Image component has the following properties:

Picture—This property specifies the image file that the component displays. The file must be uploaded to the project on the App Inventor server.
Visible—This property can be set to *showing* or *hidden*. When it is set to *showing*, the image is visible on the screen. When it is set to *hidden*, the image is not visible.
Width—This property specifies the image's width on the screen. It can be set to *Automatic*, *Fill parent*, or a specific number of pixels.

Height—This property specifies the image's height on the screen. It can be set to *Automatic*, *Fill parent*, or a specific number of pixels.

The Width and Height properties have the same settings as they do with Button and Label components. *Automatic* means that the size is set automatically to match the size of the image. *Fill parent* means that the image will be as wide and/or high as the container (such as Screen1) that the component is enclosed in. You can also specify a number of pixels for the image's width and/or height.

Tutorial 2-3 takes you through the steps of creating an Image component that displays poker cards.

VideoNote
Using the Image
Component

Tutorial 2-3:
Using the Image Component

Step 1: Make sure you have downloaded the media files from this book's companion website at www.pearsonhighered.com/gaddis. One of the media folders that you have downloaded is named Poker Cards Small. This folder contains small images of the cards in a deck of poker cards. In this tutorial you will use two of the card images.

Step 2: Start a new App Inventor project named *CardImages*.

Step 3: In the Designer, the Screen1 component will be selected in the Components column. In the Properties column, set the Title property to *Cards* and set the AlignHorizontal property to *Center*.

Step 4: In the Media column, use the *Upload File . . .* button to upload the 2_Clubs.png and 2_Diamonds.png files from the *Poker Cards Small* folder. After you have uploaded the files, the Media column should appear as shown in Figure 2-22.

Figure 2-22 The Media Column after the Image Files have been Uploaded
(*Source:* MIT App Inventor 2)

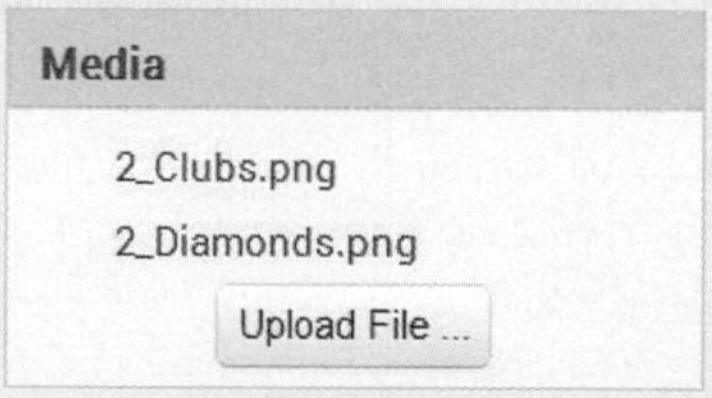

Media

2_Clubs.png

2_Diamonds.png

Upload File ...

Step 5: Find the Image component in the User Interface section of the Palette column and drag it onto the screen. This creates an Image component named Image1. Change the component's name to ImageTwoClubs. Figure 2-23 shows the Viewer and the Components column at this point.

Step 6: Make sure the ImageTwoClubs component is selected, and in the Properties column, click the Picture property. As shown in Figure 2-24, select the 2_Clubs.png image file and click *OK*. The image of a Two of Clubs card should be displayed in the Viewer, as shown in Figure 2-25.

Figure 2-23 An Image Component Added and Renamed (*Source:* MIT App Inventor 2)

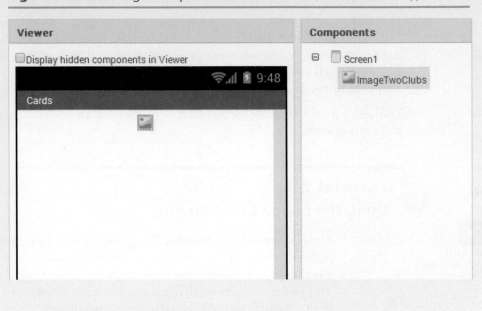

Figure 2-24 An Image Component Added and Renamed (*Source:* MIT App Inventor 2)

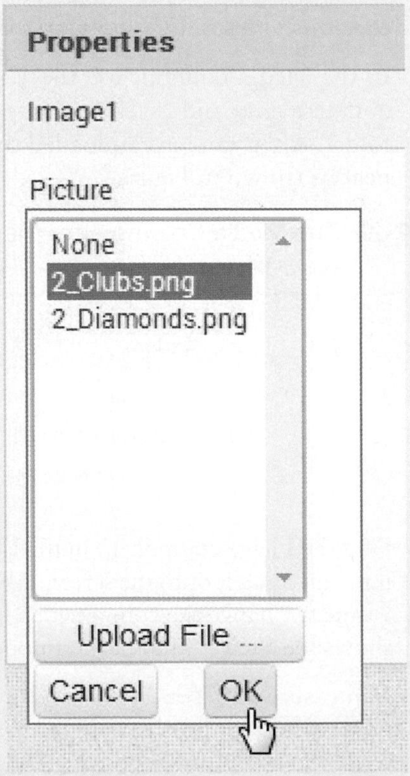

Figure 2-25 The Two of Clubs Card Displayed (*Source:* MIT App Inventor 2)

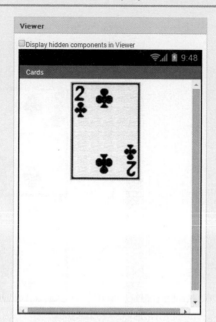

Step 7: Place another Image component on the screen, just below the first one that you created. Change the component's name to ImageTwoDiamonds and set its Picture property to 2_Diamonds.png. The Viewer should now appear as shown in Figure 2-26. If you have an emulator connected, it should appear similar to Figure 2-27.

Figure 2-26 The Two of Diamonds Card Displayed (*Source:* MIT App Inventor 2)

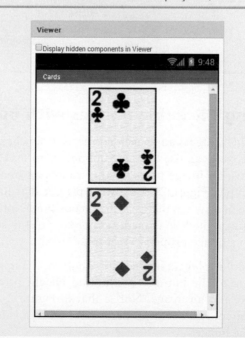

Figure 2-27 The App's Screen Displayed in the Emulator (*Source:* MIT App Inventor 2)

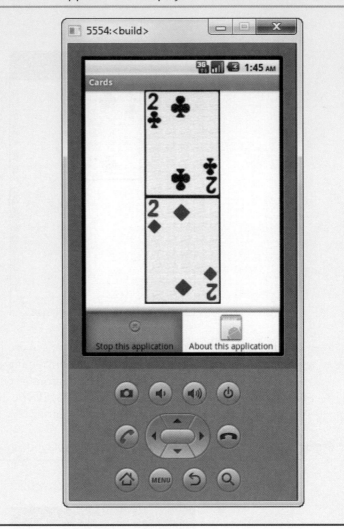

Making Clickable Images with Button components

A *clickable image* is an image that the user can click to make an action happen. In App Inventor, you can use Button components to make clickable images. Button components have an Image property that causes an image to be displayed on the button. For example, Figure 2-28 shows a project that has a Button component displaying an image of a switch that is in the up position. Notice that in the Components column the Button (which is named `ButtonSwitch`) is selected and that in the Properties column its Image property is set to `SwitchUp.png`.

When you display an image with a button, the image will be resized to fit the button according to the button's Width and Height properties. Also, buttons can display both text and an image. Notice that in Figure 2-28 the button's Text property has been cleared. If its Text property were set to a value, the text would be displayed on top of the image.

Figure 2-28 A Button Component Displaying an Image (*Source:* MIT App Inventor 2)

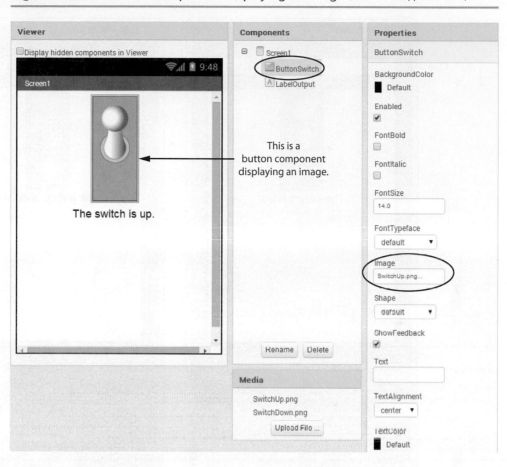

When the user clicks the ButtonSwitch component, the app performs two actions: it changes the image displayed on the button to a switch in the down position and it changes the text that is displayed in the LabelOutput component to *The switch is down*. The button's Click event handler is shown in Figure 2-29. (Of course, the image SwitchDown.png has already been uploaded to the project on the App Inventor server.) Figure 2-30 shows the app running in the emulator. The image on the left shows the emulator before the user clicks the button and the image on the right shows the emulator afterward.

Figure 2-29 The ButtonSwitch Component's Click Event Handler
(*Source:* MIT App Inventor 2)

Figure 2-30 The App Running (*Source:* MIT App Inventor 2)

Tutorial 2-4 gives you a chance to practice clickable images with Button components. In the tutorial, you will create an app with three buttons, displaying images that you can download from the book's companion website.

**VideoNote
Creating the Flags
App**

Tutorial 2-4:
Creating the Flags App

In this tutorial you will create an app that displays the flags of Finland, France, and Germany on Button components. When the user clicks any of these buttons, the name of that flag's country will appear in a Label component.

Step 1: Make sure you have downloaded the media files from this book's companion website at www.pearsonhighered.com/gaddis. One of the media folders that you have downloaded is named *Flags*. This folder contains the images of flags that you will use in this tutorial.

Step 2: Start a new App Inventor project named *Flags*.

Step 3: Set `Screen1`'s Title property to *Flags* and set its AlignHorizontal property to *Center*.

Step 4: In the Media column, use the *Upload File . . .* button to upload the `Finland.png`, `France.png`, and `Germany.png` files from the *Flags* folder.

Step 5: Add three Button components to the screen.

Step 6: Change the name of the `Button1` component to `ButtonFinland`. Clear the contents of its Text property and change its Image property to `Finland.png`.

Step 7: Change the name of the `Button2` component to `ButtonFrance`. Clear the contents of its Text property and change its Image property to `France.png`.

Step 8: Change the name of the `Button3` component to `ButtonGermany`. Clear the contents of its Text property and change its Image property to `Germany.png`. At this point, the Viewer should appear as shown in Figure 2-31.

Figure 2-31 The Flags Displayed on the `Button` Components
(*Source:* MIT App Inventor 2)

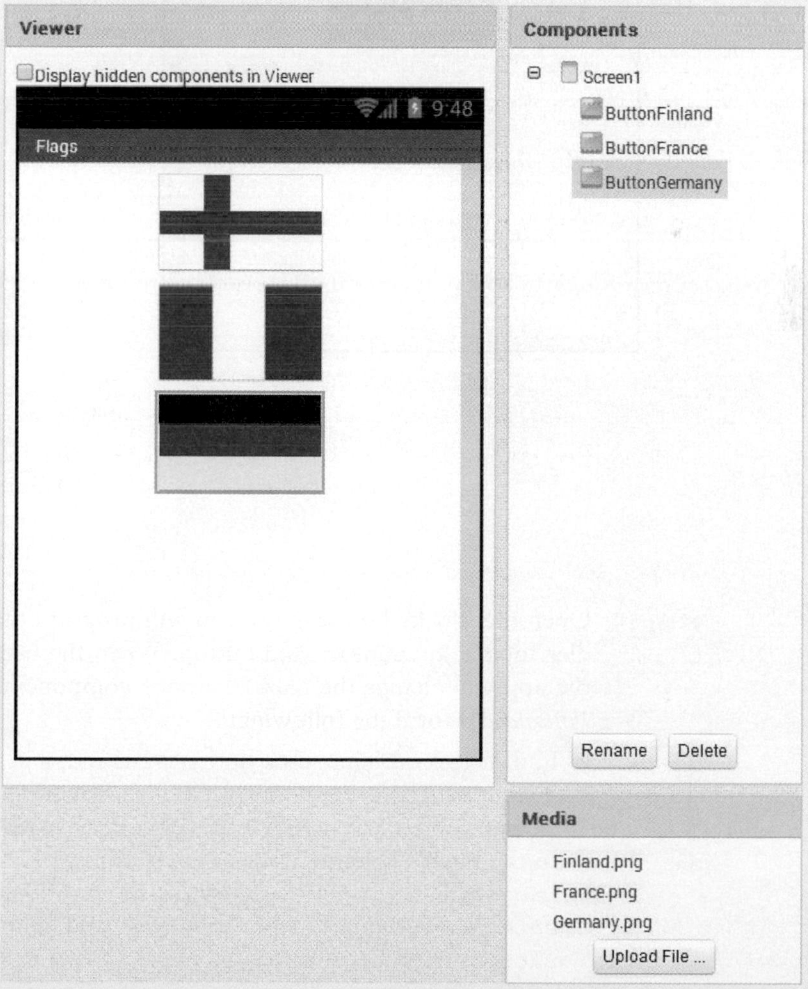

Step 9: Add a Label component below the flags. Change the component's name to LabelCountry and change its Text property to *Click a flag*. Change the FontSize property to 20 and enable the FontBold property. The Viewer should appear as shown in Figure 2-32.

Figure 2-32 The Flags and Label Displayed (*Source:* MIT App Inventor 2)

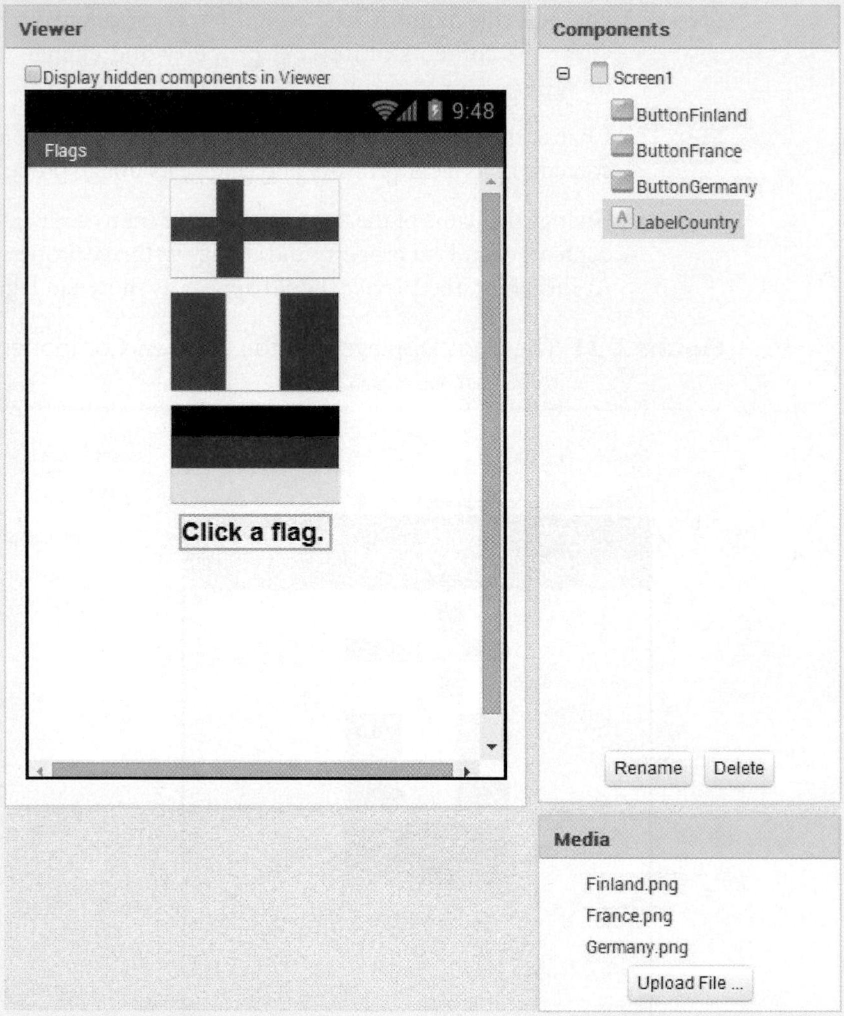

Step 10: Open the Blocks Editor. Now you will program the Click event handler for the ButtonFinland button. When the user clicks the button, the app will change the LabelCountry component's Text property to *Finland*. Perform the following:

- In the Blocks column, click ButtonFinland, and then select the when ButtonFinland.Click do block, as shown in Figure 2-33. This creates an empty when ButtonFinland.Click do block in the workspace.
- In the Blocks column, click LabelCountry, and then select the set LabelCountry.Text to block, as shown in Figure 2-34. Drag the set LabelCountry.Text to block and snap it inside the when ButtonFinland.Click do block, as shown in Figure 2-35.

- In the Blocks column, under *Built-in*, click *Text*, and then select the text string block, as shown in Figure 2-36. Drag the text string block and snap it into the socket of the set LabelCountry.Text to block, as shown in Figure 2-37.
- Change the value of the text string block to *Finland*, as shown in Figure 2-38.

Figure 2-33 Select the when ButtonFinland.Click do **Block**

(*Source:* MIT App Inventor 2)

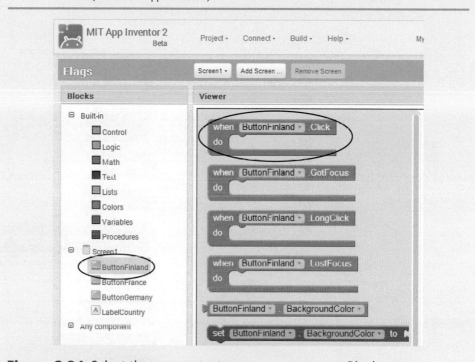

Figure 2-34 Select the set LabelCountry.Text to **Block**

(*Source:* MIT App Inventor 2)

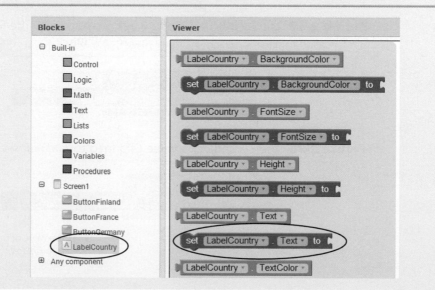

Figure 2-35 The `set LabelCountry.Text to` Block Snapped Inside the `Click` Event Handler *(Source:* MIT App Inventor 2*)*

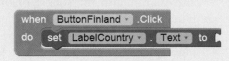

Figure 2-36 Select the Text String Block *(Source:* MIT App Inventor 2*)*

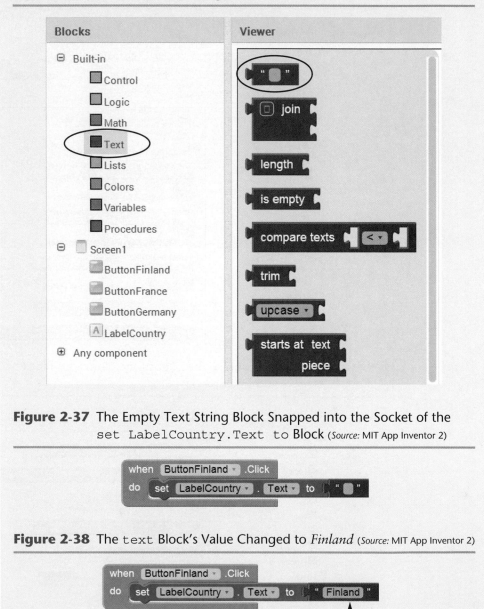

Figure 2-37 The Empty Text String Block Snapped into the Socket of the `set LabelCountry.Text to` Block *(Source:* MIT App Inventor 2*)*

Figure 2-38 The `text` Block's Value Changed to *Finland* *(Source:* MIT App Inventor 2*)*

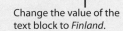

Change the value of the
text block to *Finland*.

Step 11: Repeat the procedures that you performed in Step 10 to program the Click event handlers for the ButtonFrance and ButtonGermany components. When finished, your workspace should look similar to Figure 2-39.

Figure 2-39 The Completed Blocks (*Source:* MIT App Inventor 2)

Step 12: Create a new emulator and test the app. Figure 2-40 shows the app running in the emulator, with each flag being clicked.

Figure 2-40 The App Running (*Source:* MIT App Inventor 2)

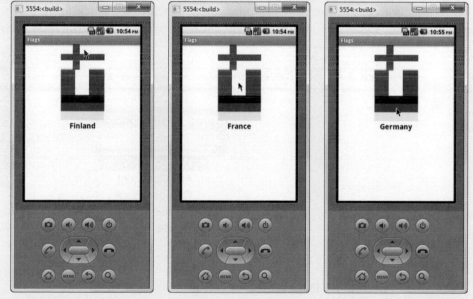

 Checkpoint

2.1 What Screen property causes an image to be displayed as the screen's background?

2.2 Where can you find a list of the media files that you have uploaded to a project?

2.3 If you want to change Screen1's background image programmatically, what block would you use?

2.4 What Image component property specifies the name of the image file to display?

2.5 What happens if a Button component's Image property specifies an image and its Text property is also set to a value?

2.2 Duplicating Blocks and Using Dropdowns

CONCEPT: You can quickly duplicate an existing block by right-clicking it, and then selecting *Duplicate* from the resulting menu. A Dropdown Block is a block that you can change so it performs a different action, or is associated with a different component.

Sometimes the easiest way to create a block is to duplicate one that you already have in the workspace. For example, if an app has several buttons, you can create a Click event handler for the first one, and then duplicate it for the remaining buttons.

When you right-click a block, the menu shown in Figure 2-41 appears. If you select *Duplicate* from the menu, a copy of the block will be created, as shown in Figure 2-42. Notice in Figure 2-42 that a red triangle with an exclamation mark (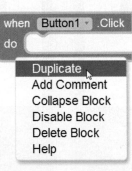) appears on both of the blocks. When this symbol appears on a block, it means the block is causing some sort of error. If you click the symbol, an error message will appear, as shown in Figure 2-43.

Figure 2-41 The Block Menu (*Source:* MIT App Inventor 2)

Figure 2-42 Duplicate Blocks (*Source:* MIT App Inventor 2)

Figure 2-43 Error Message for Duplicate Blocks (*Source:* MIT App Inventor 2)

The error message shown in Figure 2-43 is *This is a duplicate event handler for this component.* This is happening because, for each component, you can have only one event handler for each specific event. In this case, you can have only one Click event handler for each button.

This error can be easily fixed. We simply need to change one of the blocks into a `Click` event handler for a component other than `Button1`. Notice that a small down-arrow (▼) appears next to `Button1` on each of the blocks. If you click the down-arrow, a dropdown menu will appear, as shown in Figure 2-44. The dropdown menu has the names of all the components in the app that can have a `Click` event handler. In this case, it shows the names `Button1`, `Button2`, and `Button3`. If we select `Button2`, the block will become a `Click` event handler for `Button2`, as shown in Figure 2-45. Notice in Figure 2-45 that the error symbol is no longer shown on the blocks.

Figure 2-44 Changing the Duplicate Block's Component (*Source:* MIT App Inventor 2)

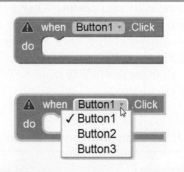

Figure 2-45 The Modified Block (*Source:* MIT App Inventor 2)

Many of the blocks in App Inventor are known as *Dropdown Blocks*, which means that they have dropdown menus that let you change the action that the block performs, or the component that the block is associated with. As you progress through this book, you will see other examples of Dropdown blocks.

Errors and Warnings

At the bottom of the workspace in the Blocks Editor is a set of "counters" that report the number of warnings and errors that are present in the workspace. Figure 2-46 shows an example. The yellow triangle (⚠) indicates warnings and the red triangle (🔺) indicates errors. A warning is usually the result of an incomplete block (such as a block with an empty socket, or a block that needs to be plugged into another block's socket). An error is something that is illegal, such as duplicate event handlers.

Figure 2-46 The Warnings and Errors Counters (*Source:* MIT App Inventor 2)

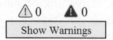

When an error occurs, a red error triangle will appear on the block or blocks that cause the error. You previously saw how to display a block's error message: you click the red triangle that appears on the block.

When warnings are present, however, the warning triangles do not automatically appear on the blocks that have the warnings. To see which blocks have warnings, you must first click the *Show Warnings* buttons that appears below the counters. This causes warning triangles to appear on the blocks that have warnings. Figure 2-47 shows an example. In the image on the left, the warning counter shows that there is one warning present. When you click *Show Warnings*, a warning triangle will appear on the offending block, as shown in the image on the right. To see the actual warning message, click the warning triangle that appears on the block, as shown in Figure 2-48. (Also notice, in Figure 2-47, that when you click *Show Warnings*, it changes to *Hide Warnings*. When you click *Hide Warnings*, the warning triangles are hidden.)

Figure 2-47 Showing Warnings (*Source:* MIT App Inventor 2)

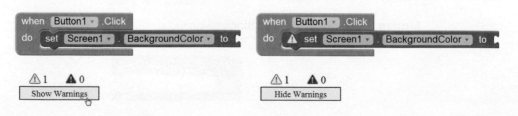

Figure 2-48 A Warning Message Displayed (*Source:* MIT App Inventor 2)

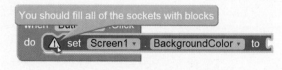

> **TIP:** You can also duplicate a block by copying and pasting it. Simply click the block to select it, press Ctrl-C to copy it to the clipboard, and then press Ctrl-V to paste it.

2.3 Sounds

CONCEPT: The Sound component is used for playing short audio files, such as sound effects, and for vibrating the phone. You use the Player component for playing longer audio files, such as songs.

App Inventor provides two components for playing sound files: The Sound component and the Player component. The Sound component is recommended for small files containing short sound effects, and the Player component is recommended for larger files, such as those containing music. Both the Sound and the Player component can make the phone vibrate. These components support a variety of sound file formats, but .mp3 and .wav are recommended.

The Sound Component

In the Designer, the Sound component is found in the Media section of the Palette, as shown in Figure 2-49. You create a Sound component like any other component: you drag it from the palette to the Viewer. Unlike other components, the Sound component is a *nonvisible component*, which means that it is not visible on the app's screen. The Sound component sits in memory and does work for the app, but it does not appear in the app's user interface.

When you drop a Sound component onto your app's screen, it appears in the area below the screen, as shown in Figure 2-50. The component also appears in the Components column, as shown in the figure. (When you create a Sound component, it will be given a default name, such as Sound1. As usual, you should change the component's name to something more meaningful.)

Sound components have a Source property that specifies the name of an audio file. The audio file must be uploaded to the App Inventor server before it can be used. You can use the Media column to upload audio files; the process is exactly

Figure 2-49 The Sound Component is in the Media Palette *(Source:* MIT App Inventor 2)

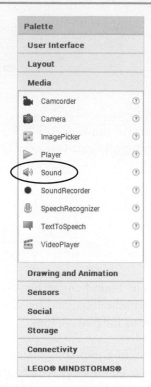

Figure 2-50 The Sound Component is a Nonvisible Component
(Source: MIT App Inventor 2)

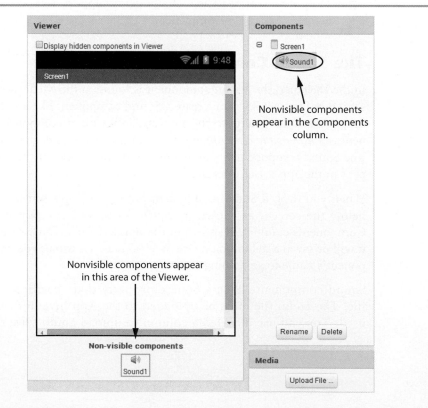

like the process of uploading image files. Alternatively, you can use the Source property to upload a file. As shown in Figure 2-51, clicking the Source property in the Properties column causes a dialog box to appear. You can either select a previously uploaded file or you can click the *Upload File . . .* button to upload a file.

Figure 2-51 The Source Property (*Source:* MIT App Inventor 2)

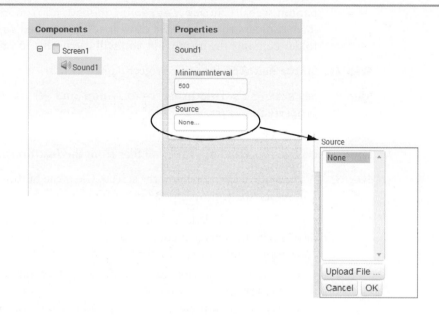

In the Blocks Editor, you use the Sound component's `Play` method to play the audio file specified by the Source property. You will find the block for the `Play` method by clicking the name of the Sound component in the Blocks column, as shown in Figure 2-52.

Figure 2-52 The Sound Component's `Play` Method (*Source:* MIT App Inventor 2)

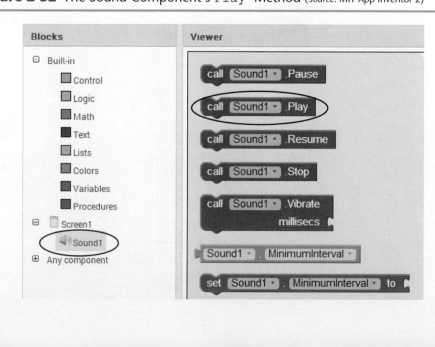

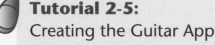

Tutorial 2-5:
Creating the Guitar App

**VideoNote
Creating the
Guitar App**

In this tutorial you will create an app that displays an image of a guitar on a Button component. When the user clicks the button, the app plays the sound of a guitar.

Step 1:   Make sure you have downloaded the media files from this book's companion website at www.pearsonhighered.com/gaddis. One of the media folders that you have downloaded is named *Instruments*. This folder contains the image that you will use in this tutorial.

Step 2:   Start a new App Inventor project named *Guitar*.

Step 3:   Set Screen1's Title property to *Guitar* and set its AlignHorizontal property to *Center*.

Step 4:   In the Media column, use the *Upload File . . .* button to upload the Guitar.png and Guitar.wav files from the *Instrument* folder.

Step 5:   Add a Button component to the screen. Clear the button's Text property and set its Image property to *Guitar.png*.

Step 6:   Open the Media palette and drag a Sound component to the Viewer and drop it onto the screen. A component named Sound1 will be created in the *Nonvisible components* area just below the screen. Perform the following:

- Use the Components column to change the component's name to SoundGuitar.
- Change the component's Source property to *Guitar.wav*.

At this point, the Viewer, Components, Media, and Properties columns should appear as shown in Figure 2-53.

Figure 2-53 The Guitar Project (*Source:* MIT App Inventor 2)

Viewer	Components	Properties
☐ Display hidden components in Viewer	⊟ ☐ Screen1	SoundGuitar
📶 🔋 9:48	📱 ButtonGuitar	MinimumInterval
Guitar	🔊 SoundGuitar	500
		Source
		guitar.wav ...
	Rename Delete	
Non-visible components	**Media**	
🔊 SoundGuitar	guitar.wav	
	guitar.png	
	Upload File ...	

Step 7: Open the Blocks Editor. Now you will program the `Click` event handler for the `ButtonGuitar` button. When the user clicks the button, the app will use the `SoundGuitar` component to play its sound file. Perform the following:

- In the Blocks column, click `ButtonGuitar`, and then select the `when ButtonGuitar.Click do` block. This creates an empty `when ButtonGuitar.Click do` block in the workspace.
- In the Blocks column, click `SoundGuitar`, and then select the `call SoundGuitar.Play` block, as shown in Figure 2-54. Drag the `call SoundGuitar.Play` block and snap it inside the `when Button Guitar.Click do` block, as shown in Figure 2-55.

Figure 2-54 The `call SoundGuitar.Play` Block (*Source:* MIT App Inventor 2)

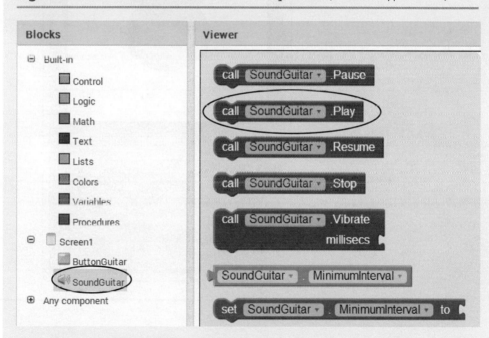

Figure 2-55 The Completed `Click` Event Handler for the `ButtonGuitar` Component (*Source:* MIT App Inventor 2)

Step 8: Create an emulator and test the app. Figure 2-56 shows the app running. When you click the image of the guitar, you should hear sound of a guitar playing.

Figure 2-56 The Guitar App Running (*Source:* MIT App Inventor 2)

Pausing, Resuming, and Stopping the Sound

In addition to the Play method, the Sound component provides other methods that control a sound that is currently playing. These methods are Pause, Resume, and Stop. Figure 2-57 shows the blocks for all of the Sound component methods. Here is a summary of these methods:

- Pause—This method pauses an audio file that is currently playing.
- Resume—After you have used the Pause method to pause an audio file, you can use the Resume method to start it playing again at the point where it was paused.
- Stop—This method stops the audio file that is currently playing

Figure 2-57 The Sound Component Methods (*Source:* MIT App Inventor 2)

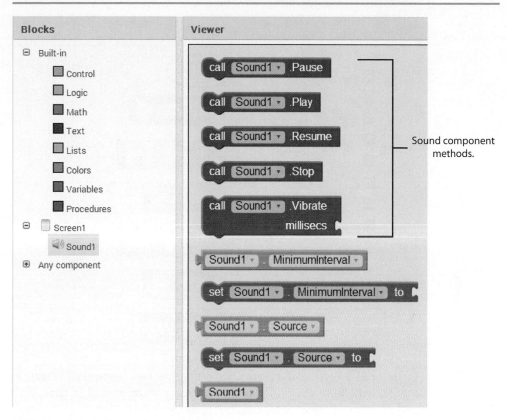

Vibrating the Phone

In addition to playing audio files, you can also use a Sound component to vibrate the phone. (Of course, the emulator doesn't vibrate. This works only if you have an actual phone connected to App Inventor.) To vibrate the phone, you call the Sound component's Vibrate method.

The Vibrate method will cause the phone to vibrate for a specified number of milliseconds. (A millisecond is 1/1000th of a second, so, a full second is 1000 milliseconds, and a half second is 500 milliseconds.)

Figure 2-58 shows an example of the Sound component's Vibrate method. Notice that a number block specifying 250 is plugged into its socket. As a result, this block will cause the phone to vibrate for 250 milliseconds, or a quarter of a second.

Figure 2-58 The Sound Component's Vibrate Method (*Source:* MIT App Inventor 2)

You use the number block any time that you need to specify a number in a program. In the Blocks column, you will find the number block under *Built-In*, in the *Math* drawer, as shown in Figure 2-59. When you create a number block, it has the default value of *0*. You can click on the value and change it to any number you need.

Figure 2-59 The Number Block (*Source:* MIT App Inventor 2)

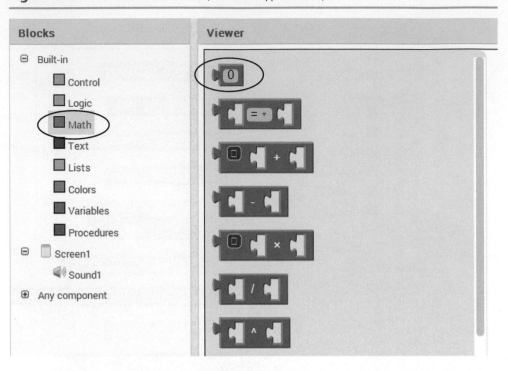

In Tutorial 2-6 you will create an app that has two buttons to vibrate the phone. One button will cause the phone to vibrate for a short period of time (250 milliseconds) and the other button will cause the phone to vibrate for a long period of time (1000 milliseconds).

VideoNote
Making the Phone
Vibrate

Tutorial 2-6:
Making the Phone Vibrate

NOTE: You will be able to test this app only if you have a smart-phone connected to App Inventor.

Step 1: Start a new App Inventor project named *Vibrate*.

Step 2: Set Screen1's Title property to *Make the Phone Vibrate* and set its AlignHorizontal property to *Center*.

Step 3: Add a Button component to the screen. Change the button's name to ButtonShortVibrate and change its Text property to *Short Vibration*.

Step 4: Add another Button component to the screen. Change the button's name to ButtonLongVibrate and change its Text property to *Long Vibration*.

Step 5:   Add a Sound component and change its name to `SoundVibration`. Figure 2-60 shows the app design at this point.

Figure 2-60 The Vibrate App *(Source:* MIT App Inventor 2)

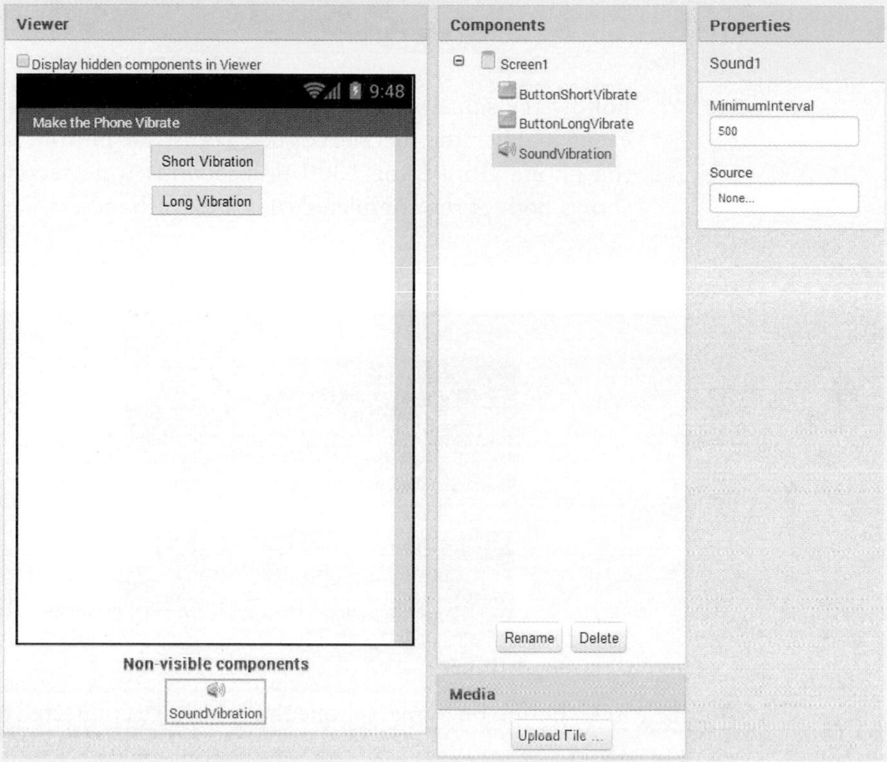

Step 6:   Now you will program the `Click` event handlers for the buttons. You will start with the `ButtonShortVibrate` button, which will make the phone vibrate for 250 milliseconds (one quarter second). Open the *Blocks Editor*, then open the *My Blocks* palette and perform the following to create the first event handler:

- Click `ButtonShortVibrate` in the Blocks column and select the `when ButtonShortVibrate.Click do` block.
- Click `SoundVibration` in the Blocks column and select the `call SoundVibration` block. Snap the block inside the `when ButtonShortVibrate.Click do` block.
- In the Blocks column, under *Built-In*, click *Math*. Select the number block (0) and snap it into the socket of the `call SoundVibration` block.
- Click the *0* value that appears in the number block and change it to *250*.

The event handler should now appear as shown in Figure 2-61.

Figure 2-61 The Completed `Click` Event Handler for the `ButtonShort-Vibrate` **Component** (*Source:* MIT App Inventor 2)

Step 7:   Follow the same procedure that you did in Step 6 to create a `Click` event handler for the `ButtonLongVibrate` button, which will make the phone vibrate for 1000 milliseconds (one second). Figure 2-62 shows both of the completed `Click` event handlers.

Figure 2-62 The Completed `Click` Event Handlers (*Source:* MIT App Inventor 2)

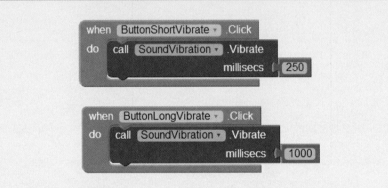

Step 8:   Test the app on a smartphone that you have connected to App Inventor.

The Player Component

The Sound component is recommended for playing short audio files (such as sound effects). If you want to play a long audio file, such as an entire song, it is recommended that you use the more efficient Player component instead. In the Designer, the Player component is found in the *Media* section of the Palette. It is similar to the Sound component. Here is a summary of its properties:

- You use the Source property to designate an audio file.
- It has a Volume property that can be set to a value from 0 through 100, to control the volume of the device's speaker.
- It has a Loop property that can cause the audio file to loop, or play repeatedly, if the property is enabled.

Here is a summary of the Player component's methods:

- You use the component's `Start` method to start the audio file playing.
- You use the component's `Pause` method to pause an audio file that is currently playing.

- You use the component's `Stop` method to stop an audio file that is currently playing.
- You use the component's `Vibrate` method to vibrate the phone a specified number of milliseconds.

In addition, when the Player component's audio file finishes playing, a `Completed` event occurs. You can create a `Completed` event handler to execute when the end of the file is reached.

> **NOTE:** The Player component can also be used to play video. However, the VideoPlayer component provides greater functionality with videos.

Checkpoint

2.6 In what section of the Palette will you find the Sound component? The Player component?

2.7 What property of the Sound component do you use to specify the name of an audio file?

2.8 How do you play a sound with the Sound component?

2.9 What Sound component method pauses the currently playing sound?

2.10 If you want to vibrate the phone for a full second, how many milliseconds will you specify to the Sound component's `Vibrate` method?

2.11 When would you choose to use the Player component instead of the Sound component?

2.4 Color Blocks

CONCEPT: In code, you use Color blocks to represent and work with colors.

Many of the user interface components in App Inventor have properties that determine the component's color. For example, Screen, Button, and Label components all have a BackgroundColor property that determines the component's background color. Button and Label components also have a TextColor property that determines the color of the text that the component displays. You can easily change the values of these properties in the Designer. You can also create code that changes the value of a color property while the app is running.

App Inventor provides a selection of Color blocks that you can use in the Blocks Editor to set the value of a color property. As shown in Figure 2-63, you click *Colors*, which appears under *Built-in*. This opens a drawer that contains blocks representing thirteen basic colors. (The two methods that appear at the bottom of the drawer are used when you want to make up your own colors.)

Figure 2-63 The `Color` Blocks (*Source:* MIT App Inventor 2)

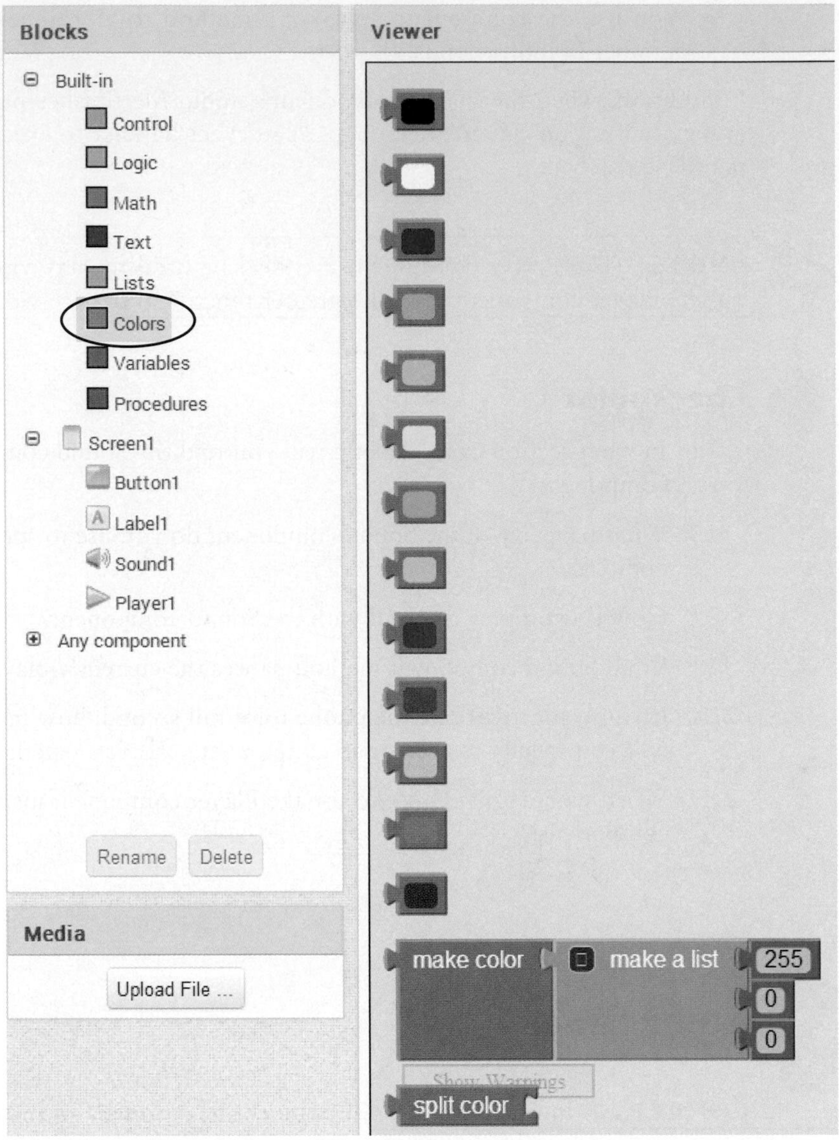

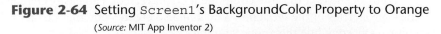

For example, Figure 2-64 shows the blocks for programmatically setting `Screen1`'s BackgroundColor property to orange and Figure 2-65 shows the blocks for setting a Button component's TextColor property to white.

Figure 2-64 Setting `Screen1`'s BackgroundColor Property to Orange

(*Source:* MIT App Inventor 2)

Figure 2-65 Setting a Button Component's TextColor Property to White
(*Source:* MIT App Inventor 2)

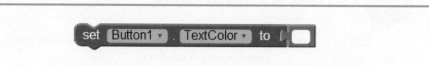

The Color blocks that are found in the Color drawer represent only a basic set of thirteen colors. You can click on a Color block, however, and open a palette of 70 colors, as shown in Figure 2-66. You can then select any color from the palette for that block.

Figure 2-66 The Color Palette (*Source:* MIT App Inventor 2)

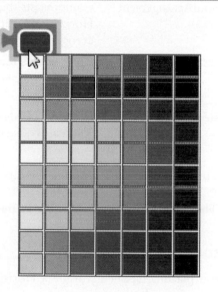

In Tutorial 2-7 you will use Color blocks to program a set of buttons that each change the screen's background color.

 Checkpoint

2.12 Where do you find the Color blocks in the Blocks Editor?

2.13 How many blocks representing basic colors does App Inventor provide in the Color drawer?

2.14 You can set property values in the Designer, using the Properties column. Why would you ever need to use Color blocks to set a color property?

2.5 Layout Components

CONCEPT: A layout component is a container that governs the positions of the components it contains.

An important part of designing an app's user interface is determining the layout of the components that are displayed in the application's windows. In App Inventor, you do not specify the exact location of a component on a screen. Instead, you let a *layout component* control the positions of components for you. Table 2-1 summarizes the layout components provided by App Inventor.

Table 2-1 Layout Components (*Source:* Pearson Education, Inc.)

Component	Summary
HorizontalArrangement	Components that are placed inside a HorizontalArrangement are arranged horizontally, across the screen.
TableArrangement	Components that are placed inside a TableArrangement are arranged in a table, with rows and columns.
VerticalArrangement	Components that are placed inside a VerticalArrangement are arranged vertically.

The layout components are found in the *Layout* section of the Palette. To use one of the components, you drag it from the Palette to the Viewer and drop it on the app's screen. Then, you place other components inside of it.

HorizontalArrangement

When you place components inside a HorizontalArrangement, the components are arranged horizontally, in a row across the screen. Figure 2-67 shows a screen that has a HorizontalArrangement component. Three Button components are inside the HorizontalArrangement. Notice that the buttons appear across the screen, horizontally.

Take a closer look at the Components column and notice the hierarchical structure. `Screen1` is the outermost component. It contains the HorizontalArrangement component, which contains the three Button components.

Also notice that the HorizontalArrangement component has Width and Height properties and each is set to *Automatic*. This means that the width and height of the HorizontalArrangement is determined by the width and height of the components inside of it.

The HorizontalArrangement component also has AlignHorizontal and AlignVertical properties. These properties determine the alignment of the components inside the HorizontalArrangement component. They work like the Screen component properties of the same name. The AlignHorizontal property can be set to *Left*, *Center*, or *Right*. The AlignVertical property can be set to *Top*, *Center*, or *Bottom*.

For example, Figure 2-68 shows three HorizontalArrangement components, each with its Width property set to *Fill parent*. The screen on the left has its AlignHorizontal property set to *Left*, the one in the middle has its AlignHorizontal property set to *Center* and the one on the right has its AlignHorizontal property set to *Right*.

> **NOTE:** The HorizontalArrangement component's AlignVertical property has no effect if the component's Height property is set to *Automatic*.

Figure 2-67 Three Buttons Inside a HorizontalArrangement *(Source:* MIT App Inventor 2)

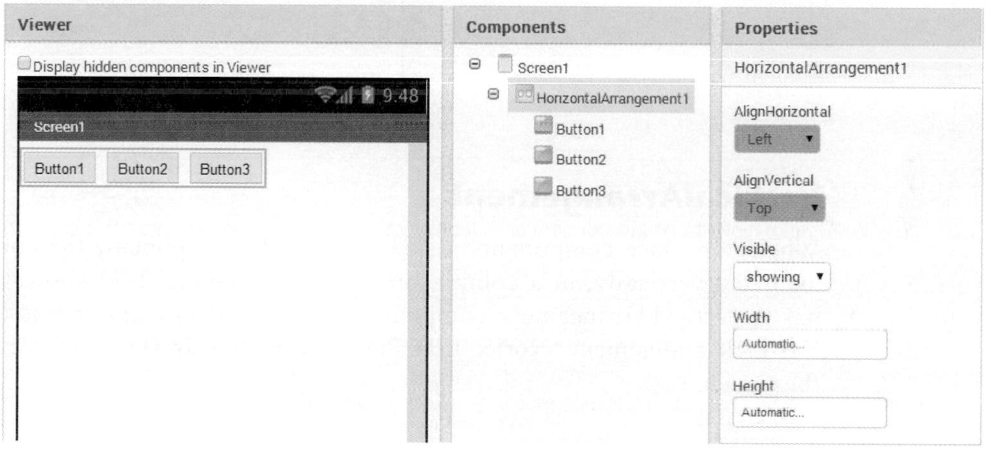

Figure 2-68 HorizontalArrangement Settings *(Source:* MIT App Inventor 2)

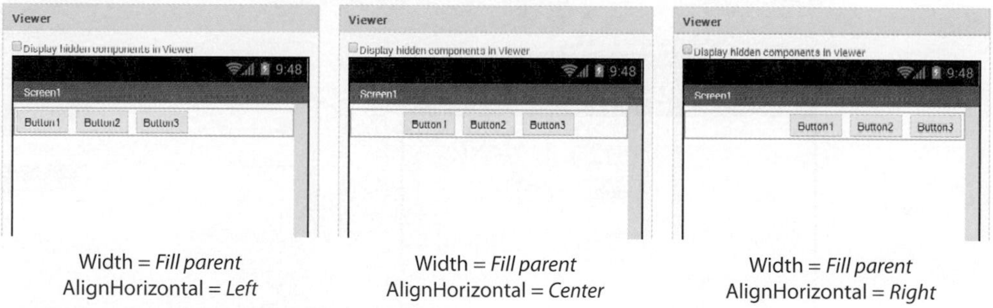

Width = *Fill parent*
AlignHorizontal = *Left*

Width = *Fill parent*
AlignHorizontal = *Center*

Width = *Fill parent*
AlignHorizontal = *Right*

TableArrangement

Components that are placed inside a TableArrangement are arranged in a grid, with rows and columns. TableArrangements have a Rows property that determines the number of rows and a Columns property that determines the number of columns. By default, the Rows and Columns properties are both set to 2. Figure 2-69 shows an example of a screen with a TableArrangement component that has 3 rows and 3 columns. The TableArrangement has a total of 9 cells, each of which can hold a component. In the figure, each cell of the TableArrangement holds a Button component.

Figure 2-69 A TableArrangement with 3 Rows and 3 Columns *(Source: MIT App Inventor 2)*

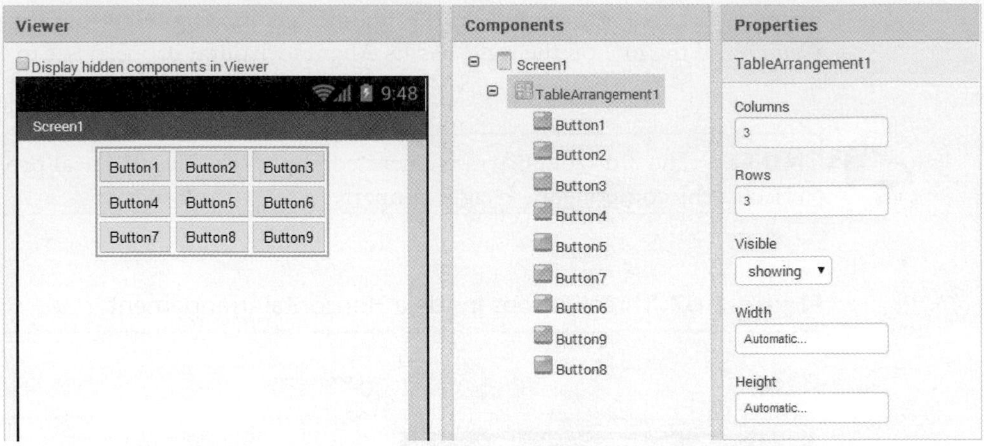

VerticalArrangement

When you place components inside a VerticalArrangement, the components are arranged vertically, in a column on the screen. Figure 2-70 shows a screen that has a VerticalArrangement component. Three Button components are inside the VerticalArrangement. Notice that the buttons appear vertically, in a column on the screen.

Figure 2-70 Three Buttons Inside a VerticalArrangement   *(Source: MIT App Inventor 2)*

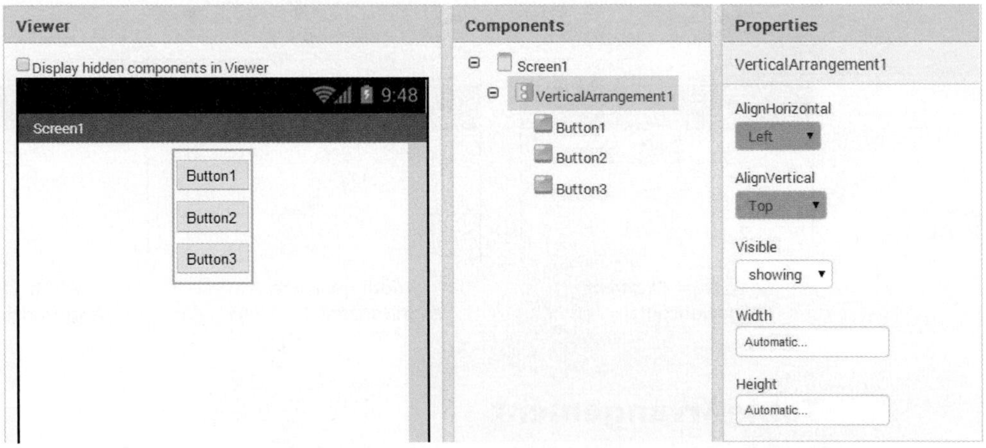

 NOTE: If you do not place a layout component on the screen, the screen acts as a VerticalArrangement.

Using Multiple Layout Components in the Same Screen

Quite often, to get the particular screen layout that you desire, you will have to use multiple layout components. You can even nest a layout component inside of another layout component. For example, Figure 2-71 shows a screen that has a TableArrangement component with a VerticalArrangement component nested inside of it. Here are some details about the components in the figure (as illustrated in Figure 2-72):

- The TableArrangement has 2 columns and 1 row.
- The Button component is in the TableArrangement's left column and the VerticalArrangement is in the TableArrangement's right column.
- The Image components are in the VerticalArrangement.

Figure 2-71 A Screen with Nested Arrangement Components (*Source:* MIT App Inventor 2)

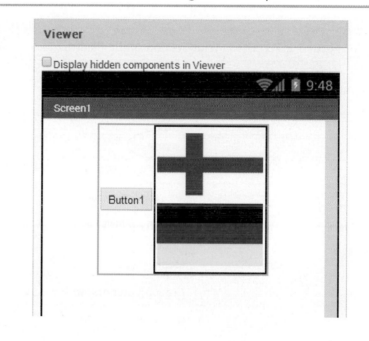

Figure 2-72 The Screen Layout (*Source:* MIT App Inventor 2)

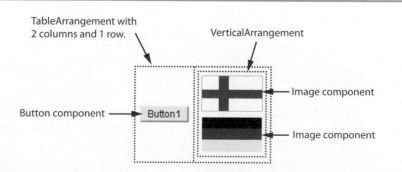

VideoNote
Using Layout
Components and
Color Blocks

Tutorial 2-7:
Using Layout Components and Color Blocks

In this tutorial you will create an app that has six buttons, each of which will change the screen's background color. The buttons will be arranged in a TableArrangement that has two columns and three rows.

Step 1:   Start a new project named *BackgroundColors*.

Step 2:   Set Screen1's AlignHorizontal property to *Center* and its Title property to *Change the Background Color*.

Step 3:   Open the *Layout* section of the Palette, as shown in Figure 2-73, and drag a TableArrangement component to the screen. This creates a TableArrangement component named TableArrangement1. (We will not change the name of this component.)

Figure 2-73 The Layout Section of the Palette (*Source:* MIT App Inventor 2)

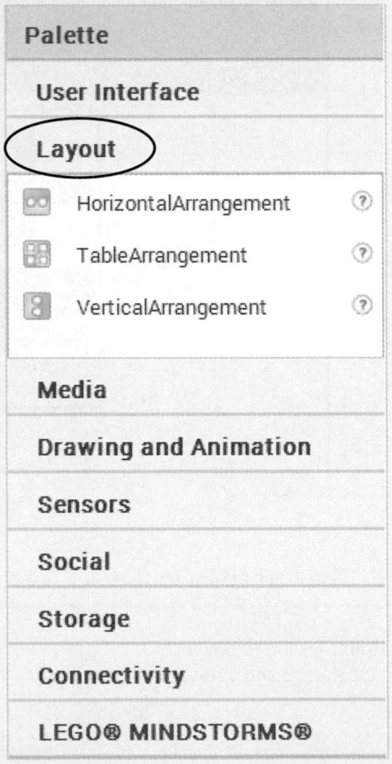

Palette
User Interface
Layout
HorizontalArrangement ?
TableArrangement ?
VerticalArrangement ?
Media
Drawing and Animation
Sensors
Social
Storage
Connectivity
LEGO® MINDSTORMS®

Step 4:   The TableArrangement1 component has properties named Columns and Rows that determine the number of columns and rows in the layout. By default both of these properties are set to 2. Change the Rows property to 3. At this point, the Viewer, Components column, and Properties columns should appear as shown in Figure 2-74.

Figure 2-74 The `TableArrangement1` Component Created
(*Source:* MIT App Inventor 2)

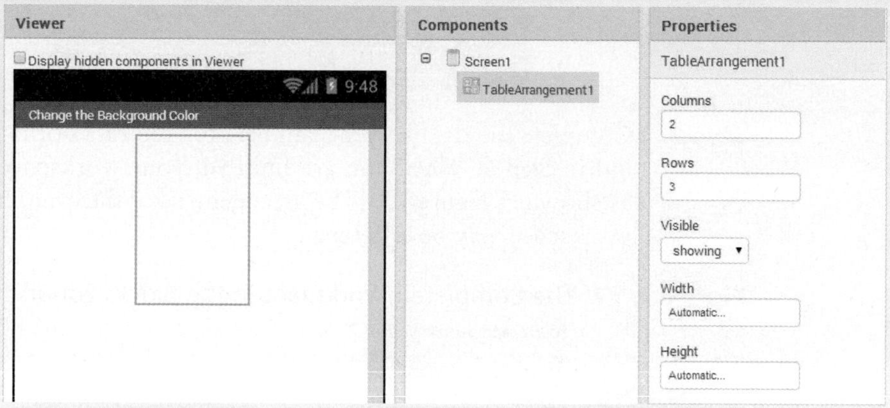

Step 5: Create six Button components and place them inside the TableArrangement. Change the names of the buttons and the values of their Text properties, as shown in Figure 2-75.

Figure 2-75 The Buttons Created and Placed Inside the TableArrangement
(*Source:* MIT App Inventor 2)

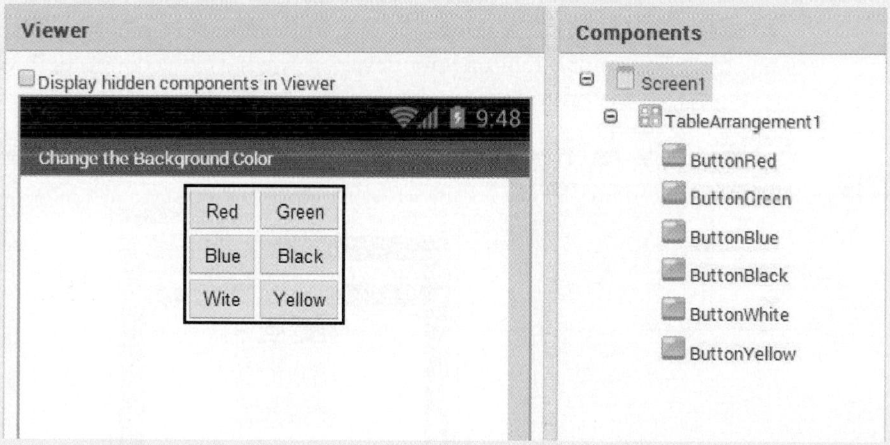

Step 6: Now you will program the `Click` event handlers for the buttons. Open the Blocks Editor and perform the following to create the first event handler:

- Click `ButtonRed` in the Blocks column and select the `when ButtonRed.Click do` block.
- Click `Screen1` in the palette and select the `set Screen1.BackgroundColor to` block. Snap the block inside the `when ButtonRed.Click do` block.
- Click *Colors*, under the *Built-In* section of the Blocks column. Select the block for the color red and snap it into the socket of the `set Screen1.BackgroundColor to` block.

The event handler should now appear as shown in Figure 2-76.

Figure 2-76 The Completed `Click` Event Handler for the `ButtonRed`
Component (*Source:* MIT App Inventor 2)

Step 7:   Complete the `Click` event handlers for the rest of the buttons, as you
did in Step 6. When you are finished, your workspace should appear
as shown in Figure 77. (The arrangement of the event handlers in your
workspace may be different.)

Figure 2-77 The Completed Workspace in the Blocks Editor
(*Source:* MIT App Inventor 2)

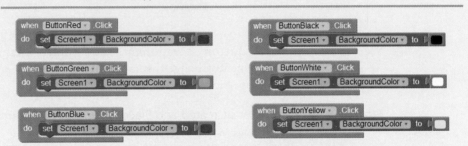

Step 8:   Figure 2-78 shows the app running in the emulator. Test the app (on the
emulator, or on your device, if you have one connected). Click each button
to confirm that it changes the screen's background to the desired color.

Figure 2-78 The App Running in the Emulator (*Source:* MIT App Inventor 2)

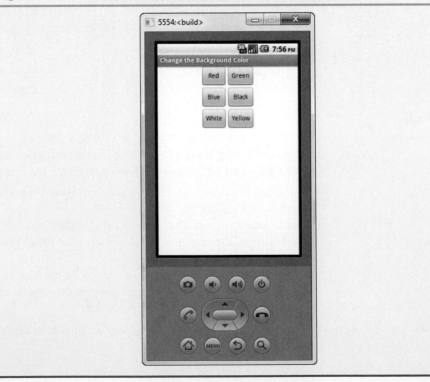

Checkpoint

2.15 How are components arranged on the screen when they are placed inside a HorizontalArrangement?

2.16 How are components arranged on the screen when they are placed inside a VerticalArrangement?

2.17 How are components arranged on the screen when they are placed inside a TableArrangement?

2.18 What is the default arrangement for the screen, if you do not place an arrangement component on it?

 2.6 Commenting Blocks

A *comment* is a note that the programmer writes into a program, explaining some part of the code. Programmers consider comments a crucial part of a program because they help someone who is reading the program's code to understand the instructions.

In the Blocks Editor, you can add a comment to any block by right-clicking the block, and then selecting *Add Comment* from the menu that pops up (as shown in Figure 2-79). This causes a small question mark (?) to appear on the block. When you click the question mark, a small note editor will appear, attached to the block. You can type any information you wish into the note editor, as shown in Figure 2-80. When you are finished, click the small question mark to hide the comment. From that point forward, you can click the question mark to pop the comment up.

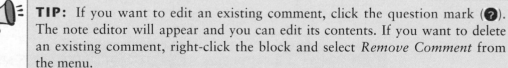 **TIP:** If you want to edit an existing comment, click the question mark (?). The note editor will appear and you can edit its contents. If you want to delete an existing comment, right-click the block and select *Remove Comment* from the menu.

Figure 2-79 Right-click a Block to Get this Menu

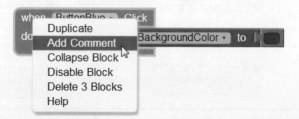

Figure 2-80 Note Editor for Comments (*Source:* MIT App Inventor 2)

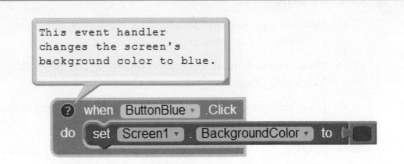

Comments do not affect the execution of your app in any way, but they are important because they make your program more understandable. Tutorial 2-8 will give you some practice working with comments. In the tutorial you will insert comments into the app that you created in the previous tutorial.

VideoNote
Adding Comments

Tutorial 2-8:
Adding Comments

Step 1: Open the BackgroundColors project that you created in Tutorial 2-7.

Step 2: Open the Blocks Editor.

Step 3: Perform the following procedure with each Click event handler:
- Right-click on the event handler block.
- Select *Add Comment* from the menu that pops up.
- Type a brief comment describing the event handler.

Figure 2-81 shows an example of your workspace after you have added comments to each event handler.

Figure 2-81 The Workspace with Comments Added (*Source:* MIT App Inventor 2)

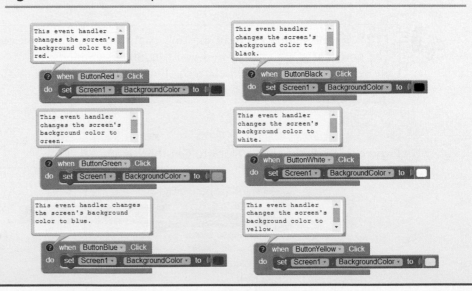

✔ **Checkpoint**

2.19 Why are comments important?

2.20 Do comments affect the way a program runs?

2.21 How do you create a comment in App Inventor?

Review Questions

Multiple Choice

1. This Screen property sets the screen's background image.
   a. Image
   b. BackgroundImage
   c. Picture
   d. Background

2. A list of media files that have been uploaded to a project is displayed in this column of the Designer.
   a. Media
   b. Components
   c. Properties
   d. Viewer

3. This Image component property specifies the name of the image file to display.
   a. Image
   b. Display
   c. Picture
   d. ImageFile

4. You can use this type of component to create a clickable image.
   a. Button
   b. Image
   c. ClickableImage
   d. ImageLink

5. This Sound component property specifies the name of an audio file.
   a. AudioFile
   b. Audio
   c. SoundFile
   d. Source

6. You call this Sound component method to play a sound.
   a. Start
   b. Play
   c. Engage
   d. Begin

7. If you want to vibrate the phone for half a second, which of these values would you plug into the socket of the Sound component's `Vibrate` method?

   a. 500
   b. 0.5
   c. 50
   d. 1/2

8. This type of arrangement formats components in a row across the screen.

   a. HorizontalArrangement
   b. LinearArrangement
   c. VerticalArrangement
   d. TableArrangement

9. This type of arrangement formats components in a column across the screen.

   a. HorizontalArrangement
   b. LinearArrangement
   c. VerticalArrangement
   d. TableArrangement

10. This type of arrangement formats components in rows and columns on the screen.

    a. HorizontalArrangement
    b. LinearArrangement
    c. VerticalArrangement
    d. TableArrangement

11. If you do not place a layout component on the screen, the screen acts as this type of arrangement.

    a. HorizontalArrangement
    b. TableArrangement
    c. VerticalArrangement
    d. A combination of TableArrangement and HorizontalArrangement

12. This is a note of explanation that is inserted into a program.

    a. Comment
    b. Argument
    c. Codenote
    d. Editing tag

Short Answer

1. If you want to display an image on an app's screen, and be able to place components on top of the image, would you use an Image component or the screen's BackgroundImage property?

2. Suppose you want to display an image as the background for an app's screen. Describe two ways that you can upload the image to the project on the App Inventor server.

3. Using blocks, how would you switch the screen's background image while the app is running?

4. How do you create a clickable image?

5. What happens if a Button component's Text property is set to a value, and the component's Image property is set to the name of an uploaded image?

6. Once you add a Sound component to a project, how do you specify a particular audio file as the component's sound source?

7. How do you play an audio file that is the source for a Sound component?

8. What is a millisecond? If you want to use a Sound component to vibrate the phone for three-fourths of a second, how many milliseconds to you specify when using the `Vibrate` method?

9. Where are the Color blocks located in the Blocks Editor?

10. Which layout component would you use in each of these situations?
    - You want to display components in a grid, with rows and columns
    - You want to display components in a row, across the screen
    - You want to display components in a column

11. Why are comments an important part of a program?

12. How do you create a comment for a block?

Exercises

1. Modify the MultipleBackgrounds app that you created in Tutorial 2-2 so it plays a sound effect each time the user switches the background image. (If you have downloaded the book's media files, you will find a Sounds folder with a variety of sound files to choose from.)

VideoNote
Creating an App to Vibrate the Phone

2. Create an app that has buttons to vibrate the phone for a quarter second, half second, three quarters of a second, and a full second.

3. Use the Designer to recreate the screens shown in Figure 2-82, Figure 2-83, Figure 2-84, and Figure 2-85. (The card images in Figure 2-85 can be found in the book's media files, in the Poker Cards Extra Small folder.)

Figure 2-82 Screen Layout for Exercise 3 (*Source:* MIT App Inventor 2)

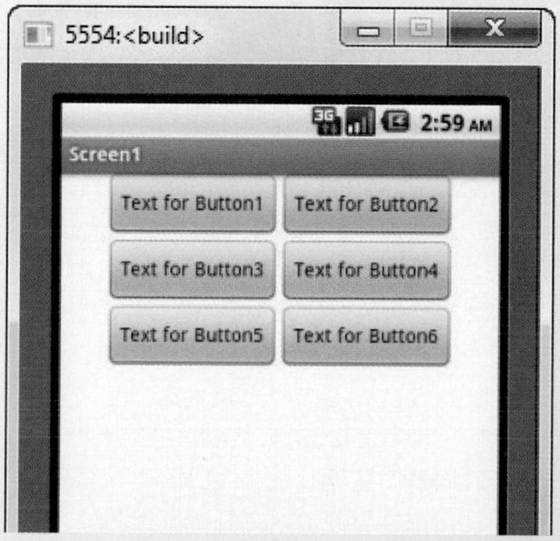

Figure 2-83 Screen Layout for Exercise 3 (*Source:* MIT App Inventor 2)

Figure 2-84 Screen Layout for Exercise 3 (*Source:* MIT App Inventor 2)

Figure 2-85 Screen Layout for Exercise 3 (*Source:* MIT App Inventor 2)

Programming Projects

1. **Clickable Number Images**

   Make sure you have downloaded the media files from this book's companion website at www.pearsonhighered.com/gaddis. In the *Numbers* folder, you will find the image files shown in Figure 2-86. Create an app that displays these as clickable images. The app should perform the following actions:

   * When the user clicks the 1 image, the app should display the word *One* in a Label component.
   * When the user clicks the 2 image, the app should display the word *Two* in a Label component.
   * When the user clicks the 3 image, the app should display the word *Three* in a Label component.
   * When the user clicks the 4 image, the app should display the word *Four* in a Label component.
   * When the user clicks the 5 image, the app should display the word *Five* in a Label component.

Figure 2-86 Image Files (*Source:* MIT App Inventor 2)

One.png   Two.png   Three.png   Four.png   Five.png

2. **Say the Number**

   Included in this book's media files, available from the book's companion web-site at `www.pearsonhighered.com/gaddis`, you will find a Sounds folder. In the Sounds folder, you will find audio files named one.wav, two.wav, and so forth. Modify the app that you created for Programming Project 1 so it plays the `one.wav` file when the user clicks the 1 image, plays the `two.wav` file when the user clicks the 2 image, and so forth.

3. **Card Identifier**

   Make sure you have downloaded the media files from this book's companion website at `www.pearsonhighered.com/gaddis`. In the *Poker Cards Extra Small* folder you will find image files for a complete deck of poker cards. Create an app displaying five different cards from the set of images. When the user clicks any of the images, the name of the card should be displayed in a Label compo-nent. Figure 2-87 shows an example of the app running. The image on the left shows the app's screen when it starts running. The image on the right shows the screen after the user has clicked the eight of diamonds card.

   Figure 2-87 Card Identifier App (*Source:* MIT App Inventor 2)

   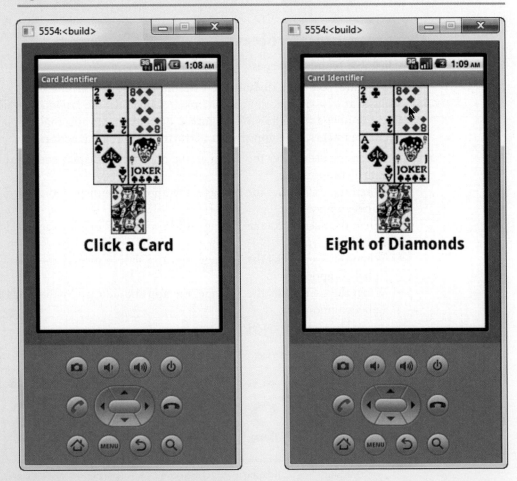

4. **Heads or Tails**

Make sure you have downloaded the media files from this book's companion website at www.pearsonhighered.com/gaddis. In the *Coins* folder you will find image files showing the heads and tails sides of a coin. Create an app with a *Show Heads* button and a *Show Tails* button. When the user clicks the *Show Heads* button, an image of the heads side of a coin should appear. When the user clicks the *Show Tails* button, an image of the tails side of a coin should appear. Figure 2-88 shows examples of how the app's screen might appear.

Figure 2-88 Heads or Tails App (*Source:* MIT App Inventor 2)

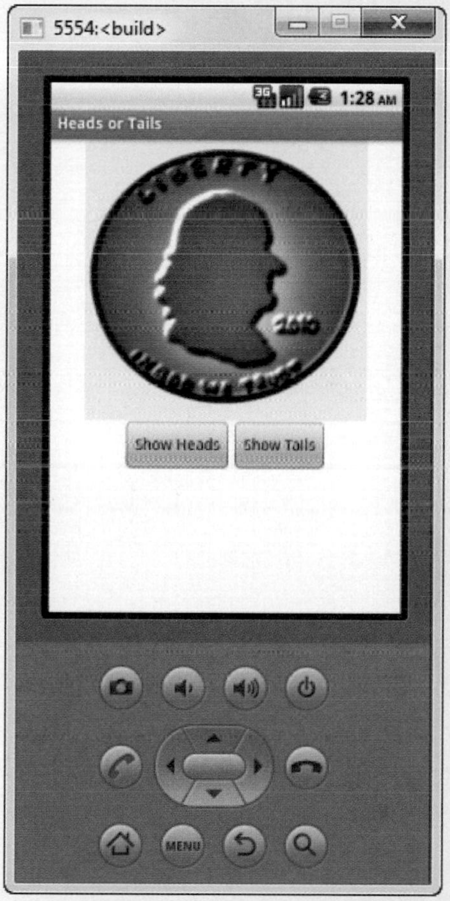

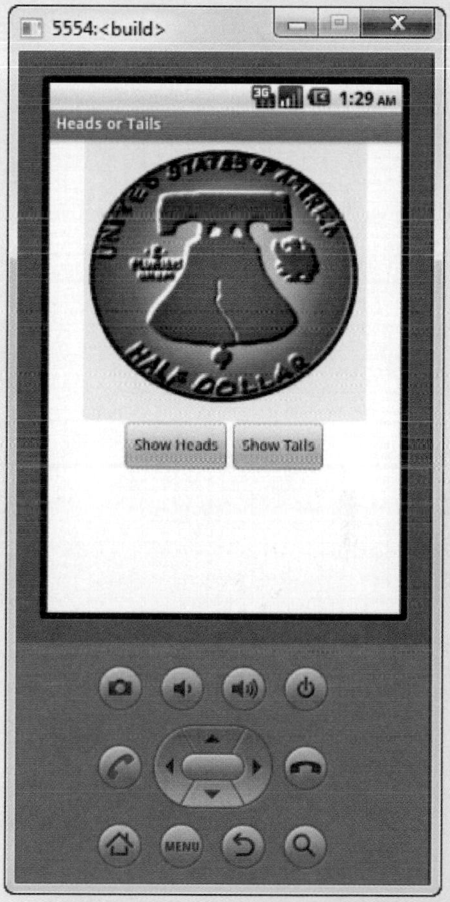

5. **Instruments**

Make sure you have downloaded the media files from this book's companion website at www.pearsonhighered.com/gaddis. In the *Instruments* folder you will find images of a guitar, a horn, and a drum. You will also find audio files for each of these instruments. Create an app that displays the instrument images, and when the user clicks an image, it plays the sound for that instrument.

6. **Audio Player**

Create an app that uses either a Sound component or a Player component to play an audio file. The app should have the following buttons:

- A *Play* button that plays the audio file
- A *Pause* button that pauses the audio file
- A *Resume* button that resumes the audio file, if it is currently paused
- A *Stop* button that stops the audio file

3 Input, Variables, and Calculations

3.1 The TextBox Component

CONCEPT: The TextBox component is a rectangular area that can display text, and can also accept keyboard input from the user.

Many of the programs that you will write from this point forward will require the user to enter data. The data entered by the user will then be used in some sort of operation. One of the primary components that you will use to get data from the user is the TextBox component.

A TextBox component appears as a rectangular area on an app's screen. When the app is running, the user can type text into a TextBox component. The app can then retrieve the text that the user entered and use that text in any necessary operations.

In the Designer, the TextBox is located in the User Interface section of the Palette. When you create TextBox components, they are automatically given default names such as `TextBox1`, `TextBox2`, and so forth. It is usually a good idea to change a component's default name to something more meaningful.

When the user types into a TextBox component, the text is stored in the component's Text property. In the Blocks Editor, if you want to retrieve the data that has been typed into a TextBox, you simply retrieve the contents of the component's Text property.

Figure 3-1 shows the screen from example project (the TextBoxDemo project) in the Viewer. Here is a summary of the components:

- `TableArrangement1`—A TableArrangement with 1 row and 2 columns.
- `LabelEnterYourName`—A Label that displays the text *Enter your name:*.
- `TextBoxName`—A TextBox component for the user to enter his or her name.
- `ButtonReadInput`—A Button component that, when clicked, reads the input that the user typed into the `TextBoxName` component, and displays that text in the `LabelOutput` component.
- `TableArrangement2`—A TableArrangement with 1 row and 2 columns.
- `LabelYouEntered`—A Label that displays the text *You entered:*.
- `LabelOutput`—A Label component that initially displays nothing. When the user clicks the `ButtonReadInput` component, the text that the user entered into the `TextBoxName` component is displayed in this label.

Figure 3-1 Example Project Using a TextBox Component (*Source:* MIT App Inventor 2)

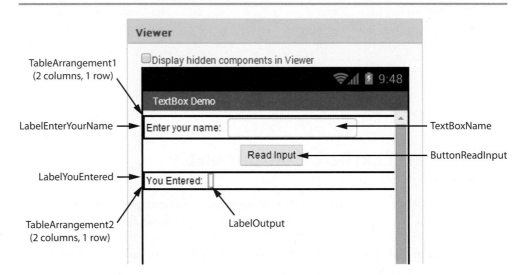

The purpose of the app is to let the user enter his or her name into the `TextBoxName` component, and then click the `ButtonReadInput` component. When the button is clicked, the text that was entered into the TextBox is displayed in the `LabelOutput` component.

Figure 3-2 shows the app running in the emulator. In the figure, the user has clicked the TextBox to select it, but has not yet entered his or her name. Notice that when

TIP: When entering TextBox input with the emulator, you can either click the keys that appear on the screen, or you can type keys on the computer's physical keyboard. Either way, you must first select the TextBox by clicking it on the app's screen.

Figure 3-2 The Example App Running in the Emulator *(Source:* MIT App Inventor 2)

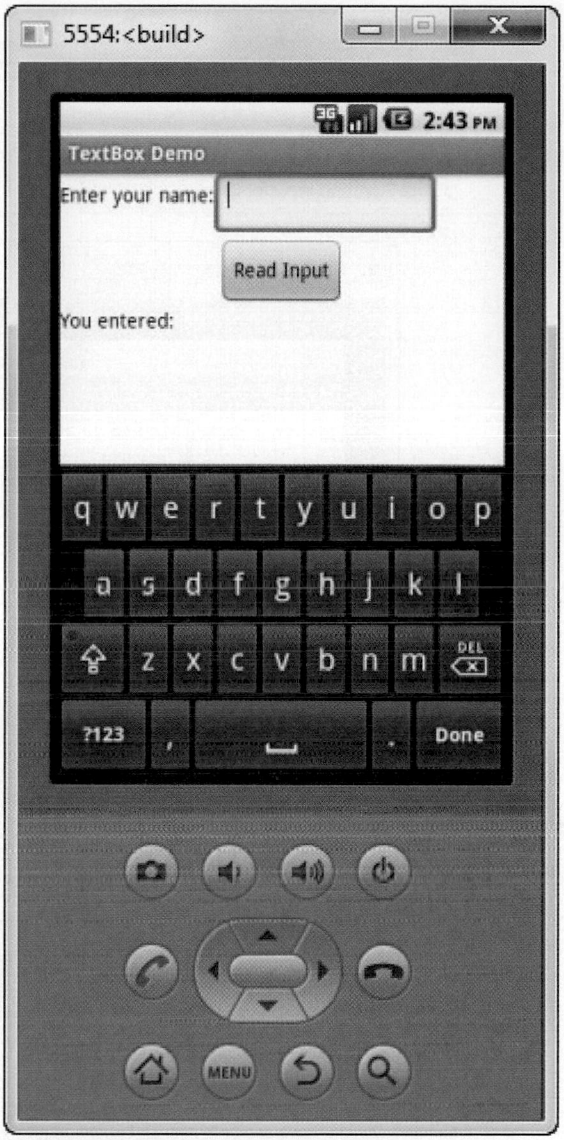

the user clicks a TextBox, the emulator's virtual keyboard pops up on the screen. The same thing happens with an actual device.

The `Click` event handler for the `ButtonReadInput` component is shown in Figure 3-2. The blocks inside the event handler set the `LabelOutput` component's

TIP: You might want to create this app on your own, as a quick exercise. After you create the `TextBoxName` component in the Designer, you will find the `TextBoxName.Text` block in the Blocks column of the Blocks Editor, in the *TextBoxName* drawer.

Figure 3-3 The `ButtonReadInput` Click Event Handler (*Source:* MIT App Inventor 2)

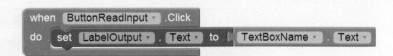

Figure 3-4 The App after the User has Entered Input and Clicked the Button
(*Source:* MIT App Inventor 2)

Text property to the value of the `TextBoxName` component's Text property. In other words, it gets the text that the user entered into the `TextBoxName` component, and displays it in the `LabelOutput` component. Figure 3-4 shows the app running in the emulator after the user has entered *Kathryn Smith* into the TextBox and clicked the button.

Other TextBox Properties

In addition to the Text property, the TextBox component has several other properties. Here is a summary:

- BackgroundColor—Sets the TextBox's background color.
- Enabled—If this property is checked in the Properties column, the user is able to enter input into the TextBox. If this property is not checked, the user cannot enter input into the TextBox. When the Enabled property is not checked, the TextBox can be used like a Label to display text.
- FontBold, FontItalic, and FontSize—These properties affect the font of the text displayed in the TextBox.
- Hint—Displays a hint for the user. When a TextBox's Text property is cleared, the value of the Hint property is displayed in light gray text inside the TextBox. This property reminds the user of what input is expected in the TextBox. (If you do not want to display a hint, simply clear this property.)
- MultiLine—If this property is checked, the TextBox will allow the user to enter multiple lines of input. If the property is not checked, the TextBox will only accept a single line of input.
- NumbersOnly—If this property is checked, the TextBox will only allow numbers to be entered.
- TextAlignment—Specifies how the text inside the TextBox is aligned. May be set to *left*, *center*, or *right*. The default value is *left*. (This property can be set only in the Designer. It cannot be set programmatically, using blocks.)
- TextColor—Sets the color of the text displayed in the TextBox.
- Visible—Specifies whether the component is visible on the screen or hidden. Can be set in the Designer to either *showing* or *hidden*.
- Width and Height—Determines the component's width and height. May be set to *Automatic*, *Fill parent*, or a specific number of pixels.

Using TextBox Components to Display Text

The primary purpose of a TextBox component is to get input from the user. TextBox components can also be used to display text, however. For example, in the `TextBoxDemo` app previously discussed, we might consider using a TextBox component instead of a Label component to display the user's name when the button is clicked. The image on the left in Figure 3-5 shows the app's screen in the Viewer. Notice that we have removed the `LabelOutput` component and replaced it with a TextBox named `TextBoxOutput`.

As you can see in the image on the right in Figure 3-5 (the app running in the emulator), the TextBox component appears clearly on the screen as a rectangular area, even when its Text property is cleared. Compare this to the Label component, which does not appear on the screen if its Text property is cleared. Sometimes it is helpful to the user to see the area on the screen where output will be displayed, even when there is no output to display. When this is the case, consider using a TextBox component instead of a Label component.

When you are using a TextBox component to display text (and not to read input), it is a good idea to uncheck the component's Enabled property. That prevents the user from selecting it and entering input into it.

If we modify the `TextBoxDemo` app to display its output in a TextBox instead of a Label, we will need to also modify the `Click` event handler for the `ButtonReadInput` component. Figure 3-6 shows the new event handler. Figure 3-7 shows the app running in the emulator after the user has entered *Kathryn Smith* into the `TextBoxName` component and clicked the button.

Figure 3-5 The Modified TextBoxDemo Project (*Source:* MIT App Inventor 2)

Figure 3-6 The Modified Click Event Handler for the `ButtonReadInput` Component (*Source:* MIT App Inventor 2)

NOTE: App Inventor also provides a PasswordTextBox component that works just like a regular TextBox, except the characters typed by the user are not displayed.

Figure 3-7 The App after the User has Entered Input and Clicked the Button
(*Source:* MIT App Inventor 2)

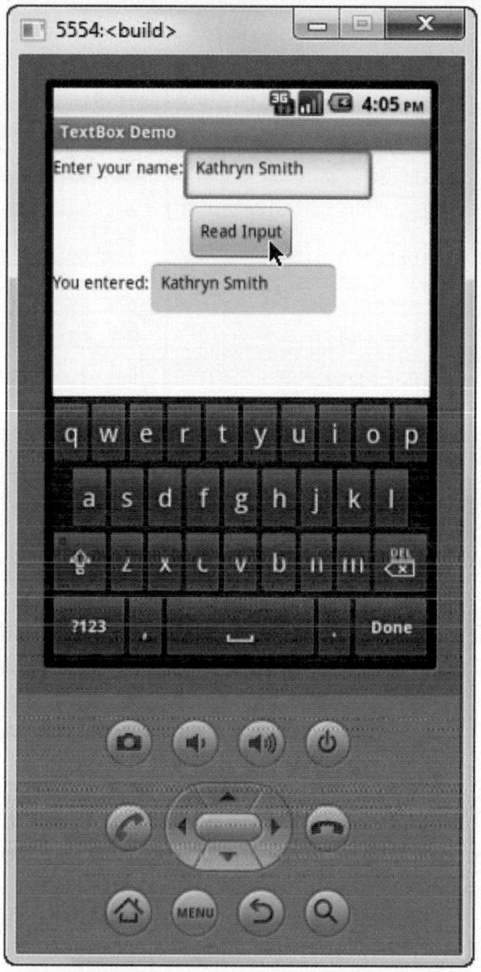

Checkpoint

3.1 What component can be used to gather text input from the user?

3.2 In code, how do you retrieve data that has been typed into a TextBox component?

3.3 What happens when you uncheck a TextBox component's Enabled property?

3.4 How do you make sure that the user enters only numbers into a TextBox?

3.2 Performing Calculations

CONCEPT: You can use math operators to write expressions that perform simple calculations. The result of a math expression can be assigned to a variable.

Most programs require calculations of some sort to be performed. A programmer's tools for performing calculations are *math operators*. In the Blocks column of the

Figure 3-8 The Math Operator Blocks (*Source:* MIT App Inventor 2)

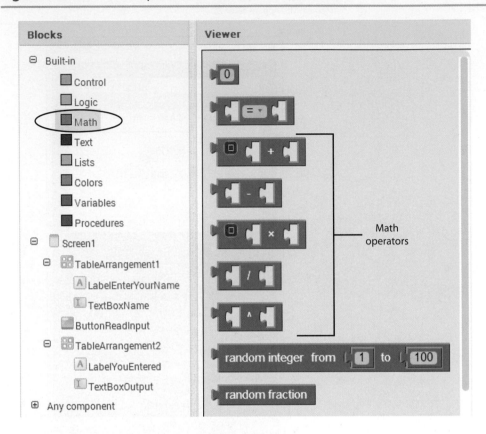

Blocks Editor, you will find the math operators by going to the *Built-In* section, then opening the *Math* drawer. This is shown in Figure 3-8. There are a lot of blocks in this drawer, but the math operators are the four blocks shown in Table 3-1.

Table 3-1 Math Operator Blocks (*Source:* Pearson Education, Inc.)

Operator	Name of the Operator	Description
	Addition	Adds two numbers and gives the result
	Subtraction	Subtracts one number from another and gives the result
	Multiplication	Multiplies one number by another and gives the result
	Division	Divides one number by another and gives the result
	Exponent	Raises one number to the power of another number and gives the result.

Notice that each of the operator blocks has its math symbol displayed in the center, along with two sockets: one on the left of the symbol, and one on the right. The two sockets are used to hold *operands*, which are the values that the operator works with. For example, Figure 3-9 shows the + operator block with two number blocks plugged in as operands: the number 10 is plugged into the left side, and the number 2 is plugged into the right side. These blocks create a math *expression* that gives the result of 10 + 2. (An expression is simply a clump of code that gives you a value.)

Figure 3-9 Using the + Operator Block (*Source:* MIT App Inventor 2)

TIP: The number block (0) is found in the *Math* drawer, which is in the *Built-in* section of the Blocks column.

The + operator block shown in Figure 3-9 calculates the result of 10 + 2, and gives us that value. However, the block is incomplete because we have to do something with the value. This means that we have to plug the + operator block into another block. For example, suppose we have a Label component named `LabelResult`, and we want to display the result of the + operator block in the label. Figure 3-10 shows how we can set the label's Text property to the value of the + operator block. As a result, the value 12 will be displayed in the label.

Figure 3-10 Displaying the Result of the + Operator in a Label (*Source:* MIT App Inventor 2)

Figure 3-11 shows other examples of how the results of operator blocks can be displayed in a Label component. The topmost blocks display the result of 600 − 200 (the label will display the value 400). The middle blocks display the result of 100 × 1.5 (the label will display the value 150). The bottom blocks display the result of 20/5 (the label will display the value 4).

Figure 3-11 Displaying the Results Various Operators in a Label (*Source:* MIT App Inventor 2)

In Tutorial 3-1 you will use a math operator block to perform a calculation. You will create an app that reads input from TextBox components, performs a calculation using the input, and displays the result of the calculation in a Label component.

Tutorial 3-1:
Calculating Fuel Economy

In the United States, a car's fuel economy is measured in miles per gallon, or MPG. You use the following formula to calculate a car's MPG:

MPG = Miles driven ÷ Gallons of gas used

In this tutorial, you will create an app that lets the user enter the number of miles he or she has driven and the gallons of gas used. The app will calculate and display the car's MPG. Figure 3-12 shows the app's screen in the Viewer, along with the names of the components. Figure 3-13 shows how the screen appears in the emulator.

When the app runs, the user enters the number of miles driven into the `TextBoxMiles` component and the gallons of gas used into the `TextBoxGallons` component.

Figure 3-12 The App's User Interface (*Source:* MIT App Inventor 2)

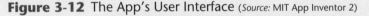

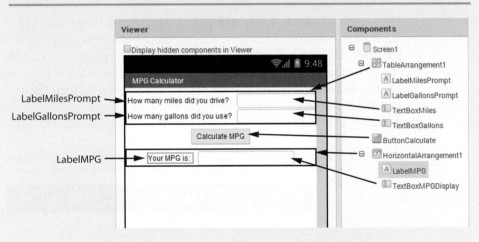

Figure 3-13 The App Running in the Emulator (*Source:* MIT App Inventor 2)

When the user clicks the `ButtonCalculate` component, the application calculates the car's MPG and displays the result in the `TextBoxMPGDisplay` component.

Step 1: Start a new project named MilesPerGallon.

Step 2: Set up the app's screen with the components shown in Figure 3-12. Refer to Table 3-2 for the relevant property settings for each component.

Table 3-2 Component property settings (*Source:* Pearson Education, Inc.)

Component	Relevant Property Settings
`Screen1`	AlignHorizontal = *Center*
	Title = *MPG Calculator*
	Scrollable = *unchecked*
`TableArrangement1`	Columns = 2
	Rows = 2
	Width = *Fill parent*
	Height = *Automatic*
`LabelMilesPrompt`	Text = *How many miles did you drive?*
`LabelGallonsPrompt`	Text = *How many gallons did you use?*
`TextBoxMiles`	Enabled = *checked*
	NumbersOnly = *checked*
	Hint = *Enter the miles*
	Width = *Automatic*
	Height = *Automatic*
`TextBoxGallons`	Enabled = *checked*
	NumbersOnly = *checked*
	Hint = *Enter the gallons*
	Width = *Automatic*
	Height = *Automatic*
`ButtonCalculate`	Text = *Calculate MPG*
`HorizontalArrangement1`	AlignHorizontal = *Center*
	Width = *Fill parent*
	Height = *Automatic*
`LabelMPG`	Text = *Your MPG is:*
`TextBoxMPGDisplay`	Enabled = *unchecked*
	Width = *Automatic*
	Height = *Automatic*

Step 3: Now you will program the `Click` event handler for the `ButtonCalculate` component. The event handler will divide `TextBoxMiles.Text` by `TextBoxGallons.Text` and store the result in `TextBoxMPGDisplay.Text`.

Open the Blocks Editor. In the Blocks column, open the *ButtonCalculate* drawer and select the `when CalculateButton. Click do` block. This creates the empty `Click` event handler shown in Figure 3-14.

Figure 3-14 Empty `Click` Event Handler for `ButtonCalculate`
(*Source:* MIT App Inventor 2)

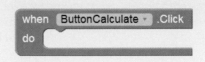

Step 4: Open the *TextBoxMPGDisplay* drawer and select the `set TextBoxMPGDisplay.Text to` block. Snap the block inside the `ButtonCalculate` component's `Click` event handler.

Step 5: Open the *Math* drawer and select the division (/) block. Snap it into the socket of the `set TextBoxMPGDisplay.Text to` block, as shown in Figure 3-15.

Figure 3-15 Division Block Snapped into Place (*Source:* MIT App Inventor 2)

Step 6: Complete the division block by snapping the `TextBoxMiles.Text` block into its left socket, and the `TextBoxGallons.Text` block into its right socket. The block should appear as shown in Figure 3-16. (You will find the `TextBoxMiles.Text` block in the *TextBoxMiles* drawer, and you will find the `TextBoxGallons.Text` block in the *TextBoxGallons* drawer.)

Figure 3-16 The Completed Event Handler (*Source:* MIT App Inventor 2)

Step 7: Test the app in the emulator or with a device. Enter 270 for the miles and 10 for the gallons. Click the *Calculate MPG* button. As shown in Figure 3-17, the app should display the MPG as 27. Experiment with other values to confirm that the app is correct.

Figure 3-17 The App Running in the Emulator (*Source:* MIT App Inventor 2)

```
5554:<build>                              □ ▣ X

                              📶 🔋 3:10 AM
   MPG Calculator
   How many miles did you drive?  270
   How many gallons did you use?  10

                  Calculate MPG

       Your MPG is:  27


    1  2  3  4  5  6  7  8  9  0

    @  #  $  %  &  *  -  +  (  )

    ALT  !  "  '  :  ;  /  ?  DEL

    ABC   .              .    Done
```

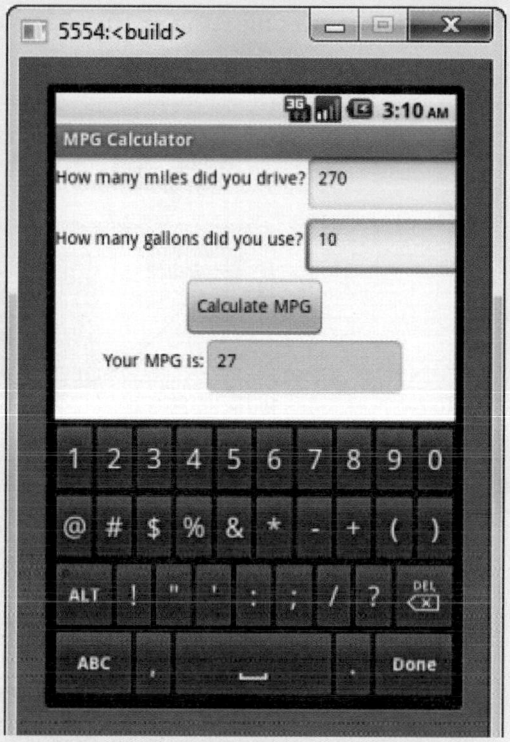

Mutator Blocks

Notice that the + and × operator blocks have a blue box (▣) in their upper-left corner. When a block has this symbol, it means that the block is a *mutator block*. A mutator block has the ability to change in some way. The + and × operator blocks have the ability to expand to accommodate additional operands.

When you create a + operator block, the block has two slots for operands. So, it can add two numbers. But what if you want to add more than two numbers? First, you click the blue box that appears in the block's upper-left corner. This causes the *mutator bubble* shown in Figure 3-18 to appear. Next, you click and drag the number block (number)

Figure 3-18 Mutator Bubble (*Source:* MIT App Inventor 2)

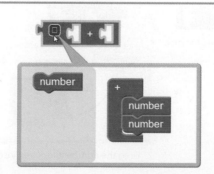

from the left side of the bubble, and insert it on the right side of the bubble as shown in Figure 3-19. This adds an additional operand to the block, as shown in Figure 3-20, allowing it to calculate the sum of three numbers. For example, Figure 3-21 shows a + operator block that gives the result of 10 + 12 + 14.

Figure 3-19 Adding an Additional Operand (*Source:* MIT App Inventor 2)

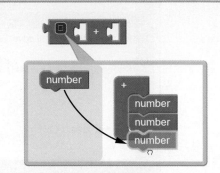

Figure 3-20 The + Block with Three Operands (*Source:* MIT App Inventor 2)

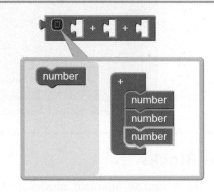

Figure 3-21 The + Block with Three Operands (*Source:* MIT App Inventor 2)

You can expand the × block in a similar way. Figure 3-22 shows how to add a third operand to the × block.

Figure 3-22 Expanding the × Block (*Source:* MIT App Inventor 2)

1 - Click the blue box.

2 - Drag the number block and insert it.

3 - The multiplication block now has three operands.

Combining Operator Blocks

You can combine operator blocks to create more complex expressions. For example, suppose you need to calculate the average of 80, 85, and 90. First you get the sum of 80 + 85 + 90. Then, you divide that sum by 3. Figure 3-23 shows how to create the expression by combining a + block with a / block. (Note that the + block that is shown in the figure has been expanded to use three operands.)

Figure 3-23 Calculating the Average of 80, 85, and 90 (*Source:* MIT App Inventor 2)

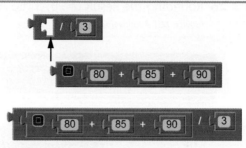

Formatting Numbers to a Specified Number of Decimal Places

You might not always be happy with the number of decimal places that a number is displayed with. For example, suppose we have a label named `LabelResult`, and we want the label to display the value of `10/3`. Figure 3-24 shows the block that we would have (inside some event handler), and the way that the result would appear on the emulator's screen. Notice that several digits are displayed after the decimal point.

Figure 3-24 Displaying the Result of `10/3` (*Source:* MIT App Inventor 2)

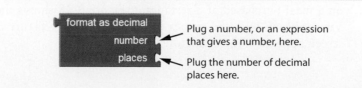

App Inventor provides a Math block named `format as decimal` that you can use to round a number to a specified number of decimal places. (When you open the *Math* drawer, you will have to scroll down, almost to the bottom of the drawer, to find the block.) The block is shown in Figure 3-25.

Figure 3-25 The `format as decimal` Block (*Source:* MIT App Inventor 2)

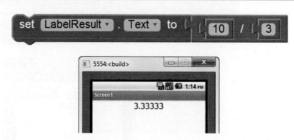

Notice that it has two sockets: *number* and *places*. The *number* socket requires a number or an expression that gives a number. This is the value that you want to round. The *places* socket requires the number of decimal places.

When you plug the desired values into the *number* and *places* sockets, the block performs the necessary rounding and gives you the result. We say that the block *returns* the result. Figure 3-26 shows how we can use the block to format the value of 10/3 to one decimal place. (Assume that the set LabelResult.Test to block shown in the figure is located inside an event handler that has executed.)

Figure 3-26 Rounding the Result of 10/3 to one decimal place

(*Source:* MIT App Inventor 2)

Figure 3-27 shows another example. Again, assume the set LabelResult.Text to block shown in the figure is located inside an event handler that has executed. The label displays the value of 123.456789 rounded to two decimal places.

Figure 3-27 Rounding the Value 123.456789 to Two Decimal Places

(*Source:* MIT App Inventor 2)

In Tutorial 3-2, you will create an app that uses a math expression to calculate the tip on a meal purchased at a restaurant, and displays the result rounded to two decimal places.

Tutorial 3-2:
Creating the Restaurant Tip Calculator App

VideoNote
Creating the
Restaurant Tip
Calculator App

In this tutorial, you will create an app that calculates a 15%, 20%, or 25% tip on a meal purchased at a restaurant. Figure 3-28 shows the app's screen in the Viewer along with the names of the components. Figure 3-29 shows how the screen appears in the emulator.

Figure 3-28 The App's User Interface (*Source:* MIT App Inventor 2)

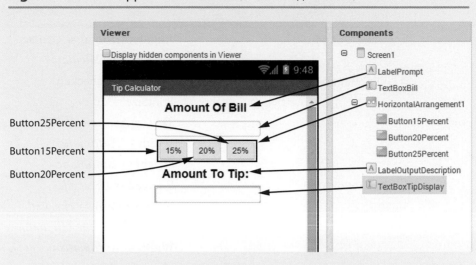

Figure 3-29 The App Running in the Emulator (*Source:* MIT App Inventor 2)

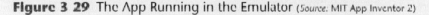

When the app runs, the user enters the total amount of the bill into the `TextBoxBill` component and then clicks one of the buttons to calculate the tip. There are three buttons; `Button15Percent` calculates a 15 percent tip, `Button20Percent` calculates a 20 percent tip, and `Button25Percent` calculates a 25 percent tip. The amount of the tip is displayed in the `TextBoxTipDisplay` component.

Step 1:   Start a new project named TipCalculator.

Step 2:   Set up the app's screen with the components shown in Figure 3-28. Refer to Table 3-3 for the relevant property settings for each component.

Table 3-3 Component property settings (*Source:* Pearson Education, Inc.)

Component	Relevant Property Settings
TBL Screen1	AlignHorizontal = *Center*
	Title = *Tip Calculator*
LabelPrompt	FontBold = checked
	FontSize = *20*
	Text = *Amount of Bill*
	Width = *Automatic*
	Height = *Automatic*
TextBoxBill	Enabled = *checked*
	NumbersOnly = *checked*
	Hint = *Enter the bill amount*
	Width = *Automatic*
	Height = *Automatic*
HorizontalArrangement1	*Keep all default property settings*
Button15Percent	Text = *15%*
	Width = *Automatic*
	Height = *Automatic*
Button20Percent	Text = *20%*
	Width = *Automatic*
	Height = *Automatic*
Button25Percent	Text = *25%*
	Width = *Automatic*
	Height = *Automatic*
LabelOutputDescription	FontBold = checked
	FontSize = *20*
	Text = *Amount To Tip:*
	Width = *Automatic*
	Height = *Automatic*
TextBoxTipDisplay	Enabled = *unchecked*
	TextAlignment = *Center*
	Width = *Automatic*
	Height = *Automatic*

Step 3: Now you will program the Click event handlers for the buttons, starting with the Button15Percent component. The event handler for the Button15Percent component will display the amount of the bill multiplied by 0.15 in the TextBoxDisplay component. The result will be rounded to two decimal places.

Open the Blocks Editor and assemble the blocks shown in Figure 3-30. When you have assembled the blocks, the `Click` event handler for the `Button15Percent` component should appear as shown in Figure 3-31.

Figure 3-30 The Blocks Needed for the `Button15Percent` Component's `Click` Event Handler (*Source:* MIT App Inventor 2)

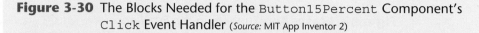

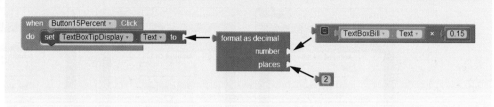

Figure 3-31 The Completed `Click` Event Handler for the `Button15Percent` Component (*Source:* MIT App Inventor 2)

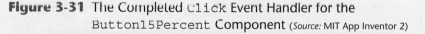

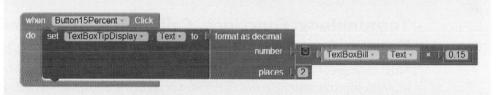

Step 4: Complete the `Click` event handlers for the `Button20Percent` and `Button25Percent` components. Figure 3-32 shows all of the completed `Click` event handlers.

Figure 3-32 The Completed `Click` Event Handlers for the Buttons (*Source:* MIT App Inventor 2)

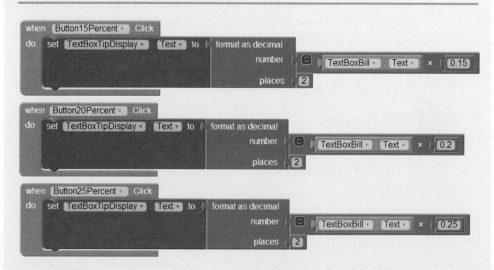

Step 5: Test the app in the emulator, or with a device. Enter *100* for the amount of the bill and click each button to see the amount of the tip. As shown in Figure 3-33, the app should display 15.00 as 15%, 20.00 as 20%, and 25.00 as 25%. Experiment with other values to confirm that the app is correct.

Figure 3-33 The App Running in the Emulator (*Source:* MIT App Inventor 2)

Terminology: Functions, Calling Functions, and Passing Arguments

Now that you have used the `format as decimal` block, we can introduce some important programming terms that you will regularly encounter. The `format as decimal` block is a special type of method known as a function. A *function* is a method that performs an operation and then gives you a value. We say that a function *returns* a value. As you already know, the `format as decimal` block rounds a number to a specified number of decimal places and returns that value.

When you execute a function (or any type of method), we say that we are *calling* it. So when you use the `format as decimal` block, you can say that you are calling the `format as decimal` function.

Quite often, functions require additional pieces of data in order to operate. These additional pieces of data are known as *arguments*. For example, the `format as decimal` function requires two arguments: the number that is to be rounded and the number of decimal places. Recall that the `format as decimal` block has two sockets for these arguments on its right edge. When we provide arguments to a function, we say that we are *passing* the arguments to the function.

 Checkpoint

3.5 What is an expression?

3.6 What is an operand?

3.7 What does the `format as decimal` block do?

3.8 What is a function?

3.9 What do you mean when you say you are calling a function?

3.10 What is an argument?

3.3 Storing Data with Variables

CONCEPT: A variable is a name that represents a value stored in the computer's memory.

Most programs store data in the computer's memory and perform operations on that data. For example, consider the typical online shopping experience: you browse a website and add the items that you want to purchase to the shopping cart. As you add items to the shopping cart, data about those items is stored in memory. Then, when you click the checkout button, a program running on the website's computer calculates the cost of all the items you have in your shopping cart, applicable sales taxes, shipping costs, and the total of all these charges. When the program performs these calculations, it stores the results in the computer's memory.

So far, the apps that you have created have stored data only in component properties. For example, a TextBox's Text property is used to hold input that the user has typed, and it can also be used to hold data that you want to display on the app's screen. A Label component's Text property is also used to hold data that you want to display.

Sometimes, you need to store data in memory without putting it in a component. For example, suppose an app needs to perform a series of calculations and save the results, but you do not want those results displayed on the screen. Instead of using component properties, you would use variables to store the results.

A *variable* is a name that represents a value that is stored in the computer's memory. For example, a program that calculates the sales tax on a purchase might use the variable name Tax to represent that value in memory. And a program that calculates the distance between two cities might use the variable name Distance to represent that value in memory. When a variable represents a value in the computer's memory, we say that the variable *holds* the value or *references* the value.

Local Variables and Global Variables

App Inventor allows you to create two types of variables: local and global. A *local variable* is created inside a method or function, and it can be accessed only by blocks that are also in that method or function. A *global variable* is created outside of all the methods and functions in the workspace, and it can be accessed by any blocks in the workspace, regardless of which method or function they belong to.

Creating a Local Variable

To create a local variable in App Inventor, you must *initialize* it. This simply means that you are storing a starting value in the variable. To create and initialize a local variable, you open the *Variables* drawer, which is in the *Built-in* section of the Blocks column. As shown in Figure 3-34, the drawer contains various blocks. You select the one that reads initialize local name to. (Notice that there are two blocks labeled this way, but they are shaped slightly differently. For now, you want to use the one that is circled in Figure 3-34.) This creates a variable initialization block in the workspace, as shown in Figure 3-35.

Figure 3-34 Creating a Variable Initialization Block (*Source:* MIT App Inventor 2)

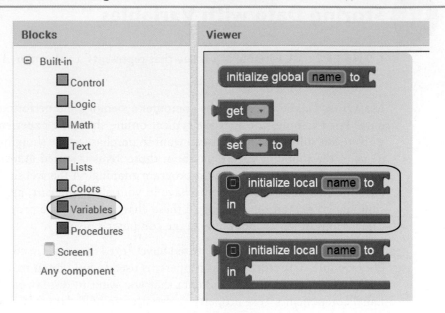

Figure 3-35 Variable Initialization Block (*Source:* MIT App Inventor 2)

Remember, local variables have to be created inside a method or function. When you create an `initialize local` *name* `to` block, you should place it inside the method or function that it will belong to. Figure 3-36 shows an `initialize local` *name* `to` block placed inside a button's `Click` event handler.

Figure 3-36 An `initialize local` *name* `to` Block Placed Inside a Button's `Click` Event Handler (*Source:* MIT App Inventor 2)

The variable initialization block isn't complete yet. We need to do two more things:

- Change the variable's name to something that describes the variable's purpose
- Assign an initial value to the variable

Changing the Variable's Name

When you create an `initialize local` *name* `to` block, the variable's default name is `name`. This isn't very descriptive, so you should change it to something that indicates what the variable is used for. For example, a variable that holds the temperature might be named `Temperature`, and a variable that holds a car's speed might be named `Speed`. You may be tempted to give variables short, nondescript names such as `x` or `b2`, but names such as these give no clue as to the purpose of the variable.

In addition, the following rules apply to variable names in App Inventor:

- The variable name must begin with an alphabetical letter.
- After the first letter, the remaining characters can be alphabetical letters, numbers, or underscore characters (_).
- You cannot have spaces in a variable name.
- Variable names must be unique within a project. You cannot have two or more variables with the same name.

To change a variable's name, simply click the word `name` that appears on the `initialize local name to` block (as shown in Figure 3-37), and type the name that you wish to give the variable. For example, in Figure 3-38 we have changed the variable's name to `Temperature`.

Figure 3-37 Changing the Variable Name (*Source:* MIT App Inventor 2)

Figure 3-38 The Variable Name Changed to `Temperature` (*Source:* MIT App Inventor 2)

Assigning an Initial Value to the Variable

When you create a variable, you must also set the variable's starting value. When we set a variable to a value, we say that we are *assigning* a value to the variable.

Notice that the variable initialization block in Figure 3-38 has a socket labeled *to*. This socket requires a value of some sort to be plugged in. The value that you plug into this socket is the variable's initial, or starting, value. The blocks that you can plug into this socket are:

- number blocks
- text string blocks
- Boolean blocks (`true` or `false`)
- List blocks (discussed in Chapter 7)
- Color blocks

For example, Figure 3-39 shows two variable initialization blocks. The upper block defines a variable named Age and sets its initial value to the number 25. The lower block defines a variable named FirstName and sets its initial value to the text *Johnny*.

Figure 3-39 Two Complete Variable Initialization Blocks *(Source:* MIT App Inventor 2)

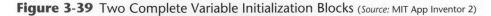

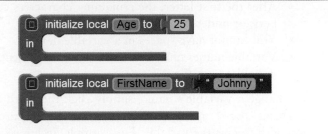

In this chapter we will use variables to hold numbers and text, so let's briefly cover the steps necessary to create a variable that is initially assigned each of those types of data.

Creating a Local Variable That Holds a Number

Suppose we have a Click event handler for a button, and inside that event handler we want to create a local variable to hold a car's speed. We also want to initially assign the number 0 to the variable. Here are the steps:

1. In the Blocks Editor, go to the *Built-in* section of the Blocks column and click *Variables*. Then select the initialize local *name* to block, as shown in Figure 3-40.

Figure 3-40 Creating a Variable Initialization Block *(Source:* MIT App Inventor 2)

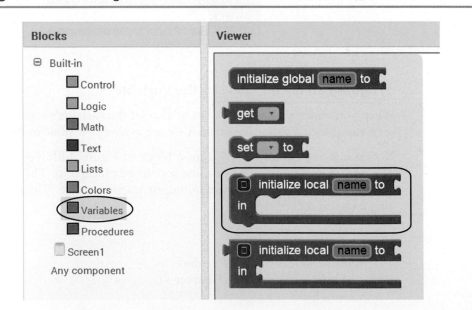

2. This creates an `initialize local` *name* `to` block in your workspace. Place the block inside the desired event handler, as shown in Figure 3-41.

Figure 3-41 Insert the `initialize local` *name* `to` Block Inside the Desired Event Handler *(Source:* MIT App Inventor 2)

3. Now you will change the variable's name to `Speed` (since this variable will be used to hold a car's speed). Click the word *name* that appears on the block (as shown in the image on the left in Figure 3-42) and change the name to `Speed` (as shown on the right in Figure 3-42).

Figure 3-42 Renaming the Variable *(Source:* MIT App Inventor 2)

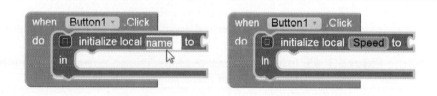

4. Now you will create a number block to assign to the `Speed` variable. Go to the *Built-In* section of the Blocks column, click *Math*, then click the number block (0). Plug the block into the *to* socket of the `Speed` variable initialization block, as shown in Figure 3-43. The variable initialization is now complete.

Figure 3-43 Assigning the Number 0 *(Source:* MIT App Inventor 2)

Creating a Variable That Holds Text

Suppose we have a `Click` event handler for a button, and inside that event handler we want to create a variable that holds the text *Dark Roast Coffee*. Here are the steps:

1. In the Blocks Editor, go to the *Built-in* section of the Blocks column, and click *Variables*. Then select the `initialize local` *name* `to` block, as shown in Figure 3-44.

Figure 3-44 Creating a Variable Initialization Block *(Source:* MIT App Inventor 2)

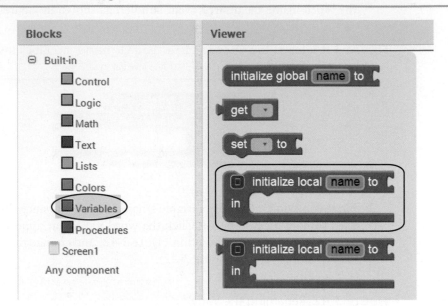

2. This creates an `initialize local` *name* `to` block in your workspace. Place the block inside the desired event handler, as shown in Figure 3-45.

Figure 3-45 Insert the `initialize local` *name* `to` Block Inside the Desired Event Handler *(Source:* MIT App Inventor 2)

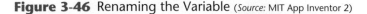

3. Now you will change the variable's name to `Beverage` (since this variable will hold the name of a beverage). Click the word *name* that appears on the block (as shown in the image on the left in Figure 3-46) and change the name to `Beverage` (as shown on the right in Figure 3-46).

Figure 3-46 Renaming the Variable *(Source:* MIT App Inventor 2)

4. Now you will create a text string block to assign to the `Beverage` variable. Go to the *Built-In* section of the Blocks column, click *Text*, then click the text string block (" "). Plug the block into the *to* socket of the `Beverage` variable

initialization block. Click the empty space that appears between the quotation marks, as shown on the left in Figure 3-47, and change the value to *Dark Roast Coffee*, as shown on the right in the figure. The variable initialization is now complete.

Figure 3-47 Assigning the Text *Dark Roast Coffee* (*Source:* MIT App Inventor 2)

Working With a Local Variable

After you have created and initialized a local variable, you can create blocks that work with the variable. The blocks that work with a local variable must be inserted inside the variable's initialization block, as shown in Figure 3-48.

Figure 3-48 Where to Insert Blocks that Work with a Variable (*Source:* MIT App Inventor 2)

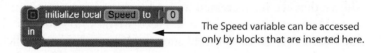

The Speed variable can be accessed only by blocks that are inserted here.

There are two instructions that you will use often when working with variables: get and set. You use a get instruction to get a variable's value, and you use a set instruction to store a value in the variable. You will find the get and set blocks in the *Variables* drawer (in the Built-in section of the Blocks column), as shown in Figure 3-49.

Figure 3-49 Blocks for Setting and Getting the Value of the Beverage Variable (*Source:* MIT App Inventor 2)

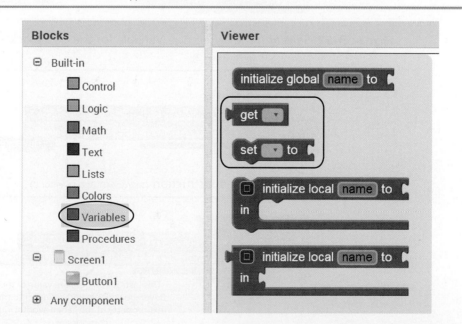

The get block returns the value of a specified variable. When you create a get block, you do two things with it:

- You plug the get block into the block that needs to get the value.
- On the get block, you select the variable that you need to get.

This is shown in Figure 3-50.

Figure 3-50 Using the get Block *(Source:* MIT App Inventor 2)

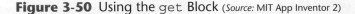

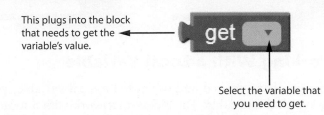

For example, suppose we have a Label component named LabelFavoriteDrink, and we want to display the value of the Beverage variable in that label. We would need to set the Label component's Text property to the value of the variable. Figure 3-51 shows that we have created a get block and we are going to plug it into the set LabelFavoriteDrink to block. Next, we need to complete the get block by selecting the Beverage variable. As shown in Figure 3-52, you click the down arrow (▼) that appears on the get block and select Beverage. Figure 3-53 shows the completed instruction.

Figure 3-51 Plugging a get Block into Another Block *(Source:* MIT App Inventor 2)

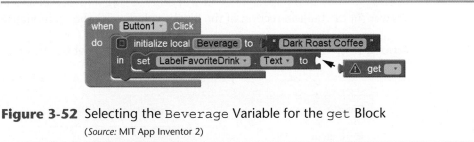

Figure 3-52 Selecting the Beverage Variable for the get Block
(Source: MIT App Inventor 2)

Figure 3-53 The Completed Instruction *(Source:* MIT App Inventor 2)

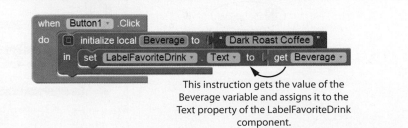

NOTE: When you create a get block, you cannot select the name of a local variable until you plug the get block somewhere inside that local variable's initialization block.

If you need to change the value of a variable, you use the set block as shown in Figure 3-54. When you create a set block for a local variable, you do the following things:

- Insert the set block into the desired variable's initialization block.
- On the set block, select the name of the variable that you want to set.
- Plug a value into the to socket of the set block.

Figure 3-54 Using the set Block *(Source:* MIT App Inventor 2)

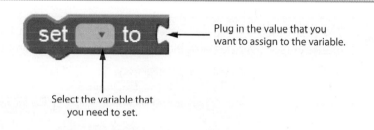

For example, suppose we have a local variable named Speed, initialized with the value 0, and we want to change its value to 75. We need to do the following things:

- Create a set block and insert it into the Speed variable's initialization block. This is shown in Figure 3-55.
- On the set block, select the Speed variable. This is shown in Figure 3-56.
- Create a number block for the value 75 and plug it into the set block. This is shown in Figure 3-57.

Figure 3-55 The set Block Created *(Source:* MIT App Inventor 2)

Figure 3-56 Selecting the Speed Variable on the set Block *(Source:* MIT App Inventor 2)

Figure 3-57 Plugging the Value 75 into the `set` Block *(Source:* MIT App Inventor 2)

NOTE: When you create a `set` block, you cannot select the name of a local variable until you plug the `set` block somewhere inside that local variable's initialization block.

TIP: A quick way to create a `get` or `set` block for a variable is to hover the mouse cursor over the variable's name in its initialization block, like this:

A popup will appear, allowing you to select a `get` or `set` block for the variable.

In Tutorial 3-3 you will create an app that uses a local variable to hold the result of a calculation.

VideoNote
Creating the
Kilometer
Converter App

Tutorial 3-3:
Creating the Kilometer Converter App

In this tutorial, you will create the *Kilometer Converter* app. The app lets the user enter a distance in kilometers into a TextBox and then converts that distance to miles and displays the results in another TextBox. The conversion formula is:

$Miles = Kilometers \times 0.6214$

Figure 3-58 shows the app's screen in the Viewer, with the names of all the components. Figure 3-59 shows the app running in the emulator.

Figure 3-58 The Kilometer Converter App (*Source:* MIT App Inventor 2)

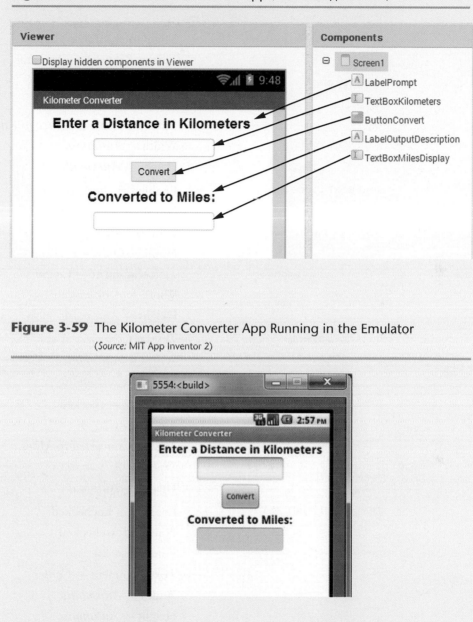

Figure 3-59 The Kilometer Converter App Running in the Emulator
(*Source:* MIT App Inventor 2)

Step 1:   Start a new project named KilometerConverter.

Step 2:   Set up the app's screen with the components shown in Figure 3-58. Refer to Table 3-4 for the relevant property settings for each component.

Table 3-4 Component Property Settings (*Source:* Pearson Education, Inc.)

Component	Relevant Property Settings
Screen1	AlignHorizontal = *Center*
	Title = *Kilometer Converter*
LabelPrompt	FontBold = checked
	FontSize = *20*
	Text = *Enter a Distance in Kilometers*
	Width = *Automatic*
	Height = *Automatic*
TextBoxKilometers	Enabled = checked
	FontBold = checked
	FontSize = *20*
	NumbersOnly = *checked*
	TextAlignment = *Center*
	Width = *Automatic*
	Height = *Automatic*
ButtonConvert	Text = *Convert*
	Width = *Automatic*
	Height = *Automatic*
LabelOutputDescription	FontBold = checked
	FontSize = *20*
	Text = *Converted to Miles:*
	Width = *Automatic*
	Height = *Automatic*
TextBoxMilesDisplay	Enabled = unchecked
	FontBold = checked
	FontSize = *20*
	TextAlignment = *Center*
	Width = *Automatic*
	Height = *Automatic*

Step 3: Now you will program the Click event handlers for the ButtonConvert component. When the ButtonConvert component is clicked, it will do the following:

- It will create a local variable named Miles, initialized to 0.
- It will multiply the value entered into the TextBoxKilometers component by 0.6214 and assign the result to the local Miles variable.
- It will display the value of the local Miles variable in the TextBoxMilesDisplay component.

Figure 3-60 shows the blocks that you will create and assemble for the Click event handler. Figure 3-61 shows how the completed Click event handler should appear.

Figure 3-60 The Blocks Needed for the ButtonConvert Component's Click Event Handler *(Source: MIT App Inventor 2)*

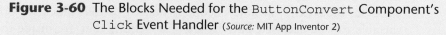

Figure 3-61 The Completed Click Event Handler for the ButtonConvert Component *(Source: MIT App Inventor 2)*

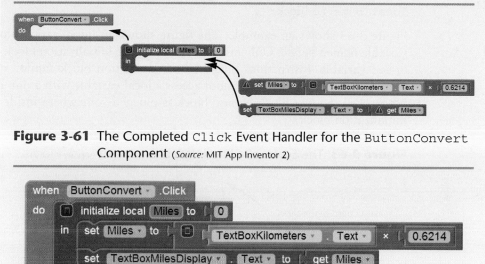

Step 4: Test the app in the emulator or with a device. Enter *100* for the kilometers and click the Convert button. As shown in Figure 3-62, the app should display 62.14 miles. Experiment with other values to confirm that the app is correct.

Figure 3-62 The App Converting 100 Kilometers to Miles *(Source: MIT App Inventor 2)*

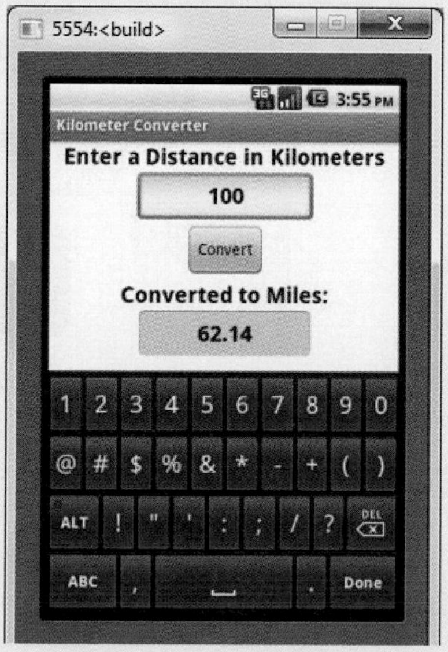

Variable Scope

Programmers commonly use the term *scope* to describe the part of a program in which a variable may be accessed. A variable is visible only to instructions inside the variable's scope. When you create a local variable with an `initialize local name to` block, the variable's scope is limited to that block. In other words, the variable can be accessed only by the instructions that are inside the `initialize local name to` block.

Figure 3-63 shows an example. The figure shows an initialization block for a local variable named `Speed`. Only instructions inside the initialization block can access the `Speed` variable. Instructions outside the initialization block cannot access the variable. This explains why you cannot access a local variable with a `get` block or a `set` block until the `get` block or `set` block is plugged somewhere inside the variable's initialization block.

Figure 3-63 The Scope of a Local Variable (*Source:* MIT App Inventor 2)

Instructions here cannot access the Speed variable.

Only instructions here can access the Speed variable.

Creating Multiple Local Variables

Sometimes you need more than one variable in a method or function. The `initialize local name to` block can be modified to create and initialize multiple variables at once. Just click the blue box (▣) that appears in the block's upper-left corner to display the mutator bubble shown in Figure 3-64. Next, you click and drag the `name`

Figure 3-64 Mutator Bubble (*Source:* MIT App Inventor 2)

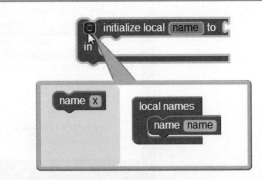

block (`name X`) from the left side of the bubble and insert it on the right side of the bubble as shown in Figure 3-65. This adds an additional variable named `x` to the block, as shown in Figure 3-66. Then you double-click the variable name to change it to something more descriptive. For example, Figure 3-67 shows an initialization block that creates two variables named `Tax` and `Total`. The last step is to plug initialization values into each variable. Figure 3-68 shows that the `Tax` and `Total` variables are initialized to the value 0.

Figure 3-65 Adding Another Variable to the Initialization Block
(*Source:* MIT App Inventor 2)

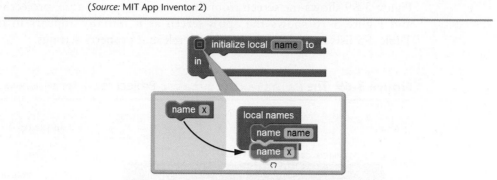

Figure 3-66 Another Variable Added to the Initialization Block (*Source:* MIT App Inventor 2)

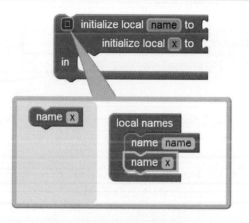

Figure 3-67 The Variable Names Changed to Tax and Total (*Source:* MIT App Inventor 2)

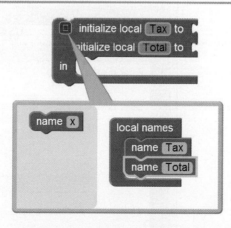

Figure 3-68 The Tax and Total Variables Initialized to the Value 0
(*Source:* MIT App Inventor 2)

Let's look at an example project that uses two local variables in an event handler. Figure 3-69 shows the screen from the `SalesTaxCalculator` project in the Viewer, and Figure 3-70 shows the app's screen as it initially appears in the emulator. Table 3-5 lists each component with its relevant property settings.

Figure 3-69 The `SalesTaxCalculator` Project (*Source:* MIT App Inventor 2)

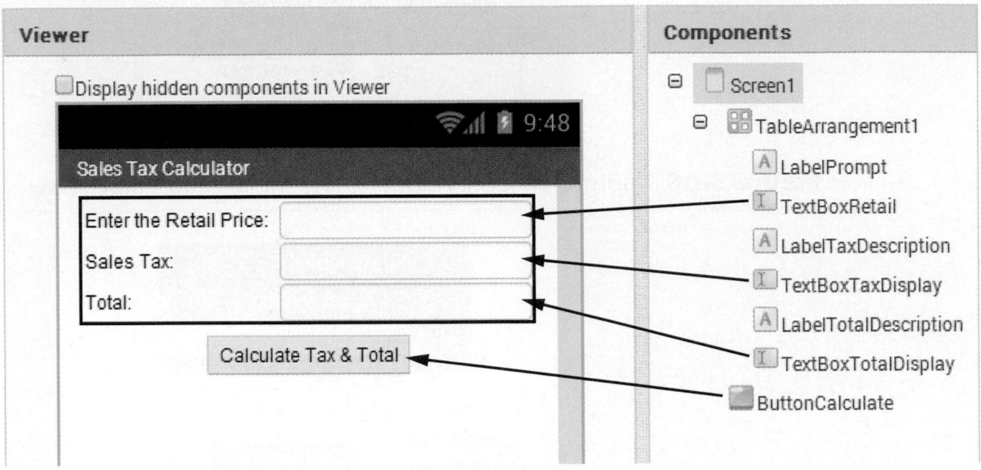

Figure 3-70 The `SalesTaxCalculator` App Running in the Emulator
(*Source:* MIT App Inventor 2)

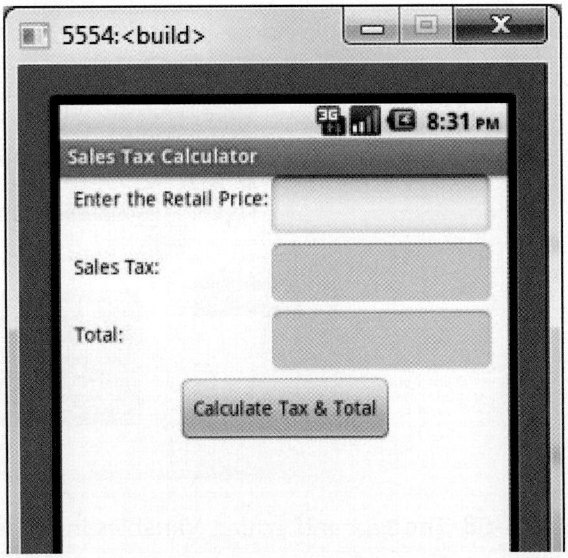

When the app is running, the user can enter the retail price of an item that is being purchased into the `TextBoxRetail` component, and then click the `ButtonCalculate` component. The app will calculate and display the sales tax (using 7% as the tax rate)

Table 3-5 Component property settings *(Source:* Pearson Education, Inc.)

Component	Relevant Property Settings
Screen1	AlignHorizontal = *Center*
	Title = *Sales Tax Calculator*
TableArrangement1	Columns = 2
	Rows = 3
	Width = *Automatic*
	Height = *Automatic*
LabelPrompt	Text = *Enter the Retail Price:*
TextBoxRetail	Enabled = *checked*
	NumbersOnly = *checked*
	Width = *Automatic*
	Height = *Automatic*
LabelTaxDescription	Text – *Sales Tax:*
TextBoxTaxDisplay	Enabled = *unchecked*
	Width = *Automatic*
	Height = *Automatic*
LabelTotalDescription	Text = *Total:*
TextBoxTotalDisplay	Enabled = *unchecked*
	Width = *Automatic*
	Height = *Automatic*
ButtonCalculate	Text = *Calculate Tax & Total*

and the total of the sale. An example screen is shown in Figure 3-71. The user has entered $100 as the retail price. The app has calculated the sales tax as $7.00 and the total of the sale as $107.00

Figure 3-71 Example Screen as the App Runs *(Source:* MIT App Inventor 2)

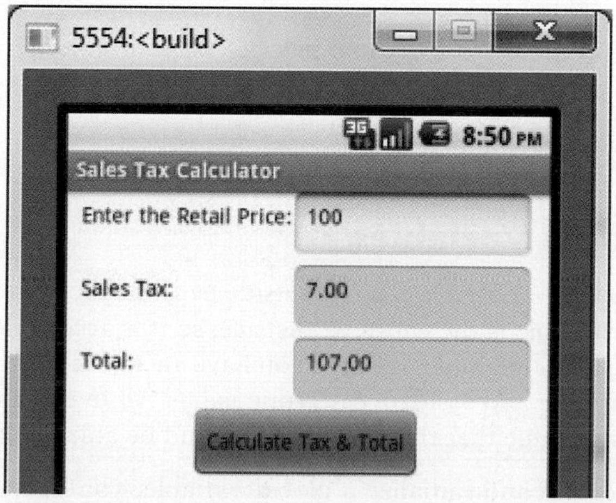

The `Click` event handler for the `ButtonReadInput` component is shown in Figure 3-72. The blocks inside the event handler set the `LabelOutput` component's Text property to the value of the `TextBoxName` component's Text property. In other words, it gets the text that the user entered into the `TextBoxName` component and displays it in the `LabelOutput` component. Figure 3-4 shows the app running in the emulator after the user has entered *Kathryn Smith* into the `TextBox` and clicked the button.

Figure 3-72 `Click` Event Handler for the `ButtonCalculate` Component

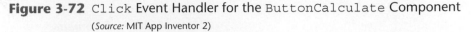

(*Source:* MIT App Inventor 2)

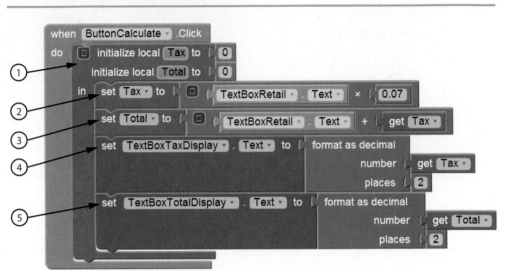

Here is a description of the blocks that are in the event handler:

1. This is an initialization block that creates and initializes two local variables: `Tax` and `Total`. Both variables are initialized to the value 0.

2. This block sets the `Tax` variable to the value of `TextBoxRetail.Text` × 0.07. (`TextBoxRetail.Text` holds the retail price that was entered by the user.)

3. This block sets the `Total` variable to the value of `TextBoxRetail.Text` + the value of the `Tax` variable.

4. This block sets `TextBoxTaxDisplay.Text` to the value of the `Tax` variable, rounded to 2 decimal places.

5. This block sets `TextBoxTotalDisplay.Text` to the value of the `Total` variable, rounded to 2 decimal places.

Global Variables

A global variable is created outside of all methods and functions. The scope of a global variable is the entire workspace, so it is accessible to all of the code in the workspace. For example, suppose you have an app with five event handlers, and you create a variable and assign it a starting value. All five of the event handlers will be able to get the value that the variable holds and be able to change the variable's value.

To create and initialize a global variable, you open the *Variables* drawer, which is in the *Built-in* section of the Blocks column. As shown in Figure 3-73, select the one that reads `initialize global` *name* `to`. This creates a global variable initialization block in the workspace, as shown in Figure 3-74.

Figure 3-73 Creating a Global Variable Initialization Block (*Source:* MIT App Inventor 2)

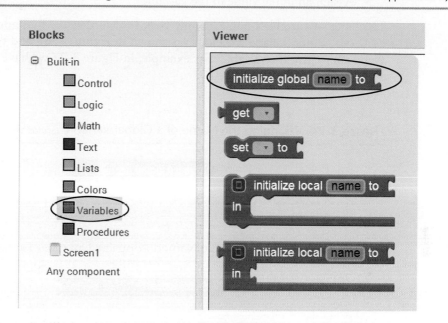

Figure 3-74 Global Variable Initialization Block (*Source:* MIT App Inventor 2)

Remember, global variables must be created outside of all methods and functions. When you create an `initialize global` *name* `to` block, you can place it anywhere in the workspace that is not inside a method or function. Figure 3-75 shows an `initialize global` *name* `to` block in a workspace that has three `Click` event handlers. Notice that the `initialize global` *name* `to` block is not inside any of the event handlers.

Figure 3-75 Global Variable Initialization Block Outside of All Methods
(*Source:* MIT App Inventor 2)

Once you have created a global variable's initialization block, you need to do two more things:

- Change the variable's name to something that describes the variable's purpose
- Assign an initial value to the variable

To change a variable's name, simply click the word *name* that appears on the ini-tialize global *name* to block (as shown in Figure 3-76), and type the name that you wish to give the variable. For example, in Figure 3-77 we have changed the variable's name to Population.

Figure 3-76 Changing the Name of a Global Variable (*Source:* MIT App Inventor 2)

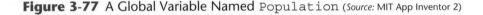

Figure 3-77 A Global Variable Named Population (*Source:* MIT App Inventor 2)

initialize global Population to

Notice that the global variable initialization block shown in Figure 3-77 has a socket labeled *to*. This socket requires a value of some sort to be plugged in. The value that you plug into this socket is the variable's initial, or starting, value. For example, Figure 3-39 shows two global variable initialization blocks. The upper block defines a variable named InterestRate and sets its initial value to the number 0.03. The lower block defines a variable named Balance and sets its initial value to the number 5,000.

Figure 3-78 Two Complete Global Variable Initialization Blocks
(*Source:* MIT App Inventor 2)

Once you have created and initialized a global variable, you can use the get block to get the variable's value and the set block to assign a value to the variable. The get blocks and set blocks can be placed in any method or function in the workspace.

In Tutorial 3-4, you will create an app that uses a global variable to hold the total of several values selected by the user.

Tutorial 3-4:
Creating the Change Counter App

VideoNote
Creating the
Change Counter
App

In this tutorial, you will create the *Change Counter* app. The app displays images of four coins, having the values 5 cents, 10 cents, 25 cents, and 50 cents. Additionally, the app will have a global variable named Total that starts with the value 0. Each time the user clicks on a coin image, the value of that coin is added to the Total variable, and then the value of the Total variable is displayed.

Figure 3-79 shows the app's screen in the Viewer with the names of all the components. Figure 3-80 shows the app running in the emulator.

Figure 3-79 The Change Counter App (*Source:* MIT App Inventor 2)

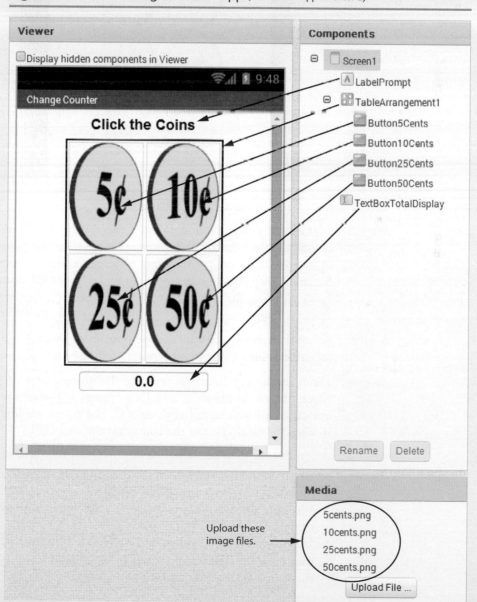

Figure 3-80 The Change Counter App Running in the Emulator

(*Source:* MIT App Inventor 2)

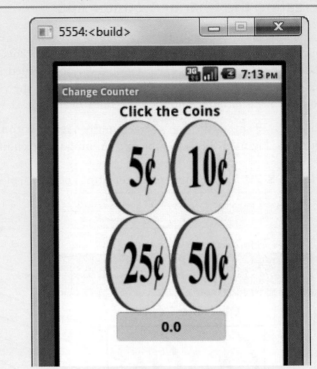

Step 1:   Start a new project named ChangeCounter.

Step 2:   Make sure you have downloaded the media files from this book's companion website at www.pearsonhighered.com/gaddis. Navigate to the location on your system where the book's media files are located. You will find a folder named *Coins* that contains several .png files. Use the Media column to upload the following image files: 5cents.png, 10cents.png, 25cents.png, and 50cents.png.

Step 3:   Set up the app's screen with the components shown in Figure 3-79. Refer to Table 3-6 for the relevant property settings for each component.

Step 4:   Open the Blocks Editor and create the global variable initialization block shown in Figure 3-81. This creates a global variable named Total and gives it an initial value of 0. The Total variable will be used to keep the total value of the coins that the user clicks.

As a reminder, these are steps to follow to create the variable initialization:

- Go to the *Built-In* section of the *Blocks* column, click *Variables*, and then select the initialize global name to block.
- Click the word *name* that appears on the block and change the name to Total.
- Go to the *Built-In* section of the *Blocks* column, click *Math*, and then click the number block (0). Plug the block into the socket of the Total variable initialization block.

Table 3-6 Component property settings (*Source:* Pearson Education, Inc.)

Component	Relevant Property Settings
Screen1	AlignHorizontal = *Center*
	Title = *Change Counter*
LabelPrompt	FontBold = *checked*
	FontSize = *20*
	Text = *Click the Coins*
	Width = *Automatic*
	Height = *Automatic*
TableArrangement1	Cols = *2*
	Rows = *2*
	Width = *Automatic*
	Height = *Automatic*
Button5Cents	Text = *clear*
	Image = 5cents.png
Button10Cents	Text = *clear*
	Image = 10cents.png
Button25Cents	Text = *clear*
	Image = 25cents.png
Button50Cents	Text = *clear*
	Image = 50cents.png
TextBoxTotalDisplay	Enabled = *unchecked*
	FontBold = *checked*
	FontSize = *20*
	Text = *0.0*
	TextAlignment = *Center*
	Width = *Automatic*
	Height = *Automatic*

Figure 3-81 Definition of the Total Variable (*Source:* MIT App Inventor 2)

initialize global Total to 0

Step 5: Now you will program the Click event handlers for the buttons, starting with Button5Cents. When the Button5Cents component is clicked, it will do the following:

- It will add 0.05 to the Total variable.
- It will display the value of the Total variable, rounded to two decimal places, in the TextBoxTotalDisplay component.

Figure 3-82 shows the completed `Click` event handler. Note that the `set` and `get` blocks are found in the *Variables* drawer of the *Built-in* section of the *Blocks* column.

Figure 3-82 The `Click` Event Handler for the `Button5Cents` Component
(*Source:* MIT App Inventor 2)

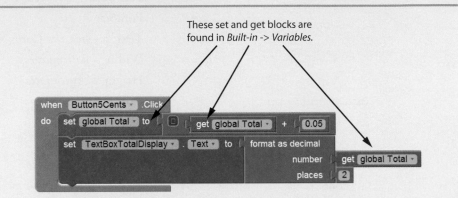

These set and get blocks are found in *Built-in -> Variables.*

Step 6: Now you will program the `Click` event handler for the `Button10Cents`. When the `Button10Cents` component is clicked, it will do the following:

- It will add 0.10 to the `Total` variable.
- It will display the value of the `Total` variable, rounded to two decimal places, in the `TextBoxTotalDisplay` component.

Figure 3-83 shows the completed `Click` event handler.

Figure 3-83 The `Click` Event Handler for the `Button10Cents` Component
(*Source:* MIT App Inventor 2)

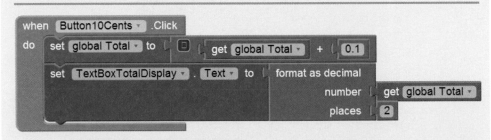

Step 7: Now you will program the `Click` event handler for the `Button25Cents`. When the `Button25Cents` component is clicked, it will do the following:

- It will add 0.25 to the `Total` variable.
- It will display the value of the `Total` variable, rounded to two decimal places, in the `TextBoxTotalDisplay` component.

Figure 3-84 shows the completed `Click` event handler.

Figure 3-84 The `Click` Event Handler for the `Button25Cents` Component
(*Source:* MIT App Inventor 2)

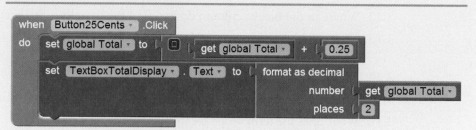

Step 8:   Now you will program the `Click` event handler for the `Button50Cents`. When the `Button50Cents` component is clicked, it will do the following:

- It will add 0.50 to the `Total` variable.
- It will display the value of the `Total` variable, rounded to two decimal places, in the `TextBoxTotalDisplay` component.

Figure 3-85 shows the completed `Click` event handler.

Figure 3-85 The `Click` Event Handler for the `Button50Cents` Component
(*Source:* MIT App Inventor 2)

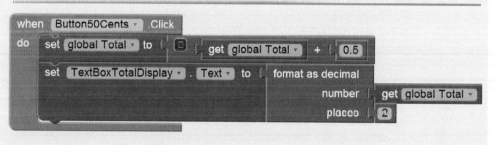

Step 9:   Test the app in the emulator or with a device. Click the coin images in any order you wish. The total shown on the app's screen should update by the correct amount each time you click a coin.

A Word of Caution About Global Variables

Most programmers agree that you should restrict the use of global variables when possible. Here are some reasons:

- Global variables make debugging difficult. Any instruction in a program can change the value of a global variable. If you find that the wrong value is being stored in a global variable, you have to track down every instruction that accesses it to determine where the bad value is coming from. In a large program with thousands of instructions, this can be difficult.
- Global variables make a program hard to understand. A global variable can be modified by any instruction in the program. If you are to understand any part of the program that uses a global variable, you have to be aware of all the other parts of the program that access the global variable.

When possible, you should create variables locally to avoid these and other problems that can arise from the use of global variables.

Checkpoint

3.11 What is a variable?

3.12 Where in the Blocks column do you find the variable initialization blocks?

3.13 How do you change a variable's name from the default name that App Inventor gives it?

3.14 How do you set a variable's initial value?

3.15 What is the purpose of the get block? What is the purpose of the set block?

3.16 What does the term scope mean?

3.17 What is the scope of a local variable? What is the scope of a global variable?

3.4 Creating Blocks with Typeblocking

CONCEPT: Typeblocking is a shortcut method for quickly creating blocks using the keyboard.

The usual way of creating a block in the workspace is to open the drawer that contains the block and then click and drag the block into the workspace. After you have created a few apps, you will become familiar with various blocks that are commonly used, and you will be able to take advantage of App Inventor's typeblocking feature.

Typeblocking is a shortcut method of creating blocks with the keyboard. In the Blocks Editor, you simply click anywhere in the workspace and type part of the name of the block that you want to create. For example, suppose you have a Button component named Button1 and you want to create a Click event handler for it. You can click anywhere in the workspace and type *click*. As shown in Figure 3-86, a popup list of

Figure 3-86 Creating a Click Event Handler with Typeblocking

(*Source:* MIT App Inventor 2)

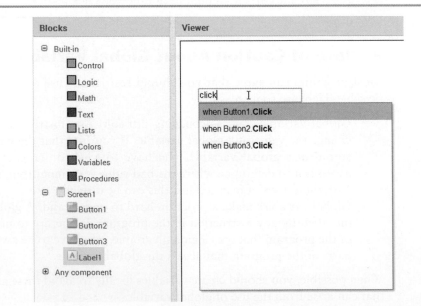

blocks will appear. Simply select the one you want from the list or press Enter when the one that you want is highlighted. The block will be created in the workspace.

You can use typeblocking to quickly create number blocks and text string blocks. For example, suppose you want to create a number block with the value 25. Simply click inside the workspace, type 25, and press Enter. This is shown in Figure 3-87.

Figure 3-87 Creating a Number Block with Typeblocking (*Source:* MIT App Inventor 2)

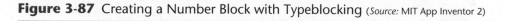

Type 25 and press Enter to create this number block.

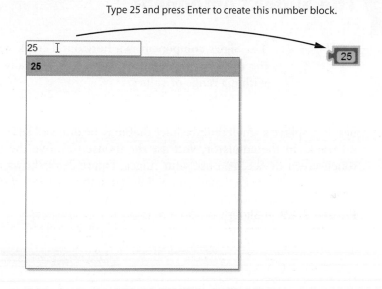

To create a text string block, click inside the workspace, type a quotation mark ("), then type the text that you want to set as the block's value, then press Enter. (Do not type an ending quotation mark, however. If you do, the ending quotation mark will become part of the text string.) Figure 3-88 shows an example. In the figure, the user has typed *"Hello World* to create a text string block with the value *Hello World*.

Figure 3-88 Creating a Text String Block with Typeblocking (*Source:* MIT App Inventor 2)

Type *"Hello World* and press Enter to create this text string block.

A good way to learn about typeblocking is to experiment with it. For example:

- You can type any of the math operators (+ - * / ^) to create math operator blocks.
- You can type *format* to create a `format as decimal` block.
- You can type the name of a color (such as *red*) to create a Color block.

3.5 The Slider Component

CONCEPT: The Slider component is a horizontal track with a thumb slider that the user can move left or right. It is typically used to adjust a value within a range of values.

The Slider component provides a visual way to adjust a value within a range of values. It displays a small thumb slider that may be dragged left or right along a horizontal track. In the emulator, you use the mouse to move the thumb slider, but on a touchscreen device, you use your finger. Figure 3-89 shows an example of a Slider component. In the Designer, you will find it in the *User Interface* section of the Palette.

Figure 3-89 A Slider Component (*Source:* MIT App Inventor 2)

The Slider component has a MinValue property and a MaxValue property that must be set to numeric values. By default, the MinValue property is set to 10.0, and the MaxValue property is set to 50.0. The MinValue property is the Slider's minimum value, and the MaxValue property is the Slider's maximum value. When the thumb slider is all the way to the left, its position is the same as MinValue. As you drag the thumb slider to the right, its position increases. When the thumb slider is all the way to the right, its position is the same as MaxValue.

Here is a summary of the Slider component's properties:

- ColorLeft—Specifies the color of the part of the horizontal track that is to the left of the thumb slider.
- ColorRight—Specifies the color of the part of the horizontal track that is to the right of the thumb slider.
- MaxValue—The Slider component's maximum value.
- MinValue—The Slider component's minimum value.
- ThumbPosition—The position of the thumb slider.
- Visible—Determines whether the component is visible on the screen. In the Designer, this can be set to either *showing* or *hidden*.
- Width—The width of the component. Can be set to *Automatic*, *Fill parent*, or a specific number of pixels.

Each time the user moves the thumb slider, a `PositionChanged` event occurs. You can create a `PositionChanged` event handler to perform an action any time the user moves the thumb slider. You create the event handler in a similar fashion for creating other event handlers: In the Blocks Editor, you open the drawer for the Slider and then select the block for the `PositionChanged` event handler. An example of this is shown in Figure 3-90, assuming we have a Slider component named `Slider1`.

Figure 3-90 Creating a `PositionChanged` Event Handler (*Source:* MIT App Inventor 2)

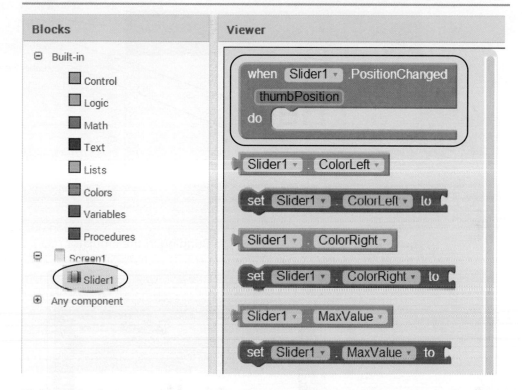

Figure 3-91 shows an empty `PositionChanged` event handler that has been created in the workspace. Notice that it has a rectangle labeled `thumbPosition`. This is a special type of local variable known as a *parameter variable*. The purpose of a parameter variable is to hold a piece of data that is passed to the event handler. When the `PositionChanged` event handler executes, the `thumbPosition` parameter variable will hold the current position of the thumb slider.

Figure 3-91 The Slider Component's `PositionChanged` Event Handler
(*Source:* MIT App Inventor 2)

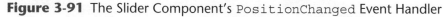

The scope of the `thumbPosition` parameter variable is the `PositionChanged` event handler. Inside the `PositionChanged` event handler you can use `get` and `set` blocks to access the `thumbPosition` parameter variable.

Let's look at an example project that uses a Slider component. Figure 3-92 shows the screen from the `SliderDemo` project in the Viewer, and Figure 3-93 shows the app's screen as it initially appears in the emulator. Table 3-7 lists each component with its relevant property settings.

Figure 3-92 The `SliderDemo` Project (*Source:* MIT App Inventor 2)

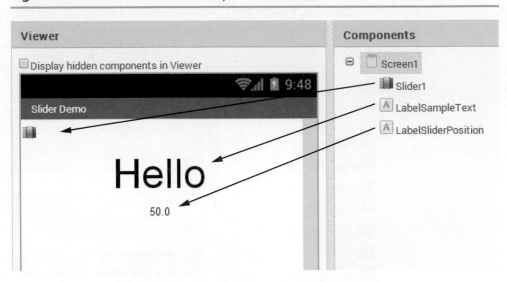

Figure 3-93 The `SliderDemo` App Running in the Emulator (*Source:* MIT App Inventor 2)

Table 3-7 Component property settings (*Source:* Pearson Education, Inc.)

Component	Relevant Property Settings
Screen1	AlignHorizontal = *Center*
	Title = *Slider Demo*
Slider1	MaxValue = 100
	MinValue = 0
	ThumbPosition = 50
	Width = *Fill parent*
LabelSampleText	Text = *Hello*
	FontSize = 50
LabelSliderPosition	Text = *50.0*

When the app is running, the user can move the thumb slider to adjust the font size of the `LabelSampleText` component. Example screens are shown in Figure 3-94. The thumb slider starts at position 50, and the label's font size starts at 50. If the user drags the thumb slider to the right, the font size increases. If the user drags the thumb slider to the left, the font size decreases. The position of the thumb slider is always displayed by the `LabelSliderPosition` component.

Figure 3-94 Example Screens as the App Runs (*Source:* MIT App Inventor 2)

Figure 3-95 shows the `Slider1.PositionChanged` event handler. Here is a description of the two sets of blocks that are in the event handler:

(1) The first set of blocks sets the `LabelSampleText` component's FontSize property to the value of the `thumbPosition` variable. For example, if the position of the thumb slider is 90, this set of blocks sets the `LabelSampleText` component's FontSize property to 90.

(2) The second set of blocks sets the `LabelSliderPosition` component's Text property to the value of the `thumbPosition` variable. This displays the thumb slider's position in the label.

Figure 3-95 The `Slider1.PositionChanged` Event Handler
(*Source:* MIT App Inventor 2)

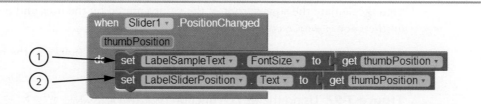

 Checkpoint

3.18 How do you set the minimum and maximum values for a Slider component?

3.19 What event occurs each time the user moves a Slider component's thumb slider?

3.20 What is the `thumbPosition` variable that is discussed in this section?

3.6 Math Functions

CONCEPT: App Inventor provides numerous advanced math functions for complex calculations.

The Math drawer in the Blocks Editor provides numerous functions that are useful for performing advanced mathematical operations. Most of them are shown in Figure 3-96. Table 3-8 gives a summary of several of the Math functions. (We will cover the random number functions in Chapter 4, so we will not go over them here.)

Figure 3-96 Math Functions (*Source:* MIT App Inventor 2)

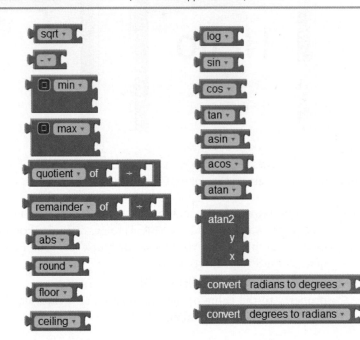

Figure 3-97 shows an example use of the sqrt block. Assume an app has a TextBox named TextBoxNumber, and the user has entered a number into it. The blocks in the figure calculate the square root of the value entered by the user and display the result in the LabelResult component.

Figure 3-98 shows another example. It sets the variable MyVar to the remainder of 17 divided by 2.

Figure 3-97 Using the sqrt Function (*Source:* MIT App Inventor 2)

Figure 3-98 Using the remainder Function (*Source:* MIT App Inventor 2)

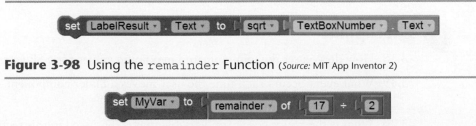

Table 3-8 Many of the Math functions (*Source:* Pearson Education, Inc.)

Math Method	Description
sqrt	Returns the square root of the argument.
—(negate)	Returns the negative of the argument.
min	Allows you to plug in multiple arguments. (When you plug a value into the slot, another slot appears.) Returns the smallest value of the given arguments.
max	Allows you to plug in multiple arguments. (When you plug a value into the slot, another slot appears.) Returns the largest value of the given arguments.
quotient	You plug in two arguments. Returns the result of dividing the first argument by the second argument. The value returned is an integer. Any fractional part of the result will be thrown away.
remainder	You plug in two arguments. Divides the first argument by the second argument and returns the remainder.
abs	Returns the absolute value of the argument.
round	Rounds the argument to the nearest integer and returns the result. If the number is halfway between two integers (such as 1.5 or 7.5), this function rounds the nearest even integer and returns the result.
floor	Returns the largest integer that is less than or equal to the argument.
ceiling	Returns the smallest integer that is less than or equal to the argument.
log	Returns the natural logarithm of the argument.
sin	Returns the sine of the argument in degrees.
cos	Returns the cosine of the argument in degrees.
tan	Returns the tangent of the argument in degrees.
asin	Returns the arc sine of the argument in degrees.
acos	Returns the arc cosine of the argument in degrees.
atan	Returns the arc tangent of the argument in degrees.
atan2	Takes two arguments, x and y. Returns the arc tangent of x / y in degrees.
convert radians to degrees	Takes an argument that is an angle in radians. Returns the argument converted to degrees.
convert degrees to radians	Takes an argument that is an angle in degrees. Returns the argument converted to radians.

Review Questions

Multiple Choice

1. When the user types into a TextBox component, the text is stored in the component's _____ property.

   a. Input
   b. Text
   c. String
   d. Data

2. The _____ property of the TextBox component determines whether the user can enter input into the component, or not.

   a. Input
   b. AllowInput
   c. Enabled
   d. ShowKeyboard

3. If the _____ property of the TextBox component is checked, the user will be able to enter only numbers.

   a. Numeric
   b. NumbersOnly
   c. DigitsOnly
   d. Numlock

4. What component is like a TextBox, but does not display the characters that the user enters?

   a. PasswordTextBox
   b. InvisibleTextBox
   c. SecureTextBox
   d. HiddenTextBox

5. The sockets on a math operator block are for _____.

   a. comments
   b. user input
   c. operators
   d. operands

6. If you want to display the number 6.1756892 rounded to 6.18, you would use this math function.

   a. `round`
   b. `format as decimal`
   c. `dollar format`
   d. `number format`

7. This is a method that performs an operation, and returns a value.

   a. function
   b. void method
   c. procedure
   d. subroutine

8. These are pieces of data that are passed to a function.
   a. specs
   b. requirements
   c. arguments
   d. metrics

9. A _____ is a name that represents a value stored in the computer's memory.
   a. tag
   b. label
   c. argument
   d. variable

10. This component is a horizontal track with a thumb slider that the user can move left or right.
   a. Slider
   b. ScrollBar
   c. HorizontalSlider
   d. ThumbSlider

Short Answer

1. In what section of the Pallete is the TextBox component located?

2. How do you prevent the user from entering input into a TextBox component?

3. How do you allow only numbers as input in a TextBox component?

4. What component would you use if you did not want the user's input to be visible on the screen?

5. What are the sockets on the left and right sides of a math operator block called?

6. What is a function?

7. What math function do you use to round a number to a specified number of decimal places?

8. What are arguments?

9. What is a variable?

10. What event happens when the user changes the position of a Slider component's thumb slider?

Exercises

1. In the Blocks Editor, use a math operator block to create an expression that gives the result of 100 + 50.

2. In the Blocks Editor, use math operator blocks to create an expression that gives the result of 100 + 50 + 10.

3. In the Blocks Editor, use math operator blocks to create an expression that gives the result of (100 + 50 + 10) / 4.

4. Modify the TipCalculator app that you created in Tutorial 3-2 to use a Slider component instead of buttons. The Slider should let the user see tip amounts between 15% and 25%.

5. In the Blocks Editor, create blocks that initialize a variable named `Age` to the value of 25.

6. In the Blocks Editor, create blocks that initialize a variable named `MiddleName` to the value of *Suzanne*.

7. Create an app with a slider that displays values in the range of 100 to 200.

8. In the Blocks Editor, create blocks that initialize a variable named `Num` to the value of the square root of 625.

VideoNote
The Average
of Three Test
Scores App

9. Create an app that lets the user enter three test scores and displays the average of the three scores.

10. Create an app that lets the user enter an angle, measured in degrees. The app should display the sine, cosine, and tangent of the angle.

Programming Projects

1. **Distance Traveled**

    Assuming there are no accidents or delays, the distance that a car travels down an interstate highway can be calculated with the following formula:

    $$Distance = Speed \times Time$$

    Create an app that allows the user to enter a car's speed in miles per hour. The application should have buttons that display the following:

    - The distance the car will travel in 5 hours
    - The distance the car will travel in 8 hours
    - The distance the car will travel in 12 hours

2. **Sales Tax and Total**

    Create an app that allows the user to enter the amount of a purchase. The program should then calculate the state and county sales tax. Assume the state sales tax is 4 percent and the county sales tax is 2 percent. The program should display the amount of the purchase, the state sales tax, the county sales tax, the total sales tax, and the total of the sale (which is the sum of the amount of purchase plus the total sales tax).

3. **Celsius and Fahrenheit Temperature Converter**

    Assuming that *C* is a Celsius temperature, the following formula converts the temperature to Fahrenheit:

    $$F = 5/9C + 32$$

    Assuming that *F* is a Fahrenheit temperature, the following formula converts the temperature to Celsius:

    $$C = 5/9(F - 32)$$

    Create an app that allows the user to enter a temperature. The app should have Button components described as follows:

    - A button that reads *Convert to Fahrenheit*. If the user clicks this button, the app should treat the temperature that is entered as a Celsius temperature and convert it to Fahrenheit.

- A button that reads *Convert to Celsius*. If the user clicks this button, the app should treat the temperature that is entered as a Fahrenheit temperature, and convert it to Celsius.

4. **Body Mass Index**

Create an app that lets the user enter his or her weight (in pounds) and height (in inches). The app should display the user's body mass index (BMI). The BMI is often used to determine whether a person is overweight or underweight for his or her height. A person's BMI is calculated with the following formula:

$$BMI = weight \times 703 \div height^2$$

5. **Cookie Calories**

A bag of cookies holds 40 cookies. The calorie information on the bag claims that there are 10 servings in the bag and that a serving equals 300 calories. Create an app that lets the user enter the number of cookies he or she actually ate and then reports the number of total calories consumed.

6. **Calorie Counter**

Create an app with a screen that resembles Figure 3-99. The screen displays the images of four fruits (a banana, an apple, an orange, and a pear) and each fruit's calories. You can find these images in the *Fruit Symbols* folder of the book's media files, available for download at www.pearsonhighered.com/gaddis.

When the application starts, the total calories displayed should be zero. Each time the user clicks one of the fruit images, the calories for that fruit should be added to the total calories, and the total calories should be displayed. When the user clicks the *Reset* button, the total calories should be reset to zero.

Figure 3-99 Calorie Counter App (*Source:* MIT App Inventor 2)

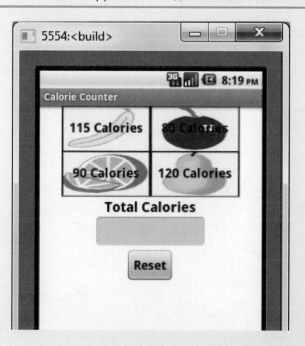

7. **Calories from Fat and Carbohydrates**

A nutritionist who works for a fitness club helps members by evaluating their diets. As part of her evaluation, she asks members for the number of fat grams and carbohydrate grams that they consumed in a day. Then, she calculates the number of calories that result from the fat, using the following formula:

$$\textit{calories from fat} = \textit{fat grams} \times 9$$

Next, she calculates the number of calories that result from the carbohydrates, using the following formula:

$$\textit{calories from carbs} = \textit{carb grams} \times 4$$

The nutritionist asks you to create an app that will make these calculations.

8. **Currency Converter**

Create an app that will convert U.S. dollar amounts to Japanese yen and to euros. To get the most up-to-date exchange rates, search the Internet using the term *currency exchange rate*. If you cannot find the most recent exchange rates, use the following:

$$1 \text{ Dollar} = 97 \text{ Yen}$$
$$1 \text{ Dollar} = 0.76 \text{ Euros}$$

Display your currency amounts rounded to two decimal places.

CHAPTER

4

Decision Blocks and Boolean Logic

TOPICS

4.1 Introduction to Decision Blocks

CONCEPT: Sometimes a program needs to "decide" whether or not to execute certain instructions. App Inventor provides three blocks for making decisions.

Computer programs work with many kinds of data. You've already created apps that work with values such as 1, 2, and 0.25. These values are numbers. You've also created apps that work with values such as *Hello* and *Enter the distance*. These are text values, which are also known as strings.

Programs can also work with the values `true` and `false`. These two values, `true` and `false`, are known as *Boolean* values, in honor of the English mathematician George Boole. In the 1800s Boole invented a system of mathematics in which the abstract concepts of true and false can be used in computations. Today, computer programming languages allow you to store the values `true` and `false` in memory and use those values in algorithms.

In a computer program, the values `true` and `false` are commonly used in decision making. Quite often, you will test a *Boolean expression* (an expression that gives either `true` or `false` as its value) and you will perform one set of instructions if the expression is `true`, or another set of instructions if the expression is `false`.

The `if then` Block

App Inventor provides the `if then` block for making decisions. In the Blocks column it is found in the *Built-in* section, in the *Control* drawer, as shown in Figure 4-1.

Figure 4-1 The Decision Blocks (*Source:* MIT App Inventor 2)

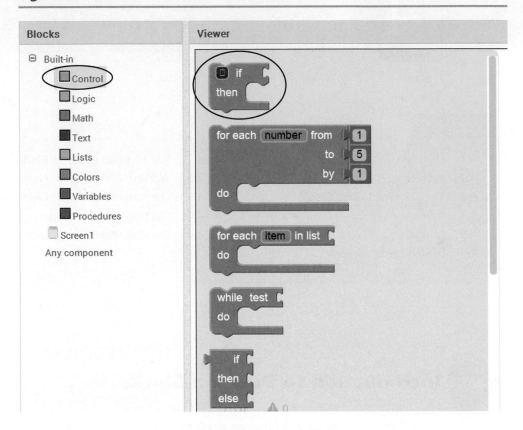

The `if then` block is shown in Figure 4-2. Notice that the `if then` block has two sockets: one for the `if` part, and one for the `then` part. The `if` socket holds a Boolean expression. If the Boolean expression is `true`, the instructions that appear in the `then` socket will be executed. If the Boolean expression is `false`, nothing happens (the instructions that appear in the `then` socket will be skipped). Figure 4-3 shows a way that might be helpful to think about the `if then` block.

Figure 4-2 The `if then` Block (*Source:* MIT App Inventor 2)

Plug a Boolean expression here.

The blocks that you plug here will be executed only if the Boolean test expression is true.

Figure 4-3 How to Think About the `if then` Block (*Source:* MIT App Inventor 2)

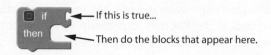

The `if then else` **Block**

The `if then` block is a mutator block. Recall from Chapter 3 that a mutator block has the ability to change in some way. When you click the blue box (▣) that appears in the upper-left corner of the block, the mutator bubble shown in Figure 4-4 appears. If you click and drag the `else` block (else) from the left side of the bubble and insert it on the right side of the bubble as shown in Figure 4-5, you change the `if then` block to an `if then else` block. Figure 4-6 shows an `if then else` block.

Figure 4-4 The `if then` Block's Mutator Bubble (*Source:* MIT App Inventor 2)

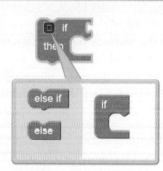

Figure 4-5 Changing the `if then` Block to an `if then else` Block
(*Source:* MIT App Inventor 2)

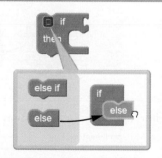

Figure 4-6 The `if then else` Block (*Source:* MIT App Inventor 2)

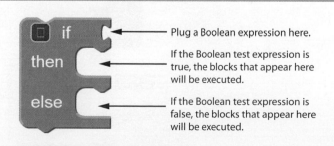

Notice that the `if then else` block has three sockets: one for the `if` part, one for the `then` part, and one for the `else` part. The `if` socket holds a Boolean expression. If the Boolean expression is `true`, the instructions that appear in the `then` socket will be executed. If the Boolean expression is `false`, the instructions that appear in the `else` socket will be executed. Figure 4-7 shows a way that might be helpful to think about the `if then else` block.

Figure 4-7 How to Think About the `if then else` Block *(Source: MIT App Inventor 2)*

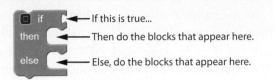

The `if then else if` Block

You can use the `if then` block's mutator bubble to change the block into an `if then else if` block. An `if then else if` block is used to test a series of Boolean expressions. In the mutator bubble, click and drag the `else if` block (else if) from the left side of the bubble and insert it on the right side of the bubble as shown in Figure 4-8. Then, drag the `else` block (else) from the left side of the bubble and insert it on the right side of the bubble as shown in Figure 4-9. This creates an `if then else if` block like the one shown in Figure 4-10.

Figure 4-8 Changing an `if then` Block to an `if then else if` Block
(Source: MIT App Inventor 2)

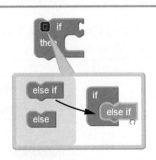

Figure 4-9 Adding an `else` Section to an `if then else if` Block
(Source: MIT App Inventor 2)

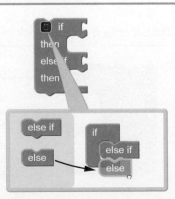

Figure 4-10 An `if then else if` Block (*Source:* MIT App Inventor 2)

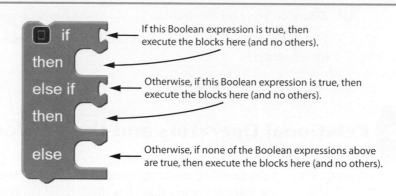

If this Boolean expression is true, then execute the blocks here (and no others).

Otherwise, if this Boolean expression is true, then execute the blocks here (and no others).

Otherwise, if none of the Boolean expressions above are true, then execute the blocks here (and no others).

When the `if then else if` block executes, Boolean expression #1 is tested. If Boolean expression #1 is true, the instructions in the `then` socket that immediately follow are executed and the rest of the block is ignored. If Boolean expression #1 is false, however, the program jumps to the very next `else if` section and tests Boolean expression #2. If it is true, the instructions in the `then` socket that immediately follow are executed and the rest of the block is then ignored. If none of the Boolean expressions are true, the instructions in the `else` socket are executed.

You can use the mutator bubble to add as many `else if` sections as you need. For example, Figure 4-11 shows an `if then else if` block that can test three Boolean expressions.

Figure 4-11 An `if then else if` Block that Can Test Three Boolean Expressions (*Source:* MIT App Inventor 2)

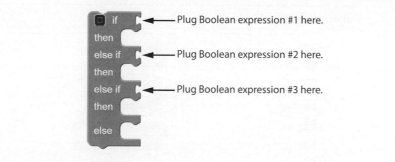

Plug Boolean expression #1 here.

Plug Boolean expression #2 here.

Plug Boolean expression #3 here.

We will take a closer look at these decision blocks, but first we must discuss Boolean expressions in greater detail.

 Checkpoint

4.1 The values `true` and `false` are what type of values?

4.2 What is a Boolean expression?

4.3 What decision blocks can you create with App Inventor?

4.4 Where do you find the decision blocks in the Blocks column?

4.5 The decision blocks have an `if` socket. What type of block do you plug into the `if` socket?

4.2 Relational Operators and the `if` Block

CONCEPT: A relational operator compares two numbers and determines whether one value is greater than, less than, equal to, greater than or equal to, less than or equal to, or not equal to the other value. The relational operators are commonly used to create Boolean expressions that are tested by decision blocks.

Typically, the Boolean expression that is tested by an `if` decision block is formed with a relational operator. A *relational operator* determines whether a specific relationship exists between two values. For example, the equal to operator (=) determines whether two values are equal. The greater than operator (>) determines whether one value is greater than another.

You access the relational operators by opening the *Math* drawer (in the *Built-in* section of the *Blocks* column) and selecting the = operator. This is shown in Figure 4-12. Once you create an = operator block, you can change it to any other relational operator by clicking the down-arrow (▼), as shown in Figure 4-13.

Figure 4-12 The Relational Operator Blocks (*Source:* MIT App Inventor 2)

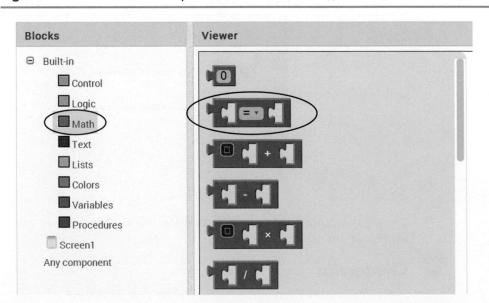

Figure 4-13 The Relational Operator Dropdown Menu (*Source:* MIT App Inventor 2)

Table 4-1 summarizes each of the relational operator blocks. Notice that each relational operator block has two sockets for operands.

Table 4-1 The Relational Operator Blocks (*Source:* Pearson Education, Inc.)

Operator Block	Description
	This is the *greater than operator*. It returns `true` if the operand on the left is greater than the operand on the right. Otherwise, it returns `false`.
	This is the *greater than or equal to operator*. It returns `true` if the operand on the left is greater than or equal to the operand on the right. Otherwise, it returns `false`.
	This is the *less than operator*. It returns `true` if the operand on the left is less than the operand on the right. Otherwise, it returns `false`.
	This is the *less than or equal to operator*. It returns `true` if the operand on the left is less than or equal to the operand on the right. Otherwise, it returns `false`.
	This is the *equal to operator*. It returns `true` if the operand on the left is equal to the operand on the right. Otherwise, it returns `false`.
	This is the *not equal to operator*. It returns `true` if the operand on the left is not equal to the operand on the right. Otherwise, it returns `false`.

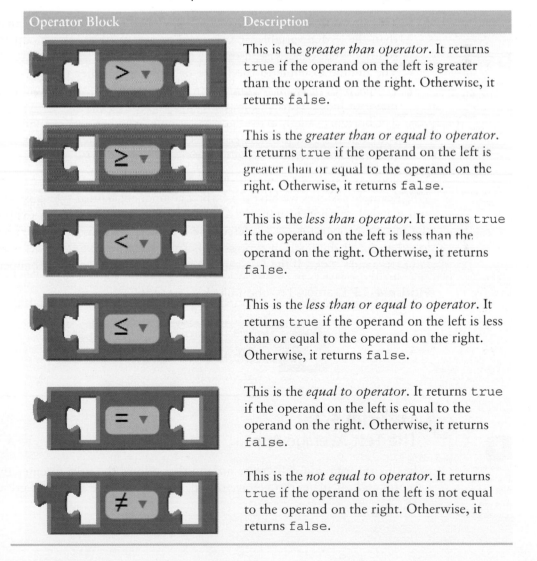

Figure 4-14 shows some examples of relational operators with operands plugged in:

Figure 4-14 Relational Operator Block Examples (*Source:* MIT App Inventor 2)

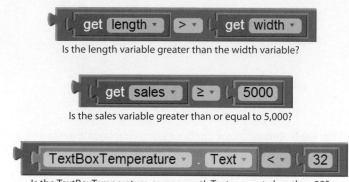

Is the length variable greater than the width variable?

Is the sales variable greater than or equal to 5,000?

Is the TextBoxTemperature component's Text property less than 32?

- The top example in the figure determines whether the `length` variable is greater than the `width` variable. If `length` is greater than `width`, the operator block returns `true`. Otherwise, it returns `false`.
- The middle example in the figure determines whether the `sales` variable is greater than or equal to 5,000. If `sales` is greater than or equal to 5,000, the operator block returns `true`. Otherwise, it returns `false`.
- The bottom example in the figure determines whether the `TextBoxTemperature` component's Text property contains a value that is less than 32.0. If it does, the operator block returns `true`. Otherwise, it returns `false`.

Now look at Figure 4-15, which shows an example of a complete `if then` block. This example assumes we have a TextBox component named `TextBoxTemperature` and a Label component named `LabelMessage`. The Boolean test expression uses the less-than operator (<) to determine whether `TextBoxTemperature.Text` is less than 32. If the Boolean expression is true, then the text *It's cold!* is assigned to `LabelMessage.Text`. If the Boolean expression is not true, nothing happens.

Figure 4-15 Example `if then` Block (*Source:* MIT App Inventor 2)

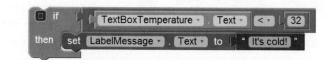

Tutorial 4-1:
The Test Average App

In this tutorial you will create an app that allows the user to enter three test scores and calculates the average of the test scores. If the average is greater than

95, the app also displays a message congratulating the user. Figure 4-16 shows the app's screen in the Viewer, along with the names of the components. Figure 4-17 shows how the screen appears in the emulator.

Figure 4-16 The App's User Interface (*Source:* MIT App Inventor 2)

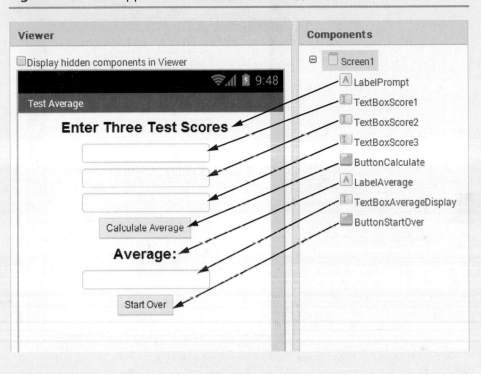

When the app runs, the user enters the three test scores into the TextBoxScore1, TextBoxScore2, and TextBoxScore1 components. When the user clicks the ButtonCalculate button, the app calculates the average of the three scores and displays the result in the TextBoxAverageDisplay component. If the average is greater than 95, the app also changes the LabelPrompt component's Text property to *Great Job!*

The app also has a button named ButtonStartOver that clears the TextBox components and restores the LabelPrompt component's Text property to the value *Enter Three Test Scores*.

Step 1: Start a new project named TestAverage.

Step 2: Set up the app's screen with the components shown in Figure 4-16. Refer to Table 4-2 for the relevant property settings for each component.

Figure 4-17 The App Running in the Emulator *(Source:* MIT App Inventor 2)

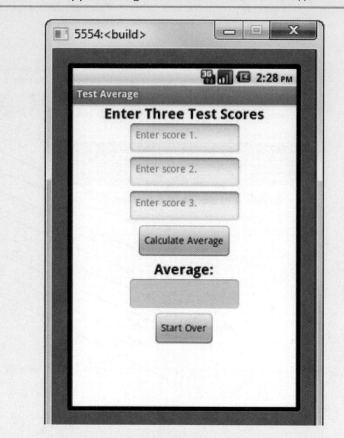

Table 4-2 Component property settings *(Source:* Pearson Education, Inc.)

Component	Relevant Property Settings
Screen1	AlignHorizontal = *Center*
	Title = *Test Average*
LabelPrompt	FontBold = *checked*
	FontSize = *20*
	Text = *Enter Three Test Scores*
	TextAlignment = *Center*
TextBoxScore1	Enabled = *checked*
	NumbersOnly = *checked*
	Hint = *Enter score 1.*
	Width = *Automatic*
	Height = *Automatic*

Component	Relevant Property Settings
TextBoxScore2	Enabled = *checked*
	NumbersOnly = *checked*
	Hint = *Enter score 2.*
	Width = *Automatic*
	Height = *Automatic*
TextBoxScore3	Enabled = *checked*
	NumbersOnly = *checked*
	Hint = *Enter score 3.*
	Width = *Automatic*
	Height = *Automatic*
ButtonCalculate	Text = *Calculate Average*
LabelAverage	FontBold = *checked*
	FontSize = *20*
	Text = *Average:*
	TextAlignment = *Center*
TextBoxAverageDisplay	Enabled = *unchecked*
	FontBold = *checked*
	FontSize = *20*
	Hint = *cleared*
	TextAlign = *Center*
	Width = *Automatic*
	Height = *Automatic*
ButtonStartOver	Text = *Start Over*

Step 3: Now you will program the blocks for the app. Open the Blocks Editor and create a Click event handler for the ButtonCalculate component, as shown in Figure 4-18. When the event handler is complete, it will calculate the average of the three test scores that were entered by the user and assign that value to the average variable. If the average is greater than 95, a special message will be displayed.

Figure 4-18 Click Event Handler Block for ButtonCalculate
(*Source:* MIT App Inventor 2)

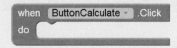

Step 4: Now you will create a local variable to hold the average of the test scores. Open the *Variables* drawer and select the initialize local *name* to block. This creates an initialization block in the workspace.

Plug the initialization block into the `ButtonCalculate.Click` event handler, as shown in Figure 4-19.

Figure 4-19 Variable Initialization Block Created (*Source:* MIT App Inventor 2)

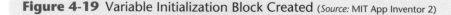

Step 5: Change the variable's name to `Average` and set the average variable's initial value to 0, as shown in Figure 4-20.

Figure 4-20 The Completed Variable Initialization Block (*Source:* MIT App Inventor 2)

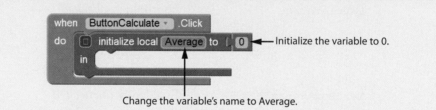

Step 6: In a different area of the workspace, assemble the blocks shown in Figure 4-21. These blocks will calculate the average of the test scores entered by the user. (Note that you will have to use the + operator's mutator bubble to add a third operand to the + operator block.) When you have the blocks assembled, they should appear as shown in Figure 4-22.

Figure 4-21 Assembling the Math Blocks to Calculate the Average
(*Source:* MIT App Inventor 2)

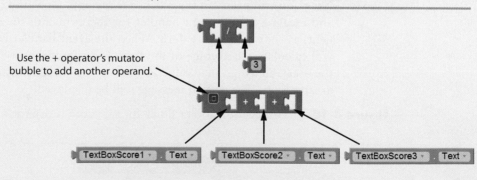

Figure 4-22 The Completed Calculation (*Source:* MIT App Inventor 2)

Step 7: You want to assign the result of the calculation to the `Average` variable. Open the *Variables* drawer, select the `set` block, and plug it into the `ButtonCalculate.Click` event handler as shown in Figure 4-23. Next, select the `Average` variable in the `set` block's dropdown. The block should now appear as shown in Figure 4-24.

Figure 4-23 The `set` Block Placed (*Source:* MIT App Inventor 2)

Figure 4-24 The Variable Name Selected in the `set` Block (*Source:* MIT App Inventor 2)

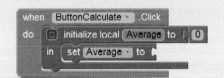

Step 8: As shown in Figure 4-25, plug the math blocks for the calculation into the socket of the `set Average to` block.

Figure 4-25 Plug the Calculation into the `set Average to` Block (*Source:* MIT App Inventor 2)

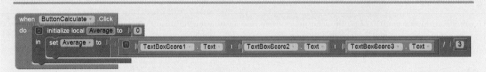

Step 9: Next, the `ButtonCalculate` component should display the average in the `TextBoxAverageDisplay` component. Add the blocks shown in Figure 4-26. (You will find the `get` block in the *Variables* drawer.)

Figure 4-26 Displaying the Average (*Source:* MIT App Inventor 2)

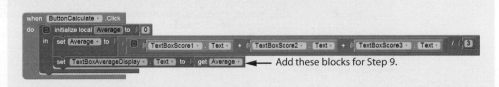

Step 10: Now you will begin assembling the `if then` block that determines whether the average is greater than 95. Open the *Control* drawer (in the *Built-in* section) and select the `if then` block. Place it as shown in Figure 4-27.

Figure 4-27 The `if then` Block Placed (*Source:* MIT App Inventor 2)

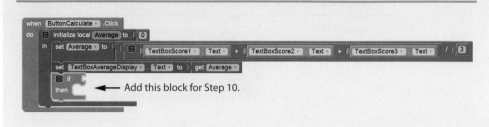

Step 11: Now create the Boolean test expression shown in Figure 4-28. Here are some hints and reminders:

- To create the > operator block, select the = block in the *Math* drawer, then use the block's dropdown to change it to a > operator block.
- You will find the `get` block in the *Variables* drawer.

Figure 4-28 The Boolean Test Expression Placed (*Source:* MIT App Inventor 2)

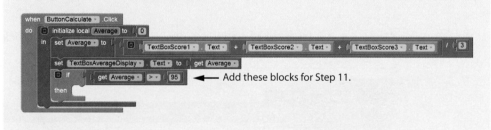

Step 12: Complete the `if then` block as shown in Figure 4-29.

Figure 4-29 The `if then` Block Completed (*Source:* MIT App Inventor 2)

Step 13: Now you will create the `Click` event handler for the `ButtonStartOver` button, as shown in Figure 4-30. When this button is clicked, the TextBox components will be cleared and the `LabelPrompt` component's Text property will be set to *Enter Three Test Scores*.

Figure 4-30 The Completed `ButtonStartOver.Click` Event Handler
(*Source:* MIT App Inventor 2)

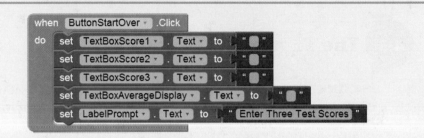

Step 14: Test the app in the emulator or on your device. First, as shown in the image on the left in Figure 4-31, enter the values 70, 75, and 80 as the test scores. Click the *Calculate Average* button and you should see the average as shown in the figure.

Next, click the *Start Over* button. The text boxes should clear. Enter the values 100, 99, and 98 as the test scores. Click the *Calculate Average* button and you should see the average as shown on the left in the figure. You should also see the message *Great Job!* displayed at the top of the screen.

Continue to test the app as you wish.

Figure 4-31 The App Running in the Emulator (*Source:* MIT App Inventor 2)

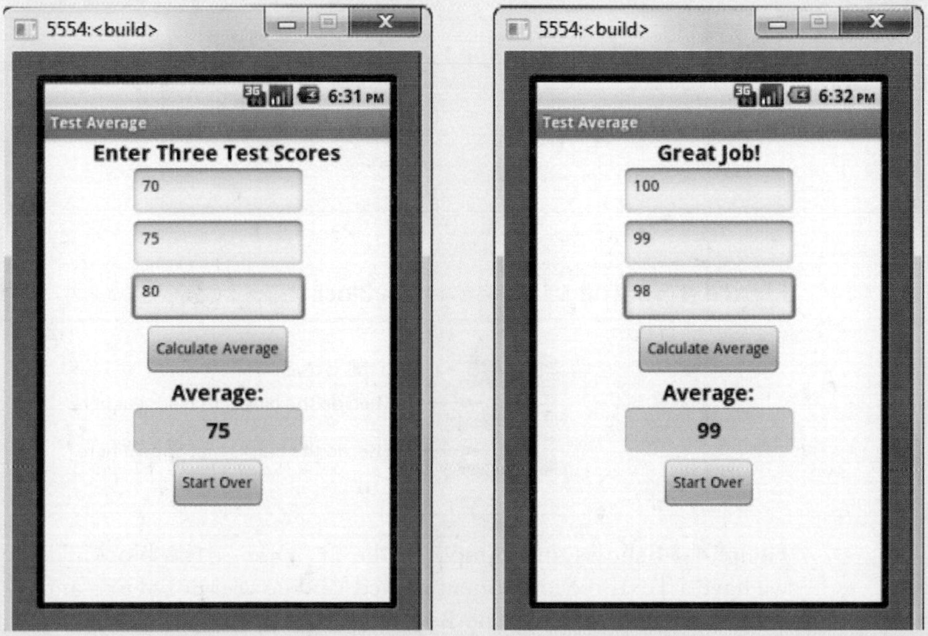

Checkpoint

4.6 What types of relationships between numeric values can you test with relational operators?

4.7 Where in the Blocks column do you find the relational operators?

4.8 When an `if then` block executes, what happens if the Boolean expression is true? What happens if the Boolean expression is false?

4.3 The `if then else` Block

CONCEPT: An `if then else` block will execute one set of blocks if its Boolean expression is true or another set of blocks if its Boolean expression is false.

As shown in Figure 4-32, you can use the `if then` block's mutator bubble to convert the block into an `if then else` block. As shown in Figure 4-33, the `if then else` block has three sockets: an `if` socket, a `then` socket, and an `else` socket. The `if` socket holds a Boolean expression. If the Boolean expression is `true`, the instructions that appear in the `then` socket will be executed. If the Boolean expression is `false`, the instructions that appear in the `else` socket will be executed.

Figure 4-32 Changing the `if then` Block to an `if then else` Block
(*Source:* MIT App Inventor 2)

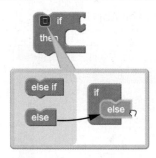

Figure 4-33 The `if then else` Block (*Source:* MIT App Inventor 2)

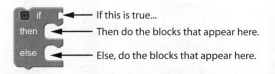

Figure 4-34 shows an example of the `if then else` block. This example assumes we have a TextBox component named `TextBoxTemperature` and a Label component named `LabelMessage`. The Boolean test expression uses the less-than operator (`<`) to determine whether `TextBoxTemperature.Text` is less than 40.0. If the Boolean expression is true, then the text *A little cold, isn't it?* is assigned to `LabelMessage.Text`. If the Boolean expression is false, the text *Nice weather we're having*! is assigned to `LabelMessage.Text`.

Figure 4-34 Example of the `if then else` Block *(Source: MIT App Inventor 2)*

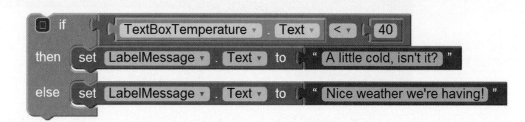

Tutorial 4-2:

Modifying the Test Average App

VideoNote
Modifying the Test Average App

In this tutorial you will modify the Test Average app that you created in Tutorial 4-1. After you modify the app, it will display the message *Great Job!* if the test score average is greater than 95, or the message *Keep Trying!* if it is not.

Step 1: Open the TestAverage project that you created in Tutorial 4-1.

Step 2: Open the Blocks Editor.

Step 3: As shown in Figure 4-35, use the `if then` block's mutator bubble to convert the `if then` block to an `if then else` block.

Figure 4-35 Converting the `if then` Block to an `if then else` Block
(*Source:* MIT App Inventor 2)

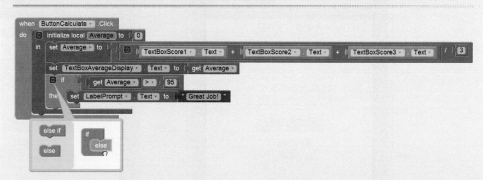

Step 4: Add the blocks shown in Figure 4-36 to the `else` socket of the `if then else` block. The `if then else` block works like this: it determines whether the value of the `Average` variable is greater than 95. If it is, the text *Great Job!* is assigned to `LabelPrompt.Text`. If it is not, the text *Keep Trying!* is assigned to `LabelPrompt.Text`.

Figure 4-36 The Modified `ButtonCalculate.Click` Event Handler
(*Source:* MIT App Inventor 2)

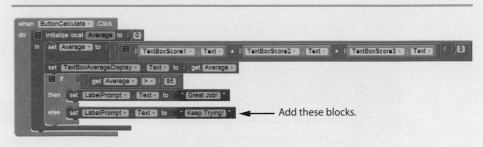

← Add these blocks.

Step 5: Test the app in the emulator or on your device. First, as shown in the image on the left in Figure 4-37, enter the values 70, 75, and 80 as the test scores. Click the *Calculate Average* button and you should see the average as shown in the figure, along with the message Keep Trying! displayed at the top of the screen.

Next, click the *Start Over* button. The text boxes should clear and the message at the top of the screen should switch back to *Enter Three Test Scores*. Enter the values 100, 99, and 98 as the test scores. Click the *Calculate Average* button and you should see the average as shown in the figure. You should also see the message *Great Job!* displayed at the top of the screen. Continue to test the app as you wish.

Figure 4-37 The App Running in the Emulator (*Source:* MIT App Inventor 2)

5554:\<build\>	5554:\<build\>
Test Average 7:59 PM	**Test Average** 7:58 PM
Keep Trying!	**Great Job!**
70	100
75	99
80	98
Calculate Average	Calculate Average
Average:	**Average:**
75	**99**
Start Over	Start Over

VideoNote
Creating the
Wages App

Tutorial 4-3:
Creating the Wages App

At a particular business, if an employee works more than 40 hours in a week, it is said that the employee has worked *overtime*. For example, an employee that has worked 45 hours in a week has worked 5 overtime hours. Employees that work overtime get paid their regular hourly pay rate for the first 40 hours plus 1.5 times their regular hourly pay rate for all hours over 40.

In this tutorial you will create an app that calculates an employee's gross pay, including overtime pay. The app allows the user to enter the number of hours worked and the hourly pay rate into text boxes. Figure 4-38 shows the app's screen in the Viewer, along with the names of the components. Figure 4-39 shows how the screen appears in the emulator.

Figure 4-38 The App's User Interface (*Source:* MIT App Inventor 2)

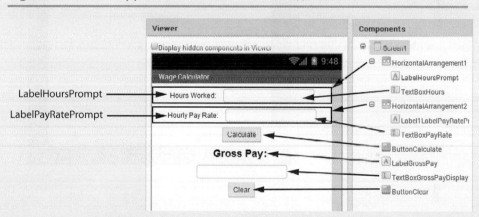

When the user clicks the `ButtonCalculate` button, the gross pay is calculated in the following manner:

> *If the hours worked is greater than 40:*
>> *regular pay = hourly pay rate × 40*
>> *overtime hours = hours worked − 40*
>> *overtime pay = overtime hours × hourly pay rate × 1.5*
>> *gross pay = base pay + overtime pay*
> *Else:*
>> *gross pa   y = hours worked × hourly pay rate*

As you can see, there are two very different calculations, depending on whether the user has worked more than 40 hours. Regardless of which calculation is used, the result is the gross pay. In this app we will use an `if then else` block to determine whether the user has worked overtime and perform the correct calculation.

Figure 4-39 The App Running in the Emulator (*Source:* MIT App Inventor 2)

Step 1: Start a new project named Wages.

Step 2: Set up the app's screen with the components shown in Figure 4-38. Refer to Table 4-3 for the relevant property settings for each component.

Table 4-3 Component property settings (*Source:* Pearson Education, Inc.)

Component	Relevant Property Settings
Screen1	AlignHorizontal = *Center*
	Title = *Wage Calculator*
HorizontalArrangement1	AlignHorizontal = *Center*
	Width = *Fill parent*
	Height = *Automatic*
LabelHoursPrompt	Text = *Hours Worked:*

Component	Relevant Property Settings
TextBoxHours	Enabled = *checked*
	NumbersOnly = *checked*
	Hint = *Hours Worked*
	Width = *Automatic*
	Height = *Automatic*
HorizontalArrangement2	AlignHorizontal = *Center*
	Width = *Fill parent*
	Height = *Automatic*
LabelPayRatePrompt	Text = *Hourly Pay Rate:*
TextBoxPayRate	Enabled = *checked*
	NumbersOnly = *checked*
	Hint = *Hourly Pay Rate*
	Width = *Automatic*
	Height = *Automatic*
ButtonCalculate	Text = *Calculate*
LabelGrossPay	FontBold = *checked*
	FontSize = *20*
	Text = *Gross Pay:*
	TextAlignment = *Center*
TextBoxGrossPayDisplay	Enabled = *unchecked*
	FontBold = *checked*
	FontSize = *20*
	Hint = *cleared*
	TextAlignment = *Center*
	Width = *Automatic*
	Height = *Automatic*
ButtonClear	Text = *Clear*

Step 3: Now you will program the blocks for the app. Open the Blocks Editor.

Step 4: Create a Click event handler for the ButtonCalculate button, as shown in Figure 4-40.

Figure 4-40 Click Event Handler for the ButtonCalculate Component

(*Source:* MIT App Inventor 2)

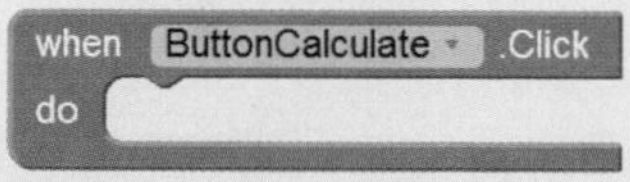

Step 5: Now you will create and initialize the local variables needed to calculate the gross pay. Create an `initialize local` *name* `to` block and, as shown in Figure 4-41, insert it into the `ButtonCalculate.Click` event handler.

Figure 4-41 The `initialize local` *name* `to` Block Created
(*Source:* MIT App Inventor 2)

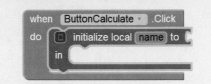

Step 6: Use the variable initialization block's mutator bubble to add three more variable names to the block. (The initialization block should have a total of four variables.) Change the variable names to those shown in Figure 4-42. Initialize each variable to the value 0.

Figure 4-42 Variable Initialization Blocks (*Source:* MIT App Inventor 2)

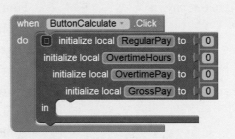

Step 7: Create an `if then` block and use its mutator bubble to change it to an `if then else` block. Insert the `if then else` block into the variable initialization block, as shown in Figure 4-43.

Figure 4-43 Begin the `ButtonCalculate.Click` Event Handler
(*Source:* MIT App Inventor 2)

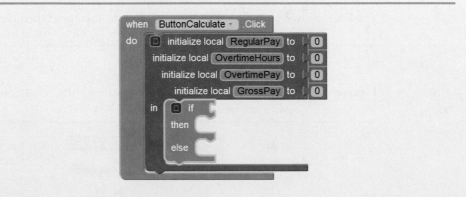

Step 8: Insert the Boolean expression shown in Figure 4-44 into the `if` socket of the `if then else` block.

Figure 4-44 Boolean Expression Created (*Source:* MIT App Inventor 2)

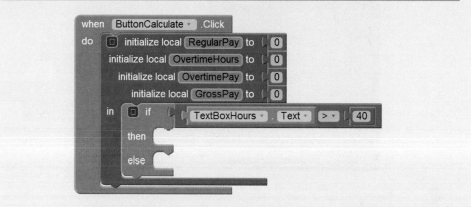

Step 9: The `if then else` block determines whether the hours worked is greater than 40. If that is true, the blocks in the `then` section will calculate the gross pay with overtime and assign the result to the `GrossPay` variable. Add the blocks shown in Figure 4-45 to the `if then else` block's `then` section.

Figure 4-45 Overtime Calculation (*Source:* MIT App Inventor 2)

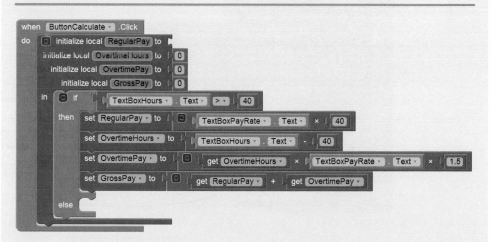

Step 10: If the hours worked is not greater than 40, the `if then else` block's `else` section will calculate the gross pay without overtime and assign the result to the `GrossPay` variable. Add the blocks shown in Figure 4-46 to the `if then else` block's `else` section.

Figure 4-46 The Completed `if then else` Block (*Source:* MIT App Inventor 2)

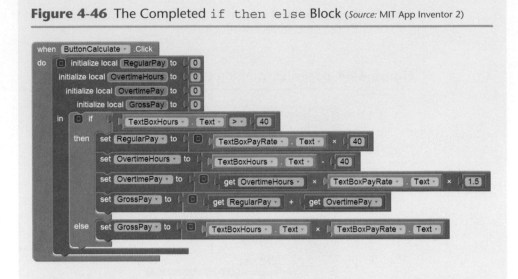

Step 11: The last action to be performed by the `ButtonCalculate` component is to display the gross pay. Add the blocks shown in Figure 4-47.

Figure 4-47 The Completed `ButtonCalculate.Click` Event Handler
(*Source:* MIT App Inventor 2)

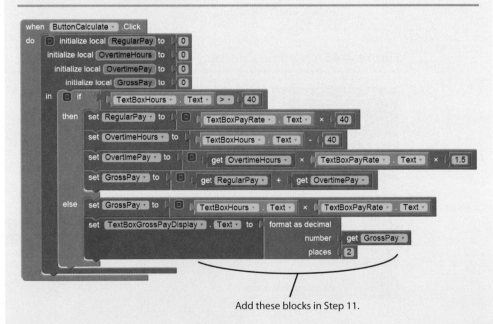

Add these blocks in Step 11.

Step 12: The `ButtonClear` button will simply clear the Text property of the `TextBox` components. Create the button's `Click` event handler as shown in Figure 4-48.

Figure 4-48 The Completed `ButtonClear.Click` Event Handler
(*Source:* MIT App Inventor 2)

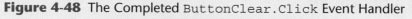

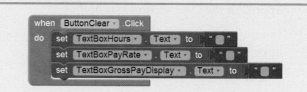

Step 13: Test the app in the emulator or on your device. First, as shown in the image on the left in Figure 4-49, enter 40 for the number of hours worked and 20 for the hourly pay rate. Click the *Calculate Gross Pay* button and the app should display 800.00 as the gross pay. No overtime hours were worked, so the gross pay is simply calculated as hours worked × hourly pay rate.

Next, click the *Clear* button. The text boxes should clear. Enter 50 for the number of hours worked and 20 for the hourly pay rate. Click the *Calculate* button and the app should display 1100 as the gross pay, as shown in the image on the right in Figure 4-38. This time, more than 40 hours were worked, so the app calculated the gross pay to include overtime pay. Continue to test the app as you wish.

Figure 4-49 The App Running in the Emulator (*Source:* MIT App Inventor 2)

5554:\<build\>	5554:\<build\>
Wage Calculator	**Wage Calculator**
Hours Worked: 40	Hours Worked: 50
Hourly Pay Rate: 20	Hourly Pay Rate: 20
Calculate	Calculate
Gross Pay:	**Gross Pay:**
800	1100.0
Clear	Clear

Checkpoint

4.9 In an `if then else` block, under what circumstances do the blocks that appear in the `then` section execute?

4.10 In an `if then else` block, under what circumstances do the blocks that appear in the `else` section execute?

4.4 A First Look At Comparing Strings

CONCEPT: The `compare texts` block compares two strings. It can determine whether one string is alphabetically less than, greater than, or equal to another string.

Figure 4-50 shows a block named `compare texts`, which is found in the *Text* drawer of the *Built-in* section of the *Blocks* column. The `compare texts` block lets you compare two strings and determine whether one string is alphabetically less than, greater than, or equal to another string. When you create the block you can select one of the comparison operators (<, =, or >) from the block's dropdown menu, as shown in Figure 4-51.

In Chapter 10 you will read more about this block, but we will take this opportunity to introduce one of them: the `compare texts` = operator.

Figure 4-50 The `compare texts` Block (*Source:* MIT App Inventor 2)

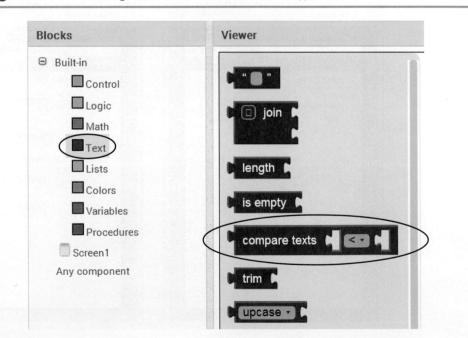

Figure 4-51 The `compare texts` Block Dropdown (*Source:* MIT App Inventor 2)

The `compare texts` `=` operator has two sockets. You simply plug two pieces of text into these sockets and the operator returns `true` if they are equal. Otherwise, it returns `false`. For example, the `if then else` block shown in Figure 4-52 compares a `TextBox`'s `Text` property to a `text` block. It works like this:

If `TextBoxSecretWord.Text` *is equal to* "*prospero*" *then*
    set `LableResult.Text` *to* "*That is the correct secret word.*"
else
    set `LableResult.Text` *to* "*That is NOT the secret word.*"

Figure 4-52 Comparing Two Strings (*Source:* MIT App Inventor 2)

```
if      compare texts   TextBoxSecretWord . Text = " prospero "
then    set  LabelResult . Text  to  " That is the correct secret word. "
else    set  LabelResult . Text  to  " That is NOT the secret word. "
```

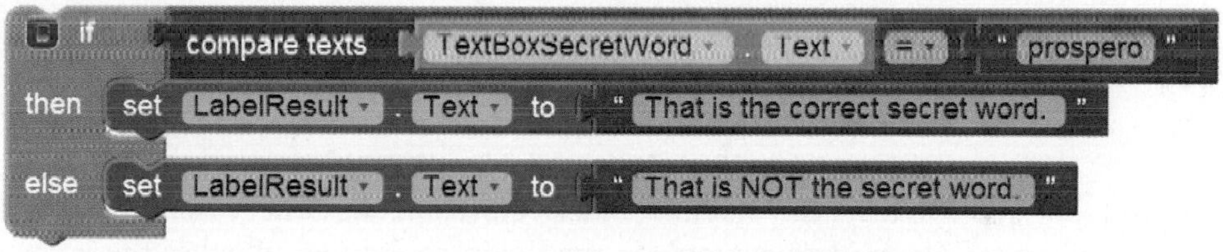

We will discuss string comparisons in greater detail in Chapter 10, but until then, you will occasionally see examples that use the `compare texts` `=` operator.

4.5 Logical Operators

CONCEPT: The logical *and* operator and the logical *or* operator allow you to connect multiple Boolean expressions to create a compound expression. The logical *not* operator reverses the truth of a Boolean expression.

App Inventor provides a set of operator blocks known as *logical operators*, which you can use to create complex Boolean expressions. Table 4-4 describes these operator blocks.

Table 4-4 Logical Operator Blocks (*Source:* Pearson Education, Inc.)

Operator Block	Description
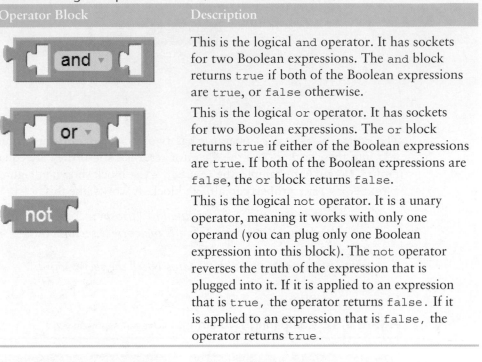	This is the logical and operator. It has sockets for two Boolean expressions. The and block returns true if both of the Boolean expressions are true, or false otherwise.
	This is the logical or operator. It has sockets for two Boolean expressions. The or block returns true if either of the Boolean expressions are true. If both of the Boolean expressions are false, the or block returns false.
	This is the logical not operator. It is a unary operator, meaning it works with only one operand (you can plug only one Boolean expression into this block). The not operator reverses the truth of the expression that is plugged into it. If it is applied to an expression that is true, the operator returns false. If it is applied to an expression that is false, the operator returns true.

Figure 4-53 shows some examples using the logical operator blocks:

- The top example in the figure determines whether the x variable is greater than the y variable, and the a variable is less than the b variable. If both expressions are true, the operator block returns true. Otherwise, it returns false.
- The middle example in the figure determines whether the x variable is equal to the y variable, OR the x variable is equal to the a variable. If either expression is true, the operator block returns true. Otherwise, it returns false.
- The bottom example in the figure negates the Boolean value of the expression x > y. If the expression is true, the operator block returns false. Otherwise, it returns true.

Figure 4-53 Logical Operator Block Examples (*Source:* MIT App Inventor 2)

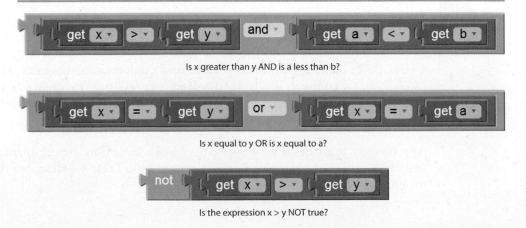

Checking Numeric Ranges with Logical Operators

Sometimes you need to determine whether a numeric value is within a specific range of values or outside a specific range of values. When determining whether a number is inside a range, it is best to use the `and` operator. For example, the `if` block shown in Figure 4-54 checks the value in `x` to determine whether it is in the range of 20 through 40.

The compound Boolean expression being tested by the `if` block in Figure 4-54 is true only when `x` is greater than or equal to 20 *and* less than or equal to 40. The value in `x` must be within the range of 20 through 40 for this compound expression to be true.

Figure 4-54 Determining Whether a Number is Inside a Numeric Range
(*Source:* MIT App Inventor 2)

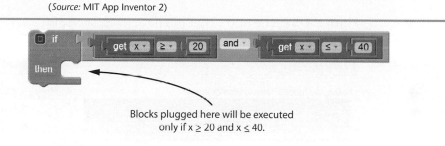

Blocks plugged here will be executed
only if x ≥ 20 and x ≤ 40.

When determining whether a number is outside a range, it is best to use the `or` operator. The `if` block shown in Figure 4-55 determines whether `x` is outside the range of 20 through 40.

Figure 4-55 Determining Whether a Number is Outside a Numeric Range
(*Source:* MIT App Inventor 2)

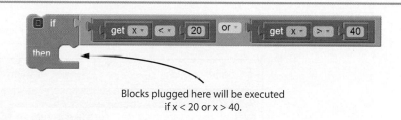

Blocks plugged here will be executed
if x < 20 or x > 40.

It is important not to get the logic of the logical operators confused when testing for a range of numbers. For example, the compound Boolean expression shown in Figure 4-56 would never test true. Obviously, `x` cannot be less than 20 and at the same time be greater than 40.

Figure 4-56 Logic Error (*Source:* MIT App Inventor 2)

Blocks plugged here will never execute!

Tutorial 4-4:
Creating the Range Checker App

In this tutorial you will create a simple app that checks a number entered by the user to determine if it is in the range of 1 through 100. Figure 4-57 shows the app's user interface in the Viewer and Figure 4-58 shows the app running in the emulator. When the app runs, the user enters a number into the `TextBoxNumber` TextBox and then clicks the `ButtonCheckNumber` button. If the number is within the range of 1 through 100 (inclusive), the app changes the `LabelStatus` component to read *Pass!* If the number is not within the range of 1 through 100, the app changes the `LabelStatus` component to read *Fail!*

Figure 4-57 The App's User Interface (*Source:* MIT App Inventor 2)

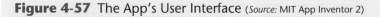

Figure 4-58 The App Running in the Emulator (*Source:* MIT App Inventor 2)

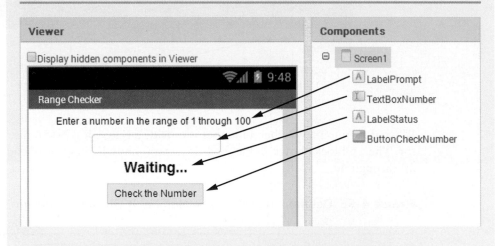

Step 1: Start a new project named RangeChecker.

Step 2: Set up the app's screen with the components shown in Figure 4-57. Refer to Table 4-5 for the relevant property settings for each component.

Table 4-5 Component property settings (*Source:* Pearson Education, Inc.)

Component	Relevant Property Settings
Screen1	AlignHorizontal = *Center*
	Title = *Range Checker*
LabelPrompt	Text = *Enter a number in the range of 1 through 100*
TextBoxNumber	Enabled = *checked*
	NumbersOnly = *checked*
	Hint = *cleared*
	Width = *Automatic*
	Height = *Automatic*
LabelStatus	FontBold = *checked*
	FontSize = *20*
	Text = *Waiting…*
	TextAlignment = *Center*
ButtonCheckNumber	Text = *Check the Number*

Step 3: Now you will program the Click event handler for the ButtonCheckNumber button. Open the Blocks Editor and create the event handler as shown in Figure 4-59.

Figure 4-59 Click Event Handler for ButtonCheckNumber
(*Source:* MIT App Inventor 2)

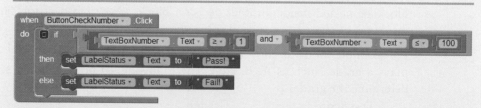

Step 4: Test the app in the emulator or on your device. First, as shown in the image on the left in Figure 4-60, enter 50 and click the button. The app should display *Pass!* Then, as shown in the image on the left, enter 101 and click the button. The app should display *Fail!* Continue to test the app with other numbers.

Figure 4-60 The App Running in the Emulator *(Source: MIT App Inventor 2)*

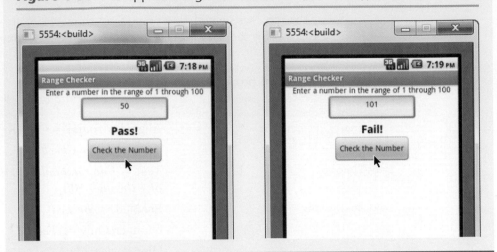

 Checkpoint

4.11 You have created a compound Booelan expression with the logical and operator. Under what circumstance will the compound expression be true?

4.12 You have created a compound Booelan expression with the logical or operator. Under what circumstance will the compound expression be true?

4.13 Describe how the logical not operator works.

4.6 Nested Decision Blocks

CONCEPT: **To test more than one condition, a decision block can be nested inside another decision block.**

It is common for a program to test a Boolean expression and, depending on the result, test another Boolean expression. This type of logic usually requires that a decision block be nested inside another decision block. (A *nested* decision block is written inside the then or else section of another decision block.)

For example, in Tutorial 4-5 you will create an app that reads a test score and displays a grade (such as A, B, etc.). The following 10-point grading scale is used to determine the grade:

Test Score	Grade
Below 60	F
60–69	D
70–79	C
80–89	B
90 and above	A

The logic of determining the grade can be expressed like this:

If the test score is less than 60, then the grade is F.
Else, if the test score is less than 70, then the grade is D.

Else, if the test score is less than 80, then the grade is C.
Else, if the test score is less than 90, then the grade is B.
Else, the grade is A.

The user will enter a numeric test score into a TextBox named `TextBoxTestScore` and the app will display corresponding grade in a TextBox named `TextBoxGradeDisplay`. Figure 4-61 shows how you will assemble the nested decision blocks.

Figure 4-61 Assembling the Nested Decision Blocks in the Grader App
(*Source:* MIT App Inventor 2)

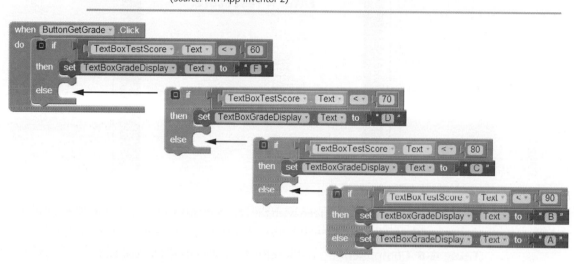

Tutorial 4-5:
Creating the Grader App

VideoNote
Creating the
Grader App

Figure 4-62 shows the Grader app's user interface in the Viewer and Figure 4-63 shows the app running in the emulator.

Figure 4-62 The App's User Interface (*Source:* MIT App Inventor 2)

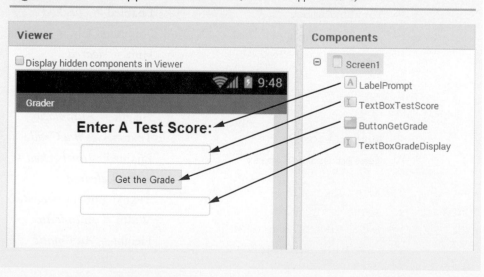

Figure 4-63 The App Running in the Emulator *(Source: MIT App Inventor 2)*

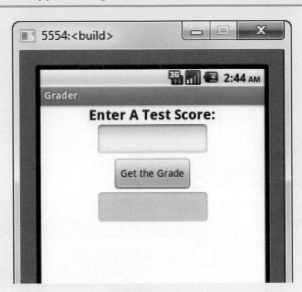

Step 1: Start a new project named Grader.

Step 2: Set up the app's screen with the components shown in Figure 4-62. Refer to Table 4-6 for the relevant property settings for each component.

Table 4-6 Component property settings *(Source: Pearson Education, Inc.)*

Component	Relevant Property Settings
Screen1	AlignHorizontal = *Center*
	Title = *Grader*
LabelPrompt	FontBold = *checked*
	FontSize = *20*
	Text = *Enter A Test Score:*
	TextAlignment = *Center*
TextBoxNumber	Enabled = *checked*
	NumbersOnly = *checked*
	Hint = *cleared*
	TextAlignment = *center*
	Width = *Automatic*
	Height = *Automatic*
ButtonGetGrade	Text = *Get the Grade*
TextBoxGradeDisplay	Enabled = *unchecked*
	Hint = *cleared*
	TextAlignment = *center*
	Width = *Automatic*
	Height = *Automatic*

Step 3: Now you will program the `Click` event handler for the `ButtonGetGrade` button. Open the Blocks Editor and create the event handler as shown in Figure 4-64. (If necessary, refer to Figure 4-61 for additional help assembling the nested `if then else` blocks.)

Figure 4-64 `Click` Event Handler for `ButtonGetGrade`
(*Source:* MIT App Inventor 2)

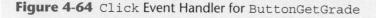

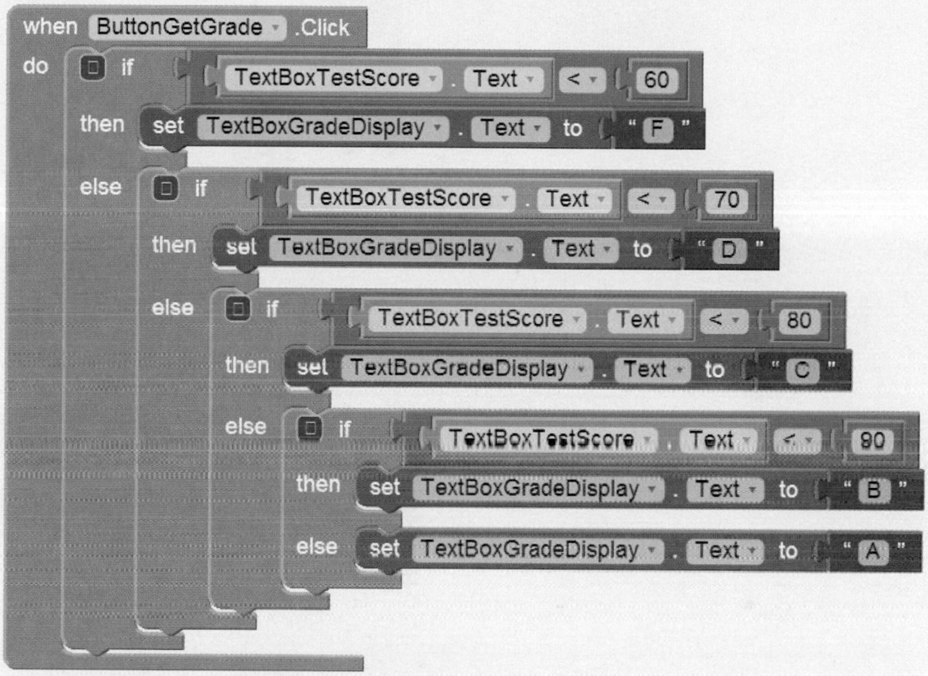

Step 4: Test the app in the emulator or on your device. Enter a variety of numeric test scores to verify the correct grades are displayed.

4.7 The `if then else if` Block

CONCEPT: The `if then else if` block tests a series of conditions. It is often simpler to test a series of conditions with the `if then else if` block than with a set of nested `if then else` blocks.

Even though the Grader app that you created in Tutorial 4-5 is a simple example, the logic of the nested decision structure is fairly complex. App Inventor provide a special version of the decision structure known as the `if then else if` block, which makes this type of logic simpler to write.

As shown in Figure 4-65, you can use the `if then` block's mutator bubble to convert the block into an `if then else` block. In the mutator bubble, click and drag the else if block (else if) from the left side of the bubble and insert it on the right side of the bubble. Then, as shown in Figure 4-66, drag the else block (else) from the left side of the bubble and insert it on the right side of the bubble. This creates an if then else if block like the one shown in Figure 4-67.

Figure 4-65 Changing an if then Block to an if then else if Block
(*Source:* MIT App Inventor 2)

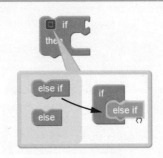

Figure 4-66 Adding an else Section to an if then else if Block
(*Source:* MIT App Inventor 2)

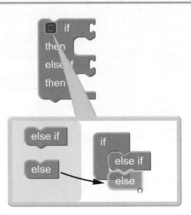

Figure 4-67 An if then else if Block (*Source:* MIT App Inventor 2)

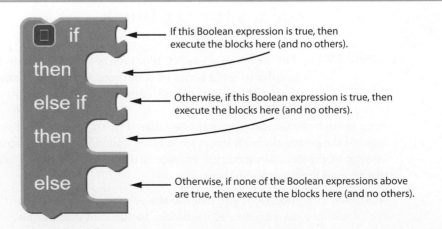

When the `if then else if` block executes, Boolean expression #1 is tested. If Boolean expression #1 is true, the instructions in the `then` socket that immediately follow are executed and the rest of the block is ignored. If Boolean expression #1 is false, however, the program jumps to the very next `else if` section and tests Boolean expression #2. If it is true, the instructions in the `then` socket that immediately follow are executed and the rest of the block is then ignored. If none of the Boolean expressions are true, the instructions in the `else` socket are executed.

You can use the mutator bubble to add as many `else if` sections as you need. For example, Figure 4-68 shows an `if then else if` block that can test three Boolean expressions.

Figure 4-68 An `if then else if` Block that Can Test Three Boolean Expressions
(*Source:* MIT App Inventor 2)

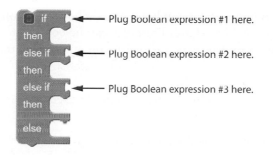

Figure 4-69 shows how the `ButtonGetGrade.Click` event handler, from the Grader app that you created in Tutorial 4-5, could be rewritten to use an `if then else if` block.

Figure 4-69 An Alternative Version of the `ButtonGetGrade.Click` Event Handler, from the Grader App (*Source:* MIT App Inventor 2)

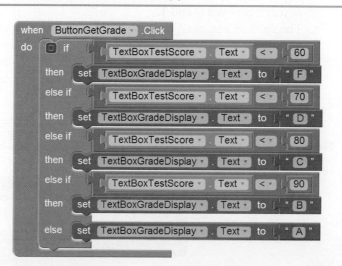

4.8 Working with Random Numbers

CONCEPT: Random numbers are used in a variety of apps. App Inventor provides math blocks that you can use in your apps to generate random numbers.

Random numbers are useful for lots of different programming tasks. The following are just a few examples.

- Random numbers are commonly used in games. For example, computer games that let the player roll dice use random numbers to represent the values of the dice. Programs that show cards being drawn from a shuffled deck use random numbers to represent the face values of the cards.
- Random numbers are useful in simulation programs. In some simulations, the computer must randomly decide how a person, animal, insect, or other living being will behave. Formulas can be constructed in which a random number is used to determine various actions and events that take place in the program.
- Random numbers are useful in statistical programs that must randomly select data for analysis.
- Random numbers are commonly used in computer security to encrypt sensitive data.

App Inventor provides the blocks shown in Figure 4-70 for generating random numbers in an app. In the Blocks Editor, the blocks are found in the *Math* drawer. Here is a summary of each block:

- The `random integer` block is a function that takes two arguments: `from` and `to`. The function returns a random integer between the two arguments (inclusively). When you create this block, App Inventor automatically provides the values 1 and 100 for the arguments, which means the function returns a value within the range of 1 through 100. You can change the `from` and `to` arguments as you wish.
- The `random fraction` block is a function that returns a random fractional number between 0 and 1.
- The `random set seed` function lets you specify a `seed` value for random number generation. You will not use this function very often, but it is helpful for testing purposes. If you call this function at the beginning of a program and always pass the same value for the `seed` argument, it will cause the program to always generate the same sequence of random numbers.

Figure 4-70 The Random Number Blocks (*Source:* MIT App Inventor 2)

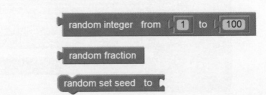

Let's look at an example app that generates random numbers. Figure 4-71 shows the screen for the RandomNumberDemo project. When the user clicks the *Generate Random Fraction* button, the app displays a random fraction between 0 and 1 (by calling the `random fraction` function). When the user clicks the *Generate Random Integer* button, the app displays a random integer within the range of 1 and 100 (by calling the `random integer` function). Figure 4-72 shows the `Click` event handlers for the two buttons and Figure 4-73 shows the app running in the emulator.

Figure 4-71 The RandomNumberDemo Project (*Source:* MIT App Inventor 2)

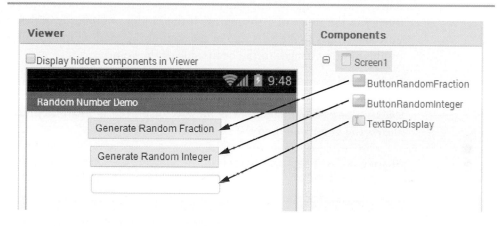

Figure 4-72 The `Click` Event Handlers (*Source:* MIT App Inventor 2)

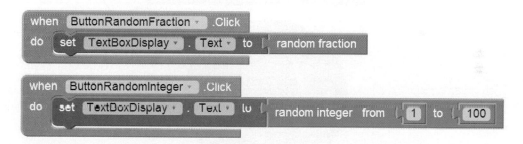

Figure 4-73 The App Running in the Emulator (*Source:* MIT App Inventor 2)

In Tutorial 4-6 you will use random numbers to determine whether the heads or tails side of a coin is facing up after the coin has been tossed.

Tutorial 4-6:
Simulating Coin Tosses

**VideoNote
Simulating Coin
Tosses**

In this tutorial you create an app that simulates the tossing of a coin. The app will display an image of a coin on a button. Each time the user tosses the coin (clicks the button) the app calls the random integer function to get a random integer in the range of 0 through 1. If the random number is 0, the image on the button changes to the tails side of the coin. If the random number is 1, the image on the button changes to the heads side of the coin.

Figure 4-74 shows the app's screen in the Viewer, with the names of all the components. Notice that the images you will upload are named Heads2.png and Tails2.png. The image that is initially displayed is Heads2.png. Figure 4-75 shows the app running in the emulator.

Figure 4-74 The App's Screen in the Viewer (*Source:* MIT App Inventor 2)

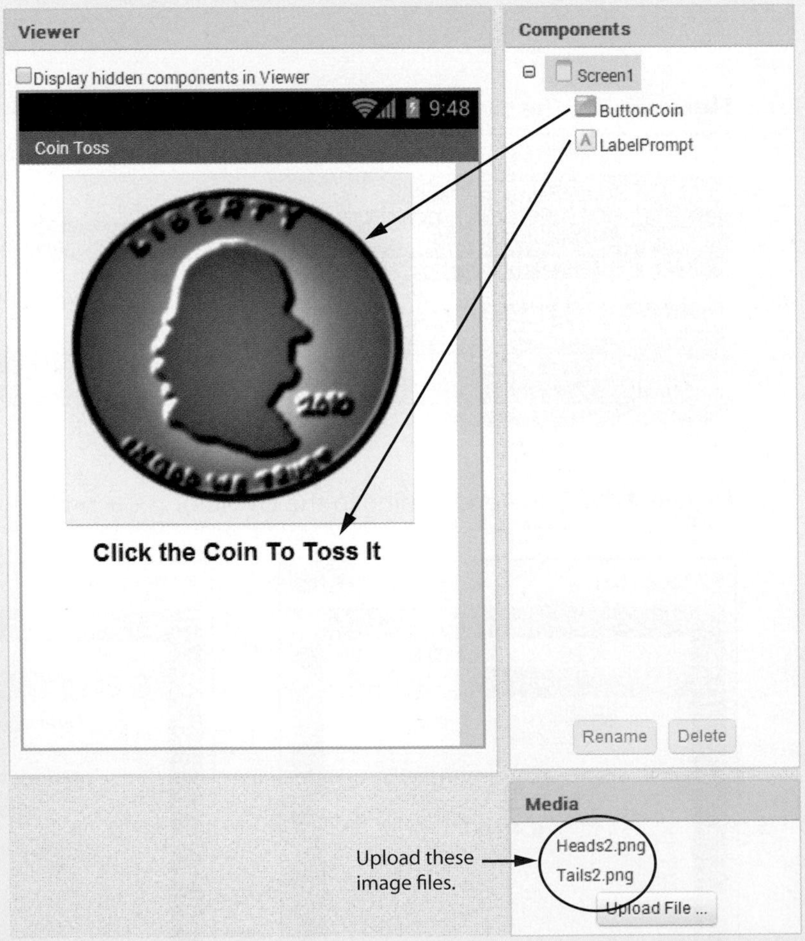

![Figure 4-74 showing the Viewer with a coin image on a button labeled "Click the Coin To Toss It", Components panel showing Screen1, ButtonCoin, LabelPrompt, and Media panel showing Heads2.png, Tails2.png with "Upload these image files." annotation]

Figure 4-75 The CoinToss App Running in the Emulator (*Source:* MIT App Inventor 2)

Step 1: Start a new project named CoinToss.

Step 2: Make sure you have downloaded the media files from this book's companion website at www.pearsonhighered.com/gaddis. Navigate to the location on your system where the book's media files are located. You will find a folder named *Coins* that contains several .png files. Use the Media column to upload the following image files: Heads2.png and Tails2.png.

Step 3: Set up the app's screen with the components shown in Figure 4-74. Refer to Table 4-7 for the relevant property settings for each component.

Table 4-7 Component property settings (*Source:* Pearson Education, Inc.)

Component	Relevant Property Settings
Screen1	AlignHorizontal = *Center*
	Title = *Coin toss*
ButtonCoin	Image = Heads2.png
	Text = *clear (blank)*
LabelPrompt	FontBold = *checked*
	FontSize = 20
	Text = *Click the Coin To Toss It*
	Width = *Automatic*
	Height = *Automatic*

Step 4: Now you will program the blocks for the app. Open the Blocks Editor and create the global variable initialization block shown in Figure 4-76. This is the variable that will hold the random number each time it is generated.

Figure 4-76 Variable Definition (*Source:* MIT App Inventor 2)

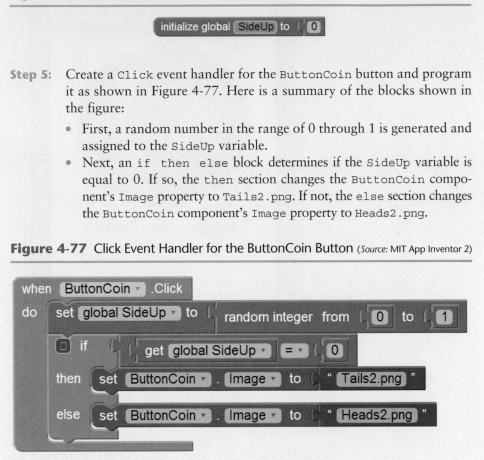

Step 5: Create a Click event handler for the ButtonCoin button and program it as shown in Figure 4-77. Here is a summary of the blocks shown in the figure:

- First, a random number in the range of 0 through 1 is generated and assigned to the SideUp variable.
- Next, an if then else block determines if the SideUp variable is equal to 0. If so, the then section changes the ButtonCoin component's Image property to Tails2.png. If not, the else section changes the ButtonCoin component's Image property to Heads2.png.

Figure 4-77 Click Event Handler for the ButtonCoin Button (*Source:* MIT App Inventor 2)

Step 6: Test the app in the emulator or on your device. Click the coin image several times. You should see the image change randomly to tails or heads.

 Checkpoint

4.14 Where are the random number blocks found in the Blocks Editor?

4.15 What does the random fraction block return?

4.16 What two arguments does the random integer function require? What does the function return?

4.9 The Screen's `Initialize` Event

CONCEPT: The `Screen1` component's `Initialize` event is triggered when the app starts running.

When an app begins running, the `Screen1` component's `Initialize` event is triggered. If you need to perform setup operations when the app starts, you can create an event handler for the `Initialize` event and perform the operations there.

To create an `Initialize` event handler for the `Screen1` component, go to the *Screen1* drawer in the *Blocks* column, as shown in Figure 4-78, and select the `when Screen1.Initialize` do block.

Figure 4-78 The `Screen1` Component's `Initialize` Event Handler
(*Source:* MIT App Inventor 2)

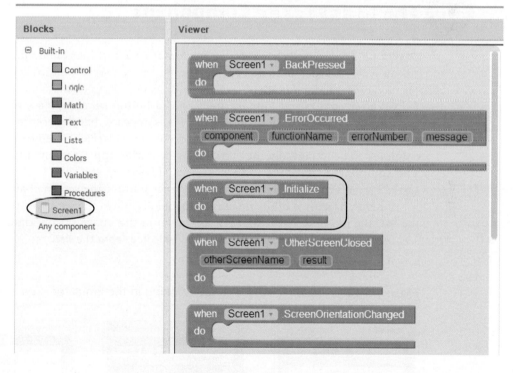

Figure 4-79 shows an example of a `Screen1.Initialize` event handler. It sets the screen's background color randomly to either blue, yellow, or green. It does this by generating a random number from 1 to 3. If the number is 1, it sets the screen color to blue. If the number is 2, it sets the screen color to yellow. If the number is 3, it sets the screen color to green.

Figure 4-79 Example `Screen1.Initialize` Event Handler (*Source:* MIT App Inventor 2)

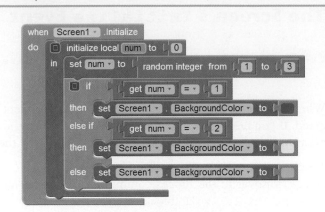

4.10 The `ListPicker` Component

CONCEPT: A ListPicker component displays a list of items and allows the user to select an item from the list.

A ListPicker component initially appears as a button on an app's screen. When the user clicks the ListPicker button, a list of items appears that the user may select from. For example, Figure 4-80 shows an example app (ListPickerDemo) running in the emulator. The image on the left shows how the app's screen initially appears. The component that looks like a button, displaying the text *Pick a Fruit*, is the ListPicker. When the user clicks the ListPicker button, the screen changes to show a list of items, as shown in the image in the middle. When the user selects an item from the list, the app's screen reappears, as shown in the image on the right. As you can see, the app displays the item that the user selected from the list.

Figure 4-80 The ListPickerDemo App Running in the Emulator (*Source:* MIT App Inventor 2)

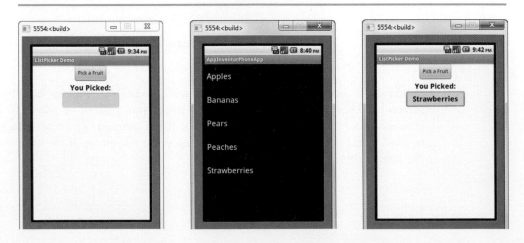

The ListPicker has all of the same properties as a Button component, plus a couple of extra ones:

- The ElementsFromString property: This property holds the list of items that is displayed when the user clicks the ListPicker. You simply type the items that you wish to appear in the component's list, separated by commas, into the ElementsFromString property. For example, Figure 4-81 shows the ListPickerDemo app in the Designer, with the ListPicker selected. You can see part of the ElementsFromString property in the figure.
- The Selection property: Once the user selects an item from the list, the selected item is copied into the Selection property.

Figure 4-81 The ListPicker Component's ElementsFromString Property
(*Source:* MIT App Inventor 2)

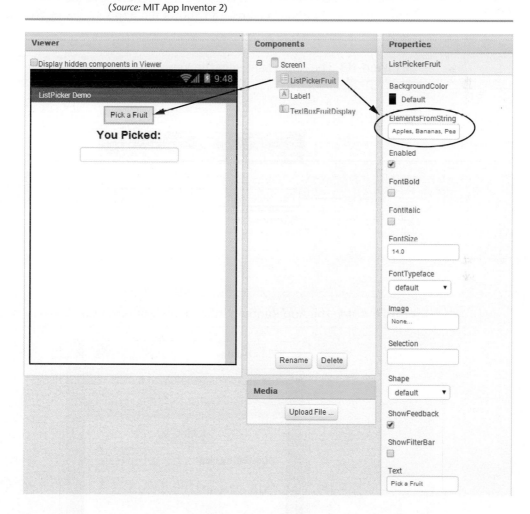

When the user selects an item from a ListPicker's list, an `AfterPicking` event is triggered. If you want to get the item that the user selected, you can create an event handler for this event. In the event handler, you can get the value of the Selection property. For example, Figure 4-82 shows the `AfterPicking` event handler for the ListPicker in the ListPickerDemo app shown in Figures 4-80 and 4-81.

Figure 4-82 The `AfterPicking` Event Handler (*Source:* MIT App Inventor 2)

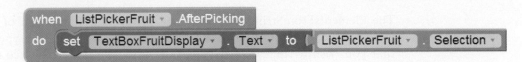

Tutorial 4-7:
Creating the Time Zone App

In this tutorial you create an app that allows the user to select a city with a ListPicker. When the user selects a city, the app displays the name of the city's time zone in a TextBox. Figure 4-83 shows the app's screen in the Viewer and Figure 4-84 shows the app running in the emulator.

Figure 4-83 The App's Screen in the Viewer (*Source:* MIT App Inventor 2)

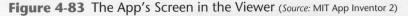

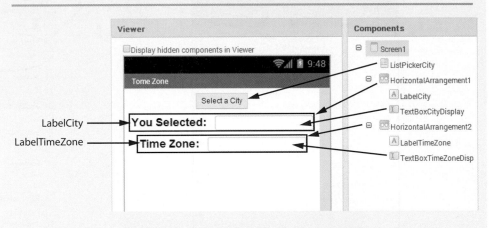

Figure 4-84 The App Running in the Emulator (*Source:* MIT App Inventor 2)

Step 1: Start a new project named TimeZone.

Step 2: Set up the app's screen with the components shown in Figure 4-83. (The ListPicker component is in the Basic palette.) Refer to Table 4-8 for the relevant property settings for each component.

Table 4-8 Component property settings (*Source:* Pearson Education, Inc.)

Component	Relevant Property Settings
Screen1	AlignHorizontal = *Center* Title = *Time Zone*
HorizontalArrangement1	*Keep default property settings*
ListPickerCity	ElementsFromString = *New York, San Francisco, Honolulu* Text = *Select a City*
LabelCity	FontBold = *checked* FontSize = *20* Text = *You Selected:*
TextBoxCityDisplay	Enabled = *unchecked* FontBold = *checked* Hint = *cleared* TextAlignment = *center* Width = *Automatic* Height = *Automatic*
HorizontalArrangement2	*Keep default property settings*
LabelTimeZone	FontBold = *checked* FontSize = *20* Text = *Time Zone:*
TextBoxCityDisplay	Enabled = *unchecked* FontBold = *checked* Hint = *cleared* TextAlignment = *center* Width = *Automatic* Height = *Automatic*

Step 3: Now you will program the AfterPicking event handler for the ListPickerCity component. Open the Blocks Editor and create the event handler as shown in Figure 4-85.

Figure 4-85 `AfterPicking` Event Handler for the `ListPickerCity` Component (*Source:* MIT App Inventor 2)

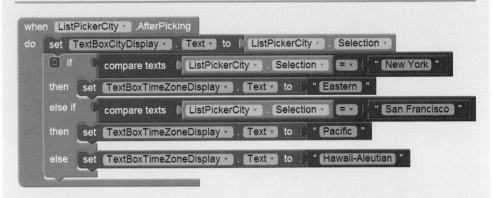

Step 4:   Test the app in the emulator or on your device. Figure 4-86 shows the list of cities that appears when you click the `ListPicker`. Figure 4-87 shows the app's screen after you have selected each of the cities.

Figure 4-86 The `ListPicker`'s List Displayed (*Source:* MIT App Inventor 2)

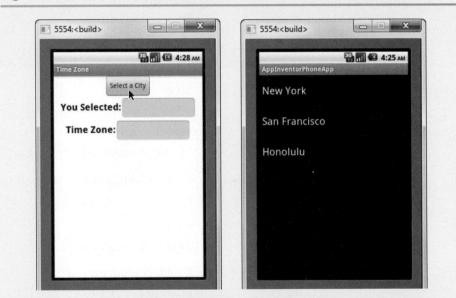

Figure 4-87 Each City Selected (*Source:* MIT App Inventor 2)

Checkpoint

4.17 How do you add items to a `ListPicker` component's list?

4.18 How do you get the item that the user selected with a `ListPicker`?

4.11 The CheckBox Component

A CheckBox component appears as a small box with some accompanying text. Figure 4-88 shows an example. A CheckBox component can be either checked, or unchecked. Clicking on an empty CheckBox causes a check mark to appear in the box. If a check mark already appears in the box, clicking it removes the check mark.

Figure 4-88 A CheckBox component

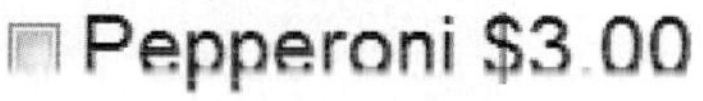

☐ Pepperoni $3.00

In the Designer, CheckBox components are found in the *User Interface* section of the Palette. CheckBox components have many properties that you are already familiar with, but the two that you will be most concerned with are the Text and the Checked properties. The Text property determines the text that is displayed next to the small box. The Checked property indicates whether the component is checked, or unchecked. When a CheckBox component is checked, its Checked property is set to true. When a CheckBox component is unchecked, its Checked property is set to false. In the Blocks Editor, you can use a decision block such as `if` or `if then else` to test a CheckBox component's Checked property and determine whether it is checked or unchecked.

NOTE: When you create a CheckBox component, its Checked property is set to `false` by default, so the component initially appears unchecked. If you want a CheckBox component to initially appear checked, you can change the `Checked` property in the Properties column.

Let's look at an example. Figure 4-89 shows the PizzaToppings app in the Designer and Figure 4-90 shows how it initially appears in the emulator. The user checks the pizza topping items and then clicks the `ButtonTotal` component to see the total cost of the selected items.

Figure 4-89 The PizzaToppings App in the Designer *(Source:* MIT App Inventor 2)

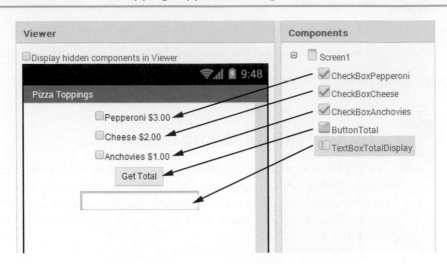

Figure 4-90 The PizzaToppings App Initially in the Emulator *(Source:* MIT App Inventor 2)

Figure 4-91 shows the app's workspace in the Blocks Editor. The app has a variable definition and a Click event handler for the ButtonTotal button. Here is a summary of the blocks that are labeled with numbers in the figure:

① This block initializes a local variable named Total, with the initial value of 0. The app uses this variable to hold the total of the items that the user has selected.

② This if then block determines whether the CheckBoxPepperoni component is checked. If so, 3.00 is added to the Total variable.

③ This if then block determines whether the CheckBoxCheese component is checked. If so, 2.00 is added to the Total variable.

④ This if then block determines whether the CheckBoxAnchovies component is checked. If so, 1.00 is added to the Total variable.

⑤ This block displays the value of the Total variable, rounded to two decimal places, in the TextBoxTotalDisplay component.

Figure 4-91 The App's Workspace in the Blocks Editor (*Source:* MIT App Inventor 2)

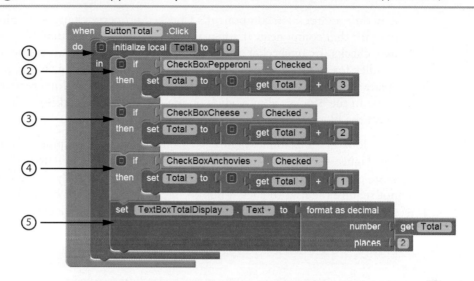

Figure 4-92 shows four different screenshots from the app running in the emulator. Each screenshot shows the app after the user has made selections and then clicked the ButtonTotal button. The total of the selected items is displayed in the TextBox. (In the upper-left screen, the user has selected no items and then clicked the button. The resulting total is 0.00.)

Figure 4-92 The App Running in the Emulator (*Source:* MIT App Inventor 2)

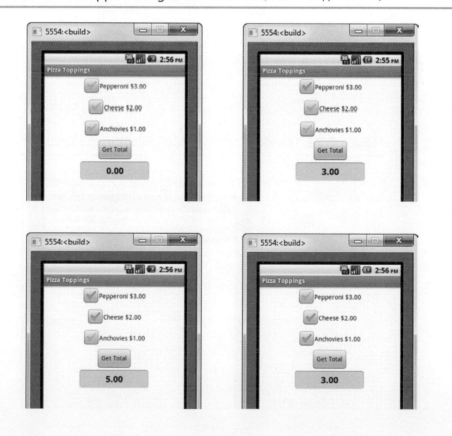

The Changed Event

Any time a CheckBox component's Checked property changes, a Changed event happens for that component. If you want some action to immediately take place when the user checks (or unchecks) a CheckBox component, you can create a Changed event handler for the component and place the desired blocks in that event handler. (You create a Changed event handler in the same manner that you create other event handlers: In the Blocks column, click on the name of the CheckBox component and then select the block for the Changed event handler.)

Let's look at an example. Figure 4-93 shows the PizzaToppings2 app in the Designer and Figure 4-94 shows how it initially appears in the emulator. This app serves the same purpose as the PizzaToppings app that we previously discussed, except it does not require the user to click a button to calculate the total cost. This app updates the total each time the user clicks one of the CheckBox components.

Figure 4-93 The PizzaToppings2 App in the Designer *(Source:* MIT App Inventor 2)

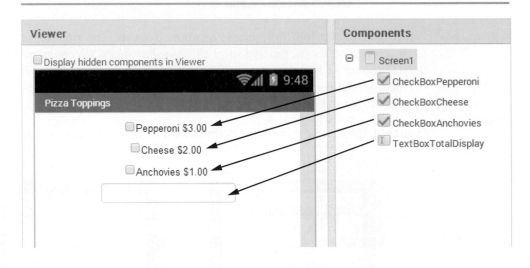

Figure 4-94 The PizzaToppings App Initially in the Emulator *(Source:* MIT App Inventor 2)

This app creates a global variable named Total, initialized to 0. The app uses this variable to hold the total of the items that the user has selected. The app also has a Changed event handler for each of the CheckBox components. Each time a CheckBox is clicked, its Changed event handler determines whether the component became checked, or unchecked, and then adjusts the value of the global Total variable accordingly. Figure 4-95 shows the initialization block for the Total variable and the Changed event handler for the CheckBoxPepperoni component.

Figure 4-95 The CheckBoxPepperoni.Changed Event Handler

(*Source:* MIT App Inventor 2)

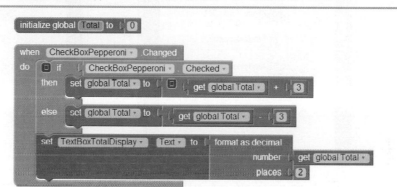

The event handler works like this:

> If CheckBoxPepperoni *is checked, then add 3.00 to the* Total *variable.*
>
> *Otherwise, subtract 3.00 from the* Total *variable.*
>
> *Display the* Total *variable rounded to two decimal places.*

Figure 4-96 shows the CheckBoxCheese.Changed and CheckBoxAnchovies. Changed event handlers, which work in a similar fashion.

Figure 4-96 The CheckBoxCheese.Changed and CheckBoxAnchovies. Changed Event Handler (*Source:* MIT App Inventor 2)

Figure 4-97 shows four different screenshots from the app running in the emulator.

Figure 4-97 The App Running in the Emulator (*Source:* MIT App Inventor 2)

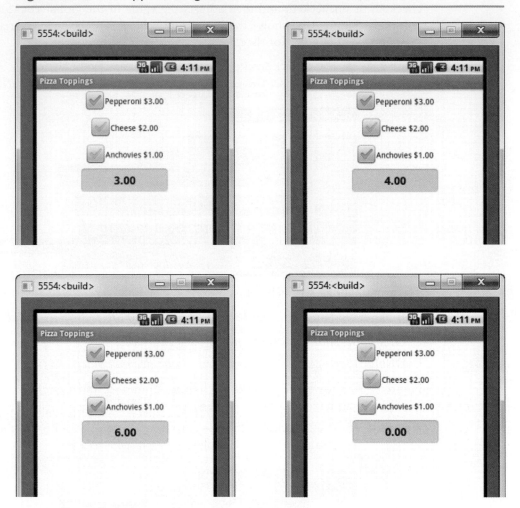

 Checkpoint

4.19 What CheckBox property determines the text that is displayed next to the component's box?

4.20 How do you determine whether a CheckBox is checked or not?

4.21 What event happens when the user clicks a CheckBox?

Review Questions

Multiple Choice

1. A(n) _____ expression has a value of either true or false.

   a. binary
   b. decision
   c. unconditional
   d. Boolean

2. The symbols >, <, and = are all _____ operators.

   a. relational
   b. logical
   c. conditional
   d. ternary

3. A(n) _____ block tests a Boolean expression and then executes a set of blocks if the expression is true. Nothing happens if the expression is false.

   a. select
   b. if then
   c. if then else
   d. ifcall

4. A(n) _____ block tests a Boolean expression and then executes one set of blocks if the expression is true, or another set of blocks if the expression is false.

   a. select
   b. if
   c. if then else
   d. ifcall

5. A(n) _____ block can test multiple Boolean expressions, executing a set of blocks depending upon which Boolean expression is true.

   a. if then else if
   b. if
   c. if then else
   d. ifcall

6. and, or, and not are _____ operators.

   a. relational
   b. logical
   c. conditional
   d. ternary

7. A compound Boolean expression created with the _____ operator is true only if all of its connected expressions are true.

   a. and
   b. or
   c. not
   d. both

8. A compound Boolean expression created with the _____ operator is true if any of its connected expressions are true.

   a. `and`
   b. `or`
   c. `not`
   d. `either`

9. The _____ operator takes a Boolean expression as its operand and reverses its logical value.

   a. `and`
   b. `or`
   c. `not`
   d. `either`

10. A _____ decision block is written inside the `then` or `else` section of another decision block.

    a. nested
    b. tiered
    c. dislodged
    d. hierarchical

11. This property holds the list of items that is displayed by a `ListPicker`.

    a. List
    b. Items
    c. Text
    d. Elementsfromstring

12. This CheckBox property determines the text that is displayed next to the component's box.

    a. Caption
    b. Selection
    c. Text
    d. Description

13. This CheckBox property is true when the CheckBox is checked, or false otherwise.

    a. Checked
    b. Selected
    c. Unchecked
    d. Completed

14. This event happens when the user clicks a CheckBox component.

    a. `Checked`
    b. `Changed`
    c. `Selected`
    d. `Clicked`

Short Answer

1. You need to test a Boolean expression and then execute one set of blocks if the expression is true. If the expression is false, you need to execute a different set of blocks. What decision block will you use?

2. Briefly describe how the and operator works.

3. Briefly describe how the or operator works.

4. Briefly describe how the not operator works.

5. When determining whether a number is inside a range, which logical operator is it best to use?

6. What is a nested decision block?

7. When does the Screen1 component's Initialize event happen?

8. How do you add items to a ListPicker's list?

9. How do you determine which item the user selected with a ListPicker?

10. In the Blocks Editor, how do you determine whether a CheckBox component is checked?

11. What event happens when the user clicks a CheckBox component?

Exercises

1. Open the Blocks Editor and define two variables, x and y. Create an if then block that determines whether the variable y is equal to 20. If it is, assign 0 to the variable x.

2. Open the Blocks Editor and define two variables, sales and commission. Create an if then block that determines whether the variable sales is greater than or equal to 10,000. If it is, assign 02 to the variable commission.

3. Open the Blocks Editor and define three variables: x, y, and z. Create an if then block that assigns 20 to the variable y and assigns 40 to the variable z if the variable x is greater than 100.

4. Open the Blocks Editor and define two variables: a and b. Create an if then else block that assigns 0 to the variable b if the variable a is less than 10. Otherwise, it should assign 99 to the variable b.

5. In the Designer, add a ListPicker to an app's screen. Change the component's name to ListPickerCities. Add the following city names to the component's list:

> New York
> London
> Paris
> Munich

6. Modify the MPG Calculator app that you created in Tutorial 3-1 (from Chapter 3) to display the message *That is an efficient auto* if the MPG is greater than 32.

7. Modify the Wages app that you created in Tutorial 4-3 in such a way that when the user works overtime, the app also displays the number of overtime hours worked, the amount of regular pay, and the amount of overtime pay.

Programming Projects

1. Roman Numeral Converter

Create an app that allows the user to enter an integer between 1 and 5 into a TextBox. The program should display the Roman numeral version of that number. If the number is outside the range of 1 through 5, the program should display an error message.

The following table lists the Roman numerals for the numbers 1 through 5.

Number	Roman Numeral
1	I
2	II
3	III
4	IV
5	V

VideoNote
The Mass and
Weight App

2. Mass and Weight

Scientists measure an object's mass in kilograms and its weight in newtons. If you know the amount of mass of an object, you can calculate its weight, in newtons, with the following formula:

$$Weight = Mass \times 9.8$$

Create an app that lets the user enter an object's mass and then calculates its weight. If the object weighs more than 1000 newtons, display a message indicating that it is too heavy. If the object weighs less than 10 newtons, display a message indicating that it is too light.

3. Magic Dates

The date June 10, 1960, is special because when it is written in the following format, the month times the day equals the year:

$$6/10/60$$

Create an app that lets the user enter a month (in numeric form), a day, and a two-digit year. The program should then determine whether the month times the day equals the year. If so, it should display a message saying the date is magic. Otherwise, it should display a message saying the date is not magic.

4. Body Mass Index Program Enhancement

In Programming Project 4 in Chapter 3 you were asked to create an app that calculates a person's body mass index (BMI). Recall from that exercise that the BMI is often used to determine whether a person is overweight or underweight for his or her height. A person's BMI is calculated with the following formula:

$$BMI = Weight \times 703 \div Height^2$$

In the formula, weight is measured in pounds and height is measured in inches. Enhance the program so it displays a message indicating whether the person has optimal weight, is underweight, or is overweight. A person's weight is considered to be optimal if his or her BMI is between 18.5 and 25. If the BMI is less than 18.5, the person is considered to be underweight. If the BMI value is greater than 25, the person is considered to be overweight.

5. **Change for a Dollar Game**

Create a change-counting game that gets the user to enter the number of coins required to make exactly one dollar. The program should let the user enter the number of pennies, nickels, dimes, and quarters. If the total value of the coins entered is equal to one dollar, the program should congratulate the user for winning the game. Otherwise, the program should display a message indicating whether the amount entered was more than or less than one dollar.

6. **Fat Percentage Calculator**

One gram of fat has 9 calories. If you know the number of fat grams in a particular food, you can use the following formula to calculate the number of calories that come from fat in that food:

$$Calories\ from\ fat = fat\ grams \times 9$$

If you know the food's total calories, you can use the following formula to calculate the percentage of calories from fat:

$$Percentage\ of\ calories\ from\ fat = Calories\ from\ fat \div total\ calories$$

Create an app that allows the user to enter:

- The total number of calories for a food item
- The number of fat grams in that food item

The app should calculate and display:

- The number of calories from fat.
- The percentage of calories that come from fat.

Also, the app's screen should have a CheckBox that the user can check if they want to know whether the food is considered low fat. (If the calories from fat are less than 30% of the total calories of the food, the food is considered low fat.)

Use the following test data to determine if the app is calculating properly:

Calories and Fat	Percentage Fat
200 calories, 8 fat grams	Percentage of calories from fat: 36%
150 calories 2 fat grams	Percentage of calories from fat: 12% (a low-fat food)
500 calories, 30 fat grams	Percentage of calories from fat: 54%

7. **Time Calculator**

Create an app that lets the user enter a number of seconds and works as follows:

- There are 60 seconds in a minute. If the number of seconds entered by the user is greater than or equal to 60, the program should display the number of minutes in that many seconds.
- There are 3,600 seconds in an hour. If the number of seconds entered by the user is greater than or equal to 3,600, the program should display the number of hours in that many seconds.

- There are 86,400 seconds in a day. If the number of seconds entered by the user is greater than or equal to 86,400, the program should display the number of days in that many seconds.

8. **Workshop Selector**

The following table shows a training company's workshops, the number of days of each, and their registration fees.

Workshop	Number of Days	Registration Fee
Time Management	2	$800
Supervision Skills	3	$1,500
Negotiation	5	$1,300

The training company conducts its workshops in the three locations shown in the following table. The table also shows the lodging fees per day at each location.

Location	Lodging Fees per Day
Chicago	$225
Dallas	$175
Orlando	$300

When a customer registers for a workshop, he or she must pay the registration fee plus the lodging fees for the selected location. For example, here are the charges to attend the Supervision Skills workshop in Orlando:

Registration: $1,500

Lodging: $300 $\times$ 3 days = *$900*

Total: $2,400

Create an app that lets the user to select a workshop from one list box and a location from another list box. When the user clicks a button, the app should calculate and display the registration cost, the lodging cost, and the total cost.

5

Repetition Blocks, Times, and Dates

5.1 The Notifier Component

A Notifier is a nonvisible component that allows an app to display dialog boxes. A *dialog box* is a small window that displays a message or prompts the user to provide some sort of input. The Notifier component can display the following types of dialog boxes:

- Message dialog—A window that displays a title and a message and waits for the user to click a button.
- Text dialog—A window that displays a title and a message, and allows the user to enter some text as input and then click an *OK* button, and optionally a *Cancel* button.
- Choose dialog—A window that displays a title and a message, and lets the user click one of two buttons, and optionally a *Cancel* button.

Figure 5-1 shows examples of each type of dialog box.

In the Designer, the Notifier component is found in the *User Interface* section of the Palette. It is a nonvisible component, and it has no properties. It does, however, provide several methods and event handlers that you can use to display dialog boxes. Let's take a closer look at how you display each type of dialog box with a Notifier.

Figure 5-1 Dialog Boxes Displayed by the Notifier Component (*Source:* MIT App Inventor 2)

The Message Dialog

A message dialog simply displays a message and waits for the user to click a button. When the user clicks the button, the dialog box closes. You display a message dialog by calling the Notifier component's `ShowMessageDialog` method.

Let's look at an example. Figure 5-2 shows the MessageDialogDemo project in the Designer. Notice that the project has a button named `ButtonMessage`, and a

Figure 5-2 The MessageDialogDemo Project in the Designer (*Source:* MIT App Inventor 2)

Notifier named `Notifier1`. When the app runs, the user clicks the button and a message dialog appears. Figure 5-3 shows the button's `Click` event handler.

Figure 5-3 The `ButtonMessage` Component's `Click` Event Handler
(*Source:* MIT App Inventor 2)

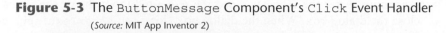

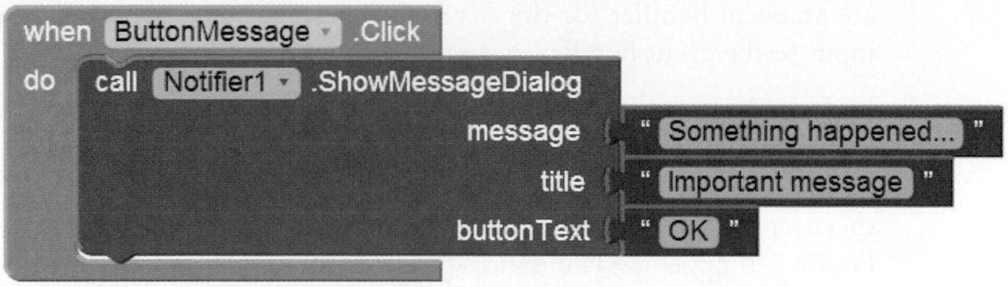

In the `Click` event handler, we call the `Notifier1.ShowMessageDialog` method. (In the Blocks Editor, you will find the block for the method in the *My Blocks->Notifier1* drawer.) Notice in Figure 5-3 that the method takes three arguments:

- `message`—The text of the message to display. In this example, the message is *Something happened . . .*
- `title`—The title to display. In this example, the title is *Important message.*
- `buttonText`—The text to display on the dialog box's button. In this example, the button text is *OK.*

Figure 5-4 shows the message dialog box displayed in the emulator. When the user clicks the *OK* button, the dialog box closes.

Figure 5-4 The Message Dialog Box (*Source:* MIT App Inventor 2)

![Screenshot of an emulator window titled "5554:<build>" showing a "Message Dialog Demo" app with a "Message" button and a dialog box displaying "Important Message", "Something happened...", and an "OK" button. Status bar shows 2:20 AM.]

The Text Dialog

A text dialog displays a message and provides a box (like a TextBox) for the user to type input. After the user has typed the requested input, he or she clicks a button to close the dialog box. When the dialog box closes, an AfterTextInput event occurs. If you want to retrieve the text that the user entered into the dialog box, you can create an event handler for the AfterTextInput event. (App Inventor passes the user's input to the event handler as an argument.)

Let's look at an example. Figure 5-5 shows the TextDialogDemo project in the Designer. Notice that the project has a button named ButtonTextDialog, a TextBox named TextBoxDisplay, and a Notifier named Notifier1. When the app runs, the user clicks the button and the text dialog shown in the image on the left in Figure 5-6 appears. The dialog prompts the user to enter his or her name. The user

Figure 5-5 The TextDialogDemo Project in the Designer (*Source:* MIT App Inventor 2)

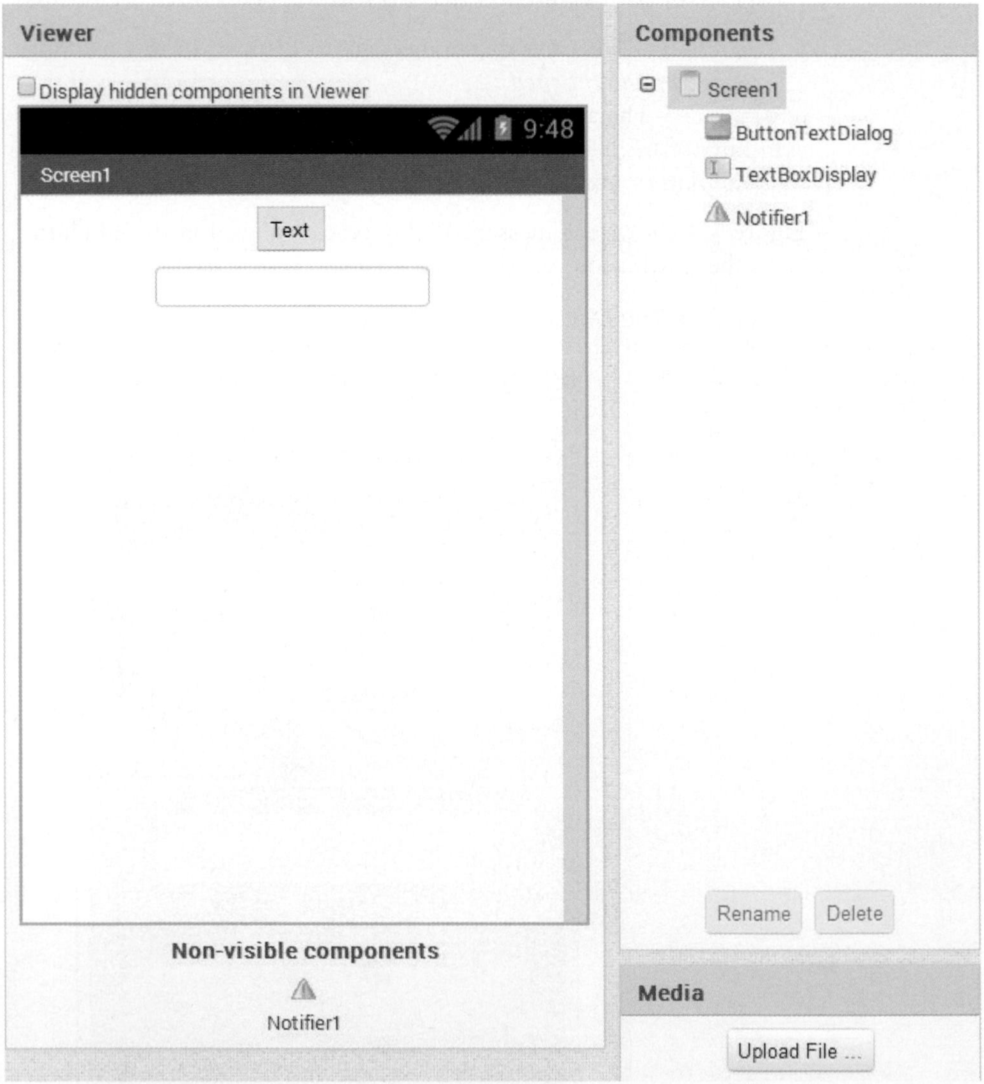

Figure 5-6 The Text Dialog Displayed (*Source:* MIT App Inventor 2)

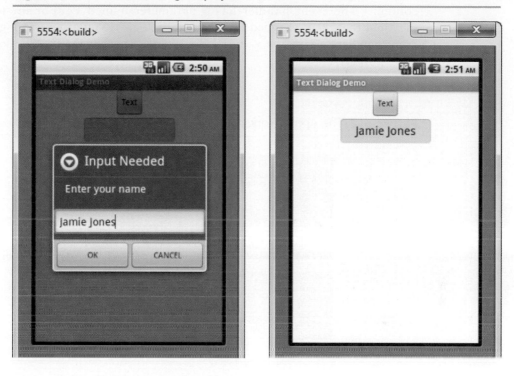

types input (in this case *Jamie Jones*) and clicks the *OK* button to close the dialog box. Notice in the image on the right in Figure 5-6 that the user's input is displayed in the `TextBoxDisplay` component.

Figure 5-7 shows the app's workspace in the Blocks Editor. Notice that we have a `Click` event handler for the `ButtonTextDialog` button and an `AfterTextInput` event handler for the `Notifier` component.

In the `ButtonTextDialog.Click` event handler, we call the `Notifier1.ShowTextDialog` method. (In the Blocks column, you will find the block for the method in the *Notifier1* drawer.) Notice in Figure 5-7 that the method takes three arguments:

- `message`—The text of the message to display. In this example, the message is *Enter your name*.
- `title`—The title to display. In this example the title is *Input Needed*.
- `cancelable`—A `true` or `false` value. If the argument is `true`, the dialog will have a *Cancel* button. If the argument is `false`, the dialog will have only an *OK* button. In this example we have plugged a `true` block in to this socket to cause a *Cancel* button to be displayed. (The `true` and `false` blocks can be found in the *Logic* drawer of the *Built-In* section of the *Blocks* column.)

When the user clicks either the *OK* or the *Cancel* button, the dialog box closes and an `AfterTextInput` event occurs. Notice in Figure 5-7 that we have created an event handler for the `AfterTextInput` event. (You will find the block for the event handler by clicking the name of the Notifier component in the *Blocks* column.) The event handler has a parameter named `response`, which holds the input that the user typed into the text dialog. As you can see in Figure 5-7, the event handler assigns the value of the response parameter to `TextBoxDisplay`'s `Text` property.

Figure 5-7 The App's Workspace in the Blocks Editor (*Source:* MIT App Inventor 2)

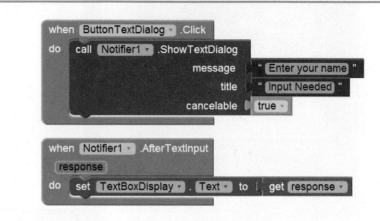

NOTE: If the user clicks the *Cancel* button on a text dialog, the value of the response parameter in the `AfterTextInput` event handler will be the text *Cancel*.

The Choose Dialog

A choose dialog lets the user make a choice by clicking one of two buttons. You can decide the text that you want to display on the buttons. For example, if you want the user to answer a yes/no question, you can display *Yes* on one button and *No* on the other. Optionally, you can also have a *Cancel* button.

When the user clicks a button on the dialog box, the dialog box closes and the `AfterChoosing` event occurs. To determine which button the user clicked, you can create an event handler for the `AfterChoosing` event. App Inventor passes the text of the button that was clicked as an argument to the event handler.

Let's look at an example. Figure 5-8 shows the ChooseDialogDemo project in the Designer. Notice that the project has a button named `ButtonChooseDialog`, a TextBox named `TextBoxDisplay`, and a Notifier named `Notifier1`. When the app runs, the user clicks the button and the choose dialog shown in the image on the left in Figure 5-9 appears. The dialog waits for the user to click the *Yes* button, the *No* button, or the *Cancel* button. Notice in the image on the right in Figure 5-9 that the user's choice is displayed in the `TextBoxDisplay` component.

Figure 5-8 The ChooseDialogDemo Project in the Designer (*Source:* MIT App Inventor 2)

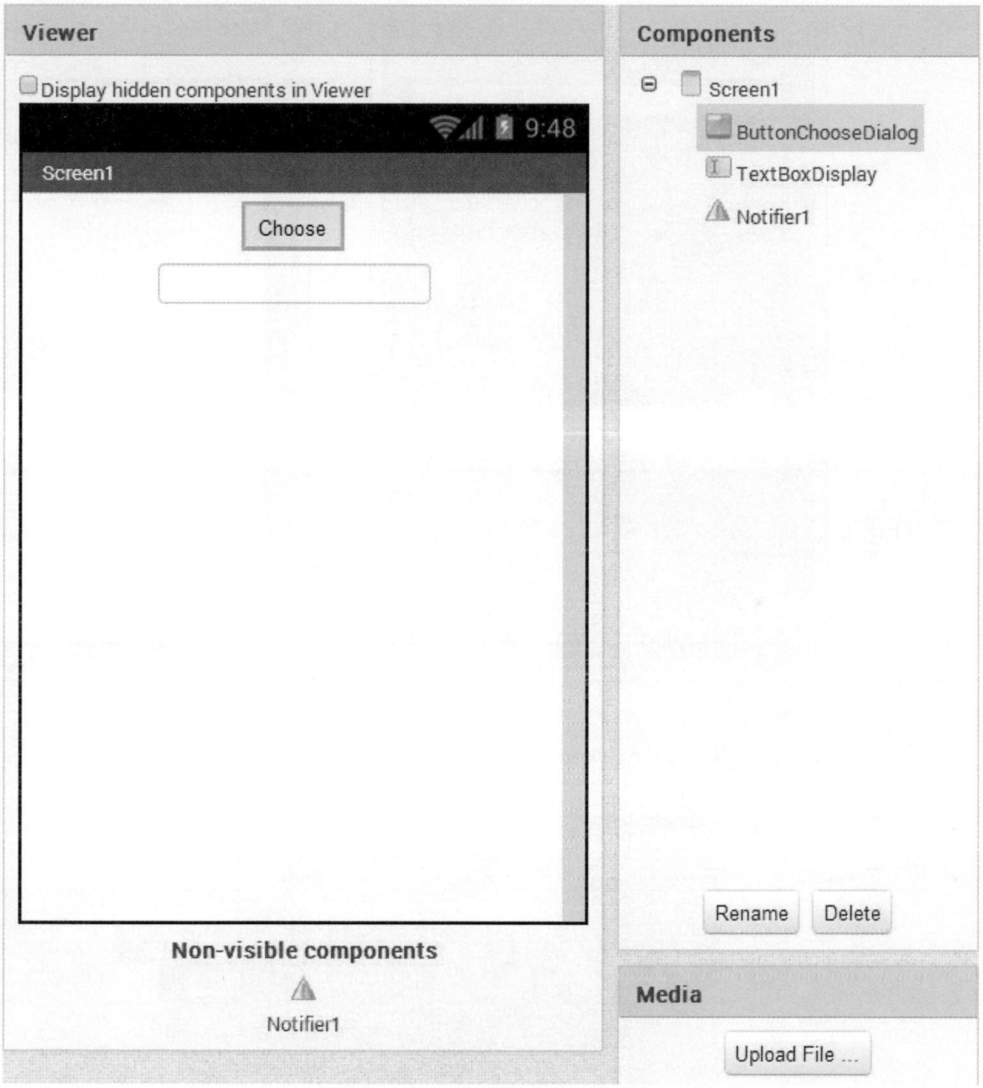

Figure 5-10 shows the app's workspace in the Blocks Editor. Notice that we have a Click event handler for the ButtonChooseDialog button and an AfterChoosing event handler for the Notifier component.

In the ButtonChooseDialog.Click event handler, we call the Notifier1. ShowChooseDialog method. (In the Blocks column, you will find the block for the method in the *Notifier1* drawer.) Notice in Figure 5-10 that the method takes five arguments:

- message—The text of the message to display. In this example, the message is *Do you want to continue?*
- title—The title to display. In this example, the title is *Confirm*.
- button1Text—The text to display on the first button. In this example, the button text is *Yes*.

Figure 5-9 The Choose Dialog Displayed (*Source:* MIT App Inventor 2)

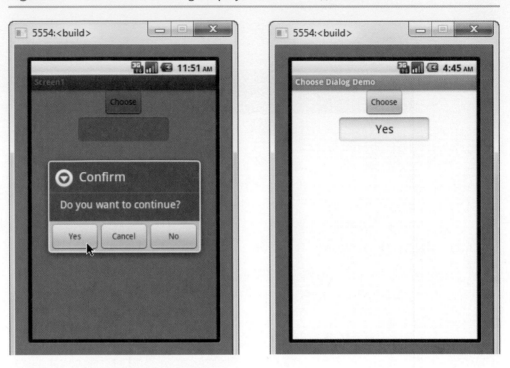

Figure 5-10 The App's Workspace in the Blocks Editor (*Source:* MIT App Inventor 2)

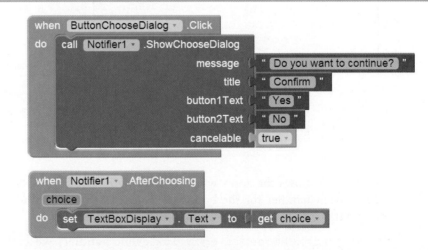

- `button2Text`—The text to display on the second button. In this example, the button text is *No*.
- `cancelable`—A `true` or `false` value. If the argument is `true`, the dialog will have a *Cancel* button in addition to the other two buttons. In this example, we have plugged a `true` block into this socket to cause a *Cancel* button to be displayed. (The `true` and `false` blocks can be found in the *Logic* drawer of the *Built-In* section of the *Blocks* column.)

When the user clicks any of the buttons on the dialog box, the dialog box closes and an AfterChoosing event occurs. Notice that in Figure 5-10 we have created an event handler for the AfterChoosing event. (You will find the block for the event handler by clicking the name of the Notifier component in the *Blocks* column.) The event handler has a parameter named choice that holds the text of the button that the user clicked. As you can see in Figure 5-10, the event handler assigns the value of the choice parameter to TextBoxDisplay's Text property.

Checkpoint

5.1 What are the three types of dialog boxes that a Notifier component can display? How do you display each type?

5.2 When does the AfterTextInput event happen?

5.3 When does the AfterChoosing event happen?

5.4 How do you retrieve the input that the user entered into a text dialog?

5.5 How do you determine which button the user clicked in a choose dialog?

5.2 The while Loop

CONCEPT: The while loop causes a statement or set of statements to repeat as long as a Boolean expression is true.

Some programming tasks involve actions that must be repeated several times. Programming languages provide special tools known as *loops* that repeat operations as many times as necessary. One of these is the while loop. The while loop gets its name from the way it works: *While a Boolean expression is true, do some task*. The loop has two parts: (1) a Boolean expression that is tested for a true or false value, and (2) a statement or set of statements that is repeated as long as the Boolean expression is true.

In the *Built-in* section of the *Blocks* column, you will find the while loop in the *Control* drawer, as shown in Figure 5-11. The while loop is shown in Figure 5-12. Notice that the while loop block has two sockets: test and do. The test socket holds a Boolean expression. When the while loop executes, the Boolean expression is tested. If the Boolean expression is true, the blocks that appear in the do socket are executed, and then the while loop starts over. If the Boolean expression is false, the while loop ends. Each time the loop executes the blocks in its do socket, we say the loop is *iterating* or performing an *iteration*.

Let's look at an example that uses a while loop to display a message dialog five times. Figure 5-13 shows the WhileLoopDemo project in the Designer. Notice that the project has a button named ButtonLoopDemo and a Notifier named Notifier1. In the emulator or an actual device, when the user clicks the button,

Figure 5-11 The `While` Loop Block (*Source:* MIT App Inventor 2)

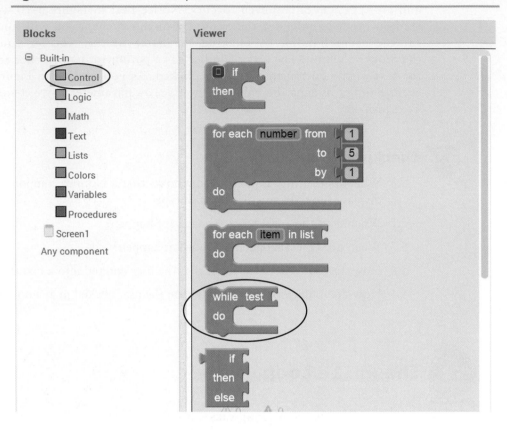

Figure 5-12 The `While` Loop (*Source:* MIT App Inventor 2)

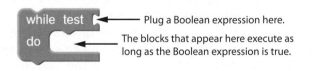

Figure 5-13 The WhileLoopDemo Project in the Designer (*Source:* MIT App Inventor 2)

the message dialog shown in Figure 5-14 is displayed. When the user clicks *OK* to close the dialog, another identical dialog is displayed. This repeats until the dialog is displayed five times.

Figure 5-14 Message Dialog is Displayed Five Times (*Source:* MIT App Inventor 2)

Figure 5-15 shows the project's workspace in the Blocks Editor. Let's take a closer look at the blocks in the project's workspace.

1. This initializes a local variable named count to the value 0. Each time the user clicks the ButtonLoopDemo button, the count variable will keep count of the number of times the message dialog is displayed.
2. This while loop uses the Boolean expression count < 5. This means that the loop will repeat as long as the value of the count variable is less than 5.
3. This block displays a message dialog.
4. This block adds 1 to the count variable.

The while Loop Is a Pretest Loop

The while loop is known as a *pretest loop*, which means it tests its condition *before* performing an iteration. Because the test is done at the beginning of the loop, you usually have to perform some steps prior to the loop to make sure that the loop executes at least once.

Figure 5-15 The Project's Workspace in the Blocks Editor (*Source:* MIT App Inventor 2)

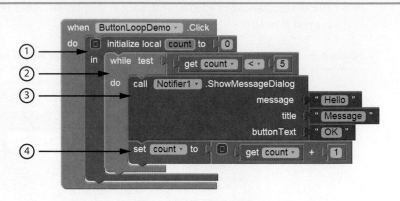

For example, in Figure 5-15, notice the first action to take place in the `ButtonLoopDemo.Click` event handler is that the `count` variable is set to the value 0. If `count` had been set to a value that is not less than 5, the loop would never execute. For example, if we had set the `count` variable to 5, or 6, or any greater value, the loop would not iterate.

An important characteristic of the `while` loop is that the loop will never iterate if its Boolean expression is false to start with. To be sure that a `while` loop executes the first time, you must initialize the relevant data in such a way that the Boolean expression starts out as `true`.

Counter Variables

In the WhileLoopDemo app, the `count` variable is set to the value 0 and then 1 is added to the `count` variable during each loop iteration. The loop executes as long as `count` is less than 5. The `count` variable is used as a *counter variable*, which means it is regularly incremented in each loop iteration. In essence, the `count` variable keeps count of the number of iterations the loop has performed.

Counter variables are commonly used to control the number of times that a loop iterates. Tutorial 5-1 will give you some practice writing a loop and using a counter variable. In the tutorial, you will write a while loop that calculates the amount of interest earned by a bank account each month for a number of months.

**VideoNote
The Ending
Balance App**

Tutorial 5-1:
The Ending Balance App

In this tutorial, you will create an app that calculates the ending balance of a savings account. The user will enter the account's starting balance and the number of months that the account will be left to earn interest. When the user clicks a button, the app will calculate the account's balance at the end of the time period. The monthly interest rate is 0.005 (i.e., 0.5%), and the interest is compounded monthly.

Figure 5-16 shows the app's screen in the Viewer along with the names of the components. Figure 5-17 shows how the screen appears in the emulator.

Figure 5-16 The EndingBalance App in the Designer (*Source:* MIT App Inventor 2)

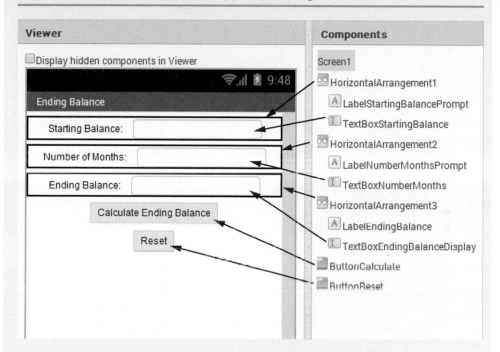

Figure 5-17 The App Running in the Emulator (*Source:* MIT App Inventor 2)

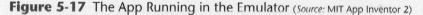

Step 1:   Start a new project named EndingBalance.

Step 2: Set up the app's screen with the components shown in Figure 5-16. Refer to Table 5-1 for the relevant property settings for each component.

Table 5-1 Component property settings (*Source:* Pearson Education, Inc.)

Component	Relevant Property Settings
Screen1	AlignHorizontal = *Center* Scrollable = *checked* Title = *Ending Balance*
HorizontalArrangement1	AlignHorizontal = *Center* Width = *Fill parent* Height = *Automatic*
LabelStartingBlancePrompt	Text = *Starting Balance:*
TextBoxStartingBalance	Enabled = *checked* NumbersOnly = *checked* Width = *Automatic* Height = *Automatic*
HorizontalArrangement2	AlignHorizontal = *Center* Width = *Fill parent* Height = *Automatic*
LabelNumberMonthsPrompt	Text = *Number of Months:*
TextBoxNumberMonths	Enabled = *checked* NumbersOnly = *checked* Width = *Automatic* Height = *Automatic*
HorizontalArrangement3	AlignHorizontal = *Center* Width = *Fill parent* Height = *Automatic*
LabelEndingBalance	Text = *Ending Balance:*
TextBoxEndingBalanceDisplay	Enabled = *unchecked* Width = *Automatic* Height = *Automatic*
ButtonCalculate	Text = *Calculate Ending Balance*
ButtonReset	Text = *Reset*

Step 3: Now you will program the blocks for the app. Open the Blocks Editor.

Step 4: Create the Click event handler for the ButtonCalculate button. Inside the event handler, create the local variable initialization block shown in Figure 5-18. The variables are needed to calculate the ending balance.

(You will need to use the initialization block's mutator bubble to add all of the necessary variables.) Here is a summary of each variable's purpose:

- The Balance variable will hold the account balance. Notice that in Figure 5-18, it is initialized with the value the user has entered into the TextBoxStartingBalance component.
- The Months variable will hold the number of months that the account will earn interest. Notice in Figure 5-18 that it is initialized with the value the user has entered into the TextBoxNumberMonths component.
- The Count variable will be used to count the months as a loop iterates. Notice that in Figure 5-18, it is initialized to the value 0.
- The InterestRate variable holds the monthly interest rate, which is 0.005.

Figure 5-18 Variable Definition Blocks *(Source:* MIT App Inventor 2)

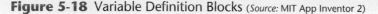

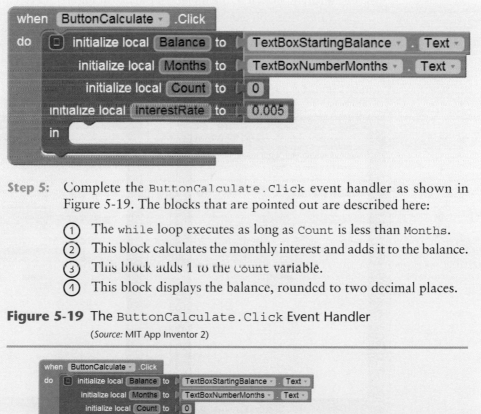

Step 5: Complete the ButtonCalculate.Click event handler as shown in Figure 5-19. The blocks that are pointed out are described here:

① The while loop executes as long as Count is less than Months.
② This block calculates the monthly interest and adds it to the balance.
③ This block adds 1 to the Count variable.
④ This block displays the balance, rounded to two decimal places.

Figure 5-19 The ButtonCalculate.Click Event Handler
(Source: MIT App Inventor 2)

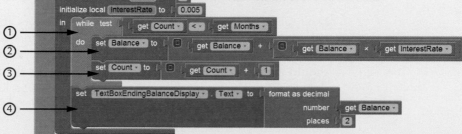

Step 6: Create the `Click` event handler for the `ButtonReset` button as shown in Figure 5-20. The event handler sets each of the TextBox components' Text properties to blank text.

Figure 5-20 The `ButtonReset.Click` Event Handler (*Source:* MIT App Inventor 2)

Step 7: Test the app in the emulator or on your device. First, enter *1000* as the starting balance and *48* as the number of months. Click the *Calculate Ending Balance* button, and 1270.49 should appear as the ending balance, as shown in the image on the left in Figure 5-21. Think about the value that you entered for the number of months. How many times did the `while` loop shown in Figure 5-19 iterate? (Answer: 48 times.)

Figure 5-21 The App Running in the Emulator (*Source:* MIT App Inventor 2)

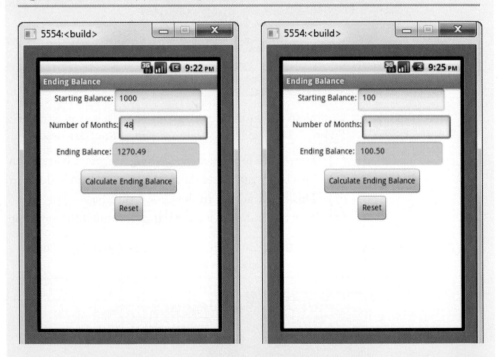

Next, click the *Reset* button to clear the TextBoxes and the ending balance. Now, enter *100* as the starting balance and *1* as the number of months. Click the *Calculate Ending Balance* button and $100.50 should appear as the ending balance, as shown in the image on the right in Figure 5-21. How many times did the `while` loop shown in Figure 5-19 iterate this time? (Answer: 1 time.)

Continue to test the app as you wish.

Infinite Loops

In all but rare cases, loops must contain a way to terminate within themselves. This means that something inside the loop must eventually make the loop's Boolean expression `false`. The loop in the EndingBalance app (Tutorial 5-1) stops when the expression `Count < Months` is `false`. If a loop does not have a way of stopping, it is called an infinite loop. An *infinite loop* continues to repeat until the program is interrupted. Infinite loops usually occur when the programmer forgets to write code inside the loop that makes the Boolean expression `false`. In most circumstances, you should avoid writing infinite loops.

The blocks shown in Figure 5-22 demonstrate an infinite loop. First, the `Count` variable is set to the value 0. The `while` loop executes as long as `Count` is less than 5. There is no code inside the loop to change the `count` variable's value, so the Boolean expression `Count < 5` is always `true`. As a consequence, the loop has no way of stopping.

Figure 5-22 An Infinite `While` Loop (*Source:* MIT App Inventor 2)

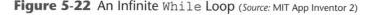

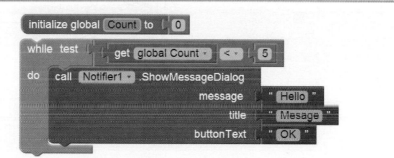

 Checkpoint

5.6   What is a loop iteration?

5.7   What is a counter variable?

5.8   What is a pretest loop?

5.9   Does the `while` loop test its condition before or after it performs an iteration?

5.10   What is an infinite loop?

5.3 The `for each` Loop

CONCEPT: The `for each` loop is designed to increment a counter variable over a range of values. It is ideally suited for problems requiring a loop that iterates a specific number of times.

The `for each` loop is ideal for situations that require a counter because it initializes, tests, and increments a counter variable. It is particularly useful for creating loops that must iterate a specific number of times.

In the Blocks column, you will find the `for each` loop in the *Control* drawer, as shown in Figure 5-23. The `for each` loop block is shown in Figure 5-24.

Figure 5-23 The `for each` Block (*Source:* MIT App Inventor 2)

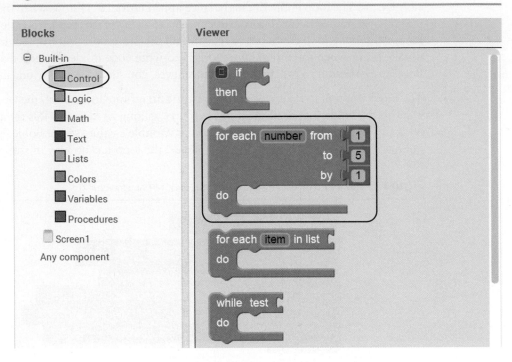

Figure 5-24 The `for each` Loop Block (*Source:* MIT App Inventor 2)

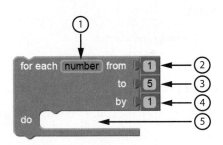

The different parts of the block are pointed out in the figure. Here is a description of each part:

① This is the loop's counter variable. When you create a `for each` loop, a variable named `number` is automatically created. The variable's scope is limited to the `for each` loop, so you cannot access it outside of the loop. In most cases, you should change the variable's name so that it is more descriptive. (To change the variable's name, simply click the existing name and then type the new name.)

② The `from` socket specifies the counter variable's starting value. When the loop begins executing, the counter variable will be set to this value. The value 1 is plugged into this socket by default, but you can change it to another value.

③ The `to` socket specifies the counter variable's ending value. When the counter variable reaches this value (or is greater than this value), the loop ends. The value 5 is plugged into this socket by default, but you can change it to another value.

④ The `by` socket specifies the amount added to the counter variable at the end of each iteration. The value 1 is plugged into this socket by default, but you can change it to another value.

⑤ The blocks that are plugged into the `do` socket will execute each time the loop iterates.

Figure 5-25 shows three very straightforward examples of the `for each` loop. In the each example, we have changed the name of the `number` variable to `Counter`. The topmost example uses the default values for each of the block's sockets. The `Counter` variable starts with the value 1 and ends with the value 5. At the end of each loop iteration, 1 is added to the `Counter` variable, so the loop will execute five times. (As the loop executes, the `Counter` variable will have the values 1, 2, 3, 4, and 5.)

Figure 5-25 Examples for the `for each` Loop (*Source:* MIT App Inventor 2)

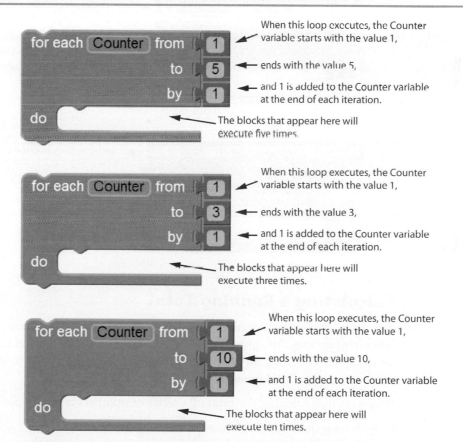

In the middle example, the `Counter` variable starts with the value 1 and ends with the value 3. At the end of each loop iteration, 1 is added to the `Counter` variable, so the loop will execute three times. (As the loop executes, the `Counter` variable will have the values 1, 2, and 3.)

In the bottom example, the `Counter` variable starts with the value 1 and ends with the value 10. At the end of each loop iteration, 1 is added to the `Counter` variable, so the loop will execute ten times. (As the loop executes, the `Counter` variable will have the values 1, 2, 3, and so forth, up to 10.)

Figure 5-26 shows two simple but less straightforward examples of the for each loop. In the top example, the Counter variable starts with the value 0 and ends with the value 5. At the end of each loop iteration, 1 is added to the Counter variable, so the loop will execute six times. (As the loop executes, the Counter variable will have the values 0, 1, 2, 3, 4, and 5.)

In the bottom example in Figure 5-26, the Counter variable starts with the value 10 and ends with the value 100. At the end of each loop iteration, 10 is added to the Counter variable, so the loop will execute ten times. (As the loop executes, the Counter variable will have the values 10, 20, 30, and so forth, up to 100.)

Figure 5-26 Examples for the for each Loop (*Source:* MIT App Inventor 2)

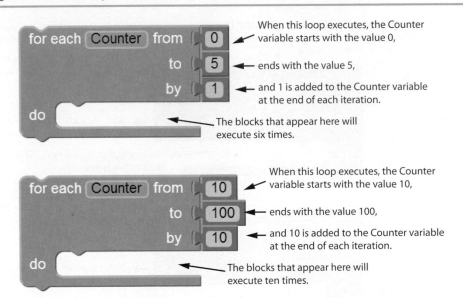

Calculating a Running Total

A *running total* is the sum of a series of numbers. Running totals are commonly calculated in programs. An application that calculates a business's total sales for a week is an example. The program would get each day's sales and add that amount to a variable that accumulates the sum of all the days' sales.

Programs that calculate the total of a series of numbers typically use two elements:

- A loop that reads each number in the series.
- A variable that accumulates the total of the numbers as they are read.

The variable that is used to accumulate the total of the numbers is called an *accumulator*. It is very important that the accumulator variable be initialized with the value 0 before the loop starts executing. Each time the loop reads a number, it adds it to the accumulator. If the accumulator starts with any value other than 0, it will not contain the correct total when the loop finishes.

In Tutorial 5-2, you will create an app that calculates the sum of a series of numbers from 1 to an upper limit specified by the user.

VideoNote
Calculating
the Sum of
Consecutive
Numbers

Tutorial 5-2:
Calculating a Sum of Consecutive Numbers

In this tutorial, you will create an app that uses a `for each` loop to calculate the sum of a series of numbers. The range will always start at 1, but the user will specify the upper limit of the range. (For example, if the user specifies 100 as the upper limit, the loop will calculate the sum of 1 through 100.)

Figure 5-27 shows the app's screen in the Viewer along with the names of the components. Figure 5-28 shows how the screen appears in the emulator.

Figure 5-27 The SumOfNumbers App in the Designer *(Source: MIT App Inventor 2)*

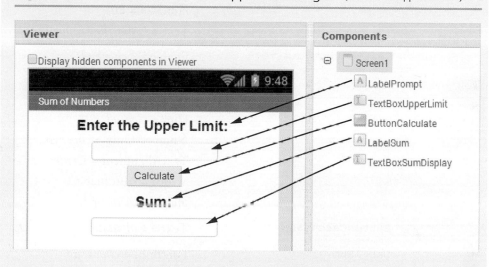

Figure 5-28 The App in the Emulator *(Source: MIT App Inventor 2)*

Step 1:   Start a new project named SumOfNumbers.

Step 2:   Set up the app's screen with the components shown in Figure 5-27. Refer to Table 5-2 for the relevant property settings for each component.

Table 5-2 Component property settings (*Source:* Pearson Education, Inc.)

Component	Relevant Property Settings
Screen1	AlignHorizontal = *Center* Title = *Sum of Numbers*
LabelPrompt	FontBold = *checked* FontSize = *20* Text = *Enter the Upper Limit:*
TextBoxUpperLimit	Enabled = *checked* FontBold = *checked* FontSize = *20* Hint = *cleared* NumbersOnly = *checked* TextAlignment = *Center* Width = Automatic Height = *Automatic*
ButtonCalculate	Text = *Calculate*
LabelSum	FontBold = *checked* FontSize = *20* Text = *Sum:*
TextBoxSumDisplay	Enabled = *unchecked* FontBold = *checked* FontSize = *20* Hint = *cleared* TextAlignment = *Center* Width = *Automatic* Height = *Automatic*

Step 3:   Now you will program the blocks for the app. Open the Blocks Editor.

Step 4:   Create the Click event handler for the ButtonCalculate button. Inside the event handler, create the local variable initialization block shown in Figure 5-29. The variables are needed to calculate the sum. (You will need to use the initialization block's mutator bubble to add an additional variable to the block.)

Figure 5-29 Variable Definition Blocks (*Source:* MIT App Inventor 2)

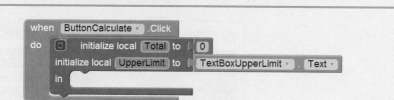

Here is a summary of each variable's purpose:

- The Total variable is the accumulator. It will hold the sum of the series of numbers. The Total variable is initialized to 0 so the loop will calculate the correct sum.
- The UpperLimit variable will hold the upper limit of the range of numbers. Notice that the UpperLimit variable is initialized with the value entered by the user into the TextBoxUpperLimit component.

Step 5: Complete the Click event handler for the ButtonCalculate button as shown in Figure 5-30. The blocks that are pointed out in the figure are described here:

① In the for each loop, the Counter variable starts at 1 and ends at the value of UpperLimit. 1 is added to the Counter variable at the end of each loop iteration.
② This adds the value of the Counter variable to the Total variable.
③ This block executes after the loop has finished. It displays the value of the Total variable in the TextBoxTotalDisplay text box.

Figure 5-30 The ButtonCalculate.Click Event Handler
(*Source:* MIT App Inventor 2)

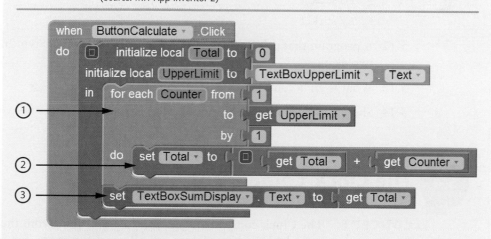

Step 6: Test the app in the emulator or on your device. First, enter *100* as the upper limit and click the *Calculate* button. You should see *5050* appear as the sum, as shown in Figure 5-31. Continue to test the app with other values as the upper limit.

Figure 5-31 The App Running in the Emulator (*Source:* MIT App Inventor 2)

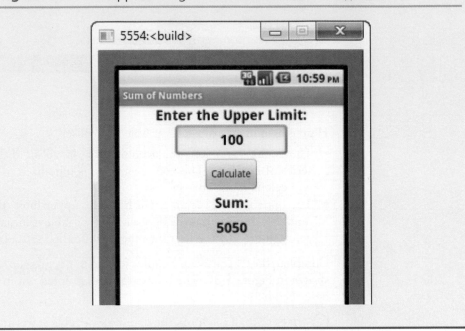

 Checkpoint

5.11 Describe the following parts of the for each loop:

- number variable
- from socket
- to socket
- by socket

5.12 A program that calculates the total of a series of numbers typically has what two elements?

5.13 What is an accumulator?

5.14 Should an accumulator be initialized to any specific value? Why or why not?

5.4 The Clock Component

CONCEPT: The Clock component gets the date and time from the internal system clock and provides methods and functions for working with dates and times. It also works as a timer that can perform operations at specific intervals.

App Inventor's Clock component allows you to get the current date and time from the device's internal clock and perform various operations with dates and times.

It also serves as a timer that performs operations at regular time intervals. It is a nonvisible component, found in the *User Interface* section of the *Palette.*

Let's first look at the Clock component as a way to get the date and time. The Clock component works with dates and times using a special value known as an instant. An *instant* is a number that represents an instant in time. An instant contains both a date and a time. If you want to know the current date and time, you call the Clock component's Now function. The Now function returns the current date and time as an instant.

You use instants to work with dates and times. For example, you can compare instants with an if then block, extract the day of the week from an instant, add seconds, minutes, and hours to an instant, and perform many other operations. However, you can't print an instant on the screen. If you want to print the date and/or time that is contained in an instant, you need to use one of the Clock functions described in Table 5-3 to format it as text.

Table 5-3 Date and Time Formatting Functions *(Source:* MIT App Inventor 2)

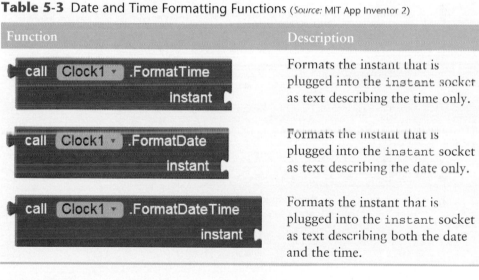

Function	Description
call Clock1 .FormatTime instant	Formats the instant that is plugged into the instant socket as text describing the time only.
call Clock1 .FormatDate instant	Formats the instant that is plugged into the instant socket as text describing the date only.
call Clock1 .FormatDateTime instant	Formats the instant that is plugged into the instant socket as text describing both the date and the time.

Let's look at the ClockDemo project as an example. When the app executes, it simply displays the time that the app started. Figure 5-32 shows the app's screen in the Designer, and Figure 5-33 shows the app's workspace in the Blocks Editor.

Notice that in Figure 5-33, the Screen1.Initialize event handler calls Clock1.Now block to get the current time as an instant. That block is plugged into the Clock1. FormatTime block, which formats the instant as text describing the time. That block is assigned to the LabelTimeDisplay.Text property, which displays the time on the screen. Figure 5-34 shows the app running in the emulator.

You can also use the Clock component as a timer that performs an operation at specific time intervals. It works like this: When the Clock component's TimerEnabled property is set to true (checked in the Properties column), a Timer event will happen at regularly scheduled intervals. The intervals are determined by the TimerInterval property, which is set to a value in milliseconds. For example, if the TimerInterval

Figure 5-32 The ClockDemo App in the Designer *(Source:* MIT App Inventor 2)

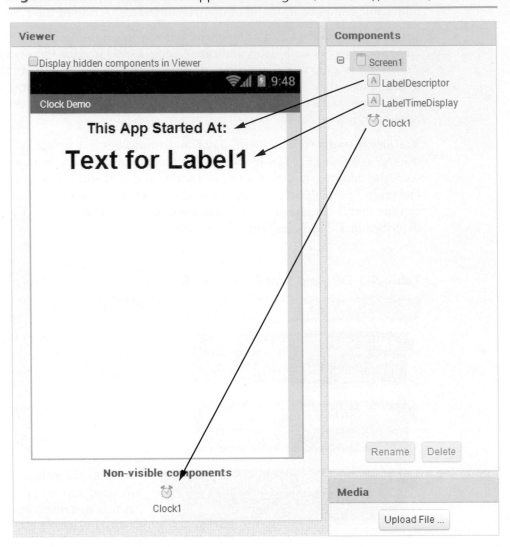

Figure 5-33 The ClockDemo Project's Workspace *(Source:* MIT App Inventor 2)

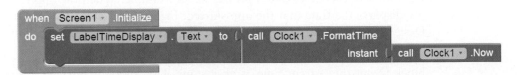

property is set to 1000 and the TimerEnabled property is set to true, then a Timer event will happen once every 1000 milliseconds (once every second).

Once you have enabled the timer and set the desired timer interval, you create an event handler for the Timer event. In the event handler, you place the blocks that you want to execute each time the Timer event occurs. To create the Timer event handler in the Blocks Editor, you go to My Blocks, click the name of the Clock component, and then select the block for the Timer event handler.

Figure 5-34 The App Running in the Emulator (*Source:* MIT App Inventor 2)

For example, suppose an app has a Clock component named `Clock1` and a Sound component named `Sound1`. The event handler shown in Figure 5-35 will play the `Sound1` component's sound every time the `Timer` event happens.

Figure 5-35 Example `Timer` Event Handler (*Source:* MIT App Inventor 2)

In Tutorial 5-3, you will create a clock app that displays the time, updated every second, on the screen.

**VideoNote
Creating a Clock
App**

Tutorial 5-3:
Creating a Clock App

In this tutorial, you will create an app that uses a Clock component to display the current time on the screen. The app will update the display once every second. You will set the Clock component's TimerInterval property to 1000 milliseconds and create a `Timer` event handler that gets the current time, formats it, and displays it.

Figure 5-36 shows the app's screen in the Viewer, along with the names of the components. Figure 5-37 shows how the screen appears in the emulator.

Figure 5-36 The MyClock App in the Designer (*Source:* MIT App Inventor 2)

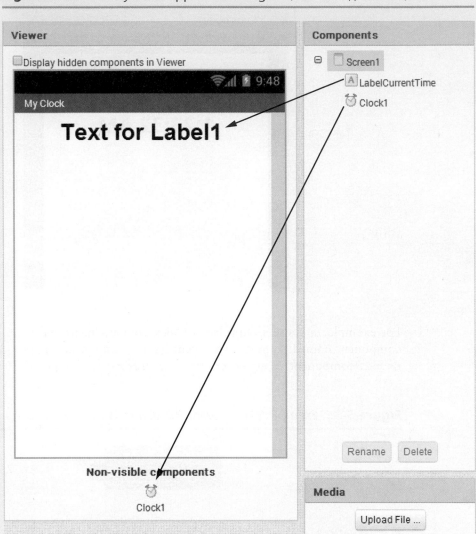

Figure 5-37 The MyClock App Running in the Emulator (*Source:* MIT App Inventor 2)

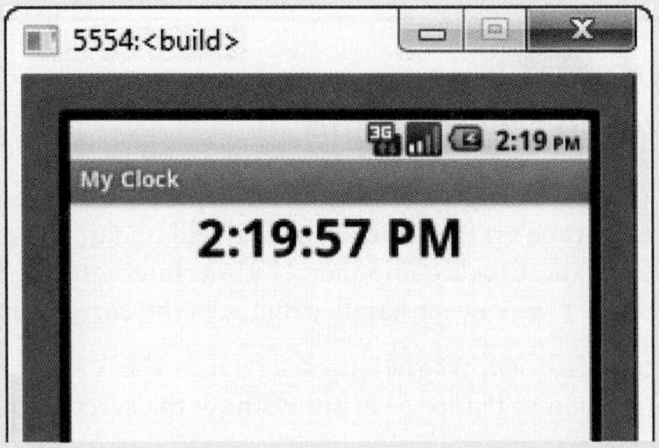

Step 1:   Start a new project named MyClock.

Step 2:   Set up the app's screen with the components shown in Figure 5-36. Refer to Table 5-4 for the relevant property settings for each component. (You do not have to change the default `Text` property for the `LabelCurrentTime` component because it will be updated automatically in the `Timer` event handler that you will create next.)

Table 5-4 Component property settings *(Source: Pearson Education, Inc.)*

Component	Relevant Property Settings
`Screen1`	AlignHorizontal = *Center* Title = *My Clock*
`LabelCurrentTime`	FontBold = *checked* FontSize = *32*
`Clock1`	TimerEnabled = *checked* TimerInterval = *1000*

Step 3:   Open the Blocks Editor. Open the *Clock1* drawer and select the block for the `Clock1.Timer` event handler.

Step 4:   Complete the event handler as shown in Figure 5-38.

Figure 5-38 The Completed `Clock1.Timer` Event Handler
    (Source: MIT App Inventor 2)

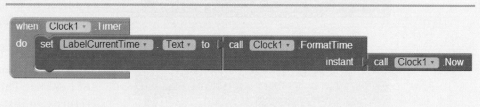

Step 5:   Test the app in the emulator or on your device. The time should update once every second.

Other Clock Methods

The Clock component provides many other methods and functions for working with dates and times. We will take a look at a few of these now, although we will not cover all of them. (You can refer to the online App Inventor documentation to learn more about the other Clock methods and functions.)

We will take a look at the Clock functions that let you add units of time to an instant to get an instant that will occur in the future.

Table 5-5 The Clock component's `Add` functions (*Source:* MIT App Inventor 2)

Function	Description
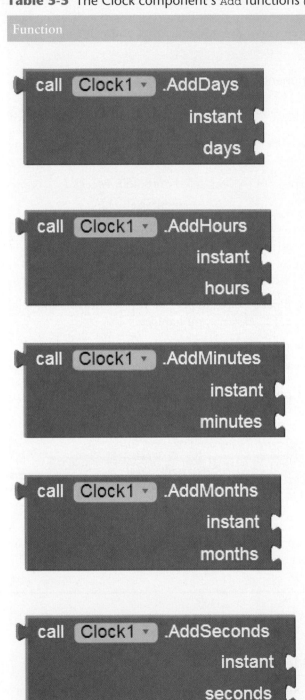 call Clock1 .AddDays / instant / days	Requires two arguments: an `instant` and a number of `days`. This function returns an instant in time that is the specified number of days after the given `instant`.
call Clock1 .AddHours / instant / hours	Requires two arguments: an `instant` and a number of `hours`. This function returns an instant in time that is the specified number of hours after the given `instant`.
call Clock1 .AddMinutes / instant / minutes	Requires two arguments: an `instant` and a number of `minutes`. This function returns an instant in time that is the specified number of minutes after the given `instant`.
call Clock1 .AddMonths / instant / months	Requires two arguments: an `instant` and a number of `months`. This function returns an instant in time that is the specified number of months after the given `instant`.
call Clock1 .AddSeconds / instant / seconds	Requires two arguments: an `instant` and a number of `seconds`. This function returns an instant in time that is the specified number of seconds after the given `instant`.

Function	Description
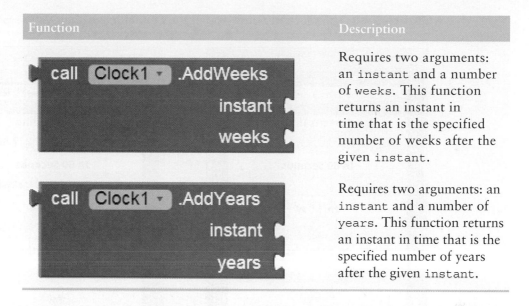	Requires two arguments: an `instant` and a number of `weeks`. This function returns an instant in time that is the specified number of weeks after the given `instant`. Requires two arguments: an `instant` and a number of `years`. This function returns an instant in time that is the specified number of years after the given `instant`.

For example, Figure 5-39 shows the ClockAddTime project in the Viewer, and Figure 5-40 shows how it initially appears in the emulator (the image on the left) and how it appears after the user has clicked the *Update* button (the image on the right). When the user clicks the *Update* button, the app displays the current date and time, the date and time 60 seconds from now, the date and time one day from now, and the date and time six months from now. Figure 5-41 shows the `ButtonUpdate` component's `Click` event handler.

Figure 5-39 The ClockAddTime Project in the Viewer (*Source:* MIT App Inventor 2)

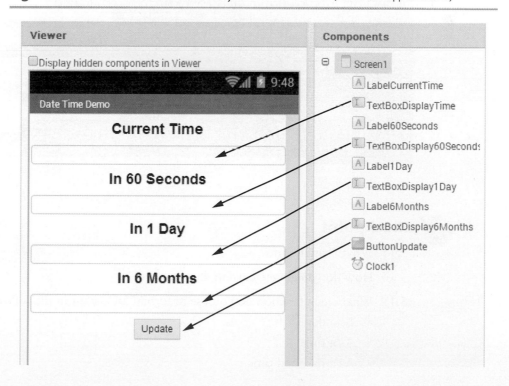

Figure 5-40 The ClockAddTime App in the Emulator (*Source:* MIT App Inventor 2)

Figure 5-41 The `Button1.Click` Event Handler (*Source:* MIT App Inventor 2)

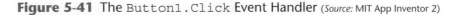
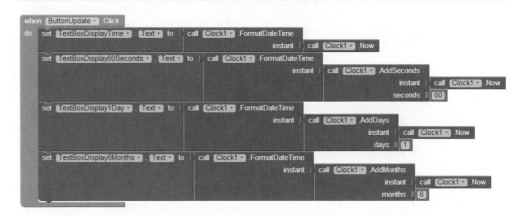

 Checkpoint

5.15 What is an instant?

5.16 How do you get the current date and time?

5.17 What clock function do you use to format an instant in the following ways?

- As a date
- As a time
- As a date and time

5.18 How do you specify the time interval for a Clock component's `Timer` event?

5.19 What Clock component function would you use to get an instant that is three days from the current date and time?

5.5 The DatePicker Component

CONCEPT: The DatePicker component appears as a button on an app's screen. When the user clicks the DatePicker button, it displays a dialog box that allows the user to select a date.

The DatePicker component (found in the *User Interface* section of the *Palette*) provides a much simpler and more reliable way for users to enter dates on a form than typing them into a TextBox. The image on the left in Figure 5-42 shows a DatePicker component before the user has clicked it. The image on the right shows how the screen appears after the user has clicked the DatePicker. A dialog box appears that allows the user to select a date.

Figure 5-42 The DatePicker Component *(Source: MIT App Inventor 2)*

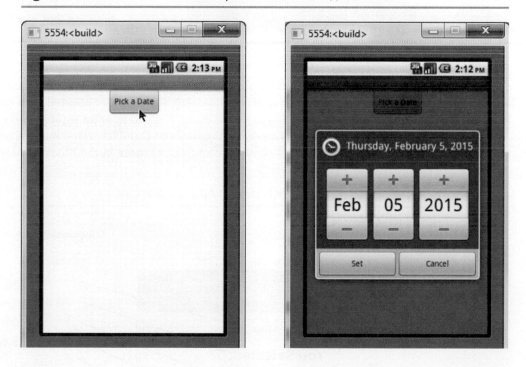

In the Designer, the DatePicker component has many of the same properties as the Button component. For example, you use the Text property to set the text that is displayed on the component. In the Blocks Editor, there are four properties in particular that you will work with. These properties are described in Table 5-6.

Table 5-6 `DatePicker` **properties** (*Source:* MIT App Inventor 2)

Property	Description
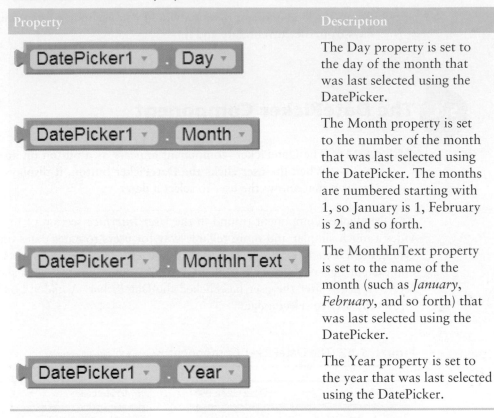 DatePicker1 . Day	The Day property is set to the day of the month that was last selected using the DatePicker.
DatePicker1 . Month	The Month property is set to the number of the month that was last selected using the DatePicker. The months are numbered starting with 1, so January is 1, February is 2, and so forth.
DatePicker1 . MonthInText	The MonthInText property is set to the name of the month (such as *January*, *February*, and so forth) that was last selected using the DatePicker.
DatePicker1 . Year	The Year property is set to the year that was last selected using the DatePicker.

When the user clicks the *Set* button in the DatePicker's dialog box, an `AfterDateSet` event occurs. If you want to retrieve the date that the user selected, you can create an event handler for the `AfterDateSet` event. Let's look at an example app that uses a DatePicker component. Figure 5-43 shows the DatePickerDemo app's screen in the Designer, and Figure 5-44 shows the app's workspace in the Blocks Editor.

Figure 5-43 The DatePickerDemo App (*Source:* MIT App Inventor 2)

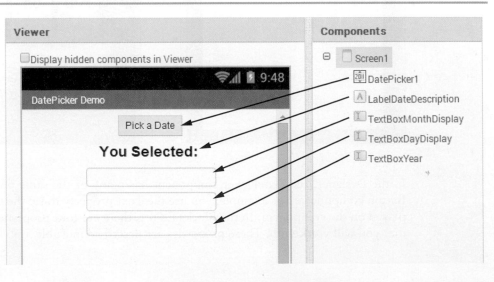

Figure 5-44 The DatePickerDemo App's Workspace in the Blocks Editor
(*Source:* MIT App Inventor 2)

Notice in Figure 5-44 that the app has one event handler: `DatePicker1.`
`AfterDateSet`. This event handler executes after the user has selected a date with the
DatePicker. It displays the name of the selected month in the `TextBoxMonthDisplay`
component, the selected day in the `TextBoxDayDisplay` component, and the selected
year in the `TextBoxYearDisplay` component.

Figure 5-45 shows an example of the app running in the emulator. The screenshot on
the left shows the app's screen as it initially appears. The user clicks the DatePicker
component and the dialog box shown in the middle screenshot appears. The user
selects a date and clicks the *Set* button. The selected date is displayed, as shown in the
screenshot on the right.

Figure 5-45 The DatePickerDemo App Running in the Emulator (*Source:* MIT App Inventor 2)

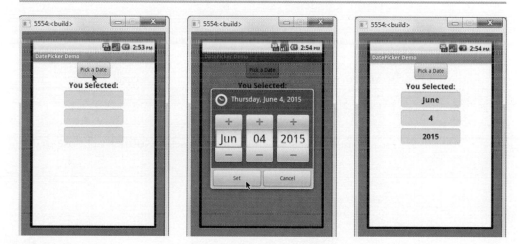

Checkpoint

5.20 What event occurs when the user clicks the *Set* button in a DatePicker's
dialog box?

5.21 What DatePicker property holds the number of the last month selected in the
DatePicker?

5.22 What DatePicker property holds the name of the last month selected in the
DatePicker?

5.23 What DatePicker property holds the day of the month that was last selected
in the DatePicker?

5.24 What DatePicker property holds the last year selected in the DatePicker?

Review Questions

Multiple Choice

1. This type of Notifier dialog simply displays a message and waits for the user to click a button.

   a. text dialog
   b. message dialog
   c. choose dialog
   d. warning dialog

2. This type of Notifier dialog displays a message and lets the user enter input.

   a. text dialog
   b. message dialog
   c. choose dialog
   d. warning dialog

3. This type of Notifier dialog displays lets the user click one of two buttons, and optionally a *Cancel* button.

   a. text dialog
   b. message dialog
   c. choose dialog
   d. warning dialog

4. This event happens when the user closes a Notifier's text dialog.

   a. `AfterText`
   b. `AfterTextInput`
   c. `TextDialogClosed`
   d. `AfterChoosing`

5. This event happens when the user closes a Notifier's choose dialog.

   a. `AfterText`
   b. `AfterTextInput`
   c. `TextDialogClosed`
   d. `AfterChoosing`

6. Each repetition of a loop is known as a(n) _____.

   a. cycle
   b. revolution
   c. orbit
   d. iteration

7. A _____ is commonly used to control the number of times that a loop iterates.

   a. counter variable
   b. test expression
   c. control clause
   d. controlled variable

8. A(n) _____ tests its condition *before* performing an iteration.

   a. preemptive loop
   b. pretest loop
   c. infinite loop
   d. logical loop

9. A(n) _____ loop has no way of ending and repeats until the program is interrupted.

   a. indeterminate
   b. interminable
   c. infinite
   d. timeless

10. A(n) _____ variable keeps a running total.

    a. sentinel
    b. sum
    c. total
    d. accumulator

11. This Clock component property specifies the time interval at which the Timer event occurs.

    a. Interval
    b. TimerInterval
    c. Timer
    d. TimerEvent

12. This Clock component function returns the current date and time as an instant.

    a. `Now`
    b. `CurrentDateTime`
    c. `CurrentInstant`
    d. `RightNow`

13. This event occurs when the user selects a date with the DatePicker component.

    a. `AfterDateSelected`
    b. `DateSelected`
    c. `AfterDateSet`
    d. `ValueSet`

14. This DatePicker component property holds the number of the last month selected by the user with the DatePicker component.

    a. Month
    b. MonthNumber
    c. SelectedMonth
    d. MonthAsANumber

15. This DatePicker component property holds the name of the last month selected by the user with the DatePicker component.

    a. Month
    b. MonthInText
    c. SelectedMonth
    d. MonthName

Short Answer

1. If you want to simply display a message to the user in a dialog box, which Notifier method would you call?

2. If you want to get some input from the user with a dialog box, which Notifier method would you call to display the dialog box?

3. If you want to use a dialog box to get a yes/no answer from the user, which Notifier method would you call to display the dialog box?

4. How many iterations will occur if the test expression of a `while` loop is false to begin with?

5. Describe the following parts of the `for each` loop:
   - `number` variable
   - `from` socket
   - `to` socket
   - `by` socket
   - `do` socket

6. What is a running total?

7. Why is it critical that accumulator variables are properly initialized?

8. What is an instant?

9. How do you get the current date and time?

10. What `Clock` component function would you use if you wanted to format an instant as text describing the time only?

Exercises

1. Create an app that displays a text dialog prompting the user to enter his or her name and then immediately displays the user's name in a message dialog.

2. Create an app that displays a choose dialog with two buttons: one labeled *Yes* and one labeled *No*. After the user clicks one of the buttons, the app should display a message dialog indicating which button the user clicked.

3. Create an app that uses a `while` loop that iterates five times. In each iteration, the app should display a random number in a message dialog.

4. Create an app that uses a `for each` loop to calculate the sum of the numbers 10, 20, 30, 40, and so forth, up to 500.

**VideoNote
The Sum of
Numbers App**

Programming Projects

1. **Pennies for Pay**

   Susan is hired for a job, and her employer agrees to pay her every day. Her employer also agrees that Susan's salary is 1 penny the first day, 2 pennies the second day, 4 pennies the third day, continuing to double each day. Create an app that allows the user to enter the number of days that Susan will work and calculates the total amount of pay she will receive over that period of time.

2. **Calculating the Factorial of a Number**

In mathematics, the notation $n!$ represents the factorial of the nonnegative integer n. The factorial of n is the product of all the nonnegative integers from 1 through n. (The factorial of 0 is 1.) For example,

$$4! = 1 \times 2 \times 3 \times 4 = 24$$

and

$$7! = 1 \times 2 \times 3 \times 4 \times 5 \times 6 \times 7 = 5{,}040$$

Create an app that lets the user enter a nonnegative integer and then uses a loop to calculate the factorial of that number. Display the factorial in a label or a text box.

3. **Time Zone App**

From east to west, the US time zones in the contiguous US are Eastern, Central, Mountain, and Pacific. Outside the contiguous US are the Alaskan Standard time zone (which is one hour behind the Pacific time zone), and the Hawaii-Aleutian time zone (which is two hours behind Alaskan Standard time).

Write an app that displays the current time in your time zone, plus the other US time zones.

(Hint: Once you get the current time as an instant, you can use the Clock component's `AddHours` function to calculate the time in the other time zones. For example, if you are in the Eastern time zone, you would add -1 hours to the current time to get the Central time, -2 hours to the current time to get the Mountain time, and so forth.)

4. **Alarm App**

Write a simple alarm app that lets the user enter a number of seconds. When the user clicks a button, the app will wait for the specified number of seconds and then play a sound.

5. **Stop Watch App**

Write a simple stop watch app that has two buttons: *Start* and *Stop*. When the user clicks the *Start* button, the app gets the current time from the system. When the user clicks the *Stop* button, the app gets the current time again and displays the number of seconds that have elapsed since the *Start* button was clicked. (Hint: You can use the `Clock` component's `duration` function to get the number of milliseconds between two instants.)

6. **Day Of The Week App**

The Clock component has a function named `WeekdayName` that takes an instant as its argument and returns the name of the day of the week for the specified instant (Sunday, Monday, etc.). Create an app that gets the current date and time and displays the name of the day of the week.

7. **Day of The Week For a Specified Date**

The Clock component has a function named `MakeInstant` that takes, as an argument, text containing a date in the form of MM/DD/YYYY. The `MakeInstant` function returns an instant representing the specified date. Create an app that lets the user enter a date in the form MM/DD/YYYY, and then displays the day of the week for that date. (Hint: Use the Clock component's `WeekdayName` function to get the name of the day of the week.)

8. **Age Calculator**

   Create an app that has two DatePicker components. The user should select his or her birthdate with the first DatePicker and some date in the future with the second DatePicker. The app should display how old the user will be on the second date.

6 Procedures and Functions

TOPICS

6.1 Modularizing Your Code With Procedures

CONCEPT: Procedures can be used to break a complex program into small, manageable pieces. A procedure simply executes a group of statements and then terminates. A procedure-with-result, which is also known as a function, returns a value to the block that called it.

In a general sense, a procedure is a collection of statements that performs a specific task. So far you have experienced procedures in the following ways:

- You have created event handlers. An event handler is a special type of procedure that responds to events, such as the clicking of a button.
- You have executed built-in procedures and functions, such as the Sound component's `Play` procedure and the `random integer` and `random fraction` functions.

In this chapter you will learn how to create your own procedures that can be executed just as you execute App Inventor's built-in procedures and functions.

Procedures are commonly used to break a problem into small, manageable pieces. Instead of writing one long procedure that contains all of the blocks necessary to solve a problem, several small procedures that each solve a specific part of the problem can be written. These small procedures can then be executed in the desired order to solve the problem. This approach is sometimes called *divide and conquer* because a large problem is divided into several smaller problems that are easily solved.

In general terms, a program that is broken into smaller units of code, such as procedures, is known as a *modularized program*. Modularization tends to simplify code. If a specific task is performed in several places in a program, a procedure can be written once to perform that task and then be executed any time it is needed. This benefit of using procedures is known as *code reuse* because you are writing the code to perform a task once and then reusing it each time you need to perform the task.

Procedures and Procedures With Results (Functions)

In this chapter you will learn to write *procedures* and *procedures with results*.

- When you call a procedure, it simply executes the blocks it contains and then terminates.
- When you call a *procedure with results*, it executes the blocks that it contains and then it returns a value back to the block that called it.

The `random integer` and `random fraction` blocks are good examples of procedures with results. Procedures with results are also known as functions, and in this book we typically use the term *function* to refer to a procedure that returns a result.

The first type of procedure that you will learn to write is the regular procedure (the type that does not return a result).

6.2 Procedures

CONCEPT: **A procedure performs a task and then terminates. It does not return a value back to the statement that called it.**

A procedure is a block that contains other blocks. To create a procedure, you must define it. In the Blocks Editor you go to the *Built-in* section of the Blocks column and then select *Procedures*. As shown in Figure 6-1, you select the `to procedure do` block from the drawer. (We will usually just refer to it as the `procedure` block.)

Figure 6-2 shows an empty `procedure` block. You insert other blocks inside the procedure block's `do` socket. When the procedure is called, the blocks that you have inserted inside the procedure will execute.

The word *procedure* that appears at the top of the block is the procedure's default name. You can click on the name to change it to something more meaningful. When you create a procedure block, you should always change its name to something that describes what the procedure does. For example, Figure 6-3 shows a procedure block after we have changed its name to `DisplayMessage`. The procedure shown in the figure is still empty but its name suggests that it will display a message. (We will see the completed procedure in a few moments.)

Figure 6-1 The `procedure` Block (*Source:* MIT App Inventor 2)

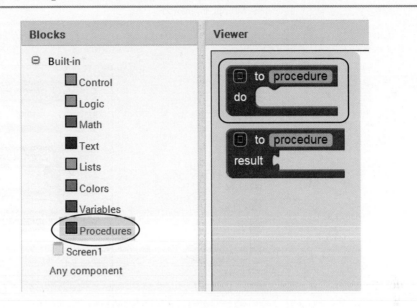

Figure 6-2 A `procedure` Block (*Source:* MIT App Inventor 2)

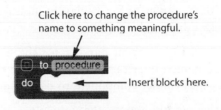

Click here to change the procedure's name to something meaningful.

Insert blocks here.

Figure 6-3 A Procedure Named `DisplayMessage` (*Source:* MIT App Inventor 2)

 NOTE: You cannot have two procedures with the same name in the same workspace. All of the procedures in the same workspace must have unique names.

You execute a procedure with a `call` block. When you create a `procedure` block, App Inventor automatically creates a `call` block for the `procedure`, which you will find by opening the Procedures drawer of the Blocks column. For example, Figure 6-4 shows the `call` block for a procedure named `DisplayMessage`. When you use a `call` block to call a procedure, the blocks that are inside the procedure are executed.

Figure 6-4 The `call` Block for a Procedure Named `DisplayMessage`
(*Source:* MIT App Inventor 2)

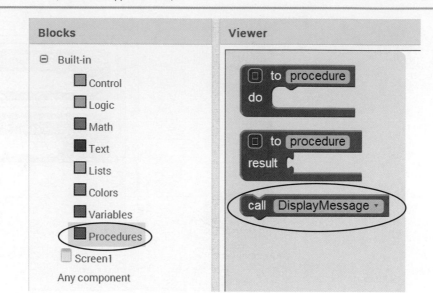

Let's look at an example app that uses a procedure. Figure 6-5 shows the ProcedureDemo app in the Designer. The app has a Button component on its screen and a Notifier component for displaying messages. Figure 6-6 shows the app's blocks in the Blocks Editor.

The app has a `Click` event handler for the `ButtonShowMessage` component and a procedure named `DisplayMessage`. Notice that the `DisplayMessage` procedure simply uses the Notifier component to display a message dialog.

Let's step through the actions that take place when the user clicks the button. Inside the `ButtonShowMessage.Click` event handler, we have a `call` block that calls the `DisplayMessage` procedure. As shown in Figure 6-7, the program jumps to the `DisplayMessage` procedure and executes the blocks inside of it. There is only one block in the `DisplayMessage` procedure, which displays a message dialog. When the procedure ends, as shown in Figure 6-7, the program jumps back to the part of the program that called the `DisplayMessage` procedure and resumes execution from that point.

Figure 6-8 shows the app running in the emulator. Screenshot 1 (the leftmost image) shows the app with the user about to click the button. Screenshot 2 (the center image) shows the message dialog that is displayed by the `DisplayMessage` procedure. The user is about to click the dialog box's *OK* button to dismiss it. Screenshot 3 (the rightmost image) shows the app's screen after the dialog box has been dismissed.

NOTE: When a program calls a procedure, programmers commonly say that the *control* of the program transfers to that procedure. This simply means that the procedure takes control of the program's execution.

Figure 6-5 The ProcedureDemo App in the Designer (*Source:* MIT App Inventor 2)

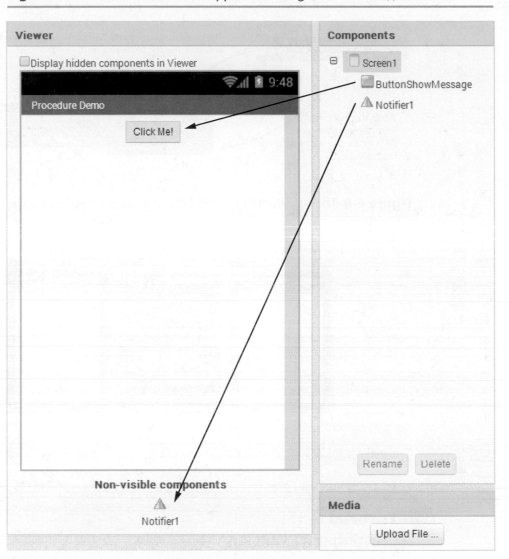

Figure 6-6 The ProcedureDemo App's Blocks (*Source:* MIT App Inventor 2)

Figure 6-7 Calling a Procedure (*Source:* MIT App Inventor 2)

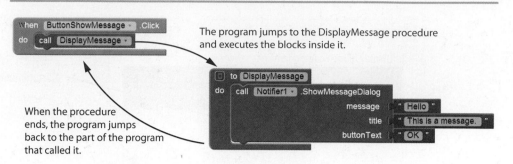

Figure 6-8 The App Running in the Emulator (*Source:* MIT App Inventor 2)

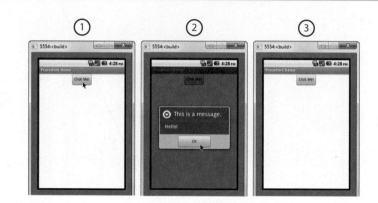

Tutorial 6-1 takes you through the process of creating a simple app that uses a procedure.

VideoNote
Creating the
Lights App

Tutorial 6-1:
Creating the Lights App

In this tutorial, you will create an app that simulates a light that can be turned on or off with a switch. Figure 6-9 shows the app's screen in the Viewer, along with the names of the components. Figure 6-10 shows how the screen appears in the emulator. Initially, the light bulb is off, as shown in the left image in Figure 6-10. When the user clicks the image of the switch, the light bulb turns on, as shown in the right image in Figure 6-10. Subsequently, each time the user clicks the switch, the bulb's state is reversed.

Notice the Media column in Figure 6-9. The following image files have been uploaded to the project:

- `LightOff.png`—This is an image of a light bulb that is off.
- `LightOn.png`—This is an image of a light bulb that is on.
- `SwitchDown.png`—This is an image of a switch that is in the down position.
- `SwitchUp.png`—This is an image of a switch that is in the up position.

Figure 6-9 The Lights App in the Designer *(Source:* MIT App Inventor 2)

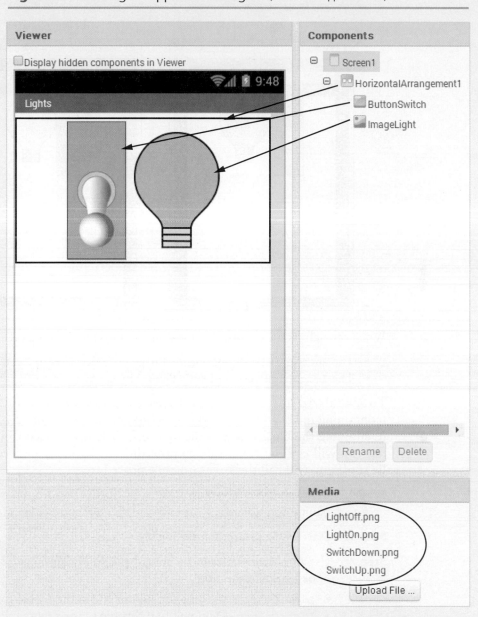

Initially, the ImageLight component's Picture property is set to LightOff.png and the ButtonSwitch component's Image property is set to SwitchDown.png. This makes the light bulb appear to be off and the switch to be in the down position.

When the light is turned on, the following actions will take place:

- The ButtonSwitch component's Image property is set to SwitchUp.png.
- The ImageLight component's Picture property is set to LightOn.png.

Figure 6-10 The App in the Emulator (*Source:* MIT App Inventor 2)

The light turned off   The light turned on

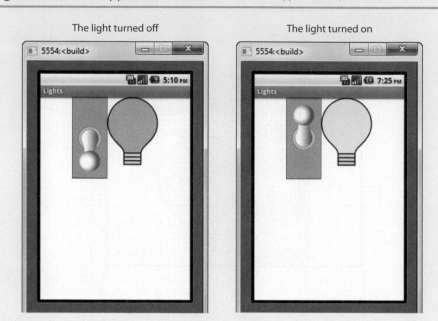

When the light is turned off, the following actions will take place:

- The `ButtonSwitch` component's Image property is set to `SwitchDown.png`.
- The `ImageLight` component's Picture property is set to `LightOff.png`.

To modularize the code, you will create a procedure named `TurnLightOn` (containing the blocks to turn the light on) and another named `TurnLightOff` (containing the blocks to turn the light off). When you need to turn the light on, you will call the `TurnLightOn` procedure and when you need to turn the light off you will call the `TurnLightOff` procedure.

Step 1: Make sure you have downloaded the media files from this book's companion website at `www.pearsonhighered.com/gaddis`.

Step 2: Start a new project named Lights.

Step 3: Use the Media column to upload the following image files from the book's media collection:
- `LightOff.png`—You will find this file in the *Lights* folder.
- `LightOn.png`—You will find this file in the *Lights* folder.
- `SwitchDown.png`—You will find this file in the *Switches* folder.
- `SwitchUp.png`—You will find this file in the *Switches* folder.

Step 4: Set up the app's screen with the components shown in Figure 6-9. Refer to Table 6-1 for the relevant property settings for each component.

Step 5: Now you will program the blocks for the app. Open the Blocks Editor.

Step 6: Create a procedure block named `TurnLightOn` by performing these steps:
- Open the *Procedures* drawer (in the *Built-in* section of the *Blocks* column) and select the `to procedure do` block. This creates an empty `procedure` block in the workspace.

Table 6-1 Component property settings (*Source:* Pearson Education, Inc.)

Component	Relevant Property Settings
Screen1	AlignHorizontal = *Center*
	Title = *Lights*
HorizontalArrangement1	AlignHorizontal = *Center*
	Width = *Fill Parent*
	Height = *Automatic*
ButtonCalculate	Text = *Cleared*
	Image = *SwitchDown.png*
ImageLight	Picture = *LightOff.png*

- Click the word *procedure* that appears at the top of the procedure block and change it to TurnLightOn.

The procedure block should now appear as shown in Figure 6-11.

Figure 6-11 The Empty TurnLightOn Procedure (*Source:* MIT App Inventor 2)

Step 7: Complete the procedure by adding the blocks shown in Figure 6-12. When this procedure is called, it will set the ButtonSwitch component's Image property to SwitchUp.png and it will set the ImageLight component's Picture property to LightOn.png.

Figure 6-12 The Completed TurnLightOn Procedure (*Source:* MIT App Inventor 2)

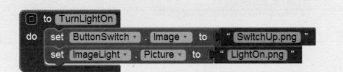

Step 8: Create a procedure block named TurnLightOff by performing these steps:
- Open the *Procedures* drawer (in the *Built-in* section of the *Blocks* column) and select the to procedure do block. This creates an empty procedure block in the workspace.
- Click the word *procedure* that appears at the top of the procedure block and change it to TurnLightOff.

The procedure block should now appear as shown in Figure 6-13.

Figure 6-13 The Empty TurnLightOff Procedure (*Source:* MIT App Inventor 2)

Step 9: Complete the procedure by adding the blocks shown in Figure 6-14. When this procedure is called, it will set the `ButtonSwitch` component's Image property to `SwitchDown.png` and it will set the `ImageLight` component's Picture property to `LightOff.png`.

Figure 6-14 The Completed `TurnLightOff` Procedure *(Source:* MIT App Inventor 2)

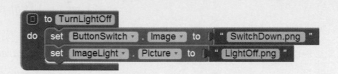

Step 10: Now you will create the `Click` event handler for the `ButtonSwitch` component. In a nutshell, the event handler will follow this logic:

> If the image of the light bulb is `LightOn.png`, then
>   Call the `TurnLightOff` procedure
> Else
>   Call the `TurnLightOn` procedure

Create the `ButtonSwitch.Click` event handler and add the `if then else` block shown in Figure 6-15. (The `compare texts` block is found in the *Text* drawer.)

Figure 6-15 Creating the `ButtonSwitch.Click` Event Handler
(Source: MIT App Inventor 2)

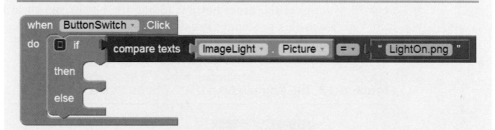

Step 11: In the `if then else` block's `then` section you want to call the `TurnLightOff` procedure and in the `else` section you want to call the `TurnLightOn` procedure. Complete the `if then else` block as shown in Figure 6-16. (You will find the `call TurnLightOff` and `call TurnLightOn` blocks in the *Procedures* drawer.)

Figure 6-16 The Completed `ButtonSwitch.Click` Event Handler
(Source: MIT App Inventor 2)

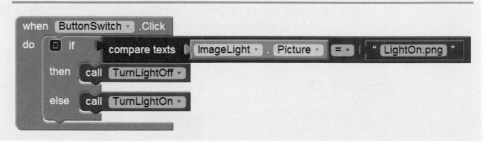

The app's complete workspace is shown in Figure 6-17.

Figure 6-17 The Complete Workspace (*Source:* MIT App Inventor 2)

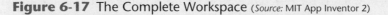

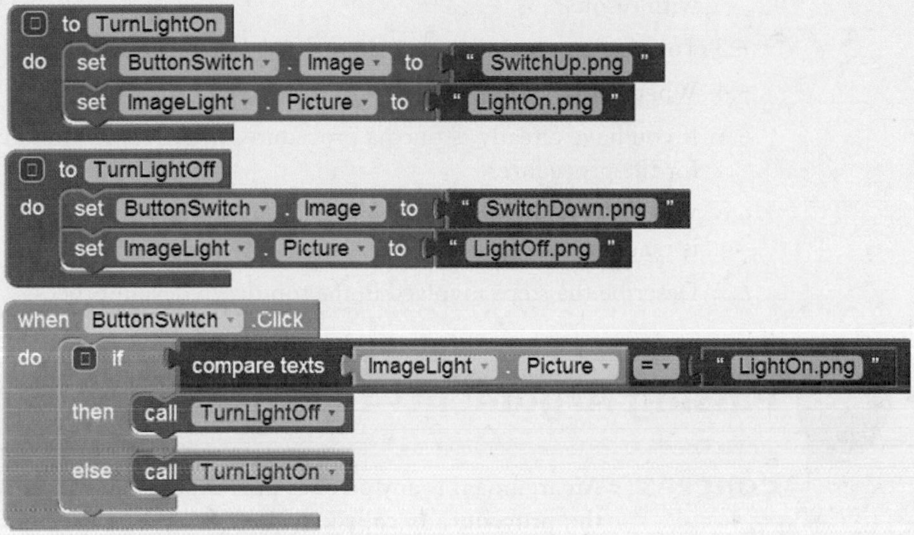

Step 12: Test the app in the emulator or on your device. Click the switch image several times to simulate turning the light on and off.

Top-Down Design

In this section, we have discussed and demonstrated how procedures work. You've seen how the program jumps to a procedure when it is called and returns to the part of the program that called the procedure when the procedure ends. It is important that you understand these mechanical aspects of procedures.

Just as important as understanding how procedures work is understanding how to use procedures to modularize a program. Programmers commonly use a technique known as *top-down design* to break down a program into procedures. The process of top-down design is performed in the following manner:

- The overall task that the program is to perform is broken down into a series of subtasks.
- Each of the subtasks is examined to determine whether it can be further broken down into more subtasks. This step is repeated until no more subtasks can be identified.
- Once all of the subtasks have been identified, they are written in code.

This process is called top-down design because the programmer begins by looking at the topmost level of tasks that must be performed, and then breaks down those tasks into lower levels of subtasks.

NOTE: The top-down design process is sometimes called *stepwise refinement*.

Checkpoint

6.1 What is the difference between a procedure and a procedure with results?

6.2 Is the `random integer` procedure an example of a procedure or a procedure with results?

6.3 To define a procedure, where do you find the `procedure` block in the Blocks Editor?

6.4 What does a `call` block do?

6.5 If you have already defined a procedure, where do you find the `call` block for the procedure?

6.6 When a procedure is executing, what happens when the end of the procedure is reached?

6.7 Describe the steps involved in the top-down design process.

6.3 Passing Arguments to Procedures

CONCEPT: An argument is any piece of data that is passed into a procedure when the procedure is called. A parameter is a variable that receives an argument that is passed into a procedure.

Sometimes it is useful not only to call a procedure, but also to send one or more pieces of data into the procedure. Pieces of data that are sent into a procedure are known as *arguments*. The procedure can use its arguments in calculations or other operations.

Figure 6-18 Arguments Passed to the `random integer` Function
(*Source:* MIT App Inventor 2)

Arguments

random integer from 1 to 100

You're already familiar with how to use arguments in a procedure call. For example, Figure 6-18 shows the random integer block, which requires two arguments. The arguments specify the minimum and maximum values for a random integer.

If you are writing a procedure and you want it to receive arguments when it is called, you must equip the procedure with one or more parameter variables. A *parameter variable*, often simply called a *parameter*, is a special variable that receives an argument when a procedure is called.

To equip a procedure block with a parameter variable, you open the procedure's mutator bubble by clicking the blue box (☐) that appears in the block's upper-left corner. Click and drag the `input` block (input: x) from the left side of the bubble and insert it on the right side of the bubble as shown in Figure 6-19. This adds a parameter variable named x to the procedure, as shown in Figure 6-20.

Remember that parameters are variables, and variables should have meaningful names. The name x is not a very descriptive name, so you should change it to something that

Figure 6-19 Adding a Parameter to a Procedure (*Source:* MIT App Inventor 2)

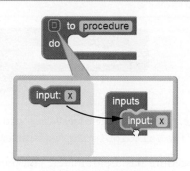

Figure 6-20 A Procedure with a Parameter Named x (*Source:* MIT App Inventor 2)

Parameter variable

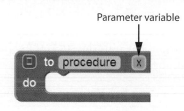

describes the parameter's purpose. (You change a parameter's name by simply clicking the name and then typing the new name.) For example, Figure 6-21 shows a procedure named `DisplayValue`. The procedure has a parameter named `ValueToDisplay`.

Figure 6-21 A Procedure with a Parameter Named `ValueToDisplay`
(*Source:* MIT App Inventor 2)

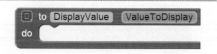

A parameter is a special type of local variable, and its scope is limited to the procedure that it belongs to. To get the value of a parameter, you must use a `get` block inside the procedure. You can use the *Variables* drawer of the Blocks column to create a `get` block, as shown in Figure 6-22, or you can hover the mouse cursor over the parameter's name, as shown in Figure 6-23.

Figure 6-22 Selecting the `get` Block from the *Variables* Drawer (*Source:* MIT App Inventor 2)

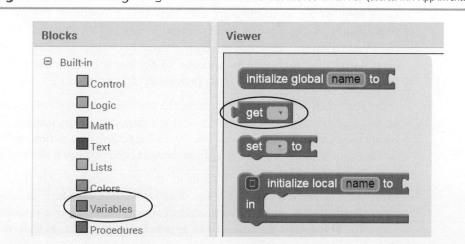

Figure 6-23 Hovering the Mouse Cursor Over the Parameter Name
(*Source:* MIT App Inventor 2)

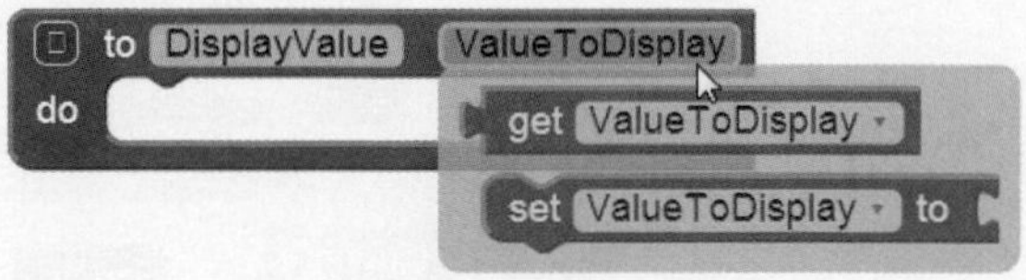

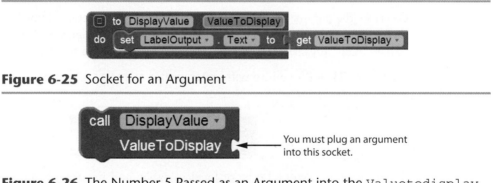

For example, inside the `DisplayValue` procedure shown in Figure 6-24, we assign the value of the `ValueToDisplay` parameter to a label's Text property.

When a procedure has a parameter, you must pass an argument into that parameter when you call the procedure. The `call` block for the procedure will have a socket with the same name as the parameter. For example, if an app has the `DisplayValue` procedure that is shown in Figure 6-24, the procedure's `call` block will have a socket named `ValueToDisplay`, as shown in Figure 6-25. When you call the procedure, you must plug an argument into the socket, as shown in Figure 6-26. In the figure, we are passing the number 5 as an argument.

Figure 6-24 Getting the Value of a Parameter (*Source:* MIT App Inventor 2)

Figure 6-25 Socket for an Argument

You must plug an argument into this socket.

Figure 6-26 The Number 5 Passed as an Argument into the `Valuetodisplay` Parameter (*Source:* MIT App Inventor 2)

Let's look at an example app that uses this procedure. Figure 6-27 shows the ArgumentDemo app in the Designer and Figure 6-28 shows the app's workspace in the Blocks Editor. The app's screen has three buttons and a `Click` event handler has been written for each one. In addition to the event handlers, the workspace has the `DisplayValue` procedure that we previously discussed.

If the user clicks the *Display 5* button, the `ButtonDisplay5.Click` event handler executes. The event handler calls the `DisplayValue` procedure, passing 5 as an argument. Inside the `DisplayValue` procedure, the `ValueToDisplay` parameter is set to the value 5. This causes the value 5 to appear in the text box, as shown in Figure 6-29.

If the user clicks the *Display 10* button, the `ButtonDisplay10.Click` event handler executes. The event handler calls the `DisplayValue` procedure, passing 10 as an argument. Inside the `DisplayValue` procedure, the `ValueToDisplay` parameter is set to the value 10. This causes the value 10 to appear in the text box, as shown in Figure 6-30.

Figure 6-27 The ArgumentDemo App in the Designer *(Source: MIT App Inventor 2)*

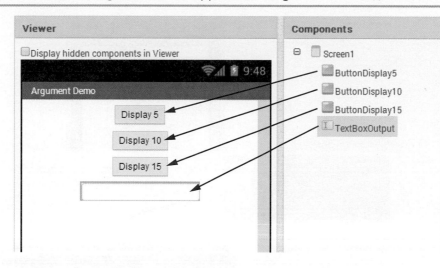

Figure 6-28 The ArgumentDemo App Workspace *(Source: MIT App Inventor 2)*

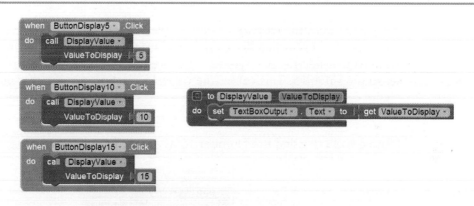

Figure 6-29 Passing the Number 5 as an Argument *(Source: MIT App Inventor 2)*

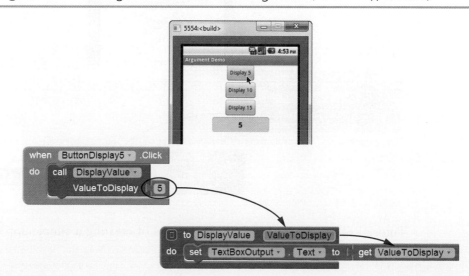

Figure 6-30 Passing the Number 10 as an Argument (*Source:* MIT App Inventor 2)

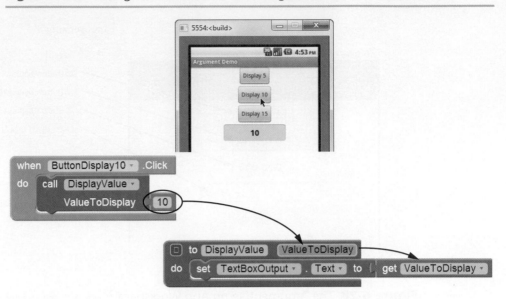

If the user clicks the *Display 15* button, the ButtonDisplay15.Click event handler executes. The event handler calls the DisplayValue procedure, passing 15 as an argument. Inside the DisplayValue procedure, the ValueToDisplay parameter is set to the value 15. This causes the value 15 to appear in the text box, as shown in Figure 6-31.

Figure 6-31 Passing the Number 15 as an Argument (*Source:* MIT App Inventor 2)

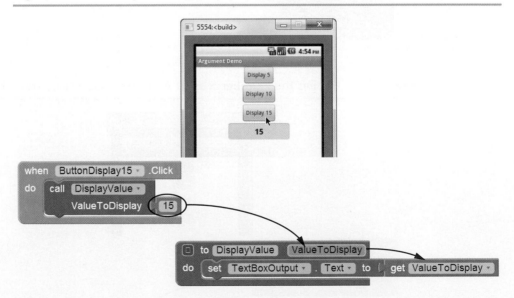

Tutorial 6-2 takes you through the process of creating a simple app that passes an argument to a procedure.

VideoNote
Creating the
AreaCircle App

Tutorial 6-2:
Creating the AreaCircle App

The formula for calculating the area of a circle is:

$$area = Pi \times r^2$$

where *Pi* is the value 3.14 and *r* is the radius of the circle.

In this tutorial you will create an app that lets the user enter a circle's radius, click a button, and see the circle's area. Figure 6-32 shows the app's screen in the Viewer, along with the names of the components. Figure 6-33 shows how the screen appears in the emulator.

Figure 6-32 The AreaCircle App in the Designer (*Source:* MIT App Inventor 2)

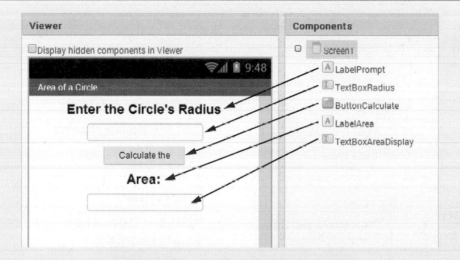

Figure 6-33 The AreaCircle App in the Emulator (*Source:* MIT App Inventor 2)

Step 1: Start a new project named AreaCircle.

Step 2: Set up the app's screen with the components shown in Figure 6-32. Refer to Table 6-2 for the relevant property settings for each component.

Table 6-2 Component property settings (*Source:* Pearson Education, Inc.)

Component	Relevant Property Settings
Screen1	AlignHorizontal = *Center*
	Title = *Area of a Circle*
LabelPrompt	FontBold = *Checked*
	FontSize = *20*
	Text = *Enter the Circle's Radius*
TextBoxRadius	FontBold = *Checked*
	FontSize = *20*
	Hint = *Radius*
	NumbersOnly = *Checked*
	TextAlignment = *Center*
ButtonCalculate	Text = *Calculate the Area*
LabelArea	FontBold = *Checked*
	FontSize = *20*
	Text = *Area:*
TextBoxAreaDisplay	Enabled = *Unchecked*
	FontBold = *Checked*
	FontSize = *20*
	Hint = *Cleared*
	TextAlignment = *Center*

Step 3: Open the Blocks Editor.

Step 4: Now you will create a procedure that accepts the radius of a circle as an argument and uses that argument to calculate the area of the circle. The procedure will display the area in the TextBoxAreaDisplay component.

Create a procedure block named DisplayArea by performing these steps:

- In the Blocks column, open the Procedures drawer and select the to procedure do block. This creates an empty procedure block in the workspace.
- Click the word *procedure* that appears at the top of the procedure block and change it to DisplayArea.

Step 5: Now you will add a parameter variable to the `DisplayArea` procedure block. The parameter will accept the radius of a circle. Perform the following:

- Open the procedure block's mutator bubble by clicking the blue box (▫) that appears in the block's upper-left corner.
- Click and drag the input block (input: X) from the left side of the bubble and insert it on the right side of the bubble as shown in Figure 6-34. This adds a parameter variable named x to the procedure.

Figure 6-34 Adding a Parameter Variable to the `DisplayArea` Procedure
(*Source:* MIT App Inventor 2)

- Change the name of the parameter to r. The `procedure` block should now appear as shown in Figure 6-35.

Figure 6-35 The `DisplayArea` Procedure with its Parameter `r`
(*Source:* MIT App Inventor 2)

Step 6: Complete the `DisplayArea` procedure as shown in Figure 6-36. The blocks calculate the area of the circle, using the parameter r as the radius, and assign the result to the `TextBoxAreaDisplay` component's Text property.

Figure 6-36 The Completed `DisplayArea` Procedure (*Source:* MIT App Inventor 2)

Step 7: Create a `Click` event handler for the `ButtonCalculate` component, as shown in Figure 6-37. The event handler calls the `DisplayArea` procedure, passing `TextBoxRadius.Text` as an argument.

Figure 6-37 The Completed `Click` Event Handler for the `ButtonCalculate` Component (*Source:* MIT App Inventor 2)

Step 8: Test the app in the emulator, or on your device. Enter several values as the radius, such as the ones shown in Figure 6-38, to confirm that the app is working.

Figure 6-38 The App Running in the Emulator (*Source:* MIT App Inventor 2)

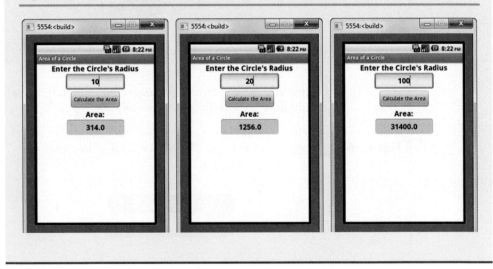

 Checkpoint

6.8 What is an argument?

6.9 What is a parameter variable?

6.10 How do you add a parameter to a procedure block?

6.11 To use a parameter inside a procedure, what type of block do you use? Where do you find this block in the Blocks Editor?

6.12 When you call a procedure that has a parameter, how do you pass an argument?

6.4 Returning Values From Procedures

CONCEPT: A procedure with result (also known as a function) is a procedure that returns a value to the part of the program that called it.

A procedure with result, or function, is like a regular procedure in the following ways:

- It contains a group of statements that perform a specific task.
- When you want to execute the function, you call it.

When a function finishes, however, it returns a value to the part of the program that called it. The value that is returned from a procedure can be used like any other value: it can be assigned to a variable, displayed on the screen, used in a mathematical expression (if it is a number), and so on.

You have already used several functions that are built into App Inventor. For example, the `random integer` function, shown in Figure 6-39, returns a value. To use the value that is returned from the `random integer` function, you plug it into another block. Figure 6-40 shows an example in which the `random integer` function is plugged into a variable's `set` block. As a result, the value that is returned from the `random integer` function is assigned to the variable.

Figure 6-39 The `random integer` Function Returns a Value *(Source:* MIT App Inventor 2*)*

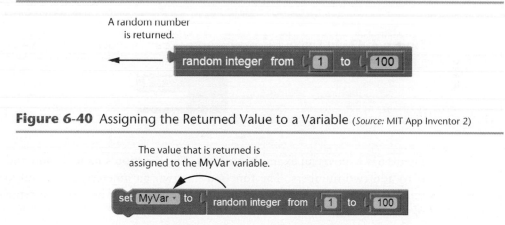

Figure 6-40 Assigning the Returned Value to a Variable *(Source:* MIT App Inventor 2*)*

In App Inventor, you create a function in the same way that you create a regular procedure, with two exceptions:

- You use the `to procedure result` block instead of the `to procedure do` block.
- You must plug a value into the block's `result` socket. This is the value that is returned from the procedure.

The `to procedure result` block is in the *Procedures* drawer, as shown in Figure 6-41. Figure 6-42 shows an empty `to procedure result` block. Notice that the block has a `result` socket. The value that is plugged into the `result` socket is returned from the function.

Figure 6-41 The `to procedure result` Block (*Source:* MIT App Inventor 2)

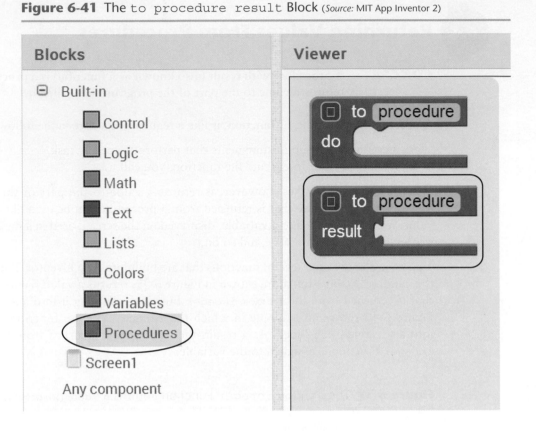

Figure 6-42 An Empty `to procedure result` Block (*Source:* MIT App Inventor 2)

Figure 6-43 shows an example function. The function's name is `Add` and its purpose is to add two numbers. The function has two parameters, `Num1` and `Num2`, so you must pass two arguments when you call the function. The function returns the value of `Num1 + Num2`.

Figure 6-43 An Example Function (*Source:* MIT App Inventor 2)

Of course, the `Add` function shown in Figure 6-43 is for only demonstration purposes. It isn't necessary to write a function for adding numbers, but this serves as a simple example to show you how functions work. Let's look at a complete app that uses the

Add function. Figure 6-44 shows the FunctionDemo app in the Designer. The app lets you enter your age into TextBoxAge1 and your best friend's age into TextBoxAge2. When you click the *Calculate Combined Age* button, the app displays the sum of the two ages in TextBoxCombinedAgeDisplay. Figure 6-45 shows an example of the app running in the emulator.

Figure 6-44 The FunctionDemo App in the Designer (*Source:* MIT App Inventor 2)

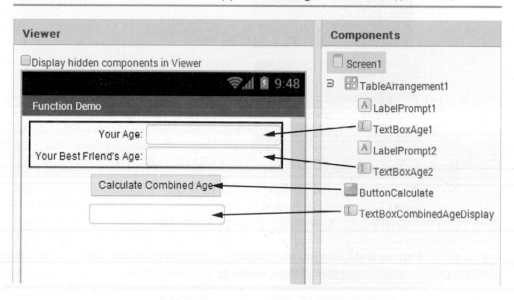

Figure 6-45 The FunctionDemo App Running in the Emulator (*Source:* MIT App Inventor 2)

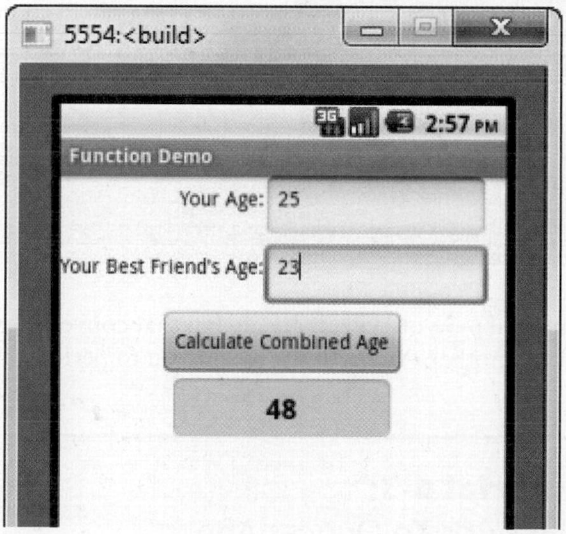

Figure 6-46 shows the app's workspace in the Blocks Editor. At the top of the workspace is the Add function that we previously discussed. Below that is the Click event handler for the `ButtonCalculate` component. In the event handler we set the `TextBoxCombinedAge` component's Text property to the value that is returned from the `Add` function. The arguments that are passed to the `Add` function are the Text properties of the `TextBoxAge1` and `TextBoxAge2` components.

Figure 6-46 The FunctionDemo App's Workspace in the Blocks Editor

(*Source:* MIT App Inventor 2)

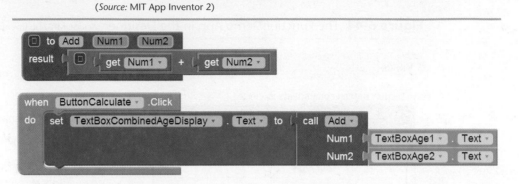

In the example of the app running in the emulator, in Figure 6-45, the user entered the value 25 into `TextBoxAge1.Text` and 23 into `TextBoxAge2.Text`. Figure 6-47 shows how these are passed as arguments to the `Add` function, and how the function returns a value back to the block that called it.

Figure 6-47 Arguments Passed to the `Add` Function and a Value Returned

(*Source:* MIT App Inventor 2)

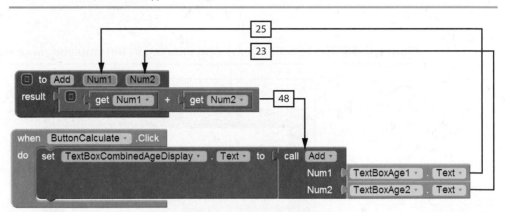

In Tutorial 6-3 you will create an app that converts a value from one unit of measurement to another. You will use a function to perform the conversion.

**VideoNote
Creating the Cups
To Ounces App**

Tutorial 6-3:
The Cups To Ounces App

Cups and fluid ounces are common units of measurement for food items. Sometimes, when a recipe calls for an item measured in cups, you find that in the grocery store the item is sold in fluid ounces. To know how much you need to purchase for the recipe, you need to convert the required number of cups to fluid ounces. The formula is:

$$ounces = cups \times 8$$

In this tutorial you will create the *CupsToOunces* app. Figure 6-48 shows the app in the Designer and Figure 6-49 shows the app running in the emulator. The app lets you enter a number of cups into the TextBoxCups component, click the ButtonConvert button, and see the equivalent number of fluid ounces displayed in the TextBoxOuncesDisplay component.

Figure 6-48 The CupsToOunces App in the Designer *(Source:* MIT App Inventor 2)

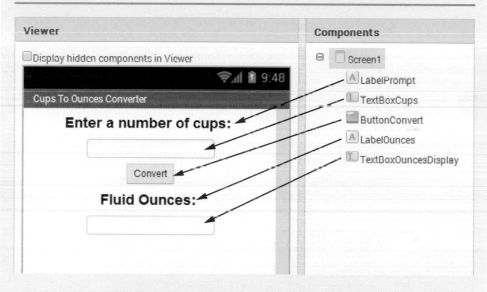

Figure 6-49 The CupsToOunces App in the Emulator *(Source:* MIT App Inventor 2)

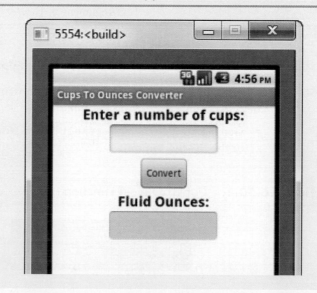

Step 1: Start a new project named CupsToOunces.

Step 2: Set up the app's screen with the components shown in Figure 6-48. Refer to Table 6-3 for the relevant property settings for each component.

Table 6-3 Component property settings (*Source:* Pearson Education, Inc.)

Component	Relevant Property Settings
Screen1	AlignHorizontal = *Center*
	Title = *Cups To Ounces Converter*
LabelPrompt	FontBold = *Checked*
	FontSize = *20*
	Text = *Enter a number of cups:*
TextBoxCups	FontBold = *Checked*
	FontSize = *20*
	Hint = *Cups*
	NumbersOnly = *Checked*
	TextAlignment = *Center*
ButtonConvert	Text = *Convert*
LabelOunces	FontBold = *Checked*
	FontSize = *20*
	Text = *Fluid Ounces:*
TextBoxOuncesDisplay	Enabled = *Unchecked*
	FontBold = *Checked*
	FontSize = *20*
	Hint = *Cleared*
	TextAlignment = *Center*

Step 3: Now you will program the blocks for the app. Open the Blocks Editor.

Step 4: Create the CupsToOunces function as shown in Figure 6-50. Here are detailed steps for creating the function:

- Get the to procedure result block from the *Procedures* drawer in the *Blocks* column.

Figure 6-50 The CupsToOunces Function (*Source:* MIT App Inventor 2)

- Change the name of the procedure to CupsToOunces.
- Open the procedure block's mutator bubble and create a parameter variable named Cups.
- Create the math expression using a multiplication (×) block and plug it into the function's result socket.

Step 5: Create a Click event handler for the ButtonConvert component, as shown in Figure 6-51. In the event handler you set the TextBoxOuncesDisplay component's Text property to the value that is returned from the CupsToOunces function. The TextBoxCups.Text property is passed as an argument to the function.

Figure 6-51 The Completed Click Event Handler for the Buttonconvert Component (*Source:* MIT App Inventor 2)

Step 6: Test the app in the emulator or on your device. Enter several values as the number of cups, such as the ones shown in Figure 6-52, to confirm that the app is working correctly.

Figure 6-52 The App Running in the Emulator (*Source:* MIT App Inventor 2)

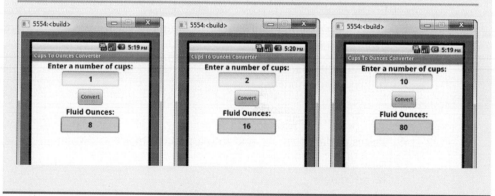

 Checkpoint

6.13 What is the difference between a regular procedure and a function?

6.14 What block do you use to create a function? Where is the block found in the Blocks Editor?

6.15 In a function's block, what is the name of the socket that holds the function's return value?

Review Questions

Multiple Choice

1. In general terms, a program that is broken into smaller units of code, such as procedures, is known as a(n) _____.

   a. object-oriented program
   b. modularized program
   c. procedural program
   d. procedure-driven program

2. Writing the code to perform a task once and then reusing it each time you need to perform the task is a benefit of using procedures called _____.

   a. code reuse
   b. the single use philosophy
   c. procedure recycling
   d. code reprocessing

3. This is another name for a procedure that returns a result.

   a. valuable procedure
   b. function
   c. generator procedure
   d. operator procedure

4. You use this type of block to execute a procedure.

   a. `perform`
   b. `execute`
   c. `invoke`
   d. `call`

5. Programmers commonly use a technique known as _____ to break down program into procedures.

   a. prototyping
   b. procedure modeling
   c. program division
   d. top-down design

6. Pieces of data that are sent into a procedure are known as _____.

   a. arguments
   b. references
   c. procedure variables
   d. data entries

7. A(n) _____ is a special variable that receives an argument when a procedure is called.

   a. reference variable
   b. argument variable
   c. parameter variable
   d. procedure variable

8. You create functions with this type of block.

   a. `to procedure do`
   b. `function`

c. `functionProcedure`

d. `to procedure result`

9. This type of block has a `result` socket.

a. `to procedure do`

b. `function`

c. `functionProcedure`

d. `to procedure result`

Short Answer

1. What do you call a procedure that executes the statements it contains and then returns a value back to the statement that called it?

2. What does a `call` block do?

3. What is another name for the top-down design process?

4. What is the relationship between arguments and parameter variables?

5. How do you create a parameter variable in a procedure?

6. What is the purpose of the `result` socket in a function?

Exercises

1. Modify the AreaCircle app that you created in Tutorial 6-2. Add a procedure that clears the two TextBoxes that appear on the app's screen. Add a Button to the screen that calls the procedure.

2. Create an app that has three Label components. Create two procedures: one that displays your name in all three Labels, and another that clears the contents of all three Labels. Add Buttons to the app's screen that call each procedure.

3. Open the Wages app that you created in Chapter 4's Tutorial 4-3.

4. Create an app that lets the user enter a number of miles and converts the input to kilometers using the following formula:

$$kilometers = miles \times 1.60934$$

The app should have a function that accepts the number of miles as an argument and returns the number of kilometers.

Programming Projects

1. **Retail Price Calculator**

   Create an app that lets the user enter an item's wholesale cost and its markup percentage. It should then display the item's retail price. For example:

   VideoNote
   Creating the Retail Price Calculator App

   - If an item's wholesale cost is 5.00 and its markup percentage is 100 percent, then the item's retail price is 10.00.
   - If an item's wholesale cost is 5.00 and its markup percentage is 50 percent, then the item's retail price is 7.50.

The app should have a function named `CalculateRetail` that receives the wholesale cost and the markup percentage as arguments and returns the retail price of the item.

2. **Falling Distance**

When an object is falling because of gravity, the following formula can be used to determine the distance the object falls in a specific time period:

$$d = 1/2 \, gt^2$$

The variables in the formula are as follows: d is the distance in meters, g is 9.8, and t is the amount of time in seconds that the object has been falling. Create an app that allows the user to enter the amount of time that an object has fallen and then displays the distance that the object fell. The app should have a function named `FallingDistance`. The `FallingDistance` function should accept an object's falling time (in seconds) as an argument. The function should return the distance in meters that the object has fallen during that time interval.

3. **Kinetic Energy**

In physics, an object that is in motion is said to have kinetic energy. The following formula can be used to determine a moving object's kinetic energy:

$$KE = 1/2 \, mv^2$$

In the formula KE is the kinetic energy, m is the object's mass in kilograms, and v is the object's velocity in meters per second. Create an app that allows the user to enter an object's mass and velocity and then displays the object's kinetic energy. The app should have a function named `KineticEnergy` that accepts an object's mass (in kilograms) and velocity (in meters per second) as arguments. The function should return the amount of kinetic energy that the object has.

4. **Calories from Fat and Carbohydrates**

A nutritionist who works for a fitness club helps members by evaluating their diets. As part of her evaluation, she asks members for the number of fat grams and carbohydrate grams that they consumed in a day. Then, she calculates the number of calories that result from the fat, using the following formula:

Calories from Fat = Fat Grams × 9

Next, she calculates the number of calories that result from the carbohydrates, using the following formula:

Calories from Carbs = Carb Grams × 4

Create an app that will make these calculations. In the app, you should have the following functions:

- `FatCalories`—This function should accept a number of fat grams as an argument and return the number of calories from that amount of fat.
- `CarbCalories`—This function should accept a number of carbohydrate grams as an argument and return the number of calories from that amount of carbohydrates.

5. **Present Value**

Suppose you want to deposit a certain amount of money into a savings account, and then leave it alone to draw interest for the next 10 years. At the end of

10 years you would like to have $10,000 in the account. How much do you need to deposit today to make that happen? You can use the following formula, which is known as the present value formula, to find out:

$$P = \frac{F}{(1 + r)^n}$$

The terms in the formula are as follows:

- P is the *present value*, or the amount that you need to deposit today.
- F is the *future value* that you want in the account. (In this case, F is $10,000.)
- r is the *annual interest rate*.
- n is the *number of years* that you plan to let the money sit in the account.

Write a function named `PresentValue` that performs this calculation. The function should accept the future value, annual interest rate, and number of years as arguments. It should return the present value, which is the amount that you need to deposit today. Demonstrate the function in an app that lets the user experiment with different values for the formula's terms.

6. **Rock, Paper, Scissors Game**

Create an app that lets the user play the game of Rock, Paper, Scissors against the Android device or emulator. The app should work as follows.

1. When the app begins, a random number in the range of 1 through 3 is generated. If the number is 1, then the device has chosen rock. If the number is 2, then the device has chosen paper. If the number is 3, then the device has chosen scissors. (Don't display the device's choice yet.)

2. The user selects his or her choice of rock, paper, or scissors. (To get this input you can use Button components displaying some of the artwork that you will find in the book's media files.)

3. The device's choice is displayed.

4. A winner is selected according to the following rules:

- If one player chooses rock and the other player chooses scissors, then rock wins. (The rock smashes the scissors.)
- If one player chooses scissors and the other player chooses paper, then scissors wins. (Scissors cuts paper.)
- If one player chooses paper and the other player chooses rock, then paper wins. (Paper wraps rock.)
- If both players make the same choice, the game must be played again to determine the winner.

Be sure to modularize the app into procedures and functions that perform each major task.

7. **Joe's Automotive**

Joe's Automotive performs the following routine maintenance services:

- Oil change—$25.00
- Lube job—$20.00
- Radiator flush—$30.00

Joe also performs other non-routine services and charges for parts and labor ($30 per hour). Create an app that displays the total for a customer's visit to Joe's. The app's screen should resemble the one shown in Figure 6-53.

Figure 6-53 Joe's Automotive App *(Source:* MIT App Inventor 2)

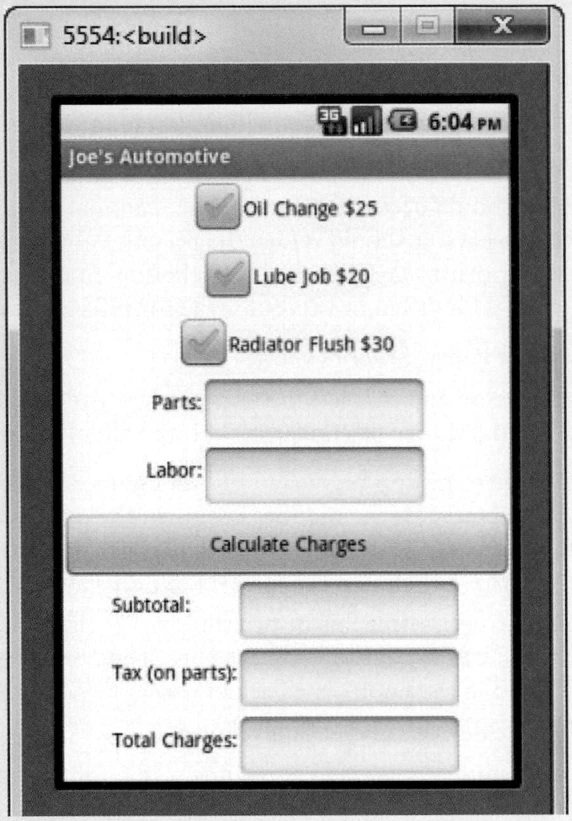

The app should have the following functions:

- `OilLubeCharges`—Returns the total charges for an oil change and/or a lube job and/or a radiator flush.
- `OtherCharges`—Returns the total charges for other services (parts and labor), if any.
- `TaxCharges`—Returns the amount of sales tax, if any. Sales tax is 6% and is only charged on parts. If the customer purchased services only, no sales tax is charged.
- `TotalCharges`—Returns the total charges.

7 Lists

7.1 Creating a List

CONCEPT: A list is a single object that contains multiple items of related data. You can think of a list in App Inventor just as any other list you use in everyday life such as a grocery or to-do list. Another common list we use often on our smartphones is our contact list. We use our contact list for phone calls, emails, text messages, and other interactions.

A *list* is an object that contains multiple data items. To create a list in App Inventor you first need to create a *variable*. Recall that you create variables in the Blocks Editor by choosing the `initialize global name to` block located in the *Variables* drawer. The list variable will hold the list of multiple items. As always, you should give the variable a meaningful name that describes the purpose of the list.

Once you create a variable to store the list, you then need to begin creating the list. To create a list in App Inventor, you need to plug the `make a list` block into the list variable. The `make a list` method is located in the *List* drawer.

Next, you can begin adding items to your list. You can add text, numbers, and Boolean values to your list. You can mix the data types in a list and have some text, some numbers, and so forth. You can also add variable data. To add a text item to your list, you

Figure 7-1 Create a Variable that Holds a List *(Source:* MIT App Inventor 2)

Variable name

will simply drag a text block (from the *Text* drawer), change the value to the data that you wish to add to the list, and plug it in. You will take the same series of steps for the other data types.

Figure 7-2 Add a Text Item to a List *(Source:* MIT App Inventor 2)

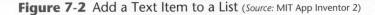

There are two simple steps to make your list visible in App Inventor. You must use a component such as a Label to display your list, and you must have an event that populates that Label once the list is created. The `Screen.Initialize` event will work if you want to show the list when your application loads.

Let's take a look at the app you will develop in Tutorial 7-1. Figure 7-3 shows the app in the Designer. There are two Labels added, one for the title *Contacts* so that it is clear what we are displaying, and then another to hold the list. The `LabelContactList`'s Text property is set to a blank string to start with.

Figure 7-3 Create a List–Design View *(Source:* MIT App Inventor 2)

In Figure 7-4, we have created a list of names using the `make a list` block. We put the names in simple text blocks, plugged those into the `make a list` block, and then stored the entire list in a variable named `ContactList`. Notice the variable is named in such a way that it describes what the list is: a contact list.

We used the `Screen1.Initialize` event to set the `LabelContactList.Text` property to the value of the `ContactList` variable. By using the `Screen.Initialize` event, the Label on the Screen will be populated with the three names as soon as the application loads in the emulator or on your device.

Figure 7-4 Creating a List–Blocks Editor (*Source:* MIT App Inventor 2)

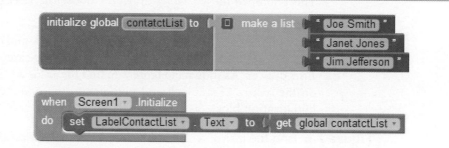

Tutorial 7-1:
Creating a List

VideoNote
Creating a List

Step 1: Create a new project in App Inventor. Drag two Labels from the *User Interface* Palette and place them on the Screen.

Step 2: Rename the Labels. Recall that components should have meaningful names that indicate both the type of component (in this case, Label) and the purpose of the component. Rename the Labels by selecting Label1 in the Components column and click *Rename*. Name it LabelTitle. Then, select Label2 and click *Rename*. Name that one LabelContactList.

Your completed Design Screen should look like Figure 7-3.

Step 3: Open the Blocks Editor

Step 4: Create a variable in the Blocks Editor to hold the list. First, under the *Built-In* category on the left hand side of the screen, click *Variables*.

Figure 7-5 Add a variable Block (*Source:* MIT App Inventor 2)

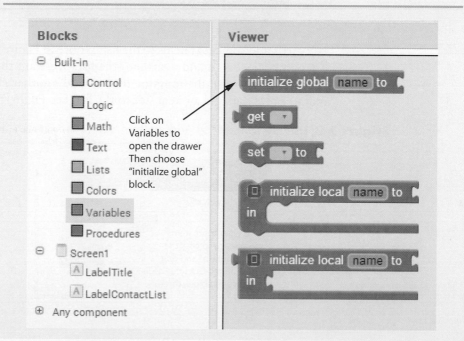

This will open the *Variables* drawer. Choose the `initialize global name to` block to add it to the workspace.

Step 5: Click on the `initialize global name to` block and change its name to `contactList`. Next, click *Lists* under *Built-In* category to open the *Lists* drawer. As shown in Figure 7-6, find the `make a list` block. Click on the `make a list` block and plug it into the `contactList` variable initialization block, as shown in Figure 7-7.

Figure 7-6 Find the `make a list` Block (*Source:* MIT App Inventor 2)

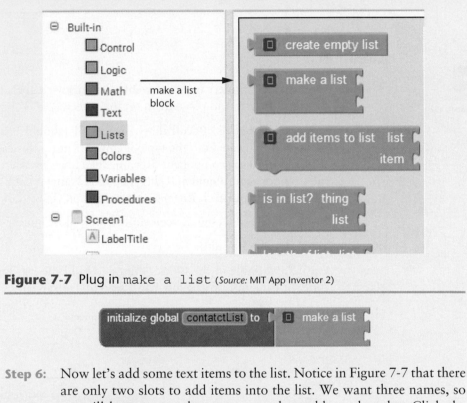

Figure 7-7 Plug in `make a list` (*Source:* MIT App Inventor 2)

Step 6: Now let's add some text items to the list. Notice in Figure 7-7 that there are only two slots to add items into the list. We want three names, so we will have to use the mutator tool to add another slot. Click the mutator tool and add an item slot to the list. See Figure 7-8.

Figure 7-8 Use the Mutator to Add an Item Slot (*Source:* MIT App Inventor 2)

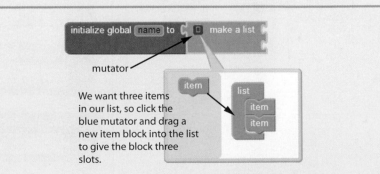

As shown in Figure 7-9, in the *Built-In* category, click *Text*. Choose the text block.

Click the text block three times so that we can add three names to our list.

Figure 7-9 Add Text Items to the List *(Source:* MIT App Inventor 2)

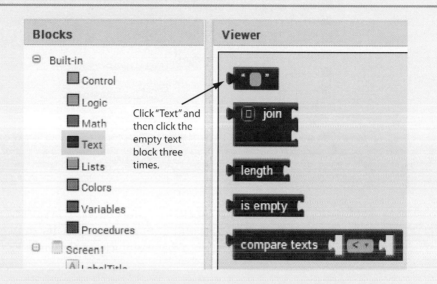

Step 7: Now change the values of the text blocks to three names you'd like on your contact list. For now, we will put both first and last name in each block. When you are finished with your names, plug them into the list as shown in Figure 7-10.

Figure 7-10 Create Your List *(Source:* MIT App Inventor 2)

Step 8: We have a list! However, if you were to test the app now, you would not see anything on your device or emulator. We need to display the contents of the list in a component, such as a Label. That's why you created the `LabelContactList` component. To display the list contents in the Label, we need to assign the List to the Label's Text property.

We also need an event. Without an event, the app does not know *when* to set the Text property with the contents. For our example, we will use the `Screen1.Initialize` event. This event fires when you start the app, and its purpose is to load the screen. Click `Screen1` to open its drawer. Look for the `Screen1.Initalize` event and then click it to add it to your blocks editor. See Figure 7-11.

Figure 7-11 Open the `Screen1` Component's Drawer *(Source:* MIT App Inventor 2)

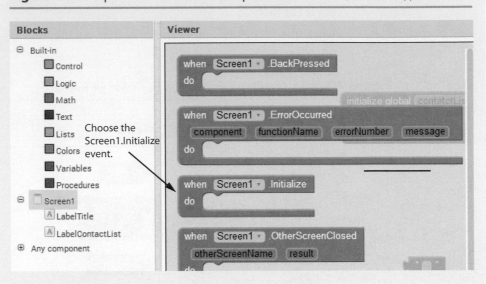

Next, find the block for your `LabelContactList`'s Text property. Click `LabelcontactList` to open its drawer. Find the set `LabelContactList.Text` to block, as shown in Figure 7-12.

Figure 7-12 Find `Set LabelContactList.Text to` *(Source:* MIT App Inventor 2)

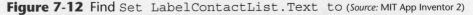

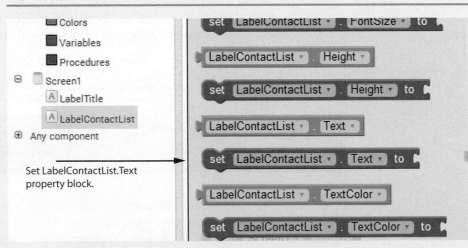

Next, plug that block into the `Screen1.Initialize` event block.

Step 9:   The last step in this tutorial is to plug in the value of the `contactList` (this is the list with the three names) into the set `LabelContactList.Text` to block. To do this, we need to hover over the name `contactList` in the `initialize global contactList` to block. Once you hover over the name, choose the `get global contactsList` block. That block holds the value, or contents, of the list. See Figure 7-13.

Figure 7-13 Find the `get global contactsList` Block (*Source:* MIT App Inventor 2)

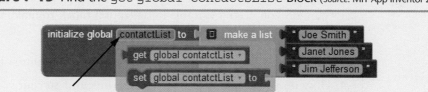

Hover over contactList, then choose the "get global contact list" block.

Plug that into the `set LabelContactList to` block, as shown in Figure 7-14.

Figure 7-14 Complete `set LabelContactList.Text to` Block
(*Source:* MIT App Inventor 2)

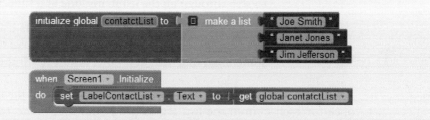

Step 10: Now it's time to run and test your app on your device or emulator. Your output will look something like Figure 7-15.

Figure 7-15 Display Your List (*Source:* MIT App Inventor 2)

Contacts:
(Joe Smith Janet Jones Jim Jefferson)

Notice while our list displays, it doesn't look exactly like we expect it to. This is because App Inventor, by default, displays list items horizontally, from left to right, enclosed in a set of parentheses. We will address this issue in the next section and show how we can display it in a sequential vertical list by iterating through the list.

Checkpoint

7.1 Why do you need a variable initialization block to make a list?

7.2 What kinds of data can you add to a list?

7.3 Can you have a list that has both number items and text items?

7.4 How do you display a list on the App Inventor screen?

7.2 Iterating Over a List with the `for each` Loop

CONCEPT: Iteration means to repeat the same process over and over until you reach the result you are looking for. To iterate a list generally means to step through all the list items, one at a time, until you reach the end.

In this section, we will iterate through lists using the `for each` loop. You can think of it this way: For each item in my list, I am going to do something, one item at a time, until I reach the last item.

The `for each` loop is designed to work with a list. When the loop executes, it iterates once for each item in the list. Figure 7-16 shows how the `for each` block appears when you create it in the Blocks Editor.

Figure 7-16 The `for each` Loop *(Source: MIT App Inventor 2)*

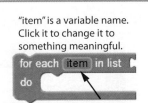

Notice that the `for each` block has a variable named `item` after the words "for each." This is a variable that represents each individual item in your list as you iterate through it. For example, if the list you are looping through is a list of contacts, you might rename this variable `contact` rather than `item`. Then you can use that variable inside the loop to process the current contact in your list. The slot at the top right requires a variable that holds a list.

The `for each` loop executes in the following manner: The `item` variable is assigned the first value in the list, and then the blocks that appear inside the `for each` block are executed. Then, the `item` variable is assigned the next value in the list, and the blocks that appear inside the `for each` block are executed again. This continues until the `item` variable has been assigned the last value in the list.

Of course, as previously mentioned, it is a good idea to change the name of the `item` variable to something that better describes the values that it will hold.

Test Scores Example

Before we begin to modify our Contact List app, let's take a look at another example and examine the anatomy of the `for each` loop.

In the Test Scores example, a list of a class's test scores is created and stored to a variable named TestScores. We will use a `for each` loop to iterate through the list and accumulate the sum of the scores. After the sum is calculated, we will divide that number by the number of items in the list to determine the class average. Last, we will populate the label on the design screen with the average so that it will display on the app.

Consider the design in Figure 7-17. Notice two labels: one to prompt the user and one to show the average of the class test scores.

Figure 7-17 Test Scores App Design (*Source:* MIT App Inventor 2)

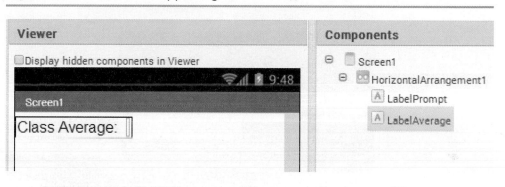

Next, consider the code shown in the blocks in Figure 7-18.

Figure 7-18 Test Scores Code in the Blocks Editor (*Source:* MIT App Inventor 2)

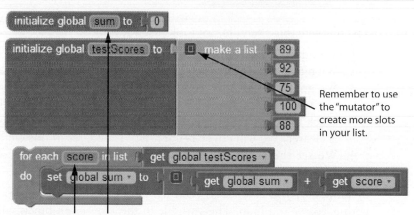

In Figure 7-18, notice the following:

1. We create a variable named testScores to hold the list.
2. We make the list and populate the scores with number blocks rather than text blocks.
3. We create a variable named sum to hold the sum of numbers.
4. As previously mentioned, the `for each` block has an `item` variable and also requires a block, which is a variable that holds a list, to be plugged into it. The variable that is renamed score will hold a value from the list as the loop iterates. By default, App Inventor names that block `item`, but we have changed its name to `score`, which is a much more descriptive name. In this example, in the first iteration **score** = 89, in the second iteration **score** = 92, and so forth.
5. The block get global testScores represents the list that holds the scores, and its "get" block is plugged into the `for each` block.

After the for each iterates through the list, the sum variable will equal all the test scores added together. This is a good start, but we are still missing a few things.

First we need to keep track of how many scores we have, and then of course we need to attach the for each loop to an event to make it run. Last, we will need to divide the sum by the number of tests and place that back into the Text property of the Label. Take a look at Figure 7-19.

Figure 7-19 Calculating the Average (*Source:* MIT App Inventor 2)

To complete this example, we took just a few more steps:

1. We added a variable named count, for the count.
2. We plugged the for each loop into the Screen1.Initialize event.
3. We added a statement to count by one in each iteration and assign the result to the count variable. (Note: we could have simply used the length of list block to determine the number of tests, but using a count variable at this point is clearer. We will cover length of list later in this chapter.)
4. We set the result of the sum variable divided by the count variable to the LabelAverage.Text property.

In summary, you can access each list item individually by iterating through the list with a for each loop. The variable in the for each block will hold an individual list item's value, and this variable will change with each iteration (to match the item in the list). The block plugged into the for each loop is the name of the variable that holds the list. This tells the for each loop which list it is going to iterate through.

Contact List Example

Let's go back to our contact list. In order to view the list vertically, with one name per line, we need to step through the list and treat each item in the list individually. Again, the way to do this is to *iterate or step through the list, one item at a time.*

We are going to print out each list item's value (i.e., the name) with the *return character* \n, one at a time, so that there will be only one name on each line. The *return character* \n (also known as the *new line escape sequence*) used in a program is the same as typing the Enter or Return key for the carriage return on your keyboard. It will advance you to the next line on your screen.

We will need to make the changes in the Blocks Editor, as shown in Figure 7-20.

Figure 7-20 Adding the Carriage Return (*Source:* MIT App Inventor 2)

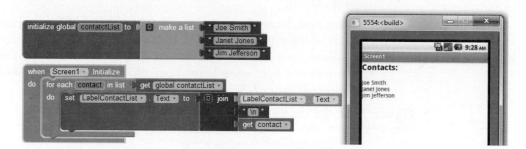

In Figure 7-20, you will see that we iterate through our list one item at a time and use the `join` block to add the item plus the return character \n to the Label's Text property. Because we are not outputting the entire list all at once, we will not see the items enclosed in parentheses as before.

VideoNote
Iterating Over a
List with the for
each Loop

Tutorial 7-2:
Iterating Over a List with the `for each` Loop

In this tutorial, we will iterate through our contact list and display each name one by one so that our list is displayed vertically.

Step 1:   Slide the block `set LabelContactList.Text` to out of the `Screen1.Initialize` event. Click *Control* to open its drawer. Select the `for each` loop block, as shown in Figure 7-21.

Figure 7-21 The `for each` Loop Block (*Source:* MIT App Inventor 2)

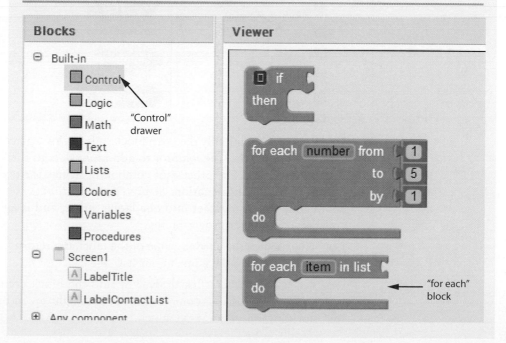

Step 2:   Now notice the variable `item` in the `for each` block. Change this to `contact` or something that is meaningful to represent each item in your list.

Next, find the `get global contactList` block, which represents the value of your list. Remember: hover over the word `contactList` in its declaration block to find its "get" block. Plug that into the bottom block of the `for each` loop. Your Blocks Editor screen should look similar to Figure 7-22.

Figure 7-22 Set Up the `for each` Block (*Source:* MIT App Inventor 2)

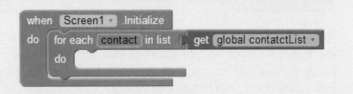

Step 3:   We now have to do a bit of formatting on our text output, using the `join` block and the return key using `\n` to advance to the next line of our label.

To find the `join` block, click *Text* to open the drawer. Click the `join` block in it to place it in your Blocks Editor. See Figure 7-23.

Figure 7-23 Find the `join` Block (*Source:* MIT App Inventor 2)

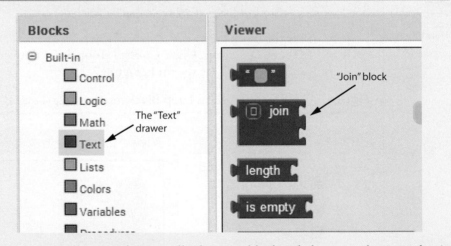

You'll notice that initially the `join` block only has two places to plug in a value. You will use the *mutator* to add more slots to the list, like we did in Figure 7-8. The process of combining strings (or text) together is called string concatenation. *String concatenation* is the process of combining strings together into one larger string, and is an important concept in computer programming.

Let's concatenate the current value of the label, the return key `\n`, and the current value of the name in our list.

Open the *LabelContactList* drawer to find the block containing the value of the label, `LabelContactList.Text` (light green block). Plug this block into the `make text` block.

1. Open the *Text* drawer and choose a text block. Double-click on the empty center of the block and change its value to \n by typing over it.
2. Hover over the loop variable `contact` (see Figure 7-22) and select the `get contact` block. Plug that block into the third slot of the `join` block. See Figure 7-24.

Figure 7-24 Formatting the List Elements *(Source:* MIT App Inventor 2)

Hover over "contact" to find the "get contact" block.

Step 4:   Test your app on the emulator or device and notice the new result:

Figure 7-25 A Better Looking List *(Source:* MIT App Inventor 2)

Checkpoint

7.5 What is the significance of the variable block plugged into the top of the `for each` block? What does this variable represent with each iteration of the `for each` loop?

7.6 How does the `for each` iteration help us display a list in App Inventor?

7.7 Consider our Test Scores example: what would be the impact if both text and number data were in the list?

7.8 What sequence of characters are used as the return character? What kind of block (data type) do you use to hold this sequence?

7.3 Selecting an Item

CONCEPT: If you would like to choose a particular item in the list to work with, you can use the `select list item` block. List items each have an **index**, or place in the list. The first item is at index 1, the second is index 2, and so forth. Once you know the index of the item you wish to select, you can extract the item easily using the `select list item` block.

Figure 7-26 `select list item` **Block** (*Source:* MIT App Inventor 2)

Being able to select an item from a list is essential so that we can interact with or use the information of an individual item in the list. For example, if we want to call or text a person in our contact list, we must first select that individual and then place the call or send a message.

In order to select an item from the list, we must know its index. Later we will learn about searching lists, but for now we need to assume that we will know the index of the item to select.

We must be careful not to try and select an index that is not in the range of the list. For example, if you only have 10 items in a list and you try to select the item at position 11, your app will crash. To avoid this, we can use the list's `length of list` function to determine how many items are in the list and then use if/then logic to stop the attempt if it is out of range.

To demonstrate this concept, we are going to modify the Contact List app in the following ways:

1. We will add a number to the left of each name to show the index or place in the list.
2. We will add a Label and TextBox for the user to select a contact by entering the index of the person they would like to select.
3. We will add a Button to the design and create an event handler to do the selection.
4. We will display back to the user the contact they selected.
5. We will add logic to check the length of the list before trying to select an item so that we can avoid a crash if the selection is out of range.

VideoNote
Selecting an Item
in a List

Tutorial 7-3
Selecting an Item in a List

Step 1: First we need to display the index of each item in the list so that the user knows the index of the contact that they want to select. So, we'll modify the program output to show the number and then the name. For example:

1. Jim Jefferson
2. Janet Jones
3. Joe Smith

To do this, we will need a variable for the index to display. In the Blocks Editor, go to the *Variables* drawer and click on a variable initialization block. Rename it `contactNum`. Set the initial value of the variable to 1, as shown in Figure 7-27.

Figure 7-27 `contactNum` **Variable** (*Source:* MIT App Inventor 2)

initialize global `contactNum` to 1

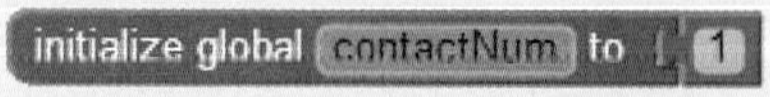

Step 2: Now we will modify the `LabelContactList` output so the index number, followed by a period and a space, appears before the name, as described in Step 1. In the `Screen1.Initialize` event handler, modify the `join` block as shown in Figure 7-28.

You will need to use the `join` block's mutator tool to add two more slots to the block. (It may be easiest to unplug all of the existing items from the `join` block, and then add them back one by one.)

To find the `get global contactNum` block, hover over the variable name `contactNum` in the variable initialization block shown in Figure 7-27.

To make the period, go to the *Text* drawer and click on a regular text block. Double-click in the middle and then type a period *and a space*.

Figure 7-28 Add Item Number to List (*Source:* MIT App Inventor 2)

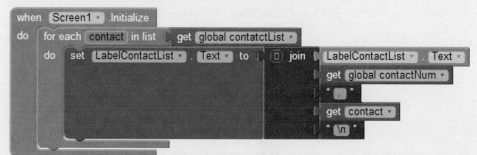

If you test your app now, you'll see that the number before each name is the number one. To fix this, we need to *increment* the `contactNum` variable with each loop iteration.

To increment means to add to a number (or up its value), generally by one. To change the `contactNum` to match the actual index of the list item, we need to add one to the previous value of `contactNum` after each time a name is displayed.

To do this, create the block shown in Figure 7-29, which adds one to the value of `contactNum`, and then stores that result back to the `contactNum` variable, as shown in Figure 7-29.

Figure 7-29 Increment the Contact Number (*Source:* MIT App Inventor 2)

set global contactNum to get global contactNum + 1

Next, place this block after each display of the name and before the end of the `for each` block, as shown in Figure 7-30.

Figure 7-30 Format Output (*Source:* MIT App Inventor 2)

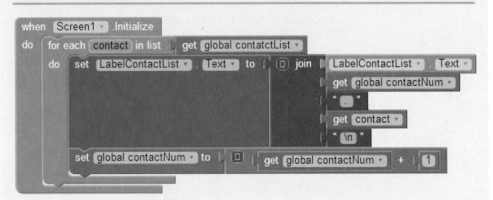

Now, test and run your app to ensure that your numbers and contacts display correctly as in Figure 7-31.

Figure 7-31 A Numbered List (*Source:* MIT App Inventor 2)

5554:<build>

8:54 AM

Screen

Contacts:
1. Joe Smith
2. Janet Jones
3. Jim Jefferson

Step 3: Now let's give the user the ability to pick one of these contacts by entering the associated index.

We will need to go to the Designer and add several components to make this possible. See Figure 7-32.

1. Add a HorizontalArrangement component to your design and populate it with a Label and a TextBox. Rename the Label component to `LabelSelectIndex` and the TextBox to `TextBoxIndex`. Change the Label's Text property to *Enter Contact Number:*. Clear the TextBox's Text property and change the Hint to *Enter number*.
2. Under the `HorizontalArrangement1` component, add a Button and change the name of the Button to `ButtonSelect`. Change the Button's Text property to *Select*.
3. Add another HorizontalArrangement below the Button and add two Labels to it. Rename the Labels to `LabelPrompt` and `Label Selection`. Change `LabelPrompt`'s Text property to *You Selected:* and clear the Text property of the second label.

Compare your design with Figure 7-32.

Figure 7-32 Select Contact Design Screen (*Source:* MIT App Inventor 2)

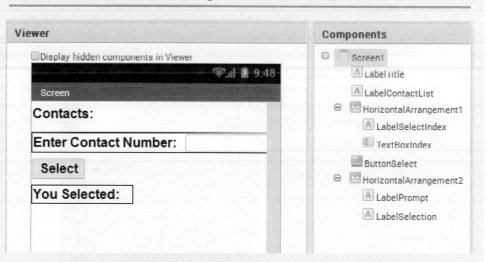

Step 4: Now we can put in the code to select the item. Go back to the Blocks Editor, open the *ButtonSelect* drawer, then click the `when ButtonSelect.Click do` block.

Step 5: Find the `set LabelSelection.Text to` block in the *LabelSelection* drawer, and insert that into the button click event from Step 4.

Step 6: Find the `select list item` block in the *List* drawer and plug that into the block from Step 5.

Step 7: Plug the required elements—the `get global contactList` and the `TextBoxIndex.Text` blocks—into the `select list item` block.

The `get global contactList` is found by hovering over the name `contactList` in the `initialize global contactList` block, and the `TextBoxIndex.Text` is in the *TextBoxIndex* drawer.

(`TextBoxIndex.Text` represents the value that the user types into the user interface.)

Check your work to make sure the Button's `Click` event block looks similar to Figure 7-33.

Figure 7-33 `ButtonSelect.Click` Event (*Source:* MIT App Inventor 2)

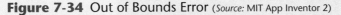

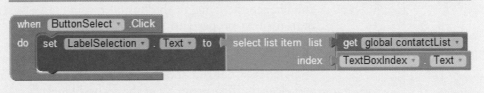

Step 8: Run and test your app in the emulator or on your device. Enter a number between one and three and see how the correct item is displayed.

Step 9: Now run your app and enter a number that is over 3. Note the error that is displayed. See Figure 7-34. How can you use decision logic to avoid this error? We will consider that next.

Figure 7-34 Out of Bounds Error (*Source:* MIT App Inventor 2)

The `length of list` Function

Being able to determine the length of a list before processing begins can be helpful in many ways. For example, if you think about the Test Scores example in section 7.2, rather than accumulating the number of test scores we iterated through, we could have just used the `length of list` function. Also, as you are about to see, we often use the `length of list` function to avoid common errors that try to access an item in a list that does not exist.

Tutorial 7-4:
Using the `length of list` Function

This tutorial is a continuation of Tutorial 7-3. We begin by adding the logic to first ensure that the value typed in by the user is in fact a number. We will use the `is a number` block that you will find in the *Math* drawer. Then we will make sure that if it is a number, the number is not too large for the list. If there are errors, we will prompt the user to enter the correct input. Figure 7-35 shows how the `ButtonSelect.Click` event handler should appear when you are finished with this tutorial.

Figure 7-35 Validate with `is a number` and `length of list`
 (*Source:* MIT App Inventor 2)

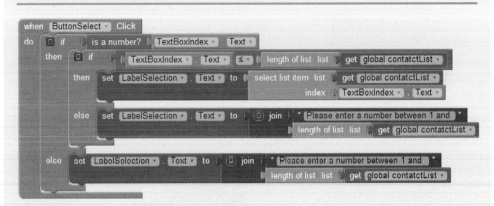

Step 1:   Go to the *Control* drawer and pull out two `if then` blocks. See Figure 7-36.

Figure 7-36 Find the `if then` Blocks (*Source:* MIT App Inventor 2)

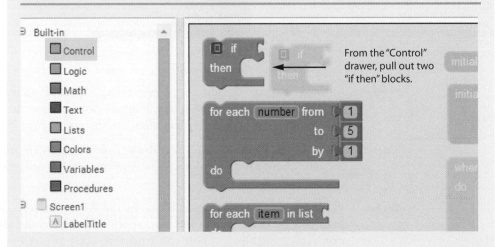

Step 2:   Use the mutator tool to change the blocks to `if then else` blocks. See Figure 7-37.

Figure 7-37 Change the Blocks to `if then else` (*Source:* MIT App Inventor 2)

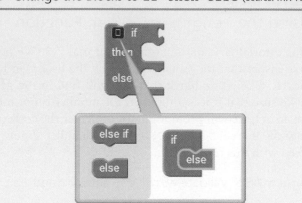

Step 3: Place one inside the other's `then` socket. Then, place this nested `if then else` block in the `ButtonSelect.Click` event handler, as shown in Figure 7-38.

Figure 7-38 Nested `if then else` Statement (*Source:* MIT App Inventor 2)

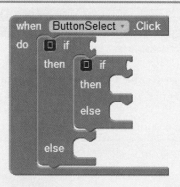

Step 4: In the *Math* drawer, find the `is a number?` block. Plug it into the test socket of the outer `if else` block. Plug the value of the `TextBoxIndex.Text` into the `is a number` function as shown in Figure 7-40.

Step 5: Find the `join` block in the *Text* drawer. Pull out an empty text block as well. Change the text block to prompt the error message *Please enter a number between 1 and*.

Step 6: Find the `length of list` block in the *Lists* drawer, as shown in Figure 7-39. Place that in the workspace and plug in the `get global contactList` block. (You can find the `get global contactList` block by hovering the mouse cursor over the word `contactList` in the variable's initialization block.)

Figure 7-39 Find the `length of list` Block (*Source:* MIT App Inventor 2)

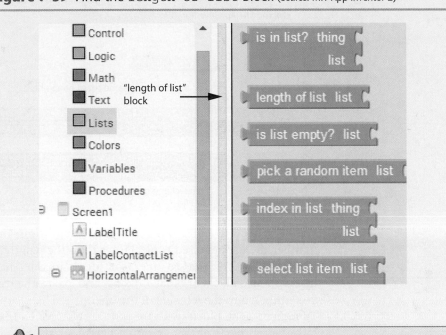

TIP: If there is a block or series of blocks in your editor that you need to re-use, you can select the block (which will include any blocks that are plugged into it) and copy and paste them to save time by using right-click->copy (or Ctrl-C) and then right-click->paste (or Ctrl-V).

Compare your work with Figure 7-40.

Figure 7-40 Program the Error Message (*Source:* MIT App Inventor 2)

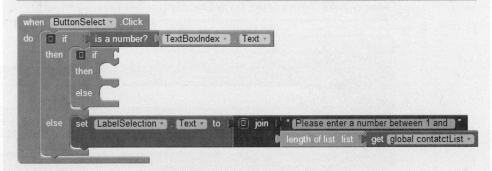

Step 7: Now, select the `set LabelSelection.Text to` block that you see in Figure 7-40 and copy and paste it. Plug the copy into the `else` of the inner `if then`. See Figure 7-41.

Figure 7-41 Program the *Number Out of Range* Error Message
(*Source:* MIT App Inventor 2)

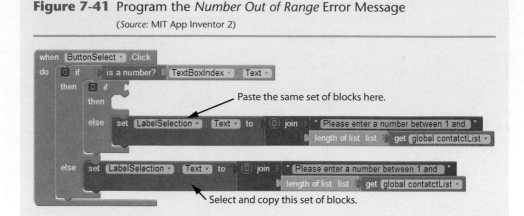

Step 8:   We now need to enter our second test condition, making sure the number the user entered is not larger than the length of the list. Find the less-than-or-equal-to operator block in the *Math* drawer and insert it into the workspace. Copy and paste the `TextBoxIndex.Text` block into the left side of the operator. Then, copy and paste the `length of list` block (with the `get global contactList` argument) into the right side of the operator. The block should appear as shown in Figure 7-42.

Figure 7-42 The Completed Test Condition (*Source:* MIT App Inventor 2)

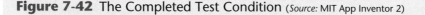

Plug the completed test condition into the test socket of the inner `if then` block, as shown in Figure 7-43.

Figure 7-43 Completed Error Handling (*Source:* MIT App Inventor 2)

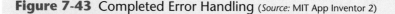

Step 9:   Last, let's plug in the block to execute when the input is valid. Populate the `LabelSelection.Text` with the item selected from the list as in the last tutorial. See Figure 7-44.

Figure 7-44 Complete Button Click Event (*Source:* MIT App Inventor 2)

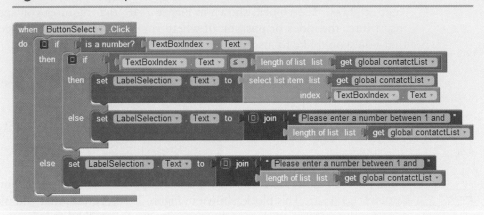

 NOTE: Actually, we are still missing some error handling. What if the user enters a zero or negative number? We'll save that one for our chapter exercises.

Checkpoint

7.9 What happens if we try to select an item in the list that is not there or out of range?

7.10 What is a list index? Why is it important to be sure the variable in the index field of the select list item is a number?

7.11 How can knowing the length of a list help us avoid errors?

7.4 Inserting and Appending Items

CONCEPT: Adding items to a list comes in two different forms. You can add items to the end of the list, and you can add items somewhere in the middle of the list. Adding to the end of a list is called appending. You can append either a single item or an entire list of items. Adding items somewhere in the middle of a list is called inserting.

When we append to a list, we add either a single item or several items to the end of a list. With App Inventor, we can use the add items to list block, as shown in Figure 7-45, to add a single item at a time. This block requires the name of the list that is being added to and the item to add.

Figure 7-45 add items to list Block (*Source:* MIT App Inventor 2)

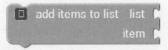

Inserting items into a list means to place new items somewhere specific in the list. For example, you may want to insert an item in position 3. App Inventor has an `insert list item` block, shown in Figure 7-46, that requires you specify the list to insert into, the index or position of where you want to insert, and then the new item that you would like to insert.

Figure 7-46 `insert list item` **Block** (*Source:* MIT App Inventor 2)

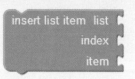

To append an entire list to the end of a list, App Inventor has a function block named `append to list`. This block, shown in Figure 7-47, requires that you plug in two lists. `list1` is the list to append to, and `list2` is the list that will be added to the end of `list1`.

Figure 7-47 `append to list` **Block** (*Source:* MIT App Inventor 2)

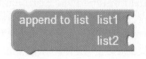

To demonstrate adding items to a list, consider an app that allows the user to enter grocery items to a list. We will provide the user with a TextBox to enter an item and a Button to click to execute the `add items to list` function. See Figure 7-48.

Figure 7-48 Add Item Design Screen (*Source:* MIT App Inventor 2)

Viewer	Components	Properties
☐ Display hidden components in Viewer	⊖ ☐ Screen1	TextBoxItem
📶 9:48	⊖ 🔲 HorizontalArrangement1	BackgroundColor
Screen1	🔲 TextBoxItem	⬛ Default
☐ [Add]	🔲 ButtonAdd	Enabled
	Ⓐ LabelGroceryList	☑
		FontBold
		☐
		FontItalic
		☐
		FontSize
		14.0
		FontTypeface
		default ▼
		Hint
		Enter Item

In Figure 7-48 there is a TextBox for the grocery item, a Button to add an item to the list, and a Label (`LabelGroceryList`) to output the list. For this example, we will simply display the entire list each time the user adds an item. Remember, list contents will be shown enclosed in a set of parentheses.

Now examine the blocks shown in Figure 7-49.

Figure 7-49 Add Item Blocks Editor (*Source:* MIT App Inventor 2)

These are the steps to create the blocks shown in the figure:

1. First, create a global variable, `groceryList`, and plug in the `create empty list` block to define the variable as a list. The `create empty list` block is used when you want to let App Inventor know that the variable will hold a list, but you aren't ready to populate it yet. Since we are going to let the user populate the list, we leave it empty to start.

2. Next, use the `when ButtonAdd.Click do` event handler to call the `add items to list` function. This function will allow you to add one or multiple items, but each item is added individually when this function executes.

3. Plug `get global groceryList` and `TextBoxItem.Text` (this is what the user entered) into the `add items to list` argument slots. This adds the item that the user entered to the `groceryList` list.

4. Clear out the `TextBoxItem.Text` property so the user can add another item if he or she chooses, and then redisplay the `groceryList` that now contains the new item.

Tutorial 7-5:
Add Items to a List

VideoNote
Adding Items to a List

This tutorial will walk us step-by-step through the grocery list example previously described, and it explains how to append items to a list.

Step 1: Design the user interface as shown in Figure 7-50.

1. Add a HorizontalArrangement and put a TextBox and a Button side-by-side.

2. Rename the TextBox to `TextBoxItem` and change the Hint property to *Enter Item*.

3. Rename the Button to `ButtonAdd` and change the Text property to *Add*.

4. Add a Label under the HorizontalArrangement and delete the Text property contents. Rename the Label to `LabelGroceryList`.

5. Compare your design to Figure 7-50.

Figure 7-50 Add Item Design (*Source:* MIT App Inventor 2)

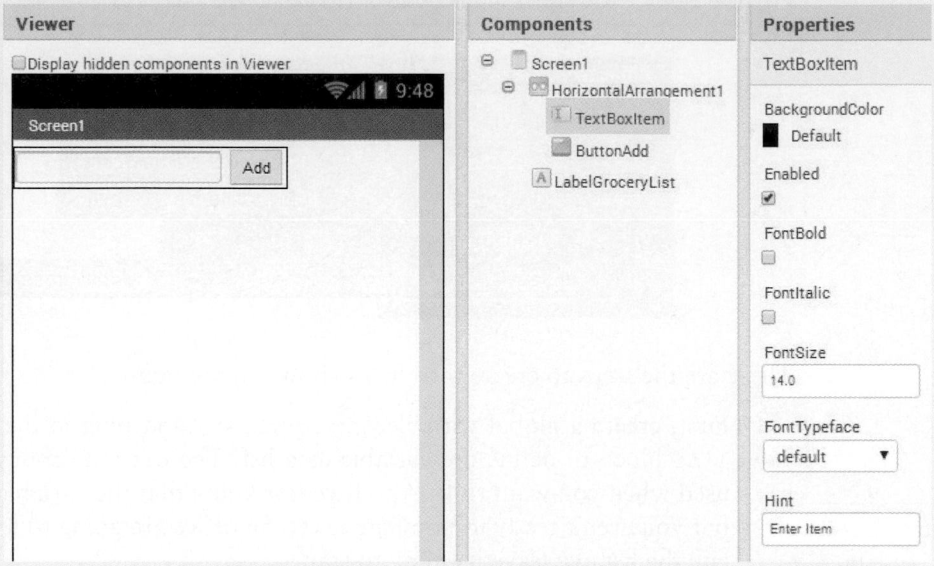

Step 2: Open the Blocks Editor and create the variable to hold the list. Remember, to do this, you click on the *Variables* drawer, then click `initialize global name to`. Once the variable initialization block is in the Blocks Editor, click on the word `name` and change the name to `groceryList`.

Step 3: Once you have a variable to hold your list, find the `create empty list` block by opening the *Lists* drawer. Click on the `create empty list` block and plug it into the `groceryList` variable initialization block.

Compare your workspace to Figure 7-51.

Figure 7-51 Declare and Initialize the `GroceryList` Variable
(*Source:* MIT App Inventor 2)

Step 4: Now program the Button's `Click` event handler. Go to the *ButtonAdd* drawer. Choose the `ButtonAdd.Click` event to place it in the editor.

Step 5: When the user clicks the *Add* button, we want to retrieve the input that was typed into the TextBox and add it to the end of the list. So, we need the `add items to list` block, which is located in the *List* drawer. Plug that into the `when ButtonAdd.Click do` event handler as shown in Figure 7-52.

Figure 7-52 The `add items to list` Block in the `ButtonAdd.Click do` Event
(*Source:* MIT App Inventor 2)

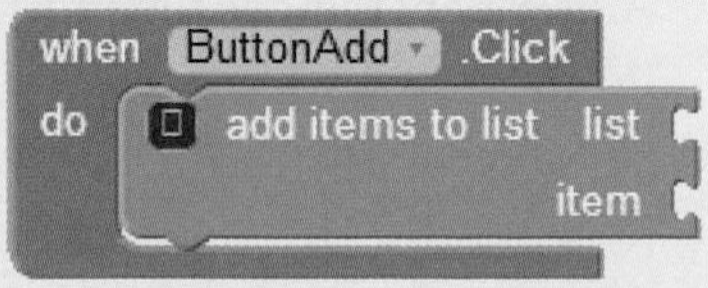

Step 6: Next we want to give the add item to list function the name of the list and the item to add. Find the get global groceryList block (by hovering the mouse cursor over the word groceryList in its initialization block), and plug that into the first argument slot of the add items to list function. Compare your workspace to Figure 7-53.

Figure 7-53 Provide the List Argument (*Source:* MIT App Inventor 2)

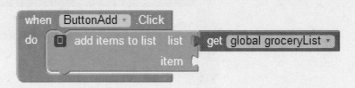

Step 7: Now grab the TextBoxItem.Text block from the *TextBoxItem* drawer. Plug that in as the item to add to the list. Compare your workspace to Figure 7-54.

Figure 7-54 Add Item to List (*Source:* MIT App Inventor 2)

Step 8: We have our item added to the list now, but we need to format the TextBox and display the list. To do this, go to the *TextBoxItem* drawer and select the set TextBoxItem.Text to block to place it in the workspace. Plug it in under the add item to list function. Then, go to the *Text* drawer and click the empty text block. Plug that into the set TextBoxItem.Text to block to clear the TextBox for the user.

Step 9: To display the list, we need to set the label LabelGroceryList to the value of the list (global ContactList block). Go to the *LabelGroceryList* drawer, click the set LabelGroceryList.Text to block, and plug that in under the block in Step 8. Then, plug the get global groceryList block into it.

Compare your Blocks Editor to Figure 7-55.

Figure 7-55 Clear the Textbox and Set Label (*Source:* MIT App Inventor 2)

Step 10: Test your app. Start and/or connect to your device or emulator and add a few items.

Figure 7-56 Run Your App *(Source:* MIT App Inventor 2)

Inserting Items into a List

Inserting an item into a list means to place an item in a specific position in the list. We use the `insert list item` block to accomplish this, and we need to know beforehand the index, or position, of where we want to insert the item.

The item will be inserted at the position we tell it, and the item that was in that place beforehand will move down, as will every item whose index is higher than the insertion point. For example, let's say we have a list with milk, bread, and eggs. Bread is at position two. If we use the `insert list item` block and give it two as the index and *jam* as the item to insert, our list will now be *milk, jam, bread, eggs*. *Jam* took over position two, *bread* is now at position three, and so on.

Appending to a List

Appending to a list is similar to adding items, except that you append an entire list to the end of another list using the `append to list` block.

To demonstrate this, consider an app that has two lists, `List1` and `List2`, and we want to add the entire `List2` to the end of `List1`. Now `List1` will contain the contents of both lists.

Consider the design screen in Figure 7-57.

We will populate two lists in the Blocks Editor. `List1` will contain *milk*, *eggs*, and *butter*. `List2` will contain *apples*, *lemons*, and *oranges*. We will display the contents of those lists on the emulator using the `Screen1.Initialize` event.

Figure 7-57 Append Lists Design (*Source:* MIT App Inventor 2)

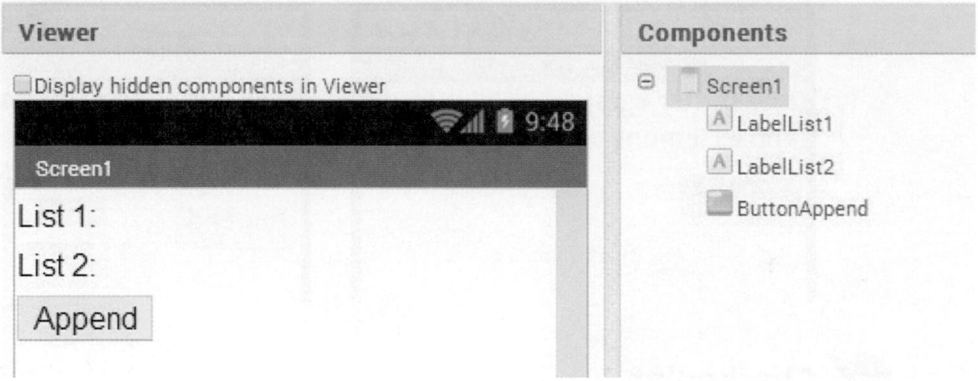

Then we will append List2 to List1 in the ButtonAppend.Click event handler. List1 will be modified and now contain *milk*, *butter*, *eggs*, *apples*, *lemons* and *oranges*. List2 will not change. Figure 7-58 shows the blocks for this example.

To create the blocks shown in Figure 7-58, take the following steps:

1. First, two variables, List1 and List2, are created to hold the lists.
2. The make a list function block is used to create the initial lists: see Figure 7-58.
3. The Screen1.Initialize event is used to display the lists in the Labels when the app loads.
4. The ButtonAppend.Click event is used to append List2 to the end of List1 and then redisplay the modified List1. See the Screen display after the Button is clicked in Figure 7-59.

Figure 7-58 Append List Blocks Editor (*Source:* MIT App Inventor 2)

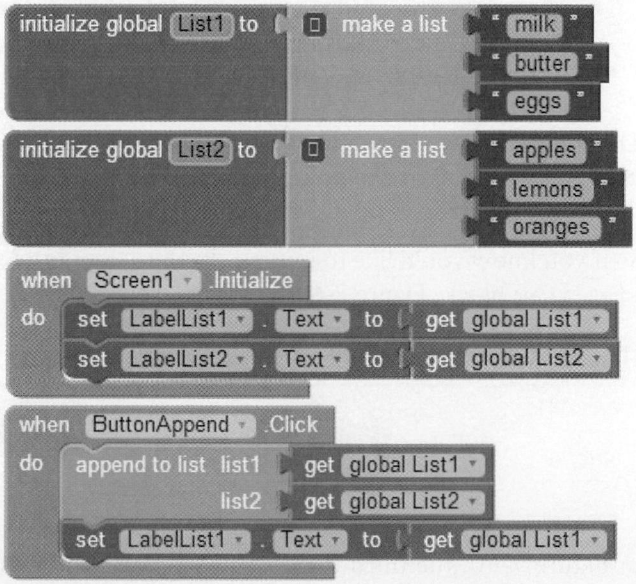

Figure 7-59 Before and After the Append (*Source:* MIT App Inventor 2)

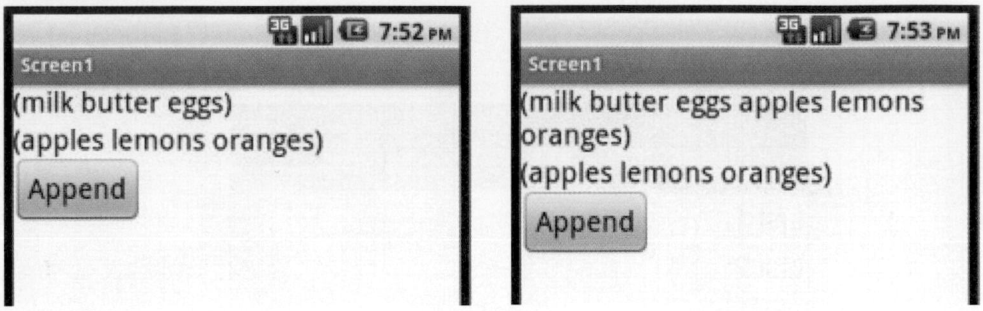

Checkpoint

7.12 What is the difference between adding and inserting items in a list?

7.13 If an item is inserted into a list at position ten, what happens to the item that was in that position before the insert?

7.14 When you append ListA to ListB, what happens to ListA? What happens to ListB?

7.15 If you want to add one item to the end of a list, which block will you use, the add item to list or append item to list?

7.5 Removing Items

CONCEPT: Removing an item from a list is just as it sounds; it is deleting an item from the list. Remember that each item in a list has an index, or a position, in that list. When an item is removed, the indexes are recalculated starting from position one, and each item in the list after the deleted item will have a new index based on the new position.

To remove an item from a list, you simply need to know the position in the list for the item you would like to remove. Remember, the first item in the list is at position one, the next at position two, and so forth.

So if you know you'd like to remove the third item in a list, you would use the remove list item block. Figure 7-60 shows an example.

Figure 7-60 Remove a List Item (*Source:* MIT App Inventor 2)

remove list item list [get global List1 ▾]
index [3]

In Figure 7-60, the third item is removed and the item originally in position four now is in position three.

Let's look at another grocery list example. This time, we will create a list of five items and use the `for each` loop to display the list vertically and with the associated number, which will show the index position (recall section 7.2).

We will add a TextBox so that the user can choose what item to remove, and then we will provide a *Remove* Button. Once the item is removed, we will redisplay the list with the number to show the new index positions. Figure 7-61 shows an example of the app's design.

Figure 7-61 Remove Item Design (*Source:* MIT App Inventor 2)

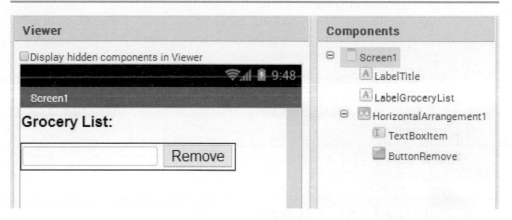

In Figure 7-61 we have a Label, `LabelTitle`, for the "Grocery List:" prompt. The Label, `LabelGroceryList`, is used to display the list. We also have a TextBox and Button so that the user can indicate which item (by the index number) they would like to remove from the list.

The Blocks Editor workspace is shown in Figure 7-62.

Figure 7-62 Remove Item and Display List (*Source:* MIT App Inventor 2)

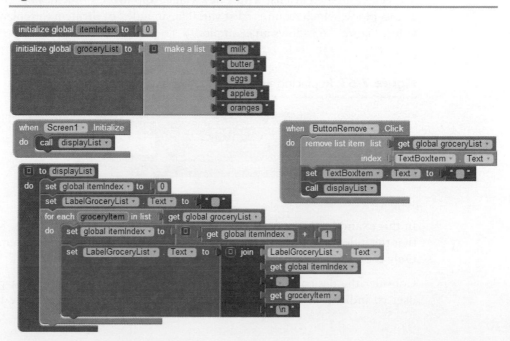

1. Two variables are created: one to store the list (groceryList), and one to store the index, or position (itemIndex).
2. Two events are used: the Screen1.Initialize and the ButtonRemove. Click.
3. Both the initialize and button click events will need to display the list item-by-item, so we will put that code into a procedure that can be called multiple times.
4. The procedure will first clear out the LabelGroceryList component's Text property and set the index to zero.
5. The for each loop iterates through the list, displaying the grocery list index and item one at a time.
6. The ButtonRemove.Click event will remove an item from a list, clear out the input field (TextReplaceItem), and then call the displayList procedure to redisplay the new list.

In the next section, we will demonstrate replacing an item and walk through a tutorial on both removing and replacing.

7.6 Replacing Items

CONCEPT: Replacing an item in a list means to change the value of one item to a new value. The index positions are unchanged and the size of the list is unchanged. Simply, the item which is replaced will be updated with a different value than before.

To replace an item in a list with a new value, App Inventor includes a replace list items block, which requires a list variable, an index of the item to replace, and a new value. Figure 7-63 shows an example.

Figure 7-63 Replacing an Item (*Source:* MIT App Inventor 2)

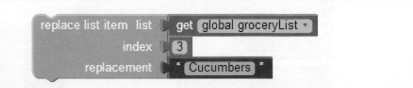

In this example, the item in position 3 will be changed to *Cucumbers*. Keep in mind that the indexes of the list items will not change as they do when you remove an item. Only the value of the item will be changed.

Consider the design in Figure 7-64. In this screen design, we have a place for the user to indicate the index, or position, of the item they would like to replace in

Figure 7-64 Grocery List App Screen Design (*Source:* MIT App Inventor 2)

Viewer	Components
☐ Display hidden components in Viewer	⊟ ☐ Screen1
📶 🔋 9:48	Ⓐ LabelTitle
Screen1	Ⓐ LabelGroceryList
Grocery List:	⊟ 🔲 HorizontalArrangement1
Replace: [ ]	Ⓐ LabelReplacePrompt
With: [ ]	Ⓣ TextBoxReplaceItem
Replace	⊟ 🔲 HorizontalArrangement2
	Ⓐ LabelWithPrompt
	Ⓣ TextBoxNew
	🖼 ButtonReplace

a grocery list, and a TextBox field for the value of the new item. There is also a Button that causes the item to be replaced and then redisplays the list.

Let's take a look the blocks for this example, shown in Figure 7-65.

Figure 7-65 Blocks in the Grocery List App (*Source:* MIT App Inventor 2)

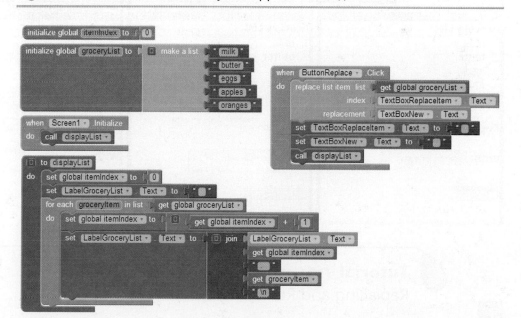

This figure contains essentially the same blocks as section 7.5, Removing Items. The only difference is the `ButtonReplace.Click` event handler shown in Figure 7-66.

Figure 7-66 `ButtonReplace.Click` **Event Handler** (*Source:* MIT App Inventor 2)

```
when  ButtonReplace  .Click
do    replace list item  list      get  global groceryList
                         index      TextBoxReplaceItem  .  Text
                         replacement  TextBoxNew  .  Text
      set  TextBoxReplaceItem  .  Text  to  "  "
      set  TextBoxNew  .  Text  to  "  "
      call  displayList
```

In Figure 7-66 we use the `replace list item` function block and supply it with the `groceryList` for the list, `TextReplaceItem.Text` for the index (this is the number that the user will type in), and the `TextBoxNew.Text` for the replacement. The `TextBoxNew.Text` will hold the value that the user entered for the replacement text.

Just like the Remove Items example in section 7.5, once we replace the item, we should clear out `TextReplaceItem.Text` and `TextBoxNewItem.Text` and then call the procedure to redisplay the list.

Figure 7-67 shows this app as it runs.

Figure 7-67 Replace Item Test (*Source:* MIT App Inventor 2)

Screen1 9:13 PM	Screen1 9:15 PM	Screen1 9:15 PM
Grocery List:	**Grocery List:**	**Grocery List:**
1. milk	1. milk	1. milk
2. butter	2. butter	2. butter
3. eggs	3. eggs	3. green beans
4. apples	4. apples	4. apples
5. oranges	5. oranges	5. oranges
Replace: Item number to replace	**Replace:** 3	**Replace:** Item number to replace
With: Name of new item	**With:** green beans	**With:** Name of new item
Replace	Replace	Replace

Tutorial 7-6:
Replacing and Removing List Items

VideoNote
Repalcing and
Removing List Items

In this tutorial we are going to write an app that will allow a user to remove or replace items in a grocery list. We will set up the list with several items and then give the user the ability to select an item to remove or replace. If the user chooses to replace an item, a TextBox will be available for the new value to be entered.

Step 1: Create the design with the components shown in Figure 7-68.

Figure 7-68 Replace and Remove Design (*Source:* MIT App Inventor 2)

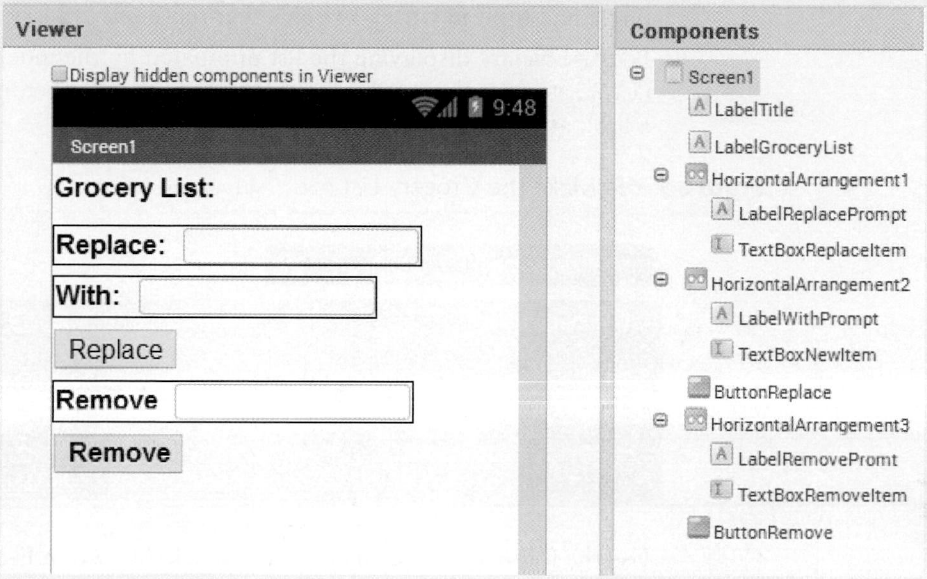

Viewer	Components

Display hidden components in Viewer

📶 🔋 9:48

Screen1

Grocery List:

Replace:

With:

Replace

Remove

Remove

Components:
- ⊖ 🔲 Screen1
  - Ⓐ LabelTitle
  - Ⓐ LabelGroceryList
  - ⊖ 🔘 HorizontalArrangement1
    - Ⓐ LabelReplacePrompt
    - Ⓘ TextBoxReplaceItem
  - ⊖ 🔘 HorizontalArrangement2
    - Ⓐ LabelWithPrompt
    - Ⓘ TextBoxNewItem
  - 🔲 ButtonReplace
  - ⊖ 🔘 HorizontalArrangement3
    - Ⓐ LabelRemovePromt
    - Ⓘ TextBoxRemoveItem
  - 🔲 ButtonRemove

1. Place a Label for the title *Grocery List:*. Change the Label's name to `LabelTitle`, its font size to 20, and its Text property to *Grocery List:*.
2. Place a Label beneath the title to display the grocery list, name it `LabelGroceryList`, change its font size to 20, and clear the Text property contents.
3. Add a HorizontalArrangement component and place a Label and TextBox inside it. Name the Label `LabelReplacePrompt`, change its font size to 20, and its Text property to *Replace*. Name the TextBox `TextBoxReplaceItem`, change its font size to 20, clear its Text property, and change the Hint property to *Item number to replace*.
4. Add another HorizontalArrangement component and place a Label and TextBox inside it. Name the Label `LabelWithPrompt`. Change its font size to 20 and its Text property to *With:*. Name the TextBox `TextBoxNewItem`, change its font size to 20, clear its Text property, and change the Hint property to *Name of new item*.
5. Add a Button, name it `ButtonReplace`, and change its Text property to *Replace*.
6. Add another HorizontalArrangement component and place a Label and TextBox inside it. Name the Label `LabelRemovePrompt`, change its font size to 20, and change its Text property to *Remove*. Name the TextBox `TextBoxRemoveItem`, change its font size to 20, clear its Text property, and change the Hint property to *Item number to remove*.
7. Add a Button, name it `ButtonRemove`, and change its Text property to *Remove*.

Step 2: Recall that we need a variable to hold our list of grocery items. Once our variable is created, we should use the `make a list` function block and fill it in with text items that represent grocery items.

Because we are displaying the list numbered by the index of each item (1., 2., etc.) we also need a variable to hold the number, or index. Take a look at Figure 7-69.

Figure 7-69 Make the Grocery List (*Source:* MIT App Inventor 2)

Use the following steps to create the blocks shown in Figure 7-69:

1. Go to the *Variables* drawer and select an `initialize global name to` block. Do this twice so that you have two in your workspace.
2. Change the name of the first variable to `groceryList` (click on the word *name* and type `groceryList` on top of it).
3. Change the name of the second variable to `itemIndex`.
4. Go to the *Lists* drawer and select the `make a list` block. Plug that into the `initialize global groceryList to` block.
5. Go to the *Text* drawer and select a text block. Repeat or copy and paste the block in the Blocks Editor until you have five text blocks. Change their names to your favorite grocery items. Plug the items into the `make a list` function block.
6. Go to the *Math* drawer, click on the number block, change the value to zero, and plug it into the `itemIndex` variable block to initialize this variable to zero.

Step 3: In this step you will program the `for each` loop shown in Figure 7-70, to iterate and display the list. When you complete this loop, you will

Figure 7-70 Display the Grocery List (*Source:* MIT App Inventor 2)

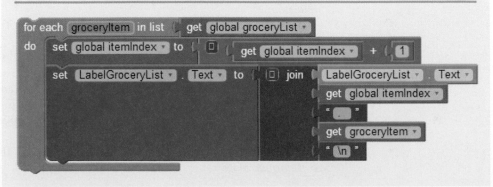

plug it into a procedure block so it is called each time the user updates the grocery list by replacing or removing items.

1. Go to the *Control* drawer and select a `for each item in list` block. Rename the `item` element that is named at the top of the loop to `groceryItem` (double click and type over the word `item`).

2. Hover over the name `groceryList` in the `initialize global groceryList to` block. Once you hover over the name, choose the `get global groceryList` block. That block holds the value, or contents, of the list. Plug it into the slot at the top of the loop.

3. Hover over the name `itemIndex` in the `initialize global item Index to` block. Once you hover over the name, choose the `get global itemIndex` block. Increment it by one by using a Math plus block (+), a Math number block, and the `get global itemIndex` block. Figure 7-71 shows how the block should appear. Plug this block structure into the `for each` loop block.

Figure 7-71 Increment Item (*Source:* MIT App Inventor 2)

set global itemIndex ▾ to | ▢ (get global itemIndex ▾ + | 1)

4. Now, in the *LabelGroceryList* drawer, find the `set Label GroceryList.Text to` block and plug that in the `for each` loop under the `itemIndex` increment block. In the *Text* drawer, select the `join` block and plug in the following: `LabelGroceryList.Text`, `get global itemIndex`, a text block containing a period with a space, a `get groceryItem` block, and a text block containing the carriage return \n. See Figure 7-72.

Figure 7-72 Set Grocery List Label (*Source:* MIT App Inventor 2)

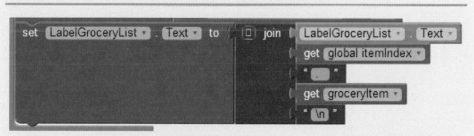

Step 4: Create a procedure called `displayList` to display the items in the list. By creating a procedure, we can call it multiple times after each update.

The first steps in this procedure are to reset the `itemIndex` to 0 and the `LabelGroceryList.Text` to blank so that our list starts from scratch.

Then we will plug in the `for each` loop from Step 3, and that's it!

1. Go to the *Procedures* drawer and select a `to procedure do` block (you do not need a `procedure with result`). Double click on the name *procedure* and rename it to `displayList`.

2. Hover over the name `itemIndex` in the `initialize global itemIndex to` block to get a `set global itemIndex` block.

3. Plug a number block (from the *Math* drawer) set to 0 into the `set global itemIndex` block. Plug that into the procedure. (See the first set of blocks in the `to displayList` procedure in Figure 7-73.)

4. Next, pull out a `set LabelGroceryList.Text to` block from the *LabelGroceryList* drawer and an empty text block from the *Text* drawer. Plug those blocks together, and then plug the resulting block into the procedure. (See the second set of blocks inside the `to displayList` procedure in Figure 7-73.)

5. Now, take the `for each` block from Step 4 and plug it in as shown in Figure 7-73.

Figure 7-73 Create `displayList` Procedure (*Source:* MIT App Inventor 2)

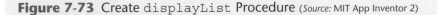

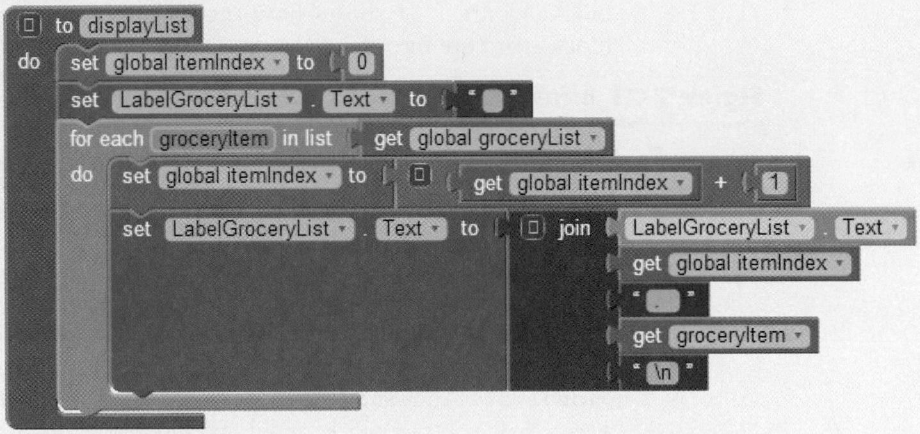

Step 5:   Now you will create the `Screen1.Initialize` event handler. Open the drawer *Screen1* and select the `Screen1.Initialize` block. Next, open the *Procedures* drawer and select the `call displayList` block. Plug the procedure call block into the `Screen1.Initialize` event handler. The Blocks Editor workspace should have the components shown in Figure 7-74.

Run and test your app. As shown in Figure 7-75, it should display the list and show the TextBoxes and Buttons. The Buttons will not work yet; we just want to make sure that the list is showing.

Step 6:   Now let's make the *Replace* Button work by creating the blocks shown in Figure 7-76. You will use the `ButtonReplace.Click` event handler and the `replace list item` block. You will also clear the two TextBoxes (to clear any existing user input) when the *Replace* Button is pressed.

The last block in the `ButtonReplace.Click` event handler will be to call the `displayList` procedure so that the new list with the item removed is displayed.

1. Find the `when ButtonReplace.Click do` event handler in the *ButtonReplace* drawer and place it in the workspace.

Figure 7-74 Call the `displayList` Procedure from the `Screen1.Initialize` Event Handler (*Source:* MIT App Inventor 2)

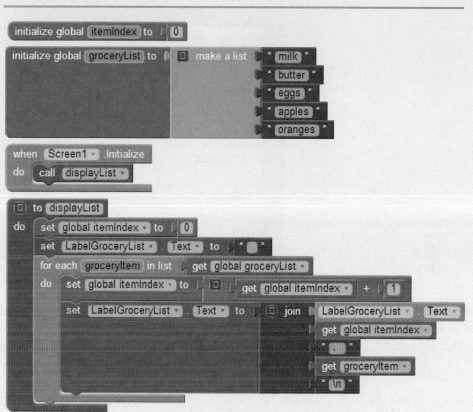

2. Find the `replace list item` block in the *List* drawer; place it inside the `ButtonReplace.Click` event handler.

3. Plug in the `get global groceryList` block found by hovering over `groceryList` in its variable initialization block.

4. Plug the `TextReplaceItem.Text` block into the `index` slot; this is the index that the user typed into the TextBox. It can be found in the *TextBox ReplaceItem* drawer.

5. Plug the `TextBoxNewItem.Text` block into the `replacement` slot. This block is found in the *TextBoxNewItem* drawer.

6. Now find the `set TextReplacementItem.Text to` and the `set TextBoxNewItem.Text to` blocks and place them in the editor. From the *Text* drawer, pull out two empty text blocks. Plug the text blocks into the `set` blocks, and plug those in under the `replace list item` block.

7. Find the `call displayList` block in the *Procedures* drawer and place it as the last item in the `Click` event handler.

Run and test your app. Now you should be able to choose an item by its number and replace it with another item.

Figure 7-75 The First Run (*Source:* MIT App Inventor 2)

Grocery List:
1. milk
2. butter
3. eggs
4. apples
5. oranges

Replace: Item number to replace

With: Name of new item

Replace

Remove Item number to remove

Remove

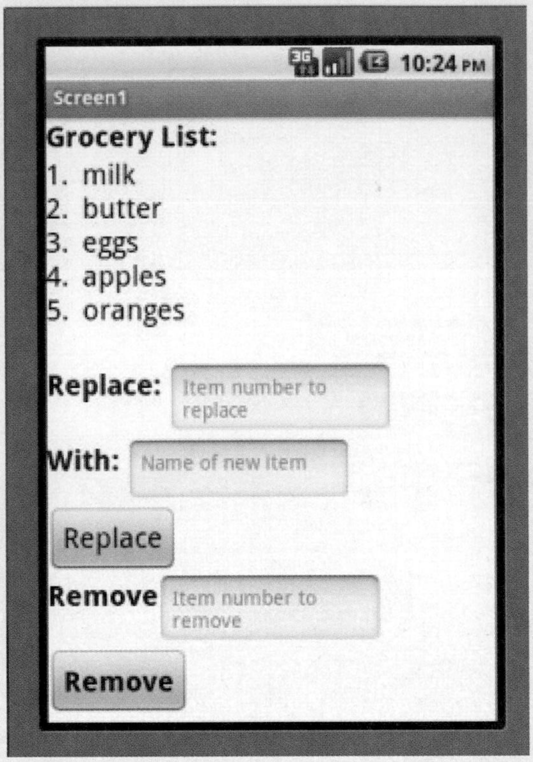

Figure 7-76 `ButtonReplace.Click` Event Handler (*Source:* MIT App Inventor 2)

Step 7: Now you will program the *Remove* Button to remove an item from a list. As with the *Replace* button, you will need to reset the screen elements and call the `displayList` procedure to redisplay the list with the item removed. Figure 7-77 shows the blocks that you will create.

1. Find the `when ButtonRemove.Click do` event handler in the *Button Remove* drawer and place it in the workspace.

2. Find the `remove list item` block in the *List* drawer and place it inside the `ButtonRemove.Click` event handler.

Figure 7-77 Remove Button (*Source:* MIT App Inventor 2)

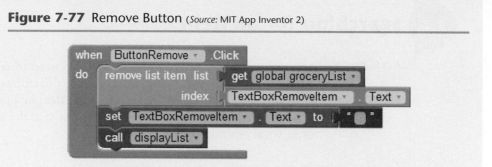

3. Now find the set TextRevmoveItem.Text to and place it in the workspace. From the *Text* drawer, pull out an empty text block. Plug the text block into the set TextRevmoveItem.Text to block and plug those in, under the remove list item block.

4. Find the call displayList block in the *Procedures* drawer and place it as the last item in the ButtonRemove.Click event handler.

Finally, your full workspace for this app should look like that shown in Figure 7-78.

Figure 7-78 Replace and Remove Items Complete Blocks Editor
(*Source:* MIT App Inventor 2)

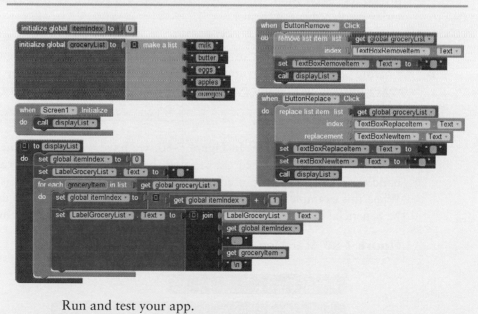

Run and test your app.

 Checkpoint

7.16 What is the difference between inserting and replacing items in a list? What happens to the indexes of the items in a list when we replace an item?

7.17 What happens to the indexes of list items when we remove an item in a list?

7.18 What are the elements that a remove list item block requires? What about the replace list item block? How are they similar and how are they different?

7.7 Searching for an Item

CONCEPT: Often we will encounter large lists and will need to search for a particular item. Remember that items in a list each have an index, or position, in the list. When we search for an item in a list, generally we are interested in two things: Does the item exist in the list? If so, where or in what position is it?

To search a list in App Inventor, we will be interested in two new blocks from the *List* drawer, `is in list?` and `index in list`.

Figure 7-79 Searching Blocks (*Source:* MIT App Inventor 2)

Both of these blocks require that you plug a "thing" in to search for and a list to search in.

The `is in list?` block will return a `true` or `false` value and is often used as an if/then test expression. The `index in list` will return an integer representing the index or placement in the list.

NOTE: It is important to consider checking first to see if the item is in the list before asking for the position. By ensuring that the item is in the list, we avoid unwanted results and/or processing if there is no position for the `index in list` block to return.

Let's look at an example. In Figure 7-80, we have a variable named `position`, a list with a few items named `List1`, and the `when Screen1.Initialize do` event handler. These blocks are used to find the position of *Jam*, which is not in the list. When this example runs, the result is simply 0. It does not cause an error, but it may be beneficial to check whether or not the item exists first, as shown in Figure 7-81.

Figure 7-80 Searching For an Item (*Source:* MIT App Inventor 2)

Figure 7-81 Checking if an Item Exists (*Source:* MIT App Inventor 2)

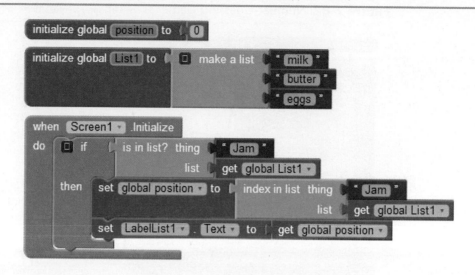

By adding the check `is in list?` before trying to find the position, we avoid any processing time if the value is returned `false` and the item does not exist in the list (recall that if the test condition is `false`, the blcoks in the `then` socket are never cxccutcd).

VideoNote
Creating a Number-Guessing Game

Tutorial 7-7:
Creating a Number-Guessing Game

In this tutorial, we will use a `for range` loop to generate a list of ten numbers with a value between 1 and 25. We will then ask the user to enter a number between 1 and 25 and check to see if the number is in the list. If the number is in the list, we will display *Win!* and display the index of the number (the position in the list). If the number is not in the list, we will display *Try Again*.

Examine the blocks shown in Figure 7-82. In the figure, we have a procedure named `loadlist` that uses a `for each number from` loop to build a list of ten random numbers whose values are between one and twenty-five. We also create a list variable (in this example, `numbersList`) by initializing with a `create empty list` block. Using an empty list block will initialize the variable as a list type, even if there are no items in the list yet.

In the Button's `Click` event handler, we first call the `loadList` procedure to build the list. In case the list was previously loaded, we will set it back to empty before we load it again. Then we use an `if then else` block to check if the item that the user entered is in the list of random numbers using the `is in list?` block. If the item is in the list, we populate a Label with *Win! The position is* and then show the user the position in the list. If the item is not in the list, we display *Try Again* in the Label. Last, we clear the Label so that the user can try again.

Figure 7-82 Number-Guessing Game (*Source:* MIT App Inventor 2)

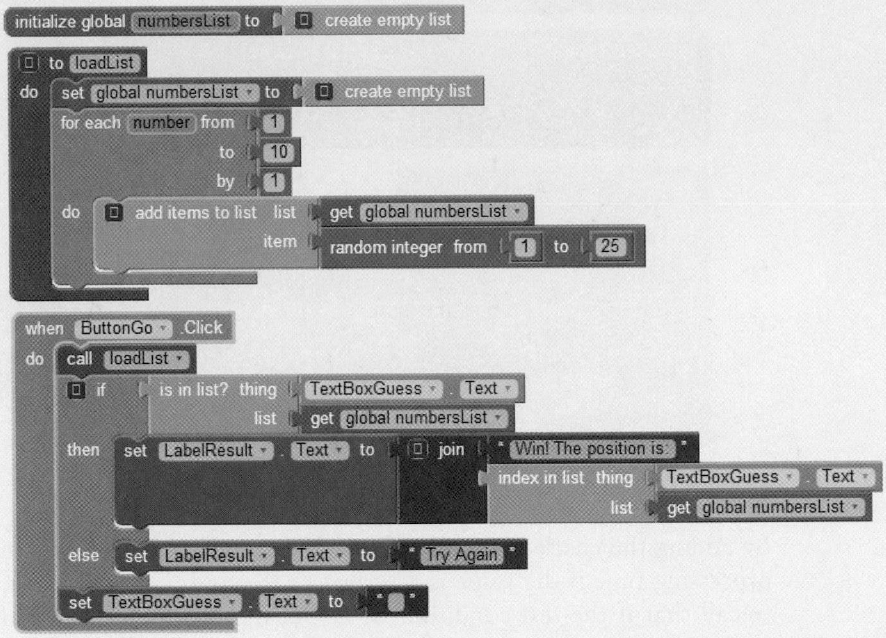

NOTE: The list will be randomly generated with each button click, so the user is guessing against a new list each time.

Step 1: Design the user interface with the following elements: A Label to prompt the user to guess a number between 1 and 25, a HorizontalArrangement with a TextBox and Button, and a Label to show the results. Figure 7-83 shows an example.

Figure 7-83 Guessing Game Design (*Source:* MIT App Inventor 2)

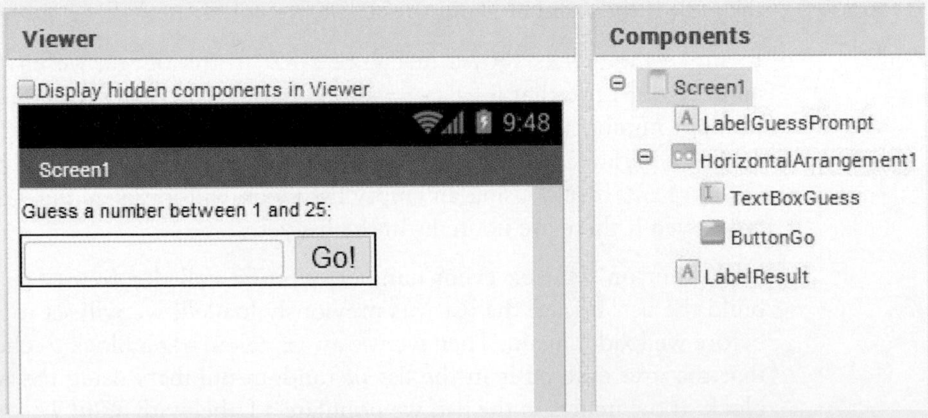

Step 2: In the Blocks Editor, go to the *Variables* drawer to find an `initialize global name to` block. Change the name to `numbersList`, go to *List*, and select a `create empty list` block. Plug that into the `initialize global numbersList to` block. See Figure 7-84.

Figure 7-84 Initialize `numbersList` (*Source:* MIT App Inventor 2)

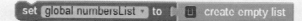

Step 3: Go to *Procedures* to select a `to procedure do` block. Change the name to `loadList`.

Step 4: Hover over the `numbersList` variable declaration block (Figure 7-84) and find the `set global numbersList to` block. Plug a `create empty list` block into it and place it in the `loadList` procedure. We do this so that if the user wants to try again, the list will be emptied out before it is reloaded. See Figure 7-85.

Figure 7-85 Reset `numbersList` (*Source:* MIT App Inventor 2)

set global numbersList ▾ to create empty list

Step 5: Go to the *Control* drawer and add a `for each number from` loop to the procedure. Give it a `from` value of 1, a `to` value of 10, and a `by` value of 1 using *Math* number blocks. See Figure 7-86.

Figure 7-86 `for each number from` Loop (*Source:* MIT App Inventor 2)

for each number from 1
to 10
by 1
do

Compare your blocks editor to Figure 7-87.

Figure 7-87 Guessing Game Blocks Editor (*Source:* MIT App Inventor 2)

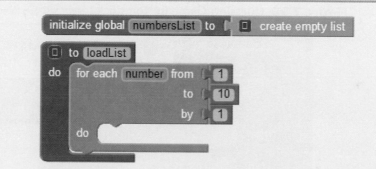

Step 6: Go to the *List* drawer and select an `add items to list` block.

Step 7: Now find the `random integer from to` block in the *Math* drawer, plug in the number 1 in the `from` slot and the number 25 in the `to` slot. Your procedure is complete and should be set up like Figure 7-88.

Figure 7-88 The Guessing Game Procedure (*Source:* MIT App Inventor 2)

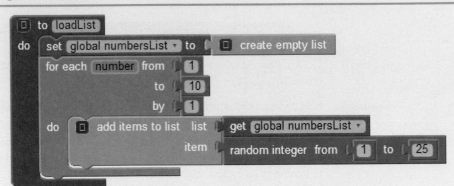

Step 8: Next we need to program the Button's Click event handler. Go to the *ButtonGo* drawer and find the when ButtonGo.Click do block in the ButtonGo drawer. Select it to place it on the blocks editor.

Step 9: Go to the *Procedures* drawer and select the call loadList block, plug that into the when ButtonGo.Click do block. Under that, place an if then else block, found in the *Control* drawer. Remember, you will have to use the mutator tool to add the "then" portion of the block. See Figure 7-90.

Figure 7-89 An if then else Block (*Source:* MIT App Inventor 2)

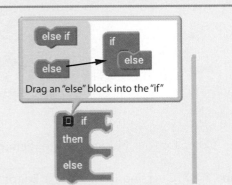

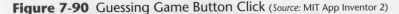

Figure 7-90 Guessing Game Button Click (*Source:* MIT App Inventor 2)

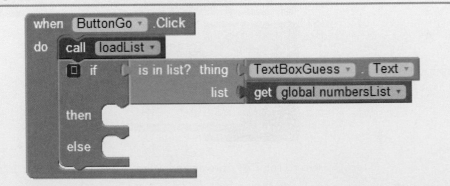

Step 10: Find a is in list? block in the *List* drawer and plug it into the if slot of the if then else block. For the thing slot of the is in list?, place

the `TextBoxGuess.Text` value block and the `get global numberList`, which can be found by hovering over its initialization block (Figure 7-85).

Compare your Button's `Click` event handler with Figure 7-90.

Step 11: Now you will program the `then` and `else` slots. For the `then` slot, you will create the block structure shown in Figure 7-91. To create these blocks, set the `LabelResult` component's Text property to a `join` block that joins the text *Win! Position:* with the `index in list` block. The `index in list` block will need two parameters, the `TextGuess.Text` block and the list variable `numbersList`.

Figure 7-91 (*Source:* MIT App Inventor 2)

Plug the block structure shown in Figure 7-91 into the `then` section.

For the `else`, simply fill in the `LabelResults.Text` block with a *Try Again* text block.

Step 12: The last thing we need to do is clear the TextBox before the user tries again. Simply set `TextGuess.Text` to an empty text block.

Compare your completed Blocks Editor to Figure 7-92.

Figure 7-92 Number-Guessing Game Blocks Editor (*Source:* MIT App Inventor 2)

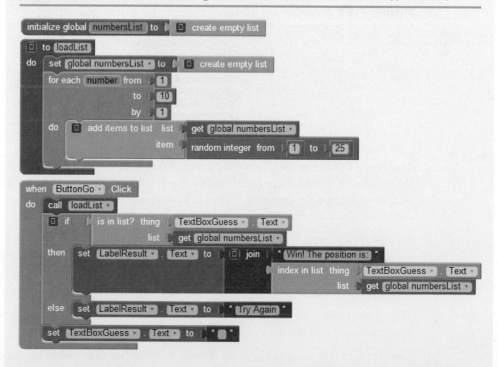

Test your app on the emulator or your device.

Pick Random Item

Another useful List block is the `pick random item` block. This block requires that you give it a list to pick from and will return a random index. This random picking, like the random number generator in the guessing game, is useful in gaming and simulation projects. It will allow the device to generate different scenarios (like a different list each time we run the Number-Guessing Game) which allows for interesting and challenging gaming apps.

Checkpoint

7.19   When we are searching a list, why do `is in list?` and `position in list` go hand in hand?

7.20   What happens if you use the `position in list` block without checking `is in list?` first? What will the `position in list` return if an item is not found?

7.8   Other List Functions

App Inventor provides other blocks that can be used to create and write lists. For example, you can consider a comma-separated value file, or CSV. This is a standard file format and can be read and written to by App Inventor with the List CSV blocks.

The blocks do what their name implies and are as follows:

Figure 7-93 *(Source:* MIT App Inventor 2)

The first, `list to csv row` block, will take a list and return text that represents a single row of comma-separated values. Each list item will have quotes around it and will be separated by commas. There is no line separator in the text that the `list to csv row` block returns.

The `list to csv table` block assumes that each item in the list is a text block of comma-separated values and that each list item will represent an entire row. For example, list item one may be *eggs, ham, bacon, toast,* which will represent a row. There is a line separator written after each list item to indicate a new row.

The `list from csv row` block will return a list made from comma-separated values. Each item in between the commas will be a single list item.

The `list from csv table` block will make a list that holds an entire row of the table in each list item.

Review Questions

Multiple Choice

1. What data type(s) can you use in a list?

   a. text block
   b. number
   c. Boolean
   d. All of the above

2. To create a list, you need to use this block:

   a. `insert list item`
   b. `append to list`
   c. `make a list`
   d. `add items to list`

3. To iterate through a list, you need to use this type of block:

   a. `iterate list`
   b. `for range`
   c. `range list`
   d. `for each`

4. What is the character sequence to display a carriage return?

   a. `ret`
   b. `cgrt`
   c. `\n`
   d. None of the above

5. To find out how many items are in a list, you will need to use this block:

   a. `list count`
   b. `list number`
   c. `size of list`
   d. `length of list`

6. The `select list item` block returns:

   a. The value of the list item
   b. The index of the list item
   c. A Boolean value
   d. Nothing

7. The `is in list item` block returns:

   a. The value of the list item
   b. The index of the list item
   c. A Boolean value
   d. Nothing

8. When the `append to list` block is used:

   a. It will add a single or more items to the end of a list
   b. It will add a single item anywhere in the list
   c. It will add and entire list to the end of a list
   d. It will add an entire list to the beginning of a list

9. When the `add item to list` block is used:

   a. It will add a single or more items to the end of a list
   b. It will add a single item anywhere in the list
   c. It will add and entire list to the end of a list
   d. It will add an entire list to the beginning of a list

10. When the `insert list item` block is used:

   a. It will add a single or more items to the end of a list
   b. It will add a single item anywhere in the list
   c. It will add and entire list to the end of a list
   d. It will add an entire list to the beginning of a list

Short Answer

1. What are the steps you need to take in order to create a list and display it on your App Inventor user interface (app screen)?

2. Why do you have to iterate through a list in order to display each item one at a time?

3. Why should you check to see if the variable that holds the list is actually a list before you try to select an item from it?

4. What happens if your list is only ten items long and you attempt to retrieve an item at index fifteen?

5. When you insert an item into position three in a list, what happens to the item that was previously in position three? What about the item that was originally in position four?

6. When you remove an item in a list, how does it impact the indexes of the items that remain in the list?

Exercises

1. **Select an Item**

   Complete Tutorial 7-3, Selecting an Item, and modify it to ensure that the user enters a valid index between one and the length of the list.

2. **Animals**

   Write an app that has a list of your favorite animals (at least five, created in the Blocks Editor). Allow the user of your app to insert animals at the beginning of the list. Display the list after each insert. Be sure to display each animal with their associated index. See Tutorial 7-2.

3. **Animals Modification 1**

   Modify the Animals app to allow the user to choose where in the list they want to insert the next animal. Have Buttons for "Insert at the Beginning" and "Add to End", and a TextBox and "Insert Here" Button to insert in the middle of the list. Be sure to put the TextBox and "Insert Here" Button in a HorizontalArrangement and use the Hint property of the TextBox to prompt the user to enter the index.

4. **Animals Modification 2**

Modify the Animals project in Exercise 2 to allow the user to remove animals.

5. **Animals Modification 3**

Modify the Animals project in Exercise 2 to allow the user to replace animals.

6. **Number Guessing**

Complete Tutorial 7-7, Number-Guessing Game, to allow the user to put in three numbers instead of one. Then, let the user know which, if any, are in the hidden list and what the found indexes are.

Chapter Projects

**VideoNote
Creating the Entrée
List App**

1. **Entrée List**

Write an application that will allow a restaurant chef to make a list of the week's entrees. Start with a blank list in the Blocks Editor and allow the chef to enter each entrée. As each item is added, display the new list.

2. **Weekly Special**

Complete Exercise 1, Entrée List. Then, allow the chef to pick a random entrée as the weekly special.

As long as there are more than two items in the list, show a button to choose weekly special. Once a weekly special has been randomly picked, be sure to show the special on your app screen (you should have a label that indicates a weekly special, and then a label to display the selected entrée).

3. **Grocery CRUD application**

CRUD sounds bad, but in computer science it is an acronym that means Create, Read, Update, and Delete. When we add, insert, and append, we are in the **create** processes (creating the list), as well as when we manually create a list using the *make a list* block. You can think of displaying the list as **reading** the list. Replacing can be thought of as the **update** processes. Finally, removing items is the **delete** portion of the CRUD acronym.

Write a complete CRUD application for a Grocery List. Review Tutorial 7-6. Start with a blank list and allow a user to add, insert, replace, and remove items. After each change to the list, redisplay the new list. Be sure that each grocery item is displayed with its associated index. Use HorizontalArrangements to lay out your screen effectively.

4. **Parallel Lists**

Our contact list leaves a bit to be desired: phone numbers, for example. We could add the phone number in the same item as each name, but then we will not be able to treat it separately in order to make a phone call or other perform any other operation on it.

Consider the concept of parallel lists. This means that item one in the first list relates to item one in the second list. Item two in list one relates to item two in list two, and so forth.

If we have a list of names and each name has a corresponding phone number in the same position (index) but in a separate list, then we can consider the name and number lists parallel.

Write an app which creates contact parallel lists, with one list holding the names and one holding the phone numbers (this can be done in the Blocks Editor with `make a list` blocks).

Include a procedure that will iterate through both lists and display the contacts with the index, name, and number:

Jane Smith 336-555-1212

John Evans 765-333-4545

Hint: You only need one `for each` loop.

Use the Screen Initialize event to call the procedure and display the list on the user interface.

5. **Lottery Game**

Write an application that simulates a lottery. See Project 4 for a description of Parallel Lists.

Create a list of five random digits between 0 and 9. Name the list *WinningDigits*. This list should be created during the Screen1. Initialize Event.

Then, create another blank list named GuessedList that will be populated by the user.

Prompt the user to enter five digits between 0 and 9. The design should have 5 labels to prompt the user for each guess and 5 TextBoxes for a place to enter their guesses. There should also be a "Go" button that kicks off the game. You will also need two additional labels to present the results.

During the *Go* Click Event, call a procedure that compares the two arrays and displays back to the screen both the WinningDigits List and the GuessedList, indicating how many matches there are.

8 Storing Data on the Device

TOPICS

8.1 App Inventor Storage Components

Most of the applications that we create will have data that needs to be saved or *persisted*. For example, the contact list on your smart phone or tablet is saved on your device. This is good, because if it weren't, you would have to re-enter your contacts each time you started your device. It simply would not be practical.

Much data in the real world is stored in files or databases. Databases are structured files that hold data in an organized way so that computers can read the information quickly. Some examples of data stored in databases that you may already access are your online banking, online stores, Facebook pages, and Twitter posts.

App Inventor provides several ways to store and interact with data. The File component allows you to read and write files on your device. With the File component, you can create new files, read and modify existing files, and save files to your device. The TinyDB component allows you to store a list of tag-value pairs. The FusionTablesControl is a powerful control that allows you to interact with *Google's Fusion Tables*, a robust online data management tool. Finally, you can also store tag-value pair data with the TinyWebDB component. This component is similar to TinyDB, except that the data is stored in the cloud and sharable between applications (more on this in section 8.4 and Chapter 13).

In this chapter, we will cover the components that store data on your device: the File and the TinyDB components.

8.2 The Application Sandbox

Application Isolation

Each Android application runs in its own isolated space, or *sandbox*. The isolation of applications does not permit applications to share resources, which allows for effective security measures. This means that without specific permissions, applications cannot see, read, or write to each other's files and programs. Sandboxing, or separating and isolating, protects your application from being adversely impacted by other applications on the device.

You can think of this sandbox as a protected folder on your device for each application. All the files in that folder are isolated from other folders on the device unless there are specific permissions set.

This concept of application isolation is important to understand before we begin learning how the File and TinyDB components work when they store information on the device. The TinyDB only stores information in the sandbox. By default, the File component stores files in this sandbox too. However, the File component can write to your device's SD card as well.

8.3 File Component

CONCEPT: App Inventor allows you to read, create, and modify files on your device. You can store files in the private application folder or on the SD card in your device. You can also read files packaged with another application, assuming the correct permissions are granted.

Reading and writing files, often referred to as file input/output, is an important topic in computer programming. It's important to learn how to create files within a program, and then save them for later use or processing.

App Inventor's File component is a nonvisible component. Once it is added to a project, its blocks are able to save, read, append to, and delete files. You simply need to provide the blocks with the name of the file you want to interact with. Let's take a look at the component and its blocks.

File Component Methods and Events

The File component's methods include `SaveFile`, `AppendToFile`, `Delete`, and `ReadFrom`. The `ReadFrom` method reads text from a file and causes a `GotText` event to occur. To access the text that was read from the file, create a `GotText` event handler.

Figure 8-1 File Component (*Source:* MIT App Inventor 2)

Palette	Viewer
User Interface	
Layout	
Media	
Drawing and Animation	
Sensors	
Social	
Storage	
📄 File	⑦
🌼 FusiontablesControl	⑦
🥟 TinyDB	⑦
🔼 TinyWebDB	⑦
Connectivity	
LEGO® MINDSTORMS®	

The "File" component

Figure 8-2 SaveFile Method (*Source:* MIT App Inventor 2)

The SaveFile method block does just what it says; it saves a file. This is also the method used to create a new file. It has two necessary parameters: the text information that makes up the file and the file's name. Both parameters require string arguments. It's important to remember how you name a file, so you can retrieve it later. It's also important to note that if a file with the same name already exists, *this block will overwrite* the file with the new information.

If you name a file *without* a preceding forward slash (/), the file will be saved in the application sandbox. If you put a forward slash, it will be saved to the device's SD card. So */theFile.txt* will be stored in the root folder of the SD card, */sdcard/ theFile.txt*. If you simply name it *theFile.txt* it will be stored in the root folder of the application sandbox.

Figure 8-3 Delete Method (*Source:* MIT App Inventor 2)

The Delete method deletes a file. You only have to provide the file name. If the file name starts with a (/), App Inventor will delete the file from the SD card (if it's found, of course), otherwise it will delete the file from the application sandbox.

Figure 8-4 AppendToFile **Method** (*Source:* MIT App Inventor 2)

The AppendToFile method will add text to the *end* of an existing file. You need to provide the text you want to append and the name of the file that you want to append it to.

Figure 8-5 ReadFrom **Method** (*Source:* MIT App Inventor 2)

The ReadFrom method will open and read the contents of an existing file. It will invoke the GotText event handler, which will give you access to the contents of the file. Call this method, and then create a GotText event handler to do any processing on the file.

Figure 8-6 shows the GotText event handler. This block is used to process the file contents after the ReadFrom method is called. If the file indicated in the ReadFrom block exists, the GotText event is fired. To access the contents of the file, you need to find the get text block. You do this by hovering the mouse cursor over the text parameter of the GotText block, and clicking the get text block, as shown in Figure 8-7. Note that you can change the text parameter name in the GotText block if you choose to.

Figure 8-6 GotText **Event Handler** (*Source:* MIT App Inventor 2)

Figure 8-7 Finding the get text **Block** (*Source:* MIT App Inventor 2)

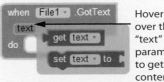

Hover over the "text" parameter to get the contents.

Creating a File

Let's look at an example of how we can use these blocks to create and save a file.

VideoNote
Creating a File

Tutorial 8-1:
Creating a File

To create a file in App Inventor, we will first need a place for the user to enter the text that we want to save in the file. For this, we will use a multiline TextBox. We will also need a place for the user to specify the name of the file (another TextBox) and an event handler to invoke the save process. (We will use a Button in this example.)

Consider the design in Figure 8-8.

Figure 8-8 Design Components to Save a File *(Source: MIT App Inventor 2)*

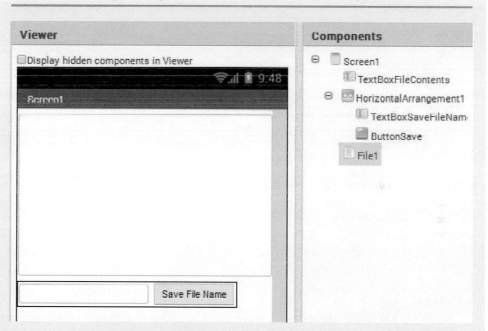

Step 1: Start a new project in App Inventor.

Step 2: From the *Storage* Palette, add a nonvisible File component to your project.

Step 3: From the *User Interface* Palette, add a TextBox to your screen.

Step 4: Rename the TextBox `TextBoxFileContents`.

Step 5: Change the following properties of the `TextBoxFile` component:
- Change the Hint property to *enter file contents*
- Click the MultiLine checkbox to enable that property
- Clear out the Text property
- Set the Height property to 200 pixels

See Figure 8-9.

Figure 8-9 `TextBoxFileContents` **Property Settings** (*Source:* MIT App Inventor 2)

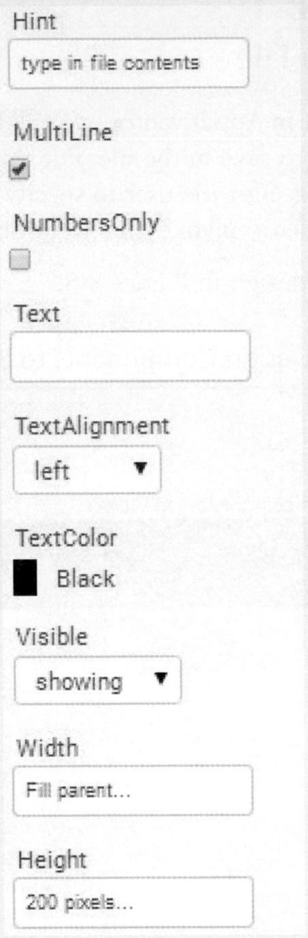

Hint

type in file contents

MultiLine

☑

NumbersOnly

☐

Text

TextAlignment

left ▼

TextColor

■ Black

Visible

showing ▼

Width

Fill parent...

Height

200 pixels...

Step 6: From the *Layout* Palette, add a HorizontalArrangement to the screen under the TextBox.

Step 7: From the *User Interface* Palette, add a TextBox and a Button to the HorizontalArrangement.

Step 8: Rename the TextBox `TextBoxFileName`. Clear out the Text property and set its Hint property to *enter file name*.

Step 9: Rename the Button `ButtonSave` and set its Text property to *Save File*. Compare your design to Figure 8-8.

Step 10: Let's program the blocks. Open the Blocks Editor and take a look at Figure 8-10.

Step 11: Find the `ButtonSave.Click` event in the *ButtonSave* drawer and select it.

Figure 8-10 The `ButtonSaveFile` Event Handler (*Source:* MIT App Inventor 2)

Step 12: In the *File1* drawer, find the `File1.SaveFile` block and place it in the `Click` event handler that you just created.

Step 13: In the *TextBoxFileContents* drawer, find the `TextBoxFileContents.Text` block and plug this into the `text` argument slot of the `File1.SaveFile` method block.

Step 14: In the *TextBoxSaveFileName* drawer, find the `TextBoxSaveFileName.Text` block and plug that into the `fileName` argument slot. See Figure 8-11.

Figure 8-11 Program the `File1.SaveFile` Block (*Source:* MIT App Inventor 2)

The contents of this text box will be saved as the file contents.

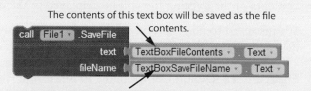

A file with the name supplied in this text box will be written to the device.

Step 15: Create the `set TextBoxFileContents.Text to` and the `set TextBoxSaveFileName to` blocks and plug empty text blocks into them so that after each save, the components are re-set. This helps the user see that their save was completed.

Figure 8-12 Reset the User Interface Components (*Source:* MIT App Inventor 2)

Step 16: Compare your blocks to Figure 8-10, then run and test your app on your device or emulator. Remember your file names so that you can retrieve them, as shown in Tutorial 8-2!

Tutorial 8-1 shows how you can store files to your device. The text that is typed into the TextBox will be the contents of the file.

 Checkpoint

8.1 What does it mean to persist data? Why is it necessary?

8.2 What are some applications that you commonly use that have data stored in databases?

8.3 When we click the "Save File" Button from Tutorial 8-1, what is stored to the device? Where?

 8.4 Retrieving a File

Now that we have begun storing files, let's see how to retrieve the file so that the application from Tutorial 8-1 makes a little more sense.

Tutorial 8-2:
Retrieving a File

**VideoNote
Retrieving a File**

To retrieve a file, we need to give App Inventor the name of an existing file. This tutorial is a continuation of Tutorial 8-1. We will modify Tutorial 8-1 so that a user can enter a file name and choose to load that file. If the user loads a file, the contents of the existing file will be displayed in the multiline TextBox.

We just need to add a couple of things to the previous design. Take a look at the design in Figure 8-13.

Figure 8-13 Design Components to Retrieve a File *(Source: MIT App Inventor 2)*

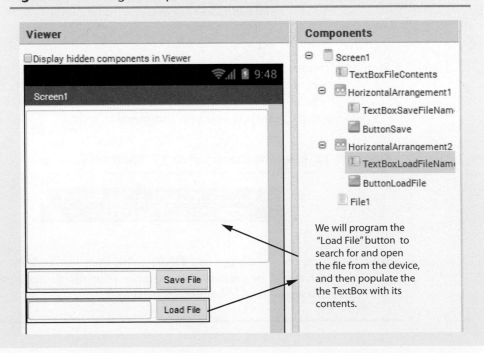

Step 1:   Open the project from Tutorial 8-1 in App Inventor.

Step 2:   From the *Layout* Palette, add a HorizontalArrangement to the screen under the save file components.

Step 3:   From the *User Interface* Palette, add a TextBox and a Button to the HorizontalArrangement.

Step 4:   Rename the TextBox to `TextBoxLoadFileName`. Clear out the Text property and set its Hint property to *file name to retrieve*.

Step 5:   Rename the Button to `ButtonLoadFile` and set its Text property to *Load File*. Compare your design to Figure 8-13.

Step 6:   Let's program the blocks. Open the Blocks Editor and take a look at Figure 8-14.

Figure 8-14 Program Blocks to Retrieve a File *(Source: MIT App Inventor 2)*

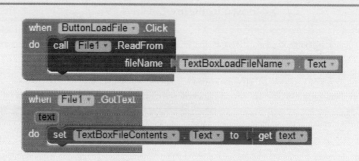

Remember that retrieving a file is usually a two-step process. First, you read the contents of the file, and then you perform some process on the file's contents. We are going to read the file requested and then we are going to display the contents in the TextBox as our "processing" step.

Step 7:   First find the `ButtonLoadFile.Click` event handler in the *ButtonLoadFile* drawer and place it in the editor.

Step 8:   Next, go to the *File1* drawer and select the `File1.ReadFrom` method block and place it into the `ButtonLoadFile.Click` event handler.

Step 9:   Now find the `TextBoxLoadFileName.Text` block in the *TextBoxLoadFileName* drawer and plug it into the `File1.ReadFrom` block as shown in Figure 8-15.

Figure 8-15 ButtonLoadFile.Click Event *(Source: MIT App Inventor 2)*

Step 10: Now find the `File1.GotText` block in the *File1* drawer and place it in the editor. Remember that as soon as the `ReadFrom` method finishes reading the file, the `GotText` event handler is automatically invoked.

Step 11: Find the set `TextBoxFileContents.Text` to block and plug that into the `GotText` event handler. See Figure 8-16.

Figure 8-16 (*Source:* MIT App Inventor 2)

Step 12: Now we need to populate that Text property with the contents of the file. Hover the mouse cursor over the `text` parameter of the `GotText` event handler, and then click on the `get text` block when it comes up as shown in Figure 8-17.

Figure 8-17 Find the `get text` Block (*Source:* MIT App Inventor 2)

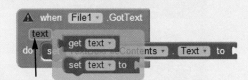

Hover over "text" and click the "get text" block.

Step 13: Once you have the `get text` block, plug it into the set `TextBoxFileContents.Text` to block, as shown in Figure 8-18.

Figure 8-18 The `File1.GotText` Block (*Source:* MIT App Inventor 2)

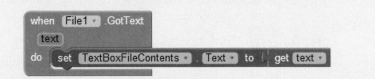

Step 14: Compare your blocks to Figure 8-14, then run and test your application on your device or emulator. Save a couple of files, and then load a couple of files. Remember your file names so you can load them in!

Appending a File

Next, we are going to demonstrate appending to a file. App Inventor's `File.Append` block appends text to the end of an existing file. Behind the scenes, it accomplishes the following steps: retrieves the existing file, modifies it by appending text to it, and then re-saves the file.

Let's take a look in Tutorial 8-3. We will continue on from Tutorials 8-1 and 8-2.

Tutorial 8-3:
Appending a File

VideoNote
Appending a File

To append a file, we need to give App Inventor the name of an existing file, as well as the text that we want to add to the end of it. This tutorial is a continuation of Tutorial 8-2. We will modify the app so a user can enter a file name, and choose to append the text typed in the multiline TextBox to the end of the file.

This time we are again going to add a HorizontalArrangement that contains a TextBox and a Button.

Step 1: Open the project from Tutorial 8-2 in App Inventor.

Step 2: From the *Layout* Palette, add a HorizontalArrangement to the screen under the existing HorizontalArrangment that contains the TextBox and Button to load the file.

Step 3: From the *User Interface* Palette, add a TextBox and a Button to the HorizontalArrangement.

Step 4: Rename the TextBox `TextBoxAppendTo`. Clear out the Text property and set its Hint property to *file to append to*.

Step 5: Rename the Button `ButtonAppend` and set its Text property to *Append File*. Compare your design to Figure 8-19.

Figure 8-19 Design Components to Retrieve a File (*Source:* MIT App Inventor 2)

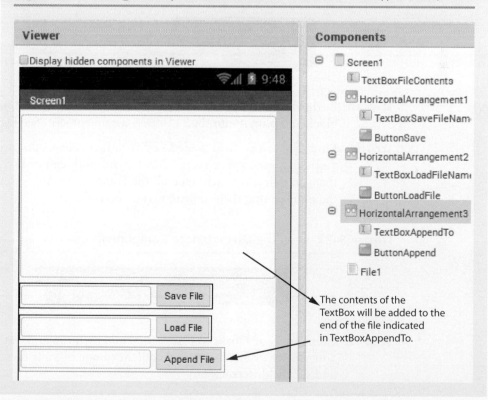

Step 6:   Let's program the blocks. Open the Blocks Editor and take a look at Figure 8-20.

Figure 8-20 The `ButtonAppend.Click` Event Handler (*Source:* MIT App Inventor 2)

Step 7:   First, find the `ButtonAppend.Click` event in the *ButtonAppend* drawer and select it.

Step 8:   In the *File1* drawer, find the `File1.AppendToFile` block and place it in the `Click` event handler that you just created.

Step 9:   In the *TextBoxFileContents* drawer, find the `TextBoxFileContents.Text` block, and plug it into the `text` argument slot of the `File1.AppendToFile` method block, as shown in Figure 8-21.

Figure 8-21 Program the `File1.AppendToFile` Block (*Source:* MIT App Inventor 2)

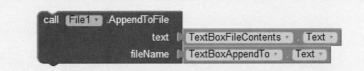

Step 10:   In the *TextBoxAppendTo* drawer, find the `TextBoxAppendTo.Text` block and plug it into the `fileName` argument slot. See Figure 8-21.

Step 11:   Find the `set TextBoxFileContents.Text to` and the `set TextBoxAppendTo.Text to` blocks and plug empty text blocks into them so that after each append, the components are re-set. This helps the user see that their append was completed.

Figure 8-22 Reset the User Interface Components (*Source:* MIT App Inventor 2)

Step 12:   Compare your blocks to Figure 8-20 and then run and test your app on your device or emulator. Add content to one of your files, then load it and see the differences!

8.5 TinyDB

CONCEPT: App Inventor allows you to store data on your device by using a database called TinyDB. This database lives on your device and allows you to store data in tag-value pairs. Using TinyDB will allow your app to store data and then retrieve it later. This ability to save data is essential to most useful mobile applications.

App Inventor provides a database called TinyDB. Being able to store and retrieve data will allow you to create applications that may be more practical and useful. Think back to the grocery list application we wrote in Chapter 7. To make the app more useful, we should keep the grocery list items persisted (or stored), so that when we get to the physical grocery store, we can start our app back up and see what we need to buy.

You should only have one TinyDB per application. You can add more, but they will use the same data storage space, so you won't get the effect of two separate storage spaces. This is also true if you have multiple screens in your application.

Because of the isolation described in Section 2, each TinyDB can only be seen by the application it applies to, and you cannot share the data store between two different applications. So, in a nutshell, you should only have one TinyDB per app and you cannot share it with another application. To share data between apps, you should use TinyWebDB, covered in Chapter 13.

To use TinyDB in your App Inventor project, you will need to add it to your application by dragging the TinyDB component from the *Storage* Palette. It will be added as a nonvisible component, as shown in Figure 8-23.

Figure 8-23 TinyDB Component (*Source:* MIT App Inventor 2)

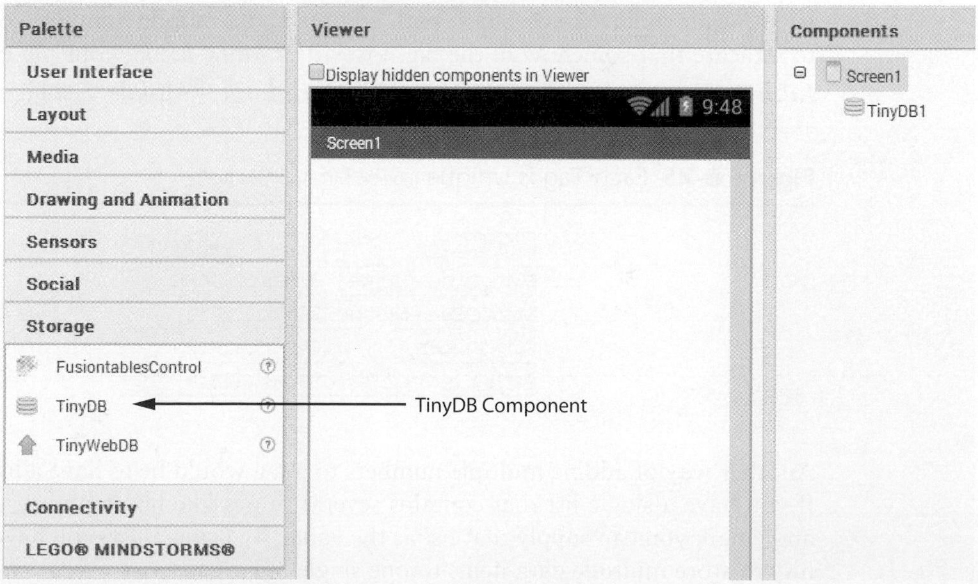

Checkpoint

8.4 How many TinyDB components should you have in a mobile application? Why?

8.5 Can you share TinyDB data between applications?

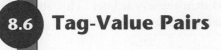 **Tag-Value Pairs**

CONCEPT: A tag-value pair consists of a tag and a value. The tag is used to identify the data item and the value is the data that you want to associate with that tag. In a TinyDB, the tag is a text item and the value can be any data type (number, text, Boolean, or list). The tag is unique in each TinyDB and cannot be entered twice. If you try to store the same tag with a different value, the original value will be overwritten.

You can picture a TinyDB as a table of tags and values. For example, in Figure 8-24 a TinyDB for contacts might hold a name as the tag and a phone number as the value.

Figure 8-24 TinyDB with Tag-Value Pairs *(Source:* MIT App Inventor 2)

Tag	Value
Mark Little	336-555-4343
Carrie Crum	919-555-1212
Patrick Jefferson	910-346-1818

Take a look at Figure 8-24 and note that each tag must be unique. For example, Mark Little has only one value: a phone number. You cannot add another value for Mark Little in the TinyDB table. If you try, his existing number will be overwritten. If you want to have two values, both a home and a mobile number, you would have to indicate that somehow in the tag. Instead of *Mark Little*, your tag could be *Mark Little—Home* and then you could add a *Mark Little—Mobile*. See Figure 8-25:

Figure 8-25 Each Tag is Unique *(Source:* MIT App Inventor 2)

Tag	Value
Mark Little - Home	336-555-4343
Mark Little - Mobile	336-555-7668
Carrie Crum	919-555-1212
Patrick Jefferson	910-346-1818

Another way of adding multiple numbers to a tag would be to have a list as the value. If you have a single list that contains several values like home phone, mobile phone, and email, you can supply that list as the value. By using a list, you have the opportunity to store multiple data items to one single tag.

8.7 Storing a Tag-Value Pair

To store data, App Inventor provides the `TinyDB.StoreValue` block. This block requires that you supply a tag and an associated value. Once you've added a TinyDB component to your project, you find this block in the *TinyDB1* drawer.

Figure 8-26 `StoreValue` Block (*Source:* MIT App Inventor 2)

Tutorial 8-4:
Storing Names and Phone Numbers

Let's write an app that will store the names and associated phone number shown in Figure 8-24.

First, take a look at Figure 8-27 for the user interface design.

Figure 8-27 `TinyDB` User Interface (*Source:* MIT App Inventor 2)

☐ Display hidden components in Viewer

Components
- ⊖ ☐ Screen1
  - TextBoxTag
  - TextBoxValue
  - ButtonSave
  - A LabelShowTinyDB
  - TinyDB1

Screen1

📶 🔋 9:48

Save

Non-visible components

TinyDB1

Rename   Delete

Media

Upload File

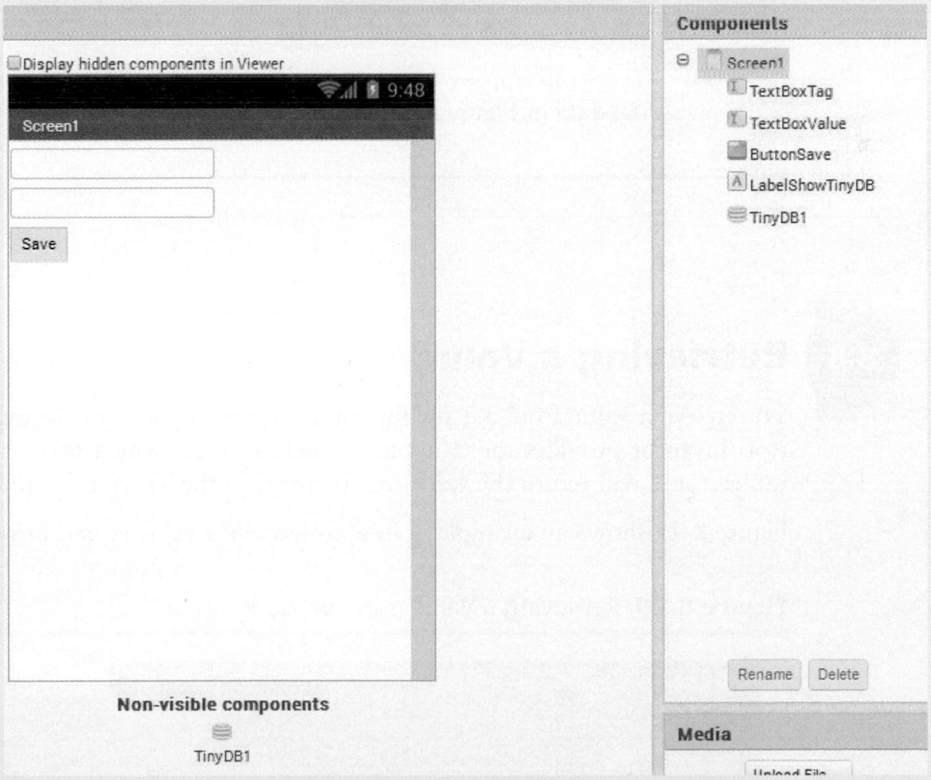

Step 1:   Add two TextBoxes, rename them TextBoxTag and TextBoxValue. Change the Hint property for TextBoxTag to *Enter Tag*. Change the Hint property for TextBoxValue to *Enter Value*.

Step 2:   Add a Button to your Screen and change the name to ButtonSave. Change the Text property of your Button to *Save*.

Step 3:   Add a Label and change the name to LabelShowTinyDB. (We will use this later to display the contents of the TinyDB.)

Step 4:   From the *Storage* Palette, drag a TinyDB component to your app and note that it will be added as a nonvisible component.

Step 5:   In the Blocks Editor, create the blocks shown in Figure 8-28. Drag the when ButtonSave.Click do block onto the editor and then plug in the call TinyDB1.StoreValue method block. Plug in TextBoxTag. Text as the tag argument and the TextBoxValue.Text as the valueToStore argument.

Figure 8-28 TinyDB Blocks Editor (*Source:* MIT App Inventor 2)

Step 6:   Test your app by running it on your device or emulator and entering the data in Figure 8-24.

8.8 Retrieving a Value

To retrieve a value from a TinyDB, you must provide it with the tag of the element. App Inventor provides the TinyDB.GetValue block, which takes in the tag as parameter and will return the value that is stored in the TinyDB for that tag.

Figure 8-29 shows an example of how to retrieve a value stored in your TinyDB.

Figure 8-29 Retrieving a Value (*Source:* MIT App Inventor 2)

This figure shows how to use the `TinyDB1.GetValue` block to retrieve the value for Mark Little (the tag). It joins the value returned with a plain text prompt and then stores it to the Label's Text property. Assuming the data in Figure 8-2 was stored in the TinyDB, the resulting Label would show *Mark Little: 336-555-4343*.

Notice the slot for `valueIfTagNotThere`. This slot gives you the ability to provide a default value if the tag happens to not be in the TinyDB. In Figure 8-7, the slot is an empty text block, however, we could have put *Not found* or *0* in that slot, depending on what we want to display when the tag is not in the TinyDB.

Tutorial 8-5:
Storing and Retrieving Values

VideoNote
Storing and
Retrieving Values

Let's create an app that allows the user to enter any number of products and prices that they wish. They will also have the ability to look up a product and see the associated price.

First, we need a place for the user to add products and store them to the TinyDB. Let's give the application two TextBoxes to enter the product name (tag) and price (value). We will also provide a *save* Button which we can use to store the tag and value.

Next, we need to provide a lookup mechanism for the user. We will provide a TextBox so the user can enter the product name (tag) and a *find* Button that we can use to retrieve the price (value).

Figure 8-30 shows the app's screen design.

Figure 8-30 Product Design Screen (*Source:* MIT App Inventor 2)

Viewer	Components
☐ Display hidden components in Viewer	⊟ ☐ Screen1
⬜ 📶 🔋 9:48	A LabelTitle
Screen1	⊟ ▦ HorizontalArrangement1
Products and Prices	I TextBoxProduct
[_____] : [_____]	A LabelColon
Save	I TextBoxPrice
Look up:	⬜ ButtonSave
[_____] Find	A LabelLookUp
Price:	⊟ ▦ HorizontalArrangement2
	I TextBoxTag
	⬜ ButtonFind
	A LabelPrice
	▤ TinyDBProducts

Step 1: Add a Label for the title, rename it `LabelTitle`, and replace the Text property with *Products and Prices*. Make the font size 20 and boldface.

Step 2: Add two HorizontalArrangement components. In the first, put a TextBox, a Label, and another TextBox. Name the first TextBox `TextBoxProduct`, name the Label `LabelColon` and the second TextBox, `TextBoxPrice`. Replace the Hint property of the `TextBoxProduct` with *Enter Product Key*, replace the Text property of the Label with a colon (:), and replace the Hint property of `TextBoxPrice` with *Price*.

Step 3: Drag a Button and a Label between the two HorizontalArrangement components. Name the Button `ButtonSave` and change the Text property to *Save*. Drag a Label in between the save Button and the second HorizontalArrangement. Rename it `LabelLookUp` and change the font size to 20, bold, and set the Text property to *Look Up:*.

Step 4: Add a TextBox and a Button to the second HorizontalArrangement. Name the TextBox `TextBoxTag` and change the Hint property to *Enter Product*. Name the Button `ButtonFind` and replace the Text property with *Find*.

Step 5: Add a Label under the second HorizontalArrangement to display the price. Name it `LabelPrice` and set the Text property to *Price:*.

Step 6: Add a TinyDB to your project and name it `TinyDBProducts`. Compare your design to Figure 8-30.

Now let's program the Blocks Editor as shown in Figure 8-31

Figure 8-31 Product Blocks Editor (*Source:* MIT App Inventor 2)

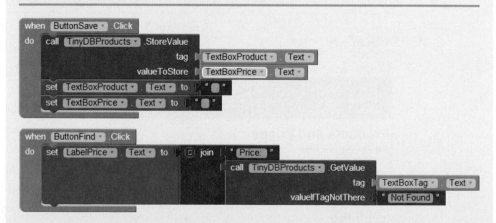

Step 7: Drag the when `ButtonSave.Click` do and when `ButtonFind.Click` do blocks from the *ButtonSave* and *ButtonFind* drawers.

Step 8: Program the when `ButtonSave.Click` do event handler:
- Find the `TinyDBProducts.StoreValue` block under its drawer and plug in the Text property blocks for the `TextBoxProduct` and the `TextBoxPrice`, as shown in Figure 8-31.

- Once the save is complete, we should clear out the TextBoxes so that the user can easily add another. Find the `set TextBoxProduct.Text to` and the `set TextBoxPrice.Text to` blocks in their associated drawers.
- Set each to a blank text block and add them to the `when ButtonSave.Click do` event handler, as shown in Figure 8-31.

Step 9: Program the `when ButtonFind.Click do` event handler:

- Find the `set LabelPrice.Text to` block and place it in the `ButtonFind.Click` block.
- Find the `TinyDBProducts.GetValue` block in the *TinyDBProducts* drawer.
- Plug the `TextBoxTag.Text` block into the `TinyDBProducts.GetValue` block.
- Place a text block with the value *Not Found* in the `valueIfTagNotThere` slot.
- Use a `join` block to join the *Price:* prompt text block and the value returned by the `TinyDBProducts.GetValue` block.
- Plug the joined text blocks into the `set LabelPrice.Text to` block.

Test and run your application. Notice that once you save the price of a product, you can later find the price by typing the product name or key into the TextBox and clicking the find Button. If this app were packaged and deployed to your android device the TinyDB would be persisted and you would have access to the price information for as long as the app lives on your phone. Using your emulator, your products and prices will stay available only during the life of the emulator session.

Checkpoint

8.6 What is the purpose of the `valueIfTagNotThere` parameter of the TinyDB `GetValue` Block?

8.7 What must you provide to retrieve a value from a TinyDB?

8.9 Tag-Value Pairs when the Value is a List

Now let's consider creating a list of information about our tag. You can create this list and then store it as the value of the tag in your TinyDB. This will allow you to store more information about your contact in your database.

To demonstrate this, you will create another Contact application, but this time you will gather the contact's name, home phone, mobile phone, and email. You will make a list of the home phone, mobile phone, and email, and store it as the value for the name, which we will use as the tag.

For this application, it will be important to create each contact's list in a consistent manner. For example, the first element in each list should always be the home phone, the second should be the mobile phone, and the third should always be the email address. This is important so that when we retrieve the values, we can be sure that data is in the correct place.

VideoNote
Storing a List
as a Value in
a Tag-Value Pair

Tutorial 8-6:
Storing a List as a Value in a Tag-Value Pair

First, let's design and code the elements we need to add our contact. We will ask the user for a name, home phone, mobile phone, and email address. We will have an *Add* Button, which we will use as the event to save the information to the TinyDB. Before saving the data, we will store the phone numbers and email values to a list. Figure 8-32 shows the app's screen.

Figure 8-32 Add Contact Interface (*Source:* MIT App Inventor 2)

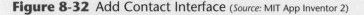

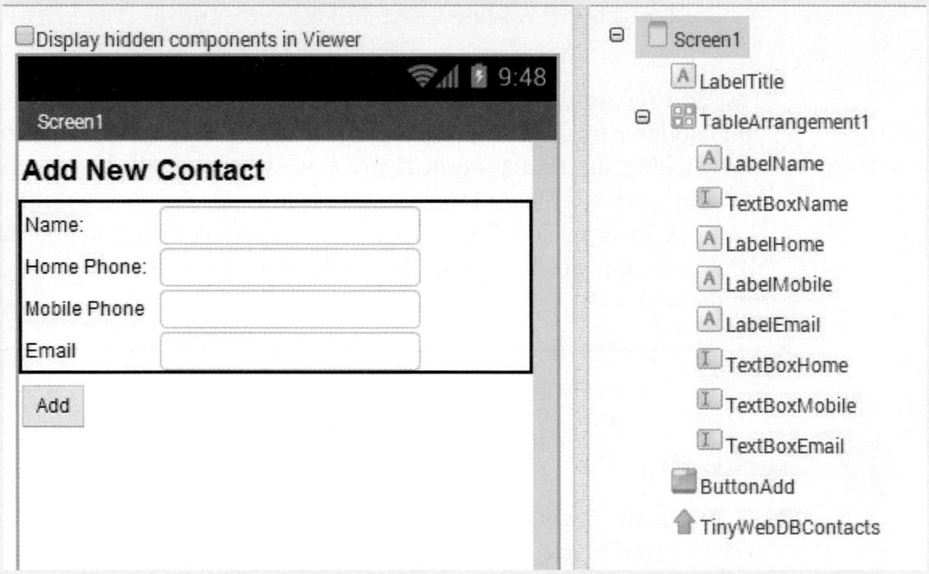

Step 1: Add a Label and change the Text property to *Add New Contact*. Change the font size to 20 and mark it as bold.

Step 2: Add a TableArrangement from the *Layout* Palette. Set the Columns property to 2 and the Rows property to 4 to give the arrangement two columns and four rows.

Step 3: Add four TextBoxes. Rename the first `TextBoxName` and change the Hint property to *Enter Name*. Rename the second `TextBoxHomePhone` and change the Hint property to *Enter Home Phone*. Rename the third `TextBoxMobilePhone` and change the Hint property to *Enter Mobile Phone*. Rename the fourth `TextBoxEmail` and change the Hint property to *Enter Email*.

Step 4: Add a Button, rename it `ButtonAdd`, and change the Text property to *Add Contact*.

Step 5: Add the TinyDB to the project and rename it `TinyDBContacts`.

Step 6: Program the blocks to add a contact to your TinyDB. Open the Blocks Editor, create a variable, `ContactInfo`, and plug in the `create empty list` block found in the *Lists* drawer. This will let App Inventor know that `ContactInfo` will store a list. See Figure 8-33.

Figure 8-33 Contact Info Variable (*Source:* MIT App Inventor 2)

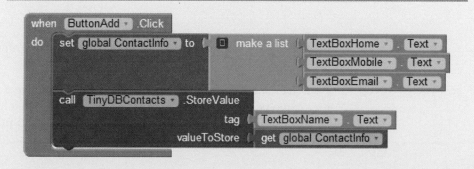

Step 7: Now you will program the `when ButtonAdd.Click do` event handler. When the user clicks the *Add* Button, we want to store the values they typed in for the home phone, mobile phone, and email into a list and store it to the `ContactInfo` variable. Then, we will save the name as the tag and `ContactInfo` as the value to your TinyDB.

  Go to *ButtonAdd* and select the `when ButtonAdd.Click do` block.

Step 8: Hover over the variable name `ContactInfo` in the `initialize global ContactInfo` block and select a `set global ContactInfo to` block. Go to the *List* drawer and select the `make a list` block, plug that into the `ContactInfo` block and then plug the `ContactInfo` block into the `when ButtonAdd.Click do` block.

Step 9: Add the `TextBoxHomePhone.Text`, `TextBoxMobile.Text`, and the `TextBoxEmail.Text` blocks into the `make a list` block.

Step 10: Now store the information to the TinyDB by going *to TinyDBContacts* and selecting the `TinyDBContacts.StoreValue` block. Plug in the `TextBoxName.Text` block as the `tag` value and `global ContactInfo` block as the `valueToStore` value. You can find the `global ContactInfo` block by hovering over the variable name `ContactInfo` in the `initialize global ContactInfo` block.

  Compare your `when ButtonAdd.Click do` event with Figure 8-34.

Figure 8-34 Add Contact Button (*Source:* MIT App Inventor 2)

Step 11: You can run and test your application now, but you'll notice that you need to clear out the TextBoxes after you save a contact to make your application more user-friendly. Set each TextBox's Text property to an empty text block, as seen in Figure 8-35. Plug this set of blocks into the when `ButtonAdd.Click` do event handler at the bottom under the `TinyDB.StoreValue` block.

Figure 8-35 Clear the Textboxes (*Source:* MIT App Inventor 2)

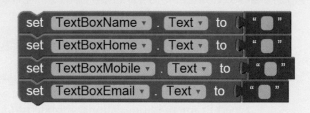

Your Button event is complete when the when `ButtonAdd.Click` do event handler resembles Figure 8-36.

Figure 8-36 `ButtonAdd.Click` Event (*Source:* MIT App Inventor 2)

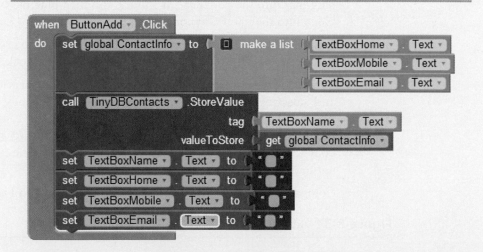

Step 12: Run and test your application using the emulator or a device and save a few contacts.

Step 13: Now let's modify the interface as described in Figure 8-37 so that a user can type in a name, press the *Find* Button, and then have that contact's information pulled back out of the TinyDB and presented back onto the device.

Figure 8-37 Add Find Function to Design *(Source: MIT App Inventor 2)*

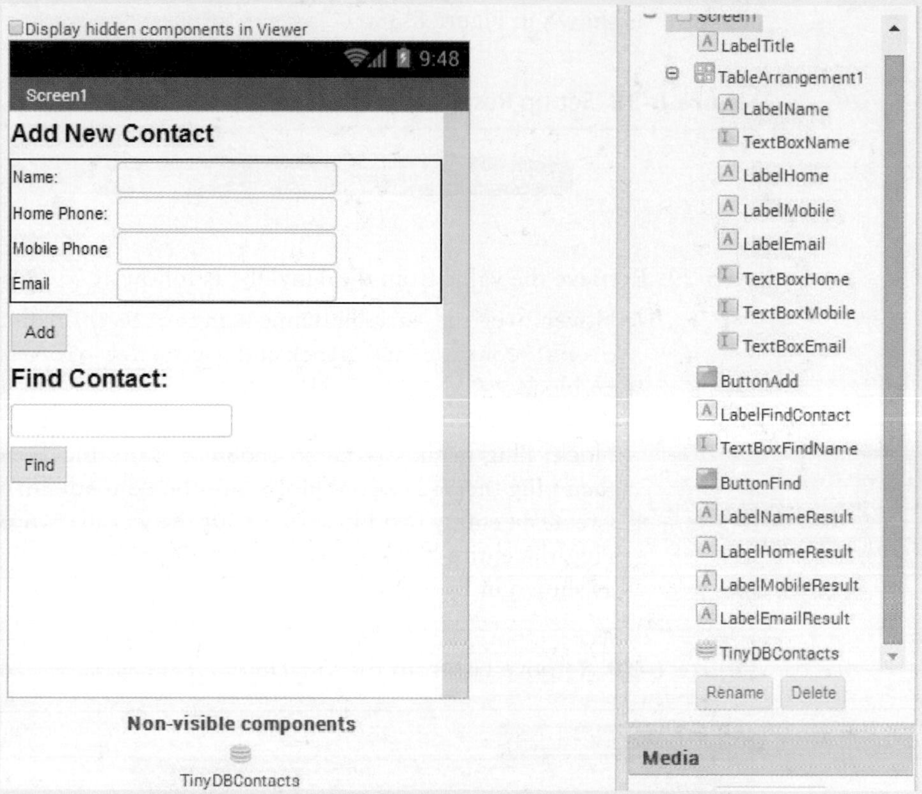

Step 14: Add a Label, rename it `LabelFindContact`, and change its Text property to *Find Contact*. Set the font size to 20 and mark it as bold.

Step 15: Add a TextBox, rename it `TextBoxFindName`, and set the Hint property to *Enter Name*.

Step 16: Add a Button, rename it `ButtonFind`, and set the Text property to *Find*.

Step 17: Add four Labels and rename them `LabelName`, `LabelHomePhone`, `LabelMobilePhone`, and `LabelEmail`. Clear the Text properties of each.

Step 18: Now you will program the `when ButtonFind.Click do` event handler. When the user clicks the *Find* Button, we will first retrieve the value from the TinyDB using the name that was entered as the tag. Because the value was stored as a list, we will have to iterate through the list to extract the values. As we extract each value, we will populate the Labels on the interface (Figure 8-37).

Go to *ButtonFind* and select the `when ButtonAdd.Click do` block.

Step 19: Now let's set up an empty list variable to hold the results (name, home number, mobile number, and email) after we search and find a value in the TinyDB. Go to the *Variables* drawer, select an `initialize` global name to block, click on name and rename the variable Results, and plug a create empty list block from the *Lists* drawer as shown in Figure 8-38.

Figure 8-38 Set up Results Variable (*Source:* MIT App Inventor 2)

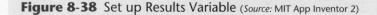

Step 20: Retrieve the value from the TinyDB, as follows:

- Hover over the variable name ContactInfo in the initialize global ContactInfo block and select a set global ContactInfo to block.
- Go to *TinyDBContacts* and select the TinyDBContacts.GetValue block. Plug in the TextBoxFindName.Text block as the tag, and then plug the get value block into the ContactInfo block.
- Create an empty text block to use for the valueIfTagNotThere slot.
- Plug the entire block into the when ButtonFind.Click do block, as shown in Figure 8-39.

Figure 8-39 Retrieve List from the TinyDB (*Source:* MIT App Inventor 2)

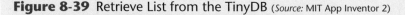

Step 21: Now you will fill in the LabelNameResult.Text property with the contact name. This will clarify who was last searched for. Find the set LabelNameResult to block and plug in the TextBoxFindName.Text.

Figure 8-40 Set up the Name Results Label (*Source:* MIT App Inventor 2)

Step 22: Now we want to pull out the information in the *list* that we stored as our *value* for the *tag*. Remember that the first item in the list was the home phone, the second item was the mobile phone, and the third item was the email address. We can use the select list item in list block from the *Lists* drawer to retrieve the items and populate the appropriate Labels.

- Find the set `LabelHomeResult.Text` block from its drawer and place it in the Blocks Editor.
- In the *Lists* drawer, select the `select list item in list` block and plug it into the set `LabelHomeResult.Text` block.
- Hover over the variable name `Results` in the `initialize global Results` block and select a `get global Results` block. Plug that into the `select list item in list` block in the first slot.

Because the home number is the first thing stored in the results list, use a `number 1` block for the `index` argument.

Step 23: Repeat Step 22 for set `LabelMobileResult.Text` and `LabelEmailResult.Text`, but be sure to change the index arguments to 2 and 3 respectively. Compare your blocks to 8-41.

Figure 8-41 Label Setter Blocks (*Source:* MIT App Inventor 2)

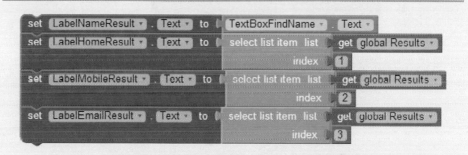

Step 24: Place the Label set blocks into the `ButtonFind.Click` event handler as shown in Figure 8-42.

Figure 8-42 Complete `when ButtonFind.Click do` Event Handler
(*Source:* MIT App Inventor 2)

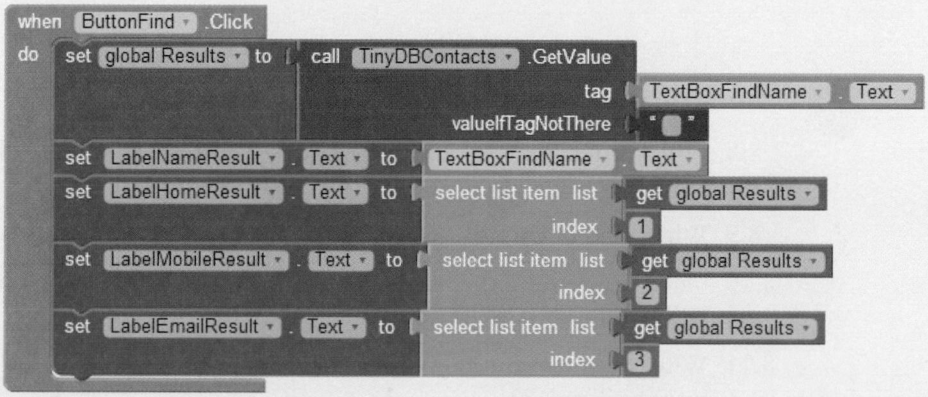

Compare your code blocks to Figure 8-43.

Figure 8-43 Tutorial 8-5 Complete Workspace (*Source:* MIT App Inventor 2)

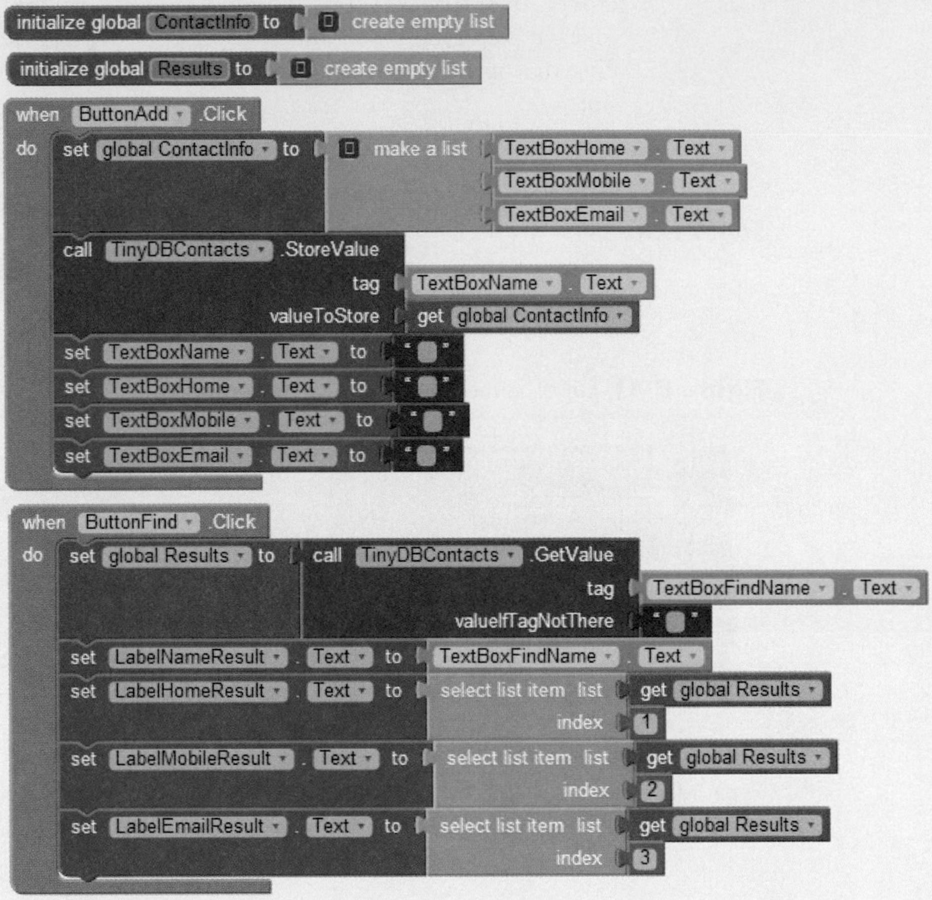

initialize global `ContactInfo` to `create empty list`

initialize global `Results` to `create empty list`

when `ButtonAdd` .Click
do set `global ContactInfo` to `make a list` `TextBoxHome` . `Text`
`TextBoxMobile` . `Text`
`TextBoxEmail` . `Text`
call `TinyDBContacts` .StoreValue
tag `TextBoxName` . `Text`
valueToStore get `global ContactInfo`
set `TextBoxName` . `Text` to `" "`
set `TextBoxHome` . `Text` to `" "`
set `TextBoxMobile` . `Text` to `" "`
set `TextBoxEmail` . `Text` to `" "`

when `ButtonFind` .Click
do set `global Results` to call `TinyDBContacts` .GetValue
tag `TextBoxFindName` . `Text`
valueIfTagNotThere `" "`
set `LabelNameResult` . `Text` to `TextBoxFindName` . `Text`
set `LabelHomeResult` . `Text` to select list item list get `global Results`
index `1`
set `LabelMobileResult` . `Text` to select list item list get `global Results`
index `2`
set `LabelEmailResult` . `Text` to select list item list get `global Results`
index `3`

Checkpoint

8.8 Why would you want to store a list as the value of your TinyDB tag? What are the advantages?

8.9 What kind of variable will you need to retrieve a list from your TinyDB?

8.10 Once you retrieve the list and store it to your variable, what additional steps will you need to take to extract the list elements?

8.11 Why is it important to know how your list was created before it was stored into the TinyDB?

8.10 TinyDB Across Multiple Screens

CONCEPT: Many applications that we use have more than one screen. App Inventor makes it easy to create multiple screen applications, but consideration should be taken of how media and storage components (like TinyDB) are impacted. Storage and media components are shared on the application level and shared between screens.

Remember the application sandbox, or application isolation, concept from section 1, which explains that each application has a single storage space that is isolated from other applications. However, when you add media or storage components to an application, those same components are visible to all the screens in that application sandbox. For example, if you add picture files for Screen1 of your app, those same files are available in Screen2—you don't have to upload them twice.

We are going to create an application that uses the ListPicker to choose an instrument, (drum, guitar or horn) on the first screen. Once an instrument is chosen, the app will forward to a second screen that shows an image of the instrument and a button, which will play a sound file. We will use a TinyDB to store information about the instrument's picture and sound file names.

The ListPicker's elements will be populated from the TinyDB on the first screen. The picture and sound files will be retrieved from the same TinyDB on the second screen.

Figure 8-44 Get All Tags *(Source: MIT App Inventor 2)*

App Inventor provides a procedure block for the TinyDB that returns a list of all tags (see Figure 8-44). We will use this block to populate the ListPicker's elements. This block is very helpful because it will show you all of the tags that are currently stored in your TinyDB.

Figure 8-45 Clear All *(Source: MIT App Inventor 2)*

There is also a ClearAll block for the TinyDB that will clear all elements from the storage space. When working with the emulator, you may notice that information from previous applications is left stored in the TinyDB. So, if you want "fresh" elements in your TinyDB, you should clear it out.

Adding a Second Screen

To add a second screen in App Inventor, you simply click the *Add Screen* Button at the top of the Designer or Blocks Editor.

Figure 8-46 Add Screen (*Source:* MIT App Inventor 2)

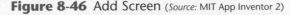

Once you click the *Add Screen* Button, you will be prompted to name the new screen. You can name it something meaningful or leave it Screen2, as shown in Figure 8-47.

Figure 8-47 Name the New Screen (*Source:* MIT App Inventor 2)

New Screen
Screen name: Screen2
Cancel   OK

> **NOTE:** You can, and probably should, rename additional screens, however, you cannot rename Screen1. You can change the Title of Screen1, so that it displays nicely on your app, but the name Screen1 is unchangeable.

Each screen has its own unique Designer and Blocks Editor spaces. To switch between the two, you click the *Screen1* Button (next to the *Add Screen* button) and it will drop down with a list of each screen in the application. In Figure 8-48, notice that the example shown is an app with two screens, Screen1 and Details.

Figure 8-48 Switching between Screens during Development (*Source:* MIT App Inventor 2)

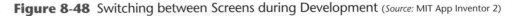

There are a few noteworthy blocks that allow you to programmatically navigate between screens at runtime. The blocks are found in the *Control* drawer of the Blocks Editor. When placed in an appropriate event handler, these blocks will allow your app to load and unload the different screens of your application. See Figure 8-49.

Figure 8-49 Navigating between Screens at Runtime (*Source:* MIT App Inventor 2)

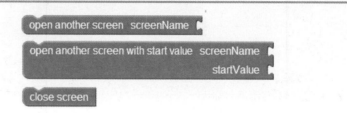

The first block in Figure 8-49 allows you to simply load a different screen by supplying its screen name. The second block allows you to send a start value to that screen. This start value can be a Text, Number, or List component. Finally, there is a `close screen` block that will allow you to close the current screen and return to the previous screen.

> **NOTE:** Applications with multiple screens work best when deployed to a device. Tutorial 8-7 will work best if you download your project's .apk file to your device and install it, rather than work with the companion website or the emulator. This is especially true if you are sending values from one screen to another. The following tutorial passes values between screens, so it's best to download and install the .apk. Downloading an .apk file is simple; to learn more about deploying the .apk to your device, see http://appinventor.mit.edu/explore/ai2/share.html.

Tutorial 8-7:
TinyDB across Multiple Screens

First, let's design and code the elements we need to invoke the ListPicker. It will be a very simple interface with a single HorizontalArrangement and a ListPicker component.

Step 1: Add a HorizontalArrangment from the *Layout* Palette. Set the Width property to *Fill parent* and the Height property to 250 pixels. Set the AlignHorizontal property to *Center* and the AlignVertical property to *Center*. See Figure 8-51.

VideoNote
TinyDB Across
Multiple Screens

Figure 8-50 Instrument Application Interface (*Source:* MIT App Inventor 2)

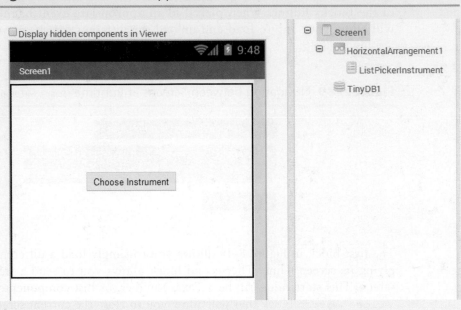

Figure 8-51 HorizontalArrangement Properties (*Source:* MIT App Inventor 2)

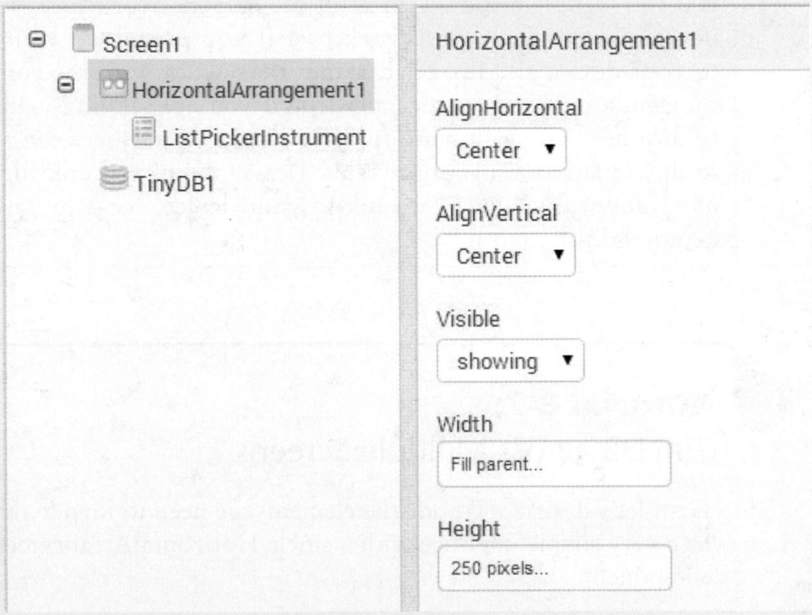

Step 2:   Add a ListPicker component to the HorizontalArrangement. Rename the ListPicker to *ListPickerInstrument*. Set the Text property to *Choose Instrument*. See Figure 8-52.

Figure 8-52 Add and Rename `ListPicker` (*Source:* MIT App Inventor 2)

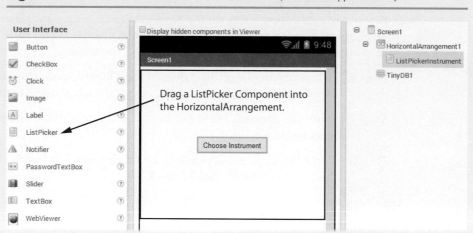

Step 3: Add a TinyDB from the *Storage* Palette to your application.

Step 4: Upload image and sound files. Download the following files from the companion website to your computer:

- drum.png
- drum.wav
- guitar.png
- guitar.wav
- horn.png
- horn.wav

Step 5: Upload the files through the *Media* panel into your application.

> **TIP:** Unfortunately you can only upload one file at a time. See Figure 8-53.

Figure 8-53 Media Files (*Source:* MIT App Inventor 2)

Media

drum.png

drum.wav

guitar.png

guitar.wav

horn.png

horn.wav

Upload File ...

Now let's program the blocks for Screen1.

Before the application starts (in the Screen1.Initialize event), a TinyDB will be populated with a tag and a value for each instrument. The value will be a list containing the instrument's picture and sound file names.

Step 6: Clear out any lingering values in the TinyDB space from other practice applications. (This is especially necessary when using the emulator.)

Step 7: Find the Screen1.Initialize event handler block and place it in the Blocks Editor.

Step 8: Find the TinyDB1.ClearAll block and place it inside the Screen1. Initialize block. See Figure 8-54.

Figure 8-54 Clear TinyDB1 (*Source:* MIT App Inventor 2)

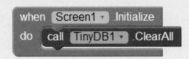

Step 9: Now we will store the information for each instrument into our TinyDB. See Figure 8-55.

Figure 8-55 Store Instrument Information (*Source:* MIT App Inventor 2)

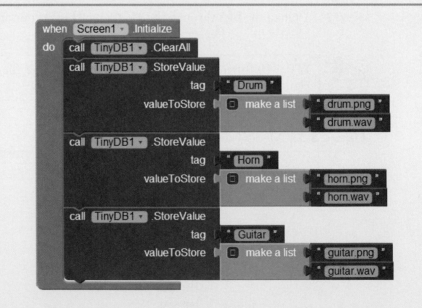

Step 10: For each instrument, use a TinyDB1.StoreValue block. Plug a Text block containing the tag into the tag slot. The tag for the drum will be

Drum, the tag for the guitar will be *Guitar* and the tag for the horn will be *Horn*. See Figure 8-55.

Step 11: Create three `make a list` blocks from the *Lists* drawer. Set up each with the name of the picture file as the first element and the sound file as the second element. It's important that the picture is always first and the sound is always second. You can switch the order as long as you do the same for all three instruments. Be sure there are no spelling mistakes!

Step 12: Plug each of the `make a list` blocks in the `valueToStore` slot of the appropriate `TinyDB1.StoreValue` block, as shown in Figure 8-55.

Step 13: Now that we have our TinyDB populated, use the `TinyDB.GetTags` block to populate the `ListPicker`'s elements, as shown in Figure 8-56.

Figure 8-56 Populate `ListPicker` (*Source:* MIT App Inventor 2)

set ListPickerInstrument ▾ . Elements ▾ to | call TinyDB1 ▾ .GetTags

Step 14: Place the block from Figure 8-56 at the bottom of the `Screen1.Initalize` event. See Figure 8-57. For testing purposes, you can run the app on the emulator or companion website after this step. Notice how the ListPickers' elements are populated with the tags stored in the TinyDB.

Figure 8-57 Completed `Screen1.Initialize` Event Handler
(*Source:* MIT App Inventor 2)

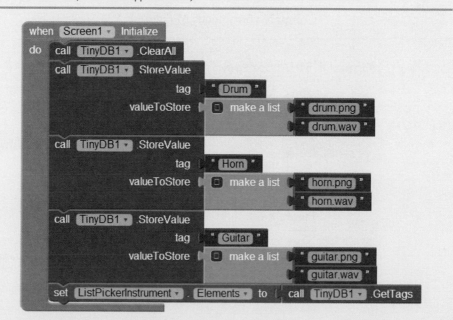

Step 15: Next we are going to program the `ListPicker.AfterPicking` event. This event is fired once the user selects an item on the list. We will need the `ListPickerIntrument.AfterPicking` block, found in the *ListPickerInstrument* drawer. See Figure 8-58.

Figure 8-58 `ListPickerInstrument.AfterPicking` Block
(*Source:* MIT App Inventor 2)

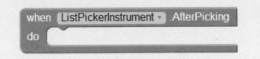

Step 16: Once the user has selected an instrument, the `AfterPicking` event is fired. Now open the second screen (which we will develop in a moment) and send it a start value of the instrument that was selected.

Find the `open another screen with start value` block, located in the *Control* drawer.

Step 17: Place the block inside the `ListPickerInstrument.AfterPicking` block. Plug a Text block that is set to the string *Details* into the `screenName` slot (this is the same name we will give our new, or second, screen). Plug a `ListPickerInstrument.Selection` property value block into the `startValue` slot. This will send the value of whatever the user selected to the `Details` screen. For example, if a user selects *Drum* from the ListPicker, *Drum* will be the start value that is sent to the second screen.

Compare your blocks to Figure 8-59.

Figure 8-59 `AfterPicking` Event (*Source:* MIT App Inventor 2)

when `ListPickerInstrument` `.AfterPicking`
do `open another screen with start value` screenName `" Details "`
startValue `ListPickerInstrument` . `Selection`

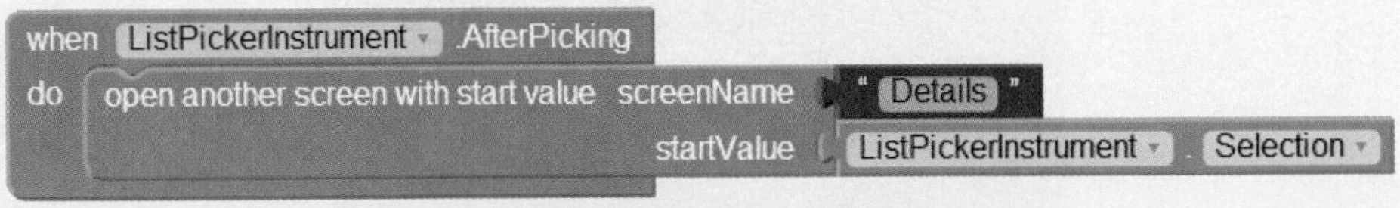

Step 18: We are now finished with `Screen1`. Compare your blocks to Figure 8-60.

Step 19: Now let's develop the second screen. Press the *Add Screen* button at the top of the App Inventor site. Name the new screen *Details*, as shown in Figure 8-61.

Figure 8-60 Complete `Screen1` Blocks (*Source:* MIT App Inventor 2)

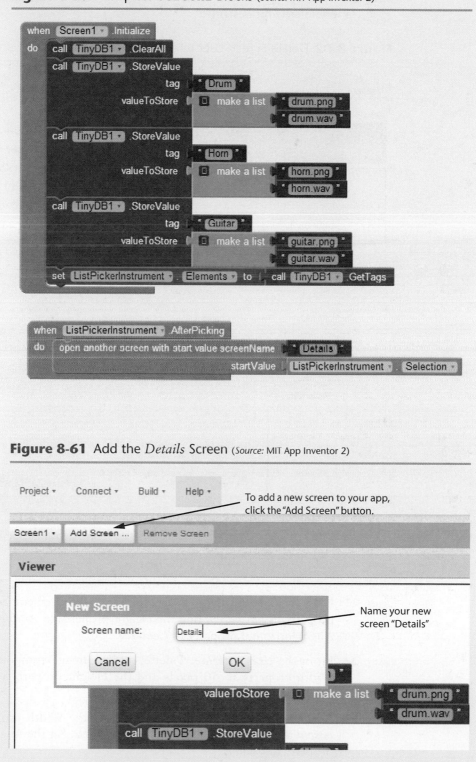

Figure 8-61 Add the *Details* Screen (*Source:* MIT App Inventor 2)

Step 20: Let's design the user interface for Screen2. Follow Figure 8-62 to complete your design.

Figure 8-62 Details Screen User Interface (*Source:* MIT App Inventor 2)

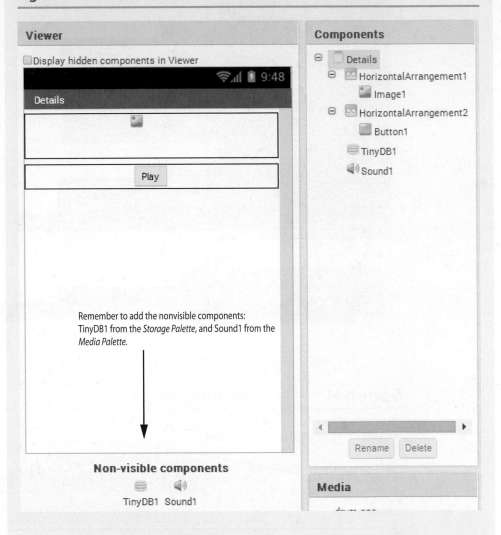

Step 21: From the *Layout* Palette, add a HorizontalArrangement. Set the Width property to *Fill parent* and the Height property to *Automatic*. Set the AlignHorizontal property to *Center*.

Step 22: From the *User Interface* Palette, add an Image component. Set the Width property to 50 pixels and the Height property to 50 pixels. Leave the Picture property set to *None*.

Step 23: Add another HorizontalArrangment. Set the Width property to *Fill parent* and the Height property to *Automatic*. Set the AlignHorizontal property to *Center*.

Step 24: From the *User Interface* Palette add a Button into the second HorizontalArrangement. Set the Text property to *Play*.

Step 25: From the *Storage* Palette, add a TinyDB component to the design.

Step 26: From the *Media* Palette, add a Sound component to the design. Compare your design to Figure 8-62.

> **NOTE:** Even though it seems that we've added two different TinyDB components, they actually share the same storage space and act like one component.

Step 27: Program the `Details.Initialize` event block. See Figure 8-63.

Figure 8-63 The `Details.Initialize` Event Block (*Source:* MIT App Inventor 2)

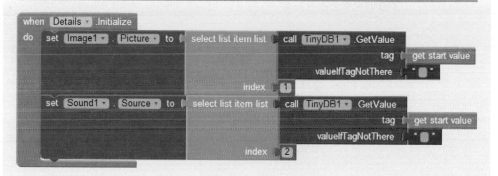

Step 28: Find the `Details.Initialze` block in the *Details* drawer. Click to place it in the Blocks Editor. See Figure 8-64.

Figure 8-64 Add the `Details.Initialize` Event Block (*Source:* MIT App Inventor 2)

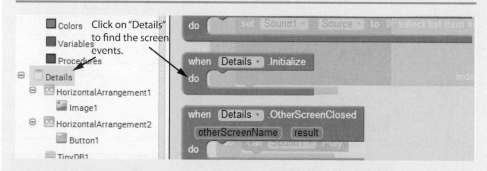

Step 29: Add two `get start value` blocks, found in the *Control* drawer.

Step 30: Add two empty text blocks, found in the *Text* drawer.

Step 31: Add two `TinyDB1.Get Value` blocks, found in the *TinyDB1* drawer. Plug in the `get start value` blocks into each `tag` slot and the empty text blocks into each `valueIfTagNotThere` slot. See Figure 8-65.

Figure 8-65 `TinyDB1.GetValue` Blocks (*Source:* MIT App Inventor 2)

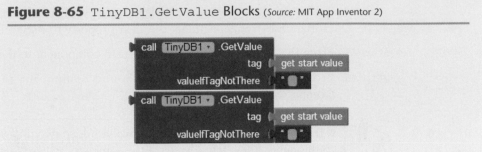

Step 32: Create two `select list item` blocks, found in the *Lists* drawer. Plug the `TinyDB1` blocks shown in Figure 8-65 into the top slot. See Figure 8-66.

Figure 8-66 `select list item` Blocks (*Source:* MIT App Inventor 2)

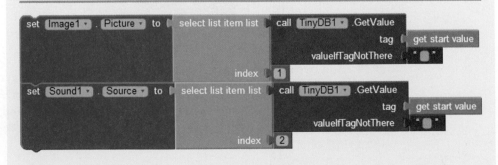

Step 33: For the first `select list item` block, plug a number 1 block in the item slot. For the second `select list item` block, plug a number 2 block in the `index` slot. See Figure 8-66.

Step 34: Now find the `set Image1.Picture to` block from the *Image1* drawer and plug in the first set of blocks shown in Figure 8-66.

Step 35: Create the `set Sound1.Sound to` block, found in the *Sound1* drawer, and plug in the second set of blocks from Figure 8-66. Figure 8-67 shows how the blocks should appear at this point.

Figure 8-67 Set Image and Sound Properties (*Source:* MIT App Inventor 2)

Step 36: Place the block set shown in Figure 8-67 into the `Details.Initialize` block and compare your blocks to Figure 8-63.

Step 37: Program the `Button1.Click` event. Find the `Button1.Click` event handler in the *Button1* drawer and place it in the Blocks Editor.

Step 38: Place a `call Sound1.Play` block in the `Button1.Click` event. Find the `call Sound1.Play` in the *Sound1* drawer. Place it into the `Button1.Click` event. See Figure 8-68.

Figure 8-68 `Button1.Click` Event (*Source:* MIT App Inventor 2)

Step 39: Build and download the .apk to your device and test your app! Compare your complete `Details` Screen Blocks Editor workspace to Figure 8-69.

Figure 8-69 Complete Details Screen Blocks (*Source:* MIT App Inventor 2)

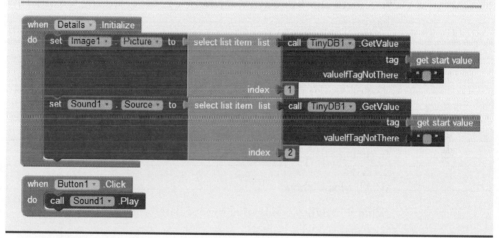

Review Questions

Multiple Choice

1. What application(s) store data into a database?
   a. Facebook
   b. Twitter
   c. Online banking applications
   d. All of the above

2. Which database does App Inventor provide for data storage on a device?
   a. SmallDB
   b. TinyDB

c. TinyWebDB

d. MyAppDB

3. How many databases should you have per App Inventor application:

a. One

b. Two

c. As many as you wish

d. None

4. How many App Inventor applications can share a single data store?

a. One

b. Two

c. As many as you wish

d. None

5. How many values can you have for a single tag in a TinyDB?

a. One

b. Two

c. As many as you wish

d. None

6. If you attempt to store a value for a tag that is already in your TinyDB, what will happen?

a. You will have two entries for the same tag

b. You will have no entries for the same tag

c. You will have one entry for the tag

d. Your program will not run

7. What data type(s) must the value be in a tag-value pair?

a. Number

b. String

c. List

d. All of the above

8. What TinyDB block is used to save data to a TinyDB?

a. `AddInfo`

b. `StoreValue`

c. `SaveInfo`

d. None of the above

9. To store information to a TinyDB, you must provide which item(s)?

a. Tag

b. Number and tag

c. Number and value

d. Tag and value

10. Which TinyDB block is used to retrieve a value from a TinyDB?

a. `GetInfo`

b. `GetData`

c. `GetValue`

d. `FindValue`

Short Answer

1. Give three examples of how a database can make mobile applications more practical and useful.

2. What would happen if you include two TinyDBs into an App Inventor project? Would you get errors? What would be the effect?

3. There can only be one value per tag in a TinyDB. Why do you think this is?

4. What is the advantage of storing a list as the value of a tag in a TinyDB? Can you think of any potential problems with this approach?

5. Why are Android applications isolated from each other? How can this protect your application? How does it limit your application?

6. If you want to share data between applications, where must that data live? What kind of database can you use for shared data between App Inventor applications?

Exercises

1. **Vehicle VIN Number**

   Review Tutorial 8-4. Write a similar app that stores a vehicle's VIN number and make. Which value should be the tag? Why?

2. **Vehicle VIN Number Modification 1**

   Review Tutorial 8-5. Expand the VIN number application from Exercise 1 to allow your user to type in a VIN and find the make of the vehicle.

3. **Vehicle VIN Number Modification 3**

   Review Tutorial 8-6. Expand the VIN project further by adding the ability to store the make, model, and year of the vehicle.

4. **Contact List Modification**

   Review Tutorial 8-6, step 11. What would happen if we did not clear the labels each time?

5. **Product/Price Modification**

   Modify the Product/Price application from Tutorial 8-5 so that the user can search for and determine the price of a product and how many are in stock.

Chapter Projects

1. **Daily Special**

   Write an application that allows a restaurant manager to enter the seven daily specials and store the information into a TinyDB using the day of the week as the tag and the special entered on the screen as the value. Provide a search underneath the entry portion that will allow the user to enter the day of the week in a textbox, click a button, and see the special for that day.

   See Tutorial 8-5 for a similar example.

VideoNote
Creating the
Daily Special App

2. **Yards to Meters**

Use a loop to generate the conversion of yards, from one yard up to one thousand. Allow the user of your application to enter the number of yards to convert and display the resulting number of meters.

    a. Use a `for range` loop in the `Screen.Initialize` event, iterating from 1 to 1000. During each iteration store the loop iteration number and the value of that multiplied by .9144 (the yard to meters conversion factor). For example, on the first iteration the tag will be 1 and value will be .9144. On the second iteration, the tag will be 2 and the value will be 2 * .9144, or 1.8288, and so forth.

    b. Include a TextBox for the user to enter the yards (a whole number between 1 and 1000), a button as the event trigger, and a Label to store the result

    c. On the `Button.Click` event, retrieve the meters from the TinyDB and populate the result Label.

3. **Product By SKU (Stock Keeping Unit)**

Often products are stored in databases by a unique identifier called an SKU. An SKU is generally a string of characters and letters.

Write a Product application that generates a TinyDB on `Screen.Initialize` of five or more SKUs and associated product names, prices, and quantity in stock. When storing items to the TinyDB, the tag should be the SKU of the product and the value should be a List containing the name, price, and quantity in stock.

Provide the user an interface allowing entry of a SKU, an search Button, and Labels to show the resulting product information.

4. **Custom Colors**

App Inventor provides us with several built-in colors to work with, which you can see in the *Color* drawer in the Blocks Editor. Behind the scenes, App Inventor colors are stored as numbers. The color black is actually stored as the number –16777216. You can see the number of a color by printing the color out as text. See Figure 8-70.

Figure 8-70 Determining the Number of a Color *(Source: MIT App Inventor 2)*

To create a color in App Inventor you can use the `make color` block found in the *Color* drawer. You will need to provide the block three or four elements, the numbers for the amount of red, green, and blue in the color and optionally the number for the opacity, or transparency. Each of the four numbers needs to be in the range of 0 through 255. You can use the Web to search for

RGB color charts. For example, the color Dark Orchid has the RGB value of 153-50-204. These numbers represent the amount of red, green, and blue, respectively. The optional fourth number represents the opacity, which is the transparency of the color. If you supply 0 for this value, the color will be completely transparent and will not be visible. If you supply the maximum value of 255, the color will be completely solid and block out anything that it covers.

5. **Make a Color**

    To make a color, you first need to create a list with the three or four numbers. You can use the mutator to change the number of parameters the make color block accepts. They must be in the proper order of red, green, blue, and opacity. To make a semi-transparent Dark Orchid you can follow the steps below:

    Step 1: Create a variable to hold your color. Name it *DarkOrchid*.

    Step 2: Find the make color block in the *Colors* drawer. Plug this in as the value of your DarkOrchid variable.

    Step 3: Create your list. Go to the *List* drawer and select the make a list block. Supply the list with the RGB colors for Dark Orchid. Plug the list into the make color block in the components slot. See Figure 8-71.

Figure 8-71 Make a Color *(Source:* MIT App Inventor 2)

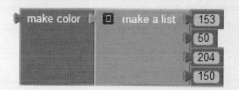

You can use the chart below (Figure 8-72) as reference or create your own colors to write an application that will store several custom colors by their name and number. Allow users to find the number for a certain color by searching the color's name. Include a component on the screen that displays the color in addition to the number that represents it.

See full color chart: http://beta.appinventor.mit.edu/learn/reference/blocks/colorchart.html.

5. **Load and Display Contact List TinyDB**

    Complete Tutorial 8-6 and review Tutorial 8-7. Modify Tutorial 8-3 by adding a ListPicker component at the bottom. This ListPicker should load all the contacts that are stored in the TinyDB to a list that the user can choose from.

    Once the contact is chosen, forward the user to a second screen that shows the detailed information (Name, Home Number, Mobile Number, and Email). Use the TinyDB.GetTags block.

Figure 8-72 Partial App Inventor Color Chart (*Source:* MIT App Inventor 2)

App Inventor Color Chart

(with thanks to James Laroche)

This chart gives the App Inventor numeric codes for a variety of colors.

Color Name	Color	App Inventor Color Number
AliceBlue		-984833
AntiqueWhite		-332841
Aqua		-16711681
Aquamarine		-8388652
Azure		-983041
Beige		-657966
Bisque		-6972
BlanchedAlmond		-5171
BlueViolet		-7722014
Brown		-5952982
BurlyWood		-2180985
CadetBlue		-10510688
Chartreuse		-8388864
Chocolate		-2987746
Coral		-32944
CornflowerBlue		-10185235
Cornsilk		-1828

TIP: Make your app more user-friendly by enabling the ShowFilterBar property. This allows the user to begin typing in a contact, and as they do, the list will filter appropriately.

CHALLENGE: To your second screen, add the nonvisible PhoneCall component. If you are running on a device, have the app place a call to the phone numbers relevant to the contact shown on the second screen. Don't call them *too* many times!

6. **Notes App**

   Complete Tutorials 8-1 through 8-3, and 8-7. Write an app that stores text notes as files in your application sandbox.

   Each time the user saves or appends to a note, store the file name to a TinyDB.

   Add a ListPicker to the bottom of the screen in Tutorial 8-3. The elements should be the files that the user has stored using the app.

   When the user chooses a file (or a "note"), open up that note for editing on a new screen. Allow the user to save modifications to the note and transfer control back to the original screen. Do not ask the user to re-enter the filename.

9 Graphics and Animation

9.1 The Canvas Component

CONCEPT: The Canvas is an App Inventor component that allows you to create two-dimensional graphics. You can use the Canvas to draw points, lines, and circles in different colors and sizes. You can also use ImageSprites on the Canvas. ImageSprites are images or animations that can move around on the Canvas.

Many of the mobile applications that we write will require some sort of graphics or animation. For example, most games require animation, moving images or touch screen interaction. With App Inventor, games are fun and easy to create, but the graphic and animation functionality can be applied to many other types of applications too. To get started, the first component to learn is the Canvas.

The App Inventor Canvas component is the starting point for creating graphics and animations. It allows us to create games and other graphical applications because it is touch-sensitive and allows us to move images and animations around.

The Canvas, found in the *Drawing and Animation* Palette, is like a sub-panel inside the Screen component. It is a rectangular panel with a specified height and width. The locations inside a Canvas are represented in pixels by a pair of x, y coordinates.

415

The x coordinate is the number of pixels from the left edge of the Canvas. The x coordinates at the left edge are 0, and they increase as you move to the right across the Canvas. The y coordinate is the number of pixels down, from the top edge of the Canvas. The y coordinates at the top edge of the Canvas are 0, and they increase as you move down the Canvas. This is illustrated in Figure 9-1.

Figure 9-1 The Canvas Coordinate System (*Source:* Tony Gaddis/Pearson Education, Inc.)

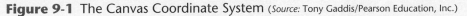

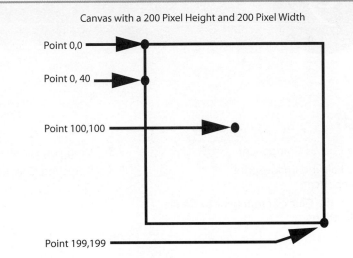

Canvas with a 200 Pixel Height and 200 Pixel Width

Point 0,0

Point 0, 40

Point 100,100

Point 199,199

Figure 9-1 shows that the top left corner of the Canvas is point 0, 0 because it is zero pixels from the left edge and zero from the top edge. The point 0, 40 is down a bit on the left edge (the x coordinate is zero pixels away from the left edge, and the y coordinate is 40 pixels down from the top). The point at 100, 100 is at the approximate center of the Canvas because it is both 100 pixels to the right of the left edge and 100 pixels down from the top edge.

Canvas Properties

The Canvas component has several properties, but as you can see in Figure 9-1, the Height and Width properties are important because they set the size of the Canvas, which is the stage of your application. By setting the Canvas's Height equal to 200 you are making the Canvas 200 pixels tall; likewise, setting the Width equal to 200 makes the Canvas 200 pixels wide. You can also set the Height and Width to *Fill parent,* which will set it to equal the Height and/or Width of your Screen1 component.

The PaintColor property sets the color for the points, lines, and circles that are drawn on the Canvas.

There are two properties that we can use to set the background of the Canvas, BackgroundColor and BackgroundImage. If we set the BackgroundColor, the color we specify will fill in the entire background of the Canvas. To set the background of the Canvas to be an image, we must first upload the image to our App Inventor project. Uploading an image for the BackgroundImage property is covered in Tutorial 9-1.

You can set all of these properties, Height, Width, PaintColor, BackgroundColor, and BackgroundImage at design-time or programmatically in the Blocks Editor.

Drawing Methods

Once you add a Canvas component to your design, you will find method blocks in the Blocks Editor that will allow you to draw on the Canvas. These are found in the *Canvas1* drawer.

The `DrawPoint` method block will draw a one-pixel point on the Canvas. It requires that you specify where on the Canvas to draw it by supplying the x, y coordinates.

The `DrawCircle` method block will draw a circle on the Canvas. The circle is drawn filled in with the color specified by the PaintColor property value. The method requires that you tell it where to draw the circle by supplying the x, y coordinates of the center of the circle. This method also requires that you give it a radius in pixels so that it knows how big to draw the circle. If you give it a value of 1 for the radius, you will have a very small, two-pixel-wide circle. If you give it a large value, such as 100, you will have a very large circle that is 200 pixels wide and 200 pixels tall.

The `DrawLine` method block will draw a line in the color specified by the PaintColor property. This method needs to know at what point to start and at what point to end, so it needs two sets of x, y coordinates. The `DrawLine` method also uses the LineWidth property, which sets the width of the line in pixels.

The `Clear` method block clears all graphics from the Canvas except for the background image.

Touch and Dragged Event Handlers

The Canvas component's `Touched` event handler acts just as it sounds: it will execute when a user touches the Canvas. It records the x, y coordinates where it was touched. Using this event will allow you to do something programmatically when the screen is touched—for example, draw a circle at the point where the user touched the screen, as you will see in our first tutorial. If the Canvas has a sprite and the sprite is touched, this event handler will set the `touchedSprite` parameter to `true`.

Figure 9-2 Touched Event Handler *(Source: MIT App Inventor 2)*

Figure 9-3 Dragged Event Handler *(Source: MIT App Inventor 2)*

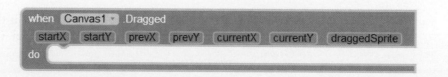

The Dragged event handler will execute when a user drags across Canvas. This event handler will record where the drag started and where it ended by keeping track of the x, y coordinates. If the user drags from the top left corner to the bottom right corner of a 200 by 200 pixel Canvas, the previous (prevX, prevY) coordinates are 0, 0 and the current coordinates (currentX, currentY) are updated as the drag occurs and finally ends with 199, 199. This event handler also has a startX and startY set of coordinates which indicates the position where the user first touched the screen. There is also a Boolean variable named draggedSprite that is set to true if the user drags a sprite on the Canvas.

There are more properties, methods, and events to learn and explore in the Canvas component, but this gives us enough information to start drawing some graphics!

**VideoNote
Drawing on the
Canvas**

Tutorial 9-1:
Drawing on the Canvas

In this tutorial, we will introduce the Canvas component by accomplishing the following tasks:

1. Add the Canvas to the Screen
2. Set the Height and Width properties
3. Set the BackgroundImage property
4. Set the PaintColor property
5. Use the Touched event handler to draw circles
6. Use the Dragged event handler to draw lines
7. Use the Clear method to clear the Canvas

Step 1: Start a new project, and in the Designer drag a Canvas component from the *Drawing and Animation* Palette to the screen.

Step 2: In the Properties panel, set the Width property to *Fill parent* and the Height property to 200.

Step 3: Download the BlueGradient.png file from the companion website. Save it on your computer in a place that you will remember. Then, set the background image by clicking on the BackgroundImage property in the *Properties* panel. You will then get a dialog box, as shown in Figure 9-4.

Click the *Upload file* button and browse to select the BlueGradient. png file.

NOTE: For this tutorial you can use any image that you wish; you will still be able to complete the following steps just fine.

Step 4: Be sure you have the Canvas component selected in the Designer and click the PaintColor property in the *Properties* panel. Change the color to *Green*.

Figure 9-4 Background Image Dialog Box *(Source:* MIT App Inventor 2)

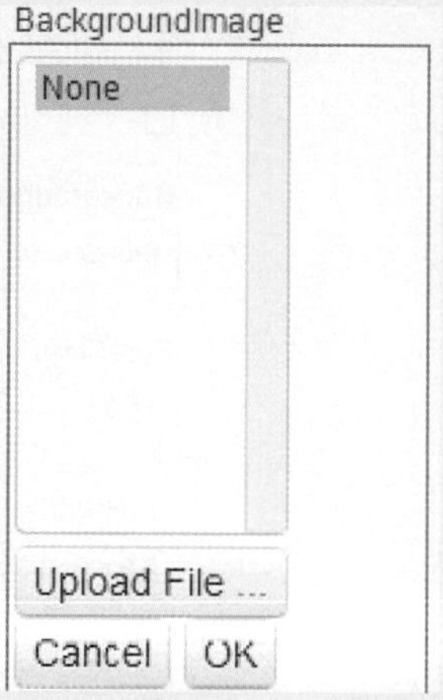

Step 5: Drag a Button from the *User Interface* Palette to the screen beneath the Canvas and rename it `ButtonClear`. Set the Button's Text property to *Clear*.

Step 6: Compare your Viewer and Components column with Figure 9-5 and your Canvas properties with Figure 9-6.

Figure 9-5 Viewer and Components *(Source:* MIT App Inventor 2)

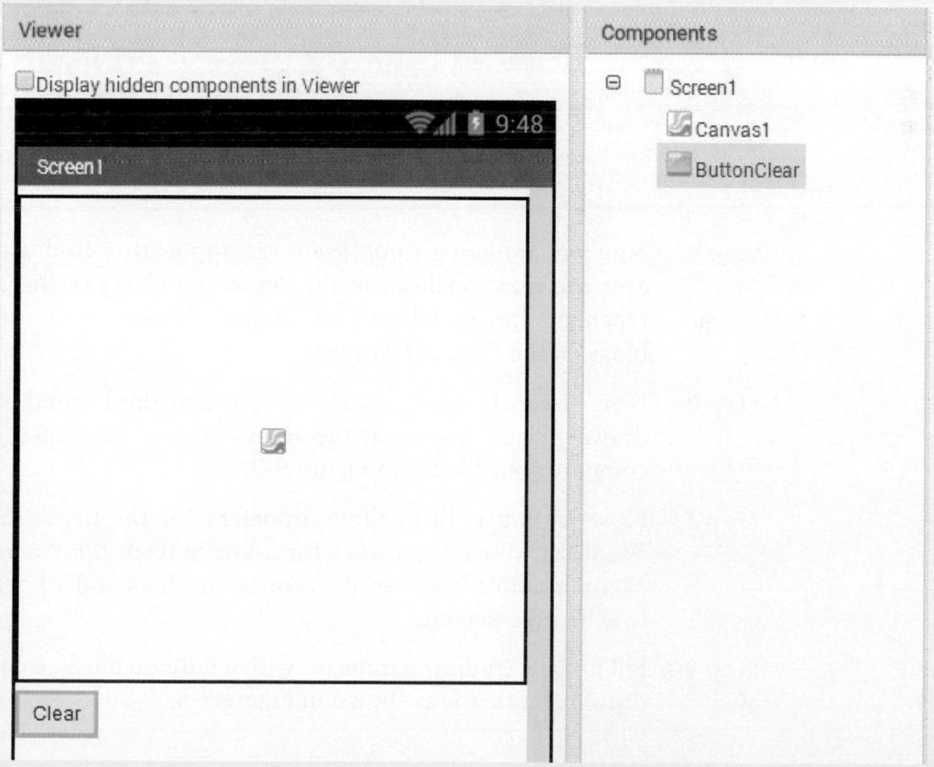

Figure 9-6 Canvas Properties Panel (*Source:* MIT App Inventor 2)

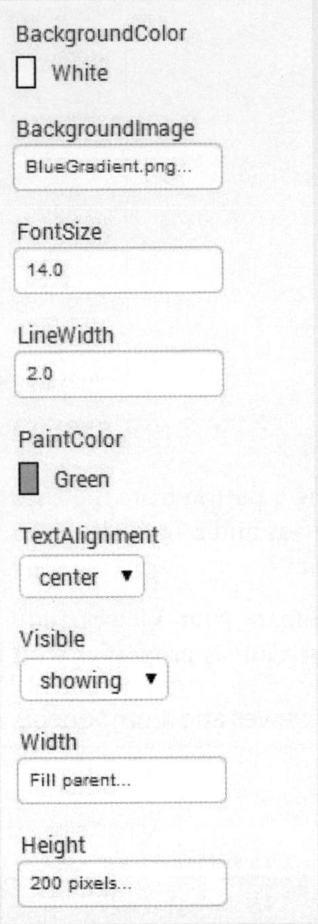

BackgroundColor

☐ White

BackgroundImage

BlueGradient.png...

FontSize

14.0

LineWidth

2.0

PaintColor

▨ Green

TextAlignment

center ▼

Visible

showing ▼

Width

Fill parent...

Height

200 pixels...

Step 7: Now we are going to program the application to draw circles wherever the user touches (on the device) or clicks (using the emulator). Open the Blocks Editor and select the when Canvas1.Touched do block in the *Canvas1* drawer.

Step 8: Now select the Canvas1.DrawCircle method found in the *Canvas1* drawer. Place that inside the when Canvas1.Touched do block and compare your blocks to Figure 9-7.

Step 9: Now we must fill in the parameters for the DrawCircle method. We want to use the values for x and y from the Canvas1.Touched event handler because it records the location of where the user touched the screen.

Step 10: Fill in the r (radius) parameter with a number block, found in the *Math* drawer, set to 15, as shown in Figure 9-8.

Figure 9-7 Touched Event Handler (*Source:* MIT App Inventor 2)

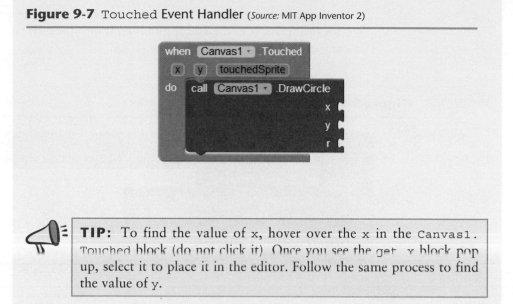

TIP: To find the value of x, hover over the x in the Canvas1. Touched block (do not click it). Once you see the get x block pop up, select it to place it in the editor. Follow the same process to find the value of y.

Figure 9-8 Complete Touched Event Handler (*Source:* MIT App Inventor 2)

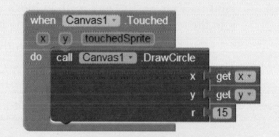

Step 11: Next, let's program the Canvas1.Dragged event handler to draw a line when a user drags their finger across the device or when a mouse is dragged while using the emulator. Find and select the when Canvas1. Dragged do block in the *Canvas1* drawer.

Step 12: Find and select the Canvas1.DrawLine method block and place it in the when Canvas1.Dragged do block. Notice that it needs four parameter values for the starting point (x1, y1) and the ending point (x2, y2). Recall from the description of the Canvas1.Dragged event handler (Figure 9-3) that the prevX and prevY parameter values indicate where the drag started and the currentX and currentY indicate where it is going. Hover over these parameters on the Canvas1. Dragged block, remember not to click them, and wait for the get blocks to pop up. Once you see the `get` block for the parameter, click it to place it in the editor and plug it into the correct slot of the `Canvas1.DrawLine` method.

Figure 9-9 Complete `Dragged` Event Handler (*Source:* MIT App Inventor 2)

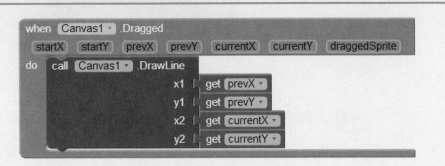

Step 13: Now you will program the *Clear* Button to clear the Canvas. Find the `when ButtonClear.Click do` block in the *ButtonClear* drawer. Select it to place it in the workspace.

Step 14: Find the `Canvas1.Clear` method block in the *Canvas1* drawer. Place it in the `when ButtonClear.Click do` block.

Compare your Blocks Editor for this tutorial to Figure 9-10.

Figure 9-10 Tutorial 9-1 Complete Blocks Editor (*Source:* MIT App Inventor 2)

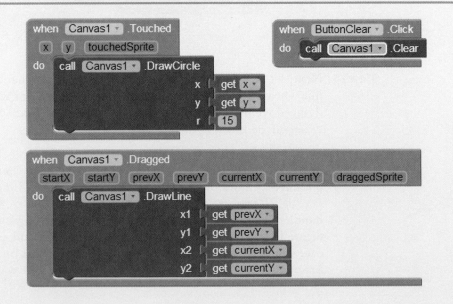

Step 15: Run and test your application on your device or emulator. See if you can draw some flowers, or a face, as shown in Figure 9-11.

Figure 9-11 Draw (*Source:* MIT App Inventor 2)

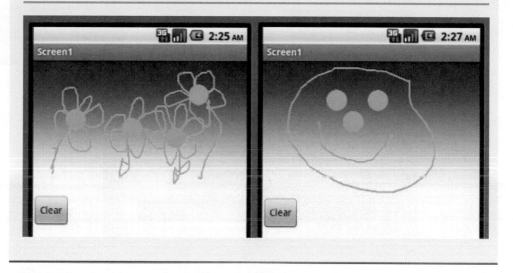

Drawing Using Specific Values

The examples shown in Tutorial 9-1 use the x, y values associated with the Touched and Dragged event handlers. You can also hard code or use variable data to draw on a Canvas.

For example, if you'd like to draw a line from the coordinates 20, 20 to 20, 40 when the user presses a Button, you can supply the DrawLine method block with those specific values, as shown in Figure 9-12.

Figure 9-12 Drawing with Hard Coded Values (*Source:* MIT App Inventor 2)

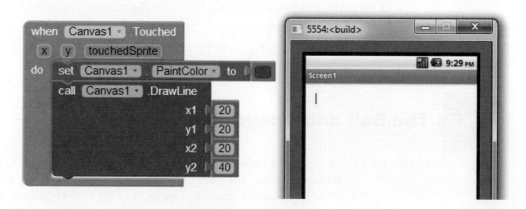

In Figure 9-12 you see that we can specifically tell the DrawLine method block where to draw the line. Which points will you need to complete a red square in this example? How many DrawLine method calls will you need?

You can also use variable data with the drawing methods. Take a look at the example in Figure 9-13.

Figure 9-13 Drawing with Variable Data (*Source:* MIT App Inventor 2)

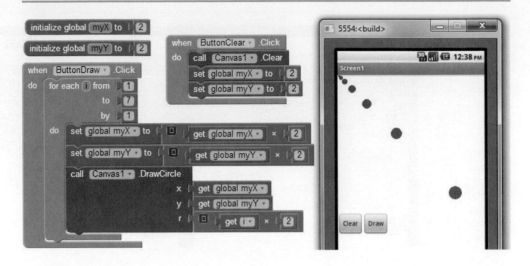

In this `DrawCircle` example, we set up two variables for the x and y coordinates. We also use a variable i, the `for range` loop counter, for the radius. The result in the emulator shows that the coordinates are variable (the circles are drawn across the screen) and that the radius is variable (the circles get bigger).

 Checkpoint

9.1   On a 300 by 300 pixel Canvas, what are the x, y coordinates of the top right corner? What are the coordinates of the bottom left corner?

9.2   What are the coordinates of the mid-point of a 160 by 160 pixel Canvas?

9.3   When calling the `DrawLine` method from the `Dragged` event handler, where do we find the `prevX` and `prevY` blocks to connect to the `x1` and `y1` sockets?

9.4   Using the example in Figure 9-12, give the coordinates to complete a square.

9.2 The Ball and ImageSprite Component

CONCEPT: A sprite is a two-dimensional graphic, picture, or animation that can be moved about the Canvas. Even though it is a separate object, when your application is running a sprite, it looks as if it is part of the Canvas.

App Inventor has two different types of sprite components. The first is the Ball component, which is essentially a two-dimensional circle that can move around the Canvas. The second is the ImageSprite component, which acts very similar to the

Ball component, except that rather than looking like a ball, you select an image for it to display. Both of these components are found in the *Animation* Palette, in the Designer.

Whether you use the Ball or ImageSprite component, you can touch it, move it, bounce it, and drag it. Balls and ImageSprites can also interact with each other and the edges of the Canvas by colliding with each other and reaching the edges.

NOTE: All of the methods and event handlers for the Ball component work the same for the ImageSprite component. The components vary in only a few properties.

The Ball and ImageSprite Component Properties

The sprite components have X and Y properties that indicate the sprite's position on the Canvas. These properties hold the x and y coordinates of the sprite's top left corner. This must be taken into consideration when moving the sprite so you do not attempt to move it off of the Canvas. For example, assume you have a Canvas that is 300 by 300 pixels, and a sprite that is 20 by 20 pixels. If you want to position the sprite in the Canvas's lower-right corner, you would position it at the coordinates 279, 279.

The sprite components also have properties that tell it them how to behave. These are Interval, Heading, and Speed, summarized here:

- The Interval property sets how *often* the sprite will move, and is in milliseconds. For example, 1,000 milliseconds equal one second, so the larger you set this property, the slower your sprite will move.
- The Heading property will set the direction of the sprite in degrees. So, 90 (degrees) will set the direction of the sprite to straight up, 180 will set the direction to left, 270 is down and 0 is right. For example, if you want the sprite to move from the bottom left corner to the top right corner in a straight line of a 200 by 200 pixel canvas, you will set the Heading to 45.
- The Speed property is the number of *pixels* to move each interval. So, if you have your Speed set to 10 and the Interval set at 1,000 milliseconds, your sprite will move 10 pixels every second (in the direction set by the *Heading*).

The Ball Component Properties

You can change how the Ball sprite appears by changing some of its basic properties. Change the PaintColor property to set the color, the Radius property to set the size, and the Visible property to either show or hide it.

The Ball and ImageSprite Component Methods

The sprite components have a `Bounce` method that simulates the sprite bouncing off an edge or corner. It is important that we first understand edges before using this method.

Edges

Edges are represented by numbers and are used in both the Bounce method and the EdgeReached event handler. The edges are represented as follows:

- North or Top Edge = 1
- South or Bottom Edge = −1
- East or Right Edge = 3
- West or Left Edge = −3
- Northeast Edges = 2
- Southwest Edge = −2
- Southeast Edge = 4
- Northwest = −4

Figure 9-14 Bounce with East Edge (*Source:* MIT App Inventor 2)

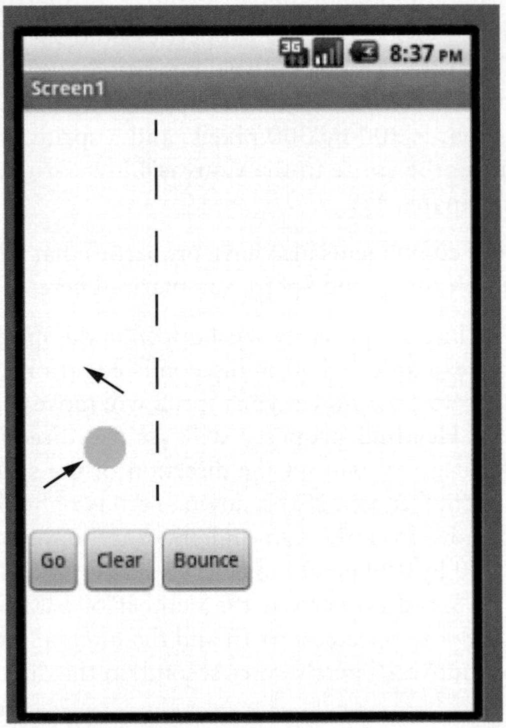

Assume we are using a Ball component, and the *Bounce* Button shown in the figure calls the Bounce method with a number 3 as the edge parameter. At the point in which it is invoked, the Bounce method will act as if there is an East edge to bounce off of (represented in Figure 9-14 by the dotted line). The Ball will appear to bounce off of it and travel in the opposite direction.

The MoveTo method will allow you to move the sprite to a specific x, y coordinate on a Canvas. For example, assume that you have a 200 by 200 pixel Canvas. You can use the `MoveTo` method to put the sprite in the approximate center by assigning 90 to both the `X` and `Y` parameters (assuming the Ball radius is 10).

Sometimes sprites may accidentally move out of bounds (off of the Canvas). You can use the `MoveIntoBounds` method block to put them back onto the Canvas.

There is one additional method block, the Boolean `CollidingWith` method, that we will cover later in this Chapter in Section 9.5, Detecting Collisions.

The Ball and ImageSprite Component Events

The `Dragged` event handler has the same arguments and works the same as the Canvas `Dragged` event handler. See Figure 9-3. This event will be executed when a user drags the sprite with their finger or mouse and will keep track of where the drag began and where it ended. It will hold these values in the `prevX`, `prevY`, `currentX`, and `currentY` argument values.

Figure 9-15 `EdgeReached` Event Handler (*Source:* MIT App Inventor 2)

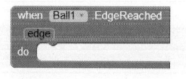

The `EdgeReached` event handler is executed when the sprite reaches an edge of the Canvas. The `edge` argument value will indicate which edge was reached by a number. See the number representation of edges above Figure 9-14. If the bottom edge was reached, the `edge` argument would have a value of -1.

Like the Canvas `Touched` event handler, the sprite `Touched` event handler will execute when the sprite is touched and will record the x, y coordinates of the position where the touch occurred.

Figure 9-16 `Flung` Event Handler (*Source:* MIT App Inventor 2)

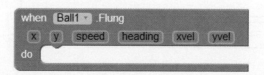

A fling is a quick swipe of the Canvas and will invoke the `Flung` event handler. The event records the x, y coordinates of where the fling started and also provides the x and Y velocities of the fling (`xvel` and `yvel`). The `speed` and `heading` values of the flung `Ball1` are also available.

Tutorial 9-2:
Bouncing Ball

**VideoNote
Bouncing Ball**

Let's create an app that will make a ball bounce around a Canvas. We will also let the user control when to start over, speed up, and slow down. We will give the user a Button that will bounce the ball down from wherever it is at the time.

Step 1: Design the user interface. Start a new project and add a Canvas to the screen

Step 2: Add a HorizontalArrangement under the Canvas and then add four Buttons to it.

Step 3: Rename your Buttons and set their Text properties to match Figure 9-17.

Figure 9-17 Screen Design (*Source:* MIT App Inventor 2)

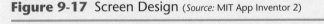

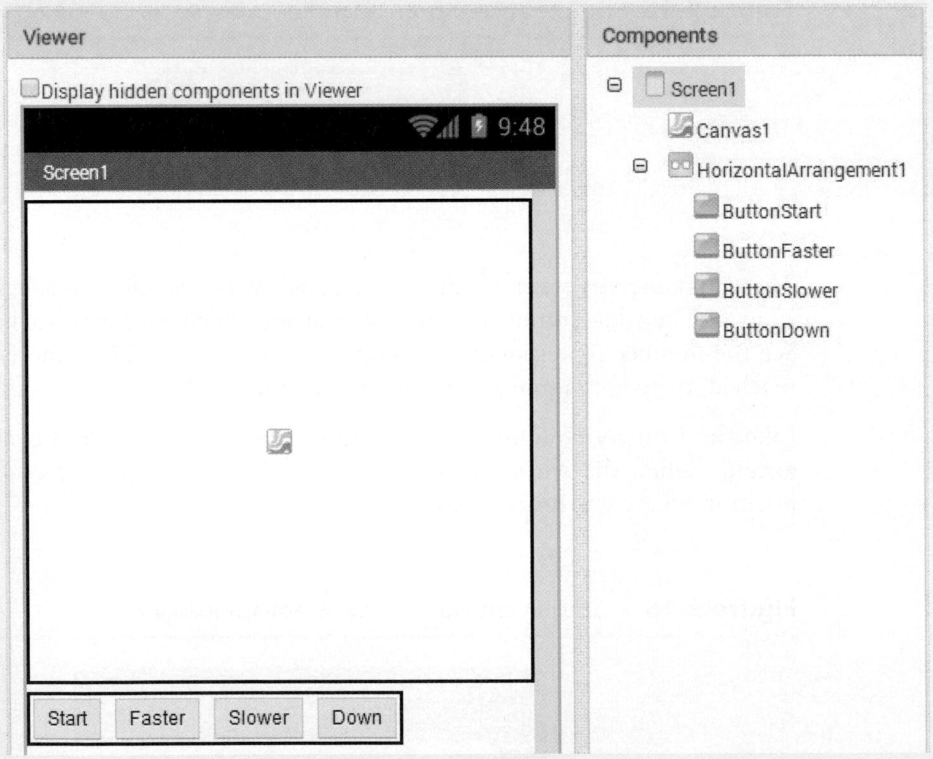

Step 4: Add a Ball component (from the *Drawing and Animation* Palette) to the Canvas and set the properties as shown in Figure 9-18.

Set the Heading to 45 degrees, the Interval to 500 (half second), the color to Magenta (or whatever you wish), the Radius to 10 and the x, y coordinates to 0, 0.

Figure 9-18 Ball Component Properties (*Source:* MIT App Inventor 2)

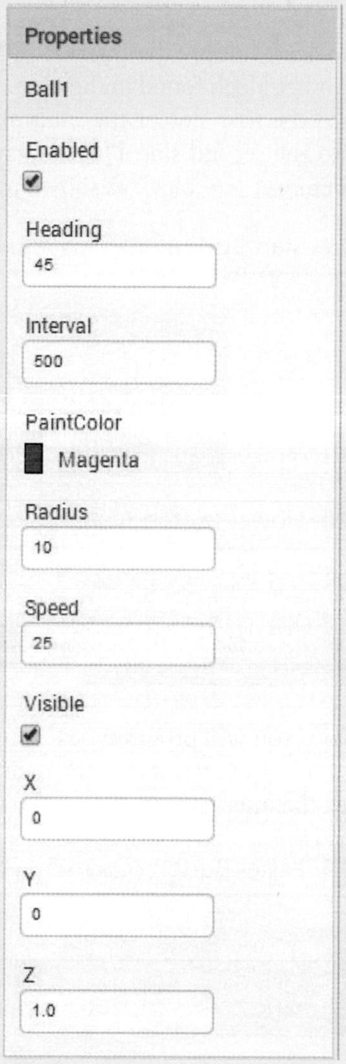

Properties

Ball1

Enabled
☑

Heading
45

Interval
500

PaintColor
⬛ Magenta

Radius
10

Speed
25

Visible
☑

X
0

Y
0

Z
1.0

Step 5: Now Let's program the blocks, starting with the `when ButtonStart.Click do` event handler. Open the *ButtonStart* drawer and find the `when ButtonStart.Click do` block. Open to the *Ball1* drawer and select three method blocks: `set Ball1.Interval to`, `set Ball1.X to` and `set Ball1.Y to`. Place all three in the `when ButtonStart.Click do` event handler. From the *Math* drawer, select three `number` blocks and set the first two to zero and the third to 500. Plug the zeros into the `X` and `Y` slots, and the 500 into the `Interval` slot as shown in Figure 9-19.

Step 6: Now you will program `Ball1` to move slower. Remember that the higher the interval the slower `Ball1` will move. So, we will simply increase the interval by two times each time the user clicks the Slower Button.

(You can also decrease the Speed to accomplish this step, but we are going to manipulate the Interval in this example.) Open the *Ball1* drawer and find the `set Ball1.Interval` and the value of `Ball1.Interval to` blocks. Multiply the Interval by 2 by using a multiplication block and a number block found in the *Math* drawer. Plug the `Ball1.Interval`block into the first slot of the multiplication block, and the number 2 block into the second slot. Plug the multiplication block into the `set Ball1.Interval to` block as shown in Figure 9-20.

Figure 9-19 Start Button (*Source:* MIT App Inventor 2)

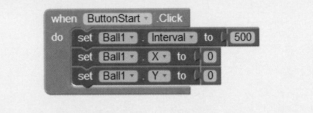

Figure 9-20 Slower Button (*Source:* MIT App Inventor 2)

Step 7: Now you will program `Ball1` to move faster. This step is almost identical to Step 6, but it uses the division math operation instead. We want to cut the interval in half to make the Ball travel faster. See Figure 9-21.

Figure 9-21 Faster Button (*Source:* MIT App Inventor 2)

Step 8: Now let's program `Ball1` to bounce on any of the edges it reaches. Find the `Ball1.EdgeReached` event handler in the *Ball1* drawer. Inside that event, place a `Ball1.Bounce` method block, also found in the *Ball1* drawer. Plug a `get edge` block (found by hovering the mouse cursor over the `edge` parameter) into the `edge` socket of the `Bounce` method block. Compare your event handler to Figure 9-22.

Figure 9-22 Bounce the Ball (*Source:* MIT App Inventor 2)

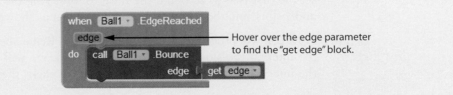

Step 9: The last action we need to program is the bounce down which happens when the user presses the `ButtonDown` Button. In the `when ButtonDown.Click do` event handler, call the `Ball1.Bounce` method. The call is similar to what we did in Step 8, but instead of using the value of the `edge` argument we will just put in a number 1 block which represents the top edge.

Figure 9-23 Bounce Down (*Source:* MIT App Inventor 2)

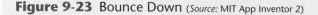

Step 10: Compare your blocks to Figure 9-24.

Figure 9-24 Tutorial 9-2 Complete Blocks Editor (*Source:* MIT App Inventor 2)

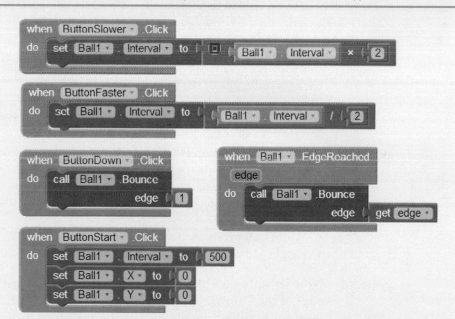

Step 11: Run and test your application on your device or emulator. Test speeding `Ball1` up and slowing it down. What happens when you click the `ButtonDown` Button quickly and consecutively?

ImageSprite Component Properties

The ImageSprite component essentially works the same as the Ball component. The differences stem just from the appearance of the sprite. For example, instead of a radius, there are Height and Width properties to indicate the size in pixels. There is also no PaintColor property because the sprite is associated with an image.

The image is indicated in the Picture property. As with other images in App Inventor, you must upload the image to App Inventor before you use it. The ImageSprite has a Boolean Rotates property. If the value is set to true, the image will rotate in the direction of the Heading property.

Tutorial 9-3:
Fishbowl - Using the ImageSprite Component

VideoNote
The Fishbowl App

In this tutorial, we will simulate a fish swimming in a bowl. After this tutorial, the fish will swim around, inside and outside of the bowl. We will learn how to keep the fish in the bowl with skills learned in Sections 9.3 and 9.4.

You will need to download two image files, `Fishbowl.png` and `Fish.png`, from this book's companion website (go to www.pearsonhighered.com/gaddis).

Step 1: Start a new project and add a Canvas to the screen. Set the Canvas component's Width to *Fill parent* and the Height to 300 pixels. Set the BackgroundImage of the Canvas to `Fishbowl.png`.

Step 2: Add an ImageSprite component to the Canvas. Change its name to `ImageSpriteFish`. Set the properties as follows:
- Heading - 300 degrees
- Interval - 100 milliseconds
- Picture - `Fish.png`
- Rotates - checked (true)
- Speed - 10
- Width - 60 pixels
- Height -30 pixels

Step 3: Now let's program the fish to switch directions when it reaches the edge of the Canvas. Use the when `ImageSpriteFish.EdgeReached` do event handler from the *ImageSpriteFish* drawer. Inside that event handler, place an `ImageSpriteFish.Bounce` method block, also found in *ImageSpriteFish* drawer. Plug a `get edge` block (found by hovering the mouse cursor over the `edge` parameter) into the `edge` socket of the `Bounce` method block. Compare your event handler to Figure 9-25.

Step 4: Run and test this app on your device or emulator. Notice that the ImageSprite component works similar to the Ball sprite. However, note how the nose of the fish points in the direction it is traveling due to the Rotates property being set to *true*. Figure 9-26 shows an example of the app running in the emulator.

Figure 9-25 Swimming Fish (*Source:* MIT App Inventor 2)

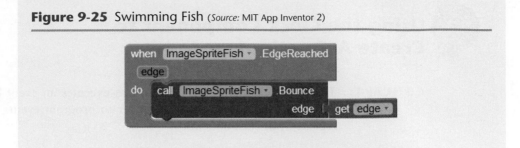

Figure 9-26 ImageSprite Rotates (*Source:* MIT App Inventor 2)

 Checkpoint

9.5 What is the purpose of the sprite Heading property? If you want your sprite to move down and left across the Canvas, what value would you use for the Heading?

9.6 Why is there no PaintColor property for the ImageSprite component?

9.7 If you want your sprite to speed up, do you increase or decrease the Interval property?

9.8 If you want to make your sprite appear to bounce away from an edge to its left, what numeric value will you plug into the edge slot?

9.9 What method will you use if your sprite moves off of the Canvas and you want it back on?

9.10 What is the purpose of the Rotates property?

9.3 Using the Clock Component to Create Animations

CONCEPT: The Clock Component is a timer that executes an event based on a time interval. You can use this timer to program events to happen repeatedly at each interval.

App Inventor's Clock component is found in the *User Interface* Palette and acts as a nonvisible component in your application. It has three properties and one event handler, `Timer`. The App Inventor Clock component also has many methods to show and manipulate dates. This chapter's coverage of the component will focus on the properties and the `Timer` event handler.

Clock Component Properties

The TimerEnabled property can be `true` or `false`. If it is set to `true`, the `Timer` event handler will execute repeatedly at the currently set interval. If this property is set to `false` (meaning the timer is disabled), the `Timer` event handler will not execute.

The TimerInterval is the interval period for the `Timer` event handler. Its value is in milliseconds. For example, if it is set at 1000, the `Timer` event handler will execute every second. If it is set at 500, the `Timer` event handler will execute every one-half second.

The TimerAlwaysFires property, if set to `true`, will cause the `Timer` event handler to execute even if the application is not active on the screen and is running behind the scenes on your device.

Clock `Timer` Event Handler

The `Timer` event handler is the only event handler that the Clock component has. If the `TimerEnabled` property is set to `true`, this event handler executes at each interval specified by the TimerInterval property.

VideoNote
Crack the Egg

Tutorial 9-4:
Crack the Egg

To demonstrate how the Clock can be used for animations, we are going to create a farm game where eggs randomly move around the screen at a set interval. The goal is to crack the eggs.

We will programmatically change the ImageSprite's Picture and Enabled properties and use the `MoveTo` method block when the sprite is touched.

You will need three images from the book's companion website: `farm.png`, `egg.png`, and `brokenEgg.png`.

Step 1: Start a new project and add a Canvas component. Set the Width to 300 pixels and the Height to 300 pixels. Set the BackgroundImage to `farm.png`.

Step 2: Add three ImageSprites. Set all of their Picture properties to the same picture, `egg.png`. Rename them `ImageSpriteEgg1`, `ImageSpriteEgg2` and `ImageSpriteEgg3`. Make sure they are all enabled, but do not worry about the Heading, Interval and Speed properties. We will handle their movement with the Clock.

Step 3: Drag a Clock component from the *User Interface* Palette onto the screen. Make sure the TimerEnabled property is checked and set the TimerInterval property to 1000.

Compare your design with Figure 9-27. Do not worry about the initial position of the eggs.

Figure 9-27 Crack the Egg Design (*Source:* MIT App Inventor 2)

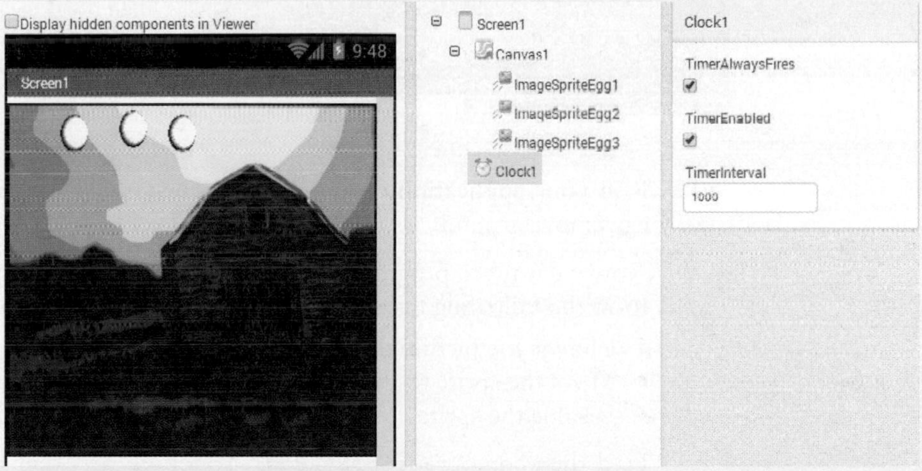

Step 4: Now you will program the actions that randomly move the eggs at the set time interval. Open the Blocks Editor and Find the `when Clock1.Timer do` event handler in the *Clock1* drawer. Place it in your editor.

Step 5: Find the `ImageSpriteEgg1.MoveTo` method block in the *ImageSpriteEgg1* drawer. Select it and place it inside the `when Clock1.Timer do` event handler.

Step 6: For the x parameter of the `MoveTo` method, randomly generate a number between 0 and 267 using the `random integer from 1 to 100` block (found in the *Math* drawer). Change the 100 value to 267 and the 1 value to zero. Do the same for the y parameter.

Step 7: Complete steps 5 and 6 for the other sprites, `ImageSpriteEgg2` and `ImageSpriteEgg3`.

Compare your workspace to Figure 9-28.

Figure 9-28 Randomly Move the Eggs (*Source:* MIT App Inventor 2)

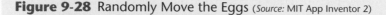

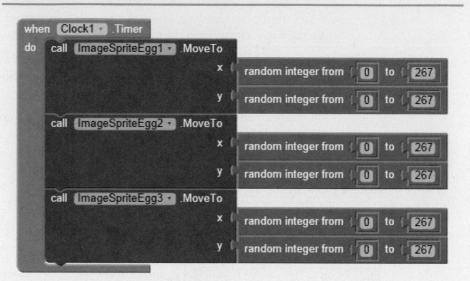

Step 8: Run your application on the emulator or your device and watch the eggs move around!

Step 9: Now we want to program each sprite's `Touched` event handlers to perform the following tasks:

- Change the picture to a broken egg
- Move the sprite to the bottom of the screen
- Disable the sprite

Find the `when ImageSpriteEgg1.Touched do` event handler in the *ImageSpriteEgg1* drawer and place it in the blocks editor.

Step 10: Find the `ImageSpriteEgg1.MoveTo` method block in the *ImageSpriteEgg1* drawer, and place it inside the `ImageSpriteEgg1.Touched` event handler. Keep the `x` parameter the same as when it was touched. To do this, create a `get x` block (found by hovering the mouse cursor over the `x` parameter of the `Touched` event handler) and plug it into the `x` socket of the `MoveTo` method block. Then, plug a number block with the value 261 (the `brokenEgg.png` is 38 pixels tall) into the `y` socket. This step will drop the egg straight down.

Step 11: Find the `set ImageSpriteEgg1.Picture to` block in the *ImageSpriteEgg1* drawer. Use an empty text block and change the value to `brokenEgg.png`. Plug the text block in the socket. See Figure 9-29.

Step 12: Disable the ImageSprite by setting its Enabled property to `false`. Compare your work to Figure 9-29.

Figure 9-29 Egg Touched Event Handler (*Source:* MIT App Inventor 2)
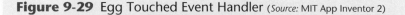

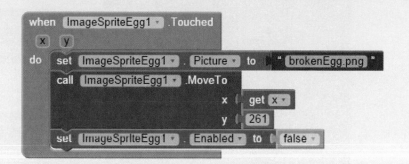

Step 13: Repeat Steps 10 through 12 to program the event handlers for the `ImageSpriteEgg2.Touched` and `ImageSpriteEgg3.Touched` events.

TIP: To repeat Steps 10 through 12, you may want to select the entire set of blocks in Figure 9-29 and duplicate it by right-clicking and choosing "duplicate" or by using copy and paste. Then, you will simply need to change `ImageSpriteEgg1` in the new set of blocks to `ImageSpriteEgg2` using the drop-down menu (remember to change all four). You can repeat these steps for `ImageSpriteEgg3`.

Step 14: Now let's program the `Timer` event handler to move the egg only if it is enabled. Find an `if then` block in the *Control* drawer. Use the value of the `ImageSpriteEgg1.Enabled` property found in the *ImageSpriteEgg1* drawer. Put the `MoveTo` method block inside the `if then` block as shown in Figure 9-30.

Figure 9-30 Test for Enabled (*Source:* MIT App Inventor 2)

Step 15: Create similar `if then` blocks that call the `ImageSpriteEgg2.MoveTo` and the `ImageSpriteEgg3.MoveTo` methods. Your `Timer` event handler should now look like Figure 9-31.

Figure 9-31 Updated `Timer` Event Handler (*Source:* MIT App Inventor 2)

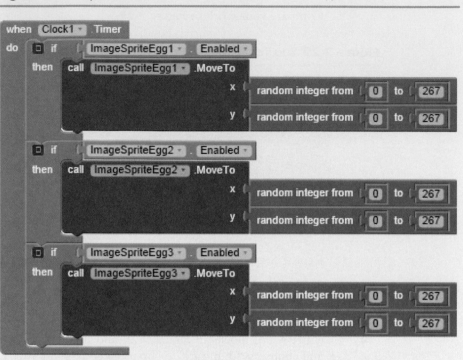

Step 16: Figure 9-32 shows the completed workspace. Run and test your application, and try to break all the eggs!

Figure 9-32 Tutorial 9-4 Complete Blocks Editor (*Source:* MIT App Inventor 2)

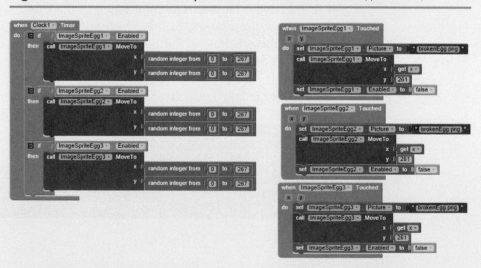

We will expand this game in the Exercises and Projects at the end of the Chapter.

Checkpoint

9.11 How can you make this game more challenging? How can you keep score and track levels? When you increase difficulty will you make the sprites move faster? Will you add more sprites to the Screen?

9.12 Assume you want to allow the user to pause the game. What property would you set in which component?

9.13 In Tutorial 9-4, when you randomly generate the x and y coordinates of a sprite, why can you start at 0 but only go to 267 for the 300 by 300 pixel Canvas?

 9.4 # Dragging Sprites

To drag a sprite, we use the `Dragged` event handler in conjunction with the `MoveTo` method block. As the sprite is dragged, we update the `MoveTo` method's x and y arguments with the value of the `currentX` and `currentY` values. An example is shown in Figure 9-33.

Figure 9-33 Using the `Dragged` Event Handler and the `MoveTo` Method Block
(*Source:* MIT App Inventor 2)

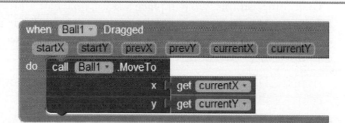

Figure 9-33 shows the `Ball1` sprite's `Dragged` event handler used with the `Ball1.MoveTo` method. Recall that a sprite's `Dragged` event handler will keep track of where the drag started with `prevX` and `prevY` values, and also keeps track of the current x and y values as it goes along. We can use the `currentX` and `currentY` values (*remember these are found by hovering the mouse cursor over the `currentX` and `currentY` parameters of the `Ball1.Dragged` event handler*) to move the ball as the drag occurs.

VideoNote
Drag Ball sprite
Example

Tutorial 9-5:
Drag Ball Sprite Example

To demonstrate an example of dragging sprites, let's create an app that allows us drag a ball around a Canvas.

Step 1: Start a new project and add a Canvas to the Screen. Make the Canvas 300 by 300 pixels by setting the Height and Width properties.

Step 2: Place a Ball sprite onto the Canvas, set the Heading to 45, the Speed to 10 and the Interval to 100. Make sure it is enabled and visible.

Step 3: In the Blocks Editor, create the blocks shown in Figure 9-33. Find the `Ball1.Dragged` event handler and the `Ball1.MoveTo` method in the *Ball1* drawer. To find the `get currentX` and `get currentY` blocks, hover the mouse cursor over the parameters in the `Ball1.Dragged` event handler.

Step 4: Run and test your app on your device or emulator. Drag the ball around and watch it move!

Tutorial 9-6:
Drag the Ball into the Box

VideoNote
Drag the Ball into the Box

This tutorial will allow us to practice dragging a Ball sprite into a box. Once the ball is in the box, it will disappear.

To accomplish this, we will place a static image of a box on the Canvas. We will then use the Clock component to continually check the position of the ball, and if it happens to be positioned anywhere over the box, we will disable it and make it nonvisible, simulating it being placed in the box.

Step 1: Drag a Canvas onto the screen and make both the Height and Width 300 pixels.

Step 2: Download `box.png` from the book's companion website. Place an ImageSprite on the Canvas and set the Height and Width to 50 pixels. Set the Picture property to `box.png` and set both the X and Y properties to 150. Rename the ImageSprite to `ImageSpriteBox`.

Step 3: Place a Ball sprite on the Canvas. Set the Heading to 45, the Interval to 0 and the Speed to 0 (because we only want this ball to move when we drag it). Set the X coordinate to 90 and the Y coordinate to 90.

Step 4: Add a HorizontalArrangement below the Canvas. Add three labels and rename them `LabelX`, `LabelComma` and `LabelY`. Set the Text property of `LabelX` to *X*, `LabelComma` to a comma, and `LabelY` to *Y*.

Step 5: Add a Button to the HorizontalArrangement, rename it `ButtonReset`, and set its Text property to *reset*.

Step 6: Add a Clock component to your screen. Make sure the TimerEnabled property is checked and set the TimerInterval to 40.

Compare your Design to Figure 9-34.

Figure 9-34 Drag Ball into Box Design (*Source:* MIT App Inventor 2)

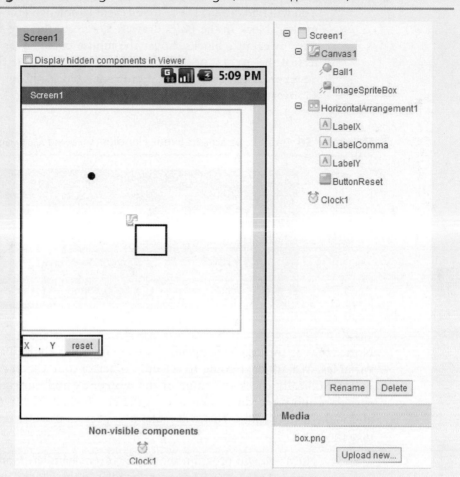

Step 7: In this step you will create the global variables shown in Figure 9-35. These global variables will hold the currentX and currentY values. We already have the currentX and currentY values in the Dragged event handler, but we also need to access these values elsewhere. To create the global variables, open the *Variables* drawer and click on the initialize global name block twice. Name the first one gCurrentX and the second gCurrentY. From the *Math* drawer, get two number blocks and set them each to zero. Plug the number blocks into the sockets of the gCurrentX and gCurrentY initialization blocks.

Figure 9-35 Initialize Global Variables (*Source:* MIT App Inventor 2)

initialize global gCurrentX to 0

initialize global gCurrentY to 0

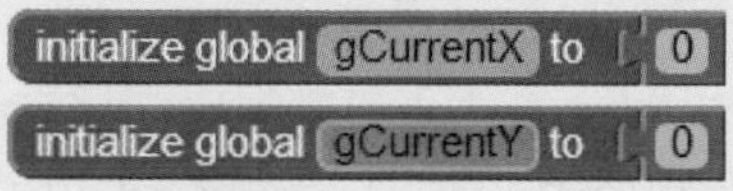

Step 8:   Program the `Ball1.Dragged` event handler as shown in Figure 9-36. You will find the `Ball1.Dragged` event handler and the `Ball1.MoveTo` method block in the *Ball1* drawer. To create the `get currentX` and `get currentY` blocks, hover the mouse cursor over those parameters of the `Ball1.Dragged` event handler. To create the `set global gCurrentX` and `set global gCurrentY` blocks, hover the mouse cursor over those variables' global initialization blocks.

Figure 9-36 `Ball1.Dragged` **Event Handler** (*Source:* MIT App Inventor 2)

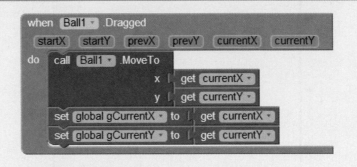

Notice that as the drag is happening, we are updating the values in our global variables. We are next going to set up a timer on our Clock component that will periodically check the value of the `currentX` and `currentY`. If the Ball sprite's x and y coordinates move over the box ImageSprite, we will disable it and make it nonvisible. This will make it appear as if we've dropped the ball into the box.

Step 9:   Now you will program the `Timer` event handler. Find and select the `when Clock1.Timer do` event handler in the *Clock1* drawer.

Step 10:   Find and select the `set LabelX.Text to` and the `set LabelY.Text to` blocks from their respective drawers, the *LabelX* drawer and *LabelY* drawer. Assign the value of `gCurrentX` and `gCurrentY` to the `LabelX` and `LabelY` label's Text properties, respectively. Place these blocks in the `Clock1.Timer` event handler, as shown in Figure 9-37.

Figure 9-37 `Clock1.Timer` **Event Handler** (*Source:* MIT App Inventor 2)

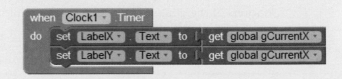

Step 11:   You aren't done, but take a minute to run and test on your phone or emulator. Watch the X and Y Labels change as you drag the ball around.

Step 12: Now we are going to use a timer to see if the Ball sprite is in the same location as the box. Because the box's top left corner is at position 150, 150 on the Canvas and the box is 50 pixels tall and wide, we are going to check and do the following:

If the x coordinate of the Ball is greater than 150 *and* less than 200 *and* the y coordinate of the Ball is greater than 150 *and* less than 200 then we want to make the Ball disappear (because the ball will be over the box). **Note:** In this set of blocks, you want to use the `global gCurrentX` and `gCurrentY` values.

Set up your `if then` block like Figure 9-38. The most efficient way to check the range of both the X and Y coordinate values is to use nested `if then` blocks. The first is the outer `if then` block checking the X coordinate range. If that passes, then we check for the Y coordinate range. If both conditions pass, the Ball is over the box. When the Ball is over the box, we want to simulate it "disappearing" by making it invisible and disabling it.

Figure 9-38 Determining if the Ball is Over the Box (*Source:* MIT App Inventor 2)

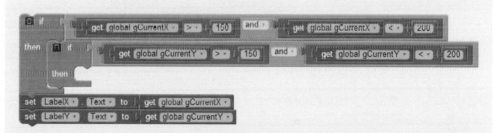

Step 13: Put the blocks shown in Figure 9-38 inside the `Clock1.Timer` event handler. From the *Ball1* drawer, find and select the `set Ball1.Enabled to` and the `set Ball1.Visible to` blocks, and set them both to `false`. Place the two statements in the `then` portion of the inner `if then` block, as shown in Figure 9-39.

Figure 9-39 Completed Timer Event (*Source:* MIT App Inventor 2)

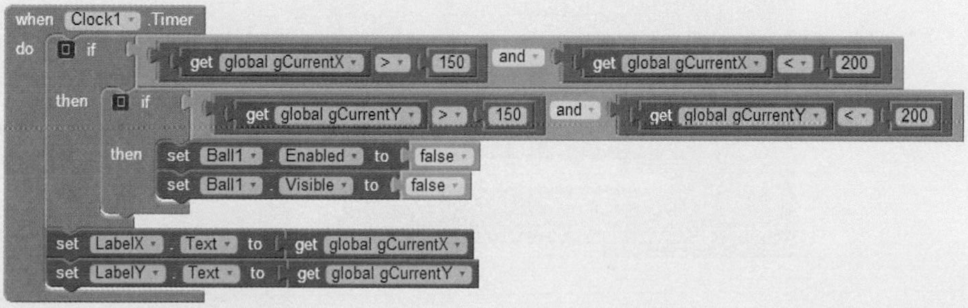

Step 14: Now you will program the `ButtonReset.Click` event handler as shown in Figure 9-40. Find the `ButtonReset.Click` event handler in the *ButtonReset* drawer and place it in the editor. In the *Ball1* drawer, find the following blocks and place them in the `ButtonReset.Click` event handler:

- `set Ball1.Enabled to`, plug a logic `true` block into its socket
- `set Ball1.Visible to`, plug a logic `true` block into its socket
- `set Ball1.X to`, plug a number 20 into its socket
- `set Ball1.Y to`, plug a number 20 into its socket
- `set gCurrentX`, plug a number 20 into its socket
- `set gCurrentY`, plug a number 20 into its socket

Figure 9-40 Reset Button (*Source:* MIT App Inventor 2)

Step 15: Run and test your app. As an exercise, consider adding more Ball sprites.

Figure 9-41 Tutorial 9-6 Complete Blocks Editor Workspace
(*Source:* MIT App Inventor 2)

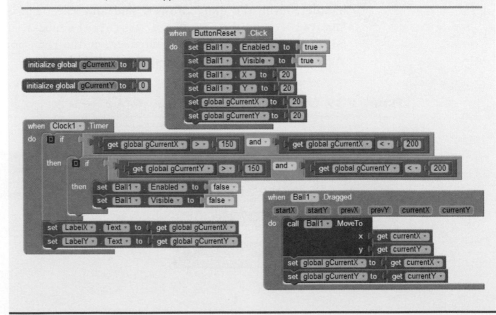

9.5 Detecting Collisions

CONCEPT: You can detect when a sprite collides with another component. You can detect the specific component that a sprite collides with and then program your animation to do various things upon this collision such as play sound, change images, update scores, and more.

The App Inventor sprite components have `CollidedWith` and `NoLongerCollidingWith` event handlers. A sprite's `CollidedWith` event handler will execute when any collision happens, regardless of which component it collides with. Therefore, if you are interested in exactly what your sprite collided with, you must have an `if then` block inside the event handler to determine what it collided with.

You may not have noticed, but in each component's drawer, the last block shown is the `component` block for that particular component. The `component` block is simply a block that represents that component. Assume we have an `ImageSpriteBalloon1` component in our design. Figure 9-42 shows how its `component` block appears.

Figure 9-42 Component Block for `ImageSpriteBalloon1` (*Source:* MIT App Inventor 2)

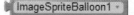

You will use `component` blocks to determine which component was hit in a collision. Next, let's also assume that our project has an `ImageSpriteDart` that we want to pop the balloon with.

Figure 9-43 `CollidedWith` Event (*Source:* MIT App Inventor 2)

```
when  ImageSpriteDart ▾ .CollidedWith
  other
do    ⊡ if        get other ▾  = ▾    ImageSpriteBalloon1 ▾
      then   set  LabelHit ▾ . Text ▾  to  “ I hit a balloon! ”
```

In Figure 9-43, you see that the `ImageSpriteDart.CollidedWith` event handler has a parameter named `other`. The `other` parameter refers to the `other` component that the `ImsgeSpriteDart` has collided with. We can get the value of the `other` parameter and compare it with the `ImageSpriteBalloon1` component's `component` block to determine whether the two have collided.

If you simply want to detect that your sprite collided with something, and you don't care what it is, you use this event handler without the `if then` block.

Let's make two sprites collide.

Figure 9-44 Colliding Sprites Design (*Source:* MIT App Inventor 2)

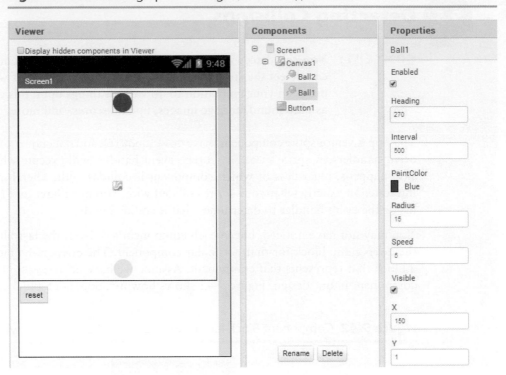

Notice in this design we have two Ball sprites, one blue and one yellow. They each have an Interval of 500, Radius of 15, and Speed of 5. They are also lined up together on the x coordinate value of 150. The Canvas size is set to *Fill parent* for the Width, and its Height is 300 pixels.

The blue ball will travel straight down; its Heading property is set to 270. The yellow ball will travel straight up; its Heading is set to 90.

In the Blocks Editor, we will program the application to turn both balls green when the collision occurs. We will also set one's direction to 0 and the other's to 180 so that they will appear to bounce off in different directions.

In Figure 9-45, you see that we use the `Ball1.CollidedWith` event handler to change the balls to green and switch their direction. See Figure 9-46 for a depiction of the application.

Figure 9-45 Programming the Collision (*Source:* MIT App Inventor 2)

```
when  Ball1 . CollidedWith
other
do   set  Ball1 . PaintColor  to  [    ]
     set  Ball2 . PaintColor  to  [    ]
     set  Ball1 . Heading  to  [ 0 ]
     set  Ball2 . Heading  to  [ 180 ]
```

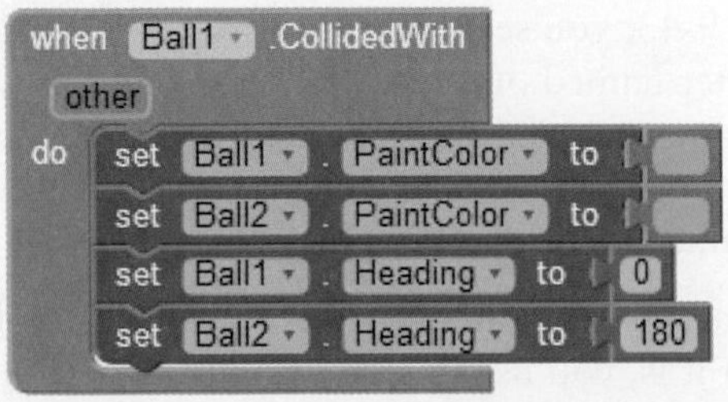

Figure 9-46 Colliding Ball Sprites (*Source:* MIT App Inventor 2)

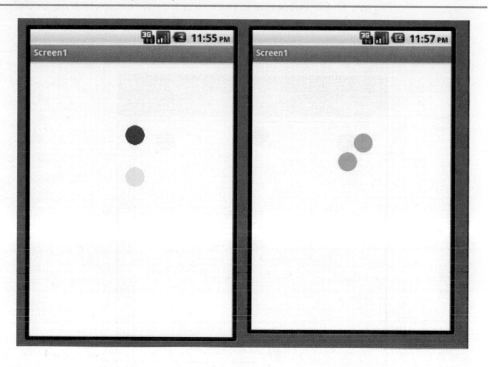

Tutorial 9-7:
Popping Balloons

You will need to download three images from the book's companion website, Balloon.png, Spiral.png, and Dart.png.

In this tutorial, we are going to simulate three balloons falling from the sky. We are giving the user a dart to pop the balloons. The balloons will travel straight down at different speeds. The user can drag the dart from left to right and when the drag is stopped, the dart will travel straight up to pop the balloon (we hope).

The app's user interface will appear as shown in Figure 9-47.

Step 1: Add a Canvas component to the screen and set the Width to 300 and the Height to 300.

Step 2: In the *Media* panel, upload the three images. Balloon.png, Spiral. png, and Dart.png.

Step 3: Add four ImageSprite components from the *Drawing and Animation* Palette to the Canvas. Align them as shown in Figure 9-47. Rename the sprites ImageSpriteDart, ImageSpriteBalloon1, ImageSpriteBalloon2, and ImageSpriteBalloon3.

Figure 9-47 Balloon and Dart User Interface (*Source:* MIT App Inventor 2)

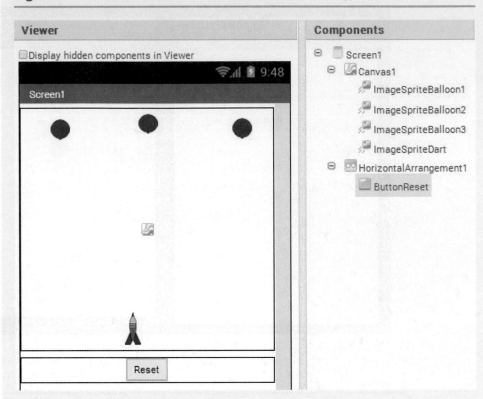

Step 4: Set the Picture property of the balloon sprites to `Balloon.png` and set the Picture property of the dart sprite to `Dart.png`.

Step 5: The Height and Width of the balloon sprites should be 25 pixels. The Height of the dart sprite should be 40 and the Width 20.

Step 6: The Heading of the balloon sprites should all be set at 270 (straight down). The Heading for the dart should be 90 (straight up).

Step 7: Set the Interval for the balloon sprites to 500. Set the Interval of the dart sprite to 100.

Step 8: Set the Speed properties of the balloon sprites to various values. For example, set one to 5, one to 7, and one to 10. Set the Speed of the dart to zero.

Step 9: Add a HorizontalArrangement (from the *Layout* Palette) under the Canvas, set its Width to *Fill parent*, and then set the AlignHorizontal property to *Center*.

Step 10: Place a Button (from the *User Interface* Palette) in the HorizontalArrangement. Rename it to `ButtonReset` and change the Text property to *Reset*.

Step 11: Now you will program the `Dragged` event handler, as shown in Figure 9-48, to allow the user to drag the dart sprite left and right. In the *ImageSpriteDart* drawer, find the `Dragged` event handler and the `MoveTo` method block. Place them in the editor and place the `MoveTo` method block inside the `Dragged` event handler.

Figure 9-48 Drag the Dart Sprite Side to Side (*Source:* MIT App Inventor 2)

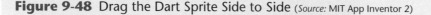

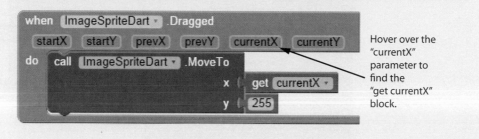

Hover over the "currentX" parameter to find the "get currentX" block.

Step 12: For the x socket of the `MoveTo` method, hover the mouse cursor over the `currentX` parameter in the `Dragged` event handler, and then click the `get currentX` block. Use a number block set to the value 255 for the y socket. By using an unchanging number for the y argument, we allow the user to drag side to side but not upwards.

Figure 9-49 Dart `TouchUp` Event Handler (*Source:* MIT App Inventor 2)

Step 13: In the *ImageSpriteDart* drawer, find the `TouchUp` event handler and the `set` blocks for the Heading, Interval and Speed properties. Set the properties according to Figure 9-49. The `TouchUp` event handler will execute when the user lets go of the drag. This is the point where we want to let the dart fly up the screen to pop a balloon.

Step 14: In the *ImageSpriteDart* drawer, find the CollidedWith event handler and the `set ImageSpriteDart.Picture to` method block.

Step 15: Place an `if then` block inside the event handler, and use the *Math* `equals` block to compare the `other` argument with the `component` blocks of each of the balloon sprites. Remember each component's `component` block is the last block in its drawer.

Figure 9-50 The `CollidedWith` Event Handler (*Source:* MIT App Inventor 2)

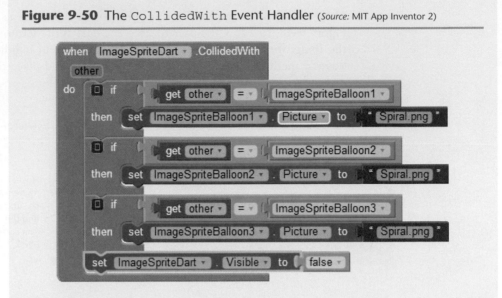

Figure 9-51 Test Which Component Collided With (*Source:* MIT App Inventor 2)

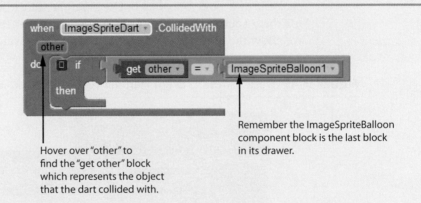

Hover over "other" to find the "get other" block which represents the object that the dart collided with.

Remember the ImageSpriteBalloon component block is the last block in its drawer.

Step 16: Place two more `if then` blocks inside the event handler. Use the `equals` block (from the *Logic* drawer) to compare the `other` argument with the `component` blocks of the other balloon sprites. It may be easiest to copy and paste the first `if then` block and then change the value of the `component` blocks to `ImageSpriteBalloon2` and `ImageSpriteBalloon3`. This is shown in Figure 9-52.

Step 17: For each balloon sprite, place their `set ImageSprite.Picture` property blocks in the proper `if then` condition. If a balloon has been hit, we are going to temporarily change its Picture property to a red spiral, helping indicate to the user that it has been hit.

Step 18: Change the Visible property of `ImageSpriteDart` to `false` to temporarily hide it.

Compare your blocks with Figure 9-50.

Figure 9-52 Test the Other Components (*Source:* MIT App Inventor 2)

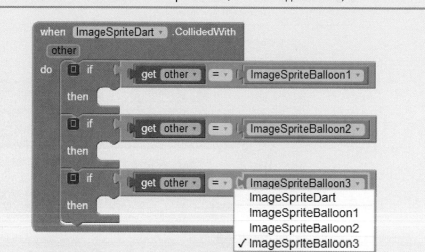

Figure 9-53 Dart Top Edge Reached (*Source:* MIT App Inventor 2)

Step 19: Now you will program the `ImageSpriteDart.EdgeReached` event handler as shown in Figure 9-53. When the dart hits the top edge of the Canvas (remember that the top edge is "1"), we want to put it back down to the bottom so the user can try again. In the *ImageSpriteDart* drawer, find and select the `EdgeReached` event handler, the `set Speed to` property block, and the `MoveTo` method block.

Step 20: In the *Control* drawer select an `if then` block and place it in the `ImageSpriteDart.EdgeReached` event handler. For the `test` socket use a *Math* `equals` block to determine if the value of the edge is equal to one. You can find the `get edge` block by hovering the mouse cursor over the `edge` parameter of the `EdgeReached` event handler.

Step 21: In the `if then` block's `then` socket, set the Speed property of the dart sprite to 0 to stop it, and move the dart to the x and y coordinates 100 and 255 respectively. (See Figure 9-53.) This will stop the sprite and place it back to the bottom of the screen.

Figure 9-54 The `NoLongerCollidingWith` Event handler
(*Source:* MIT App Inventor 2)

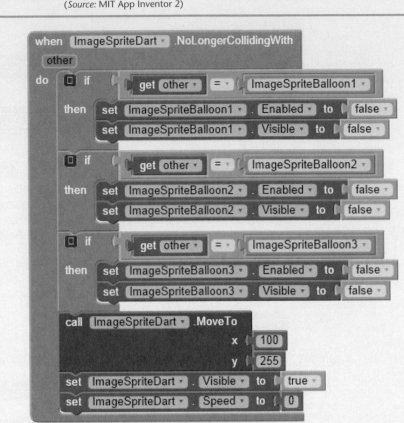

Step 22: Now you must program the application to take away the balloons and disable them once they have been popped. You are about to program the `ImageSpriteDart.NoLongerCollidingWith` event handler shown in Figure 9-54. In the *ImageSpriteDart* drawer, find the `NoLongerCollidingWith` event handler, the `MoveTo` method, the set `Visible` to property block, and the set `Speed` to property block.

Step 23: Program the first `if then` block shown in Figure 9-54. This `if then` block determines whether a collision has ocurred with `ImageSpriteBalloon1`. Use the `equals block` from the *Logic* drawer to compare the `get other` block (hover the mouse cursor over the `other` parameter to find that block) with the *ImageSpriteBalloon1* component block (remember this is the last block in the *ImageSpriteBaloon1* drawer).

Find the *ImageSpriteBalloon1* set `Enabled` to and set `Visible` to property blocks and set them both to `false` in the `if then` block. At this point the event handler should appear as shown in Figure 9-55.

Figure 9-55 Disable ImageSpriteBalloon1 (*Source:* MIT App Inventor 2)

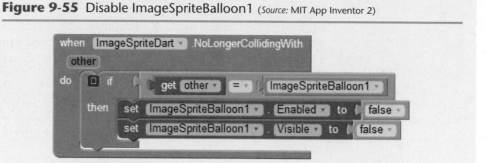

Step 24: Grab two more `if then` blocks from the *Control* drawer, or use copy and paste by copying the `if then` block from Figure 9-55, to program the conditions for `ImageSpriteBalloon2` and `ImageSpriteBalloon3` (see Figure 9-56).

Figure 9-56 Disable `ImageSpriteBalloon2` and `ImageSpriteBalloon3`
(*Source:* MIT App Inventor 2)

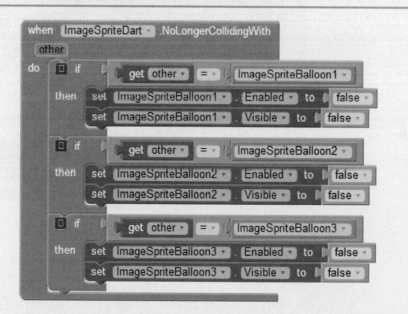

Step 25: For each of the balloons, place their `set Visible to` and `set Enabled to` blocks in the proper `if then` block. Set each of these properties to `false` as shown in Figure 9-56. Take care to make sure that each balloon block is in the proper spot. (It's easy at this point to mix the blocks up because they look similar, especially if you are using the copy and paste approach.)

Step 26: Use the dart sprite's `MoveTo` method block to place it toward the bottom of the screen at X, Y coordinates of 100, 255. Set the dart sprite's Visible property to `true` and set the Speed property to zero. The `NoLongerCollidingWith` event handler should now match Figure 9-54.

Step 27: The last event handler we need to program is the `Click` event hander for the *reset* Button, as shown in Figure 9-57. In the *ButtonReset* drawer, find the `ButtonReset.Click` event handler and place it in the editor.

Figure 9-57 Reset the Game (*Source:* MIT App Inventor 2)

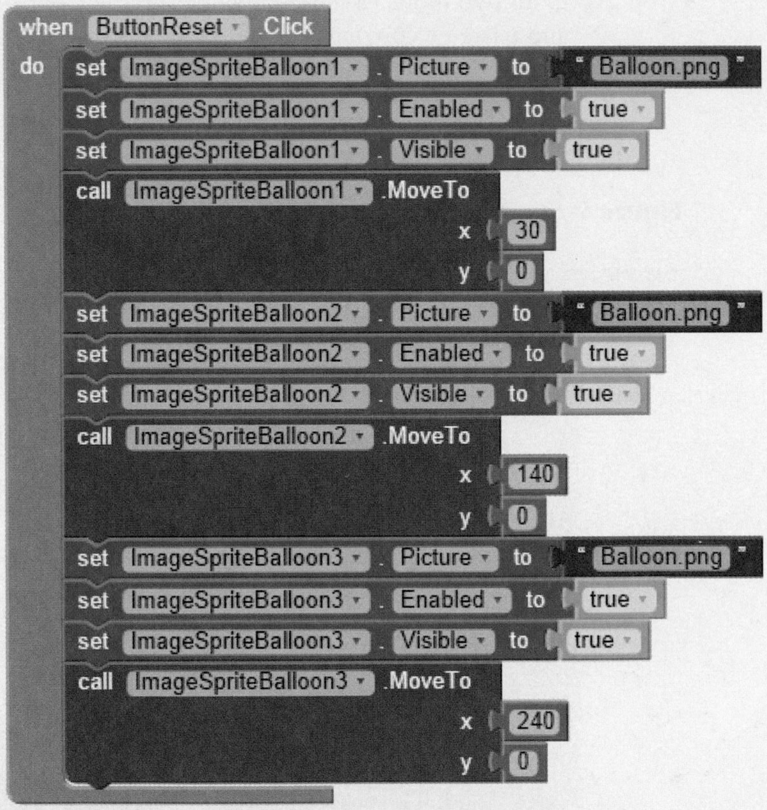

Step 28: For each of the balloon ImageSprites, find their Picture, Enabled and Visible property `set` blocks, and place them in the `ButtonReset.Click` event handler. Reset them as shown in Figure 9-57 by setting their Picture property back to a balloon and their Enabled and Visible properties to `true`.

Step 29: For each of the balloon ImageSprites, use their `MoveTo` methods to place them back at the top of the screen in their starting positions (see Figure 9-57).

Step 30: That's it! The complete Blocks Editor is shown in Figure 9-58. Run and test your game on your device or emulator. Begin thinking about how you can keep score and increase difficulty.

Figure 9-58 Tutorial 9-7 Complete Blocks Editor *(Source:* MIT App Inventor 2*)*

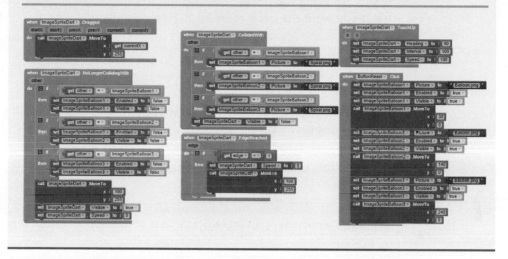

Review Questions

Multiple Choice

1. What is the X, Y coordinate position of the top right corner of a 100 × 100 pixel Canvas?

    a. 0,0
    b. 0,99
    c. 99,0
    d. 99,99

2. What is the X, Y coordinate position of the bottom right corner of a 100 × 100 pixel Canvas?

    a. 0,0
    b. 0,99
    c. 99,100
    d. 99,99

3. What properties are used to set the size of the Canvas?

    a. Height
    b. Width
    c. A and B
    d. Neither A nor B

4. The PaintColor property sets the colors for which of the following?

   a. Lines
   b. Points
   c. Circles
   d. All of the above

5. If you are using the `DrawPoint` method to draw a circle, what Radius will you use if you want the circle to be 10 × 10 pixels in size?

   a. 1
   b. 5
   c. 10
   d. None of the above

6. If you want a sprite to travel straight to the left, what number will you use as the Heading property value?

   a. 0
   b. 90
   c. 180
   d. 270

7. What property makes an ImageSprite face in the direction that it is heading?

   a. Facing
   b. Rotates
   c. Looks
   d. None of the above

8. An ImageSprite's X, Y coordinates represent where the sprite's ___ is relative to the Canvas?

   a. Middle
   b. Top right
   c. Top left
   d. Bottom right

9. A Ball sprite's X, Y coordinates represent where the Ball's ___ is relative to the Canvas?

   a. Middle
   b. Top right
   c. Top left
   d. Bottom right

10. If a Ball sprite reaches the left edge of the screen, that edge is represented by which number?

    a. 1
    b. 3
    c. −1
    d. −3

11. If an ImageSprite reaches the bottom edge of the screen, that edge is represented by which number?

    a. 1
    b. 3

c. −1

d. −3

12. What event is invoked when a user does a very quick swipe across the screen?

a. `Swiped`

b. `Dragged`

c. `Flung`

d. `Toss`

13. What event is used to determine if two sprites run into each other?

a. `Hit`

b. `Collide`

c. `CollidedWith`

d. `HitSprite`

Short Answer

1. What does it mean when we set the Canvas Height and Width to *Fill parent*?

2. When we use the `Dragged` event, we have access to the current x and y coordinates as the drag is happening. If we want to use these values, where do we find the blocks to use?

3. If we use a `for range` loop block to loop 100 times and we set the radius of a circle that we draw with each iteration equal to the loop counter, what will happen?

4. Why does a Ball sprite *not* have Height and Width properties? Why does an ImageSprite *not* have the PaintColor property?

5. How do the Interval, Speed and Heading properties work together to move a sprite? What happens if the `Speed` is set to zero?

6. Why is there a `NoLongerCollidingWith` event? What might you handle in this event?

Exercises

1. **Change Line Width**

   Complete Tutorial 9-1. Add buttons on the bottom of the screen for three different line widths: 1 pixel, 10 pixels, and 20 pixels. If the user clicks one of the buttons, change the LineWidth property accordingly. Practice drawing with the different widths.

2. **`TouchedDown` and `TouchedUp`**

   VideoNote
   TouchedDown and
   TouchedUp

   The sprite's `TouchedDown` event executes when a user first touches the sprite. The sprite's `TouchUp` event executes when a sprite's touch has stopped (finger or mouse is lifted).

   Program a Ball sprite on a Canvas. Use the `TouchedUp` and `TouchedDown` events to make the ball yellow while it is being touched or dragged and then green when it is let go.

3. **Which Edge?**

Program a Canvas with a Ball sprite that Bounces off any edge that it reaches. Put a Label under the Canvas that populates with a message each time an edge is reached. For example, when the Ball sprite reaches edge 1, set the Label's Text property to hit the top edge. Program for all four outer edges of the Canvas.

4. **Flashing Ghosts**

Download `ghost.png` from the companion website. Program a `Canvas` with five ImageSprites, using the ghost image for each of them. Set their size to 35 × 50. Use a Clock component to toggle the sprites visibility property every half-second.

5. **Flashing Ghosts 2**

Complete Exercise 4 and then use the Clock component to randomly move each of the ghosts when they are not visible.

6. **Change Color**

Program a Canvas with a Ball sprite. As the user drags the ball, change the color based on which area of the Canvas it is on. If it is on the left half, make the ball green. If it is dragged over to the right half of the Canvas, make the ball blue. Use the Clock component, the `Dragged` event, and the `MoveTo` method. See Tutorial 9-4.

7. **Change Color 2**

Expand Exercise 6 by changing the color of the ball based on which quadrant it is in. For example, if the ball is dragged to the top left quadrant, change it to red. Change the colors as follows:
- Top Left - Red
- Top Right - Blue
- Bottom Left - Yellow
- Bottom Right - Green

Chapter Projects

1. **Keep the Fish in the Bowl**

Complete Tutorial 9-3. Review Tutorial 9-5. Expand the Fishbowl project to keep the fish in the bowl. There are different approaches you can take.

One might be to find the approximate coordinates to keep the fish in the bowl. For instance, if the Y value falls below a certain number, the fish will be out of the bowl. Use the clock's timer to check coordinates and the manually bounce off an edge if it has gone too far. For example, stop the fish from going too high by having it bounce off of a North edge. Stop to the fish from going too far to the left, right, or bottom in the same manner.

Another approach may be to use clear (no image) ImageSprites outlining the bowl, then use the colliding and bounce events to keep the fish in the bowl. Make sure your ImageSprites are at least a pixel in width.

2. **Primary Colors**

Write an application that has nine Ball sprites each with a radius of 10: three red, three blue, and three yellow. Have the Balls bounce around a 300 × 300 pixel

Canvas. (Hint: Use the `EdgeReached` event and the `Bounce` method, and set your Interval, Speed and Direction appropriately.) Use a Clock Timer and collision detection to change the sprites to their mixed color if they collide. (Blue and Yellow = Green, Red and Yellow = Orange, and so forth.) Once a ball has collided and changed color, have it drop to the bottom of the Canvas. If a sprite collides with a ball that is already mixed, take no action.

3. **Balloons**

   Complete Tutorial 9-6, Popping Balloons. Enhance this game by keeping score and a level of difficulty. Score as follows:

   - If a balloon is popped, add 3.
   - If a balloon hits the ground, subtract 5.
   - If the score is above 20, add three more balloons and make some drop faster. (Hint: Add the extra balloons at the start, but disable them and make them nonvisible until you need them.)
   - If the score drops below 10, change it back to level 1 with three balloons.

   Show both the score and the level on the screen beneath the Canvas

4. **Trap the Ghosts**

   Download the `haunted_house.png` and the `ghost.png` from the companion website.

   Build a game where you drag the moving ghosts into the haunted house.

   Combine skills learned in this Chapter to accomplish the following:

   - Put a Canvas on your screen. Set the Width to *Fill parent*, and the Height to 300 pixels.
   - Set the BackgroundImage property to `haunted_house.png`.
   - Add three ghost ImageSprites and set their Width to 25 pixels and Height to 50 pixels.
   - Use a `Clock` Timer event handler to move the ghosts randomly around the Canvas. Set the Timer Interval to 1 second.
   - Allow the user to drag a ghost (if they can catch it) to the location between the windows of the Haunted House, where you expect the front door to be.
   - If the user can get the ghost to the front door, disable it and make it nonvisible.
   - Allow the user to reset the game.

5. **Catch the Eggs**

   ForYou will need four images from the companion website, `farm.png`, `egg.png`, `basket.png`, and `brokenEgg.png`.

   Design your game similar to Tutorial 9-4, Crack the Egg, where a Canvas is added with a background image of `farm.png`. Make your Canvas fill the parent for the Width property and 300 for the Height.

   Program five egg ImageSprites to move down the Canvas, from the top, at various speeds.

   Provide one basket ImageSprite starting out toward the bottom of the Canvas. Set its Height and Width to 30 pixels each. Use the `Dragged` event with the `MoveTo` method to allow the user to drag the basket to catch some eggs.

If the basket and an egg collide, disable the egg and up the score. If the egg reaches the bottom, crack it and leave it there.

Allow the user to reset the screen after all eggs are disabled.

Keep and show the score by adding 3 if an egg is caught and subtracting 5 if an egg hits the ground. Keep the score even after the screen is reset.

Use Tutorials 9-4, 9-5, and 9-6 for reference.

10 Working with Text

10.1 Concatenating Strings

CONCEPT: To concatenate simply means to join or link together. To concatenate strings means to join strings together. You can concatenate two strings or more to make a single string.

To concatenate two strings in App Inventor you use the Text **join** block. The **join** block has parameter sockets that will allow you to join multiple text blocks together; the values will be appended in order. These blocks can either be literal, like the word *hello*, or the number five, or can be variable blocks.

You can find the `join` block in the *Text* drawer. See Figure 10-1.

Figure 10-1 The Text `join` Block *(Source:* MIT App Inventor 2)

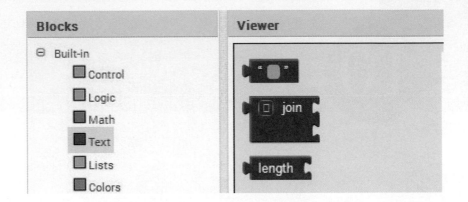

As stated previously, the `join` block appends text in order. Consider Figure 10-2. The first text block is "Hi" and the second is " Sam" (notice the preceding space). The result of this join will be "Hi Sam". If there were not a space either after the word "Hi" in the first block, or before the word "Sam" in the second block, the words would run together and the result would be "HiSam".

Figure 10-2 Concatenation *(Source:* MIT App Inventor 2)

The `join` block makes use of the mutator tool and allows for more slots of text to join. See Figure 10-3.

Figure 10-3 Using the Mutator to Add More Slots *(Source:* MIT App Inventor 2)

Any block that is plugged into the `join` block will be treated as text. For example, if you join the number 12 with the word "hello", the resulting string will be "12hello". If both arguments are numbers, they are still treated as strings. For example, concatenating the string "12" and the string "17" will result in the string "1217", not the number 29 (29 would be the result of plugging 12 and 17 into the math addition block).

Concatenating String Literals (or Text Blocks)

In programming terminology, a *string literal* is a sequence of characters that is written into an application's code. In App Inventor, you use the text block to create a string literal.

In Figure 10-4 we are joining two string literals, or text blocks. The first text block plugged into the join block contains the five characters H-e-l-l-o. This, joined with the text block containing the characters W-o-r-l-d, results in "HelloWorld", as shown on the emulator.

Figure 10-4 Join Two String Literals (*Source:* MIT App Inventor 2)

Notice that there is no space between "Hello" and "World". This is because the join block concatenates the two string literals into one string literal and will not place a space between them.

We can add a space between "Hello" and "World" in a few different ways. One would be to add a space at the end of the word "Hello". This would work fine but may not be the best solution. An additional solution would be to create another string literal containing just a space and then joining that in the middle of the other two.

To join three string literals with App Inventor, you first need to use the mutator to build a join block with three slots (remember Figure 10-3). Then you make the text blocks that you want to join together, in this case *Hello* and *World*. Take a look at Figure 10-5.

Figure 10-5 Joining Three String Literals (*Source:* MIT App Inventor 2)

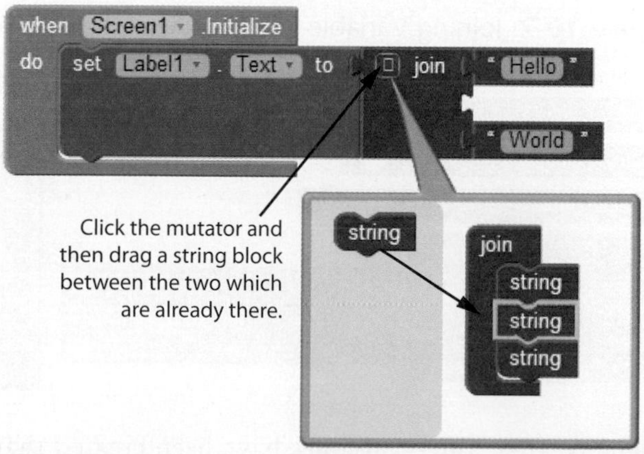

Once you have the slots that you need, add a text block containing a single space (" ") in the middle of "Hello" and "World". See Figure 10-6.

Figure 10-6 Adding a Space (*Source:* MIT App Inventor 2)

Figure 10-6 shows a space between the words "Hello" and "World". To complete the `join` blocks shown follow the steps:

Step 1: Make a text block with a single space. Go to the *Text* drawer and select a text block. By default, the text block already contains the single space that you need, you won't need to change it.

Step 2: Join the word "Hello" with the space. Go to the *Text* drawer and select the `join` block, plug in the word "Hello" and the text block with a single space.

Step 3: Use the mutator tool to add a third slot to the `join` block. See Figure 10-5. Go to the *Text* drawer and find another text block. Fill it in with the word "World".

You can join as many string literals as you wish, but beware, it won't take long before your `join` blocks will be really large! If you find this is the case, consider storing your strings into variables and then concatenate the variable strings.

Concatenating Variable Strings

You can also concatenate variables. If you have variables that contain strings you simply plug the variable's `get` block into the `join` block the same way we did with the text blocks. The resulting string will be made up of the values of the variables. Look at Figure 10-7.

Figure 10-7 Joining Variable Strings (*Source:* MIT App Inventor 2)

In Figure 10-7, three variables have been created that contain text. Note that the text block plugged into the `string2` variable contains a blank space. Next, you see that we join the variables `string1`, `string2` first, and then join those with `string3`.

Because these blocks are variables and not literals, the value of each variable is used to create the resulting string "Hello World".

Remember, to find the value of a variable, you hover the mouse cursor over the name of the variable in its initialization block. When you see the `get` and `set` blocks pop-up for the variable, click on the block you need. For an example, look at Figure 10-8, which explains how to find the `get global string1` variable block, which holds the *value* of `string1`.

Figure 10-8 Finding a Variable's `get` Block *(Source:* MIT App Inventor 2)

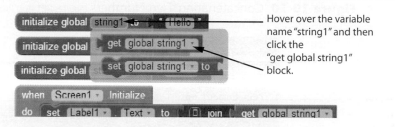

Concatenating Strings with Numbers

As previously stated, when you use the `join` block for concatenation, all data plugged into it will be treated as text. For example, if you have a number block that contains the value 12, the `join` block treats it as a string literal with the characters "1" and "2".

Treating all data as text may have unexpected results, so it is important to understand the effect of concatenating numbers with strings, numbers with numbers, and also the effect of concatenating Boolean values.

To demonstrate the effect of concatenating strings with numbers, see Figure 10-9.

Figure 10-9 Concatenating a Number and a String *(Source:* MIT App Inventor 2)

In this figure, you'll notice that we have two variables, `string1` and `number1`. Even though the variable `number1` is a number, the concatenation still works, but the number is treated as text.

Concatenating Two Numbers

It's important to understand the difference between concatenating two numbers versus adding two numbers. When you mathematically add the numbers 12 and 17, of course the result will be the number 29. However, when you concatenate the string "12" with the string "17", the result will be a string containing the characters *1-2-1-7*. This is not the same as the number 1,217. You cannot perform math operations on the resulting string.

Examine Figure 10-10, which demonstrates concatenating numbers. Here you can see the effect of concatenating two numbers.

Figure 10-10 Concatenating Two Numbers (*Source:* MIT App Inventor 2)

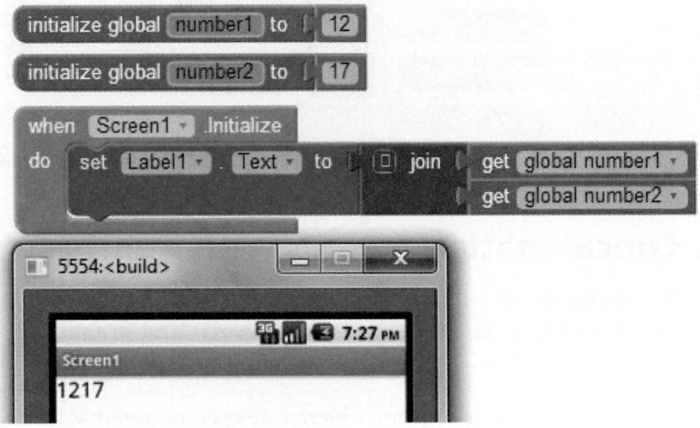

Concatenating Boolean Values

Boolean blocks are also treated as text if they are concatenated. For example, if you concatenate the word "Hello" with a Boolean `true` block, your resulting string will be "Hellotrue".

If you were to concatenate the Boolean block `true` with the Boolean block `false`, the resulting string will be "truefalse". This is shown in Figure 10-11.

Figure 10-11 Concatenating Two Boolean Values (*Source:* MIT App Inventor 2)

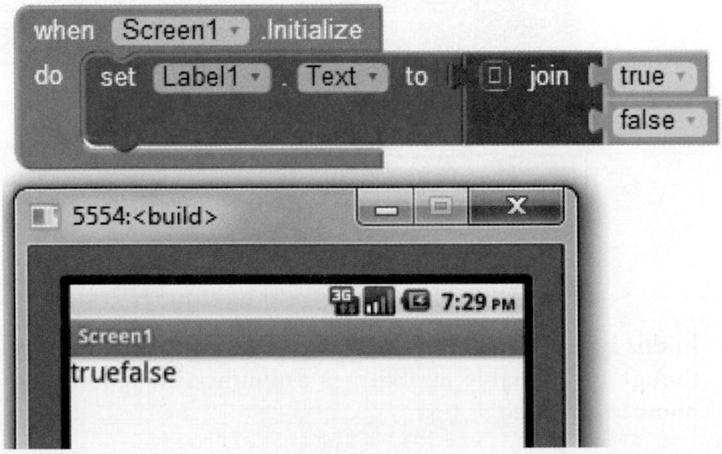

Checkpoint

10.1 When the Text `join` block is used, all elements are treated as what data type?

10.2 What is the result of concatenating the numbers 100 and 200?

10.3 What is the result of concatenating two variables?

10.4 What would the result be if you concatenate four Boolean blocks, each with the value of `true`?

10.2 Comparing Strings

CONCEPT: We can perform string comparison operations that allow us to determine whether two strings are equal or not. We can also use these comparison operations to determine if a string is greater than or less than another. These comparison functions serve many purposes, including data validation and ordering or alphabetizing lists of strings.

We can compare two strings to determine whether they are equal, whether one is greater than the other or whether one is less than another. An example of comparing two strings for equality would be password verification. An example of using the greater than or less than comparison would be to alphabetize a list of names.

The `compare texts` Block

App Inventor provides the `compare texts` block, which will allow us to determine whether two strings are equal or whether one is less than or greater than the other. The `compare texts` block is in the *Text* drawer. See Figure 10-12.

Figure 10-12 Compare Texts Block (*Source:* MIT App Inventor 2)

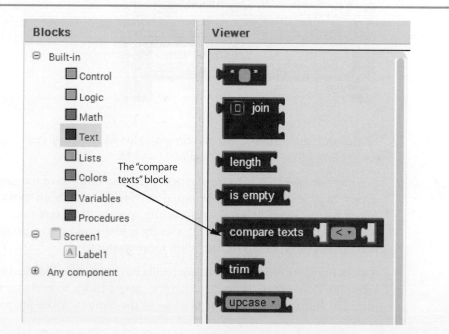

To change the operator so that it tests for equality, less than, or greater than, you click on the down arrow in the middle of the block. See Figure 10-13.

Figure 10-13 Change the Operator (*Source:* MIT App Inventor 2)

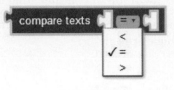

Equal Strings

As shown in Figure 10-13, we use the compare texts block to determine whether two strings are equal. This block requires that you plug in two text blocks to compare and it will return true or false based on the result of the comparison. Just like the Text join block, if you plug in a number or other data type, the compare texts block will treat it as text.

For two strings to be equal they must be identical. This includes *case sensitivity*, meaning "Hello" is different than "hello" because of the uppercase "H" in the first string and lowercase in the second. See Figure 10-14.

Figure 10-14 String Equality and Case Sensitivity (*Source:* MIT App Inventor 2)

Notice in Figure 10-14 how the return value of the compare texts block is false when comparing "Hello" to "hello".

In order for two strings to be identical they also must have the same number of characters. So, "Hello" will not be equal to "Hello " (with an extra space at the end). Actually, the word "Hello" without the space will be less than the word "Hello " with the space. This is because, if a string is identical up to a point, the shorter string will always be less than the one with more characters.

After we remove the extra space, we finally have two truly identical strings. Figure 10-16 shows an example of using the compare texts block to evaluate two strings that are identical and returns the value of true to the Label1.Text property.

Figure 10-15 Extra Space in Otherwise Equal String (*Source:* MIT App Inventor 2)

These strings look equal, but there is actually an extra space in the second one.

Figure 10-16 Equal Strings (*Source:* MIT App Inventor 2)

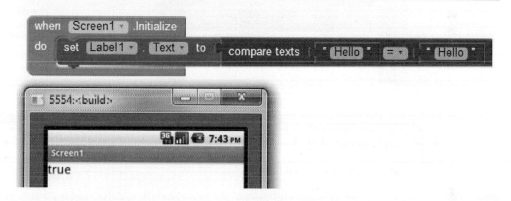

Greater Than or Less Than Comparisons

In computing, every printable character has an associated number represented in the ASCII table. ASCII stands for the *American Standard Code for Information Interchange* and is a set of 128 numeric codes that represent the English letters, various punctuation marks, and other characters. For example, the ASCII code for the uppercase letter A is 65. When you type an uppercase A on your computer keyboard, the number 65 is stored in memory.

In case you are curious, the ASCII code for uppercase B is 66, for uppercase C is 67, and so forth. Uppercase letter values are less than their corresponding lowercase values. For example, the lowercase "a" is 97. Therefore the lowercase "a" is greater than the uppercase "A". You can research the Web if you'd like to see the full ASCII table.

This numerical representation of characters is what allows us to determine whether one string is greater than or less than another. Characters are compared one by one, meaning the first characters of each string are compared, the second two are compared, and so forth until there is a difference. As soon as there are different characters in the same position of the string the determination is made about which string is greater than or less than.

So, when we compare "Hello" and "hello", the "H" and "h" are compared first and right away we have different characters. At this point it is determined that "Hello" is less than "hello". Keep in mind that the string "Hello There" is also less than "hello", even though it has more characters. This is because the first character that is different in the two strings determines which string is greater-than or less-than the other string.

As shown in Figure 10-17 we can change the operator of the `compare texts` block to change whether we want test for equal, less than or greater than. Figure 10-17 shows that "Hello" computes to a value less than "hello".

Figure 10-17 Less than String Comparison (*Source:* MIT App Inventor 2)

VideoNote
Comparing Strings

Tutorial 10-1:
Comparing Strings

In this tutorial we will create an app that allows the user to enter two strings. We will let the user know whether the first string is equal to, less than, or greater than the second. We will also use the text `join` block to format our output to the user.

Consider the design in Figure 10-18.

Figure 10-18 Tutorial 10-1 Design (*Source:* MIT App Inventor 2)

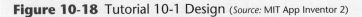

Step 1:   Place two TextBoxes on the screen, rename them to `TextBox-FirstString` and `TextBoxSecondString`. Change the Hint property of the first to *enter string one* and the Hint property of the second to *enter string two*.

Step 2:   Put a Button on the screen under the two TextBoxes and rename it `ButtonCompare`. Change its Text property to *Compare*.

Step 3:   Put a Label under the Button and rename it `LabelResult`. Clear its Text property.

Compare your design to Figure 10-18.

Step 4:   Now let's program the blocks. Consider Figure 10-19.

Figure 10-19 Tutorial 10-1 Blocks (*Source:* MIT App Inventor 2)

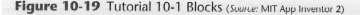

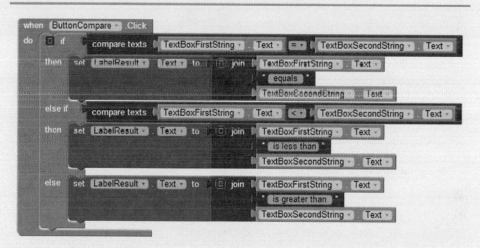

Step 5:   Find the `when ButtonCompare.Click do` event handler and place it in the workspace.

Step 6:   Program the `if then else if` decision block. Notice Figure 10-19. First we will check to see if the strings are equal. If they are, then we will populate the Label and move on. If they are not equal, we will have an `else if` slot to determine whether the first is less than the other. If so, then we will populate the Label and be done. If that condition is `false`, we will then deduce that the first string is greater than the other, so in the final `else` slot, we populate the Label that way.

To find and program the `if then else if` block, first go to the *Control* drawer and select the `if then` block. See Figure 10-20.

Figure 10-20 if then **Block** (*Source:* MIT App Inventor 2)

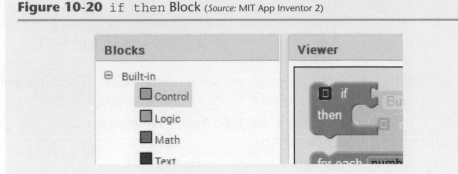

Step 7: Use the if then block's mutator to set it up to handle an else if and a final else condition as shown in Figure 10-21.

Figure 10-21 Set Up the if then else if (*Source:* MIT App Inventor 2)

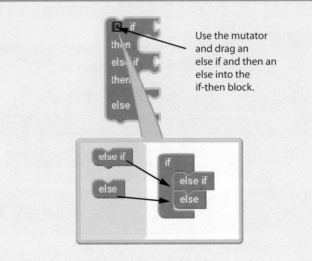

Step 8: Plug the if then else if block into the ButtonCompare.Click event.

Step 9: From the *Text* drawer, select the compare texts block and place it in the editor.

Step 10: Plug the compare texts block into the first if condition slot and change the operator to =. See Figure 10-22.

Figure 10-22 The Compare Texts Block (*Source:* MIT App Inventor 2)

Step 11: From the *TextBoxFirstString* drawer, find the `TextBoxFirstString.` `Text` block and place it in the first slot of the `compare texts` block.

Step 12: From the *TextBoxSecondString* drawer, find the `TextBoxSecondString.` `Text` block and place it in the second slot of the `compare texts` block.

 TIP: Copying and pasting block sets will speed up this tutorial. Once you get the blocks in Figure 10-23 done, consider copying and pasting that set (and just change the operator) for your other comparison.

Figure 10-23 `compare texts` **Block** (*Source:* MIT App Inventor 2)

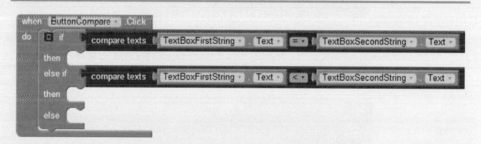

Step 13: Copy and paste your `compare texts` block and change the operator in the second one to *less than*. Plug this set into the `else if` slot as shown in Figure 10-24.

Figure 10-24 `compare texts` **Less than** (*Source:* MIT App Inventor 2)

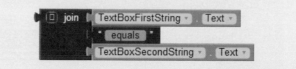

Step 14: Now that our testing is done, we can program the actions we want to perform if the strings are equal, or if the first string is less than the second string, or if the first string is greater than the second string.

You want to use the text `join` block to create a string that you can display on the screen. The desired result is to show the user the first string concatenated with the word(s) *equals, is less than,* or *is greater than,* and then concatenated with the second string. For example, if the user typed in "Hello" and "Hello" the app will display "Hello is equal to Hello". If the user types in "Hello" and "hello" the app will display "Hello is less than hello". Figure 10-25 shows the `join` block for the condition where the two stings are equal.

Figure 10-25 Join for the Equals is `true` Condition (*Source:* MIT App Inventor 2)

Step 15: Create a `set LabelResult.Text to` block, and plug the `join` block that you created in Step 14 into its socket. Figure 10-26 shows the resulting blocks.

Figure 10-26 Populate the `LabelResult.Text` Property

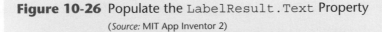
(*Source:* MIT App Inventor 2)

Step 16: Now, copy and paste (twice) the block set shown in Figure 10-26. Change the middle text block that reads "equals" to "is less than" in one, and "is greater than" for the other. You should have the blocks shown in Figure 10-27.

Figure 10-27 The Results Blocks Sets (*Source:* MIT App Inventor 2)

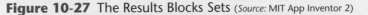

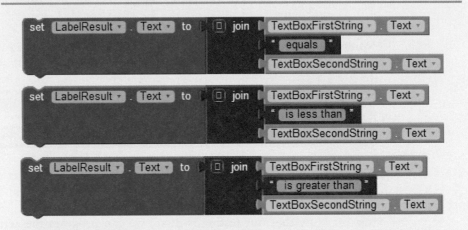

Step 17: Plug each result block set from Figure 10-27 into the appropriate condition of the `if then else if` statement. See Figure 10-28.

Figure 10-28 Tutorial 10-1 Complete Blocks Editor (*Source:* MIT App Inventor 2)

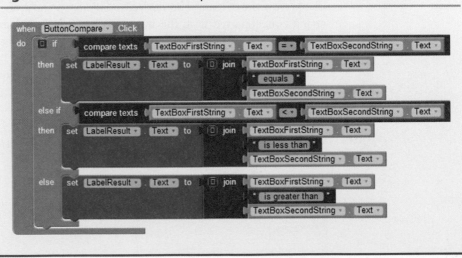

Checkpoint

10.5   Explain the numerical representation of characters in the ASCII table. How does this allow us to compare strings?

10.6   What does it mean when two strings are equal?

10.7   If you have two strings that are the same except one string is in uppercase and the other is in lowercase, which is greater?

10.8   What data type does the `compare texts` block return?

10.3 Trimming a String

CONCEPT: Sometimes we need to remove spaces surrounding a string. Trimming a string means to remove any leading or trailing spaces from it. Leading spaces are blank space characters before a string begins. Trailing spaces are the spaces after the string ends.

When we are working with data from a user interface or file, we need to remove unwanted spaces in order to effectively use the data. For example, remember that "*Hello*" with no spaces is not equal to "*Hello* " with a trailing space. Even though technically these strings are not equal, in practical terms, they both read "*Hello*" so we may want to treat them as equal.

Unwanted spaces can be a result of human error (typos), an issue with how data is stored in a file, or how the data is extracted. In order to accommodate for unwanted spaces we can use the `trim` function block. This block will remove both leading and trailing spaces from a string and return the resulting string. For example, using the `trim` block with the string "Hello ", with the trailing space, will return "Hello" with no space. See Figure 10-29 for an example of using the `trim` function block.

Figure 10-29 Using the `trim` Function Block (*Source:* MIT App Inventor 2)

Notice in Figure 10-29 that there are a few leading and trailing spaces surrounding the string literal. However, once the string is trimmed, the spaces are gone and the result is shown on the emulator.

By trimming unwanted spaces from a string, we can ensure that our data is accurate and our comparison functions return the result we expect. Keep in mind that this will depend on your business rule, or the problem you are trying to solve. There are times when you may not want to trim strings, such as for password verification.

It is also important to note that trimming only removes leading and trailing spaces and not any spaces within the string. For example, trimming the " Hello" "World " text block in Figure 10-29 does not remove the space between " Hello" and "World ".

One final thing to consider is that like the comparison blocks, all data plugged into a `trim` function block will be treated as text—you can plug in a number for example, but the program will treat it as if it were a `text` block.

10.4 Converting Case

CONCEPT: Converting case means to convert a lowercase letter to an uppercase letter or vice versa. When you convert the case of a string, you will convert all of the alphabetic letters in the string into either all uppercase or all lowercase letters.

App Inventor has a function block that we can use to convert the case of a string: the `upcase` / `downcase` block found in the *Text* drawer. This function block takes one text argument and returns the same string converted with all alphabetic letters either in uppercase (`upcase`) or lowercase (`downcase`) letters. See Figure 10-30.

Figure 10-30 upcase / downcase **Block** (*Source:* MIT App Inventor 2)

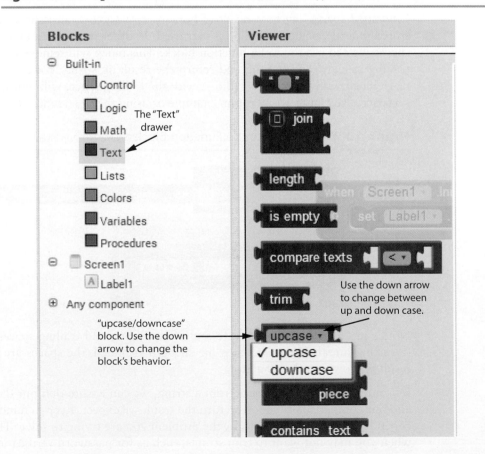

If you convert a string to uppercase with the upcase block, the function will return the string with all capital letters. "Hello World" will convert to "HELLO WORLD". Because the *H* and the *W* were already in uppercase, no changes were made to those characters. See Figure 10-31.

Figure 10-31 Converting Case of a String (*Source:* MIT App Inventor 2)

It shows in Figure 10-31 that converting a string with mixed case letters to uppercase will result in all alphabetic letters in uppercase. Conversely, using the downcase option will convert the string so that all the letters in the string are lowercase.

It's important to note that any character in a string conversion that is not an alphabetic character will be unaffected by the upcase and downcase function blocks. See Figure 10-32.

Figure 10-32 Only Alphabetic Characters Convert (*Source:* MIT App Inventor 2)

Figure 10-32 shows that converting a string that contains characters other than alphabetic characters will leave the non-alphabetic characters unaffected.

Tutorial 10-2:
Trim and Convert to Format Tags

App Inventor comes with a database in the *Storage* Palette that we can use to store data called TinyDB. Information stored to a TinyDB must be a tag-value pair. Recall that the tag is a unique identifier for a record of data you want to store. For example, for product data your key may be a SKU (Stock Keeping Unit), for vehicle data it may be a VIN number, for a contact the key may be an email address, phone number, or a name.

It may be beneficial to ensure that a key stored to the TinyDB does not have leading or trailing spaces. After all, if a key is put in with spaces surrounding it, those same spaces will have to be in the string to retrieve the data. Let's also consider that we may want to allow the user to search for a key without worrying about being case sensitive. To handle this, we will convert the tag to all uppercase letters and trim any spaces before we save the tag.

Figure 10-33 shows the user interface for the app that you will create in this tutorial.

Figure 10-33 User Interface (*Source:* MIT App Inventor 2)

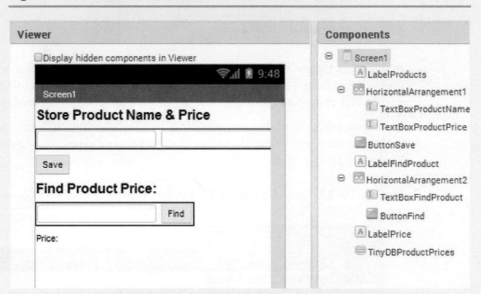

Step 1:   Add a Label to the Screen, rename it `LabelProducts`. Change its Text property to *Store Product Name & Price*.

Step 2:   Add a HorizontalArrangement and place two TextBoxes inside. Rename the first TextBox to `TextBoxProductName` and change the Hint property to *product name*. Rename the second TextBox to `TextBoxProductPrice` and change the `Hint` property to *price*.

Step 3:   Add a Button under the HorizontalArrangement and rename it to `ButtonSave`. Change the Text property to *Save*.

Step 4:   Add a Label under the save Button and rename it to `LabelFindProduct`. Change the Text property to *Find Product Price*.

Step 5:   Add a HorizontalArrangement and place a TextBox and Button inside of it. Rename the TextBox to `TextBoxFindProduct` and change the Hint property to *product name*. Rename the Button to `ButtonFind` and change the Text property to *Find*.

Step 6: Add a Label under the HorizontalArrangement. Rename the Label to `LabelPrice` and change the Text property to *Price:*.

Step 7: Add a TinyDB to the project and rename it `TinyDBProductPrices`.

Step 8: Now you will program the `when ButtonSave.Click do` event handler as shown in Figure 10-34. Find and select the event handler block in the *ButtonSave* drawer.

Figure 10-34 Button Save Click Event (*Source:* MIT App Inventor 2)

Step 9: Get the `TinyDBProductPrices.StoreValue` block from the *TinyDBProductPrices* drawer. Plug it into the `ButtonSave.Click` block.

TIP: Look at Figure 10-34 and consider how copying and pasting blocks might make this tutorial quicker.

Step 10: Select an `upcase` block and a `trim` block from the *Text* drawer.

Step 11: Select the `TextBoxProductName.Text` block from the *TextBoxProductName* drawer.

Step 12: Assemble the blocks that you created in Steps 10 and 11 as shown in Figure 10-35. Then, plug the resulting set of blocks into the `tag` socket of the `TinyDBProductPrices.StoreValue` block (see Figure 10-34).

Figure 10-35 Trim String and Change to Uppercase (*Source:* MIT App Inventor 2)

trim | upcase ▾ | TextBoxProductName ▾ . Text ▾

Step 13: Copy and paste the blocks that you assembled in Step 12 (shown in Figure 10-35). Change `TextBoxProductName` to `TextBoxProductPrice`.

Step 14: Plug the resulting set of blocks into the `valueToStore` socket of the `TinyDBProductPrices.StoreValue` block. Your blocks should look like Figure 10-34.

Step 15: Now you will program the `when ButtonFind.Click do` event handler as shown in Figure 10-36. Find and select the block in the *ButtonFind* drawer.

Figure 10-36 `ButtonFind.Click` **Event Handler** (*Source:* MIT App Inventor 2)

Step 16: Select the `set LabelPrice.Text to` block from the *LabelPrice* drawer and plug it into the `ButtonFind.Click` event handler. Next, select the `TinyDBProductPrices.GetValue` block from the *TinyDBProductPrices* drawer. Plug it into the `set LabelPrice.Text to` block.

Step 17: Select an `upcase` and a `trim` block from the *Text* drawer.

Step 18: Plug in the text blocks as shown in Figure 10-36 (`trim` plugged into the `tag` socket, and `upcase` plugged into the `trim` block). This will format the input from the user by trimming any spaces and converting any letters in their input to uppercase letters.

Step 19: Select the `TextBoxProductName.Text` block, from the *TextBox-ProductName* drawer, and plug it into the `upcase` block as shown in Figure 10-36.

Step 20: Run and test your app. Try storing products with a leading or a trailing space. Try to search for a product with a mixed case string. For example, store "*Apples*" (with leading spaces), with a price of 2.99, then search for it by typing in *apPLes* and check that it retrieves the price from the TinyDB.

 Checkpoint

10.9 Name some reasons that you would want to trim strings. Can you think of situations when you would not want to trim a string?

10.10 When we combine the text blocks `upcase` and `trim`, does it matter which order they are in? Why or why not?

10.11 When you convert a string to lowercase, what happens to the characters that are not alphabetic letters? What happens to the uppercase alphabetic letters? What about the lowercase letters?

10.12 What is the result of converting a number to uppercase? What data type is the result?

10.5 Finding a Substring

CONCEPT: A substring of a string is a set of characters that exists as part of that string.

Programs commonly need to search for substrings, or strings that appear within other strings. For example, suppose you have a document open in your word processor and you need to search for a word that appears somewhere in it. The word that you are searching for is a substring that appears in a larger string, the document.

App Inventor provides two blocks that can help us find substrings. One is used to determine whether a string contains a substring (the contains block), the other will tell us where that substring begins (the starts at block).

The contains function block returns a Boolean value of true or false based on whether or not the substring exists in the string. The contains block is useful because sometimes your program will need to know simply whether or not the string contains the substring before any processing begins.

The contains function block requires two arguments, text and piece. If the value of the piece argument exists in the text argument the function will return true, if it does not exist, it will return false. Let's look at an example in Figure 10-37.

Figure 10-37 Contains Example (*Source:* MIT App Inventor 2)

This function would return false because the string *Grapes* does not exist in the string *Oranges and Apples*.

The next block that is useful for finding substrings is the starts at function block which is also found in the *Text* drawer. It requires the same two arguments as the contains block, text and piece.

Figure 10-38 Starts at Block (*Source:* MIT App Inventor 2)

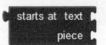

The function will return a number representing the position in the string (text parameter) where the substring (piece parameter) starts. If the substring is in the string more than once, only the position of the first occurrence is returned. If the substring does not exist in the string, the function will return zero. Let's look at an example in Figure 10-39.

Figure 10-39 Substring Example (*Source:* MIT App Inventor 2)

The function call in Figure 10-39 will return the number 8 because the substring *Orange* does exist in the string and it starts in the 8th position. The character *A* is in position 1, *p* is in position 2, and so forth. Each space will take up a position so you need to remember to count those too.

Keep in mind that both the `starts at` and `contains` blocks are *case sensitive*, meaning that the characters must be identical in the substring and string in order to find a match. For example, the substring *orange* with a lower case *o* would not be found in the *Apples Oranges Bananas* string.

 Checkpoint

10.13 Evaluate the following function calls:

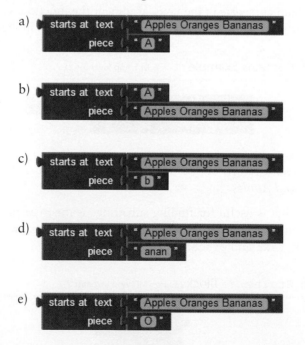

10.14 Explain the differences between the `starts at` and `contains` blocks. Explain how they similar.

10.15 Consider the parameters `text` and `piece`. Which represents the substring to search for and which represents the string to search?

10.16 How does the fact that the `starts at` and `contains` blocks are case sensitive affect whether or not a substring is found in a string?

Tutorial 10-3:
Validate an Email Address

Suppose we have an application that requires the user to enter an email address. Email addresses have a syntax that requires a name, the @ symbol, the first-level domain name, the dot (.) and then the top level domain (some familiar top level domain names are com, edu, org, and net). Generally, the format looks like this: name@domain.com.

In this tutorial we are simply going to check that the string entered by the user contains both the @ symbol and the dot. Once it is verified that the string contains those two characters, we will then check that the @ symbol comes before the dot.

> *To make this tutorial simple, we will assume that no valid email addresses contain a dot in the name. We will also skip validating that there are characters before and after the @ and dot characters. We will use other text blocks to validate the address more thoroughly later in this chapter.*

If the email address is in correct format, in our case meaning that it contains the @ symbol before a period, we will populate a Label saying *Thank you*. If those conditions are not met, we will populate the Label with *Please enter a valid email* so that the user knows to try again.

The user interface design for this project is fairly simple. As shown in Figure 10-40, we'll just have a Label, TextBox, and a Button.

Figure 10-40 User Interface *(Source: MIT App Inventor 2)*

Viewer	Components
☐ Display hidden components in Viewer	⊖ ☐ Screen1
🛜 📶 🔋 9:48	A LabelConfirmation
Screen1	TextBoxEmail
[ ]	ButtonGo
Go	

Step 1: Drag a Label from the *Basic* Palette onto the screen. Rename it `LabelConfirmation`. Clear the Label's Text property.

Step 2: Place a TextBox on the screen and rename it `TextBoxEmail`. Change the Hint property to *Enter Email*.

Step 3: Place a Button on the screen and rename it `ButtonGo`. Change the Text property to *Go*.

Step 4: Now you will program the blocks to check that both the @ symbol and a dot (.) exist in the string. We'll verify later that the @ comes before the dot.

Figure 10-41 Check for Required Characters *(Source:* MIT App Inventor 2)

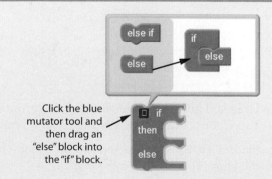

In Figure 10-41 we are using the contains blocks to verify that both characters exist in the string entered by the user and then prompt the user appropriately.

If you were to read the if then else set of blocks logically in pseudo-code or English it would sound like this:

If the `TextBoxEmail.Text` *string contains both "@" and ".", then set* `LabelConfirmation.Text` *to the string Thank you.*

Otherwise, set `LabelConfirmation.Text` *to the string Please enter a valid email.*

Step 5: Go to the *ButtonGo* drawer and select the when ButtonGo.Click do event handler.

Step 6: Go to the *Control* drawer and select an if then block. Use the mutator tool to change it to an if then else block. See Figure 10-42.

Figure 10-42 if then else Block *(Source:* MIT App Inventor 2)

Click the blue mutator tool and then drag an "else" block into the "if" block.

Step 7: Go to the *Logic* drawer and select an and block. See Figure 10-43.

Figure 10-43 The Logic and Block (*Source:* MIT App Inventor 2)

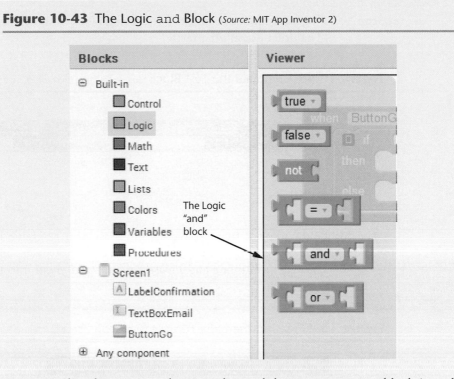

Step 8. Plug the and into the if socket and the if then else block into the ButtonGo.Click event handler. See Figure 10-44.

Figure 10-44 Insert the *Control* and *Logic* Blocks

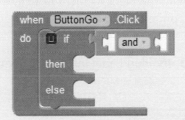

Step 9: Select two contains blocks in the *Text* drawer. Plug in the TextBox-Email.Text value block into both of the text sockets. Then make text blocks of the @ symbol and the dot and plug those into the piece sockets. Refer to Figure 10-45. (Tip: You can program just one of these block sets and then copy and paste it to make the other, just change the @ to a period.)

Figure 10-45 Check if the Symbols Exist (*Source:* MIT App Inventor 2)

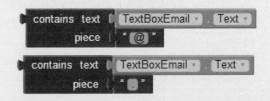

Step 10: Plug both `contains` blocks into the `and` block as shown in Figure 10-46. (The order doesn't matter.)

Figure 10-46 Complete the Test Block *(Source:* MIT App Inventor 2)

Step 11: Find and place two `set LabelConfirmation.Text to` blocks, found in the *LabelConfirmation* drawer, into the workspace and plug the text *Thank you* into one and *Please enter a valid email* into the other. See Figure 10-47.

Figure 10-47 Set up the `LabelConfirmation.Text` *(Source:* MIT App Inventor 2)

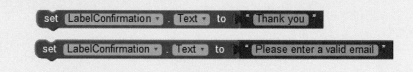

Step 12: Plug the blocks shown in Figure 10-47 into the `if then else` block. Compare your work to Figure 10-48.

Figure 10-48 Plug Label Information into the *Control* Block
(Source: MIT App Inventor 2)

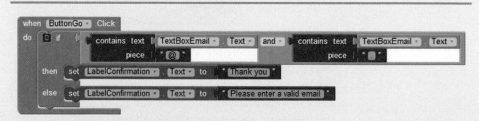

Step 13: Run and test your app with valid emails and invalid emails. Remember at this point it simply checks for a dot and the @ symbol, it doesn't check that they are in the correct order.

Step 14: Now we need to take the next step and validate that the @ symbol comes before the dot. To do this we will use the `starts at` block to tell us the position of each symbol. See Figure 10-49.

Figure 10-49 Ensuring the Order of Characters (*Source:* MIT App Inventor 2)

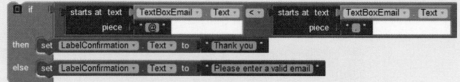

Figure 10-49 shows that we embed the `starts at` blocks (which return the position of a character) into a `less than` *Math* block. Remember the `starts at` block returns a number, so it makes sense to use the *Math* block to compare the two values.

If the position of the @ is less than the position of the dot, that means the email address is in the format that we want and we will prompt the user with "Thank you". Otherwise, the email address is not in the correct format so we will prompt the user to enter a valid email address.

Step 15: Go to the *Control* drawer and find an `if then` block and place it in the workspace.

Step 16: Use the mutator to change the block to an `if then else` block (see Figure 10-42).

Step 17: Go to the *Text* drawer and select two `starts at` blocks.

Step 18: Go to the *Math* drawer and select a math equality block (=). Change it to a less than block by clicking the down arrow and selecting the less than symbol. See Figure 10-50.

Figure 10-50 Math `less than` Block (*Source:* MIT App Inventor 2)

Step 19: Configure each argument of the math less than block as shown in Figure 10-51. This will return `true` if the @ symbol comes before the dot in the string.

Figure 10-51 Comparing the Positions (*Source:* MIT App Inventor 2)

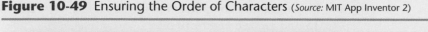

Step 20: Plug the entire comparison in the new if then else block from Steps 15 and 16. See Figure 10-52.

Figure 10-52 Program the Test Condition (*Source:* MIT App Inventor 2)

Step 21: Temporarily remove the set LabelConfirmation.Text to *Thank you* block from the first if then else block. Nest the block from Figure 10-52 into the first if then else block as shown in Figure 10-53.

Figure 10-53 Nest the if then else Blocks (*Source:* MIT App Inventor 2)

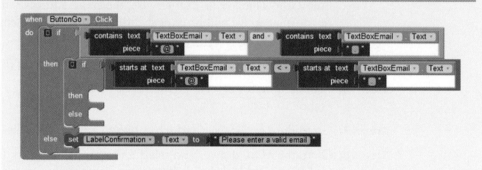

Step 22: Place the set LabelConfirmation.Text to *Thank you* block into the then slot of the inner if then else block. (See Figure 10-54.)

Step 23: Select and duplicate the set LabelConfirmation.Text to *Please enter a valid email* block and place it in the else slot of the inner if then else block. (See Figure 10-54.)

Step 24: Compare your complete tutorial with Figure 10-54. Run and test your app. Try different string combinations and ensure your app performs as expected, requiring that the email at least has the @ symbol and a dot, in that order.

Figure 10-54 Tutorial 10-3 Complete Blocks Editor (*Source:* MIT App Inventor 2)

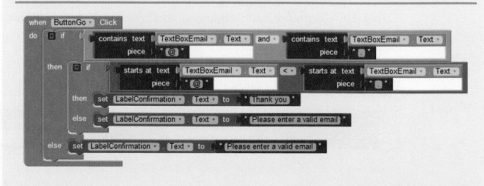

10.6 Replacing a Substring

App Inventor has a `replace all` block that returns a copy of a string, where every occurrence of a specified substring has been replaced with another string. Look at the example in Figure 10-55.

Figure 10-55 Replace All Block (*Source:* MIT App Inventor 2)

The function call in Figure 10-55 will return *barking up the right tree*. It works by searching for all occurrences of the value plugged into the `segment` socket and replacing all of those values with what is plugged into the `replacement` socket. If there were more occurrences of the word *wrong*, all of them would be replaced with the word *right*. Look at the example in Figure 10-56.

Figure 10-56 Replace All Example (*Source:* MIT App Inventor 2)

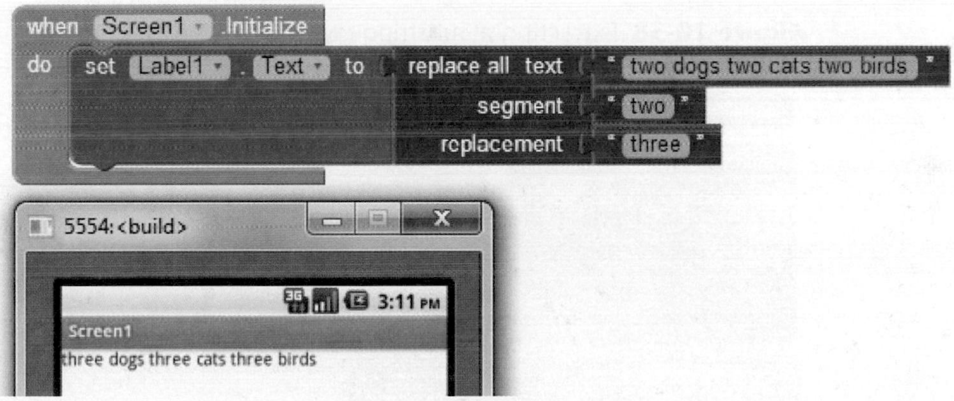

You can see in the emulator that in the retuned string all occurrences of *two* in the original string are replaced with *three*.

The `replace all` block is *case sensitive* like the other text blocks. If you accidentally plugged the text *Two*, with a capital *T*, in the `segment` socket nothing would be replaced and the string returned will match the original.

10.7 Extracting a Substring

In addition to finding and replacing substrings, you can also extract a substring from a string. To do this you will need to know the starting point and the length of the substring.

App Inventor includes the `segment` block that will allow you to extract a substring by giving it three arguments the entire string (`text`), the starting position of the substring (`start`), and the length of the substring (`length`).

Figure 10-57 Segment Block (*Source:* MIT App Inventor 2)

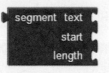

Keep in mind that both the `start` and `length` arguments of the `segment` block require numerical data.

For example, let's say you have a string of product data that contains the name, product number, and price. Also, let's assume that the product number begins with the letters "PN" and is followed by six digits. If we want to extract the product number from the string we can first find where the substring begins by using the `starts at` block. Next, because we know the product number is eight characters total, we can use the length of eight to extract the product number. See Figure 10-58.

Figure 10-58 Extracting a Substring (*Source:* MIT App Inventor 2)

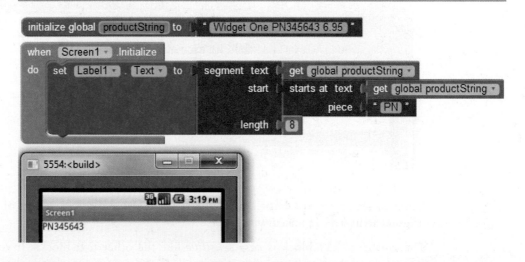

In this application we first created a variable `ProductString` to hold the product string. Then, in the `Screen.Initialize` event we populate a Label with the product number extracted from the variable `ProductString`. To extract the product number we used the `segment` block and gave it the variable that holds the string, the starting point, and the length. To determine the starting point, we used the `starts at` block, which scans the `ProductString` variable to determine where the characters *PN* occur first.

Checkpoint

10.17 What block do you use when you want to change part of a string to something else?

10.18 When you replace part of a string with a different set of characters, what information must you provide the block?

10.19 When you want to extract a substring from a string, what information must you provide to the `segment` block?

10.20 When you are extracting a substring, how does App Inventor know when to start and when to stop extracting?

10.21 When you are replacing or extracting from a string, what happens to the original string?

 ## 10.8 Splitting a Substring

App Inventor allows us to split strings into list items by providing us several split functions. There is a single `split` block, but you can change it to handle the other functions by using the drop down arrow in the middle. See Figures 10-59 and 10-60.

Figure 10-59 The `split` Block (*Source:* MIT App Inventor 2)

Figure 10-60 Accessing the Other Functions (*Source:* MIT App Inventor 2)

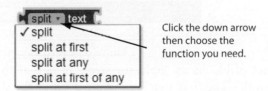

Click the down arrow then choose the function you need.

Two of these functions, the `split at first` and the `split at first of any`, return a simple two-item list. The other functions, `split`, `split at any`, and `split at spaces`, return a list that can be more than two items depending on the contents of the string and the division-point.

The *division-point* is the argument you supply to tell App Inventor where you want to split the string. For example, we may want to split a string of information separated by commas, in which case your division-point would be the comma character (,).

For the `split at first` and `split` blocks, the division point you supply will be a single string or character, like a comma, period, or word.

If you use the `split at first of any` or the `split at any` blocks, your division-point argument will be a list. Assume you want to split information in a string that is between commas and/or periods. In this case, you would make a two-item list with the division-points, a comma as one element, and a period as the other. Now you can split the string with the two division-points.

split at first

The split functions that contain the words "at first" will return the two-item lists. They will only split at the first occurrence of the division point and hence we will only have two items. Let's take a look at the `split at first` and the `split at first of any` blocks.

Figure 10-61 `split at first` Block (*Source:* MIT App Inventor 2)

This block will return a two-item list. You can think of this set of blocks as "Split the string in two at the first occurrence of a comma." The first element will be *A* and the second will be the string *E, I, O, U*. Notice that the comma that was the division-point of the split has been removed from the result.

Figure 10-62 `split at first of any` Block (*Source:* MIT App Inventor 2)

The `split at first of any` block will return a two-item list also. You can think of this set of blocks as "Split the string in two at the first occurrence of a comma or a period." The first step is to make a list of the division-points and store it to a List variable. Then use the List variable as the division-point in the `at` argument of the block.

In this example, the split function returns a two-item list. It will split the string in two at the first occurrence of a comma or period. Look at the `vowels` variable closely (A E.I, O, U, y). The first occurrence of a comma or period happens to be between the *E* and *I*, so the first element will be *A E* and the second element will be *I, O, U, y*.

Notice again that the division-point is removed from the result.

split

Next, let's look at the `split` and `split at any` functions. The difference between these functions and the `split at first` blocks is that these functions will split the string at *all* locations of the division-point.

The `split` function block shown in Figure 10-63 will return a list of 5 elements (A E I O U). The division-point is a comma, so any information in the list that is between commas will be a separate list item. This set of blocks reads "split the contents of the `vowels` variable by commas."

Figure 10-63 `split` Block (*Source:* MIT App Inventor 2)

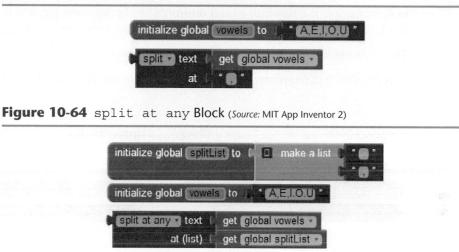

Figure 10-64 `split at any` Block (*Source:* MIT App Inventor 2)

In Figure 10-64 you'll notice that both commas and periods separate the vowels. Because both the comma and period are in the list of things to split by (`spiltList` variable) the list that is returned from the `split at any` block will have five elements (A E I O U). The logic of this set of blocks can be read as "split the contents of the `vowels` variable at each comma or period."

split at spaces

You can certainly use a space character as your division point with the split blocks covered so far, but App Inventor also provides a `split at spaces` function that will make it a little easier to split a text block by spaces. It only requires one string argument and it will return a list of the items between any spaces in the string.

Figure 10-65 Split at Spaces (*Source:* MIT App Inventor 2)

In Figure 10-65, the `split at spaces` function block will return a list of 5 elements (A E I O U) with no spaces. This is because the spaces are the division-points, which are excluded from the result.

Length of a String

We often will need to know the length of a string, especially after splitting a string. We may want to know how long each substring is or if a string is empty. App Inventor provides two blocks that will help us determine the length of a string. The first is a simple Boolean block that will let us know if a string is empty or not, the `is empty` block. The second is the `length` block. The `length` block will return a number equal to the number of characters in the string.

Often, your program will need to know if a string is empty or not before you try to process it further. Look at the example in Figure 10-66.

In this example the function would return `false` because the name is not empty. This block is often used in conjunction (as the test argument) with an `if-then` block.

The example in Figure 10-67 shows the `length` block.

This function will return the number 5 because there are five characters in the name *Sally*.

Figure 10-66 `is text empty` **Block**
(*Source:* MIT App Inventor 2)

Figure 10-67 `length` **Block**
(*Source:* MIT App Inventor 2)

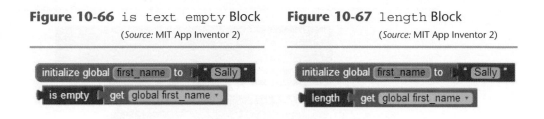

Checkpoint

10.22 Evaluate the following function calls by identifying the items in the resulting lists:

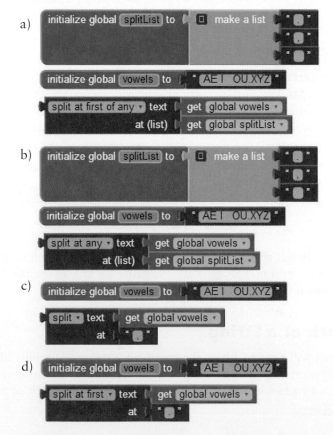

10.23   Explain the term *division-point*. What happens to the division-point characters in a string after a `split` or `split at any`?

10.24   Explain how the `split at first` and the `split at first of any` blocks perform differently than the `split` or `split at any` blocks.

10.25   Why doesn't the `split at spaces` block require that you give it a division-point argument?

10.26   What would the `length` function return if you supplied it with a text block containing *Go the Whole 9 Yards*.

Tutorial 10-4:
Validating Email – Valid Name and Top-Level Domain

VideoNote
Validating Email –
Valid Name and
Top-Level Domain

We are going create another application to validate an email address. This time, we are going to focus on making sure that the user supplies a name (at least two characters long) before the @ symbol and that they have entered a top-level domain (after the last dot) which must also be least two characters long.

There is more to validating an email address, but this is an example of how you can use the `split` blocks to examine a string. Later, we will have exercises and projects to validate further that a host is entered and that the email address starts with an alphabetic letter.

The first three steps are exactly like those in Tutorial 10-3. If you've already completed that tutorial you can start from that project and save a little time.

The user interface design for this project is fairly simple. We'll just have a Label, TextBox and Button. See Figure 10-68.

Figure 10-68 User Interface *(Source: MIT App Inventor 2)*

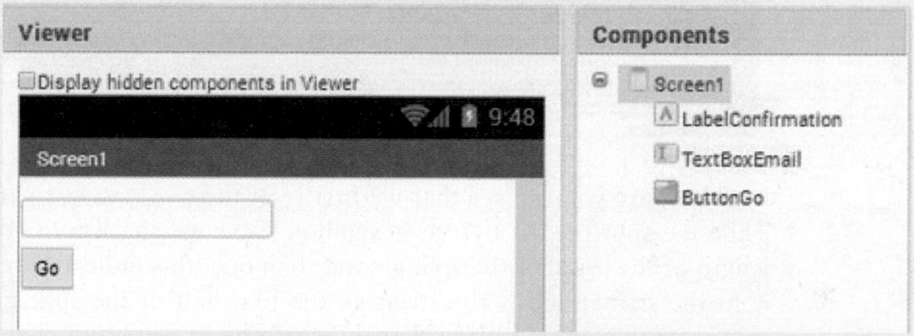

Step 1:   Drag a Label from the *Basic* Palette onto the screen. Rename it `LabelConfirmation`. Clear the Text property.

Step 2:   Place a TextBox on the screen and rename it `TextBoxEmail`. Change the Hint property to *Enter Email*.

Step 3:   Place a Button on the screen and rename it `ButtonGo`. Change the Text property to *Go*.

Step 4:   Open the Blocks Editor. The first thing we will need to do is create a Boolean variable that will store whether or not the email address is valid. Create the variable as shown in Figure 10-69.

Figure 10-69 Initialize `emailValid` Boolean Variable (*Source:* MIT App Inventor 2)

initialize global `emailValid` to `false`

Step 5: Go to the *Variables* drawer and choose an `initialize global to` block. Change the name to `emailValid`.

Step 6: Go to the *Logic* drawer and find a `false` block, plug that into the `emailValid` variable. (See Figure 10-69.)

Step 7: Now you will create a variable to hold the list that is returned when we split the email input. Go to the *Variables* drawer and choose an `initialize global to` block. Change the name to `emailList`.

Figure 10-70 EmailList Variable (*Source:* MIT App Inventor 2)

initialize global `emailList` to `create empty list`

Step 8: We need to plug in a `create empty list` block from the *List* drawer to make this a List variable.

Validate the Name

In the following steps you will create a procedure that validates the name. When you are finished, the procedure will look like Figure 10-71.

Figure 10-71 Validate Name Procedure (*Source:* MIT App Inventor 2)

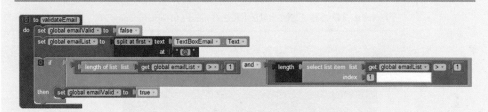

In this figure you can see that we first reset the `emailValid` variable to `false`. Then we split the list by the @ symbol. Next we check two conditions; is the length of the list after the split greater than one (this indicates that the @ symbol is in the string) and is the string in the first half of the split greater than one character (we are requiring that the name be at least two characters). If those conditions are met, we can safely set the `EmailValid` variable to `true`.

Step 9: Go the *Procedures* drawer and choose a `to procedure do` block. See Figure 10-72.

Step 10: Click on the name *procedure* and change the name to `validateName`. We will use this procedure to set the value of the `emailValid` to either `true` or `false` based on whether there is an @ symbol and that there is text before the @ symbol. See Figure 10-73.

Figure 10-72 The `to procedure do` Block (*Source:* MIT App Inventor 2)

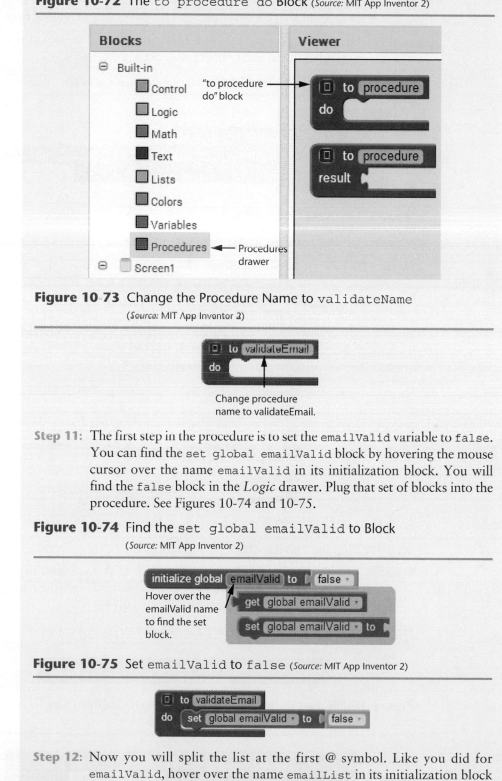

Figure 10-73 Change the Procedure Name to `validateName`
(*Source:* MIT App Inventor 2)

Change procedure
name to validateEmail.

Step 11: The first step in the procedure is to set the `emailValid` variable to `false`. You can find the `set global emailValid` block by hovering the mouse cursor over the name `emailValid` in its initialization block. You will find the `false` block in the *Logic* drawer. Plug that set of blocks into the procedure. See Figures 10-74 and 10-75.

Figure 10-74 Find the `set global emailValid to` Block
(*Source:* MIT App Inventor 2)

initialize global emailValid to false

Hover over the
emailValid name
to find the set
block.

get global emailValid

set global emailValid to

Figure 10-75 Set `emailValid` to `false` (*Source:* MIT App Inventor 2)

to validateEmail
do set global emailValid to false

Step 12: Now you will split the list at the first @ symbol. Like you did for `emailValid`, hover over the name `emailList` in its initialization block to find the `set global emailList to` block.

Step 13: Go to the *Text* drawer and select the `split` block, change it to `split at first` and plug it into the `set global emailList to` block from Step 12.

Step 14: Put the `TextBoxEmail.Text` block in the `text` argument slot and the @ symbol in the `at` argument slot. See Figure 10-76.

Figure 10-76 Split the Email Address *(Source:* MIT App Inventor 2*)*

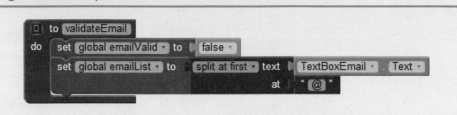

Step 15: Go to the *Control* drawer and select an `if-then` block.

Step 16: Go to the *Logic* drawer select an `and` block.

Figure 10-77 The Logic `and` Block *(Source:* MIT App Inventor 2*)*

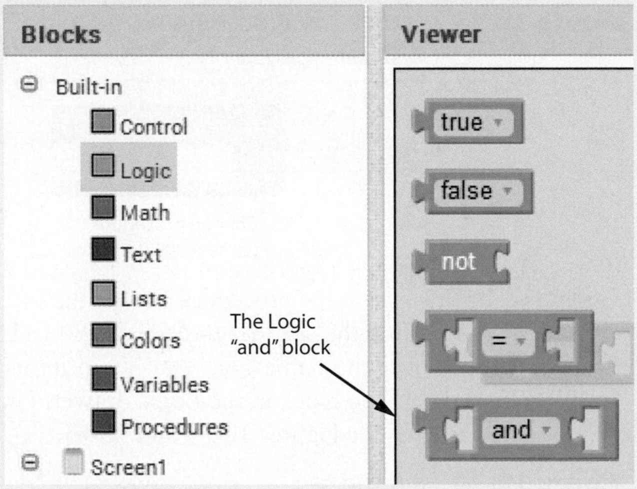

Step 17: Plug the `and` into the `if-then` block.

Step 18: Now let's program the two conditions: *Is there a name in front of the @ symbol?* and *Is it more than one character long?* (the name needs to be at least two). See Figure 10-78 and 10-79.

Figure 10-78 Test if Text is Before the @ Symbol *(Source:* MIT App Inventor 2*)*

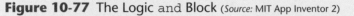

Figure 10-79 Test if the Length of the Name is Greater Than 1
(Source: MIT App Inventor 2*)*

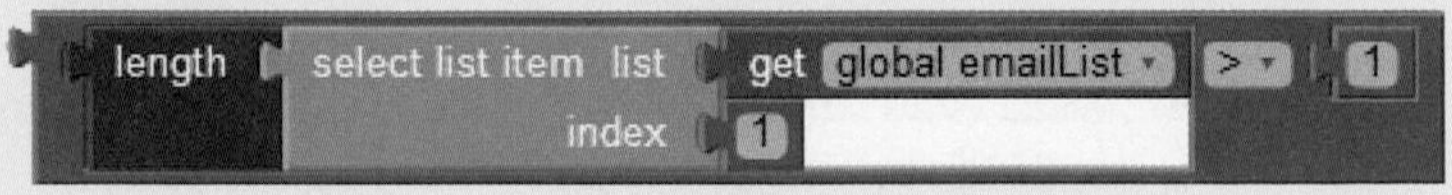

In Figure 10-78 we determine that there is indeed an @ symbol in the string if the length of emailList is greater than one. Remember that we split the string using the @ symbol as the division-point. If there is not an @ symbol in the string, then the list will be one element long and this test will not return true.

Step 19: Go to the *Math* drawer and create a greater than block.

Step 20: Go to the *List* drawer and select the length of list block.

Step 21: Hover the mouse cursor over the name emailList in its initialization block and get the get global emailList block.

Step 22: Go to the *Math* drawer and select a number block, change its value to 1.

Step 23: Configure the blocks in Steps 19–22 as shown in Figure 10-78.

Step 24: Go to the *Math* drawer and find a greater than (>) block.

Step 25: Go to the *Text* drawer and find the length block.

Step 26: Go to the *List* drawer and find the select list item block.

Step 27: Hover the mouse cursor over the name emailList in its initialization block and get the get global emailList block.

Step 28: Go to the *Math* drawer and select two number blocks, change their values to 1.

Step 29: Configure the blocks in Steps 24–28 as shown in Figure 10-79.

Step 30: Plug both test conditions into the *Logic* and block, as shown in Figure 10-80.

Figure 10-80 Test the Name Length (*Source:* MIT App Inventor 2)

Step 31: If both test conditions are true, set the emailValid variable to true. Compare your work so far with Figure 10-71.

Validate the Top-Level Domain

In the following steps you will create the blocks to validate that the top level domain is at least two characters. First, you will create the variable shown in Figure 10-81, naming it topDomain and setting it equal to a blank text block.

Figure 10-81 topDomain Variable (*Source:* MIT App Inventor 2)

initialize global topDomain to [" "]

Step 32: Go to *Variables* and choose an initialize global name to block. Change the name to topDomain.

Step 33: Go to the *Text* drawer and find an empty text block plug it into the topDomain initialization block. See Figure 10-81.

The top-level domain name will come after the *last* dot in the string. So, we will use the split block with a dot as the division-point. We will then use the length of the resulting list to select the last item in the list, which should be at least two characters long. Look at the procedure in Figure 10-82.

Figure 10-82 Validating the Top-Level Domain (*Source:* MIT App Inventor 2)

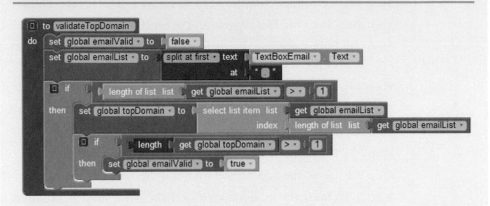

In the procedure in Figure 10-82 we first re-set the emailValid variable to false. Then we create a list of the string elements split by all dots in the string. Once we verify that the resulting list is greater than one (validating that the string does contain a dot), we can select the last item in the list to isolate the last portion (substring) of the string to validate the domain. Once that substring is extracted we can then verify that its length is at least two characters long.

Step 34: Go to the *Procedures* drawer and choose a to procedure do block Change the name to validateTopDomain. The block should appear as shown in Figure 10-83.

Figure 10-83 validateTopDomain **Procedure Block** (*Source:* MIT App Inventor 2)

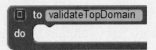

Step 35: The first step in the procedure is to set the emailValid variable to false. You can find the set global emailValid block by hovering the mouse cursor over the name emailValid in its initialization block, and you will find the false block in the *Logic* drawer. Plug that set of blocks into the procedure as shown in Figure 10-84.

Figure 10-84 (*Source:* MIT App Inventor 2)

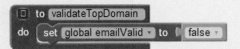

Step 36: Split the list at the first period. Like you did for emailValid, hover the mouse cursor over the name emailList in its initialization block to find the set global emailList to block.

Step 37: Go to the *Text* drawer and select the `split` block, change it to `split at first`, and plug it into the `set global emailList to` block from Step 12.

Step 38: Plug the `TextBoxEmail.Text` block into the `text` argument slot and the period into the `at` argument slot. See Figure 10-85.

Step 39: Go to the *Control* drawer and select an `if then` block.

Figure 10-85 Split the Email Address (*Source:* MIT App Inventor 2)

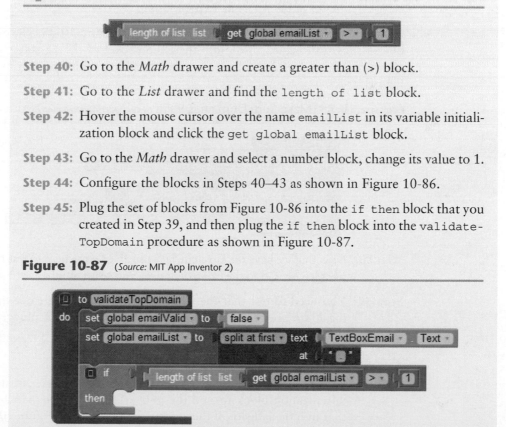

The condition that you will test in the `if then` block is shown in Figure 10-86. This will determine whether there is a period (or dot) in the string. Remember that we split the string using the period as the division-point. If the string contains a period, the length of `emailList` will be greater than one. If the string does not contain a period, the list will contain only one element.

Figure 10-86 Test if Text is Before the Period (*Source:* MIT App Inventor 2)

Step 40: Go to the *Math* drawer and create a greater than (>) block.

Step 41: Go to the *List* drawer and find the `length of list` block.

Step 42: Hover the mouse cursor over the name `emailList` in its variable initialization block and click the `get global emailList` block.

Step 43: Go to the *Math* drawer and select a number block, change its value to 1.

Step 44: Configure the blocks in Steps 40–43 as shown in Figure 10-86.

Step 45: Plug the set of blocks from Figure 10-86 into the `if then` block that you created in Step 39, and then plug the `if then` block into the `validateTopDomain` procedure as shown in Figure 10-87.

Figure 10-87 (*Source:* MIT App Inventor 2)

If the `length of list` test shown in Figure 10-87 is true, we can assume that the string contains a dot. We can extract the string after the last dot by selecting the *last* item in the list. We can then test this substring to ensure that it is at least two characters long. Look at Figure 10-88.

Figure 10-88 Get Last Item in List (*Source:* MIT App Inventor 2)

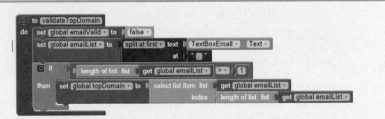

Step 46: To select the last item in the list, create a `select list item` block found in the *List* drawer.

Step 47: Find the `get global emailList` block by hovering the mouse cursor over the name `emailList` in its variable initialization block. Plug it into the `list` socket of the `select list item` block.

Step 48: Next, create a `length of list` block from the *List* drawer. Plug another `get global emailList` block into it, and plug these combined blocks into the `index` socket of the `select list item` block. See Figure 10-88.

Step 49: Now we need to assign the last list item to our variable `topDomain`. Find the `set global TopDomain to` block by hovering the mouse cursor over the name `topDomain` in its variable initialization block. Plug the set of blocks from Step 48 into it.

Compare your work for Steps 46 through 49 to Figure 10-88. Place the set of blocks shown in Figure 10-88 into the `then` socket of the `if` statement that is shown in Figure 10-87. At this point, the procedure should appear as shown in Figure 10-89.

Figure 10-89 Make Sure Domain is Valid (*Source:* MIT App Inventor 2)

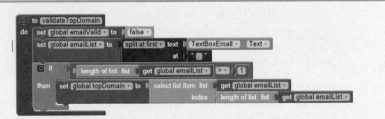

Step 50: Now that we have the last item, let's use an `if` statement to test that it is the right length. Go to the *Control* drawer and select another `if then` block.

Step 51: You need to test that the length of `topDomain` is greater than 1. Use the *Math* greater than block and a number 1 block plugged into the right socket.

Step 52: Go to the *Text* drawer and find a `length` block.

Step 53: Hover the mouse cursor over the name `topDomain` in its variable initialization block to find the `get global topDomain` block. Plug that into the left slot of the greater than block. See Figure 10-90.

Step 54: Place this set of blocks into the socket of the `if then` block from Step 51.

Figure 10-90 (*Source:* MIT App Inventor 2)

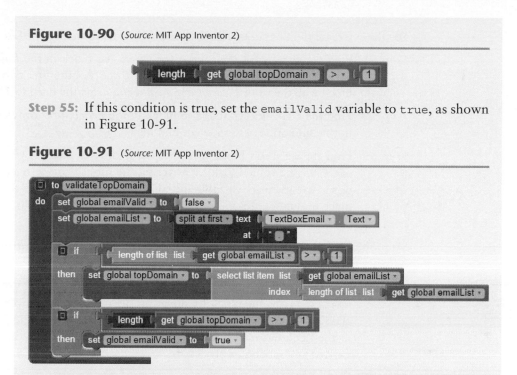

Step 55: If this condition is true, set the `emailValid` variable to `true`, as shown in Figure 10-91.

Figure 10-91 (*Source:* MIT App Inventor 2)

Now that we have the procedures written, we will need to call them. We will use the `ButtonGo.Click` event handler as shown in Figure 10-92.

Figure 10-92 Call the Procedures in `ButtonGo.Click` (*Source:* MIT App Inventor 2)

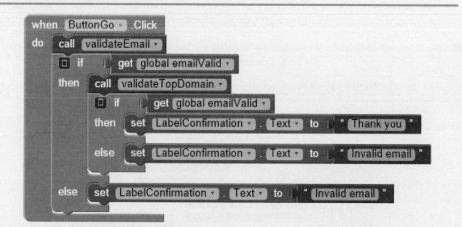

As shown in Figure 10-92, each time the button is clicked we will perform the following steps:

- Call `validateEmail`
- If `emailValid` is false, set the `LabelConfirmation.Text` to *Invalid email*
- If `emailValid` is true, call `validateTopDomain`
- If `emailValid` is false, set the `LabelConfirmation.Text` to *Invalid email*
- If `emailValid` is still true, set the `LabelConfirmation.Text` to *Thank you*

Step 56: Create the `ButtonGo.Click` event block from the *ButtonGo* drawer.

Step 57: Find the `set LabelConfirmation.Text to` block in the *LabelConfirmation* drawer. You will need three of these. Set the first two to a text block with the value *Please enter a valid email*. Set the third to *Thank you*.

Step 58: Find the `call validateName` block in the *Procedures* drawer. Place it in the `ButtonGo.Click` event handler.

Step 59: Find the `if then` block in the *Control* drawer and the `get global emailValid` value block by hovering the mouse cursor over the name `emailValid` in its variable initialization block. Connect the two and place in the `ButtonGo.Click` event handler, under the block that calls the `validateName` procedure.

Step 60: Find the `call validateTopDomain` block in the *Procedures* drawer. Place it in the `if then` block.

Step 61: Create an `if then` block from the *Control* drawer, and a `get global emailValid` value block by hovering the mouse cursor over the name `emailValid` in its initialization block. Connect the two and place them in the `ButtonGo.Click` event handler, under the block that calls the `validateTopDomain` procedure.

Step 62: Place the `set LabelConfirmation.Text to` *Thank you* block into the `then` socket from Step 61.

Step 63: Place the other `set LabelConfirmation.Text to` blocks in the other two `then` slots.

Compare your `ButtonGo.Click` event blocks to Figure 10-92.

Step 64: Run and test your app on your device or emulator. Test valid and invalid scenarios.

Figure 10-93 shows the entire Blocks Editor for Tutorial 10-4.

Figure 10-93 Tutorial 10-4 Complete Blocks Editor *(Source:* MIT App Inventor 2)

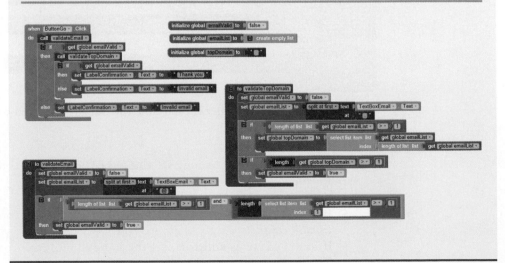

Review Questions

1. To concatenate two strings you will need to use this type of block:

   a. `concatenate`
   b. `join`
   c. `add`
   d. None of the above

2. What data types can you place in a `join` block?

   a. `number`
   b. `text`
   c. `Boolean`
   d. All of the above

3. What is the result of joining the numbers 150 and 450?

   a. 600
   b. 700
   c. 150450
   d. 1,50450

4. Which statement shows the greater string first?

   a. *Hello, hello*
   b. *hello, Hello*
   c. *hello, hi*
   d. *Hello, Hello There*

5. What is the result of using the `upcase` block with the string *hello my name is Sally*?

   a. *Hello my name is Sally*
   b. *Hello My Name Is sally*
   c. *HELLO MY NAME IS SALLY*
   d. None of the above

6. What is the result of using the `contains` block with *Four score and seven years ago* as the `text` argument and *score* as the `piece` argument?

   a. 6
   b. 5
   c. True
   d. False

7. What is the result of using the `starts at` block with *Four score and seven years ago* as the `text` argument and *score* as the `piece` argument?

   a. 6
   b. 5
   c. True
   d. False

8. What is the result of using the `contains` block with *Four score and seven years ago* as the `text` argument and *f* as the `piece` argument?

   a. 0
   b. 1
   c. True
   d. False

9. What is the result of using the starts at block with *Four score and seven years ago* as the text argument and *f* as the piece argument?

   a. 0
   b. 1
   c. True
   d. False

10. What block is used for replacing all occurrences of a substring within a string with something else?

    a. replace
    b. replace *all*
    c. replace *next*
    d. replace string

11. If you want to extract a date in the format mm/dd/yyyy from a string and you know the date starts at the third position of the string, you would use:

    a. The segment block with 1 as the start and 3 as the length
    b. The segment block with 1 as the start and 8 as the length
    c. The segment block with 3 as the start and 8 as the length
    d. The segment bock with 3 as the start and 10 as the length

12. Suppose you use the split at first function, using the string *one, two, three, four, five* as the text and a comma (,) as the division point. How many elements are in the resulting list?

    a. 1
    b. 2
    c. 4
    d. 5

13. Suppose you use the split function, using the string *one, two, three, four, five* as the text and a comma (,) as the division point. How many elements are in the resulting list?

    a. 1
    b. 2
    c. 4
    d. 5

14. What is the value of the second element in the list when you use the split at first function, using the string *one, two, three, four, five* as the text and a comma (,) as the division point?

    a. *two,*
    b. *two*
    c. *, two*
    d. *two, three, four, five*

15. Suppose you use the split at any function, using the string *apples, bananas. green beans. carrots, beets* as the text, and the division-point list includes a comma and a period. How many items will the resulting list have?

    a. 2
    b. 5
    c. 6
    d. 7

Short Answer

1. What is the effect of concatenating two numbers?

2. What role does the ASCII table and the numeric representation of characters play when we compare strings?

3. Why is it important to trim strings before evaluating them?

4. What happens to special characters and numbers when they are used in an `upcase` or `downcase` block?

5. Does App Inventor provide a block that will allow you to replace just the first instance of a substring with something else? If not, what steps would you take to handle this scenario?

6. Explain the `length` parameter used in the `segment` block. Explain the `start` parameter.

7. Explain the difference between the `split` blocks that contain the words "at first" and those that don't.

8. Explain the difference between the `split` blocks that contain the words "at any" and those that don't.

Exercises

1. Create an application that asks for a string of characters. Have a Button on the screen that will return the same string to a Label with all of the occurrences of the letter "t" in uppercase.

2. Create an application that asks for a string of characters. Have a Button on the screen that will return the last five characters of the string to a Label.

3. Create an application that asks for a first name. Have a Button on the screen that will then check the name entered. Prompt the user accordingly to a Label if the name is empty, too short (require two or more characters), or too long (don't go over 15).

4. Store a list of usernames and passwords in a TinyDB. Create an application that requires a username and password.
   a. Allow the usernames entered to have extra leading or trailing spaces and have them be case insensitive.
   b. Make the passwords be case sensitive and do not allow for leading and/or trailing spaces.
   c. Provide a Button as the event to check the login.
   d. Prompt to the screen whether the login is successful or not. If the login is not successful, indicate whether it's the username or password, or both, that is incorrect.

5. After completing Tutorials 10-3 and 10-4, combine the two by adding a third procedure in Tutorial 10-4 to handle the validation that was accomplished in 10-3.

6. Add functionality in Tutorial 10-4 to validate that there is a host name provided between the @ symbol and the last dot. Ensure that the host name is at least three characters long.

7. Store a list of names and birthdates to a TinyDB or list. Allow the user to search for a name and then extract and display their birth year only.

Projects

1. **Alphabetize Names**

   Write an application that will take three names as input. Provide a Button for the user to submit their entries. Return the strings to the screen in alphabetical order.

   TIP: Convert the strings to upper case before alphabetizing, but return them to the screen in mixed-case (first letter capital).

2. **Validate SSN**

   Write an application that takes a Social Security Number in as input, in the format XXX-XX-XXXX, where all X's are digits. Validate by splitting the string at the dashes, and then validate that the characters are numeric and each segment is the correct length.

3. **Remove Characters**

   Write an application that will take a string of input that has commas, periods, question marks, and spaces. Provide a Button to kick of the application. Return a string with all of the commas, periods, question marks, and spaces removed from the string. For example, the input *Hi, my name is Sally. What is yours?* would return *HimynameisSallyWhatisyours*.

4. **Find Product Information**

   Write an application that extracts a product name, the SKU, and the price from a string of product information. Assume that the name starts at position one and goes until the first space. The SKU starts with characters *SKU* and continues until the next space. The price starts at the dollar sign and will go until two characters after the next period. So, if the input is *WidgetX PromotionZ SKU1234 $3.99333-4454*, the application would display *WidgetX SKU1234 $3.99*.

5. **String Guessing Game**

   Create a string guessing game. Start by storing a string in a variable and show the user only dashes for the letters. Also, present a clue. For example, you may have *Man's best friend* as the clue and three dashes _ _ _ on the screen for the user to guess (of course, our word in this example is *Dog*). Allow the user to enter one character at a time pressing a Button to submit their guess. If they guess a letter in the string, fill in the letter. If our string is *Dog* and they guess an "*o*", then show _o_ on the Label. Let the user know if they have guessed right or wrong and let them also know when they've completed the word.

   TIP: Consider using the segment block to redefine your string as you go along from _- _- _ , to _- o- _ , to d-o- _ and finally d-o-g (as an example).

11

Text to Speech and Text Messaging

11.1 The TextToSpeech Component

CONCEPT: Smartphone Text to Speech is a technology that allows your app to speak text words and phrases based on of text input.

The App Inventor TextToSpeech component is found in the *Media* Palette. This component uses advanced technology that allows your app to "speak" a block of text. This is a powerful component, and it is very easy to use.

As you will see by its properties, you can set the language and the country of the TextToSpeech component, allowing your app to be usable in several different languages.

TextToSpeech Component Properties

Language and Country

The TextToSpeech component has properties that you can set for the language and country. The pronunciation of a word may be different depending on the combination of these two properties. For example, if we select English as the language and the United States as the country and ask our app to speak the word "Hello", it may sound quite different than if we used English combined with Australia.

The languages that are supported are Czech, Spanish, German, French, Dutch, Italian, Polish, and English. To select a language, you set the Language property to the three-letter

509

Table 11-1 Example language and country codes (*Source:* Tony Gaddis/Pearson Education, Inc.)

Language	Countries
eng (English)	AUS (Australia)
	CAN (Canada)
	GBR (Great Britain)
	USA (United States of America)
	and others...
spa (Spanish)	ESP (Spain)
	USA (United States of America)
fra (French)	BEL (Belgium)
	FRA (France)
	CAN (Canada)
	and others...
ita (Italian)	CHE (Switzerland)
	ITA (Italy)

code that stands for that language. Then, to select a country, you set the Country property to the three-letter code that stands for that country. Table 11-1 shows a few examples of language and country codes. (A complete list of the codes can be found in the Component Reference, Appendix D.)

For example, to select English as the language and the United States as the country, you would set the Language property to *eng* and the Country property to *USA*. To select French as the language and Canada as the country, you would set the Language property to *fra* and the Country property to *CAN*.

NOTE: The Language codes are in lowercase letters and the Country codes are in uppercase.

Figure 11-1 shows that in code, you use a text block to set the values of the Language and Country properties.

Figure 11-1 Setting Language and Country in Code (*Source:* MIT App Inventor 2)

TIP: Keep in mind that App Inventor does not translate text. So if you want to say *Hello* in English you supply it the text block *Hello*, but if you want to say the greeting in Spanish you must give it the text block in Spanish, *Hola*.

NOTE: If you fail to set the language and/or country code, or supply an invalid code, your app won't stop; it will simply use the default Text to Speech settings on your device or keep the previous programmatic setting.

Pitch and Speech Rate

The TextToSpeech component also has properties that you can set for the pitch and speech rate of the speech. The Pitch property will lower or raise the pitch of the speech based on a number that you give it between 0 and 2. If you set it to zero, the voice is low-pitched. If you set it to 2, the voice is high-pitched. The SpeechRate property will either slow down the rate at which the speech is spoken or speed it up. Again, you can give it values between 0 and 2. If you set this property to zero, the speech is very slow, and conversely setting it to 2 will make the speech very fast!

Figure 11-2 shows how you would set your properties to have the speech as slow and low as possible.

Figure 11-2 Slow and Low (*Source:* MIT App Inventor 2)

The `Speak` Method Block

The `TextToSpeech.Speak` method makes the app speak. It has one argument, `message`, that you must supply it. Whatever is plugged into the `message` socket will be spoken when this method is invoked.

The `Speak` method block will interpret blocks of different types such as text, numbers, lists, and Boolean and variable data. For example, if you create a number variable named `test` and give it the value *123*, plugging the value of the `test` variable into the `message` socket will result in the app speaking "one hundred twenty-three." The example in Figure 11-3 programs the app to speak the word *Hello There*.

Figure 11-3 `Speak` Method with Literal Text (*Source:* MIT App Inventor 2)

Figure 11-4 demonstrates how to use a global variable as the message for the `Speak` method. It matches the example mentioned previously and will speak the message "one hundred twenty-three."

Figure 11-4 `Speak` Method with Variable Data (*Source:* MIT App Inventor 2)

If you were to use a math expression such as 5*5 as the message argument, the expression would be evaluated first and the result would be for the app to speak "twenty-five."

TextToSpeech **Event Handlers**

App Inventor provides two event handlers associated with the TextToSpeech component, the BeforeSpeaking and AfterSpeaking event handlers. They are self-explanatory and simply allow processing to occur directly before the Speak method block executes and directly after. We will show an example of using these events in Tutorial 11-1.

VideoNote
Text to Speech

Tutorial 11-1:
Text to Speech

This will be a simple tutorial demonstrating the TextToSpeech.Speak method with a phrase (entered by the user) and will show how and when the BeforeSpeaking and AfterSpeaking events can be used. It will also allow the user to choose the pitch and speech rate. Refer to Figure 11-5 as you design the user interface for this app.

Figure 11-5 User Interface (*Source:* MIT App Inventor 2)

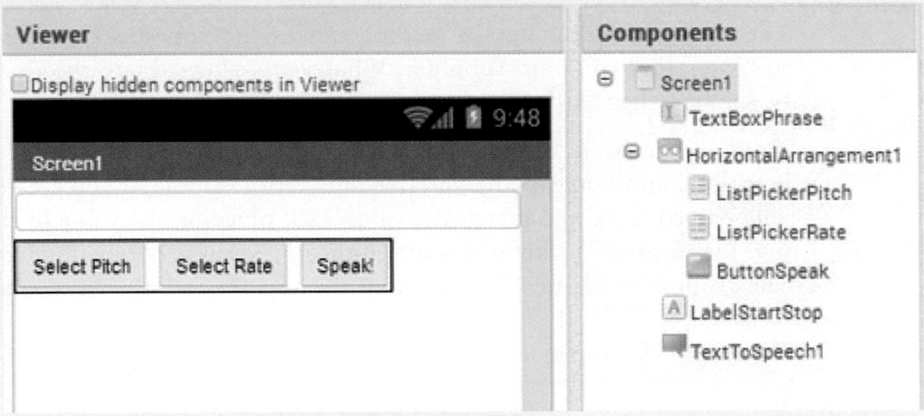

Step 1: Start a new App Inventor project named TextToSpeechDemo.

Step 2: In the Designer, go to the *Media* Palette and drag the TextToSpeech component onto the screen. Notice it is a nonvisible component.

Step 3: From the *User Interface* Palette, add a TextBox to your screen. Rename it *TextBoxPhrase*. Set the Width property to *Fill parent*. Clear the Text property and set the Hint property to *enter a phrase*.

Step 4: From the *Layout* Palette, add a HorizontalArrangement.

Step 5: From the *User Interface* Palette, add a ListPicker to your Horizontal-Arrangement. Rename it *ListPickerPitch*. Set its ElementsFromString property to *Low, Regular, High*. Change its Text property to *Select Pitch*. See Figure 11-6.

Figure 11-6 Set the ElementsFromString Property *(Source:* MIT App Inventor 2)

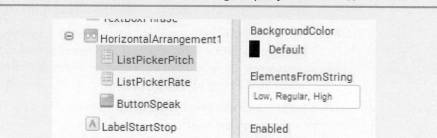

Step 6: Repeat Step 4 to add another ListPicker to your HorizontalArrangement. Rename it *ListPickerRate.* Set its ElementsFromString property to *Low, Regular, High.* Change its Text property to *Select Rate.*

Step 7: From the *User Interface* Palette, add a Button to your Horizontal-Arrangement. Rename it *ButtonSpeak* and change its Text property to *Speak!*

Step 8: Add a Label beneath the HorizontalArrangement, rename it LabelStartStop, and clear the contents of its Text property. Compare your design to Figure 11-5.

Step 9: Open the Blocks Editor and create an event handler for the Screen1. Initialize event. We will use this event to set the language to English and the country to the United States. (Alternatively, you can set it to any language and country as you like.) See Figure 11-7.

Figure 11-7 Screen1.Initialize Event *(Source:* MIT App Inventor 2)

Step 10: To demonstrate the BeforeSpeaking event, let's program the event handler to populate our Label with the text *Starting speech....* Select the BeforeSpeaking event handler in the *TextToSpeech1* drawer to place it in the editor.

Step 11: Select the set LabelStartStop.Text to block in the *LabelStartStop* drawer. Place this block inside the BeforeSpeaking event handler.

Step 12: Create a text block containing the words *Starting speech...* and plug it into the Label's socket as shown in Figure 11-8.

Figure 11-8 BeforeSpeaking Event Handler *(Source:* MIT App Inventor 2)

Each time the method `TextToSpeech1.Speak` is called, the event handler in Figure 11-8 will execute *before* the actual speaking begins.

Step 13: Now you will program the `AfterSpeaking` event handler. This event handler is executed when the `TextToSpeech1.Speak` method completes. You will program this event handler to change the `LabelStartStop` to show *Stopped*.

Select the `AfterSpeaking` event handler in the *TextToSpeech1* drawer to place it in the editor.

Step 14: Select the `set LabelStartStop.Text to` block in the *LabelStartStop* drawer. Place this block inside the `AfterSpeaking` event handler.

Step 15: Create a text block with *Stopped* as its value and plug it into the Label's socket. See Figure 11-9.

Figure 11-9 `AfterSpeaking` **Event Handler** (*Source:* MIT App Inventor 2)

Step 16: Examine Figure 11-10. We are now going to program the `ListPickerPitch.AfterPicking` event handler.

Figure 11-10 `ListPickerPitch.AfterPicking` **Event Handler**
(*Source:* MIT App Inventor 2)

Notice that we set the `TextToSpeech1.Pitch` property equal to the `ListPickerPitch.SelectionIndex` *minus* 1. This is because we programmed three elements for the ListPicker: *Low*, *Regular*, and *High*. If the user selects *Low*, the `SelectionIndex` is 1. *Regular* is 2 and *High* is 3. Remember, however, that the Pitch property accepts a range from 0 to 2. Therefore we have to subtract 1 from the SelectionIndex property's value.

Step 17: Go to the *ListPickerPitch* drawer and select the `ListPickerPitch.AfterPicking` block.

Step 18: Go to the *TextToSpeech1* drawer and select the set `TextToSpeecch1.Pitch` block and place it in the `AfterPicking` event handler.

Step 19: From the *Math* drawer, select a *subtraction* block. Plug it into the set `TextToSpeecch1.Pitch to` block.

Step 20: Go to the *ListPickerPitch* drawer and select the `ListPickerPitch.SelectionIndex` block. Place it in the left-hand side of the *subtraction* block.

Step 21: Place a number 1 block in the right-hand side of the *subtraction* block. Compare your work to Figure 11-10.

The next set of blocks is very similar to the blocks in Figure 11-10. It's just a different ListPicker; everything else is the same.

Step 22: Go to the *ListPickerRate* drawer and select the `ListPickerRate.AfterPicking` block.

Step 23: Go to the *TextToSpeech1* drawer, select the set `TextToSpeech1.SpeechRate` block, and place it in the `AfterPicking` event handler.

Step 24: From the *Math* drawer, select a *subtraction* block. Plug it into the set `TextToSpeech1.Rate to` block.

Step 25: Go to the *ListPickerRate* drawer and select the `ListPickerRate.SelectionIndex` block. Place it in the left-hand side of the *subtraction* block.

Step 26: Place a number 1 block in the right-hand side of the *subtraction* block. Compare your work to Figure 11-11.

Figure 11-11 `ListPickerRate.AfterPicking` Event Handler
(*Source:* MIT App Inventor 2)

Step 27: The final step is to program the `ButtonSpeak.Click` event handler. Examine Figure 11-12.

Figure 11-12 `ButtonSpeak.Click` Event Handler (*Source:* MIT App Inventor 2)

Step 28: In the *ButtonSpeak* drawer, select the `ButtonSpeak.Click` event handler.

Step 29: In the *TextToSpeech1* drawer, select the `TextToSpeech1.Speak` method to place it into the `ButtonSpeak.Click` event handler.

Step 30: From the *TextBoxPhrase* drawer, select the `TextBoxPhrase.Text` block and plug it into the `Speak` method block. This will make the app "speak" the message that the user types into the TextBox. Compare your entire blocks editor to Figure 11-13.

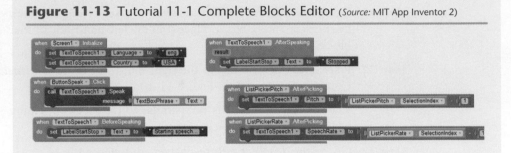

Figure 11-13 Tutorial 11-1 Complete Blocks Editor (*Source:* MIT App Inventor 2)

Step 31: Run the app on your device or emulator and test it! It's fun to play around with the different rate and pitch combinations!

Checkpoint

11.1 What do you think an app would speak based on the set of blocks in Figure 11-14?

Figure 11-14 Example `TextToSpeech` **Block** (*Source:* MIT App Inventor 2)

11.2 Are country codes for the TextToSpeech component set in lowercase letters or uppercase? What about the language codes?

11.3 Assume you have a variable that indicates which language your app speaks in. You want your app to say *Hello* if it's set to English and *Hola* if it's set to Spanish. If the variable is set to one, your app will speak in English. If it is set to two, your app will speak in Spanish. Where might you put the logic to set the appropriate language and text?

11.4 If you want your app to "speak" the same word in different languages, why do you need a separate text block for the word in each different language?

11.2 Texting Component

└─ CONCEPT: Text messaging with a smartphone means sending short lines of text to another device.

Many of us rely on text messaging to communicate with our families, friends, and colleagues throughout each day. Text messaging is a powerful capability of a mobile device, and App Inventor provides blocks for us to program apps that both send and receive text messages.

NOTE: For best results, use a device such as a smartphone to execute apps built with the Texting Component. If you have a Google Voice account, the emulator will work. Otherwise, this section assumes that you have a device with text messaging capabilities to run your applications. For more information about Google Voice, see https://support.google.com/voice/answer/115061?hl=en

The App Inventor Texting Component is found in the *Social* Palette, and it is surprisingly easy to use. This component has one method, one event handler, and just a few properties. The Texting component uses the `SendMessage` method to send a message. The `MessageReceived` event handler executes when the device receives an incoming text.

Texting Component Properties

The Message property holds the message text that the `SendMessage` method will send. Before sending a message, you set the Message property to a value that can be literal text, a variable, a list, a number, or a Boolean value. Like the TextToSpeech component's `Speak` message argument, any block or set of blocks plugged into its socket is evaluated first and then treated as text.

Figure 11-15 shows an example of setting the message to the value of a variable. This example will send the text "Hi There!" once the `SendMessage` method is called (not shown yet). Of course there are other things that will need to be set, like the text's destination phone number.

Figure 11-15 Texting `Message` Property (*Source:* MIT App Inventor 2)

```
initialize global message to " Hi There! "

when Screen1 .Initialize
do   set Texting1 . Message to get global message
```

The PhoneNumber property holds the phone number of the recipient of the message. This property is a text string of digits that can include only digits, dashes, dots, and parentheses. It should not include any other special characters or alphabetic characters, including spaces.

Figure 11-16 shows an example valid phone number. Notice that it is a text block, not a number block, and that it only contains numbers, dashes, and parentheses. Note that any dashes, parentheses, and dots are allowed, but they are actually ignored by the `SendMessage` method.

Figure 11-16 PhoneNumber Property (*Source:* MIT App Inventor 2)

```
set Texting1 . PhoneNumber to " (333)-555-1212 "
```

You can set your app to ignore messages, receive them only when your app is running, or receive them even if your app is not active using the ReceiveEnabled property. This property takes the numeric values 1, 2, and 3, which are defined as follows:

- 1-Off
- 2-Foreground
- 3-Always.

If this property is set to 1, the app will ignore all messages. If set to 2, messages will be received when the app is running, but not when the app is inactive. If set to 3, the app will receive the messages while running and queue the messages if it is not running or inactive. If the messages are queued, the actions in the `MessageReceived` event handler will happen when the app becomes active. This may result in several messages being processed at once.

Figure 11-17 shows a combination of blocks you might use to set a "do not disturb" feature in your app. The blocks test the value of a variable, and based on the result will set the ReceivedEnabled property to 1, which means to ignore all messages.

Figure 11-17 `ReceivingEnabled` **Property** (*Source:* MIT App Inventor 2)

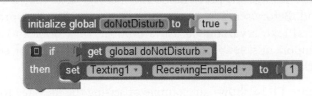

`SendMessage` **Method**

The Texting component has one method, `SendMessage`. When you call this method, your device will send a text message to the phone number set in the PhoneNumber property. The message it sends to that device will be whatever is stored in the Message property. It is important to remember to set *both* the PhoneNumber and Message properties before calling the `SendMessage` method. Figure 11-18 shows an example.

Figure 11-18 Using the `SendMessage` Method (*Source:* MIT App Inventor 2)

By examining Figure 11-18, we see how to set the phone number and message that we want to send before calling the `SendMessage` method. These properties can be set elsewhere in an app, but you may often see the blocks together, as shown in Figure 11-18.

The `MessageReceived` **Event Handler**

The `MessageReceived` event handler is executed when a text message is received by your device. Based on the ReceivingEnabled property value (previously described), this event will listen for text messages when the app is active or dormant.

Figure 11-19 shows an example of an application that has a Texting component and a TextToSpeech component. This example shows how to program the app to speak text messages as they are received.

Figure 11-19 `MessageReceived` **Example** (*Source:* MIT App Inventor 2)

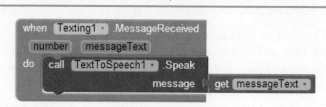

The `MessageReceived` event handler gives app developers a chance to program behavior when a text message comes in. For example, let's say we don't want to be distracted at work with unimportant text messages, but we want to hear anything that comes from family. We can use this event handler to program an app that will filter incoming messages. Using a TextToSpeech component, we will program the app so that it will speak text messages from family members and ignore all others. This way, we can set our phone beside us and hear any important messages rather than picking up the phone to look at who the text message is from and what it says. We will create this app in Tutorial 11-3, and it will demonstrate using the `MessageReceived` event handler to listen for, filter, and speak messages.

 Checkpoint

11.5 Which palette is the Texting component found in?

11.6 If the ReceivingEnabled property is set to 2 and the app is not running, will it eventually respond to messages? What about if it's set to 3?

11.7 What two things must you do before calling the `SendMessage` method?

11.8 What will happen if you assign the PhoneNumber property a string of digits representing a phone number, but you leave out the parentheses and dashes?

 11.3 Receiving Text Messages

If you'd like your app to "do" something when text messages come in, you simply add the Texting component to your project and use the `MessageReceived` event handler. The `MessageReceived` event handler will execute when a text message is received.

Figure 11-20 shows another example of the `MessageReceived` event handler. Notice that the event handler has two parameters, `number` and `messageText`. The `number` parameter stores the phone number from which the message was sent, and the `messageText` parameter is the text that was sent.

Figure 11-20 `MessageReceived` **Event Handler** (*Source:* MIT App Inventor 2)

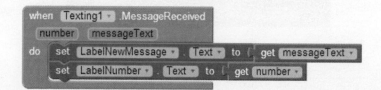

The next tutorial will demonstrate how to use this event by programming an app to filter family members' text messages and speak those out using a TextToSpeech component.

The `number` parameter you see in Figure 11-20 will hold a typical 10 digit number in the format *xxx-xxx-xxxx*. Notice three digits, a dash, three more digits, a dash, and then four digits. We want to be sure to use the same format when we are filtering for certain numbers.

Figure 11-21 shows the `MessageReceived` event handler that you will create in Tutorial 11-2. An `if then` block is used to evaluate who the text message is from, and if it meets the condition, then we use a TextToSpeech component to speak the message. (In this case, we'll make up a number: 333-444-5555. *You can use a number that you know, especially if you want to test.*)

Figure 11-21 Receiving Text (*Source:* MIT App Inventor 2)

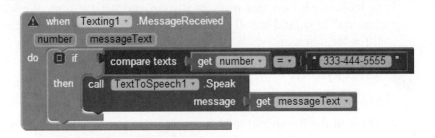

Tutorial 11-2:
Creating the Speak Messages From Family App

VideoNote
Creating the Speak Messages From Family App

Step 1: Start a new project named *SpeakMessagesFromFamily*. As shown in Figure 11-22, this app has one of the easiest interfaces we will design because there isn't anything visible on the Screen. Simply put a Texting component and a TextToSpeech component on the Screen. They will both be nonvisible. Remember the TextToSpeech component is in the *Media* Palette and the Texting is in the *Social* Palette.

Figure 11-22 User Interface (*Source:* MIT App Inventor 2)

Step 2: Open the Blocks Editor and place the `Texting1.MessageReceived` event handler, found in the *Texting1* drawer, in the editor.

Step 3: Next, we will need an `if then` block to compare the number of the message to see if it's a family member. The `if then` block is in the *Control* drawer. Select it and place it inside the `MessageReceived` event handler.

Figure 11-23 `if then` Block *(Source:* MIT App Inventor 2)

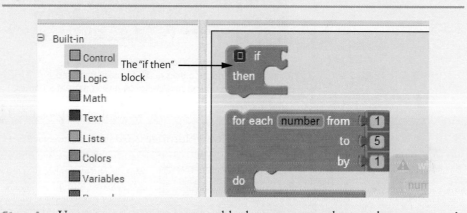

Step 4: Use a text `compare texts` block to compare the number argument's value with *333-444-5555 (or your own number for testing).*

Figure 11-24 `compare texts` Block *(Source:* MIT App Inventor 2)

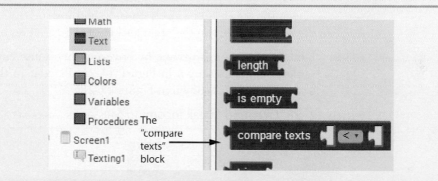

Step 5: Plug the `compare texts` block into the `if then` block in the `MessasgeReceived` handler. Click the middle of the `compare texts` block to make it an equal comparison, as shown in Figure 11-25.

Figure 11-25 Make `compare texts` Block Equal Comparison
(Source: MIT App Inventor 2)

Step 6:   To find the `get number` and `get messageText` blocks, hover the mouse cursor over the parameter names in the `MessageReceived` block, as shown in Figure 11-26.

Figure 11-26 Find the Get Number and `get messageText` Blocks
(*Source:* MIT App Inventor 2)

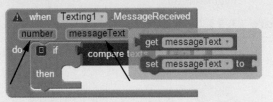

To find the get and set blocks of the MessageReceived
parameters, hover the mouse cursor over the parameter names.

Step 7:   Fill in the `compare texts` block as shown in Figure 11-27.

Figure 11-27 Filter the Phone Number (*Source:* MIT App Inventor 2)

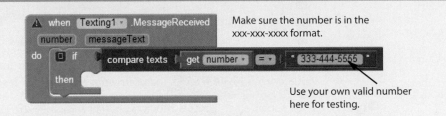

Make sure the number is in the
xxx-xxx-xxxx format.

Use your own valid number
here for testing.

Step 8:   Select the `TextToSpeech1.Speak` method in the *TextToSpeech1* drawer. Place that in the `then` socket of the `if then` block.

Step 9:   Find the `get messageText` by hovering the mouse cursor over its parameter name as shown in Figure 11-26. Place it in the socket of the `Speak` method, as shown in Figure 11-28.

Figure 11-28 Filter and Speak Incoming Messages (*Source:* MIT App Inventor 2)

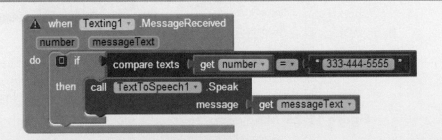

Step 10:   That's it! Run and test your app. If you are using your own number for testing, text the phone running your app and hear it speak the message you sent.

TIP: You can use the same number as the one tied to your device and "text yourself" and this app will work. Just make sure the number is correct in the `compare texts` block shown in Figure 11-28.

Sending Text Messages

Sending a text message in App Inventor is a simple process of telling the app *who* to send it to, *what* message to send, and then calling the `SendMessage` method. (Recall Figure 11-18.)

Let's look at an example of an app that sets up a list of numbers belonging to a group, like friends or family. It will allow a user to type in a message and then click a Button to send the message to everyone in the list. In the Button component's `Click` event handler, the app will use a `for each` loop to iterate through the list of numbers and send the message to each number. Take a look at Figures 11-29 and 11-30 showing the user interface and the Blocks Editor workspace for this app.

Figure 11-29 User Interface (*Source:* MIT App Inventor 2)

Figure 11-30 Blocks Editor Workspace (*Source:* MIT App Inventor 2)

NOTE: Please review the *Lists* chapter if you have trouble understanding the list or the iteration shown in Figure 11-30.

While this looks a little more complicated than Figure 11-18, the blocks used to send the message are the same. You see that we set the Texting component's Message property to the Text property of the `TextBoxMessage` TextBox. This is text entered by the user, so this will be a custom message.

Also, you will set the Texting component's PhoneNumber property set to an element in the list. When we have those two things set, we call `SendMessage`.

This app will iterate through the list and send four text messages. If you have a device, try it out; just be sure to ask your family or friends for permission to use their phone numbers (and ask them to be patient while you are testing!). You can also use your own phone number for each element in the list if you want to test with just your device.

VideoNote
Reply to Family

Tutorial 11-3:
Reply to Family

Let's expand on Tutorial 11-3 and add a response to any incoming messages from family. Recall in Tutorial 11-3 that any incoming message from family is spoken aloud using a TextToSpeech component. We are going to keep that, but add another action after calling the `Speak` method. Once the `Speak` method is called, we are going set the `Texting1.PhoneNumber` property to the number that sent the incoming message. We will set the `Texting1.MessageText` to *I heard your message. I am working now, but will call you at 5pm.* Then, we will use the `SendMessage` method to reply to our family member.

Step 1: Open your Tutorial 11-3 project and open the Blocks Editor.

Step 2: Go to the *Texting1* drawer and select three blocks, as shown in Figure 11-31:

- `set Texting1.MessasgeText to`
- `set Texting1.PhoneNumber to`
- `Texting1.SendMessage`

Step 3: Place all three in the `MessageReceived` event handler, beneath the `Speak` method, as shown in Figure 11-32.

Step 4: Be sure that you set the phone number and message text before you call `SendMessage`.

Step 5: Hover the mouse cursor over the parameter name `number` on the `Texting1.MessageReceived` block to select the `get number` block, and plug that into the `set Texting1.PhoneNumber to` block.

Step 6: Go to the *Text* drawer and select a text block. Replace the block's value with the message you want to send: *I heard your message. I am working now, but will call you at 5pm.* Plug that into the `set Texting1.Message to` block.

Figure 11-31 Finding the `Texting` Blocks (*Source:* MIT App Inventor 2)

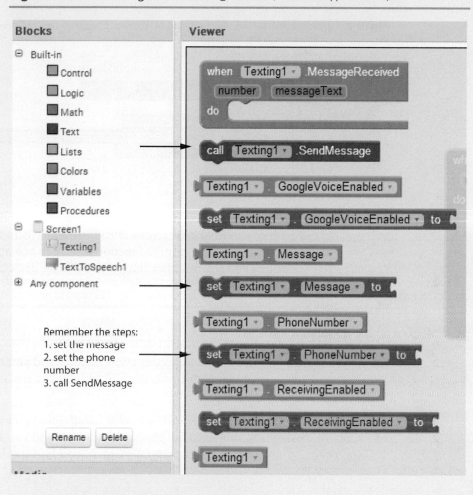

Figure 11-32 (*Source:* MIT App Inventor 2)

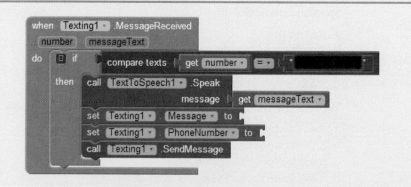

Compare your work to Figure 11-33.

Figure 11-33 Tutorial 11-43 Complete Blocks Editor (*Source:* MIT App Inventor 2)

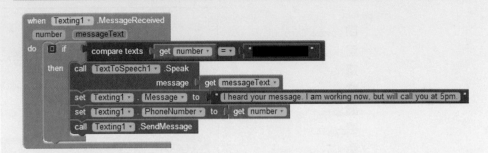

Step 7:   Run and test your app. You can run this app on your device. Ask a friend to text you (make sure your friend's number is in the if then block test condition) and test the functionality. You can also text your-self by using the same number that is tied to the device running the app, and test that way.

 Checkpoint

11.9   If you are using the MessageReceived event handler and you want to check the value of the message sent to you, what block will you use in your check, and where will you find it?

11.10   If you are using the MessageReceived event handler and you want to reply to messages coming into the phone, what block will you use to set the Texting.PhoneNumber property? Where do you find this block?

Review Questions

Multiple Choice

1. What is the proper code to use with a TextToSpeech component to speak in the Spanish language:
   a. Spanish
   b. SPANISH
   c. SPA
   d. spa

2. What is the method that is used in App Inventor to make a device speak?
   a. TextToSpeech.MessageSpeak
   b. TextToSpeech.SpeakMessage
   c. TextToSpeech.Speak
   d. TextToSpeech.Talk

3. If you want to handle some processing after the TextToSpeech component speaks, which event handler can you use?

a. `TextToSpeech.BeforeSpeaking`
b. `TextToSpeech.AferSpeaking`
c. `TextToSpeech.Last`
d. `TextToSpeech.After`

4. What will an app speak if you use a TextToSpeech component to speak the expression shown here?

a. "One hundred twenty-three"
b. "One hundred twenty-three plus one hundred twenty-three"
c. "Two hundred forty-six"
d. None of the above

5. What value do you set a Texting component's ReceivingEnabled property to if you'd like your app to ignore all messages?

a. 0
b. 1
c. 2
d. 3

6. What value do you set a Texting component's ReceivingEnabled property to if you'd like your app to receive all messages, even when your app is asleep?

a. 0
b. 1
c. 2
d. 3

7. Which strings are valid for the a Texting component's PhoneNumber property?

a. 3365556767
b. (336)5556767
c. 336-555-6767
d. All of the above

8. In which palette is the Texting component?

a. User Interface
b. Social
c. Connectivity
d. Drawing and Animation

9. What two pieces of information about an incoming text message does the `MessageReceived` event provide:

a. Time and Date
b. Time and Number From
c. Date and Number From
d. Message and Number From

10. If you want to filter incoming text messages that contain the word *love*, which event would you use, and which block would you search for the word?

    a. `TextToSpeech.AfterSpeaking` and `messageText`

    b. `Texting.RecieveMessage` and `messageText`

    c. `Texting.GotMessage` and `messageText`

    d. `Texting.MessageReceived` and `messageText`

Short Answer

1. What kind of processing might you do in the `TextToSpeech.BeforeSpeaking` event handler? What are some properties you might set in this event handler?

2. What kind of processing might you handle in the `TextToSpeech.AfterSpeaking` event handler?

3. What two properties must be set before calling the `Texting.SendMessage` method? What do you think will happen if each is not set?

4. Review Figures 11-29 and 11-30. How might you change this app to allow a user to send text messages to different groups, for example family, friends, or colleagues? How can you modify this app to store the data on your device?

5. Review Figure 11-33. How might you write an app to filter by what a message says, rather than who it is from?

Exercises

1. **Change Language**

    Write a small app that will say *Hello* or *Hola* based on the user's choice of English or Spanish.

2. **Text a Group**

    Review Figures 11-29 and 11-30. Modify this app to handle three groups: Friends, Family, and Colleagues. You will need three different buttons, but still only one text box.

VideoNote
The Forward
Message App

3. **Forward Message**

    Write an app that uses the `MessageReceived` event to forward incoming messages to a different number. Modify the message to include the "from" number at the beginning.

4. **Forward Message - Modification**

    Modify the Forward Message app from exercise 3 to only forward messages from a list of special numbers stored in a TinyDB. In the TinyDB, the *tag* is the name and the *value* is the phone number. Include the words *From Sally Smith:* at the beginning of the forwarded message (assuming *Sally Smith* is the name in the tag).

5. **Ignore and Receive Messages**

    Review Tutorial 11-3 and modify the app to:
    • Speak all messages (remove the filter by number)
    • Let the user decide to ignore messages, hold messages, and receive messages

    Provide Buttons for the user to choose their receiving options.

Chapter Projects

1. **Sayings**

   Write an app that will explain the following common sayings:
   a. An Arm and a Leg: Something that costs a lot, probably more than it seems worth.
   b. All Greek To Me: Something that is not understood because it is complex or foreign.
   c. Curiosity Killed The Cat: Means not to mettle in someone else's affairs, or it could get you into trouble.
   d. Cry Over Spilt Milk: Don't worry yourself with minor matters, or things you cannot change.
   e. Go Out On a Limb: Take a risk for a good cause.
   f. Right Off the Bat: Right away.
   g. Jumping the Gun: Acting too soon, before you understand the consequences.

   Use a VerticalArrangement and show a Button for each saying. When the user presses the Button for a saying, have the app speak the explanation given.

2. **English to Spanish, Spanish to English**

   Write an app that stores English to Spanish Translations in a TinyDB:
   - Hello: Hola
   - Goodbye: Adiós
   - How are you: Cómo estás
   - What time is it: Qué hora es

   Program app so that the user can choose their native language. If they choose Spanish, program the app to have buttons with the Spanish words and phrases from the TinyDB. Once they choose a word or phrase, populate the English spelling in a Label, and speak the word in English.

   Conversely, if they choose English as their native language, show the English words and phrases as Buttons. If they choose a word or phrase, populate a Label with the Spanish spelling, and say the word in Spanish.

3. **Wake Up**

   Write an app that will send a text message to a friend every morning at 6 AM that says *Wake Up and remember to feed the dog.*

   Add the Clock component to your project and set the interval to 100,000. Also add the Texting component.

   On each interval, check the current hour of the day; the current hour is determined by using the Clock component's Hour method with the Now method plugged into its socket. Put the current hour in the first socket of a *Math equals* block, and *Math* number 6 in the other socket. Use an if then block to handle the comparison in order to determine if it is 6 AM.

   If the condition is met:
   - Set the interval up to 3,600,000 - one hour. From this point on, we only want to check every hour.
   - Set the Message property of the text to *Wake up and remember to feed the dog.*
   - Set the PhoneNumber property to the appropriate phone number
   - Send the message

> **NOTE:** You may need to modify the hour from 6 AM to your current hour for testing. Also, if you are using the emulator, the time may be a few hours different from your current time.

4. **I Landed**

   Write an app that will let a user type in a location on their phone in a TextBox. Once they are done typing, they will hit a Button that says *I Landed*. This button will send a text message to a list of people stored in a List. The message should say *Hi, I landed in Toronto*, assuming the user typed in Toronto as the location.

5. **What's for Dinner?**

   Write an app that will receive text messages. If the text message contains the words *what* and *dinner*, reply to the message with a string entered by the user on the interface. Provide a TextBox and a Button on the interface for the user to enter the answer.

   For example, if the user is having spaghetti that night, she will type *spaghetti* in the TextBox on the interface and then hit a *submit* button. The app will listen for any text messages that come in. If a message comes in containing *what* and *dinner*, the app will automatically reply with her input of *spaghetti*. If the user did not supply an input, the reply should be *I don't know, how about you decide?*

   Have the app manipulate the text message before it looks for *what* and *dinner* so that it is case insensitive by using either the text upcase or downcase blocks.

6. **What time will you be home?**

   Write an app that will allow the user to pick a person set in a predefined family/friends list using a ListPicker (see Tutorial 11-1). Also provide a TimePicker that will allow the user to select a time.

   Provide a "send" button that will send the person selected a text message that says, "Hi, I just want to let you know that I will be home at hh:mm" (where hh is the hour and mm are the minutes).

   Challenge: Refine the app to allow the user to pick just one person or all people in the List.

   Challenge 2: Refine the app to allow the user to put in a custom method that will override the default message. If no custom message is used, keep the default message above.

12 Sensors

12.1 The LocationSensor

CONCEPT: Most smart phones have the capability to tell you the location of the device at any given time. The location is usually presented by the global latitude and longitude values and may also include the physical address. Location services must be available and enabled on a device in order for the LocationSensor to work.

The App Inventor LocationSensor can be found in the *Sensors* Palette and is a nonvisible component. Once it is added to your application, you can use it to determine your device's physical location.

 NOTE: The LocationSensor will only work with App Inventor applications that have been packaged and downloaded to a device.

There are three sources that the LocationSensor can use to obtain information: GPS, Wi-Fi, and cellular towers. GPS providers use satellite technology. Your device will need to be outside and in the line of sight (LOS) of at least three satellites to use this source. If you are in the proper LOS, your device can receive the latitude, longitude, and altitude values of its location. If you are inside a building or other structure, your device may attempt to use location information from a Wi-Fi router if you are connected to one. If your device is obtaining information from Wi-Fi, the actual latitude and longitude read is that of the Wi-Fi router. Your device can also obtain location information from cellular towers by determining the strength of the signals from the closest towers to your device. It uses the strength of the signals to determine how far away your device is from the towers and from that determines the location information.

There are many ways that you can use this sensor in your applications: to store an address to remember where you've been, to alert yourself once you are a certain distance from a specific place, to track your travels, or to notify others of your current location.

LocationSensor Component Properties

The LocationSensor has an Enabled property that must be set to true for the sensor to work. You can set this property at design-time or programmatically in the Blocks Editor.

Figure 12-1 The Enabled Property (*Source:* MIT App Inventor 2)

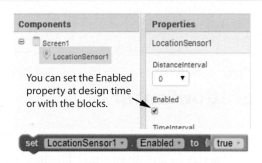

The Latitude and Longitude properties hold the latitude and longitude of the device's current location.

Figure 12-2 Latitude and Longitude Property Blocks (*Source:* MIT App Inventor 2)

There is also a property, HasLongitudeLatitude, which will indicate whether or not the device can report the latitude and longitude values. If this property is true, you will be able to see and use the latitude and longitude values.

Sometimes a device does not have the ability to show location values, or possibly location services are turned off on the device. If this is so, the value of this property will be false. Notice that there is not a set block for this property, it is read only and is determined by the device.

Figure 12-3 HasLongitudeLatitude Property Block (*Source:* MIT App Inventor 2)

LocationSensor1 . HasLongitudeLatitude

If your device has the capability, the Altitude property holds the altitude of the device. The LocationSensor provides a Boolean HasAltitude property that will be `true` if the device is able to report altitude and `false` if it cannot. Similar to the HasLongitudeLatitude property, this property is read-only because the device determines its value.

Figure 12-4 The Altitude Blocks (*Source:* MIT App Inventor 2)

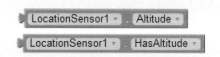

The Accuracy property holds the level of accuracy, in meters, of the device's location information. Similar to the other LocationSensor properties, there is a corresponding Boolean HasAccuracy property that can be used to check if the device is able to report accuracy. It will be `true` or `false` based on the device's capability and is read-only.

Figure 12-5 The Accuracy Blocks (*Source:* MIT App Inventor 2)

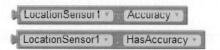

You can set the LocationSensor to update location information after the device has moved a certain distance by setting the DistanceInterval property. The interval is in meters, and if it were set to 10, the location information would be updated when the device moves *at least* ten meters from the location of the previous update. While this property can be useful, keep in mind that it does not update at every ten-meter move exactly. It only indicates that it will not update before a ten meter change. This property can also be set at design time.

Figure 12-6 The DistanceInterval Blocks (*Source:* MIT App Inventor 2)

set LocationSensor1 . DistanceInterval to

LocationSensor1 . DistanceInterval

The TimeInterval property allows you to set the minimum time interval, in milliseconds, between updates. There are 1,000 milliseconds in a second, so setting the TimeInterval property to 600,000 will cause the device to wait ten minutes before another update. Note that this does not mean the update will occur every ten minutes exactly, only that it won't happen before ten minutes have passed since the previous update. This property can also be set at design time.

Figure 12-7 The TimeInterval Blocks (*Source:* MIT App Inventor 2)

The CurrentAddress property provides the physical street address in text format. The address information is provided by Google Maps. Because it is set by Google Maps and based on the current location of the device, this property is read-only.

Figure 12-8 The CurrentAddress Block (*Source:* MIT App Inventor 2)

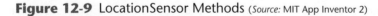

LocationSensor Component Methods

The LocationSensor has two methods, which both relate to the sensor's geocoding capabilities. Geocoding is the ability to take a given address and determine the latitude and longitude values. For example, if you were to supply a value of "1600 Pennsylvania Avenue NW, Washington, D.C." to the `LatitudeFromAddress` method, it would return the latitude of the White House, which is 38.8971. Similarly, that same text block supplied to the `LongitudeFromAddress` method will return the longitude of the White House, which is –77.03654. See Figure 12-9 for an example of how to use these geocoding methods.

Figure 12-9 LocationSensor Methods (*Source:* MIT App Inventor 2)

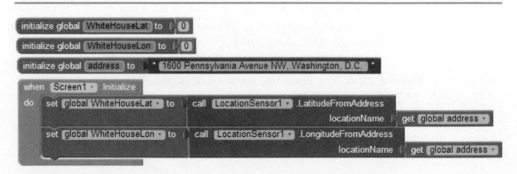

Note that you cannot use the `LatitudeFromAddress` or `LongitudeFromAddress` methods in an initialization block, as demonstrated in Figure 12-10.

Figure 12-10 Do Not Use in a Variable's Initialization Block (*Source:* MIT App Inventor 2)

Location Changed Event Handler

The LocationSensor's LocationChanged event handler executes when the application first starts and whenever the device reports a new location. The device will send the event the current latitude, longitude, and altitude as arguments (assuming those properties are supported). The values for the latitude, longitude, and altitude can be found by hovering the mouse cursor over the parameter names on the event handler block, as shown in Figure 12-11.

Figure 12-11 Finding LocationChanged Parameter Values (*Source:* MIT App Inventor 2)

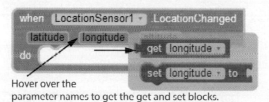

Figure 12-12 shows for an example of the LocationChanged event handler. In the figure, the event handler updates labels with the device's current latitude, longitude, and altitude each time the location is updated.

Figure 12-12 LocationChanged Event Handler (*Source:* MIT App Inventor 2)

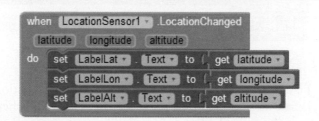

Tutorial 12-1:
Display Location

**VideoNote
Display Location**

In this Tutorial we will practice using the LocationSensor's properties to display the current location information based on the device's capabilities. We will have labels to show the latitude, longitude, altitude, and accuracy.

Before attempting to display these values, we will check the HasLongitudeLatitude, HasAltitude, and HasAccuracy properties. Take a look at Figure 12-13.

Figure 12-13 Displaying Location Information (*Source:* MIT App Inventor 2)

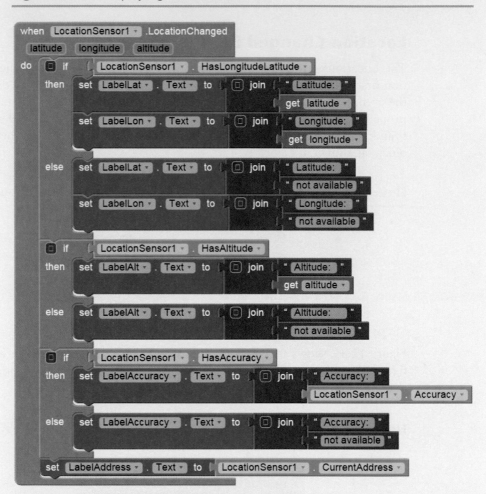

Figure 12-13 shows how to check whether the location information is available, before attempting to show the information on the phone. Rather than showing a zero for unavailable values, we will give the user a better explanation by stating that the information is not available.

Step 1: Start a new project named *DisplayLocation*. Design the user interface as shown in Figure 12-14. First, add Labels for the latitude, longitude, altitude, accuracy, and address. Rename the Labels and Text properties as shown.

Step 2: Go to the *Sensors* Palette and drag a LocationSensor component to your project.

Figure 12-14 User Interface (*Source:* MIT App Inventor 2)

Viewer	Components
☐Display hidden components in Viewer	⊖ ☐ Screen1
📶 🔋 9:48	Ⓐ LabelLon
Screen1	Ⓐ LabelLat
Longitude:	Ⓐ LabelAlt
Latitude:	Ⓐ LabelAccuracy
Altitude:	Ⓐ LabelAddress
Accuracy:	📍 LocationSensor1
Address:	

Step 3: Open the Blocks Editor and find the `LocationSensor1.`
`LocationChanged` event handler in the *LocationSensor1* drawer.

Step 4: From the *Control* drawer, create three `if then` blocks.

Step 5: Use the mutator tool to modify each of the `if then` blocks so they are
`if then else` blocks, as shown in Figure 12-15.

> 📢 **TIP:** If you are good at copying and pasting blocks, you may want to
> take a look at Figure 12-13 to determine how you might speed
> up these steps.

Figure 12-15 The Mutator Tool (*Source:* MIT App Inventor 2)

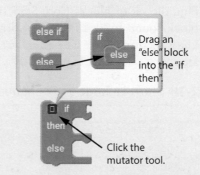

Step 6: Place the first `if then else` block in the `LocationSensor1.`
`LocationChanged` event handler block.

Step 7: Find the value of the `LocationSensor1.HasLongitudeLatitude`
property in the *LocationSensor1* drawer. Plug this block into the socket
of the `if then else` block. Remember, the `HasLongitudeLatitude`
block returns a Boolean value, so you can simply use this value as your
test. See Figure 12-16.

Figure 12-16 (*Source:* MIT App Inventor 2)

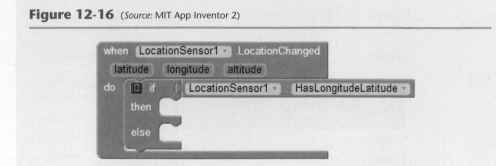

Step 8: Use a `join` block, found in the *Text* drawer, to join together a string containing *Latitude:* followed by the value of the latitude. You can find the value of the latitude by hovering the mouse cursor over the `latitude` parameter name. (Refer back to Figure 12-11.)

Figure 12-17 Configure the Label Contents (*Source:* MIT App Inventor 2)

Step 9: Plug the set of blocks from Step 8 into the `set LabelLat.Text to` block found in the *LabelLat* drawer. Place this set of blocks in the `then` section of the `if then else` block.

Step 10: Now show the longitude. Use a `join` block, found in the *Text* drawer, to join together a string containing *Longtitude:* followed by the value of the longitude. You can find the value of the longtitude by hovering the mouse cursor over the `longitude` parameter name. (Refer back to Figure 12-11.)

Step 11: Plug the set of blocks from Step 10 into the `set LabelLon.Text to` block found in the *LabelLon* drawer. Place this set of blocks in the `then` section of the `if then else` block, beneath the blocks from Step 9, as shown in Figure 12-18.

Figure 12-18 Show Latitude and Longitude (*Source:* MIT App Inventor 2)

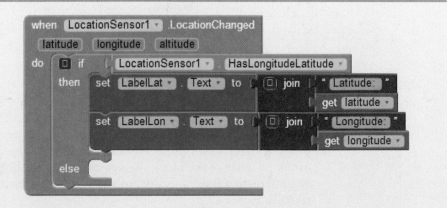

Step 12: Now program the else section of the if then else block by setting the set LabelLat.Text to and set LabelLong.Text to with text blocks explaining *Latitude: not available* and *Longitude: not available*, respectively.

Compare your first if then else block to Figure 12-19.

Figure 12-19 Show Latitude and Longitude (*Source:* MIT App Inventor 2)

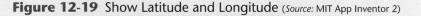

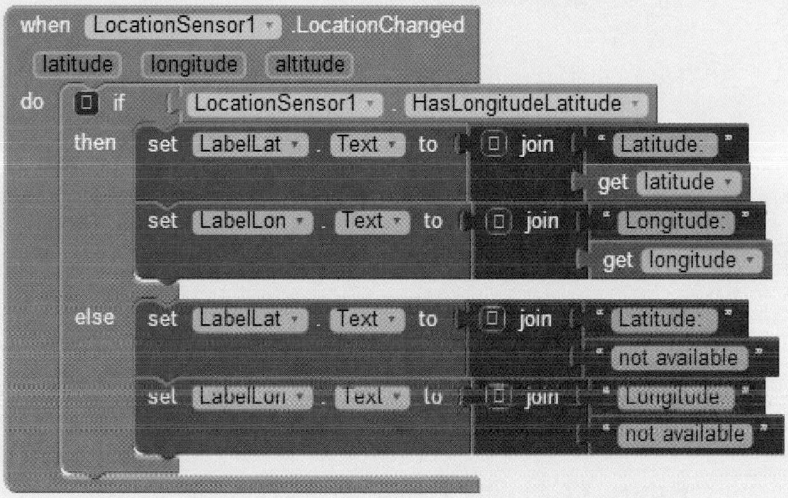

Step 13: Now program the application to show the altitude of the device. Find the value of the LocationSensor1.HasAltitude property in the *LocationSensor1* drawer. Plug this block into the test socket of the second if then else block.

Step 14: Use a join block, found in the *Text* drawer, to join together a prompt for the user, *Altitude:*, and the value of the get altitude block, which is found by hovering over the parameter name, altitude, on the LocationChanged event handler block.

Step 15: Plug the set of blocks from Step 14 into the set LabelAlt.Text to block found in the *LabelAlt* drawer. Place this set of blocks in the then section of the if then else block.

Step 16: Now program the else section of the if then else block by setting the LabelAlt component's Text property to the text *Altitude: not available*.

Compare your second if then else block to Figure 12-20.

Step 17: Now program the application to show the accuracy of the device. Find the value of the LocationSensor1.HasAccuracy property in the *LocationSensor1* drawer. Plug this block into the test socket of the third if then else block, as shown in Figure 12-21.

Figure 12-20 Show Altitude (*Source*: MIT App Inventor 2)

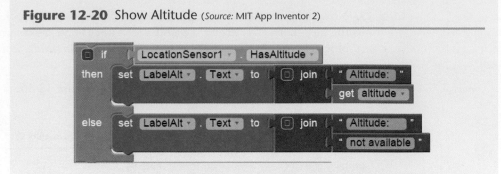

Step 18: Use a join block, found in the *Text* drawer, to join together a prompt for the user, *Accuracy:*, and the value of the LocationSensor1. Accuracy property in the *LocationSensor1* drawer.

Step 19: Plug the set of blocks from Step 18 into the set LabelAccuracy.Text to block found in the *LabelAccuracy* drawer. Place this set of blocks in the then section of the if then else block.

Step 20: Now program the else section of the if then else block by setting the LabelAccuracy component's Text property to the text *Accuracy: not available*.

Compare your third if then else block to Figure 12-21.

Figure 12-21 Show Accuracy (*Source*: MIT App Inventor 2)

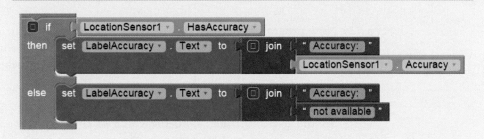

Step 21: The last step is to display the address. Find and select the block for the value of the LocationSensor1.CurrentAddress property, found in the *LocationSensor1* drawer.

Step 22: Select the set LabelAddress.Text to block, found in the *LabelAddress* drawer. Plug in the block from Step 21, and then place the resulting blocks inside the LocationChanged event handler beneath the last if then else block.

Step 23: Compare your Blocks Editor to Figure 12-22.

Step 24: To test this application you must build and package the application for your device. Go to the Build menu link at the top of the screen and either choose to provide a QR code for the .apk (you can scan and download the .apk with a QR reader) or to save the .apk to your

Figure 12-22 Tutorial 12-1 Complete Blocks (*Source:* MIT App Inventor 2)

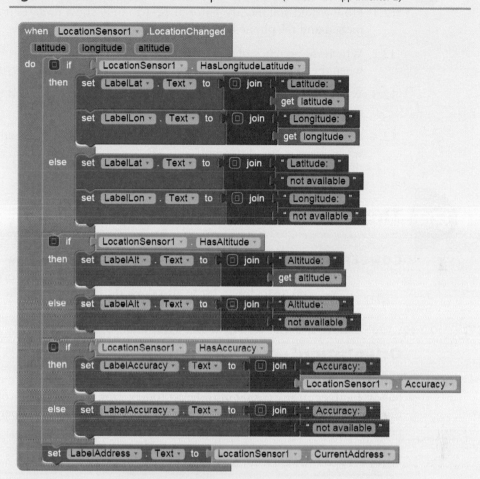

computer (you can then email it to an email address on your phone and download it that way). See Figure 12-23.

Figure 12-23 Build and Package the App (*Source:* MIT App Inventor 2)

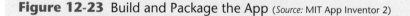

Once downloaded to your device, test the application and check if the current address is correct. Move a few meters and check that the location updates.

Checkpoint

12.1 How would you modify Tutorial 12-1 to only show updates if an hour has passed and the phone has moved at least one mile?

12.2 Why is the accuracy of the device important to know? What if you want updates when the device moves twenty meters, but your device's accuracy is fifty meters?

12.3 What will happen to your location information if the Enabled property is set to `false`?

12.4 How can you find the latitude and longitude of your home address, even when you are at a different location?

12.2 The OrientationSensor

CONCEPT: The OrientationSensor allows you to determine how a device is oriented. It will determine tilts of the device: back and forth, left to right, and up to down. It can also show the direction that the device is pointing (north, south, east, and west) in degrees.

OrientationSensor Component Properties

Similar to the LocationSensor, the OrientationSensor is a nonvisible component and has an Enabled property that must be set to `true` for the sensor to work. You can set this property at design-time by checking or unchecking it in the Properties column, or programmatically in the Blocks Editor.

Figure 12-24 Orientation Sensor `Enabled` Property (*Source:* MIT App Inventor 2)

Components	Properties
⊖ ☐ Screen1	OrientationSensor1
◁ OrientationSensor1	Enabled ☑

set OrientationSensor1 ▾ . Enabled ▾ to true ▾

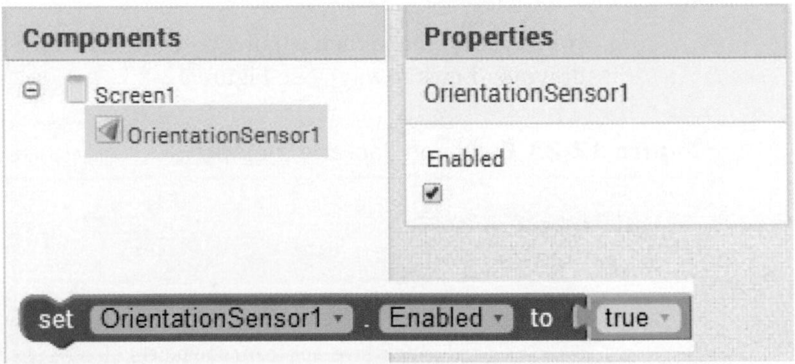

Some devices do not have an orientation sensor available, therefore App Inventor provides the read-only Boolean Available property that will be `true` or `false` depending on the device's capabilities.

Figure 12-25 The Available Property (*Source:* MIT App Inventor 2)

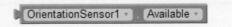

The three basic properties of this sensor are the Roll, Pitch, and Azimuth. From these three properties, the OrientationSensor also provides Magnitude and Angle properties to help in determining how much the device is being tilted and in which direction. All of these properties are read-only, because their values are set by the orientation and movement of the device.

The Roll shows the amount of tilt left to right in degrees. If the device is lying flat, the Roll is 0 degrees. As the device tilts up and onto its left side, the value increases from 0 to 90 degrees. If the device is standing straight up on the left side, the Roll is 90 degrees. Conversely, as the device is rolled up onto its right side the Roll will range from 0 to –90 degrees. If the device is standing straight up on its right side, the value of the Roll will be –90 degrees.

Figure 12-26 The Roll Property (*Source:* MIT App Inventor 2)

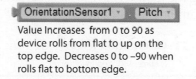

The Pitch indicates the tilt of the device from the bottom edge to the top edge. When the device is lying flat, the Pitch is zero. As the device is lifted up onto its top edge, as the bottom edge is lifted up, the value of the Pitch increases from zero to 90 degrees. If the device is standing straight up on its top edge, the Pitch is 90 degrees. If the device is tilted so that the bottom edge is down and the top is lifted up, the degrees will decrease down to –90 degrees. If the device is standing up on its bottom edge the Pitch is –90 degrees.

Figure 12-27 The Pitch Property (*Source:* MIT App Inventor 2)

The Azimuth property is the direction of the phone in degrees. For example, 0 degrees indicates it is pointing north; it will be 90 degrees if it is pointing east, 180 degrees if it is pointing south, and 270 degrees if it is pointing west.

Figure 12-28 The Azimuth Property (*Source:* MIT App Inventor 2)

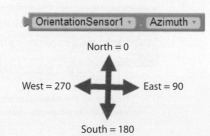

The Magnitude is used to determine how much the phone is being tilted in any direction. Remember that when the device is lying flat the Roll and Pitch are zero. The magnitude is zero also. As the degrees of the Roll and Pitch move away from zero degrees toward 90 or –90, the Magnitude increases.

The Magnitude will have a value between 0 and 1, with zero being no tilt and 1 being completely vertical. As we will see in Tutorial 12-2, the Magnitude can be used with sprites to make them move slower or faster based on the amount of tilt, similar to an object rolling on a tilting table.

Figure 12-29 The Magnitude Property (*Source:* MIT App Inventor 2)

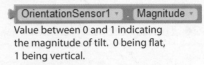

The Angle property uses the Roll and Pitch to determine in what direction the device is being tilted and returns a number that we can use to move objects in the titled direction. Like the Magnitude, we can use the angle to simulate an object rolling on a tilting table by knowing the direction to send it.

Figure 12-30 The Angle Property (*Source:* MIT App Inventor 2)

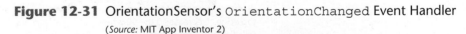

OrientationChanged **Event Handler**

The OrientationSensor's OrientationChanged event is called each time the device's orientation changes. The device will send it the azimuth, pitch, and roll as arguments and the values of these can be used within the event. Their values can be found by hovering the mouse cursor over their parameter names once the event is added to the project in the Blocks Editor.

Figure 12-31 OrientationSensor's OrientationChanged Event Handler
(*Source:* MIT App Inventor 2)

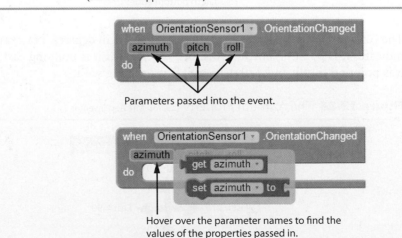

Tutorial 12-2:
Cat and Mouse

In this tutorial, we will practice using the OrientationSensor by creating a Cat and Mouse game. The tutorial will use concepts learned in Chapter 9, Graphics and Animation.

We will create an application that has a Canvas component and two ImageSprite components, one cat and one mouse. The cat sprite will move about the Canvas as the user tilts the phone, and the mouse will stay put. The further the tilt, the faster the cat will go. If the cat reaches the mouse (a collision of the two sprites) the mouse will become invisible. We will provide a reset button that makes the mouse visible again so that the user can start over.

We will also put Labels under the Canvas for all of the OrientationSensor properties. These Labels will update as the device is tilted and rotated to show how the values change.

Step 1: Start a new project named *CatAndMouse*. Make sure you have downloaded the media files from this book's companion website at www.pearsonhighered.com/gaddis. Navigate to the location on your system where the book's media files are located. You will find a folder named *Cat and Mouse* that contains the cat.png and mouse.png image files. Use the Media column to upload the files to the project.

Step 2: Add a Canvas component to the Screen. Set the Width to *Fill parent* and the Height to 300 pixels.

Step 3: Add an ImageSprite from the *Drawing and Animation* Palette onto your Canvas. Rename it ImageSpriteMouse.

Step 4: Set both the Height and Width properties to 50. Set the Image property to the mouse.png file.

Step 5: Keep the Speed set to zero; we do not want this sprite to move yet.

Set the X property to 250 and the Y property to 70.

Step 6: Add another ImageSprite from the *Drawing and Animation* Palette onto your Canvas. Rename it ImageSpriteCat.

Step 7: Set both the Height and Width properties to 50. Set the Image property to the cat.png file.

Step 8: Keep the Speed set at zero. Set the X property to 1 and the Y property to 245. Uncheck the Rotates property. Compare your design work so far to Figure 12-32.

Step 9: From the *User Interface* Palette, add a Button to the Screen under the Canvas. Rename it ButtonReset and change the Text property to *reset*.

Step 10: From the *Layout* Palette, place a TableArrangement under the ButtonReset component. Set the Columns to 2 and the Rows to 5.

Step 11: Review Figure 12-33 and add ten Labels to the TableArrangement. The first five will display the text *Roll, Pitch, Azimuth, Magnitude,* and

Figure 12-32 Cat and Mouse Design (*Source:* MIT App Inventor 2)

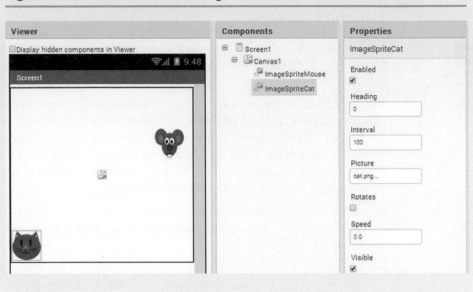

Figure 12-33 Add Labels (*Source:* MIT App Inventor 2)

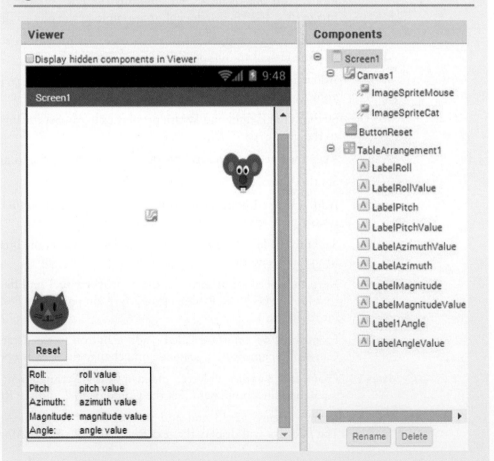

angle. Next to each of the five Labels, add a Label to display the value of the property once the application is running.

Step 12: Add an OrientationSensor component, found in the *Sensors* Palette.

Step 13: Let's begin to program the cat to move as the device is tilted. Find the `OrientationSensor1.OrientationChanged` event handler in the *OrientationSensor1* drawer and place it in the Blocks Editor.

Figure 12-34 Set the Speed to Equal the Magnitude (*Source:* MIT App Inventor 2)

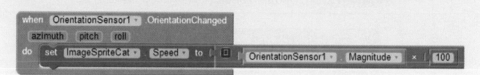

Step 14: Set the cat ImageSprite's Speed property to the Magnitude of the OrientationSensor. Go to the *ImageSpriteCat* drawer and find the `set ImageSpriteCat.Speed to` block. Place it in the `OrientationChanged` event handler as shown in Figure 12-34.

Step 15: Find the OrientationSensor's Magnitude property in the *OrientationSensor1* drawer. Recall that the Magnitude returns a value between 0 and 1. To make this more usable as a speed for the cat, use a *Math* block and multiply it by 100 to have a more accurate value. Plug this set of blocks into the `set Speed` block from Step 14.

Note: By setting the speed to the magnitude of the tilt, the cat will move faster the more the device is tilted.

Step 16: Recall that you set the direction of an ImageSprite by the Heading property. Find the `set ImageSpriteCat.Heading to` block in the *ImageSpriteCat* drawer and place it in the `OrientationChanged` event handler under the `Speed` setting.

Step 17: Find the OrientationSensor's Angle property in the *OrientationSensor1* drawer. Plug this block into the `set Heading` block from Step 16 as shown in Figure 12-9.

Note: By setting the heading equal to the OrientationSensor's angle, the cat will move in the direction the device is tilted.

Figure 12-35 Move the Cat (*Source:* MIT App Inventor 2)

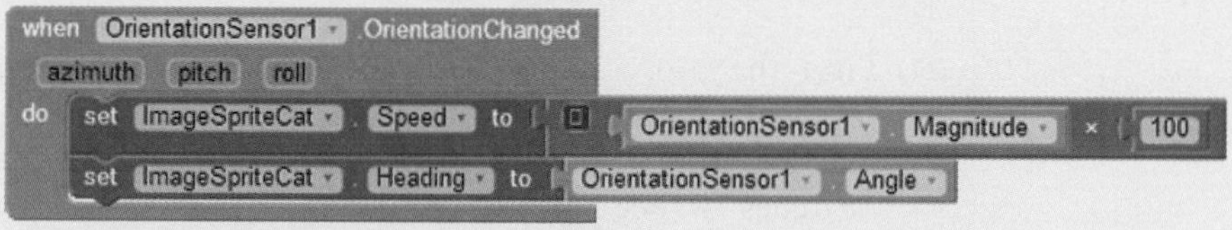

If you'd like, you can go ahead and connect your project to your device and notice how the cat moves around the Canvas based on how you tilt your device.

Step 18: Populate the value Labels by finding the blocks to set each Label's Text property in their component drawer. Place all five in the OrientationChanged event handler. Then, find the values for the event arguments, azimuth, pitch, and roll by hovering the mouse cursor over their names in the event block. Plug those values into the appropriate labels. In the *OrientationSensor1* drawer, find the value for the Magnitude (Step 11) and the Angle (Step 13) and plug them into their appropriate Labels. See Figure 12-36.

Figure 12-36 Update Labels (*Source:* MIT App Inventor 2)

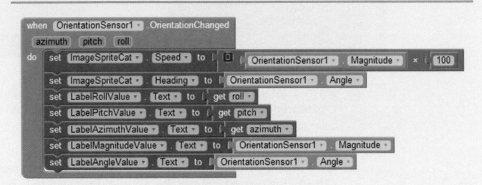

Step 19: Test your application on your device and examine the value of the Orientation Sensor properties.

Step 20: Now you will program the collision of the cat and mouse. In the *ImageSpriteCat's* drawer, find the ImageSpriteCat.CollidedWith event handler and place it in the Blocks Editor. See Figure 12-37.

Figure 12-37 CollidedWith Event Handler (*Source:* MIT App Inventor 2)

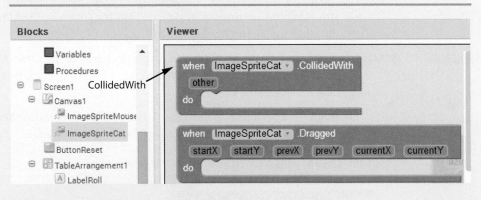

Step 21: Find the set ImageSpriteMouse.Visible to block in the *ImageSpriteMouse* drawer. Place that in the CollidedWith event and plug in a logic false block. This will hide the mouse if the cat "catches" it. See Figure 12-38.

Step 22: Program the reset Button by setting the ImageSpriteMouse.Visible to true. Go to the *ButtonReset* drawer and find the ButtonReset.Click event handler. Place it in the Blocks Editor.

Figure 12-38 Cat and Mouse Collision (*Source:* MIT App Inventor 2)

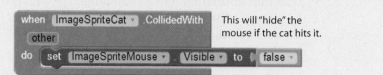

This will "hide" the
mouse if the cat hits it.

Step 23: Select the `set ImageSpriteMouse.Visible` to block in the *ImageSpriteMouse* drawer. Place that in the `ButtonReset.Click` event handler and plug in a logic `true` block. This will show the mouse again when the user resets the game.

Step 24: To reset the cat's position, you need to move the cat back to the left and bottom of the screen by updating the X and Y coordinates. Set X to 1 and Y to 245, as shown in Figure 12-39.

Figure 12-39 Button Reset (*Source:* MIT App Inventor 2)

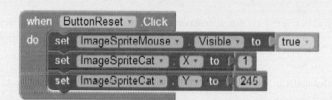

Step 25: That's it! Connect your application to your device and tilt your phone around to make the cat catch the mouse. You can try again after using the reset Button.

Figure 12-40 Tutorial 12-2 Complete Blocks Editor (*Source:* MIT App Inventor 2)

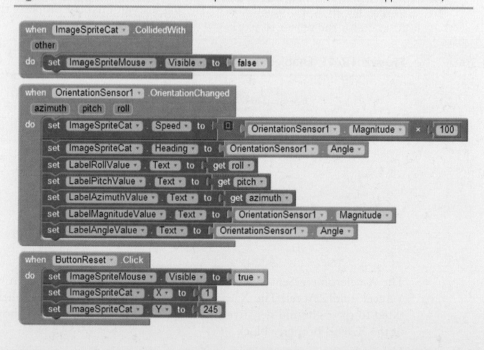

Checkpoint

12.5 Read the explanation of the Pitch property. When you lift the top edge of the phone and stand it up on the bottom edge, what is the value of the Pitch? What do you think happens to the value of the Pitch if you continue to tip the phone so that it lies flat, front-side down?

12.6 Read the explanation of the Azimuth property. What do you think the value of this property would be if the device is pointing northwest?

12.7 Which property of the OrientationSensor might you use to set the Speed of a sprite? Which would you use to set the Heading?

12.8 Why did we multiply the Magnitude by 100 in Tutorial 12-2?

12.3 The Accelerometer

CONCEPT: An accelerometer is a sensor that detects whether the device is shaking and will report the acceleration of the shake in three dimensions: the X, Y, and Z accelerations. The AccelerometerSensor component in App Inventor allows you to read the values reported by the device's accelerometer.

AccelerometerSensor Properties

The AccelerometerSensor is found in the *Sensors* Palette with the LocationSensor and the OrientationSensor. It is used to perform actions when the device is being shaken. It is a nonvisible component and has an Available property that is set to `true` if the device has an accelerometer on it. There is also an Enabled property that must be set to `true` for the sensor to work.

Figure 12-41 Enabled and Available (*Source:* MIT App Inventor 2)

The AccelerometerSensor should be both Enabled and Available in order to work.

The AccelerometerSensor has properties that return the acceleration values: XAccel, YAccel, and ZAccel. The XAccel property has a positive value when the device is tilted to the right and negative when it is tilted left. Figure 12-42 shows an example of the XAccel property block.

Figure 12-42 XAccel Property *(Source:* MIT App Inventor 2)

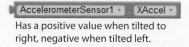

Has a positive value when tilted to
right, negative when tilted left.

The YAccel property value is positive when the bottom of the phone is raised and negative when the top is raised. Figure 12-43 shows an example of the YAccel property block.

Figure 12-43 YAccel Property *(Source:* MIT App Inventor 2)

AccelerometerSensor1 . YAccel

Has a positive value when bottom is
tilted up, negative when top is tilted up.

The ZAccel property is positive when the device is lying on its back facing upwards and negative when it is facing downwards. Figure 12-44 shows an example of the ZAccel property block.

Figure 12-44 ZAccel Property *(Source:* MIT App Inventor 2)

AccelerometerSensor1 . ZAccel

Has a positive value when facing
upwards, negative when downwards.

You can use the MinimumInterval property to set the minimum time between shakes in milliseconds. If you've programmed an action based on a phone shake, but you don't want to perform that action more than once per second, you would set the MinimumInterval to 1000 milliseconds, or one second. As a result, if someone is shaking the phone very fast, your action won't happen more than you want it to.

AccelerometerSensor Event Handlers

There are two event handlers associated with the AccelerometerSensor: the `AccelerationChanged` event and the `Shaking` event. The `AccelerationChanged` event will be executed whenever there is a change in the device's acceleration and the device will send this event the `xAccel`, `yAccel`, and `zAccel` arguments. Figure 12-45 shows an example of an `AccelerationChanged` event handler.

Figure 12-45 `AccelerationChanged` Event Handler *(Source:* MIT App Inventor 2)

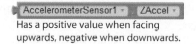

This event is triggered each time the device's
acceleration changes, and the parameters are
updated with each change.

The `Shaking` event is executed when there is a quick shake of the device and gives developers a chance to program actions based on a shake of the phone. Figures 12-46 and 12-47 demonstrate using the AccelerometerSensor's `Shaking` event handler to play music.

Figure 12-46 Shaking App User Interface (*Source:* MIT App Inventor 2)

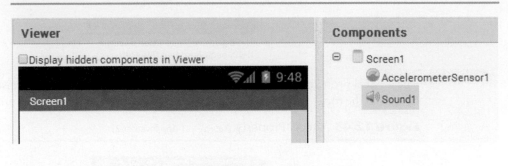

Figure 12-47 Shaking Event Handler (*Source:* MIT App Inventor 2)

In Figure 12-46, notice that an AccelerometerSensor and a Sound component are added to the project. Though not shown, the MinimumInterval for the accelerometer is set at 6000, equaling six seconds (this is about the length of the sound used in the Sound object).

If you'd like to try this example, the book's media files (available for download from the book's companion website, at `www.pearsonhighered.com/gaddis`) contain various sound files that you can set as the Source property of the Sound component, or use your own sound source.

Figure 12-47 shows how to use the `Shaking` event handler of the AccelerometerSensor to play a sound. It's very simple and a fun application to try out.

VideoNote
Shake to Clear
Canvas

Tutorial 12-3:
Shake to Clear Canvas

This tutorial will use the AccelerometerSensor to detect shaking to clear a canvas. We will create a simple application that will allow drawing on a Canvas. If the user wants to clear the Canvas and start over, they can simply give the phone a quick shake.

Step 1: Start a new project named *ShakeToClear*. Create the user interface by simply adding two components, a Canvas and an AccelerometerSensor. Examine Figure 12-48 for reference as you complete the design.

Step 2: From the *Drawing and Animation* Palette, add a Canvas to the Screen.

Step 3: Set the Canvas Width to *Fill parent* and the Height property to 300.

Step 4: From the *Sensors* Palette, add an AccelerometerSensor to the Screen. Notice it is a nonvisible component.

Step 5: Open the Blocks Editor and program the `Canvas1.Dragged` event handler. See Figure 12-49 as a reference as you program this event.

Figure 12-48 Shake to Clear Design (*Source:* MIT App Inventor 2)

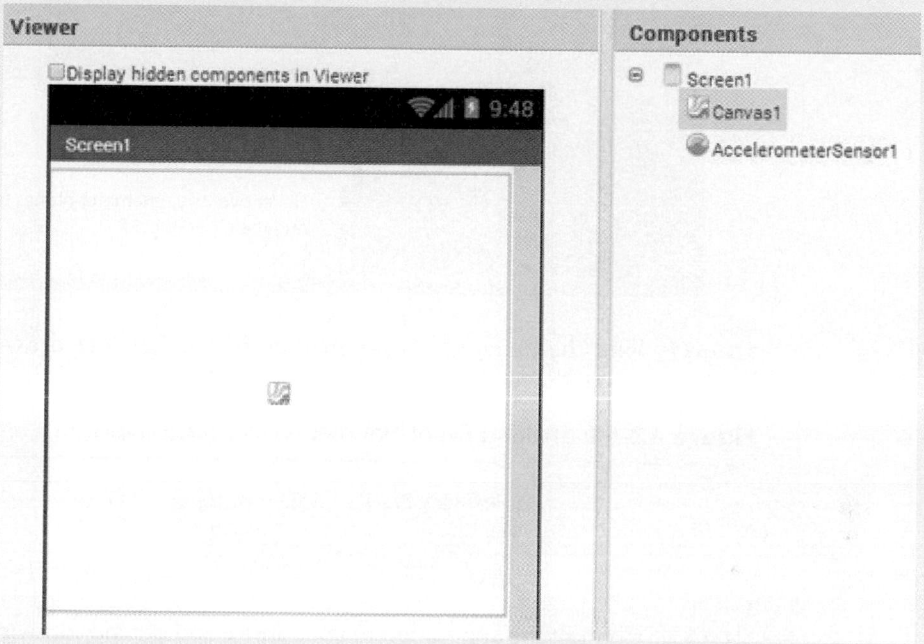

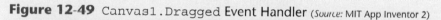

Figure 12-49 `Canvas1.Dragged` Event Handler (*Source:* MIT App Inventor 2)

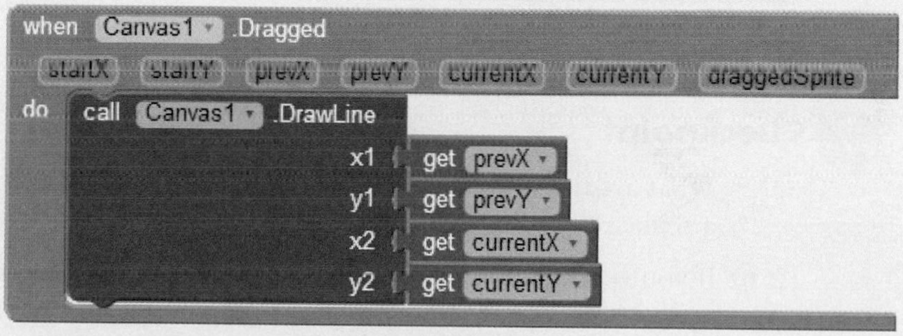

Step 6: Go to the *Canvas1* drawer and click the `Canvas1.Dragged` event handler to place it in the Blocks Editor.

Step 7: Go to the *Canvas1* drawer and click the `Canvas1.DrawLine` method. Place it inside the `Dragged` event handler.

Step 8: Find the values for `prevX`, `prevY`, `currentX`, and `currentY` by hovering the mouse cursor over their parameter names in the event handler block, as shown in Figure 12-50.

Step 9: Plug in `prevX` and `prevY` for the `x1` and `y1` arguments of the `DrawLine` method. Plug in the `currentX` and `currentY` for the `x2` and `y2` arguments. See Figure 12-49.

Step 10: Program the `Shaking` event by finding the `Accelerometer1.Shaking` event handler in the *Accelerometer1* drawer and placing it in the Blocks Editor.

Figure 12-50 Find the Argument Values (*Source:* MIT App Inventor 2)

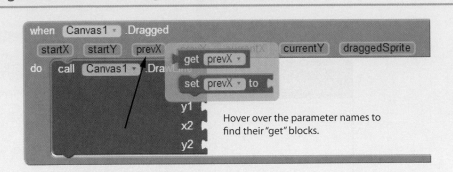

Step 11: Find the `Canvas1.Clear` method in the *Canvas1* drawer and place it inside the Shaking event handler. See Figure 12-51.

Figure 12-51 Shaking Event Handler (*Source:* MIT App Inventor 2)

Step 12: Connect the application to your device and practice drawing on the screen with your finger. When you want to, shake the device to clear the screen.

Checkpoint

12.9 What are the steps to change the Cat and Mouse game to reset the game with a shake rather than a button?

12.10 If you've programmed your application to play a 6-second music clip and you've also set the MinimumInterval to 4000 (4 seconds), what do you think will happen if the user continually shakes the phone?

12.4 Using the ActivityStarter Component to launch Google Maps

CONCEPT: You can use the ActivityStarter component to launch other apps on your device.

The ActivityStarter component allows you to open up other apps from your App Inventor project. These apps can be those that come preloaded on the phone such as the Camera App, the Internet Browser, email, and Google Maps. You can also use this component to open up apps that you've built or downloaded onto your phone. You just have to know a few parameters to get going.

We are going to demonstrate the ActivityStarter by using it to open up Google Maps. If you know the latitude and longitude of a location, you can open up Google Maps and have it zoom to that location. You can also open a more general location by simply knowing the ZIP code of the area you want to display. You can also open up a location based on an address, but because there is some formatting involved, you may find it easier to use the LocationSensor's geocoding capabilities. Simply retrieve the latitude and longitude of an address, and then use that information to open Google Maps.

ActivityStarter Properties

To open up Google Maps from your application you will need to set just a few properties of the ActivityStarter. The first is the Action property, which is a string representing the activity that will be launched. For our example, we will use the value `android.intent.action.VIEW`.

The next property that we will need to set is the ActivityClass. This value for Google Maps is `com.google.android.maps.MapsActivity`. The ActivityPackage is `com.google.android.apps.maps`.

The final property that we need to set is the DataUri. This is where we use the information we know about the address, either ZIP code or latitude and longitude values. This string is passed to Google Maps, and then that application will interpret it and decide how to open.

Recall that the latitude and longitude of the White House is 38.8971, –77.03654. We can format a string for the DataUri that looks like this:

```
geo:38.8971,-77.03654?z=23
```

The string would be fine without the `?z=23` portion of the string—this simply indicates the zoom level. You can zoom out by setting a lower number (`?z=1`) and zoom all the way in using the largest number, 23.

If you'd rather use a ZIP code in the DataUri property, you will use the `q` parameter. For example, the following specifies the ZIP code 28540:

```
geo:0,0?q=28540
```

You can use the zoom level with the ZIP code, as shown here:

```
geo:0,0?q=28540&z=10
```

This indicates that the zoom level is 10 and the ZIP code is 28540. There should be no spaces in the DataUri string.

See Figure 12-52 for a summary of the properties needed to open Google Maps zoomed into a specific location.

Figure 12-52 Google Maps App Properties for Activity Starter (*Source:* MIT App Inventor 2)

Property	Value
Action	android.intent.action.VIEW
ActivityClass	com.google.android.maps.MapsActivity
ActivityPackage	com.google.android.apps.maps
DataUri	geo:38.8971,-77.03654?z=23

VideoNote
Open Google
Maps

Tutorial 12-4:
Open Google Maps

This tutorial will demonstrate opening Google Maps and zooming into a specific location based on latitude and longitude.

Step 1: The user interface will be fairly simple with just a Button and an ActivityStarter. Drag a Button from the *User Interface* Palette onto the Screen. Rename it `ButtonOpenMap` and update the Text property to "*Open Map*".

Step 2: Add an ActivityStarter component from the *Connectivity* Palette to the project. See Figure 12-53.

Figure 12-53 User Interface (*Source:* MIT App Inventor 2)

Viewer	Components
☐Display hidden components in Viewer	⊖ ☐ Screen1
🛜.ıll 🔋 9:48	🔲 ButtonMap
Screen1	⚡ ActivityStarter1
Open Map	

Step 3: Set the properties for the ActivityStarter. Review the values in Figure 12-52 and enter them into the project as shown in Figure 12-54.

Figure 12-54 ActivityStarter Properties (*Source:* MIT App Inventor 2)

Properties

ActivityStarter1

Action

android.intent.action.VIE

ActivityClass

com.google.android.map

ActivityPackage

com.google.android.app

DataType

DataUri

geo:38.8971,-77.03654?

Step 4: Open the Blocks Editor and program the `ButtonOpenMap.Click` event handler. Go to the *ButtonOpenMap*, drawer and find the `Click` event handler and place it in the Blocks Editor.

Step 5:   Place the `ActivityStarter1.StartActivity` method inside the `ButtonOpenMap.Click` event handler. You can find the method in the *ActivityStarter1* drawer. See Figure 12-55.

Figure 12-55 Blocks Editor (*Source:* MIT App Inventor 2)

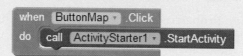

Step 6:   Connect the application to your phone and test it. Notice that Google Maps opens up zoomed in to the White House.

Review Questions

Multiple Choice

1. Where can location information come from on an Android device?
   a. GPS
   b. Wi-Fi
   c. Cellular towers
   d. All of the above

2. What LocationSensor property will tell you if the latitude and longitude values are available on your device?
   a. HasLatitude
   b. GotLatitude
   c. HasLatLong
   d. HasLongitudeLatitude

3. What LocationSensor property will tell you if the altitude value is available on your device?
   a. HasAltitude
   b. GotAltitude
   c. HasAlt
   d. None of the above

4. What property of the LocationSensor can give you the street address of a location?
   a. MyAddress
   b. Address
   c. CurrentAddress
   d. StreetAddress

5. The TimeInterval and DistanceInterval properties of the LocationSensor will set what type of intervals?
   a. The exact time and distance intervals before an update
   b. The maximum time and distance intervals before an update
   c. The minimum time and distance intervals before an update
   d. None of the above

6. The Accuracy property of the LocationSensor will give you the device's accuracy in what unit?

   a. feet
   b. meters
   c. seconds
   d. minutes

7. What properties does the OrientationSensor use to determine the tilt of a phone?

   a. Roll
   b. Pitch
   c. Azimuth
   d. All of the above

8. To simulate an object rolling on a tilting table using a sprite on a Canvas, what property of the OrientationSensor is used to increase or decrease the speed based on the severity of the tilt?

   a. Angle
   b. Speed
   c. Lift
   d. Magnitude

9. To simulate an object rolling on a tilting table using a sprite on a Canvas, what property of the OrientationSensor is used to set the direction of the sprite based on the tilt?

   a. Angle
   b. Heading
   c. Direction
   d. Azimuth

10. What event handler of the AccelerometerSensor component will detect a shake of the device?

    a. `Shake`
    b. `DeviceShaking`
    c. `Shaking`
    d. None of the above

11. What component can be used to open up the camera application on your phone?

    a. MyCamera
    b. ShowCamera
    c. Camera
    d. ActivityStarter

Short Answer

1. What does it mean to be in the line of sight to obtain location information for your device?

2. What is geocoding? What methods does App Inventor provide that enables geocoding capabilities for your applications?

3. What value is displayed when you attempt to show the altitude, but it is not available on your phone?

4. How might you use the OrientationSensor to write a compass application for your phone?

5. In Tutorial 12-2 we multiply the magnitude by 100. What differences in the application would you notice if we multiply it by 10 instead?

6. What components would you need in your project to open up you current location in Google Maps by a shake of your phone?

Exercises

1. **Show State**

   Write an application that will determine the state of the current location and prompt the user *Welcome to the state of xxxx*. For example, assume you are in North Carolina and search the CurrentAddress for the string, *NC*. If the string exists, display *Welcome to North Carolina*. Use your current state for testing. Hint: Use the *Text* contains block. How might you write an application that can determine any US state?

2. **Change Mangitude**

   Complete Tutorial 12-2. Change the multiplier of the Magnitude property (Step 11). What happens when you use a number larger than 100? What about less than 100?

3. **Change Color**

   Modify Tutorial 12-3 to change the color of the line on the Canvas when the Canvas is cleared with a shake. The Canvas will clear and the next time it is drawn upon, the color of the line will be different. Consider storing colors in a List and randomly choosing a new color each time the device is shaken.

4. **Cat and Mouse, Reset with a Shake**

   Complete Tutorial 12-2. Change it so that the application resets by a shake of the device and remove the reset button.

5. **Show Map by ZIP Code**

   Allow a user to enter a ZIP code in at text box. Add a button to launch Google Maps showing the area around the ZIP code, zoom to level 10. Hint: You will need to use a Text join block to build the DataUri string.

6. **Eiffel Tower**

   Use the Web to determine the latitude and longitude values of the Eiffel Tower. Open Google Maps up, zoomed in at level 10, showing the map area surrounding the Eiffel Tower.

7. **Shake and Send your Location**

   Write an app that will send a text message of your current location (either the street address or latitude and longitude) to a friend whenever the device is shaken. Don't text more than one time every 10 minutes.

Chapter Projects

1. **Display of Magnitude**

   Place three Ball Sprites in the bottom right corner of a Canvas that is the width of the parent and is 300 pixels tall; you can stack them on top of each other. Change the colors of each Ball sprite so that they each have their own color.

   Add an OrientationSensor to the project and each time the orientation changes, program the application to set the Ball sprite's Heading and Speed properties. The Heading property will be set to the OrientationSensor's Angle property for each Ball sprite. The Speed will be set to the Magnitude times ten for the first sprite, to the Magnitude times fifty for the second sprite, and to the Magnitude times 100 for the third sprite.

Run the application and observe how the sprites move about the canvas when the device is tilted.

VideoNote
Crossing the State Line

2. **Crossing the State Line**

Write an application that alerts you verbally (Text to Speech) when you cross a state line and enter a new state. It should say *You've now entered the state of xxxx.* Store the state codes and names in a TinyDB or parallel Lists, and use the LocationSensor to check for a new state every 20 minutes.

3. **Location Texting App**

When you are traveling, it is sometimes helpful to update another person with your current location at regular time intervals. You should never send text messages or operate your phone while you are driving, but you can create an app that performs this operation automatically. Create an app that lets the user specify a phone number and a time interval in minutes. The app should send a text message containing the phone's current location to the specified phone number at the specified time interval. (You can use the LocationSensor's CurrentAddress property to get the phone's current location.)

4. **Track your Route**

Write an application that will store your location information, latitude, longitude, and street address to a TinyDB with a shake of the phone. The tags of the pairs stored to the TinyDB should be *point1, point2,* and so on. The values should be a three-item list for the latitude, longitude, and street address. Each time you store an address, you should also increment and store the number of points stored so far. The tag would be *numberOfPointsStored* and the value will be a number.

Place a Button on the Screen that will retrieve the points in order and show the latitude and longitude values stored. (In addition to this chapter, use skills learned in Chapters 7, 8, and 10 for this project.)

5. **Show my Address**

Write an application that will allow a user to type a street address in a TextBox. Give them a Button to launch Google Maps showing that street address zoomed as close as possible. Use the geocoding methods provided in the LocationSensor.

Hint: You will need to use a *Text* `join` block to build the DataUri string.

6. **Cat and Mouse Modification**

Complete Tutorial 12-2. Add two additional mouse sprites and have all three move randomly around the Canvas every 1 1/2 seconds. Continue to use the OrientationSensor to move the cat about the canvas.

Keep score by starting at zero and adding one to the score every time a mouse is caught. Remember to remove the sprite (make it invisible and disabled) if the cat "catches" it by colliding with it.

Allow the user to reset the game by shaking the phone. When the phone is shaken, reset the score to zero and show all the mice. (See the Graphics and Animation chapter for information on ImageSprites and animation.)

CHAPTER 13

Other App Inventor Capabilities

TOPICS

13.1 Recording Audio

App Inventor provides a SoundRecorder component that allows you to record audio sounds using your device. Once a sound is recorded you can use it in various ways in your application. For example, you may want to play back sounds or store them in a List or TinyDB. The SoundRecorder component is found in the *Media* Palette and is a nonvisible component.

There are no properties associated with the recorder, but the component provides three event handlers and two methods. The two methods are `SoundRecorder.Start` and `SoundRecorder.Stop`. They are called to start and stop recording and do not have any arguments.

Figure 13-1 shows an example of an application that starts and stops recording based on Button `Click` events.

The event handlers associated with the recorder are `StartedRecording`, `StoppedRecording` and `AfterSoundRecorded`. These event handlers give developers a chance to program behaviors around the recording process.

Figure 13-1 Start and Stop Recording Methods (*Source:* MIT App Inventor 2)

If you want to perform an action as soon as recording starts you can use the `SoundRecorder.StartedRecording` event. For example, once recording has started you may want to give an indication that recording is on by flashing a message on the screen, or you may want to disable buttons until recording has stopped. Similarly, if you want to perform an action once the recording has stopped, you will use the `SoundRecorder.StoppedRecording` event.

Figure 13-2 shows an example of using the `StartedRecording` and `StoppedRecording` event handlers to enable and disable the appropriate buttons. For example, if the application is currently recording, the user should not be able to press the button to start recording, so it is disabled. Also, if the application is not recording at the time, it does not make sense to allow the stop recording button to be pressed.

Figure 13-2 Started Recording and Stopped Recording Events (*Source:* MIT App Inventor 2)

The SoundRecorder also has an `AfterSoundRecorded` event handler. This event has one argument, `sound`, which is the Sound component of the recording. This event can be used to "do" something with the SoundRecorder component. Maybe you want to store it to a variable, or into a List or TinyDB. Perhaps you want to write it to your file system. See Figure 13-3 for an example of storing the recording to a variable.

Figure 13-3 shows how to store a recording to a variable in the `AfterSoundRecorded` event handler. You can then use the variable elsewhere in your application to access the recording.

Figure 13-3 Store a Recording to a Variable (*Source:* MIT App Inventor 2)

TIP: To find the `set global mySound to` block shown in Figure 13-3, hover the mouse cursor over the name `mySound` in its initialization block. See Figure 13-4.

Figure 13-4 The `set global mySound to` Block (*Source:* MIT App Inventor 2)

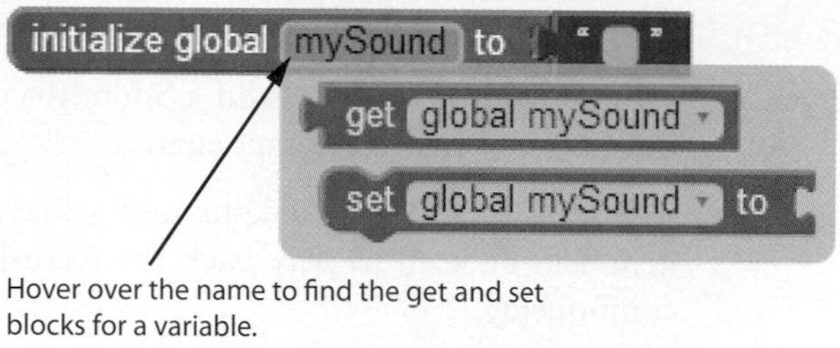
initialize global mySound to
get global mySound
set global mySound to
Hover over the name to find the get and set blocks for a variable.

TIP: To find the `get sound` block shown in Figure 13-3, hover the mouse cursor over the `sound` parameter name in the event handler block. See Figure 13-5.

Figure 13-5 The `get sound` Block (*Source:* MIT App Inventor 2)

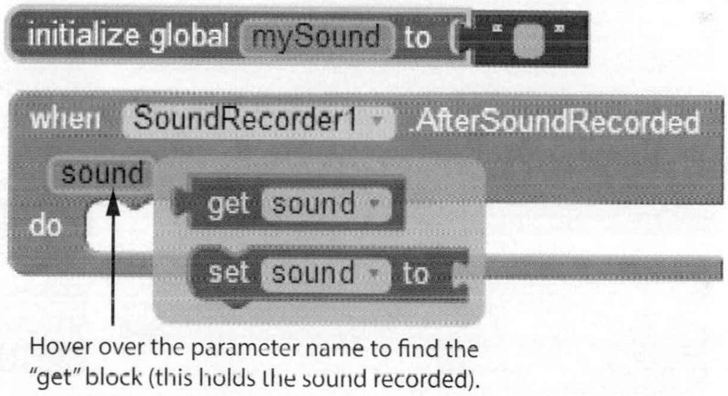
initialize global mySound to
when SoundRecorder1 .AfterSoundRecorded
sound
do
get sound
set sound to
Hover over the parameter name to find the "get" block (this holds the sound recorded).

Tutorial 13-1:
Record and Play Back Audio

VideoNote
Record and Play Back Audio

This tutorial will demonstrate a simple application that will record audio and then play back the recording.

Figure 13-6 User Interface (*Source:* MIT App Inventor 2)

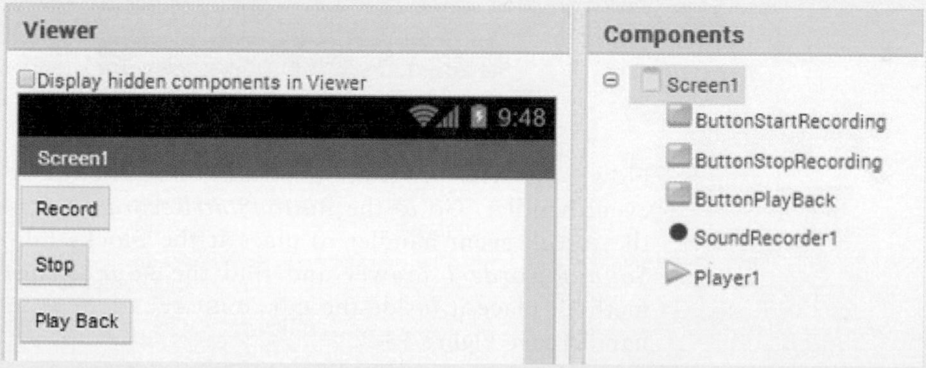
Viewer
Display hidden components in Viewer
9:48
Screen1
Record
Stop
Play Back
Components
Screen1
ButtonStartRecording
ButtonStopRecording
ButtonPlayBack
SoundRecorder1
Player1

Refer to Figure 13-4 to design the user interface for this application.

Step 1: Start a new project named *SoundRecord* and add three Buttons to the screen. Rename them `ButtonStartRecording`, `ButtonStopRecording`, and `ButtonPlayBack`. Change the Text properties to *Record*, *Stop*, and *Play Back* respectively.

Step 2: From the *Media* Palette, add a SoundRecorder component and notice that it is a nonvisible component.

Step 3: Also, from the *Media* Palette, add a Player component. This component will be used to play back the recording and is also a nonvisible component.

Refer to Figure 13-7 as you program the blocks for this tutorial.

Figure 13-7 Record and Playback Blocks Editor (*Source:* MIT App Inventor 2)

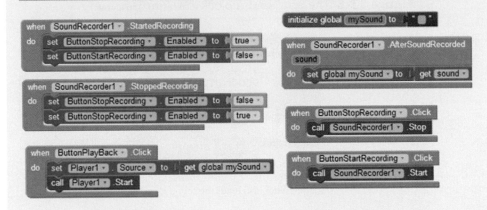

Step 4: Initialize a variable to hold the recording by going to the *Variables* drawer and select a `initalize global name to` block. Rename it to `mySound`. Go to the *Text* drawer and select an empty text block, plug that into the variable `mySound` block. See Figure 13-8.

Figure 13-8 Initialize `mySound` Global Variable (*Source:* MIT App Inventor 2)

initialize global mySound to " "

Step 5: Now you will program the `ButtonStartRecording.Click` event handler. Go to the *ButtonStartRecording* drawer and select the `Click` event handler to place it the Blocks Editor. Go to the *SoundRecorder1* drawer and find the `SoundRecorder1.Start` method, place it inside the `ButtonStartRecording.Click` event handler. See Figure 13-9.

Figure 13-9 The `ButtonStartRecording.Click` Event Handler
(*Source:* MIT App Inventor 2)

Step 6: Now you will program the `ButtonStopRecording.Click` event handler. Go to the *ButtonStopRecording* drawer and select the `Click` event handler to place it the Blocks Editor. Go to the *SoundRecorder1* drawer and find the `SoundRecorder1.Stop` method. Place it inside the `ButtonStopRecording.Click` event handler. See Figure 13-10.

Figure 13-10 The `ButtonStopRecording.Click` Event Handler
(*Source:* MIT App Inventor 2)

Step 7: Now you will program the `StartedRecording` event handler to disable the start Button and enable the stop Button. Go to the *SoundRecorder1* drawer and find the `StartedRecording` event handler and place it in the Blocks Editor.

Step 8: Go to the *ButtonStopRecording* drawer and find the `set ButtonStopRecording.Enabled to` block. Place it inside the `StartedRecording` event handler.

Step 9: Go to the *Logic* drawer and find a `true` block. Plug it into the `set ButtonStopRecording.Enabled to` block.

Step 10: Go to the *ButtonStartRecording* drawer and find the `set ButtonStartRecording.Enabled to` block. Place it inside the `StartedRecording` event handler.

Step 11: Go to the *Logic* drawer and find a `true` block. Change it to `false`, then plug it into the `set ButtonStartRecording.Enabled to` block. At this point, the event handler should appear as shown in Figure 13-11.

Figure 13-11 The `StartedRecording` Event Handler (*Source:* MIT App Inventor 2)

Step 12: Now you will program the `StoppedRecording` event handler to enable the start Button and disable the stop Button. Go to the *SoundRecorder1* drawer, find the `StoppedRecording` event handler, and place it in the Blocks Editor.

Step 13: Go to the *ButtonStopRecording* drawer and find the `set ButtonStopRecording.Enabled to` block. Place it inside the `StoppedRecording` event handler.

Step 14: Go to the *Logic* drawer and find a `true` block. Change it to `false`, then plug it into the set `ButtonStopRecording.Enabled` to block.

Step 15: Go to the *ButtonStartRecording* drawer and find the set `ButtonStartRecording.Enabled` to block. Place it inside the `StoppedRecording` event handler.

Step 16: Go to the *Logic* drawer and find a `true` block. Plug it into the set `ButtonStartRecording.Enabled` to block. At this point, the event handler should appear as shown in Figure 13-12.

Figure 13-12 The `StoppedRecording` Event Handler (*Source:* MIT App Inventor 2)

Step 17: Now you will program the `AfterSoundRecorded` event handler. Go to the *SoundRecorder1* drawer and click the event handler to place it in the Blocks Editor. Hover the mouse cursor over the `mySound` variable name in its initialization block (see Figure 13-4), and find the set `global mySound` to. Place it in the the `AfterSoundRecorded` event handler.

Step 18: Hover the mouse cursor over the parameter name `sound` in the `AfterSoundRecorded` event handler, and find the `get sound` block (see Figure 13-5). Plug that into the set `global mySound` to block. At this point, the event handler should appear as shown in Figure 13-13.

Figure 13-13 The `AfterSoundRecorded` Event Handler (*Source:* MIT App Inventor 2)

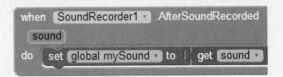

Step 19: The last step is to program the play back Button. Before the player will play, we need to give it a source. The source will be the value of the `mySound` variable. Go to the *ButtonPlayBack* drawer, find the `ButtonPlayBack.Click` event handler, and click it into place in the Blocks Editor.

Step 20: Next, go to the *Player1* drawer and find the set `Player1.Source` to block. Place it inside the `ButtonPlayBack.Click` event handler.

Step 21: Hover the mouse cursor over the `mySound` variable name in its declaration block (see Figure 13-4) and find the `get mySound` block. Plug it into the set `Player1.Source` to block.

Step 22: Finally, find the `Player1.Start` method block in the *Player1* drawer. Place it in the `ButtonPlayBack.Click` event handler as shown in Figure 13-14.

Figure 13-14 The `ButtonPlayBack.Click` Event Handler
(*Source:* MIT App Inventor 2)

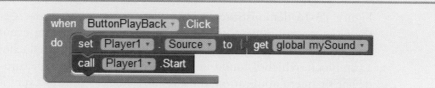

Compare your blocks to Figure 13-7 at the beginning of this tutorial.
Connect the application to your device and test the recorder!

13.2 Taking a Photo with the Phone's Camera

App Inventor has a Camera component in the *Media* Palette that will allow you to add picture-taking capabilities to your application. It works by invoking the camera on your device. Once you accept a photo from your camera application, control is passed back to your App Inventor application.

The Camera component is nonvisible and has one property, one method, and one event. The single property is the UseFront property. If this property is enabled (true) then the front-facing camera will open on the device. If there is no front-facing camera available on the device, this property will be ignored, and the camera will open as it normally does.

The single method of the Camera component is `Camera.TakePicture` and is used to invoke the device's camera.

The single event handler is `Camera.AfterPicture`. This event handler allows developers to program actions after the picture is taken. It has a single argument named `image`. The `image` is the picture that was taken, and you can use it in the `AfterPicture` event handler to store and display the image.

To demonstrate how to use the Camera component, let's look at a simple application that stores pictures to a "Wish List." Figure 13-15 shows the user interface, which has a Button, some Labels, and a Camera component.

Figure 13-15 Camera Example User Interface (*Source:* MIT App Inventor 2)

We will use the Button to invoke the camera, and we will program the application to store each picture to a Wish List. As each picture is stored, the Label on the screen will update to show how many pictures are in the list.

Figure 13-16 demonstrates using the `ButtonTakePicture.Click` event to invoke the Camera component using the `Camera1.TakePicture` event handler. Also, you see in Figure 13-16 that a list variable, `wishList`, is created using the `create empty list` block, which is found in the *List* drawer. After the picture is accepted from the device's camera application, the `Camera1.AfterPicture` event is triggered so we can perform processing on the image. In this case, we add the image to `wishList` and then update the Label on the user interface to show the picture was added.

Figure 13-16 Camera Example Blocks Editor (*Source:* MIT App Inventor 2)

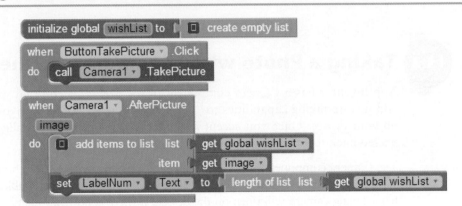

 Checkpoint

13.1 List the components and steps needed to create an application that records audio. What are some of the things you can do with audio files in your application?

13.2 In Tutorial 13-1, why do we store the sound to a global variable in the `AfterSoundRecorded` event handler?

13.3 When using the Camera component to take a picture, at what point is control passed back to your application?

13.3 The Camcorder Component

App Inventor has a Camcorder component in the *Media* Palette that will allow you to invoke the device's camcorder through your application. This component works much like the Camera component. The component starts the device's camcorder and then transfers control back to your app and raises the `AfterRecording` event handler once recording stops.

The Camcorder component is nonvisible and has one method and one event.

The single method of the Camcorder component is `Camcorder.RecordVideo` and is used to invoke the device's camcorder.

The single event handler is `Camcorder.AfterRecording`. This event handler allows developers to program actions that execute after the video is taken. It has a single argument named `clip`. The `clip` is the video that was taken, and you can use it in the `AfterRecording` event handler to store and display the video.

13.4 Using the ImagePicker Component

The ImagePicker component in App Inventor is in the *Media* Palette and acts like a special Button in your application. When clicked, the ImagePicker accesses your device's photo gallery and allows you to select a picture and then use it in your app.

The properties of the ImagePicker are similar to the Button component properties, with exception of the Selection property. The Selection property holds the name and path of the selected image, and will allow you to use the selected image in your app.

You can open the picker by clicking an ImagePicker on a user interface or by calling the `ImagePicker.Open` method programmatically in the Blocks Editor. The `Open` method is the only method of the `ImagePicker` component.

The ImagePicker has the `BeforePicking` and `AfterPicking` event handlers that can be used to perform actions before and after the process. Often developers will use the `AfterPicking` event handler to handle processing of the selected image.

VideoNote
Using the
ImagePicker

Tutorial 13-2:
Using the ImagePicker

This tutorial will display how to use the ImagePicker to select a photo from a device and then use it in an application. We will write an app that will allow the user to choose a background for a Canvas component. Figure 13-8 shows the user interface for this app in the Viewer.

Step 1:   Start a new App Inventor project and add an ImagePicker and a Canvas to the screen. Set the Width property of the ImagePicker to *Fill parent* and the Text property to *Choose Canvas Background*.

Step 2:   Set the Canvas component's Width property to *Fill parent* and the Height property to 300 pixels. Refer to Figure 13-17.

Step 3:   Figure 13-18 shows the complete blocks for this application. Pretty simple!

Go to the *ImagePicker* drawer and find the `ImagePicker1.AfterPicking` event handler. Place it in the Blocks Editor.

Step 4:   In the *Canvas1* drawer, find the `set Canvas1.BackgroundImage to` block and place it inside the `AfterPicking` event handler.

Figure 13-17 Image Picker User Interface (*Source:* MIT App Inventor 2)

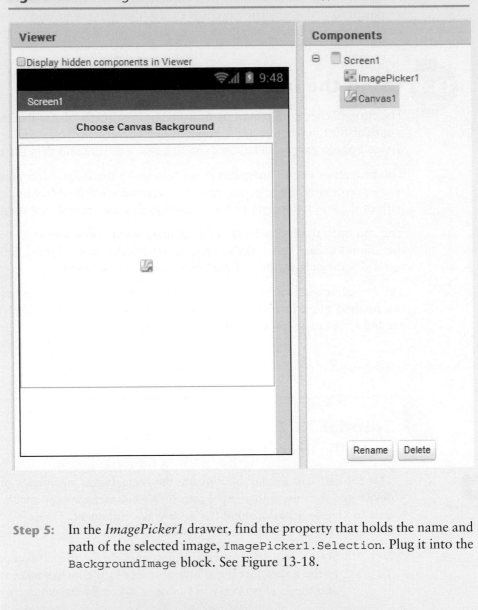

Step 5: In the *ImagePicker1* drawer, find the property that holds the name and path of the selected image, ImagePicker1.Selection. Plug it into the BackgroundImage block. See Figure 13-18.

Figure 13-18 Image Picker Blocks Editor (*Source:* MIT App Inventor 2)

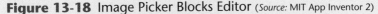

Step 6: You can test this application on your device or the emulator. See Figures 13-19 through 13-21 for a demonstration using the emulator.

Figure 13-19 Application Before Picker is Invoked (*Source:* MIT App Inventor 2)

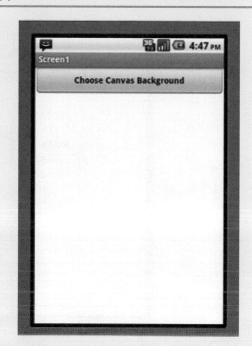

Figure 13-20 shows the picker accessing the gallery.

Figure 13-20 Application During Image Selection (*Source:* MIT App Inventor 2)

Figure 13-21 shows the selected image as the canvas background.

Figure 13-21 Canvas After Picking (*Source:* MIT App Inventor 2)

 13.5 **Playing Video**

App Inventor has a VideoPlayer component in the *Media* Palette that will allow an application to play video. You can upload your video into App Inventor the same way you upload images and sound files. App Inventor supports Windows Media Video (.wmv), 3GPP (.3gp), and MPEG-4 (.mp4) file formats for videos. Videos should be 1 MB or smaller in size, as App Inventor only allots a certain amount of space for media files per application. If your video is larger, you may encounter errors. Also, this component works best running on an actual device.

The VideoPlayer properties are Source, Visible, Height, Width, Volume, and FullScreen. The Source is the name of the video file that is uploaded into your project. The Visible property will tell your application to show video if set to true and hide it if it is set to false. The Height and Width properties control the size of the player on the Screen. The Volume property allows control of the video's volume. The FullScreen property will take over the entire screen of the application when set to true.

There are a few methods of the VideoPlayer that allow you to control the video, including Start, Pause, and SeekTo. The Start method will play the video, Pause will pause it, and the SeekTo method allows you to skip to a certain point in the video based on milliseconds. There is also a GetDuration method that will return the duration of the video in milliseconds.

There is one event handler in this component, named Completed. The Completed event handler can be used to perform any actions needed after the video has stopped. For example, if you want to be sure the video exits out of full screen mode after the video is done, you can set the FullScreen property to false in this event handler.

Tutorial 13-3:
Playing Video

This tutorial will demonstrate playing video in an App Inventor application. It will demonstrate playing, pausing, skipping to a certain point, and playing the video in full screen. You will need to download the video `SanFranStreetCar`.`wmv` from the book's companion website, or you can use your own. Just be sure the video is not larger than 1 MB.

Step 1: Start a new project named *MyVideo*. Reference Figure 13-22 to design the user interface. Find the VideoPlayer in the *Media* Palette and place it on the Screen. Set the Width to *Fill Parent* and leave the Height set to *Automatic*.

Step 2: From the *Layout* Palette, add a HorizontalArrangement and place four Button objects inside. Rename them `ButtonPlay`, `ButtonPause`, `ButtonMiddle`, and `ButtonFullScreen`. Change the Text properties to *Play*, *Pause*, *Go to middle*, and *Full Screen*, respectively.

Figure 13-22 Playing Video User Interface (*Source:* MIT App Inventor 2)

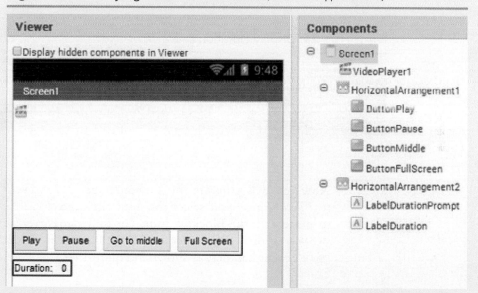

Step 3: Add another HorizontalArrangement and place two Labels inside of it. Rename the first to `LabelDurationPrompt` and change the Text property to *Duration:*. Rename the second to `LabelDuration` and set its Text property to *0* (zero).

Step 4: Now you will program the `ButtonPlay.Click` event handler. Open the Blocks Editor and go to the *ButtonPlay* drawer. Select the `Click` event handler to place it in the Blocks Editor. Go to the *VideoPlayer1* drawer and select the `VideoPlayer1.Start` method block. Place it in the `ButtonPlay.Click` event handler. At this point, the event handler should look like Figure 13-23.

Figure 13-23 Play Video (*Source:* MIT App Inventor 2)

Step 5:   In the same event handler, `ButtonPlay.Click`, you need to populate the `LabelDuration.Text` property with the duration of the video.
Find the `set LabelDuration.Text to` block in the *LabelDuration*
drawer. Place it inside the `ButtonPlay.Click` event handler, beneath
the existing blocks.

Step 6:   The duration is in milliseconds, so to display it in a way that we can
understand better, let's divide it by 1000. Go to *VideoPlayer1* and find
the `VideoPlayer1.GetDuration` method block. Plug that into the left
side of a *Math* `division` block. Plug in a number 1000 block in the
right side of the division operator. Plug this set of blocks into the `set`
`LabelDuration.Text to` block as shown in Figure 13-24.

Figure 13-24 Display Duration (*Source:* MIT App Inventor 2)

Step 7:   Now you will program the `ButtonPause.Click` event handler. Go
to *ButtonPause* and select the `ButtonPause.Click` event handler
to place it in the Blocks Editor. Go to *VideoPlayer1* and select the
`VideoPlayer1.Pause` method block. Place it in the `ButtonPause.`
`Click` event handler, as shown in Figure 13-25.

Figure 13-25 Play and Pause Events (*Source:* MIT App Inventor 2)

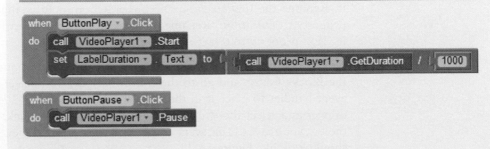

Step 8: Now you will program the `ButtonMiddle.Click` event handler to *Seek to* the middle of the video. We can do this by dividing the duration by two to reach the midpoint, and using the calculation as the `ms` argument of the `SeekTo` method.

Go to *VideoPlayer1*, find the `VideoPlayer1.SeekTo` method block and the `VideoPlayer1.GetDuration` method block. Use a *Math* division block to divide the duration in half and plug the calculation into the `VideoPlayer1.SeekTo` method block. See Figure 13-26.

Figure 13-26 Video Seek to Method (*Source:* MIT App Inventor 2)

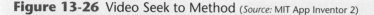

Step 9: Now let's program the *Full Screen* Button to set the `FullScreen` property to `true`. Go to *ButtonFullScreen* and select the `ButtonFull Screen.Click` event handler to place it in the Blocks Editor.

Step 10: Go to *VideoPlayer1* and find the set `VideoPlayer1.FullScreen to` block. Use a *Logic* `true` block for the argument. Place it in the `ButtonFullScreen.Click` event handler as shown in Figure 13-27.

Figure 13-27 Video Full Screen Event (*Source:* MIT App Inventor 2)

Step 11: Let's program the application to set the `FullScreen` property to `false` once the video has completed playing. Go to the *VideoPlayer1* drawer and select the `VideoPlayer1.Completed` event handler to place it in the Blocks Editor.

Step 12: Go to *VideoPlayer1*, find the set `VideoPlayer1.FullScreen to` block, and use a *Logic* `false` block for the argument. Place it in the `VideoPlayer1.Completed` event handler, as shown in Figure 13-28.

Figure 13-28 Video Completed Event (*Source:* MIT App Inventor 2)

Figure 13-29 Play Video Full Blocks Editor *(Source: MIT App Inventor 2)*

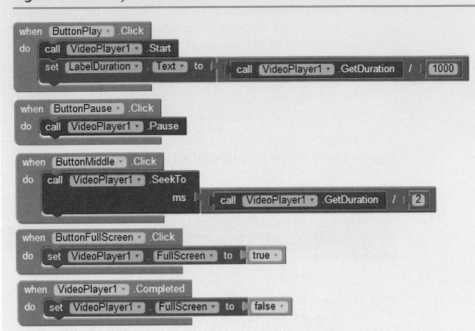

Step 13: Compare your blocks to Figure 13-29 and test your application.

 Checkpoint

13.4 When using the Camcorder component to take a video, at what point is control passed back to your application?

13.5 What kind of video file formats can you use in an App Inventor application? How large can your files be?

13.6 What does the `VideoPlayer.SeekTo` method do? How could you use this method to go back to the beginning of a video?

 13.6 Selecting Contacts from the Contact List and Placing Phone Calls

App Inventor provides three components that can be used to access the contact list on an Android device. They are the ContactPicker, the EmailPicker, and the PhoneNumberPicker. There is also a PhoneCall component that is often paired with these pickers. These components are found in the *Social* Palette.

The ContactPicker and PhoneNumberPicker Components

The ContactPicker and PhoneNumberPicker allow a user to select a contact and then use information about that contact in an app. They both appear as Buttons on the screen.

The PhoneNumberPicker will show a list of the phone numbers in the contacts list, and allow the user to select a phone number. The ContactPicker will show a list of contact names from which the user can select.

Once a contact is selected with the PhoneNumberPicker, the name, email address, phone number, and image are available to use in the app. If the ContactPicker is used, only the name, email address, and image are available. The phone number will not be.

Many of the properties of the ContactPicker and PhoneNumberPicker are similar to the Button component properties, especially those that affect how the Buttons look. However, these components have some additional properties to hold contact information such as the ContactName, EmailAddress, and Picture properties. The PhoneNumberPicker also has the PhoneNumber property. These properties' values are populated with the chosen contact's information from the device.

You can open these pickers by clicking the ContactPicker or PhoneNumberPicker Button placed on the user interface. They can also be opened by calling their Open method programmatically in the Blocks Editor. Similar to the ImagePicker, the Open method is the only method of the ContactPicker and the PhoneNumberPicker components.

These pickers both have BeforePicking and AfterPicking event handlers that can be used to perform actions before and after the picking process. The AfterPicking event handler can be used to handle processing of the selected contact. For example, assume your app creates a list of friends on your holiday shopping list. In the AfterPicking event handler, you can program the steps to store the selected contacts in a List or TinyDB.

Tutorial 13-4:
Using the Contact and Phone Number Pickers

VideoNote
Using the Contact
and Phone
Number Pickers

This tutorial will show how to use the ContactPicker and PhoneNumberPicker components to load a contact into an application. This application will not work with the emulator and needs to be run on an Android device.

Refer to Figure 13-30 to design the user interface for this application.

Figure 13-30 Contact Picker User Interface (*Source*: MIT App Inventor 2)

Viewer	Components
☐ Display hidden components in Viewer	⊖ ☐ Screen1
🛜 📶 🔋 9:48	⊖ ▦ HorizontalArrangement1
Screen1	🖼 ContactPicker1
[Pick by Name] [Pick by Phone]	📷 PhoneNumberPicker1
Name:	Ⓐ LabelName
Email:	Ⓐ LabelEmail
Phone:	Ⓐ LabelPhone
🖼	🖼 ImagePicture

Step 1: Start a new App Inventor project named *ContactAndPhoneNumber* and add a HorizontalArrangement to the screen.

Step 2: Go to the *Social* Palette and drag a ContactPicker into the HorizontalArrangement. Change the Text property to *Pick by Name*.

Step 3: Go to the *Social* Palette and drag a PhoneNumberPicker into the HorizontalArrangement. Change the Text property to *Pick by Phone*.

Step 4: Add three Labels to the Screen. Rename them `LabelName`, `LabelEmail`, and `LabelPhone`. Change their Text properties to *Name:*, *Email:*, and *Phone:* respectively.

Step 5: Add an Image component beneath the labels. Rename it `ImagePicture`. Compare your design to Figure 13-30.

Step 6: Refer to Figure 13-31 as you program the `AfterPicking` event handler of the PhoneNumberPicker. Go to the *PhoneNumberPicker1* drawer and select the `AfterPicking` event handler to place it in the Blocks Editor.

Figure 13-31 After Picking Phone Number (*Source:* MIT App Inventor 2)

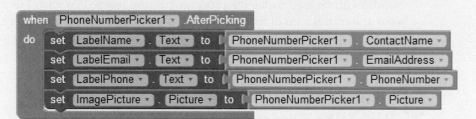

Step 7: In the *LabelName* drawer, find the set `LabelName.Text` to block and place it in the `PhoneNumberPicker1.AfterPicking` event handler.

Step 8: In the *PhoneNumberPicker1* drawer, find the `PhoneNumberPicker1.ContactName` block and plug it into the set `LabelName.Text` to block.

Step 9: In the *LabelEmail* drawer, find the set `LabelEmail.Text` to block and place it in the `PhoneNumberPicker1.AfterPicking` event handler.

Step 10: In the *PhoneNumberPicker1* drawer, find the `PhoneNumberPicker1.EmailAddress` and plug it into the set `LabelEmail.Text` to block.

Step 11: In the *LabelPhone* drawer, find the set `LabelPhone.Text` to block and place it in the `PhoneNumberPicker1.AfterPicking` event handler.

Step 12: In the *PhoneNumberPicker1* drawer, find the `PhoneNumberPicker1.PhoneNumber` block and plug it into the set `LabelPhone.Text` to block.

Step 13: In the *ImagePicture* drawer, find the set `ImagePicture.Picture` to block and place it in the `PhoneNumberPicker1.AfterPicking` event handler.

Step 14: In the *PhoneNumberPicker1* drawer, find the `PhoneNumberPicker1.Picture` block and plug it into the set `ImagePicture.Picture` to block.

Note that Steps 15-13 are similar to steps 6-12.

Figure 13-32 After Picking Contact (*Source:* MIT App Inventor 2)

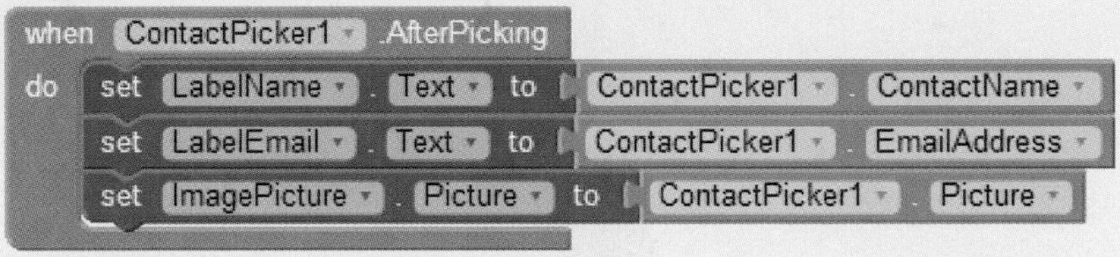

Step 15: Refer to Figure 13-32 as you program the `AfterPicking` event handler of the `ContactPicker1`. Go to the *ContactPicker1* drawer and select the `ContactPicker1.AfterPicking` event handler to place it in the Blocks Editor.

Step 16: In the *LabelName* drawer, find the `set LabelName.Text to` block and place it in the `ContactPicker1.AfterPicking` event handler.

Step 17: In the *ContactPicker1* drawer, find the `ContactPicker1.ContactName` block and plug it into the `set LabelName.Text to` block.

Step 18: In the *LabelEmail* drawer, find the `set LabelEmail.Text to` block and place it in the `ContactPicker1.AfterPicking` event handler.

Step 19: In the *ContactPicker1* drawer, find the `ContactPicker1.EmailAddress` and plug it into the `set LabelEmail.Text to` block.

Step 20: In the *ImagePicture* drawer, find the `set ImagePicture.Picture to` block and place it in the `ContactPicker1.AfterPicking` event handler.

Step 21: In the *ContactPicker1* drawer, find the `ContactPicker1.Picture` block and plug it into the `set ImagePicture.Picture to` block.

Step 22: Connect the application to your device and test both pickers.

Figure 13-33 shows an example of searching with the ContactPicker (Pick by Name), and Figure 13-34 shows an example of the results. Notice that in Figure 13-34, the phone number is not available because we used the ContactPicker.

Figure 13-33 An Example by Contact (*Source:* MIT App Inventor 2)

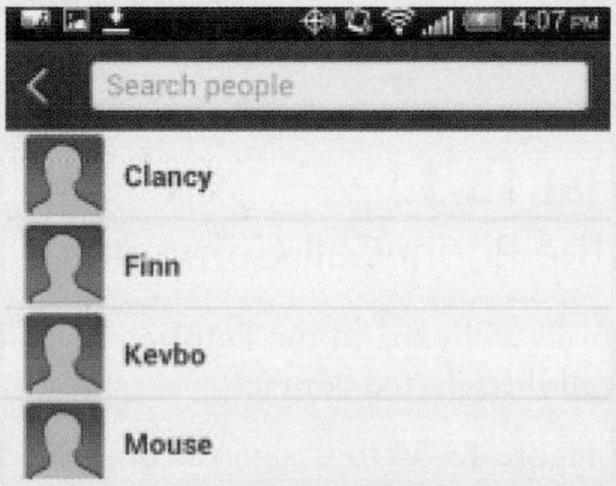

Figure 13-34 Contact Chosen by Contact Picker (*Source:* MIT App Inventor 2)

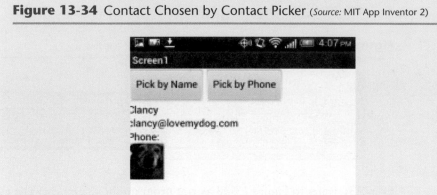

Figure 13-35 shows an example of a contact picked by phone number. Notice that the phone number *is* available because we picked using the PhoneNumberPicker.

Figure 13-35 Contact Chosen by Phone Picker (*Source:* MIT App Inventor 2)

PhoneCall Component

The PhoneCall component is often used in conjunction with the ContactPicker or PhoneNumberPicker. It is a component that will initiate a phone call to the specified number.

The PhoneCall component has one property, PhoneNumber, and one method, `MakePhoneCall`.

VideoNote
Using the
PhoneCall
Component

Tutorial 13-5:
Using the PhoneCall Component

This tutorial will expand on Tutorial 13-4. We will add the PhoneCall component to call the selected contact.

Refer to Figure 13-36 to design the user interface for this application.

Figure 13-36 PhoneCall Component (*Source:* MIT App Inventor 2)

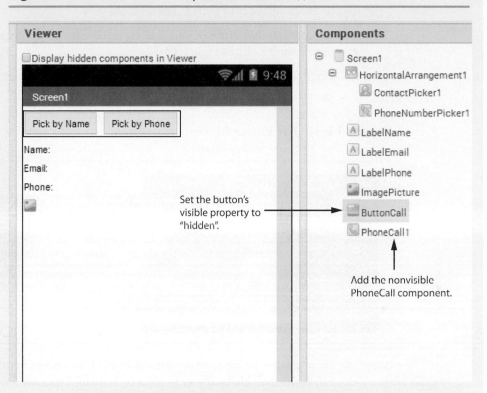

Step 1: Add a Button to the screen, rename it `ButtonCall`. Set the Text property to *Call* and set the Visible property to *hidden*.

Step 2: From the *Social* Palette, add the nonvisible PhoneCall component.

When the user uses the PhoneNumberPicker to select a contact, we want to make the *Call* button visible. In the next steps, you will add the blocks shown in Figure 13-37 to the `PhoneNumberPicker1.AfterPicking` event handler. This will make the call Button visible to the user if there is a phone number available to call.

Figure 13-37 Check If Phone Number was Retrieved (*Source:* MIT App Inventor 2)

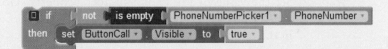

Step 3: Go to the *Control* drawer and select an `if then` block.

Step 4: Go to the *Logic* drawer and select a `not` block. Plug it in as shown in Figure 13-37. We are going to check that the phone number is not empty.

Step 5: Go to the *Text* drawer and select an `is empty` block. Plug it in as shown in Figure 13-37.

Step 6: Go to the *PhoneNumberPicker1* drawer and find the `PhoneNumberPicker1.PhoneNumber` block. Plug it into the `is empty` block as shown in Figure 13-37.

Step 7: Go to the *ButtonCall* drawer and select the set `ButtonCall.Visible` to block. Place it in the `if then` block.

Step 8: Go to the *Logic* drawer and select a `true` block. Configure and compare your blocks to Figure 13-37.

Step 9: Place the set of blocks in Figure 13-37 into the `PhoneNumber Picker1.AfterPicking` event, as shown in Figure 13-38.

Figure 13-38 The `PhoneNumberPicker1.AfterPicking` Event Handler
(*Source:* MIT App Inventor 2)

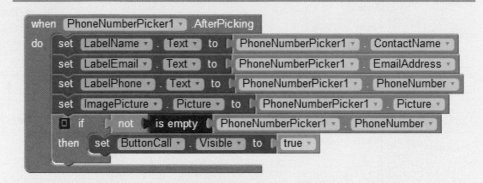

Step 10: Now we are going to program the PhoneCall component to place the call if the user clicks the `ButtonCall` Button. Examine Figure 13-39.

Figure 13-39 `ButtonCall.Click` Event (*Source:* MIT App Inventor 2)

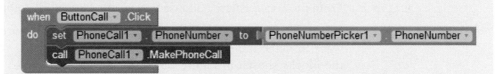

Step 11: Go to the *ButtonCall* drawer and select the `ButtonCall.Click` event handler. Place it in the editor.

Step 12: Set the value of the PhoneNumber property. Go to the *PhoneCall1* drawer and select the set `PhoneCall1.PhoneNumber` to block. Place it in the `ButtonCall.Click` event.

Step 13: Go to the *PhoneNumberPicker1* drawer and select the `Phone NumberPicker1.PhoneNumber` block. Plug it into the set `Phone Call1.PhoneNumber` to block from Step 12.

Step 14: Go to the *PhoneCall1* drawer and select the call `Phone Call1.MakePhoneCall` block. Place it in the `ButtonCall.Click` event as shown in Figure 13-39.

Step 15: Connect and test your app!

EmailPicker Component

The EmailPicker is somewhat like a TextBox in that you type into it and it has a Hint property to prompt users. As you type an email address into the EmailPicker, the email addresses in the contact list are searched and filtered, and auto-complete is used. The EmailPicker Text property contains the chosen email address. Often, the EmailPicker is used in conjunction with a Button. Once the email address is populated into the picker, the `Click` event handler of the accompanied Button is used to process the email address. The only data from the device's contact list that is loaded into the App Inventor application is the email address.

Figure 13-40 Example Email Picker User Interface (*Source:* MIT App Inventor 2)

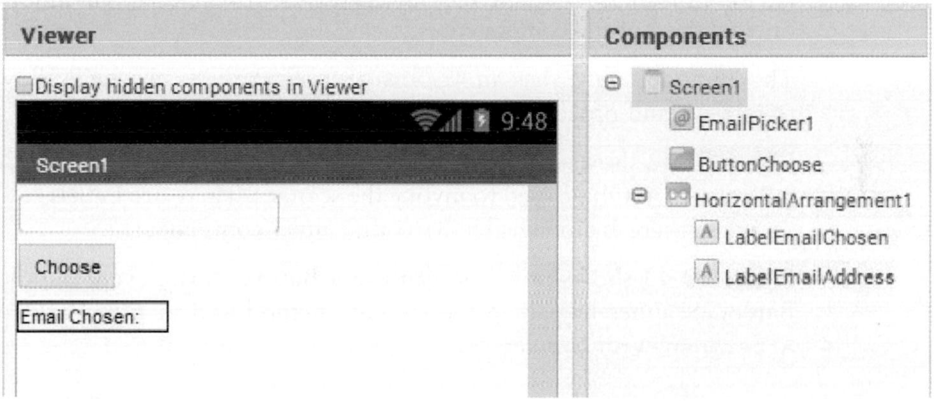

Figure 13-40 shows an example design using the EmailPicker component. Notice that a Button is used in conjunction with this picker. The Labels beneath the Button are there to show the resulting "picked" email.

Figure 13-41 shows how you might use a Button `Click` event handler to process the chosen email address.

Figure 13-41 Example Email Picker Blocks (*Source:* MIT App Inventor 2)

Checkpoint

13.7 What is the difference between a PhoneNumberPicker's Image property and a PhoneNumberPicker's Picture property?

13.8 What are the differences between the PhoneNumberPicker and the ContactPicker components?

13.9 What information does the EmailPicker provide about a contact?

13.7 Scanning a Barcode

App Inventor has a BarcodeScanner component in the *Sensors* Palette that will allow an application to scan a barcode and retrieve information based on the code.

This component uses the device's camera to scan the barcode, and in order to work, the device will need a barcode scanner program installed, such as the Barcode scanner application ZXing, which is free on the Android Market.

The BarcodeScanner is a nonvisible component. It will read both one-dimensional barcodes and QR codes. The only property the BarcodeScanner has is the Result property. It is in text format and holds results from the last successful scan.

An application invokes the BarcodeScanner by the `DoScan` method block. This is the only method of the component.

The BarcodeScanner has an `AfterScan` event handler that will allow an application to retrieve and process the result of a scan.

Figure 13-42 shows an example user interface which uses a BarcodeScanner. There is a Button that will be used to invoke the scanner. There are Labels to show the results, and then there is a nonvisible BarcodeScanner component.

Figure 13-43 shows how you can use a Button `Click` event handler to invoke the BarcodeScanner by calling the `DoScan` method and then process any results in the `AfterScan` event handler.

Figure 13-42 Example BarcodeScanner User Interface (*Source:* MIT App Inventor 2)

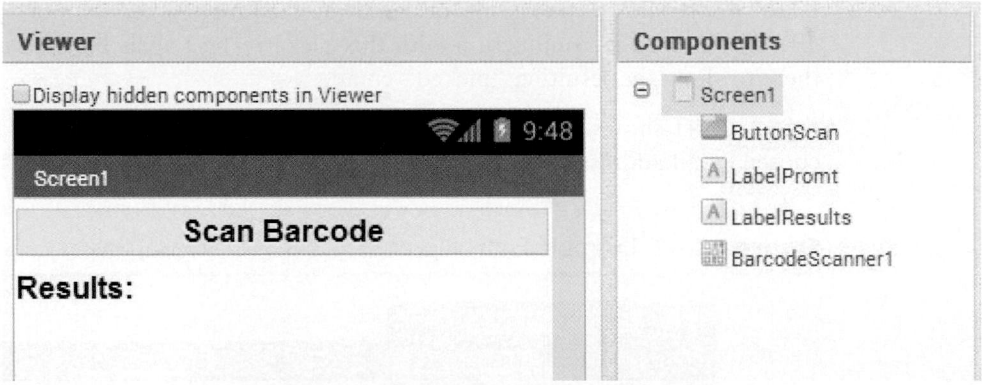

Figure 13-43 Example BarcodeScanner Blocks (*Source:* MIT App Inventor 2)

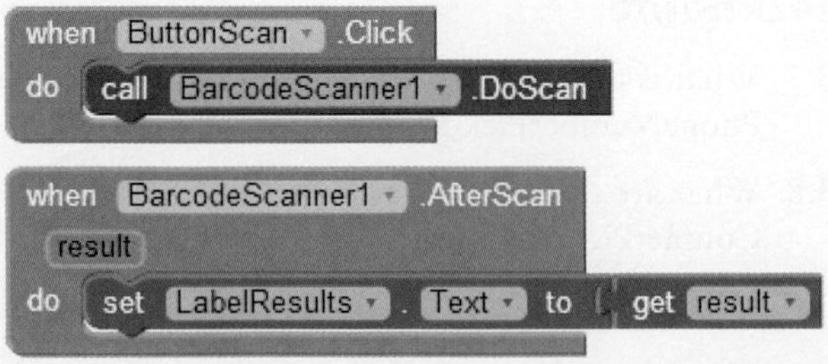

13.8 Using Voice Recognition

App Inventor's SpeechRecognizer component converts speech to text using the speech recognition feature of the Android operating system. Simply add this nonvisible component found in the *Media* Palette to your application, and you will have the capability to speak into your phone and watch it convert your message to text.

The SpeechRecognizer has one property, the Result. This property holds the text version of the last message that was recorded. To invoke the SpeechRecognizer, applications can call the `GetText` method.

After the recording stops, the `AfterGettingText` event handler is triggered. Its event handler has one parameter, `result`. This event handler is where processing on the resulting text is handled. There is also a `BeforeGettingText` event handler in which developers can perform any needed activities before the recording starts.

Tutorial 13-6:
Speak a Text Message

VideoNote
Speak a Text
Message

We are going to create an application that will use the PhoneNumberPicker to choose a phone number to send a text message to. Instead of typing the message, we are going to allow the user to speak it into the phone and display the result of the speech recognition. If the user decides the message is correct, he or she can then press an *Accept and Send* Button to send the spoken text message.

Figure 13-44 shows the completed user interface.

Step 1: Start a new App Inventor project named *SpeakATextMessage* and place a Label on the Screen. Rename it `LabelTitle`, align it centered, and change the Text property to *Speak a Text Message*. Set the Width property to *Fill parent* and set the font size to 20 pixels, *bold*.

Step 2: Add a HorizontalArrangement to the Screen. Place a PhoneNumberPicker and two Labels inside. Change the Text property of the PhoneNumberPicker to *Pick Number*. Rename the first Label to `LabelPromptNumber` and change the Text property to *Selected Number:*. Rename the second Label `LabelPhoneNumber` and empty its Text property.

Step 3: Add a Button under the HorizontalArrangement. Rename it `ButtonRecord`. Set the Width to *Fill Parent* and the Text to *Record Text Message*.

Step 4: Add a Label to display the recorded message as text. Rename it `LabelMessage`. Set the Width to *Fill Parent* and Height to 150 pixels. Change the Text property to *Message*. At this point, the app's screen should look like Figure 13-46.

Step 5: Add a Button under the `LabelMessage` component and rename it `ButtonSendText`. This Button will be pressed by the user when they are sure they want to send it. Change the Text property to *Accept and Send*.

Figure 13-44 Speech Recognition Example, User Interface
(*Source:* MIT App Inventor 2)

Figure 13-45 The Design for Steps 1 and 2 (*Source:* MIT App Inventor 2)

Figure 13-46 The Design for Steps 3 and 4 *(Source:* MIT App Inventor 2)

Viewer	Components
☐ Display hidden components in Viewer	⊖ ☐ Screen1
📶 🔋 9:48	⬜ A LabelTitle
Screen1	⊖ ▦ HorizontalArrangement1
Speak a Text Message	📷 PhoneNumberPicker1
Pick Number · Selected Number:	A LabelPromptNumber
Record Text Message	A LabelPhoneNumber
Message	🖼 ButtonRecord
	A LabelMessage

Step 6: Add the SpeechRecognizer component from the *Media* Palette.

Step 7: Add the Texting component from the *Social* Palette. Compare your design to Figure 13-44.

Refer to Figure 13-47 as you program the blocks for this tutorial.

Step 8: We need to create a variable to hold the text message after it is recorded. Go to the *Variables* drawer and choose the `initialize global name to` block. Place it in the editor and rename it `message`. Plug an empty text block into its socket.

Figure 13-47 Speak a Text Message Blocks *(Source:* MIT App Inventor 2)

Step 9: Now you will program the `PhoneNumberPicker1.AfterPicking` event handler to show the user the number that was picked. Go to the *PhoneNumberPicker1* drawer and select the `PhoneNumberPicker1.AfterPicking` event handler to place it in the editor. In the same drawer,

select the `PhoneNumberPicker.PhoneNumber` property value and place it in the editor.

Step 10: Find the `set LabelPhoneNumber.Text to` block in the *LabelPhone Number* drawer. Place it in the `PhoneNumberPicker1.AfterPicking` event handler and plug the `PhoneNumberPicker1.PhoneNumber` property into it. The event handler should appear as shown in Figure 13-48.

Step 11: Now you will create the blocks to invoke the `SpeechRecognizer1` component by calling its `GetText` method in the `ButtonRecord.Click` event handler. Go to the *ButtonRecord* drawer and select the `ButtonRecord.Click` event handler to place it in the editor. Go to the *SpeechRecogizer1* drawer and select the `GetText` method block. Place it inside the `ButtonRecord.Click` event handler, as shown in Figure 13-49

Step 12: Open the *SpeechRecognizer1* drawer and select the `AfterGettingText` event handler block. As shown in Figure 13-50, create a `set global message to` block. Plug the block into the `SpeechRecognizer1.AfterGettingText` event handler. Then, hover over the `result` parameter of the event handler and select the `get result` block. Plug it in as the argument to the `message` variable.

Figure 13-48 The `PhoneNumberPicker1.AfterPicking` Event Handler
(*Source:* MIT App Inventor 2)

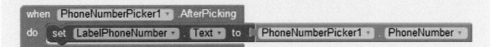

Figure 13-49 The `ButtonRecord.Click` Event Handler (*Source:* MIT App Inventor 2)

Figure 13-50 `message` Variable Initialization (*Source:* MIT App Inventor 2)

Step 13: Go to the *LabelMessage* drawer and find the `set LabelMessage.Text to` block and place it in the `SpeechRecognizer1.AfterGettingText` event handler. Hover the mouse cursor over the `result` parameter of the event handler and select the `get result` block. Plug it into the `set LabelMessage.Text to` block, as shown in Figure 13-51.

Step 14: Now we want to send the message. Go to the *ButtonSend* drawer and find the `ButtonSend.Click` event handler and place it in the Blocks Editor.

Figure 13-51 The `SpeechRecognizer1.AfterGettingText` Event Handler
(*Source:* MIT App Inventor 2)

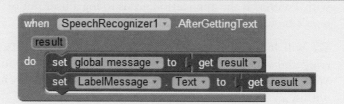

Step 15: Recall that to send a text message, we first need to set up the phone number and the message using the Texting component's PhoneNumber and Message properties. Go to the *Texting1* drawer and find both properties' "set" blocks. Place them in the `ButtonSend.Click` event handler. Set the PhoneNumber property to the `PhonePicker1.PhoneNumber` value and the `Message` property to the `get global message` block. See Figure 13-52.

Figure 13-52 Sending the Message (*Source:* MIT App Inventor 2)

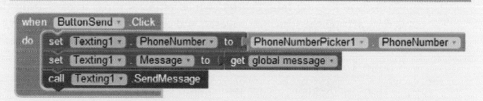

Step 16: Finally, find the `Texting1.SendMessage` method, in the *Texting1* drawer, and place it in the `ButtonSendText.Click` event handler, at the bottom.

Step 17: Compare your blocks to Figure 13-47 and connect your application to your device. Select a phone number from your contacts, record your text message, and then send it on!

13.9 Connecting to a Twitter Account

App Inventor provides a Twitter component in the *Social* Palette that will allow you to connect an application to a Twitter account. Through this component, you can search for tweets and tags, tweet messages, send direct messages to a specific user, display recent messages, follow people, and more.

In order to use this component, you will need to visit the following site to register your app:

```
http://twitter.com/oauth_clients/new
```

Once registered, you will receive a consumer key and consumer secret that you will need to use in your application. Tutorial 13-7 will show more about registering your application. These values will populate the ConsumerKey property and the ConsumerSecret property. These two properties need to be set before connecting to Twitter.

Once the key and secret are set, calling the Twitter component's `Authorize` method will transfer control to Twitter and ask the user to login. Once the user is logged in, control is transferred back to the App Inventor application, and then it can interact with Twitter. If the application needs to log a user out of Twitter, the Twitter component's `DeAuthorize` method is called.

We will look at the Twitter component's `IsAuthorized` event handler, which is triggered after a user logs in. Tutorial 13-7 will demonstrate how to register an application to obtain the key and secret and how to log into and out of Twitter within an App Inventor application.

Tutorial 13-7:
Building a Twitter Application

In this tutorial we will have two Buttons: one to log into Twitter, and one to log out. We will also have a Label that will display whether we are logged in or not. In addition to registering the application with Twitter, this tutorial will demonstrate logging into Twitter, which requires three steps: setting the *Consumer key*, setting the *Consumer secret*, and calling the `Authorize` method. It will also demonstrate how to log out of Twitter using the `DeAuthorize` method.

Step 1: Login to Twitter. Go to: http://twitter.com

Step 2: Register a new application. Go to:

http://twitter.com/oauth_clients/new and click the "Create New" button.

Step 3: You will now be on the *Create an application* page of the Twitter website. Enter the name of your application in the *Name* field. This name will be used as the source of a Tweet generated by the app. It should be no longer than 32 characters.

Step 4: Enter a description of your app in the *Description* field. This description should be 10 to 200 characters.

Step 5: Fill a URL for the website and Callback URL fields. For testing purposes, any valid URL will work, and you can use the same valid URL in both fields.

Step 6: Read and Accept the *Developer Rules of the Road*.

Step 7: Once all fields are populated on the *Create an application* page, click the *Create your Twitter application* Button at the bottom of the screen.

Step 8: Once your application is registered in Twitter, you will be forwarded to a screen with tabs at the top for *Details, Settings, API Keys,* and *Permissions*. Click on the *Details* tab at the top of the page and review your application details.

Step 9: Click on the *Settings* tab at the top of the page and review the application's settings. Click the *Allow this application to be used to*

Sign in with Twitter checkbox. Click *Update Settings* at the bottom of the page.

Step 10: Click on the *API Keys* tab at the top of the page. Copy and paste both the API key and the API secret to a safe place on your computer. You will need to know which is which and where they are, because they will be entered into your App Inventor project.

Step 11: Click on the *Permissions* tab at the top of the page. For our purposes, leave the permissions set to *Read only*.

Step 12: Now it's time to create your App Inventor project. Review Figure 13-53.

Figure 13-53 Twitter Application User Interface (*Source:* MIT App Inventor 2)

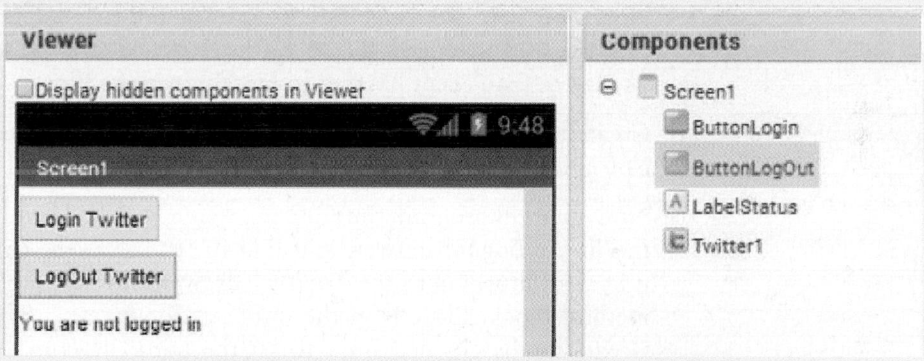

Step 13: Start a new App Inventor application and place two Buttons and a Label on the Screen. Rename the first Button ButtonLogin and change the Text property to *Login to Twitter*. Rename the second Button ButtonLogOut and change the Text property to *Log out of Twitter*. Change the Name of the Label to LabelStatus and change the Text property to *You are not logged in*.

Step 14: Go to the *Social* Palette and find the Twitter component to add to your project. Remember, this is a nonvisible component.

Refer to Figure 13-54 as you program the blocks.

Figure 13-54 Twitter Application Blocks Editor (*Source:* MIT App Inventor 2)

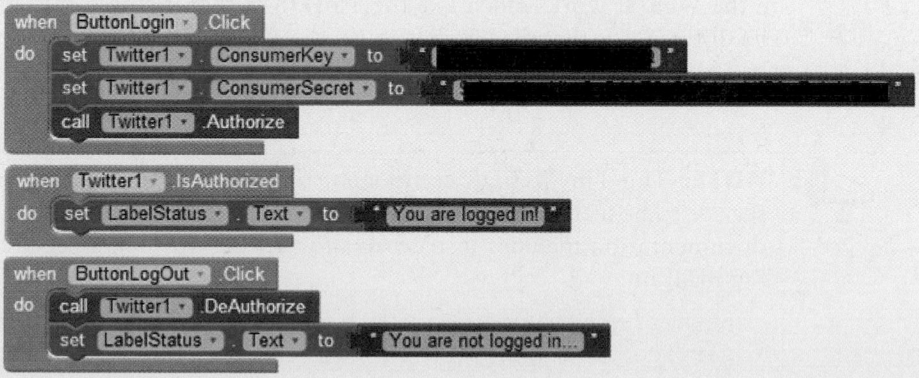

Step 15: Now you will program the `ButtonLogin.Click` event handler. Go to *ButtonLogin*, find the `Click` event handler, and place it in the Blocks Editor.

Step 16: Go to the *Twitter1* drawer and select the set `ConsumerKey` to block and the set `Twitter1.ConsumerSecret` to block. Place them in the `ButtonLogin.Click` event handler.

Step 17: Create two text blocks. Paste the saved API key into one and the API secret into the other. Plug them into the appropriate property.

Step 18: Go to the *Twitter1* drawer, and select the `Twitter1.Autorize` method block. Place it in the `ButtonLogin.Click` event handler, as shown in Figure 13-54. That's all you need to log in!

Step 19: Now you will program the `IsAuthorized` event handler to show that the user is logged in. Go to the *Twitter1* drawer, and select the `IsAuthorized` event handler to place it into the Blocks Editor.

Step 20: Create the necessary blocks to set the `LabelStatus.Text` property to *You are logged in!* Place these blocks in the `IsAuthorized` event handler.

Step 21: Now you will program the `ButtonLogout.Click` event handler. Go to the *ButtonLogout* drawer, and find the `Click` event handler to place it in the editor. Go to the *Twitter1* drawer and find the `DeAuthorize` method block. Place it in the `ButtonLogout.Click` event handler. Create the blocks necessary to set the `LabelStatus.Text` property to *You are not logged in.* Plug these blocks into the `ButtonLogout.Click` event handler, as shown in Figure 13-54.

Step 22: That's it! Compare all of your blocks to Figure 13-54 and test your application on your device or emulator.

13.10 TinyWebDB

The TinyWebDB component in App Inventor allows applications to share data stored on the Web. It works much like the TinyDB in that it stores data in tag-value pairs. The difference is that the database is on the Web, and therefore multiple applications can access it.

 NOTE: The TinyWebDB component requires that you set up a custom Web service to host the database. At the time of this writing, the online App Inventor documentation includes instructions for setting up such a service at the following location:

```
http://appinventor.mit.edu/explore/content/custom-tinywebdb-
service.html
```

The TinyWebDB component has one property, the ServiceURL which is the URL of the Web server and path of the database.

Similar to TinyDB, there is a `GetValue` method that requires you to give it a tag. Based on the tag supplied to it, the method will search the TinyWebDB for the associated value. There is also a `StoreValue` method that will store a tag-value pair.

There are three event handlers: `GotValue,` `ValueStored`, and `WebServiceError`. The `GotValue` event handler is triggered if the `GetValue` is successful and will provide the tag and value for use in the event handler. The `ValueStored` event handler is triggered when a successful store has been processed. If there is a communication error with the Web service that communicates with the database, the `WebServiceError` event handler is triggered and includes the error message.

Review Questions

Multiple Choice

1. What method of the SoundRecorder component is used to start a recording?

    a. `Record`
    b. `Go`
    c. `Start`
    d. None of the above

2. What is the event that is triggered when a recording has stopped?

    a. `DoneRecording`
    b. `AfterRecording`
    c. `AfterRecordedSound`
    d. `AfterSoundRecorded`

3. Which component allows you to take photos with the phone's camera?

    a. PictureTaker
    b. Camera
    c. ImagePicker
    d. ImageTaker

4. Which property of the ImagePicker holds the picture selected from the phone's gallery?

    a. Image
    b. Photo
    c. Picture
    d. None of the above

5. What file formats does App Inventor accept for Video?

   a. `.wmv`
   b. `.3gp`
   c. `.mp4`
   d. All of the above

6. What is the suggested file size for videos in App Inventor?

   a. 1 MB
   b. 5 MB
   c. 10 MB
   d. 25 MB

7. What properties are available for a contact when chosen with the Phone-NumberPicker?

   a. Email address
   b. Picture
   c. Phone number
   d. All of the above

8. What property is not available for a contact when chosen with the ContactPicker?

   a. Email address
   b. Picture
   c. Phone number
   d. Name

9. What properties are available for a contact when chosen with the EmailPicker?

   a. Email address
   b. Picture
   c. Phone number
   d. Name

10. What two properties must be set in an App Inventor application before attempting to connect to a Twitter account?

   a. Consumer key, Consumer secret
   b. User ID, Password
   c. Twitter Account, Twitter Password
   d. None of the above

Short Answer

1. List some common applications that use the device's camera to take pictures. What kinds of applications can you think of that might use the device's camera?

2. Why might we need to manipulate the duration of a video before displaying it to the user?

3. What are the steps to take to speak a message into a device and then have it send to a list of contacts as a text message? What components would you use, and how might the PhoneNumberPicker fit into this application?

4. What are the steps needed to log in to a Twitter account via an App Inventor application? What component(s) are needed?

5. What is the advantage of a TinyWebDB over a TinyDB?

Exercises

1. **Save Recordings**

   Write an application that allows the user to record audio and, if they accept the recording, store it to a list.

2. **Save Pictures**

   Write an application that allows a user to take pictures with the phone and, if they accept the photo (in App Inventor), save it to a list.

3. **Image Sprite**

   Write an application that will let the user select the Image for an Image Sprite.

VideoNote
The Show Spoken
Message App

4. **Show Spoken Message**

   Write an application that allows the user to speak into the phone. Once speaking is over, show the message on the Screen in text.

5. **Barcode Scanner**

   Write an application that scans the barcode of a book. Display the ISBN number on the Screen in a Label.

Chapter Projects

1. **Speaking Sprites**

   Write an application that:
   a. Includes three ImageSprites.
   b. Allows the user to use the ImagePicker to set the Image property for each sprite.
   c. Allows the user to record three audio clips for each sprite (and save them).
   d. Plays back a Sprite's recorded sound when it is touched.

   Use the ImagePicker and SoundRecoder components.

2. **Gift Shopping List**

   This application will allow a user to take a photo of a gift idea and store it in a TinyDB with the name of the person they want to buy it for.

   For example, if a user is in a store and sees a gift for Sally, they can use the ContactPicker to pick Sally's name and store it to a variable. They will then take a photo of the gift using the Camera component and store the picture to a variable.

   Once the user confirms the name and photo, store them in a TinyDB as a tag-value pair.

3. **Gift Shopping List - Modification**

   Modify the "Gift Shopping List" to show a list of the stored names and photos based on a Button click.

4. **Scan and Text ISBN**

   Write an application that will allow a user to scan a barcode of a book, and then choose a contact from their device to text message its contents to. You will need the BarcodeScanner, PhoneNumberPicker, and Texting components.

A Setting Up App Inventor

Create a Google Account

To use App Inventor, you must have a Google account. (If you have a Gmail account, then you already have a Google account, so you can skip this step.) To set up a Google account, go to www.google.com/accounts/newaccount. Figure A-1 shows how the screen appeared at the time this book was written. Simply enter the requested information, then scroll to the bottom of the screen and click *Next step*. Your Google account is now set up. Remember the username that you entered. You will need it when you log into App Inventor.

Figure A-1 The *Create a New Google Account* Screen (*Source:* Google and the Google logo are registered trademarks of Google Inc., used with permission.)

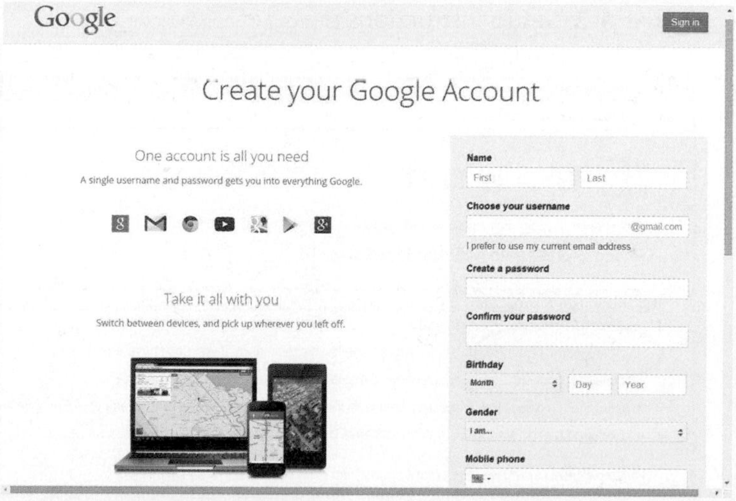

Set up App Inventor

Once you have your Google account, you can set up App Inventor. Go to the App Inventor 2 home page: http://appinventor.mit.edu/explore/. See Figure A-2.

Figure A-2 App Inventor 2 Home Page (*Source:* MIT App Inventor 2)

The screen appears in Figure A-2. Click *Get Started* and you will see a page similar to the one shown in Figure A-3. On that page, click the *Setup Instructions* link shown in the figure.

Figure A-3 Setup Instructions (*Source:* MIT App Inventor 2)

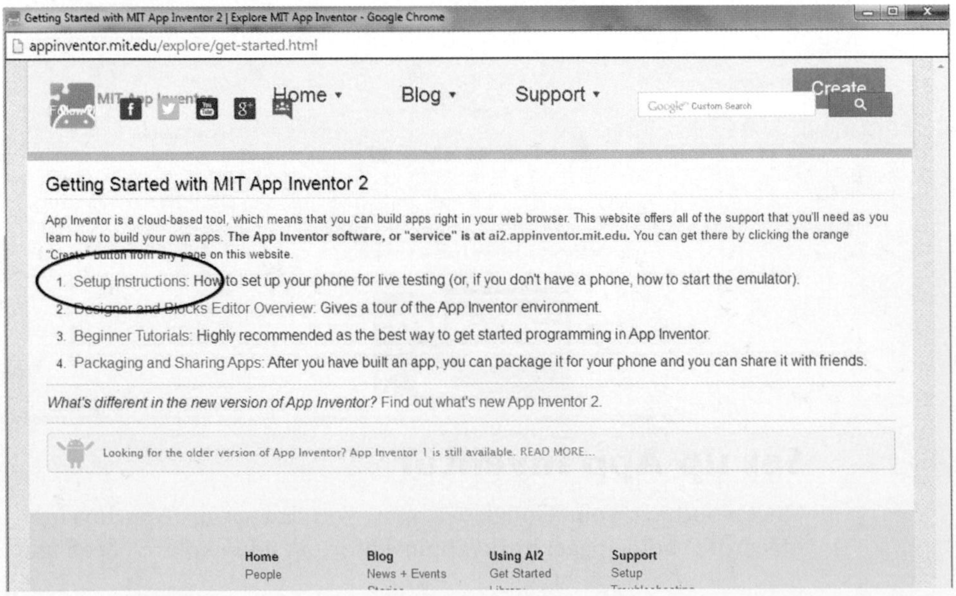

Notice in Figure A-4 that you have three options available: Connect via Wi-Fi and AI Companion (recommended), Connecting to the Emulator (if you do not have a device), and Connecting via USB (you have a device, but not Wi-Fi).

Figure A-4 Setting Up App Inventor 2 (*Source:* MIT App Inventor 2)

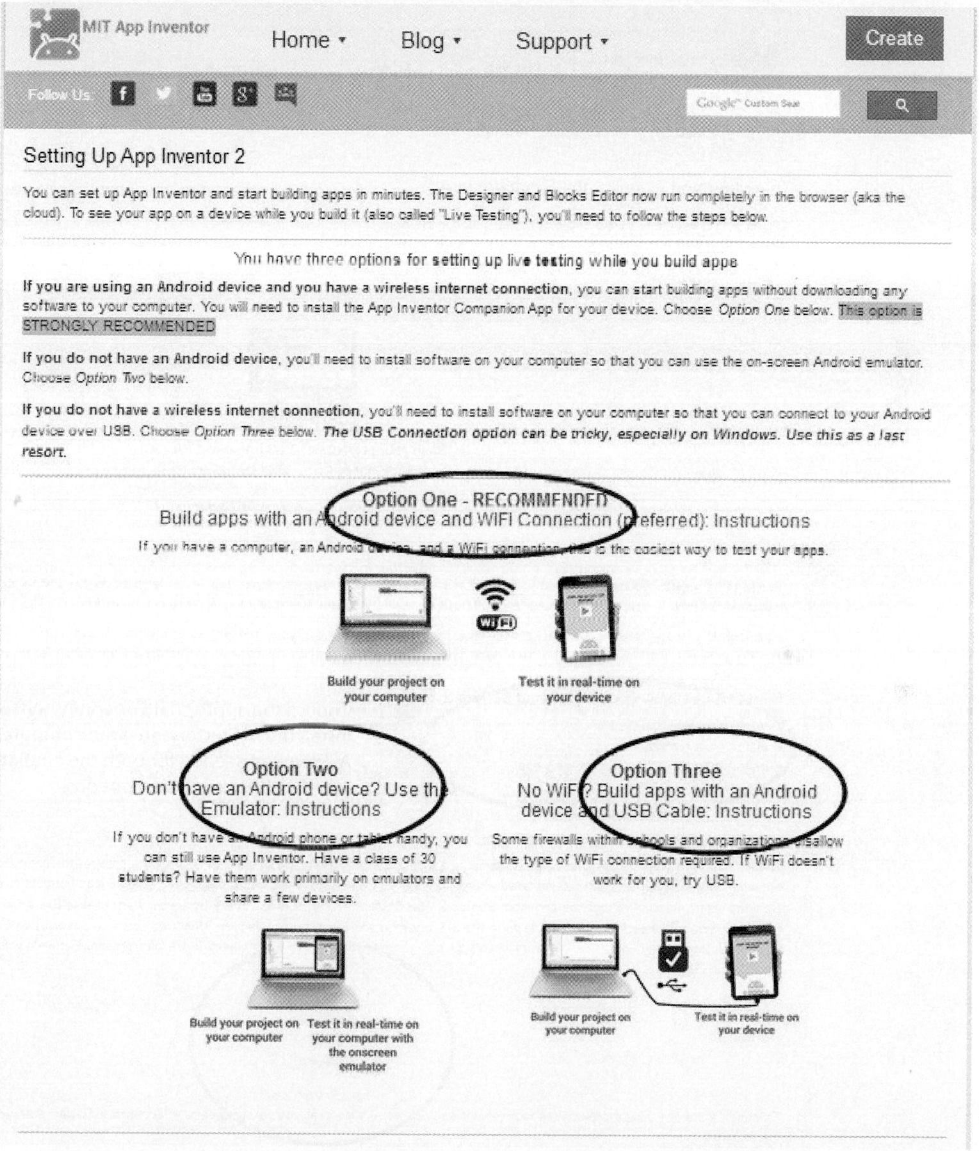

NOTE: See Appendix B for the Wi-Fi/AI Companion instructions.

Setting up the Emulator

Click on Option Two (instructions link) shown in Figure A-4. You will come to the instructions page shown in Figure A-5.

Figure A-5 Installing the AI Starter for the Emulator (*Source:* MIT App Inventor 2)

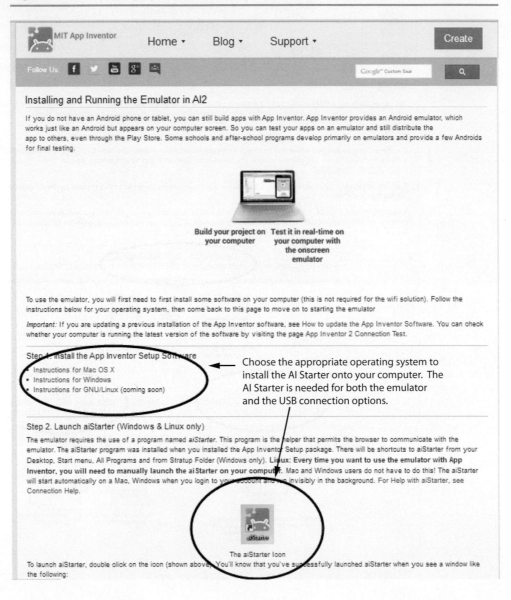

Setting up the USB

Step 1: Click on Option Three (instructions link) shown in Figure A-4. You will come to the instructions page shown in Figure A-6. Choose the appropriate operating system link and install the AI Starter by following the instructions.

Figure A-6 (*Source:* MIT App Inventor 2)

Follow Us:

Connecting to a phone or tablet with a USB cable

Build your project on your computer

Test it in real-time on your device

When you use App Inventor with a phone or tablet, that device communicates with the App Inventor software running in your computer's browser window. This communication is managed by the AI2 Companion App running on the device. The instructions below (step 2) explain how to install the companion. The Companion can communicate with your computer over a wireless connection. *This is the method strongly recommended by the App Inventor team.* It does not require any additional software to be installed on your computer. (See Option 1, under Setting up App Inventor.)

There are, however, some environments where wireless connections won't work. These include some hotels, conference centers, and schools, that configure their wireless networks to prohibit two devices on the network from communicating with each other. See How Does my Android Device Connect Over Wifi? for a short explanation.Some App Inventor users have solved this problem by purchasing a wireless router and setting up their own local network. (Also, most Macs and some PC can serve as WiFi routers that can handle a small number of machines.) But where even this is impossible, you can still use App Inventor with a phone or tablet if you connect it to the computer with a USB cable.

Setting up a USB connection can be awkward, especially on Windows machines, which need special *driver* software to connect to Android devices. (This is not the case with Mac or Linux, which do not need special drivers.) Unfortunately, different devices may require different drivers, and, outside of a few standard models, Microsoft and Google have left it to the device manufacturers to create and supply the drivers. As a consequence, that you may have to search on the Web to find the appropriate driver for your phone. App Inventor provides a test program that checks if your USB-connected device can communicate with the computer. You should run this test and resolve any connection issues before trying to use App Inventor with USB on that device.

Here are the steps for beginning to use App Inventor with the USB cable:

Step 1: Install the App Inventor Setup Software

To connect with USB, you need to first install the App Inventor setup software on your computer. (This is not required for the wifi method.) Follow the instructions below for your operating system, then come back to this page to move on to step 2

Important: If you are updating a previous installation of the App Inventor software, see How to update the App Inventor Software.

• Instructions for Mac OS X
  Instructions for Windows
  Instructions for GNU/Linux (coming soon)

You can check whether your computer is running the latest version of the software by visiting the **Connection Test Page**.

NOTE: See Appendix B for USB connection via the AI Companion instructions.

B Connecting an Android Device to App Inventor

You can run your App Inventor applications on your device while you are developing in App Inventor. To do this your device must be connected to App Inventor. Your device can connect to App Inventor two different ways: via Wi-Fi connection (AI Companion) or a USB cable.

To use Wi-Fi and the AI Companion, you need both your computer and mobile device to be connected to the *same* Wi-Fi network. You also need to be sure the AI Starter is up and running on your computer. See Appendix A: Setting Up App Inventor.

If you have a Wi-Fi connection available, it is generally advised to use this method. If you are working with several developers or more, such as in a lab environment, you may need to use USB cables if problems occur with the wireless connections.

Connecting via Wi-Fi and the AI2 Companion App

Download and install the MIT AI Companion App

Before you can connect via Wi-Fi, you must download MIT's App Inventor Companion App found on the Google Play Store.

Step 1:   Go to the Play Store on your device and search for "MIT AI2 Companion". Once the application is in the returned list, tap it to select. See Figure B-1.

Figure B-1 Search Google Play *(Source:* Google and the Google logo are registered trademarks of Google Inc., used with permission.)

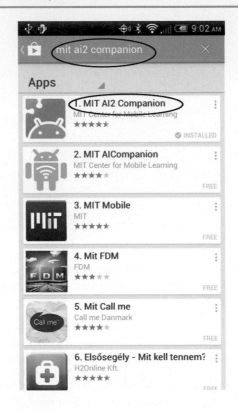

Step 2:   Tap the Install Button to install the application. See Figure B-2.

Figure B-2 Install the MIT AI2 Companion App (*Source:* Google and the Google logo are registered trademarks of Google Inc., used with permission.)

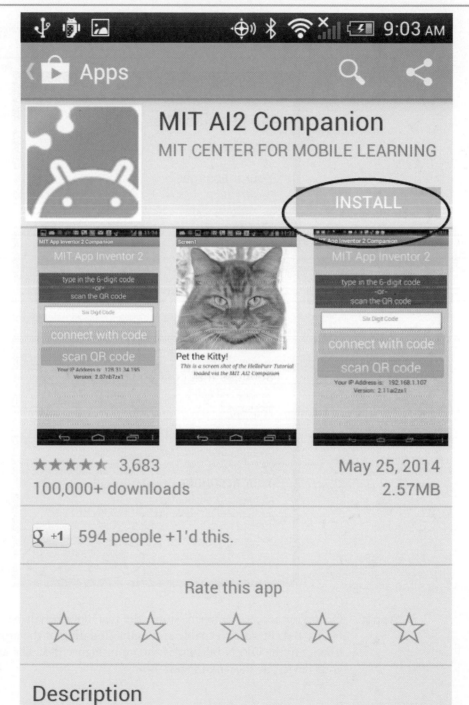

Step 3: Accept the Apps permission requirements. App Inventor needs these permissions on your device to perform various app capabilities.

Figure B-3 Accept Permissions (*Source:* Google and the Google logo are registered trademarks of Google Inc., used with permission.)

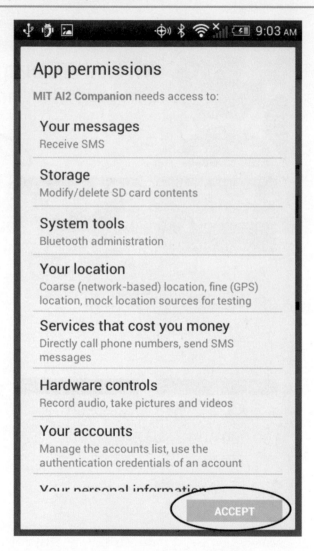

Step 4: Once you accept the permissions, the installation will begin, as shown in Figure B-4. Be sure to enable automatic updating of the app. Once it is finished, tap the OPEN button, as shown in Figure B-5. The app will open on your device, as shown in Figure B-6.

Figure B-4 Installing (*Source:* Google and the Google logo are registered trademarks of Google Inc., used with permission.)

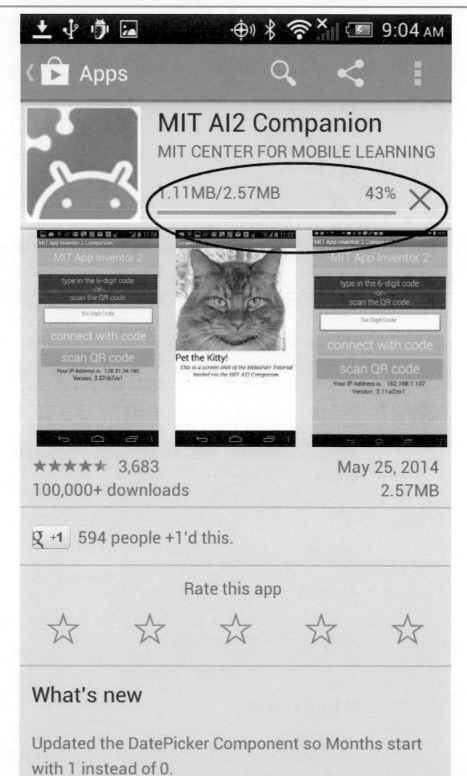

Figure B-5 Open Button (*Source:* Google and the Google logo are registered trademarks of Google Inc., used with permission.)

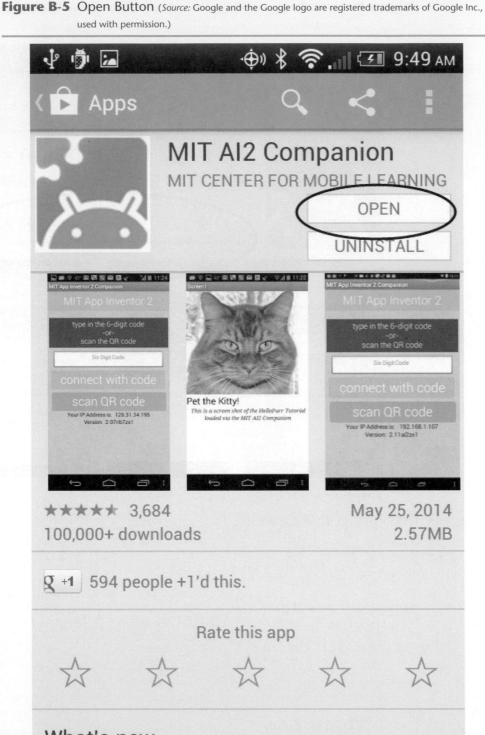

Figure B-6 AI2 Companion App Opened (*Source:* MIT App Inventor 2)

Step 5:   Now that the application is successfully installed and open on your device, let's connect it to App Inventor. Open App Inventor 2 on your computer and choose *Connect*, and then choose *AI Companion*, as shown in Figure B-7.

Figure B-7 Connect to AI Companion (*Source:* MIT App Inventor 2)

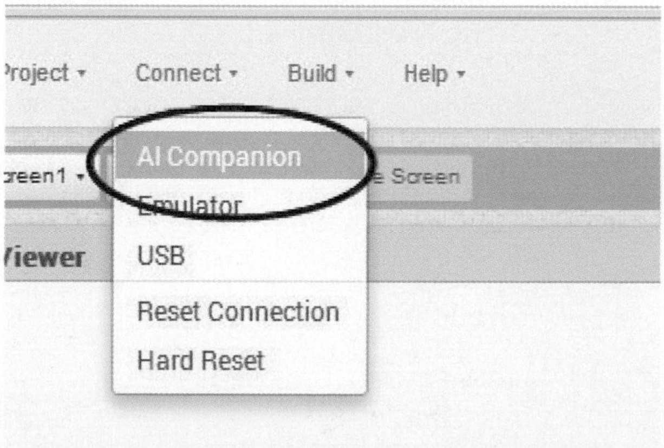

Step 6: At this point, App Inventor will generate a QR code and a text code as shown in Figure B-8.

Figure B-8 App Inventor Code (*Source:* MIT App Inventor 2)

Step 7: Choose either *Scan the QR code* from the AI Companion App on your device, or type in the code (the example code shown in Figure B-8 would be *yfcbaq*). The screen on your device should look like Figure B-9. Scanning the QR code will simply populate the code in the TextBox for you and will *automatically load your app* after the scan. You may find this approach easier. If you want to type in the code, type it in the *Six Digit Code* box and click *connect with code* to load your app.

Figure B-9 Companion App Connection (*Source:* MIT App Inventor 2)

Step 8:   Your application should now show up on your phone. If it does not, be sure that you have the latest version of the MIT AI2 Companion App and that your phone and computer are connected to Wi-Fi. You can confirm this by noticing the IP Address at the bottom of the AI2 Companion App Screen. See Figure B-9.

NOTE: If you have trouble with the Wi-Fi connection instructions, there may be a problem with your device's connection. You can read about connection issues at the following location on the App Inventor site:

http://appinventor.mit.edu/explore/support/explain-wifi-connection.html

Connecting via USB

To connect via USB, you have your device connected to your computer via USB cable. You also need to be sure the AI Starter is up and running on your computer. See Appendix A: Setting Up App Inventor.

Next, it's as simple as choosing *Connect* and then *USB* in App Inventor. See Figure B-10.

Figure B-10 Connect via USB (*Source:* MIT App Inventor 2)

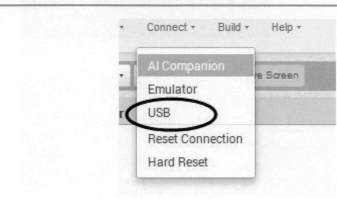

 NOTE: If you have trouble with the USB connection instructions, there may be a problem with your device's connection or the settings on your device. You can read about connection issues at the following location on the App Inventor site:

http://appinventor.mit.edu/explore/ai2/setup-device-usb.html#step2

C

Uploading Your Application to App Inventor Gallery and Google Play Store

Uploading your App to the App Inventor Gallery

The App Inventor Gallery is available at gallery.appinventor.mit.edu. The Gallery is a place where you can go to view and download other App Inventor applications, upload your own to share, learn, and collaborate with other App Inventor developers. The Gallery is an open-source environment, so you can see others' code and they can see yours. This environment fosters learning because developers can learn from each other and share their ideas.

Joining the App Inventor Gallery

Before you can upload your apps to the Gallery, you will need to join it and submit a request form. To join, use your Google account to log in at gallery.appinventor.mit.edu. At first, you won't be able to see or upload apps. You will have to request to be accepted. There is a button on the home page that will bring you to the request form to fill out. Full access should be granted within a day or two.

Once you have full access to the site, you can upload and search for applications.

Finding Apps

To find apps in the Gallery, go to the *Find Apps* menu link and notice the Search Screen. Search using keywords that relate to what you want to see. See Figure C-1.

Uploading Apps

Before you upload your application, you will need to have two files ready: the source code (.aia file) of your application and an image that will be displayed on your app's page when your application shows up on the Search Screen.

To download your source file from App Inventor, go to *My Projects* and select the project that you want to download. Then, choose *Export selected project (.aia) to my computer*. See Figure C-2.

613

Figure C-1 Find Apps in the Gallery (*Source:* MIT App Inventor 2)

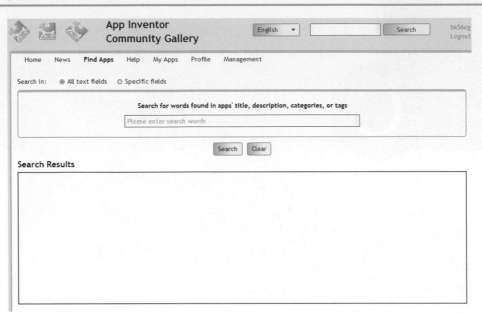

Your source will be saved to your computer as an .aia file. For example, the project shown selected in Figure C-2 would be saved as SpeakAMessage.aia. Remember where this file is saved; you will need it when you upload your app to the Gallery.

You will also need an image that represents your application. The Gallery will scale your image to a 180 by 230 pixel image. The image file size is 350 KB. Remember where this image is saved, you will need this also when you upload your app.

With your source file and image ready, go to the *My Apps* menu link in the Gallery to upload your app. You will see the *Add New Application* button as shown in Figure C-3.

Figure C-2 Download Source from App Inventor (*Source:* MIT App Inventor 2)

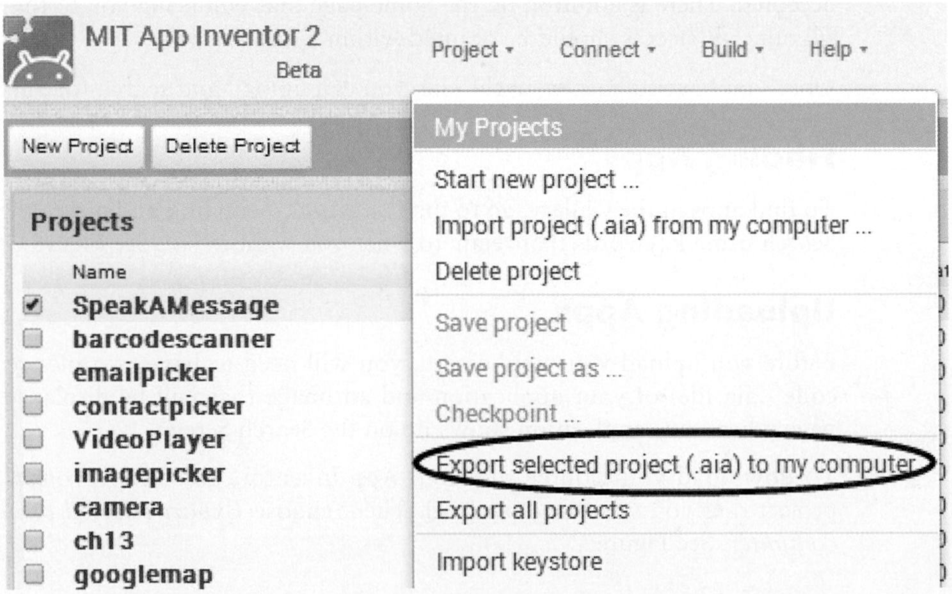

Figure C-3 Add Application (*Source:* MIT App Inventor 2)

Next, you will see the screen shown in Figure C-4, which gives you the opportunity to fill in information about your application.

Figure C-4 Information about Your App (*Source:* MIT App Inventor 2)

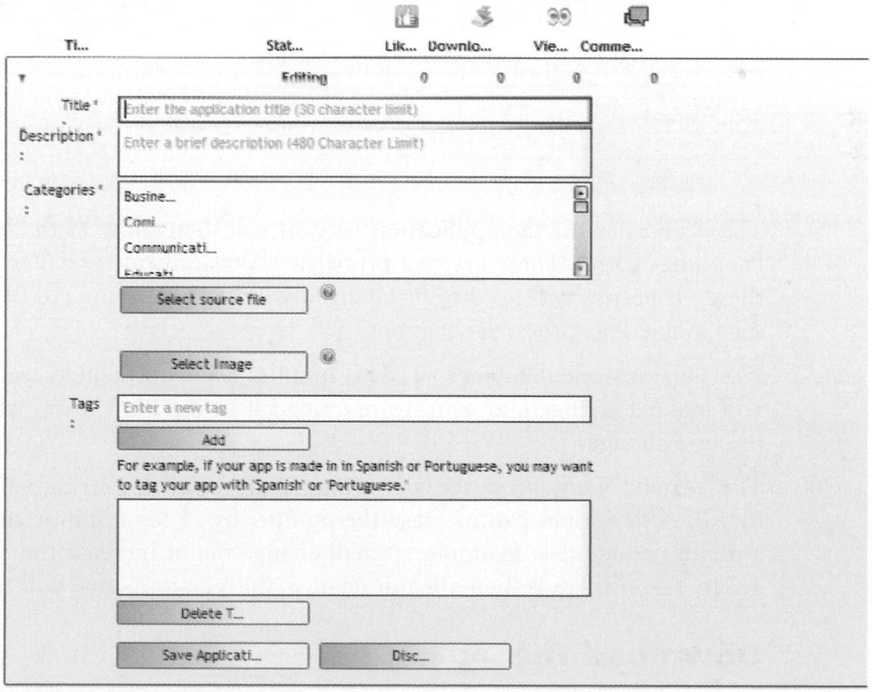

Fill in the information required and any tags you'd like to associate with your application. Required information is noted with a red asterisk. The source file will be your downloaded App Inventor .aia file. When you are done, click the *Save Application* button, and that's it! Your app will be in the Gallery to share with others.

Uploading your App to the Google Play Store

Your App Inventor apps can be uploaded for distribution on the Google Play Store. There are just a few steps to complete on your app before you are ready.

App Version

You must give your application a VersionCode number before packaging it for use on a device and uploading it to Google Play. To do this, go to the Designer and choose the `Screen1` Component in the Components column. See Figure C-5.

Figure C-5 Version (*Source:* MIT App Inventor 2)

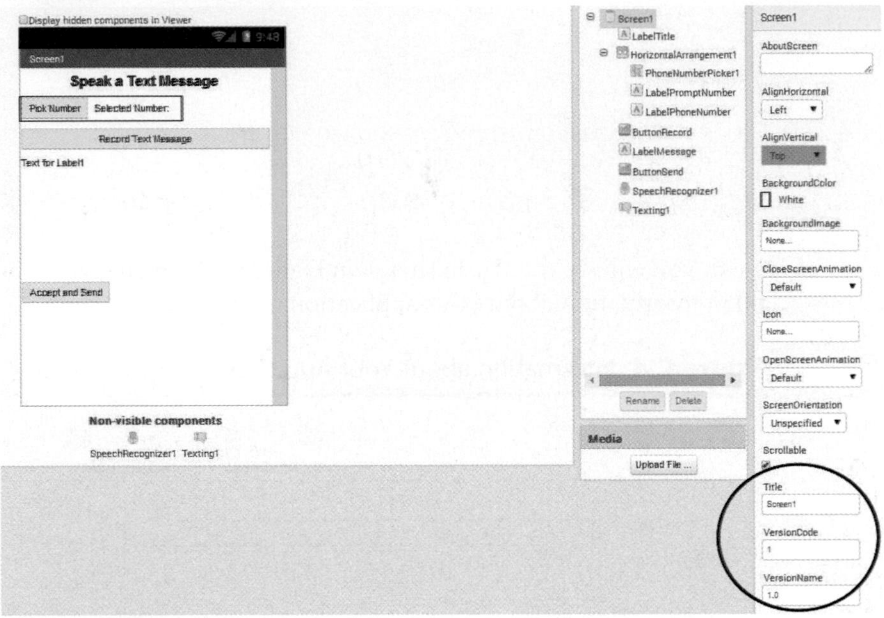

The properties for the application version will then show at the bottom right in the Properties Panel. There are two properties: VersionCode and VersionName. Both of these properties will need to be changed with each new upload of the application to the Google Play Store. See Figure C-5.

The VersionCode defaults to 1. This number needs to be increased by one each time you make a change and want to re-upload it to the Play Store, whether it is a small or large change.

The VersionName property is a string. It can hold any string value, but it defaults to 1.0. A developer can increase the number by .1 for a minor change and by 1 for a major change. For example, a small change might increase the VersionName from 1.2 to 1.3. If there is then a major change, the VersionName will be 2.0.

Download the .apk

Once your application is complete, tested, and versioned, you can download the .apk file, which will be uploaded to the Google Play Store. To download the .apk, you need to need to build the application and download it to your computer. Open the application that you want to download, at the top of the screen choose *Build*, then *App (save .apk to my computer)*. See Figure C-6.

Figure C-6 Package for Phone (*Source:* MIT App Inventor 2)

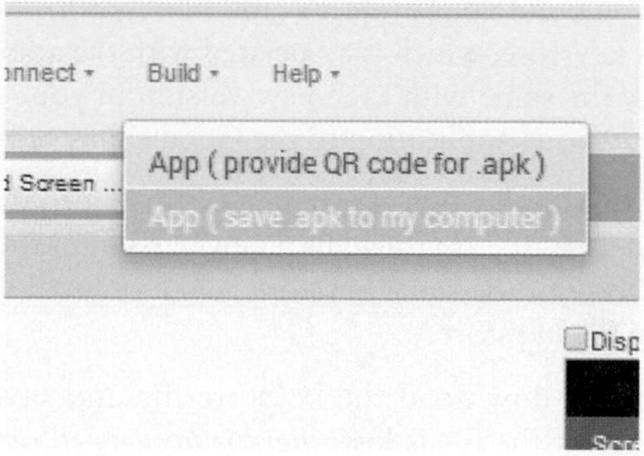

Application Backup

It is a good idea to keep safe backups of any application that is published. App Inventor projects can be backed up very easily. You simply go to *My Projects* and select the project to download by the CheckBox and then choose *Export selected project (.aia) to my computer*. See Figure C-7.

Figure C-7 Backup Source Code (*Source:* MIT App Inventor 2)

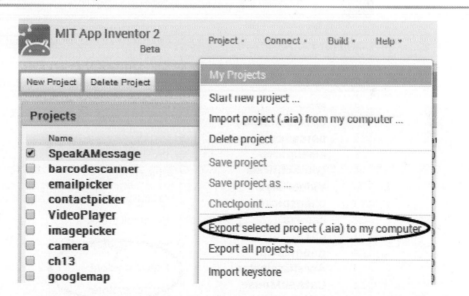

The action in Figure C-7 will create an .aia file of the source that can be saved on your computer. Keep your .aia files in a safe place. It is advisable to backup each version of your code in case you need to use a prior version. Backups are important because there is no guarantee they will always be available on the server and customers may rely on you to fix and enhance your application over time.

Application Icon

You will need an icon for your app that meets the Android icon guidelines. You can read about the guidelines here: http://developer.android.com/design/style/iconography.html.

Application Key Stores

When you build your project's .apk file, App Inventor creates a private digital key file called a keystore, which is associated with the application and your account. This key will stay the same with each new version of your application. You will need this key to upload your application to the Google Play Store.

When your application is installed on an Android device, the keystore is remembered by the device. If a user installs a new version of the application, the new version must be signed with the same keystore as the original version. It is important that you do not lose the keystore.

You should download the keystore file and save it somewhere safe that you can remember. If the file is lost, *there is no way to recover it*. There is no guarantee that your keystore will always be on the App Inventor servers, so be sure to save this file for any application that you publish to the Google Play Store.

To download the keystore, go to *My Projects* and select the project by the CheckBox and then choose *Export keystore*. See Figure C-8.

Figure C-8 (*Source:* MIT App Inventor 2)

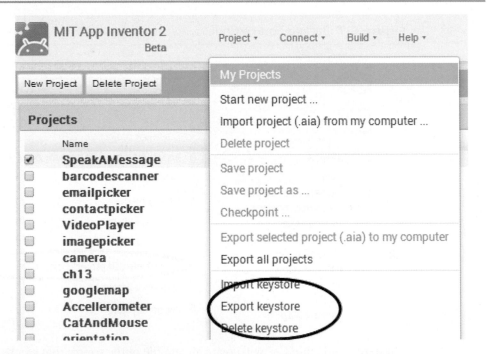

Publish Your App

You are now ready to publish your app!

To get started, you may want to read the publishing overview page at: http://developer.android.com/tools/publishing/publishing_overview.html

Another good resource for information is the launch checklist at: http://developer.android.com/distribute/googleplay/publish/preparing.html

When you are ready to publish, visit the publishing page and follow the steps at: http://developer.android.com/distribute/googleplay/publish/index.html .

D Component Reference

This appendix provides a quick reference for the App Inventor components that are covered in this book. For each component, we give a brief description of properties, events, and methods.

This book covers many, but not all, of the App Inventor components. For a complete reference covering all of the components, see the following site:

http://appinventor.mit.edu/explore/content/reference-documentation.html

AccelerometerSensor

Properties

Available: `true` if the Android device has an accelerometer available, `false` if it does not.

Enabled: If set to `true`, the Accelerometer component is enabled for use.

XAccel: X-dimension acceleration

YAccel: Y-dimension acceleration

ZAccel: Z-dimension acceleration

MinimumInterval: Property to set the minimum time between shakes in milliseconds. If you've programmed an action based on a phone shake, but you don't want to perform that action more than once per second, you would set the MinimumInterval to 1000 milliseconds, or one second. If someone is shaking the phone very fast, your action won't happen more than you want it to.

Events

AccelerationChanged (number xAccel, number yAccel, number zAccel):
This event is triggered whenever there is a change in the device's acceleration.

Shaking(): Triggered repeatedly when there is a quick shake of the device.

Methods

None

ActivityStarter

Properties

Action: The activity action. For example, `android.intent.action.WEB_SEARCH`, `android.intent.action.View` or `android.intent.action.MAIN`

ActivityClass: The activity's class name.

ActivityPackage: The activity's package name.

DataType: Data type of file associated with the activity.

DataUri: URI passed to activity, if the activity needs it.

ExtraKey: Key passed to activity, if the activity needs it.

ExtraValue: Additional value passed to activity, if the activity needs it.

Result: Returned result of the activity.

ResultName: The name used to access the returned result of the activity.

ResultType: The type of data returned from the activity.

ResultUri: URI information of data returned from the activity.

Events

`ActivityError(text message)`: Raised when error occurred using the ActivityStarter.

`AfterActivity(text result)`: Raised when the activity is complete or ended.

Methods

`text ResolveActivity()`: This method will return, as text, the name of the activity for the ActivityStarter. Often used to determine if the activity is available on a device as it will return an empty string if not.

`StartActivity()`: Invokes the activity associated with the ActivityStarter.

Ball

Properties

Enabled: If `true`, the Sprite will move when its speed is non-zero. If `false`, the Sprite will not move.

Heading: The Heading property will set the direction of the Sprite in degrees. So, 90 (degrees) will set the direction of the Sprite to straight up, 180 will set the direction to left, 270 is down and 0 is right. For example, if you want the Sprite to move from the bottom left corner to the top right corner in a straight line of a 200 by 200 pixel Canvas, you will set the heading to 45.

Interval: The Interval sets how *often* the Sprite will move in milliseconds. For example, 1,000 milliseconds equal one second, so the larger you set this property, the slower your Sprite will move.

PaintColor: Color of the Ball Sprite.

Radius: Radius of the Ball Sprite.

Speed: The Speed property is the number of *pixels* to move each interval. So, if you have your Speed set to 10, and the Interval set at 1,000 milliseconds, your Sprite will move 10 pixels every second (in the direction set by the Heading).

Visible: `true` if the Sprite is visible, `false` if hidden.

X: The Sprite's left edge's horizontal position, relative to the left edge of the Canvas.

Y: The Sprite's top edge's vertical position, relative to the left edge of the Canvas.

Z: How the sprite should be layered relative to other sprites, with higher-numbered layers in front of lower-numbered layers.

Events

CollidedWith(component other):

Raised when two Sprites collide. The collision is detected by the Sprites un-rotated position, meaning tall narrow or short wide Sprite collisions will be inaccurate.

Dragged(number startX, number startY, number prevX, number prevY, number currentX, number currentY): Raised when a Sprite is dragged by a user. The start (x,y) coordinates represent where the user first touched the Canvas. The prev (x, y) coordinates represent where the drag began. The current (x,y) coordinates indicate the current position of the Sprite. Used in conjunction with the MoveTo method to make the Sprite move.

EdgeReached(number edge): Triggered when a Sprite reaches the edge of a Canvas. If this event calls Bounce with that edge, the Sprite will appear to bounce off of the edge it reached.

The edge argument tells which edge (or corner) was reached. The edge values are as follows:

- north = 1
- northeast = 2
- east = 3
- southeast = 4
- south = −1
- southwest = −2
- west = −3
- northwest = −4

Flung(number x, number y, number speed, number heading, number xvel, number yvel):

A fling is a quick swipe of the Canvas and will invoke this event. The event records the X,Y coordinates of where the fling started and also provides the X and Y velocities of the fling (xvel and yvel). The Speed and Heading values of the flung Ball are also available.

NoLongerCollidingWith(component other):

Triggered when two collided Sprites are no longer colliding.

TouchDown(number x, number y):

Triggered when the user touches the Sprite, by placing a finger down and holding it there. x and y are the Canvas coordinates of the touch.

TouchUp(number x, number y):

Triggered when the user stops touching the Sprite, by lifting their finger from a touch. x and y are the Canvas coordinates of the touch.

Touched(number x, number y, Boolean touchedSprite):

Triggered when the user touches the Sprite, by touching and then immediately lifting their finger. x and y are the Canvas coordinates of the touch. touchedSprite is true if a Sprite is being dragged, false if not.

Methods

Bounce(number edge): Simulates the Sprite bouncing off an edge or corner. Generally, the edge argument is the one returned by EdgeReached.

Boolean CollidingWith(component other): Returns true if the calling Sprite is colliding with the other Sprite. Otherwise, returns false.

MoveIntoBounds(): If part of the Sprite moves outside of the Canvas bounds, this method is used to place the entire Sprite back on the Canvas. If the Sprite is too wide for the Canvas, it will align the Sprite on the left edge. If it is too tall, it will align the top of the Sprite along the top edge of the Canvas.

`MoveTo(number x, number y)`: Moves the Sprite's left top corner to the passed `(x,y)` coordinates.

`PointInDirection(number x, number y)`: Points the Sprite towards the point with passed `(x,y)` coordinates.

`PointTowards(component sprite)`: Points the Sprite towards point towards a specific Sprite, specified by the `sprite` argument. The new Heading will be parallel to the line joining the center points of the two Sprites.

BarcodeScanner

Properties
Result: The result after a barcode or QR is read.

Events
`AfterScan(text result)`: Raised after a successful scan.

Methods
`DoScan()`: Starts the scanner.

Button

Properties
BackgroundColor: Color of the Button background.

Enabled: If `true`, the Button is usable.

FontBold: Sets Button's text to bold.

FontItalic: Sets Button's text to display in italics.

FontSize: Sets Button's text point size.

FontTypeface: Sets Button's text font family.

Height: Button's height

Image: Path of the image to display as the Button's background.

Shape (designer only): Sets Button's shape. Values are: default, rounded, rectangular, oval. Does not apply if Image is being displayed.

ShowFeedback: Determines if a visual feedback is shown for a Button that has an Image as background.

Text: Sets the text that displays on the Button.

TextAlignment: Sets Button's text alignment. Values are left, centered, or right.

TextColor: Sets Button's text color.

Visible: Determines if Button is visible. If `true`, Button shows. If `false`, Button is hidden.

Width: Button's width

Events
`Click()`: Called when a user clicks the Button.

`GotFocus()`: Called when the user hovers over the Button and can then click it.

`LongClick()`: Called when a user long clicks the Button.

`LostFocus()`: Called when a user hovers off a Button and it is no longer clickable.

`TouchDown()`: Triggered when a Button is first touched.

`TouchUp()`: Triggered when a Button's touch ends.

Methods
None

Camcorder

Properties
None

Events
AfterRecording(text clip): Triggered after a video was recorded and provides the path of the video in the clip argument.

Methods
RecordVideo(): Records the video, and once the video is complete, this method will raise the AfterRecording event.

Camera

Properties
UseFront: Indicates if the front-facing camera should be used: true if yes, false if no. If there is no front-facing camera available, this property is ignored and the camera loads normally.

Events
AfterPicture(Text image): Triggered after a picture was taken and provides the path of the picture in the image argument.

Methods
TakePicture(): Invokes the device's camera and takes a picture and then will raise the AfterRecording event.

Canvas

Properties
BackgroundColor: The background color of the Canvas.
BackgroundImage: The file name of the Image that fills the background of the Canvas.
FontSize: The font size in pixels of text that is written on the Canvas.
Height: The height of the Canvas. This can be in pixels, set to fill the parent component or to "Automatic" which is chosen by the system.
LineWidth: The width of a line drawn on the Canvas.
PaintColor: The color of lines or circles drawn on the Canvas.
TextAlignment: Sets the alignment of text written to the Canvas to left, center, or right, set at design time only.
Visible: Determines if the Canvas is visible on the screen. This property is set to true if visible, false if hidden.
Width: The width of the Canvas. This can be in pixels, set to fill the parent component or to "Automatic", which is chosen by the system.

Events

`Dragged(number startX, number startY, number prevX, number prevY, number currentX, number currentY, Boolean draggedSprite)`:
Triggered when a user drags accross a Canvas. As a user drags across a Canvas:
- `startX` and `startY` are the Canvas coordinates where the user first touched the screen.
- `prevX` and `prevY` are the Canvas coordinates at the starting point of the drag.
- `currentX` and `currentY` are the Canvas coordinates at the current position of the drag.
- `draggedSprite` is `true` if a Sprite is being dragged, `false` if not.

`Flung(number x, number y, number speed, number heading, number xvel, number yvel, Boolean flungSprite)`:
Triggered when a user performs a fling gesture on the Canvas. A fling is a quick-swipe on the device. When there is a fling on a Canvas:
- `x` and `y` are the Canvas coordinates at the starting point of the fling.
- The `speed` is the pixels per millisecond of the fling.
- The `heading` is the direction in degrees of the fling (0–360).
- `xVel` and `yVel` indicate the velocity of the fling's vector.
- `flungSprite` is `true` if a Sprite is being flung, meaning there was a Sprite near the starting point of the fling, `false` if not.

`TouchDown(number x, number y)`
Triggered when the user touches the Canvas, by placing a finger down and holding it there. `x` and `y` are the Canvas coordinates of the touch.

`TouchUp(number x, number y)`
Triggered when the user stops touching the Canvas, by lifting their finger from a touch. `x` and `y` are the Canvas coordinates of the touch.

`Touched(number x, number y, Boolean touchedSprite)`
Triggered when the user touches the Canvas, by touching and then immediately lifting their finger. `x` and `y` are the Canvas coordinates of the touch.
`touchedSprite` is `true` if a Sprite is being dragged, `false` if not.

Methods

`Clear()`: Clears the Canvas except for the background color or image.

`DrawCircle(number x, number y, number r)`: Draws a filled in circle on the Canvas with a radius `r` and the center at the coordinates `(x, y)`.

`DrawLine(number x1, number y1, number x2, number y2)`: Draws a line between the coordinates `(x1, y1)` and `(x2, y2)`.

`DrawPoint(number x, number y)`: Draws a point at the `(x, y)` coordinates on the Canvas.

`DrawText(text text, number x, number y)`: Draws the `text` relative to the `(x, y)` coordinates using the FontSize and TextAlignment properties.

`DrawTextAtAngle(text text, number x, number y, number angle)`: Draws the `text` at the angle specified by `angle`, starting at the `(x, y)` coordinates using the FontSize and TextAlignment properties.

`number GetBackgroundPixelColor(number x, number y)`: Returns, as a number, the color at the `(x,y)` coordinates. It gets the color of a background, line, circle and drawn point at these coordinates but does not include Sprite colors.

`number GetPixelColor(number x, number y)`: Returns, as a number, the color the `(x,y)` point.

Save(): Will save a picture of the Canvas to the device. The ErrorOccured event of the Screen component will be called if the save fails.

text SaveAs(text fileName): Will save a picture of the Canvas to the device. The fileName must be provided and must have one of the following extensions: ".jpg", ".jpeg", ".png". The extension will determine the file type of JPEG or PNG.

SetBackgroundPixelColor(number x, number y, number color): Sets the color at the (x,y) coordinates to the value of color argument.

CheckBox

Properties

BackgroundColor: Color of the CheckBox's background.

Checked: If the CheckBox is checked, this property is true. It is false if it is not checked.

Enabled: If true, the CheckBox is usable and can be checked.

FontBold: Sets CheckBox's text to bold.

FontItalic: Sets CheckBox's text to display in italics.

FontSize: Sets CheckBox's text point size.

FontTypeface: Sets CheckBox's text font family.

Height: CheckBox's height.

Text: Sets the text that displays on the CheckBox.

TextColor: Sets CheckBox's text color.

Visible: Determines if CheckBox is visible. If true, CheckBox shows. If false, CheckBox is hidden.

Width: CheckBox's width.

Events

Changed(): User tapped and released check box.

GotFocus(): Called when the CheckBox becomes the focused component.

LostFocus(): Called when the CheckBox is not the focused component anymore.

Methods

None

Clock

Properties

TimerAlwaysFires: If this property is set to true, the timer will fire even if the application is not active on the screen.

TimerEnabled: If this property is set to true, the timer will fire.

TimerInterval: The timer's interval in milliseconds.

Events

Timer(): Triggered when the timer is fired.

Methods

InstantInTime AddDays(InstantInTime instant, number days): An instant in time which is the number of days, number argument, after the instant argument.

InstantInTime AddHours(InstantInTime instant, number hours): An instant in time which is the number of hours, hours argument, after the instant argument.

`InstantInTime AddMinutes(InstantInTime instant, number minutes)`: An instant in time which is the number of minutes, `minutes` argument, after the `instant` argument.

`InstantInTime AddMonths(InstantInTime instant, number months)`: An instant in time which is the number of months, `months` argument, after the `instant` argument.

`InstantInTime AddSeconds(InstantInTime instant, number seconds)`: An instant in time which is the number of seconds, `seconds` argument, after the `instant` argument.

`InstantInTime AddWeeks(InstantInTime instant, number weeks)`: An instant in time which is the number of weeks, `weeks` argument, after the `instant` argument.

`InstantInTime AddYears(InstantInTime instant, number years)`: An instant in time which is the number of years, `Years` argument, after the `instant` argument.

`number DayOfMonth(InstantInTime instant)`: A number representing the day of the month of the instant in time in the `instant` argument.

`number Duration(InstantInTime start, InstantInTime end)`: The milliseconds between instants `start` and `end`.

`text FormatDate(InstantInTime instant)`: A text representation of an instant which includes day, month, and year.

`text FormatDateTime(InstantInTime instant)`: A text representation of an instant which includes day, month, year, and time.

`text FormatTime(InstantInTime instant)`: A text representation of an instant which shows the time.

`number GetMillis(InstantInTime instant)`: Milliseconds since 1970 of the instant.

`number Hour(InstantInTime instant)`: Instant's hour of the day.

`InstantInTime MakeInstant(text from)`: Returns an instant derived from the `from` argument in the form MM/DD/YYYY hh:mm:ss or MM/DD/YYYY or hh:mm.

`InstantInTime MakeInstantFromMillis(number millis)`: An instant derived from a number of milliseconds from 1970.

`number Minute(InstantInTime instant)`: A number representing the minute of the hour.

`number Month(InstantInTime instant)`: A number (1–12) representing the month of the year.

`text MonthName(InstantInTime instant)`: Text name of the month.

`InstantInTime Now()`: The current instant from the device's time.

`number Second(InstantInTime instant)`: A number representing the second of the minute.

`number SystemTime()`: The device's time in milliseconds.

`number Weekday(InstantInTime instant)`: A number (1–7) representing the day of the week, 1 being Sunday, 2 Monday, and so on.

`text WeekdayName(InstantInTime instant)`: Text name of the day of the week.

`number Year(InstantInTime instant)`: Number representing the year of an instant.

ContactPicker

Properties

Enabled: If `true`, the ContactPicker is usable.

BackgroundColor: Color of the ContactPicker background.

ContactName: Selected contact's name.

EmailAddress: Selected contact's primary email address.

Picture: Selected contact's picture.

FontBold: Sets ContactPicker's text to bold.

FontItalic: Sets ContactPicker's text to display in italics.

FontSize: Sets ContactPicker's text point size.

FontTypeface: Sets ContactPicker's text font family.

Image: Path of the image to display as the ContactPicker background.

Shape (designer only): Sets ContactPicker's shape. Values are: default, rounded, rectangular, and oval. Does not apply if Image is being displayed.

ShowFeedback: Determines if a visual feedback is shown for a Button that as an Image as background.

Text: Sets ContactPicker's text that displays on the Button.

TextAlignment: Sets ContactPicker's text alignment. Values are: left, centered, right.

TextColor: Sets ContactPicker's text color.

Visible: Determines if ContactPicker is visible. If `true`, ContactPicker shows. If `false`, ContactPicker is hidden.

Width: ContactPicker's width

Height: ContactPicker height

Events

`AfterPicking()`: This event is triggered once the user has picked a contact.

`BeforePicking()`: This event is triggered once the user has tapped the Contact-Picker but before they have picked a contact.

`GotFocus()`: Called when ContactPicker becomes the focused component.

`LostFocus()`: Called when ContactPicker loses the focus.

Methods

`Open()`: Opens the `ContactPicker` programmatically as though it were tapped by a user.

DatePicker

Properties

BackgroundColor: The button's background color.

Day: The Day of the month that was last picked using the DatePicker.

Enabled: If `true`, the DatePicker is usable.

FontBold: Sets DatePicker font to bold.

FontItalic: Sets DatePicker font to italic.

FontSize: Sets DatePicker font's pixel size.

FontTypeface: Sets DatePicker font typeface (designer only).

Height: Sets DatePicker's height.

Image: Specifies the path of the button's image.

Month: the number of the Month that was last picked using the DatePicker. January = 1, December = 12.

MonthInText: Returns the name of the Month that was last picked using the DatePicker.

Shape: Specifies the button's shape (default, rounded, rectangular, oval). Only in the designer and only if an image is not specified.

ShowFeedback: Indicates if feedback is needed for a DatePicker with a background image.

Text: Sets the text that displays on the DatePicker.

TextAlignment: Aligns the text left, center, right. Only in designer.

TextColor: Color of Datepicker text.

Visible: Indicates if Datepicker is visible or hidden.

Width: Width of the Datepicker

Year: The Year that was last picked using the Datepicker.

Events

`AfterDateSet()`: Triggered after the user chooses a date.

`GotFocus()`: When Datepicker becomes the focused component.

`LostFocus()`: When Datepicker loses focus.

`TouchDown()`: Triggered when a button is first touched.

`TouchUp()`: Triggered when a button touch ends.

Methods

None

EmailPicker

Properties

Enabled: If `true`, the EmailPicker is usable.

BackgroundColor: Color of the EmailPicker's background.

FontBold: Sets EmailPicker's text to bold.

FontItalic: Sets EmailPicker's text to diplay in italics.

FontSize: Sets EmailPicker's text point size.

FontTypeface: Sets EmailPicker's text font family.

Text: Sets EmailPicker's text that displays on the Button.

TextAlignment: Sets EmailPicker's text alignment. Values are: left, centered, right.

TextColor: Sets EmailPicker's text color.

Hint: Shown in gray if Text property is empty.

Visible: Determines if EmailPicker's is visible. If `true`, EmailPicker's shows. If `false`, EmailPicker's is hidden.

Width: EmailPicker's width

Height: EmailPicker's height

Events

`GotFocus()`: Called when EmailPicker becomes the focused component.

`LostFocus()`: Called when EmailPicker loses the focus.

Methods

None

File

Properties
None

Events
`GotText(text text)`: Raised when the contents from a file have been read.

Methods
`AppendToFile(text text, text fileName)`: Will append the value passed in the `text` argument to the end of the file specified in the `fileName` argument. If the file does not exist, it will be created and then the text appended. Files that start with a "/" will be appended and/or created in the *sdcard* folder. Files without a "/" will be created/appended in the application folder.

`Delete(text fileName)`: Will delete the file specified in the `fileName` argument. Files that start with a "/" will be deleted from the *sdcard* folder. Files without a "/" will be deleted from the application folder.

`ReadFrom(text fileName)`: Reads text from the file specified in the `fileName` argument. Files that start with a "/" will be read from the *sdcard* folder. Files without a "/" will be read from the application folder.

`SaveFile(text text, text fileName)`: Creates and saves a file with the file name specified in the `fileName` argument. If a file already exists with the same name, the file will be overwritten. Files that start with a "/" will be saved in the *sdcard* folder. Files without a "/" will be saved in the application folder.

HorizontalArrangement

Properties
AlignHorizontal: A numeric value that indicates how the contents of the arrangement are horizontally aligned:
- 1 for left aligned
- 2 for centered
- 3 for right aligned

AlignVertical: A numeric value that indicates how the contents of the arrangement are vertically aligned:
- 1 for top aligned
- 2 for centered
- 3 for bottom aligned

Height: Height of the HorizontalArrangement in pixels.

Visible: Indicates by `true` of `false` if the HorizontalArrangement component is visible on the Screen.

Width: Width of the HorizontalArrangement in pixels.

Events
None

Methods
None

Image

Properties

Animation: To animate an image, values: ScrollRightSlow, ScrollRight, ScrollRightFast, ScrollLeftSlow, ScrollLeft, and ScrollLeftFast.

Height: Height of the Image.

Picture: File name of the picture shown by the Image component.

Visible: Determines if Image is visible. If `true`, Image shows. If `false`, Image is hidden.

Width: Width of the Image.

Events

None

Methods

None

ImagePicker

Properties

BackgroundColor: The background color of the ImagePicker.

Enabled: If `true` or set, the ImagePicker is usable.

FontBold: If set, the text on the ImagePicker bolded.

FontItalic: If set, the text on the ImagePicker is italicized.

FontSize: The point size of the text on the ImagePicker.

FontTypeface: The font family of the text on the ImagePicker.

Height: ImagePicker height in pixels.

Width: ImagePicker width in pixels.

Image: Image to display as the ImagePicker button.

Selection: File path to the image that was selected.

Text: The text on the ImagePicker button.

TextAlignment: Left, center, or right.

TextColor: The color of the text on the ImagePicker.

Visible: Indicates whether the component is visible. `true` if the component is showing and `false` if hidden.

Events

`AfterPicking()`: Triggered after a user picks an item with the ImagePicker.

`BeforePicking()`: Triggered after a user taps ImagePicker, but before an item is picked.

`GotFocus()`: Triggered when the ImagePicker gets the focus.

`LostFocus()`: Triggered when the ImagePicker loses the focus.

Methods

`Open()`: Programmatically opens the picker.

ImageSprite

Properties

Enabled: If `true`, the Sprite will move when its speed is non-zero. If `false`, the Sprite will not move.

Heading: The Heading property will set the direction of the Sprite in degrees. So, 90 (degrees) will set the direction of the Sprite to straight up, 180 will set the direction to left, 270 is down, and 0 is right. For example, if you want the Sprite to move from the bottom left corner to the top right corner in a straight line of a 200 by 200 pixel Canvas, you will set the heading to 45.

Interval: The Interval sets how *often* the Sprite will move and is in milliseconds. For example, 1,000 milliseconds equal one second, so the larger you set this property, the slower your Sprite will move.

Picture: The file name of the image associated with the Sprite, which determines the appearance of the Sprite.

Rotates: If the value is set to `true`, the ImageSprite will rotate in the direction of the Heading property. If it is `false`, it will not rotate.

Speed: The Speed property is the number of *pixels* to move each interval. So, if you have your Speed set to 10, and the Interval set at 1,000 milliseconds, your Sprite will move 10 pixels every second (in the direction set by the Heading).

Visible: `true` if the Sprite is visible, `false` if hidden.

X: The Sprite's left edge's horizontal position, relative to the left edge of the Canvas.

Y: The Sprite's top edge's vertical position, relative to the left edge of the Canvas.

Z: How the sprite should be layered relative to other sprites, with higher-numbered layers in front of lower-numbered layers.

Events

`CollidedWith(component other):`

Raised when two Sprites collide. The collision is detected by the Sprites un-rotated position, meaning tall narrow or short wide Sprite collisions will be inaccurate.

`Dragged(number startX, number startY, number prevX, number prevY, number currentX, number currentY):` Raised when a Sprite is dragged by a user. The `start (x,y)` coordinates represent where the user first touched the Canvas. The `prev (x, y)` coordinates represent where the drag began. The `current (x,y)` coordinates indicate the current position of the Sprite. Used in conjunction with the `MoveTo` method to make the Sprite move.

`EdgeReached(number edge):` Triggered when a Sprite reaches the edge of a Canvas. If this event calls `Bounce` with that edge, the Sprite will appear to bounce off of the edge it reached.

The `edge` argument tells which edge (or corner) was reached. The edge values are as follows:

- north = 1
- northeast = 2
- east = 3
- southeast = 4
- south = −1
- southwest = −2
- west = −3
- northwest = −4

`Flung(number x, number y, number speed, number heading, number xvel, number yvel):`

A fling is a quick swipe of the Canvas and will invoke this event. The event records the `x, y` coordinates of where the fling started and also provides the `x` and `y` velocities of the fling (`xvel` and `yvel`). The `speed` and `heading` values of the flung Ball are also available.

NoLongerCollidingWith(component other):
Triggered when two collided Sprites are no longer colliding.
TouchDown(number x, number y):
Triggered when the user touches the Sprite, by placing a finger down and holding it there. x and y are the Canvas coordinates of the touch.
TouchUp(number x, number y):
Triggered when the user stops touching the Sprite, by lifting their finger from a touch. x and y are the Canvas coordinates of the touch.
Touched(number x, number y, Boolean touchedSprite)
Triggered when the user touches the Sprite, by touching and then immediately lifting their finger. x and y are the Canvas coordinates of the touch. touched-Sprite is true if a Sprite is being dragged, false if not.

Methods

Bounce(number edge): Simulates the Sprite bouncing off an edge or corner. Generally, the edge argument is the one returned by EdgeReached.
Boolean CollidingWith(component other): Indicates whether there is a collision between the current and the passed other Sprite, true or false value.
MoveIntoBounds(): If part of the Sprite moves outside of the Canvas bounds, this method is used to place the entire Sprite back on the Canvas. If the Sprite is too wide for the Canvas, it will align the Sprite on the left edge. If it is too tall, it will align the top of the Sprite along the top edge of the Canvas.
MoveTo(number x, number y): Moves the Sprite's left top corner to the passed (x,y) coordinates.
PointInDirection(number x, number y): Points the Sprite towards the point with passed (x,y) coordinates.
PointTowards(component sprite): Points the Sprite towards point towards a specific Sprite, specified by the sprite argument. The new Heading will be parallel to the line joining the center points of the two Sprites.

Label

Properties

BackgroundColor: Color of the Label's background.
FontBold: Sets Label's text to bold.
FontItalic: Sets Label's text to display in italics.
FontSize: Sets Label's text point size.
FontTypeface: Sets Label's text font family.
Height: Label's height
Text: Sets the text that displays on the Label.
TextAlignment: Sets Label's text alignment. Values are left, centered, or right.
TextColor: Sets Label's text color.
Visible: Determines if the Label is visible. If true, the Label shows. If false, the Label is hidden.
Width: Label's width

Events

None

Methods

None

ListPicker

Properties

BackgroundColor: Color of the ListPicker's background.

ElementsFromString: A comma delimited string that determines the list.

FontBold: Sets ListPicker's text to bold.

FontItalic: Sets ListPicker's text to display in italics.

FontSize: Sets ListPicker's text point size.

FontTypeface: Sets ListPicker's text font family.

Height: ListPicker's height

Items: List of items, separated by commas, to display in the ListPicker.

Selection: The List element that is selected.

Text: Sets the text that displays on the ListPicker.

TextColor: Sets ListPicker's text color.

Visible: Determines if ListPicker is visible. If `true`, ListPicker shows. If `false`, ListPicker is hidden.

Width: The ListPicker's width.

Events

`AfterPicking()`: This is called after a user has selected an item from the List-Picker.

`BeforePicking()`: This is called after the user has tapped the ListPicker, but before an item is selected.

`GotFocus()`: Called when the ListPicker becomes the focused component.

`LostFocus()`: Called when the ListPicker is not the focused component anymore.

Methods

`Open()`: Invokes the ListPicker programmatically as if the user tapped it.

ListView

Properties

Elements: Text elements that determine your list.

ElementsFromString: A comma-delimited string that determines the list.

Height: The height of the list

Selection: Select text item of the ListView.

SelectionIndex: The selected index of the item selected from the ListView, starting at 1 for the first item.

ShowFilterBar: Indicates whether or not to show the filter bar. `true` will show the bar, `false` will hide it.

Visible: Determines if ListView is visible. If `true`, ListView shows. If `false`, ListView is hidden.

Width: The width of the list.

Events

`AfterPicking()`: Raised after a selection is made.

Methods

None

LocationSensor

Properties

Accuracy: Android device's accuracy level, in meters.

Altitude: If available, the Android device's altitude.

AvailableProviders: Hold the list of available service providers, for example: GPS or Network.

CurrentAddress: Android's current physical street address.

DistanceInterval:

You can set the Location Sensor to update location information after the device has moved a certain distance by setting the DistanceInterval property. The interval is in meters, and if it were set to 10, the location information would be updated when the device moves *at least* ten meters from the location of the previous update. While this property can be useful, keep in mind that it does not update at every ten-meter move exactly. It only indicates that it will not update before a ten-meter change.

Enabled: If `true`, location information of the device is available to the application.

HasAccuracy: If `true`, the accuracy of the Android device can be determined.

HasAltitude: If `true`, the altitude of the Android device can be determined.

HasLongitudeLatitude: If `true`, the longitude and latitude of the Android device can be determined.

Latitude: The latitude of the Android device.

Longitude: The longitude of the Android device.

ProviderLocked: If `true`, the device will not change service providers.

ProviderName: The name of the current service provider.

TimeInterval:

The TimeInterval property sets the minimum time interval between updates. If you set this property to 600,000 it will wait ten minutes before another update. Note that this does not mean the update will occur every ten minutes exactly, only that it won't happen before ten minutes have passed since the previous update.

Events

`LocationChanged(number latitude, number longitude, number altitude)`: Raised when the Android device reports a new location.

`StatusChanged(text provider, text status)`: If status of the service provider changes, this event will be raised.

Methods

`number LatitudeFromAddress(text locationName)`: Returns the latitude of the address passed to `locationName`.

`number LongitudeFromAddress(text locationName)`: Returns the longitude of the address passed to `locationName`.

OrientationSensor

Properties

Available: `true` if Android device has an orientation sensor available, `false` if it does not.

Enabled: If set to `true`, the OrientationSensor component is enabled for use.

Azimuth: The Android device's azimuth angle.

Pitch: The Android device's pitch angle.

Roll: The Android device's roll angle.

Magnitude

> The Magnitude is used to determine how steep the phone is being tilted in any direction. As the degrees of the Roll and Pitch move away from zero degrees toward 90 or –90, the Magnitude increases. The Magnitude will have a value between 0 and 1, with zero being no tilt and 1 being completely vertical.

Angle

> Returns the angle that determines what direction the device is being tilted and returns a number that we can use to move objects in the titled direction.

Events

`OrientationChanged(number azimuth, number pitch, number roll)`: The Orientation Sensor's `OrientationChanged` Event is called each time the device's orientation changes.

Methods

None

Notifier

Properties

None

Events

`AfterChoosing(Text choice)`: Called after the user has clicked a button in a choose dialog box. The `choice` parameter will hold the text that is displayed on the button that the user clicked.

`AfterTextInput(Text response)`: Called after the user has closed a text dialog box. The `response` parameter will hold the text that was entered as input into the dialog box.

Methods

`ShowMessageDialog(Text message, Text title, Text buttonText)`: Displays a message dialog box displaying the message and title passed as arguments. The dialog box will also have a button displaying the given button text. The button will dismiss the dialog when clicked.

`ShowChooseDialog(Text message, Text title, Text button1Text, Text button2Text, Boolean cancelable)`: Displays a choose dialog box displaying the message, title and button texts passed as arguments. If the `cancelable` parameter is `true`, the dialog box will also have a Cancel button. The `AfterChoosing` event occurs after the user clicks one of the buttons.

`ShowTextDialog(Text message, Text title, Boolean cancelable)`

Displays a text dialog box displaying the message and title passed as arguments, and an OK button. If the `cancelable` parameter is `true`, the dialog box will also have a Cancel button. The `AfterTextInput` event occurs after the user clicks dismisses the dialog.

`ShowAlert(Text message)`: Temporarily displays a message specified by the `message` parameter, which vanishes after a few seconds.

```
LogError(Text message)
LogInfo(Text message)
LogWarning(Text message)
```
These methods, intended for debugging purposes, write messages to the log files on the Android device. You use Android debugging tools, such as the Android Debug Bridge (ADB), to read these log files.

PasswordTextBox

Properties
BackgroundColor: Color of the PasswordTextBox background.

Enabled: If `true`, the PasswordTextBox is usable.

FontBold: Sets PasswordTextBox's text to bold.

FontItalic: Sets PasswordTextBox's text to diplay in italics.

FontSize: Sets PasswordTextBox's text point size.

FontTypeface: Sets PasswordTextBox's text font family.

Height: PasswordTextBox's height.

Hint: Hint for the password.

Text: Sets the text that displays on the PasswordTextBox.

TextAlignment: Sets PasswordTextBox's text alignment. Values are: left, centered, right.

TextColor: Sets PasswordTextBox's text color.

Visible: Determines if PasswordTextBox is visible. If `true`, PasswordTextBox shows. If `false`, PasswordTextBox is hidden.

Width: PasswordTextBox's width.

Events
`GotFocus()`: Called when the PasswordTextBox becomes the focused component.

`LostFocus()`: Called when the PasswordTextBox is not the focused component anymore.

Methods
None

PhoneCall

Properties
PhoneNumber: Phone number to call

Events
None

Methods
`MakePhoneCall()`: Calls the number stored in the component's PhoneNumber property.

PhoneNumberPicker

Properties
Enabled: If `true`, the PhoneNumberPicker is usable.

BackgroundColor: Color of the PhoneNumberPicker background.

ContactName: Selected contact's name.

EmailAddress: Selected contact's primary email address.

PhoneNumber: Selected contact's phone number.

Picture: Selected contact's picture.

FontBold: Sets PhoneNumberPicker's text to bold.

FontItalic: Sets PhoneNumberPicker's text to display in italics.

FontSize: Sets PhoneNumberPicker's text point size.

FontTypeface: Sets PhoneNumberPicker's text font family.

Image: Path of the image to display as the PhoneNumberPicker background.

Shape (designer only): Sets PhoneNumberPicker's shape. Values are: default, rounded, rectangular, and oval. Does not apply if an image is being displayed.

ShowFeedback: Determines if a visual feedback is shown for a Button that as an Image as background.

Text: Sets PhoneNumberPicker's text that displays on the Button.

TextAlignment: Sets PhoneNumberPicker's text alignment. Values are: left, centered, right.

TextColor: Sets PhoneNumberPicker's text color.

Visible: Determines if PhoneNumberPicker is visible. If `true`, PhoneNumberPicker shows. If `false`, PhoneNumberPicker is hidden.

Width: PhoneNumberPicker's width.

Height: PhoneNumberPicker's height.

Events

`AfterPicking()`: This event is triggered once the user has picked a contact.

`BeforePicking()`: This event is triggered once the user has tapped the Phone-NumberPicker, but before they have picked a contact.

`GotFocus()`: Called when PhoneNumberPicker becomes the focused component.

`LostFocus()`: Called when PhoneNumberPicker loses the focus.

Methods

`Open()`: Opens the PhoneNumberPicker programmatically as though it were tapped by a user.

Player

Properties

IsLooping: Indicates if media is looping or not.

IsPlaying: Indicates if media is playing or not.

Source: The file name of the audio or video file of the Player component.

Volume: Volume of the Player, a number between 0 and 100.

Events

`Completed()`: Indicates that the media is finished playing.

Methods

`Pause()`: Pauses the media file playing.

`Start()`: Starts playing the media file.

`Stop()`: Stops playing the media file.

`Vibrate(number milliseconds)`: Makes the phone vibrate (with the device's vibration motor) for the given number of milliseconds.

Screen

Properties

AlignHorizontal: Indicates how to align items horizontally on the Screen, 1 for left aligned, 2 for centered, 3 for right aligned.

AlignVertical: Indicates how to align items vertically on the Screen, 1 for top aligned, 2 for centered, 3 for bottom aligned.

BackgroundColor: The background color of the screen.

BackgroundImage: If set, the image that makes up the background of the Screen.

Height: Height of the Screen, in pixels.

Icon: This is the launch icon that shows on a phone that has installed the application. It should be around 48X48 in size and should be PNG or JPG; other formats may prevent App Inventor from packaging the application.

ScreenOrientation: The Screen orientation value requested, landscape, portrait, sensor, user, and unspecified are the common values.

Scrollable: In the Designer, a developer can check this property to indicate that the Screen is scrollable. If it is checked, a vertical scrollbar will be available for the user and the Screen height can surpass that of the device. If it is not checked, the Screen is limited to the device's screen height.

VersionCode (designer only: main screen only): The VersionCode defaults to 1. This number needs to be increased by one each time you make a change and want to re-upload it to the Play Store, whether it is a small or large change.

VersionName (designer only: main screen only): The VersionName property is a string. It can hold any string value, but it defaults to 1.0. Oftentimes a developer will increase the number by .1 for a minor change and by 1 for a major change. For example, a small change might increase the VersionName from 1.2 to 1.3. If there is then a major change, the VersionName will be 2.0.

Title: The title that will show on the upper left of the device screen when the application is running. This is usually the name of the app, but can be anything and modifiable programmatically as the app runs.

Width: Width of the Screen, in pixels.

Events

BackPressed(): Triggered when the device's Back button is pressed.

Initialize(): Triggered when the application begins, it's a good place to initialize values and other set up tasks.

ErrorOccurred(component component, text functionName, number errorNumber, text message): Triggered when an error occurs, and is currently used for errors in the following:

- LEGO MINDSTORMS Nxt* components
- Bluetooth components
- Twitter component
- SoundRecorder component
- ActivityStarter: the StartActivity is called, but no activity that corresponds to the properties
- LocationSensor: when LatitudeFromAddress or LongitudeFromAddress fails.
- Player: When setting the Source property fails.
- Sound: When setting the Source property fails or when the Play function fails.
- VideoPlayer: When setting the Source property fails.

A default notification is show by the system with a message and an error number. This event can be used to change the default message of the error using the `errorNumber` to determine which error has occurred.

`OtherScreenClosed(text otherScreenName, any result)`: Triggered when control is passed back to this `Screen` because another has closed.

`ScreenOrientationChanged()`: Screen orientation changed

Methods

`CloseScreenAnimation(text animType)`: Animation used when closing the `Screen`. Options are `default`, `fade`, `zoom`, `slidehorizontal`, `slidevertical`, and `none`.

`OpenScreenAnimation(text animType)`: Animation used when opening the `Screen`. Options are `default`, `fade`, `zoom`, `slidehorizontal`, `slidevertical`, and `none`.

Slider

Properties

ColorLeft: The color that is left of the thumb on the Slider.

ColorRight: The color that is right of the thumb on the Slider.

The Slider component has a MinValue property and a MaxValue property that must be set to numeric values. By default, the MinValue property is set to 10.0, and the MaxValue property is set to 30.0. The MinValue property is the Slider's minimum value and the MaxValue property is the Slider's maximum value. When the thumb slider is all the way to the left, its position is the same as MinValue. As you drag the thumb slider to the right, its position increases. When the thumb slider is all the way to the right, its position is the same as MaxValue.

MaxValue: Must be set to a numeric value. By default, the MaxValue property is set to 30.0, which is the Slider's maximum value and the value when the thumb slider is all the way to the right. Resetting this value will change the Thumbposition to half way between the new MaxValue and the MinValue property.

MinValue: Must be set to a numeric value. By default, the MinValue property is set to 10.0, which is the Slider's minimum value and the value when the thumb slider is all the way to the left. Resetting this value will change the Thumbposition to half way between the new MinValue and the MaxValue property.

ThumbPosition: A numeric value that is the position for the Slider's thumb. Can have values between and including the MinValue and MaxValue.

Visible: Indicates whether the Slider is visible on the Screen or not.

Width: Width of the Slider, in pixels.

Events

`PositionChanged(number thumbPosition)`: Triggered when the ThumbPosition property has changed.

Methods

None

Sound

Properties

Source: The file name of the audio file of the Sound component.

MinimumInterval: Minimum time interval before the sound is repeated.

Events

None

Methods

`Pause()`: Pauses the audio file.

`Play()`: Starts playing the audio file.

`Resume()`: Resumes a paused audio file.

`Stop()`: Stops the audio file.

`Vibrate(number millisecs)`: Makes the phone vibrate (with the device's vibration motor) for the given number of milliseconds.

SpeechRecognizer

Properties

Result: Stores the text of the latest recording.

Events

`AfterGettingText(text result)`: Raised after a recording has completed and the text is produced, the text produced is stored in `result`.

`BeforeGettingText()`: Raised immediately before the SpeechRecognizer is invoked or started.

Methods

`GetText()`: Records users speech and converts the speech to text, then raises the `AfterGettingText` when action is complete.

Spinner

Properties

Elements: The text elements to choose from.

ElementsFromString: Allows the elements to be determined from a comma-delimited string.

Height: Height of the Spinner

Prompt: The current title for the Spinner.

Selection: The current selected item in the Spinner, in text format.

SelectionIndex: The index of the selected item, starting at 1. Zero if no selection.

Visible: Determines if Spinner is visible. If `true`, Spinner shows. If `false`, Spinner is hidden.

Width: Width of the Spinner

Events

`AfterSelecting(text selection)`: Triggered after the user selects an item from the Spinner's dropdown list.

Methods

`DisplayDropdown()`: Displays the dropdown list so that a selection can be made.

TableArrangement

Properties

Columns (number-of-columns): The number of columns in the TableArrangement.

Height: Height of the TableArrangement, in pixels.

Rows (number-of-rows): The number of rows in the TableArrangement.

Visible: Indicates whether or not the TableArrangement component is visible on the Screen.

Width: Width of the TableArrangement, in pixels.

Events

None

Methods

None

TextBox

Properties

Enabled: If `true`, the TextBox is usable.

BackgroundColor: Color of the TextBox background.

FontBold: Sets TextBox's text to bold.

FontItalic: Sets TextBox's text to display in italics.

FontSize: Sets TextBox's text point size.

FontTypeface: Sets TextBox's text font family.

Height: TextBox's height

Hint: Hint for the password.

Text: Sets the text that displays on the TextBox.

TextAlignment: Sets TextBox's text alignment. Values are: left, centered, right.

TextColor: Sets TextBox's text color.

Visible: Determines if TextBox is visible. If `true`, TextBox shows. If `false`, TextBox is hidden.

Width: TextBox's width

MultiLine: Indicates by `true` or `false` whether the TextBox accepts multiple input lines. Because there is no Done key on the keyboard of a MultiLine Text-box, the application should use the `HideKeyboard` method to hide the keyboard using this type of `TextBox`.

NumbersOnly: Indicates by `true` or `false` whether this TextBox accepts only numeric values, applies to keyboard entry only.

Events

GotFocus(): Called when the TextBox becomes the focused component.

LostFocus(): Called when the TextBox is not the focused component anymore.

Methods

HideKeyboard(): Used with a MultiLine TextBox component to hide the keyboard.

Texting

Properties

GoogleVoiceEnabled: Determines if the component will be able to be used with Google Voice compatibility.

PhoneNumber: The phone number the text message will be sent to.

Message: Holds the text of the message.

ReceivingEnabled:

This property takes the numeric values 1, 2, and 3, which are defined as follows: 1-Off, 2-Foreground, and 3-Always. If this property is set to 1, the application will ignore all messages. If set to 2, messages will be received when the application is running, but not when the application is inactive. If set to 3, the application will receive the messages while running and queue the messages if it is not running or inactive. If the messages are queued, action in the `MessagedRecieved` event will happen when the application becomes active. This may result in several messages being processed at once.

Events

`MessageReceived(text number, text messageText)`

The `ReceiveMessage` event is triggered by a text message coming into your device. Based on the ReceivingEnabled property value (see property description above), this event will listen for text messages when the application is active or dormant.

Methods

`SendMessage()`: Sends the text stored in the Message property to the number stored in the PhoneNumber property.

TextToSpeech

Properties

Country: The three-character country code used for speech.

Language: The three-character language code used for speech.

Result: Path to the speech that is was generated.

Pitch: Sets the Pitch to a value between 0 and 2 where lower values lower the tone of the voice and greater values increase it.

SpeechRate: Sets the SpeechRate to a value between 0 and 2 where lower values slow down the pitch and greater values speed it up.

Events

`AfterSpeaking(Text result)`: Raised once the speech of the text is spoken, has access to the speech in the `result` argument.

`BeforeSpeaking()`: Raised immediately before the speech of the text is spoken.

Methods

`Speak(Text message)`: Speaks the text passed in the `message` argument.

Language and Country Codes

Language codes are shown in lowercase and country codes for each language are shown in uppercase.

ces (Czech)
> CZE

spa (Spanish)
> ESP
> USA

deu (German)
> AUT
> BEL
> CHE
> DEU
> LIE
> LUX

fra (French)
> BEL
> CAN
> CHE
> FRA
> LUX

nld (Dutch)
> BEL
> NLD

ita (Italian)
> CHE
> ITA

pol (Polish)
> POL

eng (English)
> AUS
> BEL
> BWA
> BLZ
> CAN
> GBR
> HKG
> IRL
> IND
> JAM
> MHL
> MLT
> NAM
> NZL
> PHL
> PAK
> SGP
> TTO
> USA
> VIR
> ZAF
> ZWE

TimePicker

A button that, when clicked, launches a pop-up dialog to allow the user to select a time.

Properties

Enabled: If true, the TimePicker is usable.

BackgroundColor: Color of the TimePicker background.

FontBold: Sets TimePicker text to bold.

FontItalic: Sets TimePicker text to diplay in italics.

FontSize: Sets TimePicker text point size.

FontTypeface: Sets the TimePicker's text font family.

Height: TimePicker height

Hour: The hour which was last picked, in 24-hour clock. 8:00 PM. will return 20.

Image: TimePicker background image.

Minute: The minute which was last picked.

Shape: Indicates the button's shape (default, rounded, rectangular, oval). Does not apply if an image is set.

ShowFeedback: Indicates if feedback should show for a TimePicker that has a background image.

Text: The Text property of the TimePicker.

TextAlignment: Sets TimePicker text alignment. Values are: left, centered, right.

TextColor: Sets TimePicker text color.

Visible: Indicates whether or not (true or false) the TimePicker is visible on the Screen.

Width: Width of the TimePicker in pixels.

Events

AfterTimeSet(): Raised when time is set.

GotFocus(): Called when the TimePicker becomes the focused component.

LostFocus(): Called when the TimePicker loses focus.

Methods

None

TinyDB

Properties

None

Events

None

Methods

StoreValue(text tag, valueToStore): Tag-value pair, the value of valueToStore is stored under the value of the tag argument.

GetValue(text tag): Searches the TinyDB for the tag argument and returns the associated value. If the tag was not found, an empty string is returned.

TinyWebDB

Properties

ServiceURL: the URL of the Web server and path of the database.

Events

GotValue(text tagFromWebDB, any valueFromWebDB): Raised when the value of a tag is retrieved successfully from the server.

ValueStored(): Raised when a value is successfully stored to the TinyWebDB on the server.

WebServiceError(text message): Raised when there is a communication error when communicating with the Web service.

Methods

GetValue(text tag): Calls the Web service and request the value of the tag passed into the method and accepts whatever the Web service returns. The service should turn the value of tag or some other indication if the value is not found.

StoreValue(text tag, any valueToStore): Calls the Web service and requests that it store the valueToStore under the tag in the TinyWebDB.

Twitter

Properties

ConsumerKey: Consumer Key generated by Twitter

ConsumerSecret: Consumer Secret generated by Twitter

DirectMessages:

The list of the most recent messages that tag the user, starting with an empty list. To populate the property with the list the program must:

1. Call the Authorize method.
2. Wait for the IsAuthorized event.
3. Call the RequestDirectMessages method.
4. Wait for the DirectMessagesReceived event.

Then the property will be populated with the direct messages retrieved and hold that list of messages until RequestDirectMessages is called again.

Followers:

The list of the followers of the user, starting with an empty list. To populate the property with the list the program must:

1. Call the Authorize method.
2. Wait for the IsAuthorized event.
3. Call the RequestFollowers method.
4. Wait for the FollowersReceived event.

Then the property will be populated with the list of followers retrieved and hold that list of messages until RequestFollowers is called again.

FriendTimeline:

The list of the twenty most recent messages of followed users, starting with an empty list. To populate the property with the list, the program must:

1. Call the Authorize method.
2. Wait for the IsAuthorized event.

3. Specify users to follow with one or more calls to the `Follow` method.
4. Call the `RequestFriendTimeline` method.
5. Wait for the `FriendTimelineReceived` event.

Then the property will be populated with the list of messages retrieved and hold that list of messages until `RequestFriendTimeline` is called again.

Mentions:

This property contains a list of mentions of the logged-in user. Initially, the list is empty. To set it, the program must:

The list mentions of the user, starting with an empty list. To populate the property with the list the program must:

1. Call the `Authorize` method.
2. Wait for the `IsAuthorized` event.
3. Call the `RequestMentions` method.
4. Wait for the `MentionsReceived` event.

Then the property will be populated with the list of mentions retrieved and hold that list of messages until `RequestMentions` is called again.

SearchResults:

The list of search results after the program.

1. Calls the `SearchTwitter` method.
2. Waits for the `SearchSuccessful` event.

SearchResults will then be equal to the parameter to `SearchSuccessful`.

Username:

If the user is authorized, this is the value of the logged in user's username.

Events

`DirectMessagesReceived(list messages)`

Triggered when messages are retrieved from the `RequestDirectMessages` method call. The list of the messages is then stored in the `messages` parameter or the Messages property.

`FollowersReceived(list followers)`

Triggered when all followers are retrieved from the `RequestFollowers` method call. The list of the followers is then stored in the `followers` parameter or the Followers property.

`FriendTimelineReceived(list timeline)`

Triggered when messages are retrieved from the `RequestFriendTimeline` method call. The list of the messages are then stored in the `timeline` parameter or the Timeline property as Lists. The Lists will each contain a status update (username message).

`IsAuthorized():`

Raised after the `Authorize` or the `toCheckAuthorized` method is called and an authorization is successful. Once this event is raised, all other methods in the component can be used.

`MentionsReceived(list mentions):`

Triggered when mentions are retrieved from the `RequestMentions` method call. The list of mentions is then stored in the `mentions` parameter or the `Mentions` property.

`SearchSuccessful(list searchResults):`

Triggered when search results are retrieved from the `SearchSuccessful` method call. The results are then stored in the `results` parameter or the Results property.

Methods

`Authorize()`: Redirects and request that user login to Twitter using the Web browser and OAuth0 protocol, assuming the user is not already authorized.

`CheckAuthorized()`: Checks if user is already authorized, and if so, causes `IsAuthorized` event handler to be called.

`DeAuthorize()`: Cancels the Twitter authorization from the application instance.

`DirectMessage(text user, text message)`:

Assuming authorization has passed, this method will send a direct and private message to the user specified in the `user` argument. The method trims the message down to 160 characters.

`Follow(text user)`: Starts following a user.

`RequestDirectMessages()`:

Assuming authorization has passed, this method requests the twenty most recent direct messages sent to the user. This method raises the `Direct MessagesReceived` event and populates the DirectMessages property to the list of messages.

`RequestFollowers()`: Retrieves the list of followers of the user.

`RequestFriendTimeline()`: Retrieves the list of the twenty most recent messages of people the user follows.

`RequestMentions()`.

Assuming authorization has passed, this method requests the twenty most recent mentions of the user. This method raises the `MentionsReceived` event and populates the Mentions property to the list of mentions.

`SearchTwitter(text query)`:

Searches Twitter for the text stored in `query`.

`SetStatus(text status)`:

Assuming authorization has passed, this method will set the user's status to the text stored in `status`. This method will trim the status to 160 characters.

`StopFollowing(text user)`: Quits following the username stored in the `user` argument.

VerticalArrangement

Properties

Visible:

If `true`, component and its contents are visible.

Height:

Vertical arrangement height (y-size).

Width:

Vertical arrangement width (x-size).

AlignHorizontal: A numeric value that indicates how the contents of the arrangement are horizontally aligned:

- 1 for left aligned
- 2 for centered
- 3 for right aligned

AlignVertical: A numeric value that indicates how the contents of the arrangement are vertically aligned:

- 1 for top aligned
- 2 for centered
- 3 for bottom aligned

Events
    None

Methods
    None

VideoPlayer

Properties

Source: The file name of the video file of the VideoPlayer component.

Visible: Indicates whether the component is visible. `true` if the component is showing and `false` if hidden.

FullScreen: Indicates whether the video is playing in full-screen mode. `true` if the component is in full screen and `false` if not.

Height: VideoPlayer height in pixels.

Width: VideoPlayer width in pixels.

Volume: A number between 0 and 100 for volume. Zero is no volume and 100 for loudest. Any number less than zero will be treated as zero. Any number greater than 100 is treated as the number 100.

Events

`Completed()`: Indicates that the video is finished playing.

Methods

`Pause()`: Pauses the video file.

`Start()`: Starts the video file.

`SeekTo(number millisecs)`: Goes to the specified milliseconds in the video file (from the beginning).

`number GetDuration()`: Returns the milliseconds of the duration of the video.

Answers to Checkpoints

Chapter 1

1.1 A computer is a device that follows instructions for manipulating and storing information.

1.2 A computer program is a set of instructions that the computer follows to perform a task.

1.3 An algorithm is a set of well-defined logical steps that must be taken in order to perform a task.

1.4 Machine language is the only language that computers understand.

1.5 Because computers only understand machine language (which consists of binary numbers), programming languages were invented to make programming easier. Programming languages consist of words, which are easier for people to understand.

1.6 False

1.7 The Designer

1.8 The part of the app that the user sees, and interacts with.

1.9 No, it does not.

1.10 The Palette provides a list of components that you can use to build your app.

1.11 The Viewer column shows a rectangular area that represents the app's screen. You design an app's user interface by dragging components from the Palette and dropping them onto the simulated screen in the Viewer.

1.12 The Components column shows a hierarchical tree listing all of the components that you have placed in your app. Each time you drag a component from the Palette and drop it onto the Viewer, an entry representing that component appears in the Component column. You can use the Component column to select any component in your app.

1.13 The Media column allows you to manage the media files (images, videos, and audio files) that you want to use in your app. Because App Inventor stores your apps in the cloud, you have to upload any media files that you want to use in an app. The Media column allows you to upload such files to the App Inventor server, download them from the server to your computer, and delete them from the server when they are no longer needed.

1.14 The Properties column lets you examine and change a component's properties.

1.15 The Blocks Editor is where you assemble code blocks that perform actions.

1.16 A code block is a shape that looks something like a puzzle piece. App Inventor provides numerous blocks that represent actions and data. You assemble code blocks in the Blocks Editor to create an app's code.

1.17 To create a new emulator, click *Connect* at the top of the screen, and then click *Emulator* on the menu that appears. It might take several minutes for the emulator to be created in the computer's memory. Once the emulator has been created and initialized, it will appear on the screen.

1.18 The My Projects screen

1.19 `Screen1`

1.20 Title

1.21 It displays text on the app's screen.

1.22 Text

1.23 Automatic, Fill parent, A Specified Number of Pixels

1.24 Click the *Rename* button at the bottom of the Components column, and then type the new name into the *Rename Component* dialog box. Default names are not very descriptive, so you should always change a component's name to something that is more meaningful. A component's name should reflect the purpose of the component.

1.25 • Component names can contain only letters, numbers, and underscores (_).
• The first character of a component name must be a letter.
• Component names cannot contain spaces.

1.26 Text

1.27 • Left – Components are aligned along the left edge of the screen
• Center – Components are aligned in the center of the screen
• Right – Components are aligned along the right edge of the screen

1.28 • Top – Components are aligned along the top of the screen
• Center – Components are aligned in the center of the screen
• Bottom – Components are aligned along the bottom of the screen

1.29 A program that waits for specific events to happen, and then it responds to those events. An event is an action that takes place, such as the user clicking a button, or sliding his or her finger across the device's screen. An incoming text message is also an event, as well as when the user tilts or shakes the phone.

1.30 They will be listed under `Screen1`, or the name of the Screen component that they belong to.

1.31 In the Blocks Palette, a drawer holds a collection of blocks.

1.32 BackgroundColor

1.33 FontSize

1.34 FontBold

Chapter 2

2.1 BackgroundImage

2.2 In the Media column

2.3 Use the set `Screen1.BackgroundImage` to block.

2.4 Picture

2.5 The text is displayed on top of the image.

2.6 Both are found in the Media section of the palette.

2.7 Source

2.8 With its `Play` block.

2.9 Pause

2.10 1000

2.11 The Sound component is recommended for short audio files. If you want to play a long audio file, such as an entire song, it is recommended that you use the more efficient Player component instead.

2.12 Go to the *Built-In* section of the Blocks column, and click *Colors*.

2.13 13 blocks

2.14 When you need to create code that changes the value of a color property while the app is running.

2.15 Components that are placed inside a HorizontalArrangement are arranged horizontally, across the screen.

2.16 Components that are placed inside a VerticalArrangement are arranged vertically.

2.17 Components that are placed inside a TableArrangement are arranged in a table, with rows and columns.

2.18 VerticalArrangement

2.19 They help someone who is reading the program's code to understand the instructions.

2.20 No

2.21 In the Blocks Editor, you can add a comment to any block by right-clicking the block, and then selecting *Add Comment* from the menu that pops up. This causes a small question mark to appear on the block. Click the question mark to open a note editor. You can type any information you wish into the note editor.

Chapter 3

3.1   TextBox

3.2   From its Text property

3.3   The user cannot enter input into it.

3.4   Check the NumbersOnly property.

3.5   A clump of code that gives you a value.

3.6   Operands are the values that the operator works with. The math operator blocks require two operands.

3.7   It returns a number rounded to a specified number of decimal places.

3.8   A function is a method that performs an operation, and then gives you a value.

3.9   Calling a function means to execute it.

3.10 A piece of data that is passed to a function or method.

3.11 A variable is a name that represents a value that is stored in the computer's memory.

3.12 Go to the *Built-In* section and click *Variables*.

3.13 Just click the name that appears on the block and type the new name.

3.14 Plug a block, such as a number block or a text string block, into the variable initialization's to socket.

3.15 The get block allows you to get a variable's value, and the set block allows you to set a variable's value (assign a value to it).

3.16 The part of a program in which a variable may be accessed.

3.17 The scope of a local variable is the variable's initialization block. The scope of a global variable is the entire workspace, so it is accessible to all of the code in the workspace.

3.18 With the Slider's MinValue and MaxValue properties

3.19 A PositionChanged event occurs

3.20 The thumbPosition block is a special type of variable known as a parameter variable. The purpose of a parameter variable is to hold a piece of data that is passed to the event handler. When the PositionChanged event handler executes, the thumbPosition parameter variable will hold the current position of the thumb slider.

Chapter 4

4.1   Boolean

4.2   An expression that gives either true or false as its value.

4.3   if then, if then else, and if then else if

4.4   Go to the *Built-In* section and open the *Control* drawer.

4.5   A Boolean expression.

4.6   Greater than, greater than or equal to, less than, less than or equal to, equal to, not equal to.

4.7   Go to the *Built-in* section and open the *Math* drawer.

4.8   If the Boolean expression is `true`, the instructions that appear in the `then` socket will be executed. If the Boolean expression is `false`, nothing happens (the instructions that appear in the `then` socket will be skipped).

4.9   If the Boolean expression is `true`, the instructions that appear in the `then` socket will be executed.

4.10   If the Boolean expression is `false`, the instructions that appear in the `else` socket will be executed.

4.11   If all of its connected expressions are `true`.

4.12   If any of its connected expressions are `true`.

4.13   It reverses the truth of the expression that is plugged into it. If it is applied to an expression that is `true`, the operator returns `false`. If it is applied to an expression that is `false`, the operator returns `true`.

4.14   Go to the *Built-in* section and open the *Math* drawer.

4.15   A random fractional number between 0 and 1.

4.16   The two arguments are `from` and `to`. The function returns a random integer between the two arguments (inclusively).

4.17   You type the items that you wish to appear in the component's list, separated by commas, into the ElementsFromString property.

4.18   You get the value of the `Selection` property.

4.19   `Text`

4.20   When a CheckBox component is checked, its Checked property is set to `true`. When a CheckBox component is unchecked, its Checked property is set to `false`. In the Blocks Editor, you can use a decision block such as `if then` or `if then else` to test a CheckBox component's Checked property, and determine whether it is checked or unchecked.

4.21   The `Changed` event.

Chapter 5

5.1   • Message dialog – A window that displays a title and a message, and waits for the user to click a button. Use the `ShowMessageDialog` method to display it.
    • Text dialog – A window that displays a title and a message, allows the user to enter some text as input, and then click an *OK* button, and optionally a *Cancel* button. Use the `ShowTextDialog` method to display it.
    • Choose dialog – A window that displays a title and a message, and lets the user click one of two buttons, and optionally a *Cancel* button. Use the `ShowChooseDialog` method to display it.

5.2 When a text dialog closes.

5.3 When a choose dialog closes.

5.4 The `AfterTextInput` event handler has a parameter named `response` that holds the input that the user typed into the text dialog.

5.5 The `AfterChoosing` event handler has a parameter named `choice` that holds the text of the button that the user clicked.

5.6 An execution of the blocks that appear in the loop.

5.7 A variable that is regularly incremented in each loop iteration. In essence, it keeps count of the number of iterations the loop has performed.

5.8 A loop that tests its Boolean expression before performing an iteration.

5.9 Before

5.10 A loop that never stops.

5.11 • `number` variable – This is the counter variable. When you create a `for each` loop, a variable named `number` is automatically created, and plugged into this socket.
   • `from` – This is the counter variable's starting value. When the loop begins executing, the counter variable will be set to this value.
   • `to` – This is the counter variable's ending value. When the counter variable reaches this value, the loop ends.
   • `by` – This is the amount added to the counter variable at the end of each iteration. The default value is 1.

5.12 • A loop that reads each number in the series.
   • A variable that accumulates the total of the numbers as they are read.

5.13 A variable that is used to accumulate a total.

5.14 It is very important that an accumulator variable be initialized with the value 0. If the accumulator starts with any value other than 0, it will not contain the correct total when the loop finishes.

5.15 A number that represents an instant in time. It contains both a date and a time.

5.16 You call the Clock component's `Now` function.

5.17 • Use `FormatDate` to format an instant as a date
   • Use `FormatTime` to format an instant as a time
   • Use `FormatDateTime` to format an instant as a date and time

5.18 With the TimerInterval property.

5.19 `AddDays`

5.20 `AfterDateSet`

5.21 `Month`

5.22 `MonthInText`

5.23 `Day`

5.24 `Year`

Chapter 6

6.1   When you call a procedure, it simply executes the blocks it contains and then terminates. When you call a procedure with result, it executes the blocks that it contains, and then it returns a value back to the block that called it.

6.2   It is an example of a procedure with result.

6.3   Go to the *Built-in* section of the Blocks column and open the *Procedures* drawer.

6.4   It causes a procedure to execute.

6.5   Go to the *Built-in* section of the Blocks column and open the *Procedures* drawer.

6.6   The program jumps back to the part of the program that called the procedure and resumes execution from that point.

6.7   • The overall task that the program is to perform is broken down into a series of subtasks.
      • Each of the subtasks is examined to determine whether it can be further broken down into more subtasks. This step is repeated until no more subtasks can be identified.
      • Once all of the subtasks have been identified, they are written in code.

6.8   A piece of data that is passed into a procedure when the procedure is called.

6.9   A special variable that receives an argument when a procedure is called.

6.10 Click the blue mutator box that appears on the `procedure` block, and drag an `input` block from the left side of the mutator bubble to the right side.

6.11 A `get` block. You will find the `get` block in the *Built-in* section of the Blocks column, in the *Variables* drawer.

6.12 The `call` block for the procedure will have a socket with the same name as the parameter. When you call the procedure, you must plug a block into the socket.

6.13 When you call a regular procedure, it simply executes the blocks it contains, and then terminates. When you call a function, it executes the blocks that it contains and then it returns a value back to the block that called it.

6.14 The `to procedure result` block, which is found in the *Procedures* drawer of the *Built-In* section of the *Blocks* column.

6.15 `result`

Chapter 7

7.1   The List needs to be stored in a variable so that it can be accessed elsewhere in the program.

7.2   You can use number, text, Boolean, and variable data.

7.3   Yes.

7.4   You use the `for each` loop to iterate through the items of the list and populate labels on the screen with the times in the list.

7.5 It represents a List item. The List item that the loop is currently on, or processing.

7.6 We can show each item individually. Without it we can only show the entire list.

7.7 The math calculation would not work.

7.8 The \n sequence is used as the return character. You use a text block to hold it.

7.9 There will be an error.

7.10 The position in the list of an item. The index is always a number; something other than a number will produce an error.

7.11 If we know the length of a List, we can be sure to avoid accessing an item that is out of range.

7.12 Adding an item means adding it to the end of the list. Inserting an item into a list means to place an item in a specific position in the list.

7.13 It will be moved to position 11.

7.14 ListA will remain unchanged. ListB will contain the elements of both ListA and ListB.

7.15 add items to list

7.16 Inserting an item into a List means to place an item in a specific position in the list. Replacing an item means to change the value of an item. The indexes of items in a list do not change when an item is replaced.

7.17 When an item is removed, the indexes are re-calculated starting from position one, and each item in the list after the deleted item will have a new index based on the new position.

7.18 The remove list item block requires the List, and the index of the item to be removed. The replace list item block requires the List, the index of the item to be removed, and the replacement value for the item.

7.19 Because it is important to consider checking first to see if the item is in the list before asking for the position. By ensuring that the item is in the List, we avoid unwanted results and/or processing if there is no position for the index in list block to return.

7.20 If the item is not found in the List, we have wasted processing time by looking for it. When the item is not found, the position in list function returns 0.

Chapter 8

8.1 Persisting data means to save it so that it can be accessed later. It is important because most applications that we use require persisted data.

8.2 Facebook, Twitter, Instagram, Vine, Online Banking, to name a few.

8.3 The contents of the TextBoxFileContents component's Text property is saved to a file on the device. The name of the file is specified by the TextBoxSaveFileName component's Text property. If the user specified a name without a preceding forward slash (/) the file will be saved in the application sandbox. If the file name begins with a forward slash, it will be saved to the device's SD card.

8.4 You can only have one. If you have more, they use the same data store space anyway and act as a single TinyDB. You may overwrite something you do not want to if you use them the wrong way.

8.5 No. A TinyDB can only be accessed by one application.

8.6 This slot provides a default value if the tag happens to not be in the TinyDB.

8.7 The element's tag

8.8 A List will allow you to store multiple items of information for one tag. For example, for a contact you can store the email, picture, and phone number into a List and use that for the value of one person (tag).

8.9 A List variable.

8.10 You will need to iterate through the List using a `for each` loop.

8.11 If you are going to use a List as a value, you must know what you are extracting when you iterate through the List. Consistency is important.

Chapter 9

9.1 The top right is 299,0 and the bottom left is 0,299.

9.2 The midpoint is approximately at 80,80.

9.3 Hover the mouse cursor over `prevX` and `prevY` parameters on the `Dragged` event handler block and select the `get` block from the resulting popup. Once you see the `get` block for the parameter, click it to place it in the editor and plug it into the correct slot of the `DrawLine` method.

9.4 40,20 and 40,40

9.5 To set the direction, in degrees, of a moving Sprite. Any number between 180 and 270, not including 180 or 270.

9.6 Because the color is set by the image associated with the ImageSprite.

9.7 Decrease

9.8 −3

9.9 `MoveIntoBounds`

9.10 To make the Sprite looks like it is moving forward, its top will rotate in the direction of the Heading.

9.11 You can decrease the Interval property of the Clock and make the eggs move faster. You can have a global variable to hold the score and increment it when an egg it cracked. Yes, and Yes you can.

9.12 Set TimerEnabled property to `false` in the Clock Component.

9.13 If you go higher than 280, the Sprite will be off of the Canvas.

Chapter 10

10.1 Text

10.2 100200

10.3 It concatenates their values as Text.

10.4 truetruetruetrue

10.5 Each character that you can type on a keyboard has a numerical representation in the ASCII Table. When we compare strings, we can use the ASCII number to compare them as we would numbers.

10.6 They are identical, with the same characters, in the same case, in the same order.

10.7 The lowercase one because lowercase letters come later than the uppercase letters in the ASCII table.

10.8 Boolean

10.9 Often we will trim strings that come from user or file input, in case there are extra spaces that we do not want. These spaces can affect string comparisons, possibly making two strings not equal, when in reality they should be. Generally, passwords should not be trimmed.

10.10 No, the order does not matter. The upcase block will change the entire string to uppercase and the trim will take of leading and trailing spaces. Because they do not affect each other, the order does not matter.

10.11 The characters that are not alphabetic letters will not be changed. Uppercase letters are changed to lowercase and the already lowercase letters are unchanged.

10.12 The numbers stay the same, the result is text.

10.13 Evaluate the following function calls:
  a) 1
  b) 0
  c) 0
  d) 16
  e) 7

10.14 The starts at will return a number expressing where the string begins, the contains returns a Boolean. They are similar because both blocks will indicate whether the substring is in the string.

10.15 piece is the string to search for and text is the string to search.

10.16 Because these blocks are case-sensitive, the piece will not be found in the text if it is not in the same case exactly.

10.17 The replace all block.

10.18 The entire original string, the segment that you want to replace and the replacement string that you want to insert.

10.19 The entire original string, the starting point of the extraction and the length of the string you want to extract.

10.20   It will start at the position in the string matching the `start` argument value, and it will stop when it reaches the number of characters of the `length` argument value.

10.21   It remains the same.

10.22   a) AE, I OU.XYZ (two elements)
         b) AE, I, OU, XYZ (four elelments)
         c) AE I OU.XYZ (one element, there is no comma in the Vowels variable)
         d) AE I OU, XYZ (two elements)

10.23   The division-point is the character at which the split occurs, for example a comma. The division-points are discarded after the split.

10.24   The `split at first` and `split at first of any` blocks only split one time. The `split` and `split at any` will split the strings as many times as there are division-point characters in the string.

10.25   Because it assumes a space division-point.

10.26   20

Chapter 11

11.1   "Two hundred forty-six."

11.2   Country codes are in uppercase, language codes are in lowercase.

11.3   In the `BeforeSpeaking` event handler.

11.4   Because App Inventor does not translate text.

11.5   The *Social Palette*.

11.6   No, if the ReceivingEnabled is set to 2 and Yes if it is set to 3.

11.7   The PhoneNumber and Message properties.

11.8   Nothing, it is fine to have a phone number without dashes and parenthesis.

11.9   The `get message` block, found by hovering the mouse cursor over the `message` parameter of the `MessageReceived` event handler.

11.10   The `get number` block, found by hovering the mouse cursor over the `number` parameter of the `MessageReceived` event handler.

Chapter 12

12.1   Set the DistanceInterval to 1610 and the TimeInterval to 3600000.

12.2   It is important to consider the device's accuracy level in your application because you may not want your app to be too sensitive or insensitive compared to the capability of the device. If your application is more sensitive than your device, you will have to adhere to the device's accuracy level and your application should handle differences gracefully.

12.3   The LocationSensor will not provide location information if its Enabled property is set to `false`.

12.4 You can use the `LatitudeFromAddress` and `LongitudeFromAddress` methods of the LocationSensor.

12.5 When you lift the top edge of the phone and stand it up on the bottom edge, the value of Pitch is –90. If you continue to tip the phone so that it lies flat, front-side down the value of the Pitch increases from –90 to zero.

12.6 135

12.7 You can use the Magnitude to set the Speed and the Angle to set the Heading of a Sprite.

12.8 The `Magnitude` is a value between 0 and 1. In order to make this a value that can be used as the Speed property of a Sprite (which is in milliseconds) we need to multiply it by 100.

12.9 Add the Accelerometer component to the project, then use the `Accelerometer.Shaking` event to clear the Canvas rather than using the Button.

12.10 There will be an echo effect; the clip will start playing again before the first one ends. You will have two audio clips playing at once.

Chapter 13

13.1 You need a SoundRecorder component to record. If you want to playback the audio, you will need a `Player` component. You can play audio files, store them to a list or TinyDB for use later.

13.2 We store the sound to a global variable so that we can use it outside of the `AfterSoundRecorded` event. The sound is only available in the `AfterSoundRecorded` event so to use it elsewhere we need to store it to a variable.

13.3 Once a user has confirmed the photo.

13.4 Once a user has completed a video recording and has confirmed the video.

13.5 App Inventor supports Windows Media Video (.wmv), 3GPP (.3gp) and MPEG-4 (.mp4) file formats for videos. Videos should be 1 MB or smaller in size

13.6 `SeekTo` will take you to a place in the video which is the given milliseconds, `ms` argument, past the start of the video. You can give it a number one for the `ms` argument to go back to the beginning.

13.7 The PhoneNumberPicker's Image property is the image that makes up the background of the picker's button. The PhoneNumberPicker's Picture property is the contact's picture from the Contact list on the device.

13.8 The ContactPicker component has properties for the contact's picture, name and email whereas the PhoneNumberPicker has properties for the contact's phone number in addition to the picture, name and email.

13.9 The EmailPicker provides just the contact's email address.

Index